EARLY CHRISTIAN DOCTRINES

S.S. = Summary
Statement

EARLY
CHRISTIAN DOCTRINES

BY

J. N. D. KELLY, F.B.A.

PRINCIPAL OF ST. EDMUND HALL, OXFORD

REVISED EDITION

1817

Published in San Francisco by

HARPER & ROW, PUBLISHERS

New York   Hagerstown   San Francisco   London

© 1960, 1965, 1968, 1978, JOHN NORMAN DAVIDSON KELLY

EARLY CHRISTIAN DOCTRINES, Revised Edition.

Library of Congress Catalog Card Number: 58-12933

ISBN 06-064334-X

The text of this book is printed on 100% recycled paper.

78 79 80 81 82 83 10 9 8 7 6 5 4 3 2

PREFACE TO THE FIFTH EDITION

In preparing this edition for the press, I have introduced much more numerous, and also much more extensive, revisions and modifications than in the last three editions; in certain sections, indeed, I have re-written whole paragraphs and pages in order to take account of fresh knowledge or of alterations in my own views. I am deeply grateful to friends for their advice, and particularly to the Revd Professor G. C. Stead, who generously suggested more than a score of the changes I have adopted. I have also thought it desirable, in order to fill a gap to which several scholars drew my attention, to insert an entirely new final chapter.

16 November 1976.

PREFACE TO THE FIRST EDITION

My object in writing this book has been the modest one of providing students, and others who may be interested, with an outline account of theological development in the Church of the fathers. The last English manual on the subject, the late J. F. Bethune-Baker's admirable *Introduction to the Early History of Christian Doctrine*, was published more than half a century ago, and although it has gone through many editions and re-printings, the original text remains substantially unaltered. Since it was written, important advances have been made in our knowledge of early Christian thought, and the theological climate is markedly different in several respects. I should like to hope that this book has taken account of some of these changes. In view of its limited purpose, however, I have had to deny myself the pleasure of investigating some of the wider problems which the evolution of dogma inevitably raises. To take but two examples, no attempt has been made here either to define the intrinsic nature of orthodoxy or to assess the impact of

Hellenism on the original Gospel. Vitally important as these, and kindred, topics are, they seemed to lie outside the scope of such a book as this, and I have been content with trying to expound the doctrines themselves as understandingly and impartially as possible.

The text contains lavish quotations (mostly in English) from, and references to, the ancient fathers and theologians, and in the footnotes I have tried to indicate the exact sources of as many of these as possible. I would seriously urge students to follow these up wherever they have the opportunity, for the only way to understand the mind of the early Church is to soak oneself in the patristic writings. References to modern authors have in general been avoided, but the discerning reader will quickly perceive how deeply indebted I am to the classic historians of dogma, such as Harnack, Tixeront, Loofs and Seeberg. The brief bibliographies appended to the chapters are of course not meant to be exhaustive, but merely to list a selection of works which I have myself found useful and which my readers might study with advantage.

It is no doubt natural, as one reaches the end of a book like this, to be conscious of a deep sense of dissatisfaction. It would have been easier, and more satisfactory, to have treated one doctrine thoroughly than so many in a summary fashion. So I hope my readers will curb their impatience if here and there they think the discussion inadequate, or if the balance between the different sections does not always seem to them well maintained. I would also take this opportunity of thanking the many friends who have supported me with their help and encouragement. Among these I would particularly mention the Rev. Dr. F. L. Cross, Lady Margaret Professor of Divinity, who read the whole book through and made countless valuable suggestions, and Etta Gullick, who was largely responsible for the index. It is also pleasant to recall that it was at Bincombe, the Somerset house of Rowley and Etta Gullick, that the first chapters were laboriously drafted and the last were typed out in their final form.

Low Sunday, 1958

CONTENTS

		PAGE
Prefaces		v
Abbreviations, etc.		xii

PART I

PROLEGOMENA

CHAP.

I. THE BACKGROUND ... 3

   1. The Patristic Epoch ... 3

   2. Judaism ... 6

   3. Religious Trends in the Roman Empire ... 11

   4. Graeco-Roman Philosophy ... 14

   5. Neo-Platonism ... 20

   6. The Gnostic Way ... 22

II. TRADITION AND SCRIPTURE ... 29

   1. The Norm of Doctrine ... 29

   2. The Primitive Period ... 31

   3. Irenaeus and Tertullian ... 35

   4. The Third and Fourth Centuries ... 41

   5. The Appeal to the Fathers ... 48

III. THE HOLY SCRIPTURES ... 52

   1. The Old Testament ... 52

   2. The New Testament Canon ... 56

   3. The Inspiration of Scripture ... 60

   4. The Unity of the Two Testaments ... 64

   5. Typology and Allegory ... 69

   6. The Antiochene Reaction ... 75

vii

PART II

THE PRE-NICENE THEOLOGY

CHAP.   PAGE

IV. THE DIVINE TRIAD   83

    1. One God the Creator   83

    2. The Church's Faith   87

    3. The Apostolic Fathers   90

    4. The Apologists and the Word   95

    5. The Apologists and the Trinity   101

    6. Irenaeus   104

V. THIRD-CENTURY TRINITARIANISM   109

    1. Introduction   109

    2. Hippolytus and Tertullian   110

    3. Dynamic Monarchianism   115

    4. Modalistic Monarchianism   119

    5. The Roman Theology   123

    6. Clement and Origen   126

    7. The Influence of Origen   132

VI. THE BEGINNINGS OF CHRISTOLOGY   138

    1. One-sided Solutions   138

    2. The Spirit Christology   142

    3. The Apologists and Irenaeus   145

    4. The Western Contribution   149

    5. The School of Alexandria   153

    6. The East after Origen   158

VII. MAN AND HIS REDEMPTION   163

    1. The Sub-Apostolic Age   163

    2. The Apologists   166

    3. The Theory of Recapitulation   170

4. The West in the Third Century 174

5. The Doctrine of Man in the East 178

6. Eastern Views of the Work of Christ 183

CHAP.

VIII. THE CHRISTIAN COMMUNITY 189

1. The Beginnings of Ecclesiology 189

2. Early Views of the Sacraments 193

3. Developments in the Doctrine of the Church 200

4. Baptism in the Third Century 207

5. Progress in Eucharistic Doctrine 211

6. The Penitential Discipline 216

PART III

FROM NICAEA TO CHALCEDON

IX. THE NICENE CRISIS 223

1. The Eve of the Conflict 223

2. The Teaching of Arius 226

3. The Theology of Nicaea 231

4. The Aftermath of Nicaea 237

5. The Nicene Party and Athanasius 240

6. The Anti-Nicenes 247

X. THE DOCTRINE OF THE TRINITY 252

1. The Return to the Homoousion 252

2. The Homoousion of the Spirit: Athanasius 255

3. The Homoousion of the Spirit: the Cappadocians 258

4. The Cappadocians and the Trinity 263

5. The Trinity in the West 269

6. The Contribution of Augustine 271

CHAP.   PAGE

XI. FOURTH-CENTURY CHRISTOLOGY   280

1. Introduction   280

2. The Arians and Eustathius   281

3. The Christology of Athanasius   284

4. Apollinarianism   289

5. The Orthodox Reaction   295

6. The Antiochene Christology   301

XII. THE CHRISTOLOGICAL SETTLEMENT   310

1. Nestorianism   310

2. Cyril of Alexandria   317

3. From Ephesus Towards Unity   323

4. The Case of Eutyches   330

5. The West and Leo   334

6. The Chalcedonian Settlement   338

XIII. FALLEN MAN AND GOD'S GRACE   344

1. The Soul's Origin   344

2. Athanasius and the Fall   346

3. The Greek Fathers   348

4. The West Before Augustine   353

5. The Doctrine of Pelagius   357

6. Augustine and Original Sin   361

7. Grace and Predestination   366

8. The Western Settlement   369

9. The East in the Fifth Century   372

XIV. CHRIST'S SAVING WORK   375

1. The Clue to Soteriology   375

2. Athanasius   377

3. Fourth-century Greek Fathers   380

4. The West in the Fourth Century   386

5. Augustine   390

6. The East in the Fifth Century   395

CHAP.
XV. CHRIST'S MYSTICAL BODY   401

1. Ecclesiology in the East   401

2. The East and the Roman See   406

3. Western Doctrines: Hilary and Optatus   409

4. Western Doctrines: Augustine   412

5. The West and the Roman Primacy   417

XVI. THE LATER DOCTRINE OF THE SACRA-
MENTS   422

1. General Theory   422

2. Baptism   428

3. Confirmation or Chrism   432

4. Penance   436

5. The Eucharistic Presence   440

6. The Eucharistic Sacrifice   449

PART IV

EPILOGUE

XVII. THE CHRISTIAN HOPE   459

1. The Tension in Eschatology   459

2. Second-century Conceptions   462

3. The Development of Dogma   464

4. Origen   469

5. Later Thought: Resurrection of the Body   474

6. Later Thought: Parousia and Judgment   479

7. Life Everlasting   485

XVIII. MARY AND THE SAINTS   490

    1. The Martyrs and Saints   490

    2. Mary in the Ante-Nicene Period   491

    3. From Nicaea to Ephesus   494

    INDEX   501

ABBREVIATIONS, ETC.

ACO   E. Schwartz, *Acta conciliorum oecumenicorum.*

LXX   Septuagint.

Mansi J. D. Mansi, *Sacrorum conciliorum nova et
           amplissima collectio.*

PG   J. P. Migne, *Patrologia Graeca.*

PL   J. P. Migne, *Patrologia Latina.*

In the citation of patristic texts the editions used have generally been those either of J. P. Migne (this applies in particular to quotations from Irenaeus) or, where available, of the Berlin Corpus of Greek fathers and the Vienna Corpus of Latin fathers. Page references have only been given when the chapter divisions were either inadequate or non-existent. In a number of cases the references are to well-known editions other than the above, and here the page has usually been set down after the editor's name. The abbreviations of the titles of journals etc. cited in the NOTES ON BOOKS should be self-explanatory.

PART I

PROLEGOMENA

CHAPTER I

THE BACKGROUND

1. *The Patristic Epoch*

THE object of this book is to sketch the development of the principal Christian doctrines from the close of the first century to the middle of the fifth. The choice of these frontiers is not so arbitrary or artificial as one might at first sight suppose. There is an obvious convenience in placing the starting-point outside the New Testament. Not only is its teaching a distinct, highly specialized field of study, but the difference of atmosphere becomes immediately apparent as one crosses from the apostolic to the post-apostolic age. At the other end the council of Chalcedon (451) saw the curtain begin to fall on the Church's first doctrinally creative period. Discussion was far from being closed; to take but one example, the Christological issue which Chalcedon had tried to settle continued as a subject of fierce controversy for generations. But, so far as the central stream of Christendom was concerned, the brilliant upsurge of fresh ideas which had distinguished the earlier centuries had spent itself. By the sixth century, both in East and West, the reign of formalism and scholasticism was well under way.

If he is to feel at home in the patristic age, the student needs to be equipped with at least an outline knowledge of Church history and patrology. Here there is only space to draw his attention to one or two of its more striking features. In the first place, he must not expect to find it characterized by that doctrinal homogeneity which he may have come across at other epochs. Being still at the formative stage, the theology of the early centuries exhibits the extremes of immaturity and sophistication. There is an extraordinary contrast, for example, between the versions of the Church's teaching given by the

3

second-century Apostolic Fathers and by an accomplished fifth-century theologian like Cyril of Alexandria. Further, conditions were favourable to the coexistence of a wide variety of opinions even on issues of prime importance. Modern students are sometimes surprised at the diversity of treatment accorded by even the later fathers to such a mystery as the Atonement; and it is a commonplace that certain fathers (Origen is the classic example) who were later adjudged heretics counted for orthodox in their lifetimes. The explanation is not that the early Church was indifferent to the distinction between orthodoxy and heresy. Rather it is that, while from the beginning the broad outline of revealed truth was respected as a sacrosanct inheritance from the apostles, its theological explication was to a large extent left unfettered. Only gradually, and even then in regard to comparatively few doctrines which became subjects of debate, did the tendency to insist upon precise definition and rigid uniformity assert itself.

Two important dividing-lines cut across the period, the one vertically and the other horizontally. The former is the difference of theological temperament between East and West. For historical reasons Rome and the churches immediately associated with her (Gaul, Spain, North Africa, etc.) developed in relative independence of the Eastern churches, and this is reflected in their creeds, liturgies and doctrinal attitude. While Greek theologians are usually intellectually adventurous and inclined to speculation, their Latin counterparts, with the exception of those subject to Eastern influences, seem by contrast cautious and pedestrian, confining themselves to expounding the traditional rule of faith. As an extreme example of this difference we need only juxtapose the conceptions of theology held by (a) Irenaeus and Tertullian, and (b) Clement and Origen, in the latter half of the second and first half of the third centuries. Deeply suspicious of, even hostile to, philosophy, the former limited the function of theology to expounding the doctrines set out in Holy Scripture; they applauded[1] the simple believers who were content with the rule of faith. The latter, on the

---

[1] E.g. Irenaeus, *haer.* 2, 26, 1; Tertullian, *de praescr.* 14, 1-3.

other hand, went so far as to distinguish two types of Christianity, with two grades of Christians corresponding to them. The first and lower type was based on 'faith', i.e. the literal acceptance of the truths declared in Scripture and the Church's teaching, while the second and higher type was described as 'gnosis', i.e. an esoteric form of knowledge. This started with the Bible and tradition, indeed was founded on them, but its endeavour was to unravel their deeper meaning, and in the light of it to explore the profounder mysteries of God and His universe and scheme of salvation; it was supposed to culminate in mystical contemplation or ecstasy. Thus they divided the faithful into simple believers, whom they tended to disparage, and 'spiritual' men, 'gnostics' or 'perfect', whom they regarded as specially privileged by God.

The horizontal dividing line coincides with the reconciliation between Church and Empire effected by Constantine I (306–337), of which the council of Nicaea (325) was the symbol. Prior to this the Church was a persecuted body, struggling to adapt itself to its environment and to fight off such foes as Gnosticism. It is to its credit that, in spite of all difficulties, it was able to produce great constructive theologians like Irenaeus and Origen. With the accession of Constantine, however, the situation radically changed. Henceforth, except for a brief interlude when Julian was sole emperor (361–3), the Church was to enjoy the often embarrassing favour of the State. The era of acute ecclesiastical controversy now began, and councils of bishops became the accepted instruments for defining dogma. As a matter of fact, Christian theology was now entering upon its first splendid summer, and the definitions hammered out against this background of controversy and often unedifying rivalries were to prove of lasting value. Because of the importance of this horizontal division, the material in this book has been arranged so as to take account of it.

Most significant of all, however, is the fact that the Church of the fathers was set in the complex cultural environment of the Roman Empire. This means that, although drawing on its own unique sources of revelation, Christian theology did not take shape in a vacuum. The atmosphere in which it had to grow and develop was crowded with religious, philosophical and even theosophical notions. To some of these it reacted violently, by others it was consciously or unconsciously affected. Some degree of familiarity with this environment is indispensable to anyone who hopes to appreciate the evolution of patristic thought, and an attempt will be made to supply this in this chapter. The reader should not expect anything like a comprehensive picture of later Judaism or of Graeco-Roman culture during the first five centuries. In the following sections a few of the more note-worthy tendencies and movements will be singled out, but even these will only be touched on briefly and in so far as they impinged upon the Church's teaching.

2. Judaism

Judaism was the cradle in which Christianity was nurtured, the source to which it was uniquely indebted. It left a deep imprint, as is generally agreed, on the Church's liturgy and ministry, and an even deeper one on its teaching. In evaluating this impact, we must take account both of Palestinian Judaism and of the Hellenized version current at Alexandria. The former can be dealt with quite briefly, for the heyday of its influence falls outside this book in the apostolic age, when it moulded the thought of all the New Testament writers. Yet, in spite of the early rupture between Christians and Jews, it would be a grave error to dismiss it as a negligible force in our period. Until the middle of the second century, when Hellenistic ideas began to come to the fore, Christian theology was taking shape in predominantly Judaistic moulds, and the categories of thought used by almost all Christian writers before the Apologists were largely Jewish. This explains why the teaching of the Apostolic Father, for example, while not strictly unorthodox, often strikes a strange note when judged by later standards. And it is certain that this 'Judaeo-Christian' theology continued to exercise a powerful influence well beyond the second century.

The two features of later Palestinian Judaism which call for mention here are its attitude to divine 'hypostases' and its heightened interest in angels. It is certain that the former, and by no means unlikely that the latter, helped to create an atmosphere of thought propitious to the development of the Christian conception of God as three-personal. Students of the Old Testament are familiar with the growing tendency there[1] visible to personify Wisdom and to assign it creative functions; and the readiness of New Testament writers like St. Paul to avail themselves of the idea in order to explain the status of Christ is also a commonplace. In later Judaism we come across a multitude of such figures—Wisdom itself (one text[2] implies that it was Wisdom to whom God said, 'Let us make man in our image', etc.), God's 'glory' or 'Presence' (Shekinah), His Word, His Spirit (sometimes[3] spoken of as God's agent in creation), and others too. It remains a matter of dispute how far they were actually hypostatized; the probability is that they were personified abstractions, or else periphrases for God Himself, and that the question of their independent subsistence was never raised. At the same time there was an enormous extension and sharpening in later Judaism of the belief in angels, the ministers of God, so frequently, and until *Daniel* anonymously, mentioned in the Old Testament. Several of them were now given personal names, and we read[4] of seven (or six) archangels. God's will in His world was executed, so popular piety liked to imagine, by them as His deputies, and there was even an angel, Uriel, appointed to regulate the movement of the stars.[5] Of particular interest, some scholars have thought, is the suggestion, of which traces can be found in several sources,[6] that in the heavenly court two angelic powers, sometimes identified as Michael and Gabriel, stand before God's throne interceding for men.

Rather closer attention must be given to the special brand of Judaism which flourished at Alexandria. In earlier days it had produced the Septuagint version of the Old Testament, and in

---

[1] Job 28, 12 ff.; *Prov.* 8, 22 ff.; *Wis.* 7, 22 ff.; *Ecclus.* 24, 1 ff.
[2] 2 Enoch 30, 8.   [3] *Judith* 16, 14; 2 *Bar.* 21, 4.
[4] E.g. *Tob.* 12, 15; 1 *Enoch* 20, 1 ff.   [5] 1 *Enoch* 75, 3.
[6] E.g. *Apoc. Mos.* 33-5.

the Christian period it proved a highly sympathetic channel for
introducing Hellenistic culture to the early Church. Greek
ideas had always attracted the Jews of that great cosmopolitan
city, set at the frontiers between East and West, and it was
here that the most thoroughgoing attempt was made to interpret Jewish theology in terms of Hellenistic philosophy. Perhaps the most notable exponent of these tendencies was Philo
(*c.* 30 B.C.–*c.* A.D. 45), who, as well as being a scholarly man with
a decidedly mystical bent, was a considerable personage in the
Jewish community at Alexandria and headed the delegation
which it sent to the Emperor Gaius in A.D. 40. An inflexible Jew
in faith and practice, he was drawn to the Greek philosophers,
especially Plato, accepting wholeheartedly the Platonic distinction between the ideal, or intelligible, and the material worlds,
but maintained that all their best ideas had been anticipated in
the Jewish Scriptures. The Pentateuch was his favourite study,
and the majority of his voluminous works are devoted to expounding it. He regarded the Bible as fully inspired in the sense
that God used its authors as passive instruments for communicating His will.[1] Two aspects of his thought are of especial
interest to students of Christian doctrine.

First, the method of allegorizing Scripture by means of
which he was able to show that the truths set forth by revealed
religion were identical with those of the philosophers. Allegorical exegesis was no novelty at that time; scholars had employed it for centuries to discover hidden meanings in the
poems of Homer and Hesiod, and with its help the Stoics (for
example, L. A. Cornutus: *fl.* A.D. 50) enabled themselves to
read their own metaphysical system out of the ancient myths.
More than a hundred years before an Alexandrian Jew, Aristobulus, had used it to explain away the cruder anthropomorphisms of the Pentateuch. Philo takes it up enthusiastically,
and contends[2] that, of the various attitudes possible to the
Mosaic Law, much the most satisfactory is to observe its
prescriptions punctiliously while at the same time striving
with the aid of allegory to grasp their deeper purport. He

[1] Cf. *quis rer. div. haer.* 66; *de spec. leg.* 1, 65.   [2] *De ebriet.* 33-93.

compares[1] the literal sense of Scripture to the shadow which the body casts, finding its authentic, profounder truth in the spiritual meaning which it symbolizes. Not that he wants to depreciate, much less abolish, the literal meaning; just as man is body and soul and must pay attention to the former as the tabernacle of the latter, so the plain historical sense merits the fullest respect.[2] By these principles he is able to explain[3] the story of Adam and Eve as a myth symbolizing the creation of the human earthy soul along with the intelligence, senses and passions, the seduction of the intelligence by pleasure and its subjection to the material order, and the ways in which it can return to its original state. This is merely one example of a method by which, while adhering strictly to the letter of the Law, he can regard it as a divinely authorized veil covering a whole complex of Greek philosophical ideas which he found intellectually congenial.

Secondly, there is his concept of the Logos, or Word. Guided by the later Platonists he so much admired, Philo taught[4] that God is utterly transcendent; He transcends even virtue, knowledge and absolute goodness and beauty, the eternal Forms which his revered master, Plato, had postulated. God is pure being ($\tau\grave{o}$ $\check{o}\nu\tau\omega\varsigma$ $\check{o}\nu$), absolutely simple and self-sufficing,[5] and can be described[6] as 'without quality' ($\check{a}\pi o\iota o\varsigma$) —which probably means that, by His transcendence, He cannot be included in any of the logical categories in which we classify finite beings. The question thus arose of His relation to the world. It was all the more urgent because Jewish theology pictured God as calling it into existence by His fiat and being directly concerned with it, while Platonism too insisted on the divine formation and governance of the universe. The contemporary Platonic solution, as we shall see, was to interpose a hierarchy of divine beings between the Supreme Good, or God, and the material order, and to regard these as ruling, or even creating, the latter. This could not commend itself to Philo, since nothing must interfere with the uniqueness of the

---

[1] De confus. ling. 190. [2] De migrat. Abrah. 89–93.
[3] Leg. alleg. passim. [4] De opif. mun. 8.
[5] De post. Caini 167; leg. alleg. 2, 2 f.; de mut. nom. 27.
[6] E.g. leg. alleg. 1, 51.

God revealed in Scripture. Instead he conceived[1] of intermediary powers (δυνάμεις) which, though their status is somewhat confused, were not so much distinct beings as God's operations considered in abstraction from Himself. Among these intermediaries the supreme and most important was the Logos, 'the eldest and most akin to God', as he calls it,[2] ' of the things that have come into existence'.

Philo's teaching about the Logos is ambiguous, even inconsistent, but its main lineaments are clear enough. As intermediary between God and the universe the Logos has a double role: it is God's agent in creation,[3] and it is also the means by which the mind apprehends God.[4] Both ideas hark back to Stoicism. We shall discover[5] that for the Stoics Logos (which also means reason or plan) was the rational principle immanent in reality, giving form and meaning to it; at the same time reality was comprehensible to men because of the presence of Logos in them. Philo has taken up the conception and linked it with his doctrine of divine transcendence. No doubt he was helped by the fact that in the Bible he read that God created the world by His word (λόγῳ), and that it was by His word that He revealed Himself to the prophets; and he was also acquainted with the Wisdom theology, according to which God first created Wisdom and then used her to create the world.   There has been much discussion whether he regarded the Logos as a personal being, but to ask this is to misconceive his position. What is important, from the point of view of his metaphysic, is that he identifies[6] the Logos with the Platonic world of Forms or archetypes, of which sensible reality is a copy. Like the Middle Platonists, he does not regard that world as self-existent, but simply as expressing the mind of the one God. Just as in man (here we again observe Stoic influences at work) there is a λόγος ἐνδιάθετος (i.e. the rational thought in the mind) and also a λόγος προφορικός (i.e. the thought uttered as a word), so the divine Logos is first of all the ideas

---

[1] Cf. quaest. in Exod. 2, 68; de Abrah. 121; de plant. 86.
[2] Leg. alleg. 3, 175.   [3] E.g. de cherub. 125-7.
[4] E.g. de migrat. Abrah. 174.   [5] See below, p. 18.
[6] De opif. mun. 20; 24.

or thoughts of God's mind, and is then projected into formless, unreal matter, making it into a real and rational universe.[1] When Philo speaks[2] of it in personal terms as 'first-begotten Son', the personification is not to be taken too seriously.

The Logos is, of course, the medium of God's government of the world. Being immanent in it as well as transcendent in the divine mind, it is 'the captain and steersman of the universe'.[3] And since it is the Platonic world of Forms, we can see how in contemplating the Logos men can come to the knowledge of God.[4] Further, when the Old Testament describes the appearance of the angel of Yahweh to the patriarchs, Philo's explanation[5] is that in fact it was the Logos.

3. Religious Trends in the Roman Empire

The world in which the Church made triumphant, if sometimes painful, headway was hungry for religion. Surviving monuments of every kind testify to the desperate longing, felt by all classes, for assurance against death and fate, redemption from evil, spiritual cleansing, union with God. To meet this need the old classical religions had little to offer. Despite periodical drives (e.g. by Augustus) to revive ancient piety, the gods of Greece and Rome had lost whatever power they had possessed to inspire. The worship of the emperor or his *genius*, fostered by Augustus and his successors, became increasingly prominent and had official backing. At best, however, it provided a channel for corporate loyalty and the sense that Providence watched over the Empire. Much more satisfying were the Oriental cults which from the first century before Christ spread rapidly across the Graeco-Roman world. Isis, Serapis and Cybele were the most fashionable divinities, winning masses of devotees and having temples erected to them at the public charge; while among soldiers the Persian god Mithras, the ally of the Sun and so the champion of light against darkness, was immensely popular. Syncretism was the product of this mutual jostling of religions; the gods of one country were identified with those of

---

[1] *De vit. Mos.* 2, 127.   [2] *De agric.* 57.
[3] *De cherub.* 36.   [4] Cf. *de confus. ling.* 97.
[5] *De somn.* 1, 232–9; *de mut. nom.* 87; *de cherub.* 3; *de vit. Mos.* 1, 66.

another, and the various cults fused with and borrowed from each other indiscriminately. The belief in the immortality of the soul, sometimes linked with the idea of the transmigration of souls taught by Pythagoras (6th cent. B.C.), and in a future judgment leading either to punishment or a blessed life with the gods, was general.

Two phenomena in this welter of superstition and genuine piety call for notice. First, the extraordinary vogue of the so-called mystery religions. This is the name given to those close-knit religious groups or fellowships into which newcomers had to be initiated by secret ceremonies ('mysteries') not communicable to outsiders. In classical times the mysteries held at Eleusis in honour of Demeter and Persephone were the most famous. The ones that were popular in our period were mostly Oriental in origin. There were mysteries of Isis, and of the great Anatolian mother-goddess Cybele and her youthful lover, the vegetation god Attis, and of others; probably the most widespread and representative were those of Mithras. All these religions had sacred meals, and in the preparatory stages great store was set by abstinences, mortifications and purifications. The rites which formed the climax of their worship were occult actions, involving carefully guarded formulae and cult objects, which imparted an uplifting revelation to the initiate and secured his mystic union with the deity. In the rites of Cybele and Attis, for example, he underwent a kind of baptism in the blood of a bull (*taurobolium*) or a ram (*criobolium*), which was slain above him,[1] and as a result felt himself 'reborn for ever'. The rites of Isis persuaded him that he had traversed the portals of death itself and had returned revivified, protected by the goddess upon whom he had gazed face to face.[2] The appeal of these mystery religions undoubtedly lay in the satisfaction they could give to the craving for an intense personal experience of the divine, with the accompanying sense of release from guilt and fear; their moral impact should not be underrated.

Secondly, the growing attraction, for educated and uneducated people alike, of a monotheistic interpretation of the

[1] Cf. Prudentius, *perist.* 10, 1011-50.   [2] Cf. Apuleius, *met.* 11, 23 f.

conventional polytheism. More and more the many gods of the pagan pantheon tended to be understood either as personified attributes of one supreme God or as manifestations of the unique Power governing the universe. The current syncretism made this process easy and natural, and at a higher level it coincided with the trend of enlightened philosophical opinion. The sophist Aristides, who lectured in Asia Minor and Rome in the middle of the second century, provides an instructive example. A series of his speeches survives celebrating individual gods, especially Asclepius, to whom he has a warm, genuine attachment; but it is evident[1] that in his eyes they all represent cosmic forces emanating from the one universal Father. Plutarch, too, the biographer and essayist (*fl.* 100), while adhering to ancestral religious practices and admitting[2] the existence of subordinate intermediary gods and demons, combines this with belief[3] in a single supreme and perfect God Who is true being. The growing use of 'Pantheos', either as an amalgam uniting the characteristics of several gods or as an adjective attached to the name of one, was symptomatic. When in 274 the emperor Aurelian instituted the state cult of Sol Invictus, he was not merely saluting the sun as protector of the Empire, but acknowledging the one universal Godhead Which, recognized under a thousand names, revealed Itself most fully and splendidly in the heavens. Apuleius (*fl.* 160) sums the matter up when he describes[4] Isis as '. . . the chiefest of the heavenly ones, the inclusive manifestation of gods and goddesses . . . whose unique divinity the whole world adores under manifold forms, with varied rites and by multifarious names'.

It is unnecessary here to dwell on particular cults in detail, *Manichaeism* but an exception must be made of Manichaeism because of its special impact on Christian thought. Its founder was the prophet Mani, who was born in Babylonia *c.* 216 and suffered martyrdom under Bahram I *c.* 277. Often classified as a Christian heresy, it was really a completely independent religion embody-

---

[1] Cf. his speeches to Asclepius, Zeus and Serapis (nos. 42, 43 and 45 in B. Keil's ed.).   [2] E.g. *de fac.* 30; *de defect. orac.* 10; 13.
[3] E.g. *de Is. et Osir.* 77 f.   [4] *Met.* 11, 5.

ing Christian, but also Buddhist and Zoroastrian, elements. Indeed, it claimed to be the only universal religion, giving in its fulness the revelation which prophets prior to Mani had only communicated fragmentarily. The elaborate, dramatic myths in which this revelation came to be clothed hardly concern us here. In essence Manichaeism was a *gnosis*, akin in some respects to the Gnosticism which will be examined later in this chapter, and as such offered men salvation by knowledge. It was founded on a radical dualism, and taught that reality consists of two great forces eternally opposed to each other, Good (that is, God, Truth, Light) and Evil, or Darkness, the latter being identified with matter. As he exists, man is tragically involved in the material order; he is fallen and lost. Actually, however, he is a particle of Light, belonging to, though exiled from, the transcendent world. He is of the same essence as God, and human souls are fragments of the divine substance. His salvation lies in grasping this truth by an interior illumination which may be spontaneous, but usually comes in response to initiation into the Manichaean fellowship; and in the process of salvation, paradoxically, God is at once redeemer and redeemed. The all-important thing was to withdraw oneself from the contamination of the flesh, matter being the fundamental evil. Such in outline was the dualist doctrine which, with its highly organized church, its graded hierarchy of adherents ('auditors', 'elect', 'priests', 'bishops', 'apostles' or 'masters'), and its corresponding degrees of asceticism, swept over Europe, Africa and Asia from the end of the third century and won such notable converts as Augustine.

4. *Graeco-Roman Philosophy*[1]

Philosophy was the deeper religion of most intelligent people; what is more important for our purpose, its concepts provided thinkers, Christian and non-Christian alike, with an intellectual framework for expressing their ideas. The two most

---

[1] As the accounts given of different thinkers in this and the following sections are quite summary, detailed references have been dispensed with.

influential types of thought in our period harked back to Platonism and Stoicism. Of the other great classical systems, Aristotelianism exerted a certain influence through its logic, and some of its principles (for example, that a supreme Mind is the ultimate cause of the universe) were absorbed by later forms of Platonism. Scepticism, which traced its ancestry to Pyrrho of Elis (*fl.* 300 B.C.), and maintained that knowledge is impossible and that suspense of judgment is the only rational attitude, enjoyed a revival with Aenesidemus (*fl.* 60 B.C.) and Sextus Empiricus (*fl.* A.D. 175) and kept up a formidable attack on dogmatism of every kind, but its appeal was to rather limited, chiefly scientific, circles. On the other hand, Epicureanism (founded by Epicurus: 341–270 B.C.), with its denial that the gods are concerned about human affairs, and its doctrine that reality is composed of an infinity of atoms in a void and that sensation is the criterion of good and evil, had lost all effective force.

The key to Plato's (*c.* 429–347 B.C.) philosophy is his theory of knowledge. Being convinced that knowledge in the strict sense is possible, but that it cannot be obtained from anything so variable and evanescent as sense-perception, he was led to posit a transcendent, non-sensible world of Forms or Ideas (εἴδη) which are apprehended by the intellect alone. His point was that, while sensation presents us with great numbers of particular objects which are constantly changing, the mind seizes on certain characteristics which groups of them possess in common and which are stable. For example, it fastens on the characteristic of beauty common to certain objects and of similarity common to others, and so reaches the Forms of beauty-in-itself and likeness-in-itself. The Forms thus resemble the universals of which modern philosophers speak, but we should notice that for Plato they had objective existence. It is an open question whether he believed there were Forms corresponding to every class of sensible things, but we do know that he regarded them as arranged in a hierarchy crowned by the most universal Form of all, the Form of the Good (later he called it the One), which is the cause of all the other Forms and of our knowledge of them. Being unchanging and eternal, the Forms alone are truly real. They transcend, and are wholly independent of, the world of particular sensible things. In fact, the latter, the world of Becoming, is modelled on the world of Forms, and particulars only are what they are in so far as the Forms are participated in, or copied, by them.

The transition to Plato's psychology and theology is easy. In his view the soul is an immaterial entity, immortal by nature; it exists prior to the body in which it is immured, and is destined to go on existing after the latter's extinction. So far from having anything to do with the world of Becoming, it properly belongs to the world of Forms (that is, of Being), and it is in virtue of the knowledge it had of them in its pre-mundane existence that it can recognize (he calls this ἀνάμνησις, or recollection) them here. It is, moreover, a tripartite structure, consisting of a higher or 'rational' element which apprehends truth and by rights should direct the man's whole life, a 'spirited' element which is the seat of the nobler emotions, and an 'appetitive' element which covers the carnal desires. As regards theology, it seems fairly certain that, in spite of the reverential language he often used of it, Plato did not regard the Form of the Good or the One as God in the ordinary sense of the word. Soul for him was the supreme directive, organizing principle, and he believed in a World-Soul animating the material universe. In *Timaeus* he pictures a Demiurge, or Craftsman, making the World-Soul (in *Philebus* they seem to be identified) and shaping the world out of pre-existent material. But we should observe that the Demiurge constructs the world according to the pattern which he contemplates in the world of Forms. He and that world seem independent of each other, so that we are left with two ultimate principles in addition to pre-existent matter.

Plato's pupil, Aristotle (384–322 B.C.), modified his master's teaching in several important respects. A feature of his logic was his analysis of the ways in which the mind thinks about things. These he called Categories, and he enumerated ten in all: substance (οὐσία—in the sense of individual thing), quantity, quality, relation, place, date, position, state, action, passivity.

Aristotle

Aristotle, however, believed that these represent not only the ways in which the mind thinks about the external world, but also the modes in which things objectively exist in that world. From this it is apparent that, unlike Plato, he was a realist and accepted the reality of the material world as we know it. Further, he sharply criticized Plato's theory of Forms. He fully agreed that there must be Forms in the sense of universals common to all particulars of a class, and also that they must be objectively real and not mere mental concepts; he was even prepared to describe them as 'secondary substances' (δεύτεραι οὐσίαι). But he objected to Plato's suggestion that they are 'separate from', or transcend, particulars. His contention was that they are actually present in particulars; in fact, the individual substance (οὐσία in the primary sense) is a compound (σύνολον) of the subject, or substratum (ὑποκείμενον, or ὕλη), and the Form. In harmony with this his psychology differed from Plato's. So far from being disparate entities, he taught that body and soul constitute a composite unity, the body being as matter to the soul and the soul, as it were, the Form of the body. As regards God, he took up Plato's thought that Soul is immortal and self-moving, the source of motion and change in all that is not soul, and expanded it into the conception of an eternal Mind which, unmoved itself, is the Prime Mover of all that exists.

Stoicism presents a very different picture. Founded by Zeno of Citium *c.* 300 B.C., it was a closely knit system of logic, metaphysics and ethics. Its lofty, if somewhat impersonal, moral ideal won it countless adherents; it taught conquest of self, life in accordance with nature (i.e. the rational principle within us), and the brotherhood of man. From the theological point of view, however, what was most remarkable about it was its pantheistic materialism. The Stoics reacted vigorously against the Platonic differentiation of a transcendent, intelligible world not perceptible by the senses from the ordinary world of sensible experience. Whatever exists, they argued, must be body, and the universe as a whole must be through and through material. Yet within reality they drew a distinction between a

Stoicism

passive and an active principle. There is crude, unformed matter, without character or quality; and there is the dynamic reason or plan (λόγος) which forms and organizes it. This latter they envisaged as spirit (πνεῦμα) or fiery vapour; it was from this all-pervading fire that the cruder, passive matter emerged, and in the end it would be reabsorbed into it in a universal conflagration. But though more ethereal than the passive matter it informed, spirit was none the less material, and the Stoics were not afraid to accept the paradox of two bodies occupying the same space which their theory entailed. This active principle or Logos permeates reality as mind or consciousness pervades the body, and they described it as God, Providence, Nature, the soul of the universe (anima mundi). Their conception that everything that happens has been ordered by Providence to man's best advantage was the basis of their ethical doctrine of submission to fate.

Thus Stoicism was a monism teaching that God or Logos is a finer matter immanent in the material universe. But it also taught that particular things are microcosms of the whole, each containing within its unbroken unity an active and a passive principle. The former, the principle which organizes and forms it, is its logos, and the Stoics spoke of 'seminal logoi' (λόγοι σπερματικοί), seeds, as it were, through the activity of which individual things come into existence as the world develops. All these 'seminal logoi' are contained within the supreme, universal Logos; they are so many particles of the divine Fire which permeates reality. This leads to the Stoic doctrine of human nature. The soul in man is a portion of, or an emanation from, the divine Fire which is the Logos. It is a spirit or warm breath pervading the body and giving it form, character, organization. Material itself, it survives the body, but is itself mortal, persisting at longest until the world conflagration. Its parts are, first, the five senses; then the power of speech or self-expression; then the reproductive capacity; and, finally, the ruling element (τὸ ἡγεμονικόν), which is reason. The soul is the logos in man, and the Stoics made an important distinction between the 'immanent logos' (λόγος ἐνδιάθετος), which is his reason considered merely as present in him, and the 'expressed logos' (λόγος προφορικός), by which they meant his reason as extrapolated or made known by means of the faculty of speech or self-expression.

Both the Stoicism and, to an even greater extent, the Platonism which flourished in the first two Christian centuries show important deviations from their classical prototypes. Each had borrowed from the other, and indeed the intellectual attitude of great numbers of educated people might be described as either a Platonizing Stoicism or a Stoicizing Platonism. Not that it would be accurate to speak of Eclecticism as holding the field. On the academic plane at any rate the two schools maintained their independence and engaged in polemics with each other. Thus the Stoicism preached by such men as Seneca (c. 4 B.C.–A.D. 65), Epictetus (c. 55–138) and Marcus Aurelius (121–80) was a distinct system of thought, although with the emphasis placed on conduct. There is discernible in it, however, alongside a theoretical allegiance to the traditional materialism, a definite movement away from the classic Stoic position. Seneca, for example, so stresses the divine perfection and goodness that he approximates to the conception of God as transcendent. Marcus Aurelius, too, divides human nature into three parts—body, animal soul (ψυχή) and intelligence (νοῦς)—and explicitly states that the last of these, the ruling part (τὸ ἡγεμονικόν) in man, is not derived, as the other two are, from the four elements which constitute matter (fire, air, water, earth). It is an offshoot (ἀπόσπασμα) from God, a spiritual substance of loftier origin than matter.

The Platonism of the period (Middle Platonism, as it is called) presents a much less coherent aspect. Generalization about it is not easy, for several diverse trends of thought were to be found in it. For example, two of its leading second-century representatives were Atticus and Albinus, the one hostile to and the other greatly influenced by Aristotelianism. As a movement, however, this revived Platonism had a strongly religious colouring. The chief objects of its adherents were to understand the truth about the divine world and, so far as their personal lives were concerned, to point the way to attaining the greatest possible likeness to God. From the theological point of view their most notable contribution was to bring together the supreme Mind which Aristotle had postulated and Plato's Good, and to equate them. So Middle Platonism was more definitely theistic than its classical forerunner; at the summit of the hierarchy of being it placed the unique Divine Mind. It retained the conception bequeathed by Plato of a transcendent world of Forms, but represented them as God's thoughts. Albinus's system was more complex. He distinguished the First Mind or God, Who is unmoved, the Second Mind or World-Intellect, through which He operates and which is set in motion by desire for Him, and the World-Soul. Celsus, the critic of Christianity whom Origen sought to answer, belonged to the same school. God, he argued, cannot have created the body, or indeed anything mortal, and only Soul can have come from Him directly;[1] and the idea of His coming down to men must be rejected as involving a change in Him, and a change necessarily for the worse.[2] In general the Middle Platonists were ready enough to allow the existence of intermediary divinities. This was only to be expected in view of the position they assigned to the supreme God. While including Him in the hierarchy of being, they nevertheless regarded Him as utterly transcendent, only to be glimpsed in occasional flashes of illumination.

5. Neo-Platonism

In Neo-Platonism the tendency to make God transcendent was carried as far as it could go. This was that fully developed system, Platonic in its main inspiration, but incorporating Aristotelian, Stoic and even Oriental elements, which flourished from the middle of the third century and with which the fathers of the second half of our period were familiar. It is best exemplified by Plotinus (205-70), the Greek-speaking Egyptian who was its founder and also one of the greatest thinkers of the ancient world.

[1] Origen, c. Cels. 4, 52; 4, 54.   [2] Ib. 4, 14.

Plotinus was, philosophically speaking, a monist, conceiving of reality as a vast hierarchical structure with grades descending from what is beyond being to what falls below being. His highest principle, or 'hypostasis', is God, more properly designated as the One. Itself beyond being, and even beyond mind (with which, it will be recalled, the Middle Platonists equated God), the One is the source from which being derives, the goal to which it ever strives to return. The process is described analogically as emanation, but it leaves the One undiminished and unchanged, just as the radiation of light from the sun does not cause it to suffer any loss. Ineffably simple, the One cannot be the subject of any attributes; we can call It good, not in the sense that it possesses goodness as a quality, but that It *is* goodness. Immediately below the One in the hierarchy comes the second hypostasis, Mind or Thought; and below and issuing from it comes the third hypostasis, Soul. Mind comprises the world of Forms, which it contemplates in its effort to return to the One; and thus multiplicity is introduced into the universe. It is the causal principle, being identified with Plato's Demiurge. Soul is divided into two: the higher soul, which is akin to Mind and transcends the material order, and the lower soul, or Nature (φύσις), which is the soul of the phenomenal world. All individual souls are emanations from the World-Soul, and like it they have a higher element which is related to Mind, and a lower element which is directly connected with the body. Matter in itself, that is, unilluminated by form, is darkness or non-being, and as such is evil.

Two features of Neo-Platonism deserve to be stressed. As expounded by Plotinus, it represents an optimistic attitude to the universe. Material though it is, the world as we know it is good in his eyes; it is created and ordered by the higher soul, and is held together by Nature. Though matter in itself is evil, the visible universe reflects the intelligible order, and as such should be accepted as the best of all possible worlds. Secondly, the religious bias of the whole Neo-Platonic conception is patent. Whatever exists is an 'overflow' of the One, and pervading all reality, at its different levels, is the ardent longing for

union with what is higher, and ultimately with the One itself. So
the human soul, fired by the heavenly Eros of which Plato spoke
in his *Symposium*, is challenged to undertake this ascent. The first
stage is one of purification; it must free itself from the body and
the beguilements of sense-perception. At the second stage it
rises to the level of Mind and busies itself with philosophy and
science, retaining, however, its self-consciousness. The final stage
consists in mystical union with the One; it is mediated by
ecstasy, and when this occurs the awareness of the distinction
between subject and object is lost. In this present life, of course,
the state of ecstasy is rarely, if ever, attained and is bound to
be short-lived; Plotinus, we are informed by his biographer
Porphyry,[1] was himself granted this experience four times only
in five years.

6. *The Gnostic Way*

One of the most potent forces operating in the Church's environment, particularly in the second and third centuries, was
Gnosticism. This is the name (from γνῶσις = knowledge) applied to an amorphous group of sects or schools of thought
about which theologians like Irenaeus, Tertullian and Hippolytus inform us. They treat it simply as a Christian heresy, an
aberration brought about by the adulteration of sound apostolic
doctrine with pagan philosophy,[2] or even astrology and Greek
mystery religions,[3] and charge[4] the Simon Magus mentioned in
Acts 8 with having originated it. Earlier scholars tended to
accept the main part of this thesis, so that A. Harnack could
describe[5] Gnosticism as 'the extreme Hellenization of Christianity'. It is true that the Gnostic systems with which we are
best acquainted were patently Christian in intention. On the
other hand, there were others (e.g. those represented by the
'Book of Baruch' cited by Hippolytus[6] and by the *Apocalypse
of Adam*) in which the Christian features were quite superficial.

[1] *Vit. Plot.* 23.
[2] E.g. Irenaeus, *haer.* 2, 14; Tertullian, *de praescr.* 7; 30.
[3] Hippolytus, *ref.* praef. 8.
[4] E.g. Irenaeus, *haer.* 1, 23, 2; 1, 27, 4; 2, praef. 1.
[5] *Dogmengeschichte*, 4 ed., 1, 250.   [6] *Ref.* 5, 24-7.

GNOSTICISM — usually Xn in intention

Further, there seems to have been a Jewish Gnosticism ante-dating the Christian; and in most Gnostic systems Jewish, more correctly heterodox Jewish, ingredients were prominent. Some of the later New Testament documents also combat what appear to be Gnostic influences. It is therefore more satisfactory to regard Gnosticism as a movement or, more precisely, tendency which was wider and older than Christianity. The product of syncretism, it drew upon Jewish, pagan and Oriental sources , and brought a distinctive attitude and certain characteristic ideas to the solution of the problem of evil and human destiny.

We can perhaps illustrate what Gnosticism was by giving a rough, composite summary[1] of the teaching current in one of its most important schools, that of the Christian Valentinus, *Valentinus* who taught at Alexandria and later at Rome in the middle decades of the second century. According to this, above and beyond the universe dwells the supreme Father, Bythos, the unbegotten Monad and perfect Aeon, and by His side Sige (Silence), who is His Ennoia (Thought). From these proceed, by successive emanations, three pairs of aeons, Nous (or Mono-genes) and Aletheia (Truth), Logos and Zoe (Life), Anthropos (Man) and Ecclesia (Church), thus completing the Ogdoad. From Logos and Zoe proceed five (the Decad), and from Anthropos and Ecclesia six (the Dodecad), further pairs of aeons. These thirty form the Pleroma, or fulness of the God-head, but the only-begotten Nous alone possesses the pos-sibility of knowing and revealing the Father. The lowest of the thirty aeons, however, Sophia, yielded to an ungovernable desire to apprehend His nature. She travailed with the guilty yearning she had conceived (Enthymesis), and would have been dissolved into the All had not Horos (Limit: also called Stauros, or Cross), appointed as guardian of the Pleroma, con-vinced her that the Father is incomprehensible. So Sophia cast away her passion and was allowed to remain within the

[1] Cf. Irenaeus, *haer.* 1, 1–8; Hippolytus, *ref.* 6, 21–37. Much light has been thrown on Valentinus's own teaching by the papyri discovered at Nag Hammadi: see *The Jung Codex* (studies by H. C. Puech, G. Quispel and W. C. Van Unnik), 1955, London.

Pleroma. Nous and Aletheia meanwhile, at the Father's behest, produce a new pair of aeons, Christ and the Holy Spirit, to instruct the aeons in their true relation to Him. Order having been thus restored, they sing the praises of the Father and produce the Saviour Jesus as the perfect fruit of the Pleroma.

But what of Sophia's monstrous birth, Enthymesis, exiled from the Pleroma and now known as a lower Sophia, or Achamoth? As she wanders about the still lifeless void, her anguish brings matter to birth, while out of her yearning for Christ she produces the 'psychic' ($\psi \upsilon \chi \iota \kappa \acute{o} \nu$) or soul-element. Then Christ has pity on her and, descending by the Cross (Horos), impresses form on her formlessness. As a result of this she gives birth to spiritual, or 'pneumatic', substance. Out of these three elements—matter, psyche and pneuma—the world then came into being. First, Sophia formed a Creator, or Demiurge, out of psychic substance as an image of the supreme Father. The Demiurge, who is in fact the God of the Old Testament, then created heaven and earth and the creatures inhabiting it. When he made man, he first made 'the earthy man', and then breathed his own psychic substance into him; but without his knowledge Achamoth planted *pneuma*, or spirit, born from herself, in the souls of certain men. This spiritual element yearns for God, and salvation consists in its liberation from the lower elements with which it is united. This is the task which the Saviour Jesus accomplishes. According to their constitution, there are three classes of men—the carnal or material, the psychic and the pneumatic. Those who are carnal cannot in any case be saved, while in order to attain redemption the pneumatic only need to apprehend the teaching of Jesus. The psychic class can be saved, though with difficulty, through the knowledge and imitation of Jesus.

This amalgam of speculation and mythology, interspersed with scriptural reminiscences, was typical of developed Gnosticim. But there were many systems or schools, differing markedly from each other. Valentinus himself, for example, seems to have taught a much simpler doctrine than that elaborated by his disciples; while it contained elements of myth, it

had contacts with Johannine Christianity. His school included
such notable figures as Heracleon (*fl.* 175), the author of an
allegorizing commentary on the Fourth Gospel which emphasized the distinctions between the supreme God and the
Demiurge and between the three classes of mankind, and
Ptolemaeus († *c.* 180), whose *Letter to Flora*[1] is an invaluable
witness to Gnostic principles of exegesis. The most important
Christian Gnostic apart from Valentinus was the Syrian-born
Basilides, who lectured at Alexandria *c.* 120–40. In his system[2]
we meet with the same conception of graded orders of existence descending from the supreme, ineffable Father, and the
same opposition between Him and the God of the Jews, the
creator of the material universe and man. Redemption consists in the coming of the Father's first-begotten, Nous, in
human form to release the spiritual element imprisoned in
men's bodies. While Christian motifs predominate here, they
play a minor part in the Gnostic Justin's 'Book of Baruch',[3]
which expounds a closely related story of redemption in the
setting of Greek myths and the Mosaic account of creation.
Again, the 'Naassene' tractate cited by Hippolytus[4] takes a
short hymn addressed to the god Attis as its text. On the
basis of this it seeks to explain the origin of man and of the
suffering to which he is heir. Other Gnostics of whom we hear
in the second century are Menander of Samaria, who is said
to have practised magic arts;[5] Satornilus (or Saturninus) of
Antioch, who emphasized the asceticism which was one possible corollary of the Gnostic contempt for matter;[6] Isidore, the
son and disciple of Basilides, whose followers deduced that the
spiritually perfect were free to be immoral;[7] and Carpocrates,
who carried this antinomianism to extreme lengths.[8] Of
Marcion, who stood much closer to the Church, an account
will be given later.[9]

[1] Cf. Epiphanius, *haer.* 33, 3–7.
[2] Cf. Irenaeus, *haer.* 1, 24; Hippolytus, *ref.* 7, 20 ff.
[3] Cf. Hippolytus, *ref.* 5, 24–7.   [4] *Ref.* 5, 1–11.
[5] Hippolytus, *ref.* 7, 28; Irenaeus, *haer.* 1, 23, 5; Eusebius, *hist. eccl.* 3, 26.
[6] Hippolytus, *ref.* 7, 28.
[7] Irenaeus, *haer.* 1, 24; Clement Alex., *strom.* 2, 20, 112; 3, 1, 1–3, 2.
[8] Irenaeus, *haer.* 1, 25; Clement Alex., *strom.* 3, 2, 5.   [9] See pp. 57 f.

To speak of Gnosticism as a movement is misleading, for that term suggests a concrete organization or church. There were, as we have seen, plenty of Gnostic teachers, each with his coterie of adherents, but there was no single Gnostic Church. On the other hand, it is clear that behind all the variegated Gnostic sects there lay a common stock of ideas which could fasten upon, adapt themselves to and eventually transform any religious movement concerned to find an answer to the problems of existence, evil and salvation. These ideas may now be briefly summarized. First, most of the Gnostic schools were thoroughly dualistic, setting an infinite chasm between the spiritual world and the world of matter, which they regarded as intrinsically evil. Secondly, when they tried to explain how the material order came into existence, they agreed in refusing to attribute its origin to the ultimate God, the God of light and goodness. It must be the result of some primeval disorder, some conflict or fall, in the higher realm, and its fabricator must have been some inferior deity or Demiurge. Where the Old Testament was accepted as authoritative, it was easy and natural to identify him with the Creator-God of the Jews. Thirdly, the Gnostics all believed that there is a spiritual element in man, or at any rate in the *élite* of mankind, which is a stranger in this world and which yearns to be freed from matter and to ascend to its true home. Fourthly, they pictured a mediator or mediators descending down the successive aeons or heavens to help it to achieve this. These ideas were expounded in a setting of elaborate pseudo-cosmological speculation, and extensive use was made of pagan myths, the Old Testament and concepts borrowed from Far Eastern religions.

In this way, then, the Gnostics sought to explain the riddle of man's plight in a universe he feels to be alien to himself. But what of the redemption they offered? Here we come to the distinctive feature which gives Gnosticism its name. In all the Gnostic systems redemption is brought about by knowledge, and it is the function of the divine mediators to open the eyes of 'pneumatic' men to the truth. 'The spiritual man', the disciples of the Valentinian Marcus declared.[1] 'is redeemed by know-

[1] Irenaeus, *haer*. I, 21, 4.

ledge'; while according to Basilides,[1] 'the Gospel is knowledge
of supramundane things'. In other words, when a man has
really grasped the Gnostic myths in all their inwardness, and
thus realizes who he is, how he has come to his present condition, and what is that 'indescribable Greatness' which is the
supreme God, the spiritual element in him begins to free itself
from the entanglements of matter. In the vivid imagery of
Valentinus's *Gospel of Truth*,[2] before he acquires that knowledge, he plunges about like a drunken man in a dazed state,
but having acquired it he awakens, as it were, from his intoxi-
cated slumbers. Irenaeus has a colourful passage[3] describing *Irenaeus*
how the possession of this esoteric knowledge—of the abysmal
Fall, of Achamoth, of the Demiurge and so forth—was
supposed to enable the Gnostic to overcome the powers
confronting him after death, and so to traverse the successive
stages of his upward journey.

It is easy to understand the fascination which the Gnostic
complex of ideas exercised on many Christians. The Church,
too, professed to offer men saving knowledge, and set Christ
before them as the revelation of the Father. There was a powerful strain in early Christianity which was in sympathy with
Gnostic tendencies. We can see it at work in the Fourth Gospel,
with its axiom that eternal life consists in knowledge of God
and of Christ, and even more clearly in such second-century
works as *2 Clement* and Theophilus's *Ad Autolycum*. As we
noticed above, Clement of Alexandria freely applied[4] the title
'gnostics' to Christians who seemed to have a philosophic
grasp of their faith. It is the existence of a genuinely Christian,
orthodox 'gnosis' side by side with half-Christian, heretical or
even non-Christian versions which in part accounts for the
difficulty in defining Gnosticism precisely. As has been shown,
many of the Gnostic teachers mentioned above sincerely regarded themselves as Christians, and there is an element of
truth in the thesis that their systems were attempts to restate
the simple Gospel in terms which contemporaries would find
philosophically, even scientifically, more satisfying. The root

[1] Hippolytus, *ref.* 7, 27, 7.   [2] Cf. *The Jung Codex*, pp. 29 ff.
[3] *Haer.* I, 21, 5.   [4] E.g. *strom.* 5, 1; 6, 3, 3; 7 passim.

incompatibility between Christianity and Gnosticism really lay, as second-century fathers like Irenaeus quickly perceived, in their different attitudes to the material order and the historical process. Because in general they disparaged matter and were disinterested in history, the Gnostics (in the narrower, more convenient sense of the term) were prevented from giving full value to the fundamental Christian doctrine of the incarnation of the Word.

EXACTLY

NOTES ON BOOKS

1. B. Altaner, *Patrologie* (Freiburg i.B., 7 ed. 1966); H. von Campenhausen, *The Fathers of the Greek Church; The Fathers of the Latin Church* (London, 1963; 1964); J. Quasten, *Patrology* (Utrecht and Brussels, 1950 contd.). 2. W. Bousset, *Die Religion des Judentums in späthellenistischen Zeitalter* (Tübingen, 3 ed. 1926); J. Daniélou, *Philon d'Alexandrie* (Paris, 1958); E. R. Goodenough, *Introduction to Philo Judaeus* (Oxford, 2 ed. 1962); G. F. Moore, *Judaism in the First Centuries of the Christian Era* (Harvard, 1927 and 1930). 3. S. Angus, *The Religious Quests of the Graeco-Roman World* (London, 1929); F. Cumont, *Les Religions orientales dans le paganisme romain* (Paris, 4 ed. 1929); T. R. Glover, *The Conflict of Religions in the Early Roman Empire* (London, 10 ed. 1923); H. Lietzmann, *A History of the Early Church*, Vols. I and II (Eng. trans.: London, 2 ed. 1949–50); H. C. Puech, *Le Manichéisme* (Paris, 1940). 4. and 5. A. H. Armstrong, *The Architecture of the Intelligible Universe in the Philosophy of Plotinus* (Cambridge, 1940); *An Introduction to Ancient Philosophy* (London, 1947); (ed.), *Later Greek and Early Medieval Philosophy* (Cambridge, 1967); E. Bevan, *Stoics and Sceptics* (Oxford, 1913); *Hellenistic Popular Philosophy* (Cambridge, 1923); F. Copleston, *A History of Philosophy*, Vol. I (London, 1946); F. M. Cornford, *Plato's Theory of Knowledge* (London, 1935); I. M. Crombie, *An Examination of Plato's Doctrines* (London, 1962); R. D. Hicks, *Stoics and Epicureans* (London, 1910); G. E. R. Lloyd, *Aristotle: the Growth and Structure of his Thought* (Cambridge, 1968); M. Pohlenz, *Die Stoa* (Göttingen, 3 ed. 1964); J. M. Rist, *Stoic Philosophy* (Cambridge, 1969); R. T. Wallis, *Neoplatonism* (London, 1972); R. E. Witt, *Albinus and the History of Middle Platonism* (Cambridge, 1937). 6. F. L. Cross (ed.), *The Jung Codex* (London, 1955); R. M. Grant, *Gnosticism and Early Christianity* (New York, 2 ed. 1966); *Gnosticism: an Anthology* (London, 1961); H. C. Puech and G. Quispel, 'Les Écrits gnostiques du Codex Jung' (art. in *Vig. Christ.*, 1954); G. Quispel, 'The Original Doctrine of Valentine' (art. in *Vig. Christ.*, 1947); F. Sagnard, *La Gnose valentinienne* (Paris, 1947); R. McL. Wilson, 'Gnostic Origins' (art. in *Vig. Christ.*, 1955); *The Gnostic Problem* (London, 1958); *Gnosis and the New Testament* (Oxford, 1968).

CHAPTER II

TRADITION AND SCRIPTURE

1. *The Norm of Doctrine*

BEFORE examining particular doctrines, there is an important preliminary question which the student must face. This concerns the attitude of the Church in the period under review to Christian doctrine itself, in particular to its sources and authority. It is easy to furnish a rough-and-ready, partial answer. Christianity came into the world as a religion of revelation, and as such claimed a supernatural origin for its message. Its ultimate source, as the theologians of the early centuries clearly perceived, lay in the Person, words and works of Jesus Christ in the context of the revelation of which He was the climax. On closer inspection, however, the problem is seen to be more complex. What is meant by Christian doctrine is the teaching of the Catholic Church from the end of the first century onwards. This at once raises the question of the media by which the original revelation was preserved and handed down in the Church. Further, the principles by which these media were interpreted call for investigation; and since interpretations were liable to differ, it seems desirable to consider the criteria by which the Church judged doctrines to be sound or erroneous, orthodox or heretical.

Broadly speaking, the problem we have raised is the problem of Tradition (as we now call it) and Scripture, i.e. of the relation between the two. Other questions are closely linked with it, such as the place accorded to reason in the formulation of Christian truth; but it will be well to confine ourselves to the central issue. God Himself, all the early theologians acknowledged, was the ultimate author of the revelation; but He had committed it to prophets and inspired lawgivers, above all to the apostles who were eye-witnesses of the incarnate Word, and they had passed it on to the Church. Hence, when asked where the authentic faith was to be found, their answer was clear and unequivocal: in a general way it was contained in the Church's continuous tradition of teaching, and more concretely in the Holy Scriptures. These were in fact the twin—as we shall see, overlapping—authorities to which Christians looked for the confirmation of their beliefs. By itself, however, this is a bald statement, and calls for a good deal of elucidation if its implications are to be grasped. What books, for example, were accepted as Scripture, and how did the Church determine her sacred canon? And what principles of exegesis did she employ? Again, the notion of tradition needs more precise definition, and some estimate must be formed of the store set by it at different epochs. We must also ask how far, if at all, tradition and Scripture counted as independent of, and supplementary to, each other. And presupposed in the whole inquiry is the deeper question of the doctrinal *magisterium* claimed for, and exercised by, the Church.

The former set of questions, concerned with the Bible and its interpretation, will be the theme of the following chapter. In the present one we shall examine more closely the Church's constant appeal to Scripture and tradition, and in the course of our inquiry shall seek to explain what she understood by tradition. At the threshold, however, the reader should be placed on his guard against an ambiguity inherent in the word. In present-day idiom 'tradition' denotes the body of unwritten doctrine handed down in the Church, or the handing down of such doctrine, and so tends to be contrasted with Scripture. In the language of the fathers, as indeed of the New Testament,[1] the term of course conveyed this idea of transmission, and eventually the modern usage became regular. But its primary significance (cf. παραδιδόναι; *tradere*), viz. authoritative delivery, was originally to the fore and always remained prominent. Hence by tradition the fathers usually mean doctrine which the Lord or His apostles committed to the Church, irrespective of

[1] E.g. *Luke* 1, 2; *1 Cor.* 11, 2; 11, 23; 15, 3; *Jude* 3.

whether it was handed down orally or in documents, and in the earlier centuries at any rate they prefer to employ other words or phrases to designate the Church's unwritten traditional teaching. The ancient meaning of the term is well illustrated by Athanasius's reference[1] to 'the actual original tradition, teaching and faith of the Catholic Church, which the Lord bestowed, the apostles proclaimed and the fathers safeguarded'.

Good

2. The Primitive Period

The generations stretching from the apostolic age to the middle of the second century have a special interest for our inquiry. This springs from the fact that, although the New Testament books were already in existence, there was as yet no officially sanctioned New Testament canon. Whence then did the Church draw her teaching, and how did she assess its soundness? For an answer we naturally look to the writings of the so-called Apostolic Fathers (Clement of Rome, Ignatius, Polycarp, the author of *2 Clement*, 'Barnabas', Hermas) and the Greek Apologists (Aristides, Justin, Tatian, Athenagoras, Theophilus). For all these Christianity seems to have implied a complex of belief and practice (in Clement's[2] phrase, 'the rule of our tradition', or in Justin's,[3] 'following God and the teaching derived from Him') which in the final resort went back to Christ Himself. But if He was the supreme teacher,[4] the immediately accessible authorities both for the facts about His Person and for His message were (a) the prophets, who had foreseen every detail of His ministry, and (b) the apostles, who had worked with Him and whom He had commissioned. This twofold appeal to the united witness of the Old Testament and the apostles was characteristic of the age; it is aptly illustrated by Polycarp's summons[5] to the Philippians to accept as their standard Christ Himself along with 'the apostles who preached the gospel to us and the prophets who announced our Lord's coming in advance'.

OT + Apostles used by early Fathers

---

[1] *Ad Serap.* I, 28.   [2] 7, 2.   [3] *Dial.* 80, 3.
[4] Cf. Justin, *1 apol.* 12, 9.   [5] *Phil.* 6, 3.

The importance of the Old Testament as a doctrinal norm in
the primitive Church cannot be exaggerated. A fuller discussion must be postponed until the next chapter; three points only
need be established at this stage. First, the doctrinal authority
ascribed to it was based on the apparently unquestioning assumption that, correctly interpreted, it was a Christian book,
and that the prophets in particular were really testifying to
Christ and His glory. Justin's insistence[1] that the Jewish
Scriptures did not belong to the Jews but to the Christians was
universally shared. Secondly, this assumption was only rendered
possible because Christians were using, consciously or unconsciously, a particular method of exegesis. This method, again,
will come in for treatment later; for the moment it is sufficient
to remark that it was not overtly contained in, or suggested by,
the Old Testament itself. The Apologists[2] who claimed that
they had become Christians merely by studying the Scriptures
(i.e. the Old Testament) were clearly going beyond what
the facts warranted. Obviously they were reading them with
eyes enlightened by the specifically Christian revelation; and
'Barnabas' admits as much when he describes[3] his Christo-
centric exegesis as a *gnosis*. But, thirdly, this principle of interpretation was no invention of the early second century. The
apostles, as we shall see, had employed it, and there is every
reason to suppose that our Lord Himself set the precedent—a
fact which Justin explicitly acknowledges.[4] In the days of the
Apostolic Fathers and the Apologists it was already traditional
in the Church, a tradition for which (again Justin is the first to
avow[5] it) the Church was on the human plane indebted to the
apostles.

The parallel doctrinal norm, the testimony of the apostles,
was equally important in theory, and of course more important
in fact. 'The apostles', wrote[6] Clement, 'received the gospel
for us from the Lord Jesus Christ. . . . Armed therefore with
their charge, and having been fully assured through the resur-

---

[1] *1 apol.* 32, 2; *dial.* 29, 2.
[2] E.g. Justin, *dial.* 8, 1; Tatian, *ad Graec.* 29.
[3] 6, 9; 9, 8; 10, 10; 13, 7.   [4] *1 apol.* 50, 12.
[5] Ib. 49, 5.   [6] 42.

rection of our Lord Jesus Christ and confirmed in the word of
God with full conviction of the Holy Spirit, they went forth
with the glad tidings.' By Justin's[1] time the idea that the
Church's message rested upon the apostles' witness to Christ
and the instructions He had given them before and after His
resurrection had been more fully worked out. It was through
the apostles, Hermas stated,[2] that the Son of God was preached
throughout the world. Hence we are not surprised to find
Ignatius,[3] a generation earlier, setting up conformity to the
Lord and His apostles as an ideal; it makes no difference that he
probably had ethical instruction primarily in mind. A practical
expression of this attitude was the keen interest taken in the
apostles' personal reminiscences of Christ. Papias, for example,
did his best[4] to discover His exact teaching by making inquiries
of 'the elders'. A further evidence of it is the high prestige enjoyed by the Pauline epistles and the gospels. Although they
had not been canonized, the number of citations from them
in this period is quite remarkable. Polycarp, for example, regarded[5] St. Paul's letter to the Philippians as the foundation-
stone of their faith; and for Justin[6] the gospels owed their
authority to their being the 'memoirs' (ἀπομνημονεύματα)
of the apostles. To them, too, he traced[7] the explanation of why
baptism was necessary, and the manner of celebrating the
eucharist.

There is no reason to infer, however, that the primitive
Church regarded the apostolic testimony as confined to written
documents emanating from, or attributed to, the apostles.
Logically, as it must have done chronologically, the testimony
stood prior to the documents, and it would be more correct to
say that the latter were valued precisely because they were held
to enshrine the former. Admittedly there is no evidence for
beliefs or practices current in the period which were not
vouched for in the books later known as the New Testament.
But there is equally nothing to suggest, and general probability

---

[1] E.g. 1 apol. 42, 4; 50, 12; 53, 3; 67, 7; dial. 53, 1.   [2] Sim. 9, 17, 1.
[3] E.g. Eph. 11, 2; Magn. 13, 1; Trall. 7, 1.
[4] Cf. Eusebius, hist. eccl. 3, 39, 3 f.   [5] Phil. 3, 2.
[6] 1 apol. 66, 3; dial. 103, 8.   [7] 1 apol. 61, 9; 66, 1-3.

makes it unlikely, that Christian teachers had these books specifically in mind on the majority of occasions when they referred to the apostolic testimony. It is much more plausible that they were thinking generally of the common body of facts and doctrines, definite enough in outline though with varying emphases, which found expression in the Church's day-to-day preaching, liturgical action and catechetical instruction, just as much as in its formal documents. It is a commonplace that the New Testament writers themselves presupposed, and on occasion quoted summaries of, this outline message or 'kerygma', which apparently existed in various forms. A similar outline seems to have been available to the writers of our period, and they, too (formal creeds were still lacking), frequently reproduce echoes of it.[1] As often as not the background of these appears to be the Church's living liturgical and catechetical tradition. It was this 'pattern of teaching',[2] whether set down in apostolic letters or gospels or embodied in the Church's propaganda or liturgical life, together with the principles of Old Testament interpretation referred to above, which they regarded as 'the teaching derived from Christ's apostles'.[3]

Three further points should be noticed. First, while Scripture (i.e. the Old Testament) and the apostolic testimony were formally independent of each other, these fathers seem to have treated their contents as virtually coincident. What the apostles saw and proclaimed as eye-witnesses, the prophets testified to beforehand in minutest detail; there was no item in the message of the former which, if one but searched the Scriptures, the prophets could not be shown to have foreseen. Secondly, the apostolic testimony had not yet come to be known as 'tradition'. Though Clement spoke[4] of 'the rule of our tradition', the term (παράδοσις) was of rare occurrence in this period. Justin used[5] it only once, and then to indicate the tradition of Jewish teachers. The cognate verb (παραδιδόναι) was much more frequent, but possessed no specialized meaning. Polycarp

[1] Cf. Ignatius, *Eph.* 18, 2; *Trall.* 9; *Smyrn.* 1, 1 f.; Polycarp, *Phil.* 2, 1; Justin *1 apol.* 13; 61, 3; 61, 10; 65, 3; 67, 2; *dial.* 63, 1; 85, 2; 126, 1; 132, 1.
[2] *Rom.* 6, 17.   [3] Justin, *1 apol.* 53, 3.
[4] 7, 2.   [5] *Dial.* 38, 2.

could speak[1] of 'the word transmitted from the beginning', and Justin of the apostles 'delivering' to the Gentiles the prophecies about Jesus,[2] or 'handing down' the institution of the eucharist.[3] More often than not, however, the context has nothing to do with Christianity; and where it has, the reference is sometimes to Christ Himself, sometimes[4] even to teaching contained in Scripture. The truth is that, although the idea was present in embryo, no single term had been earmarked to denote tradition, i.e. the authoritative handing down of doctrine, or the doctrine so handed down.

Thirdly, hints begin to appear of the theory that the Church's ministers, in virtue of their endowment with the Spirit, were the divinely authorized custodians of the apostolic teaching. Clement, for example, though not explicit on the point, seems to imply[5] that the hierarchy which succeeded the apostles inherited the gospel message which they had been commissioned to preach. The immense stress which Ignatius placed on loyalty to the episcopate finds its explanation in the fact that he regarded the bishop as the appointed guarantor of purity of doctrine. In 2 Clement[6] strict obedience to the presbyters is inculcated on the ground that their task is to preach the faith, and that their instructions are identical with those of Christ Himself.

3. Irenaeus and Tertullian

In the following half-century the Church's estimate of her doctrinal norms underwent certain adjustments. In the first place, while the Old Testament lost none of its prestige as an organ of revelation, the apostolic testimony as such was promoted in the minds of Christians to a position of supreme authority. This shift of perspective was, of course, assisted and indeed made possible by the recognition of the New Testament as fully canonical and as entitled to rank alongside the Old as inspired Scripture. Secondly, the distinction between Scripture and the Church's living tradition as co-ordinate channels of this

---

[1] Phil. 7, 2.   [2] 1 apol. 49, 5.   [3] Ib. 66, 3.
[4] E.g. Justin, 1 apol. 53, 6; dial. 42, 1.   [5] Cf. 42.   [6] 17.

apostolic testimony became more clearly appreciated, and enhanced importance began to be attached to the latter. This development was largely the by-product of the great struggle between Catholicism and the Gnostic sects which was now fully engaged. Not only did the Gnostics exploit Scripture to their own ends, but one of their techniques[1] was to appeal, in support of their speculations, to an alleged secret apostolic tradition to which they claimed to have access.

This new and more mature position is mirrored, with minor differences of emphasis, in the writings of Irenaeus (*fl.* 180) and Tertullian (*c.* 160–*c.* 220). For both[2] of them Christ Himself was the ultimate source of Christian doctrine, being the truth, the Word by Whom the Father had been revealed; but He had entrusted this revelation to His apostles, and it was through them alone that knowledge of it could be obtained. 'Through none other', wrote[3] Irenaeus, 'than those by whom the gospel reached us have we learned the plan of our salvation'; while for Tertullian[4] what was believed and preached in the churches was absolutely authoritative because it was the selfsame revelation which they had received from the apostles, the apostles from Christ, and Christ from God. Elsewhere[5] he insisted that Christians must not pick and choose doctrines according to their whims; their sole authorities were the apostles, who had themselves faithfully transmitted Christ's teaching. Both on occasion described this original message as tradition, using the word to denote the teaching delivered by the apostles, without any implied contrast between tradition and Scripture. So Irenaeus claims[6] that, however much Christians may differ in language or mental capacity, the 'force of the tradition' (i.e. the 'faith' or 'preaching' communicated by the apostles) remains one and the same; while Tertullian can refer[7] to the whole body of apostolic doctrine, whether delivered orally or in epistles, as *apostolorum traditio* or *apostolica traditio*.

---

[1] Cf. Irenaeus, *haer.* 3, 2, 1; Clement Alex., *strom.* 7, 17, 106–8; Epiphanius, *haer.* 33, 7, 9.
[2] Cf. Irenaeus, *haer.* 3, praef.; 3, 5, 1; Tertullian, *de praescr.* 13.
[3] Ib. 3, 1, 1. [4] Ib. 21. [5] Ib. 6: cf. 37.
[6] Ib. 1, 10, 2: cf. 5, 20, 1. [7] Ib. 21; *c. Marc.* 1, 21; 4 5.

But where in practice was this apostolic testimony or tradition to be found? It was no longer possible to resort, as Papias and earlier writers had done, to personal reminiscences of the apostles. The most obvious answer was that the apostles had committed it orally to the Church, where it had been handed down from generation to generation. Irenaeus believed that this was the case, stating[1] that the Church preserved the tradition inherited from the apostles and passed it on to her children. It was, he thought, a living tradition which was, in principle, independent of written documents; and he pointed[2] to barbarian tribes which 'received this faith without letters'. Unlike the alleged secret tradition of the Gnostics, it was entirely public and open, having been entrusted by the apostles to their successors, and by these in turn to those who followed them, and was visible in the Church for all who cared to look for it.[3] It was his argument with the Gnostics which led him to apply[4] the word 'tradition', in a novel and restricted sense, specifically to the Church's oral teaching as distinct from that contained in Scripture. For practical purposes this tradition could be regarded as finding expression in what he called 'the canon of the truth'. By this he meant, as his frequent allusions[5] to and citations from it prove, a condensed summary, fluid in its wording but fixed in content, setting out the key-points of the Christian revelation in the form of a rule. Irenaeus makes two further points. First, the identity of oral tradition with the original revelation is guaranteed by the unbroken succession of bishops in the great sees going back lineally to the apostles.[6] Secondly, an additional safeguard is supplied by the Holy Spirit, for the message was committed to the Church, and the Church is the home of the Spirit.[7] Indeed, the Church's bishops are on his view Spirit-endowed men who have been vouchsafed 'an infallible charism of truth' (*charisma veritatis certum*[8]).

On the other hand, Irenaeus took it for granted that the

---

[1] *Haer.* 5, praef.   [2] Ib. 3, 4, 1 f.
[3] Ib. 3, 2–5.   [4] Ib. 3, 2–5 (16 times).
[5] E.g. ib. 1, 10, 1 f.; 1, 22, 1; 5, 20, 1; *dem.* 6.
[6] Cf. *haer.* 3, 2, 2; 3, 3, 3; 3, 4, 1.
[7] E.g. ib. 3, 24, 1.   [8] Ib. 4, 26, 2: cf. 4, 26, 5.

apostolic tradition had also been deposited in written documents. As he says,[1] what the apostles at first proclaimed by word of mouth, they afterwards by God's will conveyed to us in Scriptures. Like the Apologists, he held[2] that the whole life, passion and teaching of Christ had been foreshadowed in the Old Testament; but the New was in his eyes the written formulation of the apostolic tradition (cf. ἐγγράφως παραδιδόναι[3]). For this reason his test for books belonging to it was not simply Church custom but apostolicity,[4] i.e. the fact that they had been composed by apostles or followers of the apostles, and so could be relied upon to contain the apostolic testimony. The difficulty was, of course, that heretics were liable to read a different meaning out of Scripture than the Church; but Irenaeus was satisfied[5] that, provided the Bible was taken as a whole, its teaching was self-evident. The heretics who misinterpreted it only did so because, disregarding its underlying unity, they seized upon isolated passages and rearranged them to suit their own ideas.[6] Scripture must be interpreted in the light of its fundamental ground-plan, viz. the original revelation itself. For that reason correct exegesis was the prerogative of the Church, where the apostolic tradition or doctrine which was the key to Scripture had been kept intact.[7]

Did Irenaeus then subordinate Scripture to unwritten tradition? This inference has been commonly drawn, but it issues from a somewhat misleading antithesis. Its plausibility depends on such considerations as (a) that, in controversy with the Gnostics, tradition rather than Scripture seemed to be his final court of appeal, and (b) that he apparently relied upon tradition to establish the true exegesis of Scripture. But a careful analysis of his *Adverus háereses* reveals that, while the Gnostics' appeal to their supposed secret tradition forced him to stress the superiority of the Church's public tradition, his real defence of orthodoxy

---

[1] *Haer.* 3, 1, 1. [2] Ib. 4, 33, 10-14.
[3] Ib. 3, 1, 1: cf. 3, 1, 2; 3, 10, 6; 3, 14, 2.
[4] Cf. ib. 1, 9, 2; 3, 1, 1; 3, 3, 4; 3, 10, 1; 3, 10, 6; etc.
[5] Ib. 2, 27, 2. [6] Ib. 1, 8, 1; 1, 9, 1-4.
[7] Ib. 4, 26, 5; 4, 32, 1; 5, 20, 2.

was founded on Scripture.[1] Indeed, tradition itself, on his view, was confirmed by Scripture, which was 'the foundation and pillar of our faith'.[2] Secondly, Irenaeus admittedly suggested[3] that a firm grasp of 'the canon of the truth' received at baptism would prevent a man from distorting the sense of Scripture. But this 'canon', so far from being something distinct from Scripture, was simply a condensation of the message contained in it. Being by its very nature normative in form, it provided a man with a handy clue to Scripture, whose very ramifications played into the hands of heretics. The whole point of his teaching was, in fact, that Scripture and the Church's un-written tradition are identical in content, both being vehicles of the revelation. If tradition as conveyed in the 'canon' is a more trustworthy guide, this is not because it comprises truths other than those revealed in Scripture, but because the true tenor of the apostolic message is there unambiguously set out.

Tertullian's attitude does not differ from Irenaeus's in any important respect. He was an innovator, it is true, in extending the meaning of 'tradition' to cover what had been customary in the Church for long generations. In this sense practices like the triple renunciation and triple immersion at baptism, the reception of the eucharist in the early morning, the prohibition of kneeling on Sundays and at Eastertide, and the sign of the cross could be described[4] as traditions; one tradition might even be said[5] to be at variance with another. In its primary sense, however, the apostolic, evangelical or Catholic tradition[6] stood for the faith delivered by the apostles, and he never contrasted tradition so understood with Scripture. Indeed, it was en-shrined in Scripture, for the apostles subsequently wrote down their oral preaching in epistles.[7] For this reason Scripture has absolute authority; whatever it teaches is necessarily true,[8] and woe betide him who accepts doctrines not discoverable in it.[9]

[1] Cf. ib. 2, 35, 4; 3, praef.; 3, 2, 1; 3, 5, 1; 4, praef., 1; 5, praef.
[2] Ib. 3, praef.; 3, 1, 1.   [3] Ib. 1, 9, 4.   [4] De cor. 3 f.
[5] De virg. vel. 2.   [6] C. Marc. 4, 5; 5, 19; de monog. 2.
[7] De praescr. 21.   [8] De carne Chr. 3; adv. Prax. 29.
[9] Adv. Hermog. 22; de carne Chr. 6.

But Tertullian did not confine the apostolic tradition to the
New Testament; even if Scripture were to be set on one side, it
would still be found in the doctrine publicly proclaimed by the
churches. Like Irenaeus, he found[1] the surest test of the authenticity of this doctrine in the fact that the churches had been
founded by, and were continuously linked with, the apostles;
and as a further guarantee he added[2] their otherwise inexplicable unanimity. He was emphatic[3] that no secret tradition
existed, and that it was incredible that the apostles did not
know, or failed to pass on, the revelation in its entirety.

This unwritten tradition he considered to be virtually
identical with 'the rule of faith' (regula fidei), which he preferred
to Scripture as a standard when disputing with Gnostics. By
this he did not mean, as scholars have sometimes imagined, a
formal creed, but rather the intrinsic shape and pattern of the
revelation itself. His citations[4] from it show that, fully formulated, it made explicit the cardinal truths about God the Father,
Jesus Christ and the Holy Spirit. Thus the regula was for him
what 'the canon of the truth' was for Irenaeus, although he
made more use of the concept. He states[5] explicitly that the
rule has been handed down by Christ through the apostles, and
implies[6] that it can be used to test whether a man is a Christian
or not. Further, the regula points the way to the correct exegesis of Scripture. Like Irenaeus, Tertullian is convinced[7] that
Scripture is consonant in all its parts, and that its meaning should
be clear if it is read as a whole. But where controversy with
heretics breaks out, the right interpretation can be found only
where the true Christian faith and discipline have been maintained, i.e. in the Church.[8] The heretics, he complained,[9] were
able to make Scripture say what they liked because they dis-
regarded the regula.

Not surprisingly, many students have deduced that Tertullian made tradition (i.e. the Church's unwritten teaching as

---

[1] E.g. de praescr. 21; 32; c. Marc. 4, 5.   [2] De praescr. 28.
[3] Ib. 22; 27.   [4] Cf. de praescr. 13; de virg. vel. 1; adv. Prax. 2.
[5] Apol. 47, 10.   [6] De praescr. 37.
[7] E.g. ib. 9 f.; de resurr. 21; adv. Prax. 26.   [8] De praescr. 19.
[9] De pud. 8: cf. de praescr. 12; adv. Prax. 20.

declared in the *regula*) a more ultimate norm than the Bible. His true position, however, was rather subtler and approximated closely to that of Irenaeus. He was certainly profoundly convinced[1] of the futility of arguing with heretics merely on the basis of Scripture. The skill and success with which they twisted its plain meaning made it impossible to reach any decisive conclusion in that field. He was also satisfied, and made the point even more forcibly than Irenaeus, that the indispensable key to Scripture belonged exclusively to the Church, which in the *regula* had preserved the apostles' testimony in its original shape. But these ideas, expounded in his *De praescriptione*, were not intended to imply that Scripture was in any way subordinate in authority or insufficient in content. His major premiss remained that of Irenaeus, viz. that the one divine revelation was contained in its fulness both in the Bible and in the Church's continuous public witness. If he stressed the latter medium even more than Irenaeus, elaborating the argument that it was inconceivable that the churches could have made any mistake in transmitting the pure apostolic doctrine, his reason was that in discussion with heretics it possessed certain tactical advantages. Being by definition normative, the *regula* set out the purport of the gospel in a form about which there could be no debate.

4. *The Third and Fourth Centuries*

With two main differences the attitude to Scripture and tradition which we saw emerging in the previous section became classic in the Church of the third and fourth centuries. These differences were: (a) with the passing of the Gnostic menace, the hesitation sometimes evinced by Irenaeus, and to a rather greater degree by Tertullian, about appealing directly to Scripture disappeared; and (b) as a result of developments in the Church's institutional life the basis of tradition became broader and more explicit. The supreme doctrinal authority remained, of course, the original revelation given by Christ

[1] *De praescr.* 15; 19; 37.

42   PROLEGOMENA

and communicated to the Church by His apostles. This was
the divine or apostolic 'tradition' (παράδοσις; *traditio*) in the
strict sense of the word. It was with reference to this that
Cyprian in the third century could speak[1] of 'the root and
source of the dominical tradition', or of 'the fountain-head and
source of the divine tradition', and that Athanasius in the
fourth could point[2] to 'the tradition . . . which the Lord gave
and the apostles proclaimed' as the Church's foundation-stone.
That this was embodied, however, in Holy Scripture, and
found a parallel outlet in the Church's general unwritten
teaching and liturgical life, was taken for granted, and the use
of the term 'tradition', with or without such qualifications as
'ecclesiastical' or 'of the fathers', to describe this latter medium
now became increasingly common.

There is little need to dwell on the absolute authority accorded to Scripture as a doctrinal norm. It was the Bible,
declared[3] Clement of Alexandria about A.D. 200, which, as
interpreted by the Church, was the source of Christian teaching. His greater disciple Origen was a thorough-going Biblicist
who appealed[4] again and again to Scripture as the decisive
criterion of dogma. The Church drew her catechetical material,
he stated,[5] from the prophets, the gospels and the apostles'
writings; her faith, he suggested,[6] was buttressed by Holy
Scripture supported by common sense. 'The holy and inspired Scriptures', wrote[7] Athanasius a century later, 'are fully
sufficient for the proclamation of the truth'; while his contemporary, Cyril of Jerusalem, laid it down[8] that 'with regard
to the divine and saving mysteries of faith no doctrine, however trivial, may be taught without the backing of the divine
Scriptures. . . . For our saving faith derives its force, not from
capricious reasonings, but from what may be proved out of the
Bible.' Later in the same century John Chrysostom bade[9] his
congregation seek no other teacher than the oracles of God;
everything was straightforward and clear in the Bible, and the

---

[1] *Ep.* 63, 1; 74, 10.   [2] *Ad Serap.* 1, 28.   [3] *Strom.* 7, 16, 93.
[4] E.g. *de princ.* 1, praef., 10; 1, 5, 4; 2, 5, 3.   [5] *C. Cels.* 3, 15.
[6] *De princ.* 3, 6, 6.   [7] *C. gent.* 1: cf. *de syn.* 6.   [8] *Cat.* 4, 17.
[9] *In Col. hom.* 9, 1; *in 2 Thess. hom.* 3, 4 (PG 62, 361; 485).

sum of necessary knowledge could be extracted from it. In the West Augustine declared[1] that 'in the plain teaching of Scripture we find all that concerns our belief and moral conduct'; while a little later Vincent of Lérins († c. 450) took it as an axiom[2] the Scriptural canon was 'sufficient, and more than sufficient, for all purposes'.

Meanwhile certain shifts of emphasis are discernible in the concept of tradition. Early third-century writers, like Clement of Alexandria and Origen, continued to use language about it closely akin to that of Irenaeus and Tertullian, and spoke of 'the ecclesiastical canon' or 'the canon of faith'. The position of both of them, it is true, is complicated by the fact that, in addition to the Church's public tradition, they believed they had access to a secret tradition of doctrine. Clement, who called it a γνῶσις or παράδοσις, regarded[3] it as stemming from the apostles and including quasi-Gnostic speculations, while for Origen[4] it seems to have consisted of an esoteric theology based on the Bible; in both cases it was reserved for the intellectual élite of the Church. Although Clement seems to have confused his secret Gnostic tradition with 'the ecclesiastical canon', he had clear ideas about the latter, and defined[5] it as 'the congruence and harmony of the law and the prophets with the covenant delivered at the Lord's *parousia*'. According to Origen,[6] the rule of faith, or canon, was the body of beliefs currently accepted by ordinary Christians; or again it could stand[7] for the whole content of the faith. In his usage it was equivalent to what he called 'the ecclesiastical preaching' (κήρυγμα[8]), and he meant by it the Christian faith as taught in the Church of his day and handed down from the apostles. Though its contents coincided with those of the Bible, it was formally independent of the Bible, and indeed included the principles of Biblical interpretation.[9]

[1] *De doct. christ.* 2, 14.   [2] *Common.* 2.
[3] E.g. *strom.* 6, 7, 61; 6, 8, 68; 6, 15, 131.
[4] E.g. *c. Cels.* 1, 7; *in Rom.* 6, 8; *hom. in Ios.* 23, 4; *comm. in Matt.* 10, 6.
[5] *Ib.* 6, 15, 125.   [6] *In Ioh.* 13, 16, 98.
[7] *Frag. in 1 Cor.* (in *Journ. Theol. Stud.* x, p. 42).
[8] *De princ.* 3, 1, 1.   [9] Cf. esp. *ib.* 4, 2, 2.

After Clement and Origen the idea of a 'canon of faith' gradually lost the prominence it had previously enjoyed. Other media were coming to be recognized as depositories of the Church's living doctrinal inheritance. One of these was the liturgy, which in the third century was acquiring a considerable measure of fixity. The title of Hippolytus's famous collection of services, *The Apostolic Tradition*, dating from the early third century, and also that of the much earlier *Didache* ('The Teaching of the Lord through the Twelve Apostles'), are reminders that the Church's whole liturgical apparatus, including the baptismal and eucharistic rites which entered so deeply into the ordinary Christian's devotional life, was regarded as emanating from the apostles and so as reflecting their testimony. Formal creeds, based on the solemn questions and answers at baptism and the elaborate catechetical instruction which preceded it, were now coming into regular use. The current title of the Western baptismal creed, *symbolum apostolorum*, and the widely accepted story[1] of its compilation by the Twelve, testify to the universal assumption that these brief formulae were crystallizations of the primitive apostolic doctrine. Synods and councils, particularly the ecumenical council of Nicaea (A.D. 325), played an increasingly important role after the middle of the third century, and the reverence paid to the credal statements they promulgated stemmed from the belief that they bore witness to and made explicit the faith once delivered to the saints. In close conjunction with this the practice of appealing to the orthodox fathers, whether as individuals or assembled in synods, began to develop. If the theory, so dear to Irenaeus and Tertullian, that the apostolically founded sees could be relied upon to have preserved the apostles' witness in its purity had faded, its place was being taken by a growing consciousness of the magisterial authority of the Catholic Church. The Roman church in particular (the evidence must be reserved to a later chapter) regarded itself, and was regarded by many, as in a special sense the appointed custodian and mouthpiece of the apostolic tradition.

[1] Cf. *explan. symb. ad init.* (PL 17, 1155 f.); Rufinus, *in symb. apost.* 2.

A few illustrations must suffice. Eusebius's statement,[1] when submitting his creed at the council of Nicaea, that it was based on teaching received from his episcopal predecessors, in the course of catechetical instruction and at baptism, [as well as on the Bible,] exactly reflects contemporary ideas about doctrinal authority. It was natural for him, too, when looking for depositories of the apostles' witness, to single out[2] a line of orthodox worthies of the past—Hegesippus, Dionysius of Corinth, Melito, Irenaeus, etc. So Athanasius, disputing with the Arians, claimed[3] that his own doctrine had been handed down from father to father, whereas they could not produce a single respectable witness to theirs. The Nicene faith embodied the truth which had been believed from the beginning. The fathers of Nicaea, he declared,[4] had merely ratified and passed on the teaching which Christ bestowed and the apostles proclaimed; anyone who deviated from it could not count as a Christian. A century later, as Cyril's correspondence with Nestorius and the Chalcedonian Definition reveal, the Nicene council and its creed enjoyed the prestige of unimpeachable authorities. On the other hand, Basil made[5] the liturgical custom of baptizing in the threefold name a pivot in his argument for the coequality of the Spirit with Father and Son, pleading[6] that the apostolic witness was conveyed to the Church in the mysteries as well as in Scripture, and that it was apostolic to abide by this unwritten tradition. So when Gregory of Nyssa desired to substantiate the unique generation of the Son, he explained[7] that it was enough that 'we have the tradition descending to us from the fathers, like an inheritance transmitted from the apostles along the line of holy persons who succeeded them'. In other writers, like Gregory of Nazianzus,[8] Epiphanius[9] and Chrysostom,[10] the contrast between what is handed down in writing (ἐγγράφως) and unwritten tradition (ἀγράφως) is clearly brought out. Epiphanius, it is noteworthy,

---

[1] *Ep. ad Caes.* 2 (PG 20, 1537). [2] *Hist. eccl.* 4, 21.
[3] *De decret. Nic. syn.* 27. [4] *Ad Afr.* 1; *ad Serap.* 1, 28.
[5] *De Spir. sanct.* 26; 28; 67; 71. [6] Ib. 66; 71.
[7] *C. Eunom.* 4 (PG 45, 653). [8] *Ep.* 101 (PG 37, 176).
[9] *Haer.* 61, 6. [10] *In 2 Thess. hom.* 4, 2 (PG 62, 488).

evidently regarded[1] the Roman church (his attitude was not singular) as having preserved the apostolic rule of faith uniquely intact; but the supreme expression of it, he thought,[2] was the creed sealed by the fathers gathered in session at Nicaea.

Yet, if the concept of tradition was expanded and made more concrete in these ways, the estimate of its position *vis-à-vis* Scripture as a doctrinal norm remained basically unaltered. The clearest token of the prestige enjoyed by the latter is the fact that almost the entire theological effort of the fathers, whether their aims were polemical or constructive, was expended upon what amounted to the exposition of the Bible. Further, it was everywhere taken for granted that, for any doctrine to win acceptance, it had first to establish its Scriptural basis. A striking illustration is the difficulty which champions of novel theological terms like ὁμοούσιος ('of the same substance'), or again ἀγέννητος ('ingenerate' or 'self-existent') and ἄναρχος ('without beginning'), experienced in getting these descriptions of the Son's relationship to the Father, or of God's eternal being, generally admitted. They had to meet the damning objection, advanced in conservative as well as heretical quarters, that they were not to be found in the Bible. In the end they could only quell opposition by pointing out (Athanasius[3] in the one case, and Gregory of Nazianzus[4] in the other) that, even if the terms themselves were non-Scriptural, the meaning they conveyed was exactly that of Holy Writ. The creed itself, according to Cyril of Jerusalem,[5] Augustine[6] and Cassian,[7] was a compendium of Scripture. An exception to this general attitude might seem to be Basil's reliance, mentioned above, upon tradition as embedded in the liturgy, rather than upon Scripture, to demonstrate the full deity of the Holy Spirit. Even he, however, makes it crystal clear, in the very discussion in question, that there is no contradiction between unwritten tradition and the gospel,[8] for in their traditionally transmitted teaching the fathers have only been following what Scripture itself

---

[1] *Haer*. 27, 6: cf. Ambrose, *ep*. 42, 5; Rufinus, *comm. in symb. apost*. 3.
[2] *Ancor*. 118 f. [3] E.g. *de decret. Nic. syn*. 21.
[4] *Or*. 31, 23 f. [5] *Cat*. 5, 12. [6] *Serm. ad cat*. 1.
[7] *De incarn*. 6, 3. [8] *De Spir. sanct*. 66.

implies.[1] Indeed, all the instances of unwritten tradition lacking Scriptural support which the early theologians mention will be found, on examination, to refer to matters of observance and practice (e.g. triple immersion in baptism; turning East for prayer) rather than of doctrine as such, although sometimes they are matters (e.g. infant baptism; prayers for the dead) in which doctrine is involved.

On the other hand, the ancient idea that the Church alone, in virtue of being the home of the Spirit and having preserved the authentic apostolic testimony in her rule of faith, liturgical action and general witness, possesses the indispensable key to Scripture, continued to operate as powerfully as in the days of Irenaeus and Tertullian. Clement, for example, blamed[2] the mistakes of heretics on their habit of 'resisting the divine tradition', by which he meant their incorrect interpretation of Scripture; the true interpretation, he believed, was an apostolic and ecclesiastical inheritance. An examination of Origen's references to 'the ecclesiastical canon' suggests that, while it was closely connected with and found confirmation in Holy Scripture, it also threw light on the true intent of the Scriptural writers. Athanasius himself, after dwelling on the entire adequacy of Scripture, went on to emphasize[3] the desirability of having sound teachers to expound it. Against the Arians he flung the charge[4] that they would never have made shipwreck of the faith had they held fast as a sheet-anchor to the σκοπὸς ἐκκλησιαστικός, meaning by that the Church's peculiar and traditionally handed down grasp of the purport of revelation. Hilary insisted[5] that only those who accept the Church's teaching can comprehend what the Bible is getting at. According to Augustine,[6] its doubtful or ambiguous passages need to be cleared up by 'the rule of faith'; it was, moreover, the authority of the Church alone which in his eyes[7] guaranteed its veracity.

It should be unnecessary to accumulate further evidence. Throughout the whole period Scripture and tradition ranked as complementary authorities, media different in form but

[1] Ib. 16.   [2] Strom. 7, 16, 103.   [3] C. gent. 1.
[4] C. Ar. 3, 58.   [5] In Matt. 13, 1.   [6] De doct. christ. 3, 2.
[7] C. ep. Manich. 6: cf. de doct. christ. 2, 12; c. Faust. Manich. 22, 79.

Incredibly well said

coincident in content. To inquire which counted as superior or more ultimate is to pose the question in misleading and anachronistic terms. If Scripture was abundantly sufficient in principle, tradition was recognized as the surest clue to its interpretation, for in tradition the Church retained, as a legacy from the apostles which was embedded in all the organs of her institutional life, an unerring grasp of the real purport and meaning of the revelation to which Scripture and tradition alike bore witness.

5. The Appeal to the Fathers

One final elaboration of the argument from tradition must be mentioned. In the previous section we noticed the growing tendency, in the fourth century, to appeal to the orthodox fathers of the past, as individuals or assembled in councils, as custodians and interpreters of the Church's tradition. In the fifth century the practice was greatly extended, explicit and even formal recognition being given to the authority of the succession of venerated teachers. As an offshoot of this the compilation of lists of fathers of unimpeachable prestige, with select quotations from their writings, became a favourite technique in theological debate.

Mary mother of God

For Augustine the authority of 'plenary councils' was 'most healthy'.[1] Writing to Egyptian monks in defence of the Blessed Virgin's claim to be called mother of God, Cyril of Alexandria counselled[2] them to follow in the steps of the holy fathers, since it was they who had preserved the faith handed down from the apostles and had taught Christians to believe aright. Again, he was prepared to affirm[3] that the correct doctrine of the Trinity had been expounded by 'the wisdom of the holy fathers'. As against Nestorius, he appealed[4] to 'the holy, world-wide Church and the venerable fathers themselves', claiming that the Holy Spirit spoke in them. For the more formal justification of his Christological position, he pre-

[1] *Ep.* 54, 1.
[2] *Ad monach.* (PG 77, 12; 13).   [3] *In Ioh. ev.* 4, 11 (PG 74, 216).
[4] *Adv. Nest.* 4, 2.

pared elaborate dossiers of patristic quotations, inserting them in his controversial writings[1] and producing them at the council of Ephesus.[2] A contemporary of a very different school of thought, the Antiochene Theodoret, adopted exactly the same position, speaking[3] of the orthodox faith as having been transmitted to us, 'not only by the apostles and prophets, but also by those who interpreted their writings—Ignatius, Eustathius, Athanasius, Basil, Gregory, John and the other luminaries of the world—and also by the holy fathers who before these assembled at Nicaea'. He added that any who deviated from their teaching must be labelled enemies of the truth; and elsewhere[4] explained that the Holy Spirit inspired the fathers to elucidate the darker passages of Scripture. He, too, compiled dossiers of patristic authorities, and these found their way into his *Eranistes*.[5]

These developments might suggest that the tradition of the fathers was coming to be treated as authoritative in its own right. Such a reading of the evidence would, however, be mistaken. Great as was the respect paid to the fathers, there was no question of their being regarded as having access to truths other than those already contained, explicitly or implicitly, in Scripture. In the Christological controversy, for example, Cyril's ultimate appeal[6] was always to its teaching—'the tradition of the apostles and evangelists . . . and the bearing of divinely inspired Scripture as a whole'. Theodoret for his part crystallized his position in the statement,[7] 'I yield obedience to Holy Scripture alone'. In the eyes of both of them the authority of the fathers consisted precisely in the fact that they had so faithfully and fully expounded the real intention of the Bible writers. What they found impressive was that so many famous and saintly teachers, venerated in the whole Church, were unanimous in their interpretation of Scripture and in their

---

[1] Cf. *de recta fide ad regin.*; *apol. c. Orient.* (PG 76, 1212 ff.; 316 ff.).
[2] A.C.O. I, 1, 7, 89 ff.   [3] *Ep.* 89.   [4] *Ep.* 151 (PG 83, 1440).
[5] Cf. PG 83, 81 ff.; 169 ff.; 284 ff.
[6] *De recta fide ad regin.* 2 (PG 76, 1204): cf. *quod unus sit Christus* (PG 75, 1257).   [7] *Eran.* 1 (PG 83, 48).

statement of the doctrines set forth, or at any rate implied, in it.

The results of this long evolution were codified in the middle of the fifth century by Vincent of Lérins. Learned and godly men, he states,[1] have often searched for a sure, universally applicable rule for distinguishing the truths of the Catholic faith from heretical falsehoods. What is necessary, he suggests, is a twofold bulwark, the authority of the divine law (i.e. the Bible) and the tradition of the Catholic Church. In itself, he concedes, Scripture 'is sufficient, and more than sufficient'; but because it is susceptible of such a variety of interpretations, we must have recourse to tradition. This 'norm of ecclesiastical and Catholic opinion', as he designates it, is to be identified with 'what has been believed everywhere, always and by all' (*quod ubique, quod semper, quod ab omnibus creditum est*). Thus 'we shall conform to the principle of universality if we confess as alone true the faith professed by the entire Church throughout the world; to that of antiquity if we deviate in no particular from the tenets manifestly shared by our godly predecessors and the fathers; and equally to that of consent if, relying on former ages, we make our own the definitions and opinions of all, or at any rate the majority of, bishops and teachers'.

In practice, of course, heresy itself can often invoke precedents, and the scrutiny of the past sometimes reveals important divergences of opinion. In such cases Vincent suggests[2] that the Christian will prefer the measured decision of a general council to the hastily formed or ignorant opinions of individuals or of unrepresentative groups; and, failing a general council, he will collate and examine the views of representative fathers, especially of those who, living at different times and in different parts of the world, have remained steadfast in the faith and communion of the Catholic Church. Not that Vincent is a conservative who excludes the possibility of all progress in doctrine. In the first place, he admits[3] that it has been the business of councils to perfect and polish the traditional formulae, and even concepts, in which the great truths contained in the

---

[1] *Common.* 2.   [2] Ib. 3: cf. 27.   [3] Ib. 23.

original deposit are expressed, thereby declaring 'not new doctrines, but old ones in new terms' (*non nova, sed nove*). Secondly, however, he would seem to allow for an organic development of doctrine analogous to the growth of the human body from infancy to age. But this development, he is careful to explain, while real, must not result in the least alteration to the original significance of the doctrine concerned. Thus in the end the Christian must, like Timothy,[1] 'guard the deposit', i.e. the revelation enshrined in its completeness in Holy Scripture and correctly interpreted in the Church's unerring tradition.

[1] Ib. 22: cf. *1 Tim*. 6, 20.

NOTE ON BOOKS

A. Benoit, 'Écriture et tradition chez saint Irénée (art. in *Rev. d'hist. et de phil. relig.*, 1960); J. Beumer, *Die mündliche Überlieferung als Glaubensquelle* (Freiburg-Basel-Vienna, 1962); L. Bouyer, 'Holy Scripture and Tradition as Seen by the Fathers' (art. in *East. Churches Quarterly*, 1947); Y. Congar, *Tradition and Traditions* (Eng. trans.: London, 1966); A. Deneffe, *Der Traditionsbegriff* (Münster i.W., 1931); D. van den Eynde, *Les Normes de l'enseignement chrétien dans la littérature patristique des trois premiers siècles* (Gembloux and Paris, 1937); E. Flesseman-van Leer, *Tradition and Scripture in the Early Church* (Assen, 1954); R. P. C. Hanson, *Origen's Doctrine of Tradition* (London, 1954); *Tradition in the Early Church* (London, 1962); H. Holstein, 'La Tradition des apôtres chez saint Irénée (art. in *Rech. des sc. rel.*, 1949); G. W. H. Lampe, 'Scripture and Tradition in the Early Church' (essay in *Scripture and Tradition*, ed. F. W. Dillstone, London, 1955); A. Michel, 'Tradition' (art. in *Dict. Théol. Cath.*); G. L. Prestige, *Fathers and Heretics*, chap. I (London, 1940); H. E. Symonds, 'The Patristic Doctrine of the Relation of Scripture and Tradition' (art. in *East. Churches Quarterly*, 1947); H. E. W. Turner, *The Pattern of Christian Truth*, Lectures VI and VII (London, 1954); M. Wiles, *The Making of Christian Doctrine* (Cambridge, 1967).

CHAPTER III

THE HOLY SCRIPTURES

1. *The Old Testament*

FOR the first hundred years, at least, of its history the Church's Scriptures, in the precise sense of the word, consisted exclusively of the Old Testament. The books comprising what later became known as the New Testament were, of course, already in existence; practically all of them had been written well before the first century ended, and they were familiar to and used by second-century Christian writers. They had not yet been elevated, however, to the special status of canonical Scripture. Judaism, on the other hand, had its collection of sacred, or 'holy', books long before Christianity was born. The official list, said to have been finally ratified by the so-called synod of Jamnia A.D.90-100, was virtually closed by the apostolic age, and it was natural that the Church should appropriate it. She instinctively claimed to be the new Israel, and as such the legitimate heir both of the revelation and of the promises made to the old. So when writers like Clement of Rome,[1] 'Barnabas'[2] and Justin[3] refer to Scripture ('it is written', etc.), what they have in view is almost always the Bible of the Jews. There were important groups of second-century Christians (we shall discuss them in a later section) who felt uneasy about the Old Testament, or even rejected it as completely alien to the gospel of Christ, but they stood outside the central stream of Christianity. For the Church as a whole it was a Christian book which spoke of the Saviour on every page. Nor did this reverence for it diminish when, in the later decades of the second century, the New Testament writings won their way to recognition as

---

[1] E.g. 23; 34, 6; 35, 7; 46, 2 f.   [2] E.g. 4, 7; 4, 11; 5, 4; 6, 12.
[3] *Dial.* passim.

inspired Scripture. Throughout the whole patristic age, as indeed in all subsequent Christian centuries, the Old Testament was accepted as the word of God, the unimpeachable source-book of saving doctrine.

Summary statement

It should be observed that the Old Testament thus admitted as authoritative in the Church was somewhat bulkier and more comprehensive than the twenty-two,[1] or twenty-four,[2] books of the Hebrew Bible of Palestinian Judaism. (These conventional totals were arrived at by reckoning 1 and 2 *Samuel* and 1 and 2 *Kings* as two books, the twelve minor prophets as one book, *Ezra-Nehemiah* and *1-2 Chronicles* as one book each, and, in the case of the former, by attaching *Ruth* and *Lamentations* to *Judges* and *Jeremiah* respectively.) It always included, though with varying degrees of recognition, the so-called Apocrypha, or deutero-canonical books. The reason for this is that the Old Testament which passed in the first instance into the hands of Christians was not the original Hebrew version, but the Greek translation known as the Septuagint. Begun at Alexandria about the middle of the third century B.C., this became the Bible of the Greek-speaking Jews of the Dispersion, and most of the Scriptural quotations found in the New Testament are based upon it rather than the Hebrew. For the Jews of Palestine the limits of the canon (the term is Christian, and was not used in Judaism) were rigidly fixed; they drew a sharp line of demarcation between the books which 'defiled the hands', i.e. were sacred, and other religiously edifying writings. The outlook of the Jewish communities outside Palestine tended to be much more elastic. While respecting the unique position of the Pentateuch, they treated the later books of the Old Testament with considerable freedom, making additions to some and drastically rewriting others; and they did not hesitate to add entirely new books to the permitted list. In this way *1 (3) Esdras, Judith, Tobit* and the books of *Maccabees* came to be included among the histories, and *Wisdom, Ecclesiasticus, Baruch,* the *Song of the Three Holy Children,* the *History of Susannah, Bel and the Dragon*

on the Apocrypha

---

[1] Cf. Josephus, *c. Ap.* 1, 8 (*c.* A.D. 90).
[2] Cf. 2(4) *Esd.* 14, 44-6 (*c.* A.D. 90).

(these last three 'the Additions to the Book of Daniel'), and the *Prayer of Manasseh* among the poetical and prophetic books.

In the first two centuries at any rate the Church seems to have accepted all, or most of, these additional books as inspired and to have treated them without question as Scripture. Quotations from *Wisdom*, for example, occur in *1 Clement*[1] and *Barnabas*,[2] and from *2 (4) Esdras* and *Ecclesiasticus* in the latter.[3] Polycarp[4] cites *Tobit*, and the *Didache*[5] *Ecclesiasticus*. Irenaeus refers to[6] *Wisdom*, the *History of Susannah, Bel and the Dragon* and *Baruch*. The use made of the Apocrypha by Tertullian, Hippolytus, Cyprian and Clement of Alexandria is too frequent for detailed references to be necessary. Towards the close of the second century, when as a result of controversy with the Jews it became known that they were now united in repudiating the deutero-canonical books, hesitations began to creep in; Melito of Sardes (*fl.* 170), for example, satisfied himself,[7] after a visit to Palestine, that the Hebrew canon was the authoritative one. Origen, it is true, made extensive use of the Apocrypha (as indeed of other truly apocryphal works), but his familiarity as a scholar with the Hebrew Bible made him conscious that there was a problem to be faced. A suggestion he advanced[8] was that, when disputing with Jews, Christians should confine themselves to such books as they recognized; but he added the caution that the further extension of such a self-denying ordinance would necessitate the destruction of the copies of the Scriptures currently read in the churches.

It was in the fourth century, particularly where the scholarly standards of Alexandrian Christianity were influential, that these doubts began to make their mark officially. The view which now commended itself fairly generally in the Eastern church, as represented by Athanasius,[9] Cyril of Jerusalem,[10] Gregory of Nazianzus[11] and Epiphanius,[12] was that the deutero-canonical books should be relegated to a subordinate position

---

[1] 3, 4; 27, 5. [2] 6, 7. [3] 12, 1; 19, 9. [4] 10, 2.
[5] 4, 5. [6] *Haer.* 4, 26, 3; 4, 38, 3; 5, 5, 2; 5, 35, 1; *dem.* 97.
[7] Cf. Eusebius, *hist. eccl.* 4, 26, 13 f. [8] *Ep. ad Afric.* 4 f.
[9] *Ep. heort.* 39. [10] *Cat.* 4, 33; 4, 35 f. [11] *Carm.* I, 12.
[12] *Haer.* 8, 6; 76, 5.

outside the canon proper. Cyril was quite uncompromising;[1] books not in the public canon were not to be studied even in private. Athanasius displayed greater flexibility, ruling[2] that they might be used by catechumens for the purpose of instruction. Yet it should be noted (a) that no such scruples seem to have troubled adherents of the Antiochene School, such as John Chrysostom and Theodoret; and (b) that even those Eastern writers who took a strict line with the canon when it was formally under discussion were profuse in their citations from the Apocrypha on other occasions. This official reserve, however, persisted for long in the East. As late as the eighth century we find John Damascene maintaining[3] the Hebrew canon of twenty-two books and excluding *Wisdom* and *Ecclesiasticus*, although he was ready to acknowledge their admirable qualities.

The West, as a whole, was inclined to form a much more favourable estimate of the Apocrypha. Churchmen with Eastern contacts, as was to be expected, might be disposed to push them into the background. Thus Hilary, though in fact citing all of them as inspired, preferred[4] to identify the Old Testament proper with the twenty-two books (as he reckoned them) extant in the Hebrew; while Rufinus described[5] *Wisdom, Ecclesiasticus, Tobit, Judith* and *1* and *2 Maccabees* as 'not canonical, but ecclesiastical', i.e. to be read by Christians but not adduced as authoritative for doctrine. Jerome, conscious of the difficulty of arguing with Jews on the basis of books they spurned and anyhow regarding the Hebrew original as authoritative, was adamant[6] that anything not found in it was 'to be classed among the apocrypha', not in the canon; later he grudgingly conceded[7] that the Church read some of these books for edification, but not to support doctrine. For the great majority, however, the deutero-canonical writings ranked as Scripture in the fullest sense. Augustine, for example, whose influence in the West was decisive, made no distinction between them and the

---

[1] Ib. 4, 36.   [2] Loc. cit.   [3] *De fide orth.* 4, 17.
[4] *In pss. prol.* 15.   [5] *Comm. in symb. apost.* 38.
[6] *Praef. in Sam. et Mal.*: cf. *praef. in Ezr.*; *epp.* 53, 8; 107, 12.
[7] *Praef. in lib. Sal.*

rest of the Old Testament, to which, breaking away once for all from the ancient Hebrew enumeration, he attributed[1] forty-four books. The same inclusive attitude to the Apocrypha was authoritatively displayed at the synods of Hippo and Carthage in 393 and 397 respectively, and also in the famous letter[2] which Pope Innocent I despatched to Exuperius, bishop of Toulouse, in 405.

2. The New Testament Canon

The first writer to speak unequivocally of a 'New' Testament parallel to the Old was Irenaeus.[3] But in teaching that it was inspired Scripture he was by no means an innovator. The author of *2 Peter*[4] had used language about St. Paul's letters which placed them on a level with 'other scriptures', i.e. the Old Testament, and in Ignatius's[5] eyes 'the gospel' was an equivalent authority to the 'prophets'. *2 Clement*[6] had introduced a quotation from the First Gospel with the words, 'Another scripture says'; and both 'Barnabas'[7] and Justin[8] had prefaced New Testament excerpts with the formula, 'It is written'. After Irenaeus's time, however, the fully scriptural character of the specifically Christian writings was universally acknowledged, and the description of them as the 'New Testament' (a title harking back to St. Paul's designation[9] of the Jewish Scriptures as 'the old covenant') came into vogue. Clement of Alexandria, for example, speaks[10] of 'a fresh, new Testament' being given to the new people of God; when reporting one of the Lord's utterances, he says[11] that it is 'according to the New Testament'. We have Tertullian's statement[12] that the Roman church 'associates the Law and the prophets with the evangelical and apostolic books'. He recognized[13] a twofold collection of equal authority which he called *instrumentum utriusque testamenti*, and both Testaments were on his view alike 'divine Scripture'.[14] Henceforth there could be no question that the

---

[1] *De doct. christ.* 2, 13.
[2] Text in *Journ. Theol. Stud.* xiii (1911–12), pp. 77–82.
[3] E.g. *haer.* 4, 9, 1.   [4] 3, 15 f.   [5] E.g. *Smyrn.* 5, 1; 7, 2.
[6] 2, 4.   [7] 4, 14.   [8] E.g. *dial.* 49, 5.   [9] 2 Cor. 3, 14.
[10] *Paed.* 1, 59, 1.   [11] *Strom.* 3, 11, 71: cf. ib. 6, 15, 125.
[12] *De praescr.* 36.   [13] *Adv. Prax.* 20.   [14] E.g. *de test. anim.* 5.

Christian books belonged to what were called αἱ ἅγιαι γραφαί, *sanctae scripturae* or their numerous equivalents.

The formal recognition of a fixed list, or canon, of New Testament writings can be dated about the middle of the second century. The first to draft one, so far as surviving evidence shows, was Marcion, the heretic from Sinope, on the Black Sea, who separated himself from the Catholic Church in Rome in 144. A Christian by upbringing, he declined to avail himself of the allegorical methods of exegesis current in the Church, and consequently found the Old Testament impossible to reconcile with the gospel of Christ. The legalism and strict justice of the one, he thought, and the grace and redeeming love revealed in the other, stood for two antithetically opposed conceptions of religion. Accepting the Old Testament as literally true, he concluded that there must be two Gods, a lower Demiurge who created the universe (i.e. the God of Judaism), and the supreme God made known for the first time by Christ. The kinship between his ideas and those of contemporary Gnosticism[1] cannot be denied (Irenaeus states[2] that he was a disciple of the Gnostic Cerdo), but he refrained from identifying the Demiurge with the principle of evil. His dualism, however, led him to reject the Old Testament, and it was natural that he should seek to canonize an alternative set of Scriptures for use in his church. St. Paul, so outspokenly hostile to the Law, was his hero, and he regarded such Christian writings as seemed infected with a Jewish outlook as suspect. Hence the list he drafted consisted of St. Luke's Gospel, with all seemingly Judaizing passages excised,[3] and ten Pauline epistles (all, in fact, except the Pastorals) similarly expurgated.[4]

The significance of Marcion's action should not be misunderstood. He has sometimes been acclaimed (e.g. by the great German scholar Harnack) as the originator of the Catholic canon, but this is an extravagant point of view. The Church already had its roughly defined collection, or (to be more precise) collections, of Christian books which, as we have seen,

---

[1] See above, pp. 23-26.   [2] *Haer.* 1, 27, 2.
[3] Cf. Tertullian, *c. Marc.* 4 (esp. 4, 2).   [4] Cf. id., *c. Marc.* 5.

it was beginning to treat as Scripture. The Lord's sayings, as
the use of them by St. Paul[1] and the early fathers[2] testifies, had
been treasured from the beginning, and about 150 we find
Justin familiar with all four gospels (the 'memoirs of the
apostles', as he calls[3] them), and mentioning their use in the
weekly service. If it is too much to say that they already formed
a corpus, they were well on the way to doing so. Only a
generation later Irenaeus was to speak[4] of 'the fourfold gospel'
(τετράμορφον εὐαγγέλιον) as the most natural thing in the
world, and Tatian was to piece together his 'Harmony' (*Diates-
saron*) of the four evangelists. Further, although St. Paul's
epistles took longer than the gospels to be universally ranked on
exactly the same level as the Old Testament (it is noteworthy
that none of Irenaeus's 206 quotations from them is introduced
by *scriptura ait*), everything goes to suggest, not least intrinsic
probability, that they were very early grouped together as a
collection. Ignatius, for example, states[5] that the Apostle makes
mention of the Ephesians 'in every letter'; and Polycarp's
citations from them indicate that such a collection existed at
Smyrna. There are numerous apparent echoes of them in
Clement which perhaps indicate[6] that he was acquainted with
the nucleus of one as early as 95. It is altogether more probable,
therefore, that when he formulated his *Apostolicum*, as when he
singled out the Third Gospel, Marcion was revising a list of
books currently in use in the Church than proposing such a list
for the first time.

Nevertheless, if the idea of a specifically Christian canon was
deeply rooted in the Church's own convictions and practice,
Marcion played an important part in the practical emergence
of one. What none of the great ecclesiastical centres, so far as
we know, had done, and what his initiative seems to have provoked them to do, was to delimit their lists of authorized
Christian books in a public, official way. The influence of

---

[1] *1 Thess.* 4, 15; *1 Cor.* 7, 10.
[2] E.g. Ignatius, *Smyrn.* 3, 2; Polycarp, *Phil.* 2, 3; 7, 2; Papias, *frag.* (in Eusebius, *hist. eccl.* 3, 39); Justin, *1 apol.* 14-17.
[3] E.g. *1 apol.* 66; 67; *dial.* 103; 106.   [4] *Haer.* 3, 11, 8.
[5] *Eph.* 12, 2.   [6] Cf. 47.

Montanism, an ecstatic movement which originated in Phrygia in 156 and whose founder, Montanus, and his chief associates believed themselves to be vehicles of a new effusion of the Paraclete, worked in the same direction. In the 'oracles' of their prophets the Montanists saw[1] a revelation of the Holy Spirit which could be regarded as supplementing 'the ancient scriptures' (*pristina instrumenta*). From now onwards, therefore, it became a matter of immense concern to the Church that the New Testament, as it was coming to be called, should be credited with the right number of books, and the right books. Tertullian, for example, defended against Marcion the inspired character of the four gospels[2] in their integrity and of *Acts*,[3] as well as of thirteen Pauline epistles.[4] He also recognized *Hebrews*, attributing it to Barnabas,[5] and both *1 John* and *Revelation*.[6] Yet nothing like an official catalogue appears in his works. The earliest such catalogue of which we have evidence is the Roman one contained in the so-called Muratorian fragment.[7] Late second century in date and authoritative in tone, this recognized the whole New Testament except *Hebrews*, *1* and *2 Peter*, *James* and *3 John*, assigned a place to *Wisdom* and the *Apocalypse of Peter*, admitted Hermas's *Shepherd* as useful reading, and branded Marcionite and Gnostic books as unfit for perusal 'in the Catholic Church'. The text is very corrupt, and emendations have been proposed restoring a mention of the Petrine epistles, or at any rate of *1 Peter*.

The development of the canon throughout the rest of our period makes an exceedingly complicated story, and falls outside the scope of this book. The student should refer to specialized manuals on the subject. The main point to be observed is that the fixation of the finally agreed list of books, and of the order in which they were to be arranged, was the S.S. result of a very gradual process. While the broad outline of the

---

[1] Cf. Tertullian, *de çarn. resurr.* 63.   [2] *C. Marc.* 4, 2; 4, 5.
[3] Ib. 5, 1; *de praescr.* 23.
[4] He claims the Pastorals for St. Paul in *c. Marc.* 5, 21.
[5] *De pud.* 20.   [6] Ib. 19.
[7] For the text see A. Souter, *Text and Canon of the New Testament* (2nd ed. 1954), pp. 191 ff.

canon was settled by the end of the second century, different localities continued to maintain their different traditions, and some (e.g. Alexandria in Origen's time[1]) appear to have been less partial to fixity than others. Three features of this process should be noted. First, the criterion which ultimately came to prevail was apostolicity. Unless a book could be shown to come from the pen of an apostle, or at least to have the authority of an apostle behind it, it was peremptorily rejected, however edifying or popular with the faithful it might be. Secondly, there were certain books which hovered for long on the fringe of the canon, but in the end failed to secure admission to it, usually because they lacked this indispensable stamp. Among these were the *Didache*, Hermas's *Shepherd* and the *Apocalypse of Peter*. Thirdly, some of the books which were later included had to wait a considerable time before achieving universal recognition. For example, *Hebrews* was for long under suspicion in the West, and *Revelation* was usually excluded in the fourth and fifth centuries where the school of Antioch held sway. The Western church was absolutely silent about *James* until the latter half of the fourth century, and the four smaller Catholic epistles (*2 Peter*, *2 and 3 John*, *Jude*), absent from most early lists, continued for long to be treated as doubtful in certain circles. By gradual stages, however, the Church both in East and West arrived at a common mind as to its sacred books. The first official document which prescribes the twenty-seven books of our New Testament as alone canonical is Athanasius's Easter Letter[2] for the year 367, but the process was not everywhere complete until at least a century and a half later.

3. *The Inspiration of Scripture*

From Judaism Christianity inherited the conception of the divine inspiration of Holy Scripture. Whenever our Lord and His apostles quoted the Old Testament, it is plain that they regarded it as the word of God. This comes to light repeatedly in

---

[1] Cf. R. P. C. Hanson, *Origen's Doctrine of Tradition*, 1954, ch. 8.
[2] PG 26, 1437.

the New Testament records, but is explicitly affirmed in two passages in the later epistles: (a) 'All scripture is inspired by God and is useful for teaching, reproof, correction';[1] and (b) 'No prophecy ever came by the will of man, but men spoke from God, being moved by the Holy Spirit'.[2] These sentences crystallize what was to be the Church's attitude to the Old Testament throughout the whole period covered by this book, and also towards the New Testament after it had been canonized as an authority coordinate with the Old. The several books were, as common usage expressed it,[3] 'written by the Holy Spirit'; the human author served as God's instrument, and his tongue was, in words of the Psalmist (45, 1) which were frequently applied[4] in this sense, 'the pen of a ready writer'.

It goes without saying that the fathers envisaged the whole of the Bible as inspired. It was not a collection of disparate segments, some of divine origin and others of merely human fabrication. Irenaeus, for example, is not surprised[5] at its frequent obscurity, 'seeing it is spiritual in its entirety'; while Gregory of Nyssa understands[6] St. Paul to imply that everything contained in Scripture is the deliverance of the Holy Spirit. Even Theodore of Mopsuestia, who distinguished[7] between the special inspiration of the prophets and the inferior grace of 'prudence' granted to Solomon, was not really an exception, for he was satisfied[8] that all the authors of both Testaments wrote under the influence of one and the same Spirit. Origen,[9] indeed, and Gregory of Nazianzus[10] after him, thought they could perceive the activity of the divine wisdom in the most trifling verbal minutiae, even in the solecisms,[11] of the sacred books. This attitude was fairly widespread, and although some of the fathers elaborated it more than others, their general view was that Scripture was not only exempt from error but contained nothing that was superfluous. 'There

[1] 2 Tim. 3, 16. [2] 2 Pet. 1, 21.
[3] E.g. Origen, c. Cels. 5, 60; Basil, hom. in ps. 1, 1; Jerome, in Is. 29, 9 ff.
[4] E.g Theodoret, in pss. praef. (PG 80, 865); Jerome, ep. 70, 7.
[5] Haer. 2, 28, 2. [6] C. Eunom. 7 (PG 45, 744).
[7] In Iob (PG, 66, 697). [8] In Nah. 1, 1.
[9] In ps. 1, 4 (PG 12, 1081). [10] Or. 2, 105.
[11] Cf. Origen, in Os. (PG 13, 825 ff.).

is not one jot or tittle', declared[1] Origen, 'written in the Bible which does not accomplish its special work for those capable of using it.' In similar vein Jerome stated[2] that 'in the divine Scriptures every word, syllable, accent and point is packed with meaning'; those who slighted the commonplace contents of *Philemon* were simply failing, through ignorance, to appreciate the power and wisdom they concealed.[3] According to Chrysostom,[4] even the chronological figures and the catalogues of names included in Scripture have their profound value; and he devoted two homilies to the salutations in *Romans* 16 in the hope[5] of convincing his auditors that treasures of wisdom lie hid in every word spoken by the Spirit.

What was understood by inspiration in the patristic period? In Alexandrian Judaism the popularly accepted theory had been that it was a species of possession. Philo's explanation[6] of the experience of the prophets was that, when God's Spirit seized them, they lost consciousness; they no longer knew what they were saying, or, rather, they no longer spoke but God spoke through their lips. The Christian apologist Athenagoras gives a similar account, representing[7] the prophets as prophesying in a state of ecstasy (κατ' ἔκστασιν), and the Spirit as breathing through them much as a musician breathes through a pipe. But it was the Montanists, the ecstatic sect referred to above,[8] to whom this theory particularly appealed, and their leaders, Montanus, Priscilla and Maximilla, supplied living illustrations of it, falling unconscious when they prophesied.[9] Not unnaturally, it found a vigorous defender in Tertullian[10] when he succumbed to the influence of Montanism. Again and again we catch echoes of it in the language of Catholic writers, as when Chrysostom speaks[11] of St. John and St. Paul as musical instruments played upon by the Holy Spirit, or when Ambrose describes[12] the tumultuous disturbance of the prophetic mind.

---

[1] *Hom. in Ierem.* 39, 1 (Klostermann, 197).   [2] *In Eph.* 2 (3, 6).
[3] *In Philem.* prol.   [4] *In illud, Vidi dom. hom.* 2, 2 (PG 56, 110).
[5] *In illud, Salutate hom.* 1, 1 (PG 51, 187).
[6] *Quis rer. div. haer.* 249–66; *de spec. leg.* 4, 48 f.
[7] *Leg.* 7; 9.   [8] See above, p. 59.
[9] Cf. Epiphanius, *haer.* 48, 4 ff.   [10] *C. Marc.* 4, 22; 5, 8; *de an.* 11; 21.
[11] *In Ioh. hom.* 1, 1 f.; *de Laz. conc.* 6, 9.   [12] *De Abrah.* 2, 61.

Scriptural writers not passive!

In general, however, while influenced by Philo's conceptions and freely likening the Scriptural writers to instruments, the orthodox tradition was careful to avoid the implication that their role was purely passive. Hippolytus, for example, explains[1] that when the Word moved the prophets, the effect was to clarify their vision and instruct their understanding; and Origen, rejecting all comparison between the inspired authors and the ecstatic oracles of paganism, suggests[2] that the Spirit's function was to cause the former to apprehend divine truth more clearly without in any way suspending their free will. The burden of Epiphanius's criticism[3] of the Montanists was his reminder that, in distinction from them, the true prophets of God (by whom he meant the writers of the Old and New Testaments) were in a state of normal consciousness, in full possession of their faculties, when they wrote. They understood, therefore, what they were saying; and although Scripture sometimes depicts them as falling victims to ecstasy, it would be erroneous to deduce from this that they had lost the use of their reason. Arguing on rather different lines, both Chrysostom[4] and Cyril of Alexandria[5] make much of the personal contribution of Moses, St. John and St. Paul in the actual composition of their works. In the West Jerome emphasizes[6] the normality of the prophet's condition, and underlines[7] the differences of style, general culture and background which they severally exhibit. So Augustine, discussing the activity of the evangelists, admits[8] that they used their own personal reminiscences in compiling the gospels, the function of the Spirit being to stimulate their memories and preserve them from error. It was not a case of His imparting a fresh revelation to them; rather did He regulate and control their mental powers.[9]

Unfortunately few, if any, of the fathers seem to have tried to probe the deeper problems raised by their doctrine of inspiration. With one or two exceptions we look in vain for any

S. S.

---

[1] *De Christ. et antichr.* 2.   [2] *C. Cels.* 7, 3 f.; *in Ezech.* 6, 1 f.
[3] *Haer.* 48, 1-10.   [4] *In Gen. hom.* 7, 4; 12, 1; 20, 4.
[5] *In Ioh.* 1, 10; 1, 18 (PG 73, 148; 176); *in Rom.* 7, 25; 8, 3.
[6] *In Is.* prol.   [7] *In Is.* prol.; *in Ierem.* prol.; *in Am.* prol.
[8] *Serm.* 246, 1.   [9] *De consens. evang.* 3, 30.

positive, constructive account (other than the theory of possession, the perils of which they were usually alive to) of the action of the Holy Spirit on the inspired writers. Augustine, it is true, analyses[1] at length the three principal types of vision (corporal, spiritual and intellectual) which God employed to communicate to them the things He desired them to declare. Elsewhere he points out[2] that in some cases the Spirit bestows a direct vision on the prophet, in others instructs his intelligence, and in still others (e.g. that of Caiaphas) prompts him to utter divine truth without knowing it. Theodore of Mopsuestia, again, has some original speculations on the subject. In the first place, while accepting the inspiration of the whole Bible, he argues[3] that the Holy Spirit's action varied from writer to writer; the special gift bestowed on the prophets, for example, was in a different category from the grace of prudence which Solomon possessed. Secondly, he attempts to explore the phenomenon of prophecy itself. It involved a state of ecstasy, he explains,[4] which withdrew the prophet's attention from his immediate surroundings and focused it on 'the visions so frightening and mysterious' vouchsafed him by the Spirit. The organs of sight were thus first affected, and then a verbal message might be transmitted to his sense of hearing. Suggestions like these have their value, but Augustine and Theodore were more or less isolated pioneers. The majority were content to accept the fact of the inspiration of the sacred writers, without examining further the manner or the degree of its impact upon them.

4. The Unity of the Two Testaments

The inspiration of Scripture being taken for granted, the Church had to work out the methods of exegesis to be employed in interpreting it. The fundamental issue here, as was very soon perceived, was to determine the precise relation of the Old Testament to the New, or rather (since at the earliest stage there was no specifically Christian canon), to the revelation

[1] De Gen. ad litt. 12, 1-14. [2] De div. quaest. 2, q. 1, 1.
[3] In Iob (PG 66, 697). [4] In Nah. 1, 1.

of which the apostles were the witnesses. As has already been mentioned, the solution arrived at consisted in treating the Old Testament as a book which, if it were read with unclouded eyes, would be seen to be Christian through and through. In adopting this attitude Christian theologians and teachers were merely following the example of the apostles and evangelists, and indeed of the Lord Himself. It is evident from every page of the gospel records that the incarnate Christ freely took up, applied to Himself and His mission, and in so doing reinterpreted, the key-ideas of the Messiah, the Suffering Servant, the Kingdom of God, etc., which He found ready to hand in the faith of Israel. In harmony with this the essence of the apostolic message was the proclamation that in the manifestation, ministry, passion, resurrection and ascension of the Lord, and in the subsequent outpouring of the Spirit, the ancient prophecies had been fulfilled. Whether we look to the fragments of primitive preaching embedded in *Acts*, or to St. Paul's argumentation with his correspondents, or to the elaborate thesis expounded in *Hebrews*, or to the framework of the evangelists' narratives, we are invariably brought face to face with the assumption that the whole pattern of the Christian revelation, unique and fresh though it is, is 'according to the Scriptures'. In this connexion St. Luke's story[1] of the two disciples on the road to Emmaus is highly instructive, for it presents a vivid picture of the primitive Church's conviction that all the events of Christ's earthly career, together with their profound redemptive implications, are to be understood as the fulfilment of what was written about Him 'in the law of Moses, and in the prophets, and in the psalms', and that the ultimate warrant for this conviction was His own express authorization.

As an illustration of post-apostolic practice we may cite the author of *1 Clement*. The focal-point of his thinking is the Old Testament; not only is it the source-book for Christian behaviour, but it also provides[2] the prototype of the Christian ministry and liturgy. In the second century we have Justin's

---

[1] *Luke* 24, 25-48.   [2] E.g. 43.

statement[1] to Trypho the Jew that 'the Scriptures are much more ours than yours. For we let ourselves be persuaded by them, while you read them without grasping their true import'. So the author of *The Preaching of Peter* represents[2] the apostles as saying: 'Having unrolled the books we possess, and in which the prophets mention Christ sometimes in parables, sometimes in enigmas, sometimes clearly and distinctly, we have discovered His coming, His death, His cross, all the other sufferings the Jews inflicted on Him, His resurrection, His assumption. . . . And we say nothing apart from Scripture.' 'How could we believe', Justin exclaims,[3] 'that a crucified man is the first-born of the ingenerate God, and that He will judge the whole human race, were it not that we have found testimony borne prior to His coming as man, and that we have seen that testimony exactly fulfilled?' It seems clear[4] that, if he and his contemporaries had not available a recognized anthology of proof-texts or *testimonia*, they at any rate made use of an established method of appealing to select portions of the Old Testament, particularly from Isaiah, Jeremiah, certain of the minor prophets, and the Psalms, which appeared to set forth 'the determinate counsel of God' as fulfilled in the gospel. There were others, however, who, taking their cue from Philo of Alexandria,[5] tried to make the task of interpretation easier by a lavish resort to allegory. According to 'Barnabas',[6] the fatal error of the Jews was to let themselves be beguiled by the literal sense of Scripture. What God really asked of His people was not bloody sacrifices, as the Law seemed to prescribe, but a contrite heart; not bodily fasting, but the practice of good works; not abstention from certain forms of food, but the avoidance of vices symbolized by them.[7] 'Barnabas' even detected[8] a prophecy of the Saviour's name and of His crucifixion in the number (318) of Abraham's servants, since the Greek letters for 18, viz. IH, point to 'Ιησοῦς, and that signifying 300, viz. T, stands for the cross.

---

[1] *Dial.* 29. [2] Cf. Clement Alex., *strom.* 6, 15, 128.
[3] *1 apol.* 53.
[4] Cf. C. H. Dodd, *According to the Scriptures*, 1952, pp. 126 f.
[5] See above, pp. 8 f. [6] 4, 7. [7] 9 f. [8] 9.

The orthodox assumption of the underlying unity between the old and new dispensations did not meet with acceptance with all Christians. It was repudiated, as we have seen,[1] by Marcion, who refused to admit the Old Testament as a Christian book at all. As a history of mankind and of the Jewish race it might be entirely accurate, and it might have provisional validity as a code of strict righteousness; but its author must have been the Demiurge, not the God of love revealed by Christ, and it must have been utterly superseded by the new law proclaimed by the Saviour. On the other hand, a less extreme attitude than Marcion's, but differing like his from the official one, prevailed in Christian Gnostic circles. We have a sample of this in the famous letter[2] which the Valentinian Ptolemaeus wrote about 160 to a catechumen named Flora. First, he rejects both the orthodox thesis that the Mosaic law is the work of the good God (its imperfections sufficiently refute such an idea), and the contrary thesis that it must be attributed to an *evil* Demiurge. Then he argues that the contents of the Pentateuch fall into three sections, one indeed deriving from God, but one also from Moses in his legislative capacity, and one from the elders of the people. Finally, he distinguishes three levels, as it were, in the section attributable to God. There are first those divine precepts (e.g. the Decalogue) which involve no imperfection and which Christ came, not to abolish, but to fulfil. Then there are certain mixed injunctions, partly good and partly bad (the *lex talionis* is an example), which Christ definitely superseded. Thirdly, there are what he calls 'typical' commandments, e.g. the laws relating to sacrifice and the ceremonial law generally, which have value so long as they are treated, not literally, but as types or figures. From this it should be plain that the God Who has inspired this tripartite legislation is not the absolute, unengendered Father, but His image, the just Demiurge.

While readier than Marcion to acknowledge the spiritual worth of at any rate portions of the Old Testament, Ptolemaeus was at one with him in setting a gulf between the old

---

[1] See above, p. 57.　　　[2] Cf. Epiphanius, *haer.* 33, 3-7.

dispensation and the new. Views like his were inevitable wherever the Gnostic distinction between the unknown supreme God and the Demiurge prevailed, and made it necessary for the Catholic Church to justify her own position more explicitly. Not without reason has it been claimed[1] that 'the real battle in the second century centred round the position of the Old Testament'. The outlines of this apologetic were traced by Justin, when he argued[2] that, for example, Leah and Rachel prefigured the Synagogue and the Church, or that the polygamy of the patriarchs was a mystery (οἰκονομία). The fullest statement, however, of the orthodox position is to be found in Irenaeus, one of whose favourite themes[3] is that the Law of Moses and the grace of the New Testament, both adapted to different sets of conditions, were bestowed by one and the same God for the benefit of the human race. If the Old Testament legislation appears less perfect than the New, this is because mankind had to undergo a progressive development, and the old law was designed for its earlier stages.[4] Hence we should not conclude that it was the product of a blind Demiurge and that the good God came to abolish it; in the Sermon on the Mount Christ fulfilled it by propounding a more intimate and perfect justice.[5] As for those passages which were stumbling-blocks to the Marcionites (e.g. the story of Lot, or of the spoiling of the Egyptians), what was required[6] was to look for the deeper significance of which they were figures or types. Similarly, so far from knowing only an inferior creator God, the prophets had full cognizance of all the incidents of the Incarnation,[7] and were fully apprised of the Saviour's teaching and passion.[8] The only difference is that prophecy, by its very nature, was obscure and enigmatic, divinely pointing to events which could only be accurately delineated after their historical realization.[9]

From this time onwards the continuity of the two Testaments becomes a commonplace with Christian writers. It is

---

[1] F. C. Burkitt, *Church and Gnosis*, 1932, p. 129.
[2] *Dial.* 134, 2; 141, 4.   [3] *Haer.* 3, 12, 14; 4, passim.
[4] Ib. 4, 13; 14; 38.   [5] Ib. 4, 12 f.   [6] Ib. 4, 30-1.
[7] Ib. 1, 10, 1.   [8] Ib. 4, 33, 12.   [9] Ib. 4, 26, 1.

grounded in the fact, pointed out by Theophilus of Antioch,[1] that both the prophets and the evangelists were inspired by one and the same divine Spirit. The affirmation of the oneness of God, imperilled by Gnostic speculation of every sort, was the indispensable premiss for refuting the Gnostic separation of the Testaments, and to demonstrate this oneness was the principal task of Irenaeus and his contemporaries. As a result of their efforts Tertullian can speak of 'the peace which exists between the Law and the gospel',[2] and of 'the harmony between the prophetic and the dominical utterances'.[3] If there is a difference, it does not spring from any contrariety of the Old Testament to the New, but from the fact that the latter is a drawing out of what is contained in the former, as the mature fruit is a develop-ment of its seed.[4] In Origen's eyes 'the dogmas common to the so-called Old and New Testaments' form a symphony;[5] if the one precedes and the other follows Christ's corporeal mani-festation, there is no iota of difference between them.[6] No doubt the prophets' mode of knowledge was different from that of the apostles, for they contemplated the mysteries of the Incarnation before their accomplishment; but that was a quite accidental point. The Christians who will assist at Christ's second coming will know no more of it, though their know-ledge will be different in kind, than the apostles who foretold it; and similarly the insight of the apostles must not be reckoned superior to that of Moses and the prophets.[7] The way was thus early paved for the classic doctrine which Augustine was to formulate in the epigram:[8] 'In the Old Testament the New is concealed, in the New the Old is revealed'.

5. Typology and Allegory

The method of exegesis presupposed in the preceding sec-tion has in modern times been given the convenient name 'typology'. The fathers themselves used various terms to

[1] *Ad Autol.* 3, 12.   [2] *C. Marc.* 1, 19.   [3] Ib. 4, 39.
[4] Ib. 4, 11.   [5] *In Ioh.* 5, 8.   [6] *In Matt. comm.* 14, 4.
[7] *In Ioh.* 6, 15-42.   [8] *Quaest. in hept.* 2, q. 73.

describe it, chiefly perhaps 'allegory', which was suggested to
them by St. Paul's statement[1] that the story of Abraham's two
sons was an 'allegory' of the two covenants. 'Allegory', however, is best avoided in this connexion; the word led to confusion even in the patristic age, and its accepted meaning to-day
denotes a somewhat different type of exegesis from typology.
Since the fathers employed both typology and allegory (in
its modern sense), the distinction between the two methods
needs to be clearly brought out.

description of allegory

In allegorical exegesis the sacred text is treated as a mere
symbol, or allegory, of spiritual truths. The literal, historical
sense, if it is regarded at all, plays a relatively minor role, and
the aim of the exegete is to elicit the moral, theological or
mystical meaning which each passage, indeed each verse and
even each word, is presumed to contain. A classic example is
Augustine's well-known explanation[2] of the parable of the
Good Samaritan, according to which the traveller stands for
Adam, Jerusalem for the heavenly city from which he fell,
Jericho for his resulting mortality, the thieves for the devil and
his angels, the wretched plight in which they left him for the
condition to which he was reduced by sin, the priest and the
Levite for the ineffective ministrations of the old covenant,
the Samaritan for Christ, the inn for the Church, and so on.
Allegorism was well established in Alexandrian Judaism, and
Philo, as we have seen,[3] made a systematic use of it to bridge
the chasm between the Old Testament revelation and his own
Platonizing philosophy. In the hands of such a second-century
Christian writer as 'Barnabas'[4] Philonic allegorism was able to
detect a Christian significance in the least likely passages of the
Old Testament. The Christian Gnostics were even more daring,
applying allegory to the New Testament and interpreting the
incidents of the earthly life of Jesus as a complex pattern of
symbolism mirroring the drama of the aeons. Thus when St.
John reports that the Lord 'went down to Capernaum', the
Gnostic commentator Heracleon deduces[5] from the verb 'went

---

[1] *Gal.* 4, 24.   [2] *Quaest. evang.* 2, 19.   [3] See above, pp. 8 f.
[4] See above, p. 66.   [5] Cf. Origen, *in Ioh.* 10, 48–59.

down' that Capernaum must signify the lowest stratum of reality, i.e. the world of matter, and that the reason why Christ apparently neither accomplished nor said anything there must be that the material order was uncongenial to Him.

Typological exegesis worked along very different lines. Essentially it was a technique for bringing out the correspondence between the two Testaments, and took as its guiding principle the idea that the events and personages of the Old were 'types' of, i.e. prefigured and anticipated, the events and personages of the New. The typologist took history seriously; it was the scene of the progressive unfolding of God's consistent redemptive purpose. Hence he assumed that, from the creation to the judgment, the same unwavering plan could be discerned in the sacred story, the earlier stages being shadows or, to vary the metaphor, rough preliminary sketches of the later. Christ and His Church were the climax; and since in all His dealings with mankind God was leading up to the Christian revelation, it was reasonable to discover pointers to it in the great experiences of His chosen people. This conception, it should be observed, was no invention of Christian theologians. In the Old Testament itself the events of Israel's past are construed as figures or types of realities to come; Deutero-Isaiah[1] in particular looked back to the redemption from Egypt as recapitulating, as it were, God's original victory over chaos, and looked forward to a second Exodus from captivity in the future and a renewal of creation. But a corollary of it was that typology, unlike allegory, had no temptation to undervalue, much less dispense with, the literal sense of Scripture. It was precisely because the events there delineated had really happened on the plane of history that they could be interpreted by the eye of faith as trustworthy pointers to God's future dealings with men.

Of these two methods of exegesis the characteristically Christian one was typology, which had its roots firmly planted in the Biblical view of history. In its struggle with the Marcionites the Church found it an invaluable weapon for countering

[1] E.g. 51, 9-16.

their attempt to separate the two Testaments. Naturally it posed great difficulties, the chief perhaps being that of determining, in the light of intelligible criteria, what features of the Old Testament should be regarded as genuinely 'typical'. The fathers were not always aware of, much less able to solve, these, and many of their essays in typology strike one as naïve and arbitrary; nevertheless this was the formula which, consistently though often fumblingly (often too, as we shall see, with the aid of other less legitimate principles), they applied to the interpretation of Scripture. It has been fashionable to distinguish different schools of patristic exegesis, notably the Alexandrian with its bias towards allegory, and the Antiochene with its passion for literalism. Valid though this contrast is, it should not be pressed to the extent of overlooking the underlying unity, at the deeper level of typology, of the fathers' approach to the Scriptural revelation. There was general agreement about cardinal issues, such as that Adam, or again Moses the law-giver, in a real sense foreshadowed Christ; the flood pointed to baptism, and also to the judgment; all the sacrifices of the old Law, but in a pre-eminent way the sacrifice of Isaac, were anticipations of that of Calvary; the crossing of the Red Sea and the eating of manna looked forward to baptism and the eucharist; the fall of Jericho prefigured the end of the world. The list of correspondences could be expanded almost indefinitely, for the fathers were never weary of searching them out and dwelling on them. They were united in believing that what Origen called[1] 'the Jewish mystery (or dispensation) in its entirety' was, as it were, a rehearsal of the Christian mystery.

The inherent difficulties of typology, however, made the transition to allegorism extremely tempting, especially where the cultural environment was Hellenistic and impregnated with Platonic idealism,[2] with its theory that the whole visible order is a symbolical reflection of invisible realities. Hence it is not surprising that most of the fathers injected a strain of allegory, some of them a powerful one, into their typology. Alexandria, famous in the late second and third centuries for its catechetical

---

[1] *Hom. in Ierem.* 10, 4.   [2] See above, pp. 15 f.

school, became the home of allegorical exegesis, with the great
Biblical scholar, Origen, as its leading exponent. An admirer[1]
of Philo, he regarded[2] Scripture as a vast ocean, or (using a
different image) forest, of mysteries; it was impossible to
fathom, or even perceive, them all, but one could be sure that
every line, even every word, the sacred authors wrote was
replete with meaning. Formally he distinguished[3] three levels of
signification in Scripture, corresponding to the three parts of
which human nature is composed: the bodily, the psychic and
the spiritual. The first was the straightforward historical sense,
and was useful for simple people; the second was the moral
sense, or the lesson of the text for the will; the third was the
mystical sense with relation to Christ, the Church or the great
truths of the faith. In practice Origen seems to have employed
a slightly different triple classification, comprising (a) the plain
historical sense, (b) the typological sense,[4] and (c) the spiritual
sense,[5] in which the text may be applied to the devout soul.
Thus when the Psalmist cries (3, 4), 'Thou, O Lord, art my
support, my glory, and the lifter up of my head', he explains[6]
that it is in the first place David who speaks; but, secondly, it
is Christ, Who knows in His passion that God will vindicate
Him; and, thirdly, it is every just soul who, by union with
Christ, finds His glory in God.

This is but a single example of a method of exegesis which in
Origen's hands was capable of almost infinite ramifications.
Another might be his interpretation[7] of the holocaust and sin-
offering prescribed by the Law as pointing to (a) Christ's
sacrifice, and (b) the sacrifice which each Christian, in imitation of Christ, should reproduce and accomplish in his heart.
It is evident that, working on these lines, there was no limit to
the symbolism which he was able to detect in Scripture. Indeed,
he makes[8] the point that, thanks to the allegorical method, it is

---

[1] Cf. *comm. in Matt.* 15, 3.
[2] *Hom. in Ex.* 9, 1; *in Gen.* 9, 1; *in Ezech.* 4, 1.
[3] *De princ.* 4, 2, 4 : cf. *in Matt.* 10, 14; *hom. in Lev.* 5, 5.
[4] E.g. *hom. in Num.* 8, 1 (Baehrens, 49).
[5] E.g. *in Cant.* 2 (Baehrens, 165).   [6] *Sel. in ps.* 3, 4.
[7] *Hom. in Lev.* 1, 4 f.
[8] *De princ.* 4, 2, 2; *hom. in Num.* 26, 3; *hom. in Ierem.* 12, 1.

possible to interpret it in a manner worthy of the Holy Spirit, since it would not be proper to take literally a narrative or a command unworthy of God. It is not true, as has sometimes been alleged, that he did away with the literal meaning, although he is satisfied[1] that in a number of cases it is inacceptable. He was undoubtedly prone, however, to ascribe too readily to the inspiration of the Spirit the fanciful spiritual symbolism which his fertile imagination discovered in almost every word or image of the Bible. Every proper name, every number, all the animals, plants and metals mentioned there seemed to him to be allegories of theological or spiritual truths. Finally, not only does he strive[2] to find a spiritual, in addition to the obvious factual, sense in the gospels, but he is on occasion prepared[3] to borrow the Gnostic technique of seeing in the episodes of Christ's life an image or representation of events accomplished in the spiritual realm.

Although he was primarily a loyal and orthodox churchman, the Platonizing strain in Origen's assumption that Scripture is a patchwork of symbolism cannot be disguised. His predecessor Clement, though not strictly an exegete, anticipated his method and many of his leading ideas about exegesis. He expounded[4] the theory that all the loftiest truths can only be communicated by symbols; Moses and the prophets had used them just as much as the sages of Egypt and Greece, and the religiously advanced Bible student must always be on the look-out for the deeper meaning. Underlying this doctrine was the Platonic conception, shared by Origen too, that there is a hierarchy of beings, and that the lower reflect, and can be treated as symbols of, the higher. The Alexandrian theologians who followed them, from Dionysius to Cyril, were all to a greater or lesser extent infected with their predilection for allegory; and the same can be said of the Palestinian (Epiphanius was a notable exception) and Cappadocian fathers. Through their influence the allegorizing tradition passed to the West, and is visible in the expository writings, for example, of Hilary and Ambrose.

---

[1] *De princ.* 4, 2, 5.   [2] E.g. *c. Cels.* 2, 69.
[3] E.g. *in Ioh.* 10, 9 ; 13, 59; etc.   [4] Cf. *strom.* 5 passim.

The greatest of Latin exegetes, Jerome, though in his later days he became suspicious of allegorism, accepted[1] Origen's three senses of Scripture, deeming[2] that recourse to the spiritual meaning was made necessary by the anthropomorphisms, inconsistencies and incongruities in which the Bible abounded; and Augustine employed allegory with the greatest freedom, delighting particularly in the mystical significance of names and numbers. He seems to have held[3] that the same passage of Scripture may have several different meanings, all of them willed by the Holy Spirit. In a more formal vein he listed[4] four senses of Scripture: the historical, the 'etiological' (an example is Christ's explanation in *Matt.* 19, 8 of the reasons for Moses' allowing a bill of divorcement), the analogical (which brings out the complete harmony of the Old and New Testaments), and the allegorical or figurative. His rule for determining whether the literal or the figurative sense was the more correct was that whatever can be shown to be inconsistent, if taken literally, with propriety of life or purity of doctrine must be taken figuratively. In a general way he thought[5] that no interpretation could be true which did not promote the love of God or the love of man.

6. *The Antiochene Reaction*

The tradition of allegorical exegesis was thus securely established in the Church, although most of its later exponents were more cautious than Origen and steered clear of his wilder extravagances. Nevertheless a vigorous reaction against allegorism of every sort made itself manifest in the fourth and fifth centuries. Its centre was Antioch, the ecclesiastical metropolis of Syria, where a tradition of Bible study, with meticulous attention to the text, had been fostered since the days of Lucian (martyred 312). The chief theologians concerned in this were Diodore of Tarsus (*c.* 330–*c.* 390), Theodore of Mopsuestia

---

[1] *Ep.* 120, 12: cf. *in Am.* 4, 4; *in Ezech.* 16, 31.
[2] *In Matt.* 21, 5; *in Gal.* 5, 13.
[3] *Confess.* 12, 42; *de doct. christ.* 3, 38.
[4] *De util. cred.* 5-8.   [5] E.g. *de doct. christ.* 3: esp. 3, 14; 3, 23.

(*c.* 350–428) and Theodoret (*c.* 393–*c.* 460), but practical illustrations of the Antiochene method are to be found in the sermons of such a preacher as John Chrysostom (*c.* 347–407). Despite differences of emphasis, the whole school was united in believing that allegory was an unreliable, indeed illegitimate, instrument for interpreting Scripture. The true key to its deeper spiritual message where this was not already fully explicit, as in genuine prophecy, was what they called 'insight' ($\theta\epsilon\omega\rho\iota\alpha$). By this they meant the power of perceiving, in addition to the historical facts set out in the text, a spiritual reality to which they were designed to point. Thus they accepted typology proper—indeed, the classic definition of a type as 'a prophecy expressed in terms of things' ($\dot{\eta}$ $\delta\iota\dot{\alpha}$ $\pi\rho\alpha\gamma\mu\acute{\alpha}\tau\omega\nu$ . . . $\pi\rho\sigma\phi\eta\tau\epsilon\iota\alpha$) was framed by Chrysostom[1]—but tried to rescue it from being exploited arbitrarily. For *theoria* to operate they considered it necessary (a) that the literal sense of the sacred narrative should not be abolished, (b) that there should be a real correspondence between the historical fact and the further spiritual object discerned, and (c) that these two objects should be apprehended together, though of course in different ways.

The antithesis which the Antiochenes made between allegory and *theoria* comes out in a remark of Severian of Gabbala (fl. *c.* 400) justifying the parallel he drew between the creatures 'which the waters brought forth' (*Gen.* 1, 21) and Christians regenerated by baptism. 'It is one thing', he states,[2] 'to force allegory out of the history, and quite another thing to preserve the history intact while discerning a *theoria* over and above it'. Chrysostom is bringing out the same point when he divides[3] Scriptural statements into (a) those which allow a 'theoretic' in addition to the literal sense, (b) those which are to be understood solely in the literal sense, and (c) those which admit only of a meaning other than the literal, i.e. allegorical statements. In Diodore's formula,[4] 'We do not forbid the higher interpretation and *theoria*, for the historical narrative does not

---

[1] *De poenit. hom.* 6, 4: cf. *in ps.* 9, 4.
[2] *De creat.* 4, 2 (PG 56, 459).   [3] *In ps.* 9, 4.
[4] *Praef. in pss.* (ed. L. Mariès, *Recherches de science religieuse*, 1919), p. 88.

exclude it, but is on the contrary the basis and substructure of loftier insights. .... We must, however, be on our guard against letting the *theoria* do away with the historical basis, for the result would then be, not *theoria*, but allegory.' In harmony with this he freely admitted[1] the propriety of treating Cain as prefiguring the synagogue, Abel the Church, and the spotless lamb enjoined by the Law Christ. Similarly Theodore discerned[2] in the Israelites' sprinkling of their doors with blood at the Exodus an authentic sign of our deliverance by Christ's blood, and in the brazen serpent a type of the Lord's conquest of death; while he agreed that in the experiences of Jonah God foreshadowed Christ's entombment and resurrection, and His summons of mankind to eternal life.

As the theorists of the movement, Diodore and Theodore were severest in applying its principles. The result was the elimination of all purely allegorical or symbolical exegesis from the Old and New Testaments, and the drastic limitation of both the strictly prophetic and the typological elements in the Old. Theodore, for example, refused to recognize such traditionally accepted texts as Hos. 11, 1 f.; Mic. 4, 1-3; 5, 1 f.; Hag. 2, 9; Zech. 11, 12-14; 12, 10; Mal. 1, 11; 4, 5 f. as directly Messianic; they did not conform to his rigorous criteria, and their contexts provided (he thought) a fully satisfying historical explanation. Similarly he reduced[3] the number of Psalms which he allowed to be directly prophetic of the Incarnation and the Church to four (2; 8; 45; 110). In the case of other Psalms (e.g. 21, 2; 69, 22) which had been applied to the Saviour either by the apostolic writers or by Himself, he explained[4] that they lent themselves to this use, not because they were predictive, but because His spiritual predicament has been analogous to the Psalmist's. Yet he was prepared to concede that some Psalms (e.g. 16; 55; 89) and prophecies (e.g. Joel 2, 28 f.; Am. 9, 11; Zech. 9, 9; Mal. 3, 1), although not Messianic if taken literally, could legitimately be interpreted as such in so far as

[1] Art. cit. p. 88.   [2] In Ion. praef. ; 2, 8 ff. (PG 66, 320 f.; 337-40).
[3] Cf. R. Devreesse, *Essai sur Théodore de Mopsueste* (*Studi e Testi*, 141, 1948), pp. 70 ff.   [4] E.g. *in pss.* 21, 2; 30, 6 (Devreesse, 121; 137 f.).

they were types which reached their true fulfilment in the Christian revelation. His attitude to *Canticles*, which was almost everywhere treated as an allegory of the Church, or else of the loving soul's intercourse with Christ, was equally cautious. Its plain, literal meaning, he insisted, must be given full weight, and it was in fact an epithalamium composed by Solomon to celebrate his marriage with the Egyptian princess; but there is no reason to infer, as his later critics did, that he excluded the possibility of a deeper significance as well. On the other hand, his position, like Diodore's, must be admitted to have been an extreme one. Other convinced Antiochenes, like Chrysostom and Theodoret, while loyal to the principles of the school, felt themselves free to apply them more flexibly. The former, while stating his clear preference for the literal sense, is not averse[1] on occasion from citing the figurative as well. The latter is much readier than Theodore to recognize[2] the prophetic element in the Psalms, and affirms[3] that, so far from being an actual human love-song, *Canticles* is a 'spiritual work'.

[1] Cf. *in Is.* 1, 22; 6, 6.   [2] *In pss.* prol.   [3] *In Cant.* prol.

NOTE ON BOOKS

Canon. E. C. Blackman, *Marcion and His Influence* (London, 1948); H. von Campenhausen, *The Formation of the Christian Bible* (Eng. trans.: London, 1972); J. Knox, *Marcion and the New Testament* (Chicago, 1942); M. J. Lagrange, *Histoire ancienne du canon du nouveau testament* (Paris, 1933); A. Merk, 'Origenes und der Kanon des alten Testaments' (art. in *Biblica*, 1925); A. Souter (rev. by C. S. C. Williams), *The Text and Canon of the New Testament* (London, 1956); H. B. Swete, *Introduction to the Old Testament in Greek* (Cambridge, 2 ed. 1914).

Inspiration. H. Cremer, 'Inspiration' (art in Hauck's *Realencyk.*); E. Mangenot, 'Inspiration de l'Écriture' (art in *Dict. Théol. Cath.*); W. Sanday, *Inspiration* (London, 1893); M. Wiles, *The Making of Christian Doctrine*, chap. 3 (Cambridge, 1967).

Exegesis. G. Bardy, 'Interprétation chez les pères' (art. in *Dict. de la Bible: Suppl.*); J. Daniélou, *Origen* (Eng. trans., London, 1955); *Sacramentum Futuri* (Paris, 1950); 'The Fathers and the Scriptures' (art. in *Theology*, 1954); R. Devreesse, *Le Commentaire de Théodore de Mopsueste sur les psaumes* (Vatican City, 1939); C. H. Dodd, *According to the Scriptures*

(London, 1952); R. M. Grant, *The Letter and the Spirit* (London, 1957); R. P. C. Hanson, *Allegory and Event* (London, 1959); G. W. H. Lampe, 'Typological Exegesis' (art. in *Theology*, 1953); G. W. H. Lampe and K. J. Woollcombe, *Essays on Typology* (London, 1957); H. de Lubac, 'Typologie et allégorisme' (art. in *Rech. sc. relig.*, 1947); *Histoire et esprit: l'intelligence de l'écriture d'après Origène* (Paris, 1950); J. Pépin, *Mythe et allégorie* (Paris, 1958); L. Pirot, *L'Œuvre exégétique de Théodore de Mopsueste* (Rome, 1913); M. Pontet, *L'Exégese de saint Augustin prédicateur* (Paris, 1945); A. Vaccari, 'La Θεωρία antiochena nella scuola esegetica di Antiochia' (arts. in *Biblica*, 1920 and 1934); M. Wiles, *The Spiritual Gospel*, esp. chap. 3 (Cambridge, 1960).

General. *The Cambridge History of the Bible*, vol. I (eds. P. R. Ackroyd and C. F. Evans: Cambridge, 1970): esp. chap. iii, 6 and 7; chap. iv, 9, 10 and 12; chap. v, 13–18; vol. II (ed. G. W. H. Lampe: Cambridge, 1969): esp. chaps. ii, iv and vi, 1.

CHAPTER IV

THE DIVINE TRIAD

1. *One God the Creator*

THE classical creeds of Christendom opened with a declaration of belief in one God, maker of heaven and earth. The monotheistic idea, grounded in the religion of Israel, loomed large in the minds of the earliest fathers; though not reflective theologians, they were fully conscious that it marked the dividing line between the Church and paganism. According to Hermas,[1] the first commandment is to 'believe that God is one, Who created and established all things, bringing them into existence out of non-existence'. It was He Who 'by His invisible and mighty power and great wisdom created the universe, and by His glorious purpose clothed His creation with comeliness, and by His strong word fixed the heavens and founded the earth above the waters'.[2] For Clement[3] God is 'the Father and creator of the entire cosmos', and for 'Barnabas'[4] and the *Didache*[5] 'our maker'. His omnipotence and universal sovereignty were acknowledged, for He was 'the Lord almighty',[6] 'the Lord Who governs the whole universe',[7] and 'the master of all things'.[8] The reader should notice that at this period the title 'almighty' connoted God's all-pervading control and sovereignty over reality, just as 'Father' referred primarily to His role as creator and author of all things.

These ideas derive almost exclusively from the Bible and latter-day Judaism, rarely from contemporary philosophy. Echoes of later Stoicism, however, are audible in Clement's references[9] to God's ordering of His cosmos. When we pass to

[1] *Mand.* I, I.	[2] *Vis.* I, 3, 4.	[3] 19, 2.
[4] 19, 2.	[5] I, 2.	[6] *Did.* 10, 3.
[7] *Barn.* 21, 5.	[8] *1 Clem.* 8, 2.	[9] E.g. 20; 33.

the Apologists, the infiltration of secular thought is even more
obvious. Aristides of Athens, for example, opened[1] the *Apology*
which he addressed to the emperor Hadrian (117–38), or possibly Antoninus Pius (138–61), with an outline demonstration
of God's existence based on Aristotle's argument[2] from motion.
The consideration of the order and beauty of the universe induced him to believe in a supreme Being Who was the prime
mover and Who, remaining Himself invisible, dwelt in His
creation. The fact that there was a cosmos demanded a divine
craftsman to organize it. Sovereign and Lord, He has created
everything for man; reality came to be out of nothing at the
behest of Him Who is incorruptible, unchanging and invisible.
He Himself is uncreated, without beginning or end; He has no
form, no limits, no sex. The heavens do not contain Him
(here we detect a criticism of Stoic pantheism,[3] with its identification of God with the world); on the contrary, He contains
them, as He contains everything visible and invisible. Hence
Christians 'acknowledge God as creator and demiurge of all
things . . . and apart from Him worship no other God'.[4]

In Justin the oneness, transcendence and creative role of God
are asserted in language strongly coloured by the Platonizing
Stoicism[5] of the day. It was apparently his sincere belief[6] that
the Greek thinkers had had access to the works of Moses. So
God is everlasting,[7] ineffable and without name,[8] changeless
and impassible,[9] and 'ingenerate'[10] (ἀγέννητος: a technical term
stressing His unique unoriginateness in contrast to creatures).
He is also 'the creator of the universe', the maker and Father of
all things; Himself above being, He is the cause of all existence,[11]
and Marcion was wrong in drawing a distinction between God
and the Demiurge.[12] 'We have learned', he states,[13] 'that, being
good, He created all things in the beginning out of formless
matter.' This was the teaching of Plato's *Timaeus*,[14] which Justin

[1] 1; 4.   [2] See above, p. 17.   [3] See above, p. 18.
[4] 15, 3.   [5] See above, p. 19.   [6] 1 apol. 44, 8; 59, 1.
[7] Ib. 13, 4.   [8] Ib. 9, 3; 61, 11; 63, 1.   [9] Ib. 13, 4; 25, 2.
[10] Ib. 14, 1; 2 apol. 6, 1.   [11] 1 apol. 13, 1; dial. 56, 1; 3, 5; 4, 1.
[12] 1 apol. 58, 1.   [13] Ib. 10, 2: cf. 59, 5; 67, 8.
[14] E.g. 30; 53; 69: see above, p. 16.

supposed[1] to be akin to, and borrowed from, that contained in *Genesis*. For Plato, of course, pre-existent matter was eternal, but it is improbable that Justin acquiesced in the implied dualism; what seems clear[2] is that he regarded the heaven and earth which, according to Moses, had been created first as the material out of which God formed His cosmos. A further important point he made[3] was that, in creating and sustaining the universe, God used His Logos, or Word, as His instrument.

The other Apologists were in line with Justin, although some quite definitely supported creation *ex nihilo*. As Tatian pointed out,[4] the matter out of which the universe was made was itself created by 'the sole artificer of the cosmos', and He created it through His Word. 'From nothing', declared[5] Theophilus of Antioch, 'God created whatever He willed, as He willed it'. Athenagoras, however, envisaged[6] Providence as shaping pre-existent matter. Nevertheless they all emphasized His transcendence. 'Is it not absurd', exclaimed[7] Athenagoras, 'to level the charge of atheism against us, who distinguish God from matter, and teach that God is one thing and matter another, and that they are separated by a vast chasm? For the Deity is unoriginate and eternal, to be apprehended by understanding and reason alone, whereas matter is originate and perishable.' For Theophilus[8] God was 'without beginning because uncreated', 'immutable because immortal', 'Lord because He is Lord over all things', 'Father because He is prior to all things', 'most high because He is above all things', 'almighty because He holds all things; for the heights of the heavens, the depths of the abysses and the ends of the world are in His hands'. He was particularly critical[9] of the Platonic notion of the eternity of matter, arguing that, if it were true, God could not be the creator of all things, and therefore His 'monarchy', i.e. His position as the sole first principle, must go by the board. As he expressed it, 'The power of God is manifested in this, that out of things that are not He makes whatever He pleases'.

[Margin annotation: Good Statement]

---

[1] Ib. 59.
[2] Cf. ib. 59, 5.
[3] Ib. 59; 64; *2 apol.* 6.
[4] *Or.* 5, 1-3.
[5] *Ad Autol.* 2, 4.
[6] *Supplic.* 19, 2: cf. 10.
[7] Ib. 4, 1 f.
[8] Ib. 1, 5.
[9] Ib. 2, 4.

With Irenaeus the affirmation of God as one and as creator assumed special prominence; his task was different from that of the Apologists, being to rebut the Gnostics' theory of a hierarchy of aeons descending from an unknowable Supreme God, with its corollary of a gulf between Him and the creator or Demiurge. One or two texts make his position clear. 'It is proper', he wrote,[1] 'that we should start with the first, most important proposition, viz. God the creator (*a demiurgo deo*), Who made heaven and earth and everything in them, the God Whom they (i.e. the Gnostics) blasphemously describe as an abortive product; and that we should show that there is nothing above or after Him . . . since He is alone God, alone Lord, alone creator, alone Father, and alone contains all things and bestows existence on them.' The first article of our faith, he explained,[2] is 'God the Father, increate, unengendered, invisible, one and only Deity, creator of the universe'; Christ's own words imply that the world has but one fabricator, and that He is identical with the God proclaimed by the Law and the prophets.[3] He taught[4] that God exercises His creative activity through His Word and His Wisdom, or Spirit, and was a firm believer in creation *ex nihilo*, pointing out[5] that 'men indeed cannot make anything out of nothing, but only out of material already before them; God is superior to men in this prime respect, that He Himself furnished the material for His creation although it had no previous existence'.

To establish these principles Irenaeus appeals,[6] in addition to Scripture, to our natural reason: 'Created things must necessarily draw the commencement of their existence from some first cause; and God is the commencement of all. He comes from no one, and all things come from Him. . . . Among all things is included what we call the world, and in the world man. So this world has also been created by God.' Again, he delights[7] to expose the contradiction involved in postulating a series of emanations of graded degrees of divinity: 'By the very

---

[1] *Haer.* 2, 1, 1: cf. *dem.* 4 f.   [2] *Dem.* 6.   [3] *Haer.* 2, 11, 1.
[4] Ib. 2, 30, 9; *dem.* 5.   [5] *Haer.* 2, 10, 4.
[6] *Dem.* 4: cf. *haer.* 2, 6, 1.   [7] *Haer.* 2, 1, 4.

reasoning by which they strive to show that there is a Pleroma, or God, above the creator of heaven and earth, it will be possible to maintain that there is another Pleroma above the Pleroma, another again above that, and above Bythos another ocean of deity ... and thus, their doctrine tailing off *ad infinitum*, they will always be required to conceive of other Pleromata and other Bythi.' In any case, every subordinate emanation must share the nature of its principle,[1] but the very notion of Godhead excludes a plurality of Gods. 'Either there must be one God Who contains all things and has made every creature according to His will; or there must be many indeterminate creators or gods, each beginning and ending at his place in the series. . . . But in this case we shall have to acknowledge that none of them is God. For each of them . . . will be defective in comparison with the rest, and the title "Almighty" will be reduced to nought.'[2] The Demiurge of Gnosticism cannot be God since he has another superior to himself.[3]

2. *The Church's Faith*

The doctrine of one God, the Father and creator, formed the background and indisputable premiss of the Church's faith. Inherited from Judaism, it was her bulwark against pagan polytheism, Gnostic emanationism and Marcionite dualism. The problem for theology was to integrate with it, intellectually, the fresh data of the specifically Christian revelation. Reduced to their simplest, these were the convictions that God had made Himself known in the Person of Jesus, the Messiah, raising Him from the dead and offering salvation to men through Him, and that He had poured out His Holy Spirit upon the Church. Even at the New Testament stage ideas about Christ's pre-existence and creative role were beginning to take shape, and a profound, if often obscure, awareness of the activity of the Spirit in the Church was emerging. No steps had been taken so far, however, to work all these complex elements into a coherent whole. The Church had to wait for more than three

[1] Ib. 2, 17, 7.   [2] Ib. 2, 1, 5.   [3] Ib. 4, 2, 5.

hundred years for a final synthesis, for not until the council of Constantinople (381) was the formula of one God existing in three co-equal Persons formally ratified. Tentative theories, however, some more and some less satisfactory, were propounded in the preceding centuries, and it will be the business of this chapter and the next to survey the movement of thought down to the council of Nicaea (325).

Before considering formal writers, the reader should notice how deeply the conception of a plurality of divine Persons was imprinted on the apostolic tradition and the popular faith. Though as yet uncanonized, the New Testament was already exerting a powerful influence; it is a commonplace that the outlines of a dyadic and a triadic pattern are clearly visible in its pages.[1] It is even more marked in such glimpses as are obtainable of the Church's liturgy and day-to-day catechetical practice. In the primitive period there were no stereotyped creeds of the kind that later became regular, but it is clear that, as in the apostolic age, the main theme of the Church's propaganda, as of her worship, was that God had sent His Son, the Messiah Jesus, Who had died, risen on the third day, ascended to heaven, and would return in glory. The writings of Ignatius[2] and Justin[3] suggest that this very early began to settle down in semi-fixed formularies. Often these included a reference to the Holy Spirit, the inspirer of the Old Testament prophets and the gift bestowed in these latter times on the faithful. As the second century advances, we come across more detailed citations of 'the rule of faith', i.e. the teaching inherited from the apostles and set out in freely worded summaries.[4] Sometimes these are cast in a dyadic mould and refer to the Father and the Lord Jesus Christ, but the triadic pattern, affirming belief in the Father Who created the universe, in His Son Jesus Christ, and in the Holy Spirit, gradually becomes normal. An illustration may be quoted from a treatise[5] of Irenaeus's which gives

---

[1] For a summary of the evidence see J. N. D. Kelly, *Early Christian Creeds* (London, 3 ed. 1972), chap. 1.

[2] E.g. *Eph.* 18, 2; *Trall.* 9; *Smyrn.* 1, 1 f.

[3] E.g. *1 apol.* 21, 1; 31, 7; *dial.* 63, 1; 126, 1.   [4] See above, p. 40.

[5] *Dem.* 6.

a very fair picture of intelligent catechetical instruction at this period:

> This, then, is the order of the rule of our faith. . . . God the Father, not made, not material, invisible; one God, the creator of all things: this is the first point of our faith. The second point is this: the Word of God, Son of God, Christ Jesus our Lord, Who was manifested to the prophets according to the form of their prophesying and according to the method of the Father's dispensation; through Whom (i.e. the Word) all things were made; Who also, at the end of the age, to complete and gather up all things, was made man among men, visible and tangible, in order to abolish death and show forth life and produce perfect reconciliation between God and man. And the third point is: the Holy Spirit, through Whom the prophets prophesied, and the fathers learned the things of God, and the righteous were led into the way of righteousness; Who at the end of the age was poured out in a new way upon mankind in all the earth, renewing man to God.

The baptismal rite is the liturgy with which we are best acquainted for this time, and the evidence it provides is in complete harmony with this. Whether or not baptism was administered in the apostolic age, as many New Testament texts seem to imply, in the name of Jesus, the triadic pattern was not slow in asserting itself, no doubt under the influence of the Lord's command recorded in Matt. 28, 19. So the *Didache* prescribed[1] baptism in the threefold name. Justin relates[2] that those who are to be baptized 'are conducted by us to a place where there is water, and there, in the same manner as we ourselves were regenerated, they are regenerated in turn. In the name of God the Father and master of all things, and of our Saviour Jesus Christ, they are washed in the water'. Later he adds[3] that baptism is 'in the name of God the Father and master of all things', of 'Jesus Christ, Who was crucified under Pontius Pilate', and 'of the Holy Spirit, Who foretold by the

---

[1] 7, 1-3. [2] *1 apol.* 61, 3. [3] Ib. 61, 10-13.

prophets the whole story of Jesus'. Clearly he has in mind a liturgical formula which was already stereotyped, as has Irenaeus when he reports,[1] 'We received baptism for the remission of sins in the name of God the Father, and in the name of Jesus Christ, the Son of God, Who was incarnate and died and rose again, and in the Holy Spirit of God'. A similar pattern formed the ground-plan of the doxology ('glory to the Father of all things, in the name of the Son and of the Holy Spirit') which Justin assumes[2] to have been included in the eucharistic prayer, as also of the doxology ('I glorify Thee through the everlasting and heavenly high-priest Jesus Christ, Thy beloved Son, through Whom be glory to Thee together with Him and the Holy Spirit') with which Polycarp is related[3] to have ended his prayer before his martyrdom.

The ideas implicit in these early catechetical and liturgical formulae, as in the New Testament writers' use of the same dyadic and triadic patterns, represent a pre-reflective, pre-theological phase of Christian belief. This in no way diminishes their interest and importance. It was out of the raw material thus provided by the preaching, worshipping Church that theologians had to construct their more sophisticated accounts of the Christian doctrine of the Godhead.

3. *The Apostolic Fathers*

The earliest writers we have to consider, the Apostolic Fathers, appear as witnesses to the traditional faith rather than interpreters striving to understand it. Nevertheless their deliverances, usually fragmentary and often naïve, furnish useful insight into the lines along which the Church's unconscious theology was developing; and this insight is all the more valuable because, so far from being a homogeneous group, they were the spokesmen of widely differing trends.

Little can be gleaned from the first of them, Clement of Rome. He coordinates the Three in an oath,[4] 'As God lives,

---

[1] *Dem.* 3: cf. ib. 7.   [2] *1 apol.* 65.
[3] *Mart. Polyc.* 14, 3.   [4] 58, 2.

and the Lord Jesus Christ lives, and the Holy Spirit'; and again in the question,[1] 'Have we not one God, and one Christ, and one Spirit of grace poured upon us?' As for Christ, he takes[2] His pre-existence prior to the incarnation for granted, since it was He Who spoke through the Spirit in the Psalms, and Who is 'the sceptre of majesty', i.e. the instrument through which God has ever exercised His sovereignty. He is also 'the way by which we have found salvation, the high-priest of our offering'; through Him we 'gaze up to the heights of heaven'.[3] The Holy Spirit Clement regarded[4] as inspiring God's prophets in all ages, as much the Old Testament writers as himself. But of the problem of the relation of the Three to each other he seems to have been oblivious.

2 Clement and 'Barnabas' have each special traits of their own. The former opens[5] by advising its readers to 'think of Jesus Christ as of God, as of the judge of living and dead'. He is our Saviour, and 'through Him we have known the Father of truth'.[6] In a later chapter the author lays bare his underlying conception of the relation of Christ to the Father, stating[7] that 'being first of all spirit, Christ the Lord, Who saved us, became flesh and so called us'. It seems plain that in using this language he was not, as one might be tempted to infer, confusing the Son and the Holy Spirit, for elsewhere[8] he identifies the latter with the pre-existent, spiritual Church, which he evidently regards as distinct from the pre-existent Christ. Hence, though his thought is obscure, he seems to acknowledge three—God the Father, Christ Who was spirit and became flesh, and the Holy Spirit, the heavenly Church and mother of the faithful. Hints of a similar two-level use of 'spirit' occur in 'Barnabas'. Sometimes he makes reference,[9] in traditional fashion, to the Spirit as inspiring prophets and as having prepared in advance those whom God calls; but he also speaks[10] of Christ's body as 'the vessel of spirit', presumably denoting by the word the spiritual nature of the divine element in the Lord. The chief

---

[1] 46, 6. [2] 22, 1; 16, 2. [3] 36, 1 f.
[4] 8, 1; 13, 1; 16, 2; 63, 2. [5] 1, 1. [6] Ib. 3, 1.
[7] 9, 5. [8] 14, 3. [9] 6, 14; 12, 2; 19, 7. [10] 7, 3; 11, 9

interest of his theology, however, is the prominence it gives to
Christ's pre-existence. It was He Who cooperated[1] with God
the Father at creation (the words, 'Let us make man in our
image', were addressed to Him); He conversed with Moses,
and before the incarnation received His mandate from the
Father.[2] He is 'Lord of the entire cosmos', and it is His glory
that 'all things are in Him, and unto Him'.[3]

IGNATIUS Ignatius and Hermas are rather more revealing, although
their approaches differed markedly. The centre of Ignatius's
thinking was Christ. It is true that he assigned a proper place to
the Holy Spirit. He was the principle of the Lord's virginal conception;[4] it was by Him that Christ established and confirmed
the Church's officers;[5] He was the gift sent by the Saviour, and
spoke through Ignatius himself.[6] Further, the triadic formula
occurs thrice[7] at least in his letters, the most notable example
being a picturesque simile comparing the faithful to stones
forming the temple built by God the Father; the cross of Jesus
Christ is the crane by which they are hoisted up, and the Holy
Spirit the hawser. Much more frequently, however, he speaks
of God the Father and Jesus Christ, declaring[8] that 'there is one
God, Who has revealed Himself through His Son Jesus Christ,
Who is His Word emerging from silence'. Christ is the Father's
'thought' ($\gamma\nu\omega\mu\eta$), 'the unlying mouth by which the Father
spoke truly'.[9] Ignatius even declares[10] that He is 'our God', de-
scribing[11] Him as 'God incarnate' ($\dot{\epsilon}\nu\ \sigma\alpha\rho\kappa\grave{\iota}\ \gamma\epsilon\nu\acute{o}\mu\epsilon\nu\sigma\varsigma\ \theta\epsilon\acute{o}\varsigma$) and
'God made manifest as man' ($\theta\epsilon\sigma\hat{v}\ \dot{\alpha}\nu\theta\rho\omega\pi\acute{\iota}\nu\omega\varsigma\ \phi\alpha\nu\epsilon\rho\sigma\nu\mu\acute{\epsilon}\nu\sigma\upsilon$).
He was 'in spirit ($\pi\nu\epsilon\nu\mu\alpha\tau\iota\kappa\hat{\omega}\varsigma$) united with the Father'.[12] In
His pre-existent being 'ingenerate' ($\dot{\alpha}\gamma\acute{\epsilon}\nu\nu\eta\tau\sigma\varsigma$: the technical
term reserved to distinguish the increate God from creatures),
He was the timeless, invisible, impalpable, impassible one Who
for our sakes entered time and became visible, palpable and
passible.[13] His divine Sonship dates from the incarnation.[14]

---

[1] 5, 5; 6, 12.   [2] 14, 3; 14, 6.   [3] 5, 5; 12, 7.
[4] *Eph.* 18, 2.   [5] *Philad.* inscr.   [6] *Eph.* 17, 2; *Philad.* 7, 1.
[7] *Eph.* 9, 1; *Magn.* 13, 1; 13, 2.   [8] *Magn.* 8, 2.
[9] *Eph.* 3, 2; *Rom.* 8, 2.
[10] E.g. *Eph.* inscr.; 18, 2; *Trall.* 7, 1; *Rom.* inscr.   [11] *Eph.* 7, 2; 19, 3.
[12] *Smyrn.* 3, 3.   [13] *Eph.* 7, 2; *Polyc.* 3, 2.   [14] *Smyrn.* 1, 1.

In view of this language the conclusion has sometimes been drawn[1] that, while echoing the triadic scheme made official by the baptismal formula, Ignatius was really an 'economic trinitarian', i.e. regarded God as an undifferentiated monad in His essential being, the Son and the Spirit being merely forms or modes of the Father's self-revelation, only distinguishable from Him in the process of revelation. A closer analysis, however, shows how misleading this interpretation is as an account of Ignatius's thought. This, it should be noted, was steeped in the Fourth Gospel, and its strong emphasis on the oneness of Christ with the Father reflects such Johannine texts as 1, 1 f.; 10, 30; 14, 9; 17, 5. In tracing His divine Sonship to His conception in Mary's womb, he was simply reproducing a commonplace of pre-Origenist theology; the idea did not convey, and was not intended to convey, any denial of His pre-existence. So far as Ignatius is concerned, he definitely states[2] that He 'existed with the Father before the ages', and that He 'came forth from the unique Father, was with Him and has returned to Him'. Phrases like these imply a real distinction, as do the passages[3] in which he compares the relation of deacons to the bishop, or of the church to the bishop, to that of Christ to the Father. Numerous other contexts suggest that His independence *vis-à-vis* the Father was not limited to His earthly sojourn, such as (a) the formulae[4] of greeting and farewell affixed to the letters, and (b) Ignatius's requests[5] to his correspondents to address their prayers to Jesus Christ. But the only hint he gives of the nature of this distinction within the unity of the divine spirit (πνεῦμα) is that Christ is the Father's 'thought' (γνώμη).

The atmosphere completely changes when we pass to Hermas. Preoccupied with repentance and the sovereignty of the one, creative God, he nowhere mentions the name of Jesus, and only discusses His Person in two of his *Similitudes*. The first, a parable obviously modelled on the gospel one, tells[6] the

[1] Notably by F. Loofs (cf. *Leitfaden zum Studium der Dogmengeschichte*, 5 ed. 1950, §15, 4).   [2] *Magn.* 6, 1; 7, 2.
[3] *Trall.* 3, 1; *Magn.* 6, 1; 7, 1; *Smyrn.* 8, 1.
[4] *Eph.* 21, 2; *Magn.* inscr.; *Trall.* 13, 2; *Rom.* inscr.
[5] *Eph.* 20, 1; *Rom.* 4, 2; *Smyrn.* 4, 1.   [6] *Sim.* 5, 2.

story of a land-owner who entrusted his vineyard during his
absence to a servant, and was so pleased on his return with his
management of it that, after consulting 'his well-beloved son
and heir', he decided to make him 'joint-heir' with his son.
The landowner, Hermas explains,[1] is the Creator, the estate the
world, and the servant the Son of God; the landowner's
'beloved son', we gather, is the Holy Spirit. Later, because the
Son of God seems to have been assigned altogether too lowly a
status, he amends[2] his interpretation. The servant, apparently,
was not, as the first account might appear to suggest, a mere
man, but God had caused 'the holy, pre-existent spirit' to indwell Him; it was because His flesh cooperated so willingly
and successfully with this divine spirit that God promoted Him
to be 'a partner with the Holy Spirit'. In the second of the two
Similitudes, which describes the Church under the figure of a
tower built upon an unshakable rock, the Son of God is again
identified[3] with holy spirit ('that holy spirit which spoke with
you in the likeness of the Church is the Son of God'); and
Hermas represents[4] Him as born before the world, the Father's
counsellor in His creative work, the pillar of all creation, and as
having been manifested in these latter days.

Hermas clearly envisages three distinct personages—the
master, i.e. God the Father, his 'well-beloved son', i.e. the
Holy Spirit, and the servant, i.e. the Son of God, Jesus Christ.
The distinction between the three, however, seems to date from
the incarnation; as pre-existent the Son of God is identified[5]
with the Holy Spirit, so that before the incarnation there would
seem to have been but two divine Persons, the Father and the
Spirit. The third, the Saviour or Lord, was elevated to be their
companion as a reward for his merits, having cooperated nobly
with the pre-existent Spirit which indwelt him. Hermas's
theology was thus an amalgam of binitarianism and adoptionism, though it made an attempt to conform to the triadic
formula accepted in the Church. It was still further complicated by being crossed with a totally different set of ideas. In

[1] *Sim.* 5, 5.   [2] Ib. 5, 6.   [3] Ib. 9, 1, 1.
[4] Ib. 9, 12, 1-5; 9, 14, 5.   [5] Ib. 9, 1, 1.

Son of God = Michael in Hermas?

a number of passages[1] we read of an angel who is superior to the six angels forming God's inner council, and who is regularly described as 'most venerable', 'holy', and 'glorious'. This angel is given the name[2] of Michael, and the conclusion is difficult to escape that Hermas saw in him the Son of God and equated him with the archangel Michael. Both, for example, are invested with supreme power over the people of God;[3] both pronounce judgment on the faithful;[4] and both hand sinners over to the angel of repentance to reform them.[5]

The evidence to be collected from the Apostolic Fathers is meagre, and tantalizingly inconclusive. Christ's pre-existence, it should be noted, was generally taken for granted, as was His role in creation as well as redemption. This theme, which could point to Pauline and Johannine parallels, chimed in very easily with the creative functions assigned to Wisdom in later Judaism.[6] The theory that the divine element in Christ was pre-existent spirit had wide currency and could take various forms. There is evidence also, as we observed in the preceding paragraph, of attempts to interpret Christ as a sort of supreme angel; here the influence of Jewish angelology[7] is discernible. Of a doctrine of the Trinity in the strict sense there is of course no sign, although the Church's triadic formula left its mark everywhere.

< note

4. *The Apologists and the Word*

The Apologists were the first to try to frame an intellectually satisfying explanation of the relation of Christ to God the Father. They were all, as we have seen, ardent monotheists, determined at all costs not to compromise this fundamental truth. The solution they proposed, reduced to essentials, was that, as pre-existent, Christ was the Father's thought or mind, and that, as manifested in creation and revelation, He was its extrapolation or expression. In expounding this doctrine they

---

[1] *Vis.* 5, 2; *mand.* 5, 1, 7; *sim.* 5, 4, 4; 7, 1, 5; 8, 1, 2.
[2] *Sim.* 8, 3, 3. [3] Ib. 5, 6, 4; 8, 3, 3.
[4] Ib. 8, 3, 3; 9, 5, 2–7; 9, 6, 3–6; 9, 10, 4.
[5] Ib. 8, 2, 5; 8, 4, 3; 9, 7, 1 f. [6] See above, p. 7.
[7] See above, p. 7.

had recourse to the imagery of the divine Logos, or Word,[1] which had been familiar to later Judaism as well as to Stoicism, and which had become a fashionable cliché through the influence of Philo. Others had, of course, anticipated them. In the Fourth Gospel,[2] for example, the Word is declared to have been with God in the beginning and to have become flesh in Christ, while for Ignatius[3] Christ was the Father's Word issuing from silence. The Apologists' originality (their thought was more Philonic than Johannine) lay in drawing out the further implications of the Logos idea in order to make plausible the twofold fact of Christ's pre-temporal oneness with the Father and His manifestation in space and time. In so doing, while using such Old Testament texts as *Ps.* 33, 6 ('By the word of the Lord were the heavens made'), they did not hesitate to blend with them the Stoic technical distinction[4] between the immanent word (λόγος ἐνδιάθετος) and the word uttered or expressed (λόγος προφορικός).

JUSTIN   Their teaching appears most clearly in Justin, although his theology is far from being systematic. His starting-point was the current maxim that reason (the 'germinal logos'=λόγος σπερματικός) was what united men to God and gave them knowledge of Him. Before Christ's coming men had possessed, as it were, seeds of the Logos and had thus been enabled to arrive at fragmentary facets of truth.[5] Hence such pagans as 'lived with reason' were, in a sense, Christians before Christianity.[6] The Logos, however, had now 'assumed shape and become a man' in Jesus Christ; He had become incarnate in His entirety in Him.[7] The Logos is here conceived of as the Father's intelligence or rational thought; but Justin argued[8] that He was not only in name distinct from the Father, as the light is from the sun, but was 'numerically distinct too' (καὶ ἀριθμῷ ἕτερον). His proof, which he was particularly concerned to develop against Jewish monotheism, was threefold. The Word's otherness, he thought, was implied (a) by the alleged appearances of

[1] See above, pp. 9–11; 18 f.   [2] 1, 1 ff.
[3] *Magn.* 8, 2: cf. *Eph.* 3, 2; *Rom.* 8, 2.   [4] See above, pp. 18 f.
[5] *1 apol.* 32, 8; *2 apol.* 8, 1; 10, 2; 13, 3.   [6] *1 apol.* 46, 3.
[7] Ib. 5, 4; *2 apol.* 10, 1.   [8] *Dial.* 128, 4.

God in the Old Testament (e.g. to Abraham by the oaks of Mamre), which suggest[1] that, 'below the Creator of all things, there is Another Who is, and is called, God and Lord', since it is inconceivable that 'the Master and Father of all things should have abandoned all supercelestial affairs and made Himself visible in a minute corner of the world'; (b) by the frequent Old Testament passages (e.g. *Gen.* 1, 26: 'Let us make man etc.') which represent God as conversing with another, Who is presumably a rational being like Himself;[2] and (c) by the great Wisdom texts, such as *Prov.* 8, 22 ff. ('The Lord created me a beginning of His ways etc.'), since everyone must agree that the offspring is other than its begetter.[3] So the Logos, 'having been put forth as an offspring from the Father, was with Him before all creatures, and the Father had converse with Him'.[4] And He is divine: 'being Word and first-begotten of God, He is also God'.[5] 'Thus, then, He is adorable, He is God';[6] and 'we adore and love, next to God, the Logos derived from the increate and ineffable God, seeing that for our sakes He became man'.[7]

The incarnation apart, the special functions of the Logos, according to Justin, are two: to be the Father's agent in creating and ordering the universe,[8] and to reveal truth to men.[9] As regards His nature, while other beings are 'things made' (ποιήματα[10]) or 'creatures' (κτίσματα[11]), the Logos is God's 'offspring' (γέννημα[12]), His 'child' (τέκνον[13]) and 'unique Son' (ὁ μονογενής[14]): 'before all creatures God begat, in the beginning, a rational power out of Himself'.[15] By this generation Justin means, not the ultimate origin of the Father's Logos or reason (this he does not discuss), but His putting forth or emission for the purposes of creation and revelation; and it is conditioned by, and is the result of, an act of the Father's will.[16] But this generation or emission does not entail any separation between the Father and His Son, as the analogy between human

---

[1] Ib. 56, 4; 60, 2.   [2] Ib. 62, 2.
[3] Ib. 129, 3 f.: cf. ib. 61, 3-7; 62, 4.   [4] Ib. 62, 4.
[5] 1 apol. 63, 15.   [6] Dial. 63, 5.   [7] 2 apol. 13, 4.
[8] 1 apol. 59; 64, 5; 2 apol. 6, 3.
[9] 1 apol. 5, 4; 46; 63, 10; 2 apol. 10, 1 f.; etc.   [10] 2 apol. 6, 3; dial. 62, 4.
[11] Dial. 61, 1; 100, 2.   [12] 1 apol. 21, 1; dial. 62, 4   [13] Dial. 125, 3.
[14] Ib. 105, 1.   [15] Ib. 61, 1.   [16] Ib. 61, 1; 100, 4; 127, 4; 128, 4.

reason and its extrapolation in speech makes clear. 'When we utter a word, we give birth to the word (or reason) within us, but without diminishing it, since the putting of it forth entails no abscission. We observe much the same when one fire is kindled from another. The fire from which it is kindled is not diminished but remains the same; while the fire which is kindled from it is seen to exist by itself without diminishing the original fire'.[1] Elsewhere[2] Justin uses the analogy of the impossibility of distinguishing the light from the sun which is its source in order to argue that 'this Power is indivisible and inseparable from the Father', and that His numerical distinction from the Father does not involve any partition of the latter's essence.

Tatian was a disciple of Justin's, and like his master spoke[3] of the Logos as existing in the Father as His rationality and then, by an act of His will, being generated. Like Justin, too, he emphasized[4] the Word's essential unity with the Father, using the same image of light kindled from light. 'The birth of the Logos involves a distribution (μερισμόν), but no sever-ance (ἀποκοπήν). Whatever is severed is cut off from its original, but that which is distributed undergoes division in the economy without impoverishing the source from which it is derived. For just as a single torch serves to light several fires and the light of the first torch is not lessened because others are kindled from it, so the Word issues forth from the Father's power without depriving His begetter of His Word. For ex-ample, I talk and you listen to me; but I, who converse with you, am not, by the conveyance of my word to you, made empty of my word.' At the same time Tatian threw[5] into sharper relief than Justin the contrast between the two suc-cessive states of the Logos. Before creation God was alone, the Logos being immanent in Him as His potentiality for creating all things; but at the moment of creation He leaped forth from the Father as His 'primordial work' (ἔργον πρωτότοκον). Once born, being 'spirit derived from spirit, rationality from

---

[1] *Dial.* 61, 2.   [2] Ib. 128, 3 f.   [3] *Or.* 5, 1.
[4] Ib. 5, 1 f.   [5] Ib. 5, 1.

rational power', He served as the Father's instrument in creating and governing the universe, in particular making men in the divine image.[1]

The teaching of Theophilus of Antioch followed similar lines, although he frankly used the Stoic technical terms appropriate to the underlying system of ideas. 'God', he wrote,[2] 'having His Word immanent (ἐνδιάθετον) in His bowels, engendered Him along with His wisdom, emitting Him before the universe. He used this Word as His assistant in His creative work, and by Him He has made all things. This Word is called First Principle because He is the principle and Lord of all things fashioned by Him'. Again, dealing with the sonship of the Logos, he wrote:[3] 'He is not His Son in the sense in which poets and romancers relate the birth of sons to gods, but rather in the sense in which the truth speaks of the Word as eternally immanent (ἐνδιάθετον) in God's bosom. For before anything came into being He had Him as His counsellor, His own intelligence and thought. But when God willed to create what He had planned, He engendered and brought forth (ἐγέννησε προφορικόν) this Word, the first-begotten of all creation. He did not thereby empty Himself of His Word, but having begotten Him consorts with Him always'. Like Justin, Theophilus regarded[4] the Old Testament theophanies as having been in fact appearances of the Logos. God Himself cannot be contained in space and time, but it was precisely the function of the Word Whom He generated to manifest His mind and will in the created order.

A rather fuller account is given by Athenagoras. In a famous passage,[5] after stating that the unoriginate, eternal and invisible God has created and adorned, and actually governs, the universe by His Word, he goes on to identify the Word as the Son of God. Repudiating the objection that there is something ridiculous in God's having a son, he protests that God's Son is not like the children of men, but is 'the Father's Word in idea and in actualization' (ἐν ἰδέᾳ καὶ ἐνεργείᾳ). It was by Him, and

---

[1] Ib. 7, 1 f.   [2] Ad Autol. 2, 10.   [3] Ib. 2, 22.
[4] Ib.   [5] Supplic. 10, 1 ff.

through Him, that everything was made, and the Father and the Son form a unity. 'The Son being in the Father and the Father in the Son by the unity and power of divine spirit, the Son of God is the Father's intelligence and Word' (νοῦς καὶ λόγος). To make his meaning clearer, Athenagoras then points out that, while He is God's offspring, He never actually came into being (οὐχ ὡς γενόμενον), 'for God from the beginning, being eternal intelligence, had His Word (λόγον) in Himself, being eternally rational' (ἀιδίως λογικός). A more correct account would be, that He 'issued forth' (προελθών : again the idea of λόγος προφορικός) into the world of formless matter as the archetypal idea and creative force. In support of this he quotes *Prov.* 8, 22, 'The Lord created me as a beginning of His ways for His works', without stressing, however, the verb 'created'. In a later chapter[1] he speaks of 'the true God and the Logos Who derives from Him', dwelling on the unity and fellowship which exist between Father and Son; and elsewhere[2] he describes the Son as the Father's 'intelligence, Word, wisdom'.

There are two points in the Apologists' teaching which, because of their far-reaching importance, must be heavily underlined, viz. (a) that for all of them the description 'God the Father' connoted, not the first Person of the Holy Trinity, but the one Godhead considered as author of whatever exists; and (b) that they all, Athenagoras included, dated the generation of the Logos, and so His eligibility for the title 'Son', not from His origination within the being of the Godhead, but from His emission or putting forth for the purposes of creation, revelation and redemption. Unless these points are firmly grasped, and their significance appreciated, a completely distorted view of the Apologists' theology is liable to result. Two stock criticisms of it, for example, are that they failed to distinguish the Logos from the Father until He was required for the work of creation, and that, as a corollary, they were guilty of subordinating the Son to the Father. These objections have a superficial validity in the light of post-Nicene orthodoxy, with its doctrine of the Son's eternal generation and its fully worked-out conception of hypostases or Persons; but they make no sense in the thought-atmosphere in which the Apologists moved. It is true that they lacked a technical vocabulary adequate for describing eternal distinctions within the Deity; but that they apprehended such distinctions admits of no doubt. Long before creation, from all eternity, God had His Word or Logos, for God is essentially rational; and if what later theology recognized as the personality of the Word seems ill defined in their eyes, it is plain that they regarded Him as one with Whom the Father could commune and take counsel. Later orthodoxy was to describe His eternal relation to the Father as generation; the fact that the Apologists restricted this term to His emission should not lead one to conclude that they had no awareness of His existence prior to that. Similarly, when Justin spoke of Him as a 'second God' worshipped 'in a secondary rank',[1] and when all the Apologists stressed that His generation or emission resulted from an act of the Father's will, their object was not so much to subordinate Him as to safeguard the monotheism which they considered indispensable. The Logos as manifested must necessarily be limited as compared with the Godhead Itself; and it was important to emphasize that there were not two springs of initiative within the Divine Being. That the Logos was one in essence with the Father, inseparable in His fundamental being from Him as much after His generation as prior to it, the Apologists were never weary of reiterating.

Logos one in essence with the Father

5. The Apologists and the Trinity

What the Apologists had to say about the Holy Spirit was much more meagre, scarcely deserving the name of scientific theology. This is understandable, for the problem which principally exercised them was the relation of Christ to the Godhead. Nevertheless, being loyal churchmen, they made it their business to proclaim the Church's faith, the pattern of which was of course triadic.

[1] Cf. *1 apol.* 13, 3.

On several occasions Justin coordinates the three Persons, sometimes quoting[1] formulae derived from baptism and the eucharist, and at other times echoing official catechetical teaching. Thus he counters[2] the charge of atheism brought against Christians by pointing to the veneration they pay to the Father, the Son and 'the prophetic Spirit'. Indeed, references to 'the holy Spirit' or 'the prophetic Spirit' abound in his writings; and although he was often hazy about the relation of His functions to those of the Logos, the attempts he made[3] to extract testimony to His existence as a third divine being from Plato's writings prove that he regarded the two as really distinct. According to Tatian,[4] 'the Spirit of God is not present in all, but He comes down upon some who live justly, unites Himself with their souls, and by His predictions announced the hidden future to other souls'. Athenagoras conceived[5] of the Spirit as inspiring the prophets, and was familiar[6] with the triadic formula; he even defined[7] the Spirit as 'an effluence (ἀπόρροιαν) of God, flowing from and returning to Him like a beam of the sun'. Theophilus, parting company at this point with Justin, identified[8] the Spirit with Wisdom, equating the latter with the spirit which, according to Ps. 33, 6, God used along with His Word in creation. He was the first to apply the term 'triad' to the Godhead, stating[9] that the three days which preceded the creation of sun and moon 'were types of the Triad, that is, of God and of His Word and of His Wisdom'.

Yet, as compared with their thought about the Logos, the Apologists appear to have been extremely vague as to the exact status and role of the Spirit. His essential function in their eyes would seem to have been the inspiration of the prophets. Developing this, Justin interprets[10] Is. 11, 2 ('The Spirit of God shall rest upon him') as indicating that with the coming of Christ prophecy would cease among the Jews; henceforth the Spirit would be Christ's Spirit, and would bestow His gifts and graces upon Christians. Hence it is He Who is the source of

---

[1] Cf. 1 apol. 61, 3-12; 65, 3.   [2] Ib. 6, 1 f.
[3] Ib. 60, 6 f.: cf. Pseudo-Plato, ep. 2, 312 e.   [4] Or. 13, 3.
[5] Supplic. 7, 2; 9, 1.   [6] Ib. 10, 3.   [7] Ib.
[8] Ad Autol. 1, 7; 2, 15; 18.   [9] Ib. 2, 15.   [10] Dial. 87, 2 ff.

the illumination which makes Christianity the supreme philosophy.[1] There are passages,[2] however, where he attributes the
inspiration of the prophets to the Logos; and Theophilus, too,
suggests[3] that it was the Logos Who, being divine spirit, illuminated their minds. There can be no doubt that the Apologists' thought was highly confused; they were very far from
having worked the threefold pattern of the Church's faith into
a coherent scheme. In this connexion it is noteworthy that
Justin did not assign the Holy Spirit any role in the incarnation.
Like other pre-Nicene fathers, he understood[4] the divine Spirit
and 'power of the Most High' mentioned in *Luke* 1, 35, not as
the Holy Spirit, but as the Logos, Whom he envisaged as
entering the womb of the Blessed Virgin and acting as the
agent of His own incarnation.

In spite of incoherencies, however, the lineaments of a
Trinitarian doctrine are clearly discernible in the Apologists.
The Spirit was for them the Spirit of God; like the Word, He
shared the divine nature, being (in Athenagoras's words) an
'effluence' from the Deity. Although much of Justin's language
about Him has a sub-personal ring, it becomes more personal
when he speaks of 'the prophetic Spirit'; and there is no
escaping the personal implications contained in his pleas[5] that
Plato borrowed his conception of a third One from Moses, and
that the pagan custom of erecting statues of Kore at springs was
inspired by the Scriptural picture of the Spirit moving upon the
waters. As regards the relation of the Three, there is little to be
gleaned from Justin beyond his statement[6] that Christians vener-
ate Christ and the Spirit in the second and the third ranks respectively. Athenagoras echoes this idea when he inveighs[7]
against labelling as atheists 'men who acknowledge God the
Father, God the Son and the Holy Spirit, and declare both Their
power in union and Their distinction in order' (τὴν ἐν τῇ τάξει
διαίρεσιν). This order, or τάξις, however, was not intended
to suggest degrees of subordination within the Godhead; it

---

[1] Ib. 4, 1.   [2] *1 apol.* 33, 9; 36, 1.   [3] *Ad Autol.* 2, 10.
[4] *1 apol.* 33, 4 ff.: cf. *dial.* 100, 5 f.   [5] *1 apol.* 60, 6; 64, 1 ff.
[6] Ib. 13, 3.   [7] *Supplic.* 10, 3.

belonged to the Triad as manifested in creation and revelation.
Theophilus, with his doctrine of God's Word and His Wisdom
(he probably preferred 'Wisdom' to 'Spirit' because of the
persistent ambiguity of the latter term), provides a fairly
mature example of their teaching. In spite of his tendency[1] to
blur the distinction between the Word and the Spirit, he really
had the idea of the holy Triad fixed firmly in his mind. He
envisaged God as having His Word and His Wisdom eternally
in Himself, and generating[2] Them for the purpose of creation;
and he was also clear[3] that when God put Them forth He did
not empty Himself of Them, but 'is forever conversing with
His Word'. Thus the image with which the Apologists worked,
viz. that of a man putting forth his thought and his spirit in
external activity, enabled them to recognize, however dimly,
the plurality in the Godhead, and also to show how the Word
and the Spirit, while really manifested in the world of space
and time, could also abide within the being of the Father, Their
essential unity with Him unbroken.

6. Irenaeus

The theologian who summed up the thought of the second
century, and dominated Christian orthodoxy before Origen,
was Irenaeus. He for his part was deeply indebted to the
Apologists; although he was more of a self-conscious churchman than they, more openly attached to and more ready
to parade the Church's threefold 'rule of faith', the framework
of his thinking remained substantially the same as theirs. Thus
he approached God from two directions, envisaging Him both
as He exists in His intrinsic being, and also as He manifests
Himself in the 'economy', i.e. the ordered process of His self-
disclosure. From the former point of view God is the Father
of all things, ineffably one, and yet containing in Himself from
all eternity His Word and His Wisdom. In making Himself
known, however, or in exerting Himself for creation and redemption, God extrapolates or manifests these; as the Son and

---

[1] See above, p. 102.   [2] *Ad Autol.* 2, 10; 2, 22.   [3] Ib. 2, 10.

the Spirit, They are His 'hands', the vehicles or forms of His self-revelation. Thus Irenaeus could claim[1] that 'by the very essence and nature of His being there is but one God', while at the same time 'according to the economy of our redemption there are both Father and Son'—and, he might easily have added, Spirit. Where he was in advance of the Apologists, from whom he also diverged in his deliberate avoidance of philosophical jargon, was (a) in his firmer grasp and more explicit statement of this notion of 'the economy', and (b) in the much fuller recognition which he gave to the place of the Spirit in the triadic scheme.

In the first section we noticed the emphasis Irenaeus placed on the uniqueness and transcendence of the Father, the author of whatever exists. Nevertheless, 'being altogether mind and altogether Word, God utters what He thinks and thinks what He utters. His thinking is His Word, and His Word is His intelligence, and the Father is that intelligence comprising all things'.[2] More briefly, 'since God is rational, He created whatever was made by His Word'[3] (in the original there was no doubt a play on λογικός and λόγος). Here we have the conception, so familiar from the Apologists, of the Logos or Word as God's immanent rationality which He extrapolates in creation etc. Unlike them, however, Irenaeus rejects[4] the favourite analogy between God's utterance of His Word and the declaration of human thought in speech on the ground that He is identical with His Word. In fact, taking his cue from *Is.* 53, 8 (LXX: 'Who shall explain His generation?'), he repudiates all attempts to explore the process by which the Word was begotten or put forth. He also throws[5] into much more striking relief than they the Word's co-existence with the Father from all eternity. The inference has been very generally drawn from this that he taught a doctrine of eternal generation, especially as he sometimes speaks[6] of the *Son* being always with the Father. Too much, however, should not be read into such remarks, for

---

[1] *Dem.* 47. [2] *Haer.* 2, 28, 5: cf. ib. 1, 12, 2.
[3] *Dem.* 5. [4] *Haer.* 2, 28, 4-6: cf. ib. 2, 13, 8.
[5] E.g. ib. 2, 30, 9; 3, 18, 1; 4, 20, 1. [6] E.g. ib. 2, 30, 9; 4, 20, 3.

in his usage 'Son' was little more than a synonym for 'Word'. The conception of eternal generation would be hard to square with the framework of ideas he inherited from the Apologists, and it is strange that, if he was responsible for it, his devoted disciple Hippolytus[1] did not reproduce it. What seems decisive is that he nowhere mentions the doctrine as such. He certainly conceived of the Word's relationship to the Father as eternal, but he had not reached the position of picturing it as generation.

With the Son Irenaeus closely associated the Spirit, arguing[2] that, if God was rational and therefore had His Logos, He was also spiritual and so had His Spirit. Here he showed himself a follower of Theophilus[3] rather than Justin, identifying the Spirit with the divine Wisdom, and thereby fortifying his doctrine of the third Person with a secure Scriptural basis.[4] Thus he states[5] that 'His Word and His Wisdom, His Son and His Spirit, are always by Him', and that it was to them that God addressed the words, 'Let us make man etc.' That 'His Wisdom, i.e the Spirit, was with Him before the world was made', he finds[6] proved by Solomon's statements in *Prov.* 3, 19, and 8, 22 ff., viz. 'By Wisdom God established the earth', and, 'The Lord created me a beginning of His ways etc.' Thus the Word and the Spirit collaborated in the work of creation, being, as it were, God's 'hands'.[7] This image, doubtless reminiscent of *Job* 10, 8, and *Ps.* 119, 73 ('Thy hands have made me and fashioned me'), was intended to bring out the indissoluble unity between the creative Father and the organs of His activity. It was the function of the Word to bring creatures into existence, and of the Spirit to order and adorn them.[8] So he writes,[9] 'It is the Word Who establishes things, i.e. gives them body and bestows the reality of being upon them, and the Spirit Who gives order and form to these different powers'.

Creation, of course, does not exhaust the functions of the Word and the Spirit. It is by the Word, and the Word alone, that the Father reveals Himself: 'He is ineffable, but the Word

[1] See below, p. 112.   [2] *Dem.* 5.   [3] See above, pp. 102; 104.
[4] E.g. *Ps.* 33, 6; *Wis.* 1, 6; 9, 1 f.; 9, 17.   [5] *Haer.* 4, 20, 1.
[6] Ib. 4, 20, 3.   [7] E.g. ib. 4, praef. 4; 5, 1, 3; 5, 5, 1; 5, 6, 1; *dem.* 11.
[8] E.g. *haer.* 4, 20, 2.   [9] *Dem.* 5.

declares Him to us'.[1] The Johannine basis of this theology is
apparent, and it finds characteristic expression in such statements as,[2] 'The Son reveals the knowledge of the Father
through His own manifestation, for the Son's manifestation is
the making known of the Father'; and, 'What is invisible in the
Son is the Father, and what is visible in the Father is the Son'.
So in the Old Testament theophanies (here he was in full agreement with Justin) it was really the Word Who spoke with the
patriarchs.[3] In the incarnation the Word, hitherto Himself invisible to human eyes, became visible and disclosed for the first
time that image of God in the likeness of which man was
originally made.[4] As for the Spirit, it was He 'through Whom
the prophets prophesied, and the fathers learned the things of
God, and the righteous were led into the way of righteousness,
and Who at the end of the age was poured out in a new way ...
renewing man unto God'.[5] The Spirit's role is indeed essential,
for 'without the Spirit it is impossible to behold the Word of
God ... since the knowledge of the Father is the Son, and the
knowledge of the Son of God can only be obtained through the
Spirit; and according to the Father's good pleasure the Son
ministers and dispenses the Spirit to whomsoever the Father
wills, and as He wills'.[6] Our sanctification is indeed wholly the
work of the Spirit, for it is 'the Spirit of the Father Which
purifies a man and raises him to the life of God'.

Naturally the Son is fully divine: 'the Father is God, and the   *< Great*
Son is God, for whatever is begotten of God is God'.[7] The
Spirit, too, although Irenaeus nowhere expressly designates
Him God, clearly ranked as divine in his eyes, for He was
God's Spirit, ever welling up from His being.[8] Thus we have
Irenaeus's vision of the Godhead, the most complete, and also
most explicitly Trinitarian, to be met with before Tertullian.
Its second-century traits stand out clearly, particularly its
representation of the Triad by the imagery, not of three
coequal persons (this was the analogy to be employed by the

[1] *Haer.* 4, 6, 3.   [2] Ib. 4, 6, 3; 4, 6, 6.
[3] E.g. ib. 4, 9, 1; 4, 10, 1.   [4] Ib. 5, 16, 2.   [5] *Dem.* 6.
[6] Ib. 7.   [7] Ib. 47.   [8] Cf. *haer.* 5, 12, 2.

*Irenaeus — Most explicit Trinitarian before
Tertullian.*

post-Nicene fathers), but rather of a single personage, the Father Who is the Godhead Itself, with His mind, or rationality, and His wisdom. The motive for this approach, common to all Christian thinkers of this period, was their intense concern for the fundamental tenet of monotheism, but its unavoidable corollary was a certain obscuring of the position of the Son and the Spirit as 'Persons' (to use the jargon of later theology) prior to their generation or emission. Because of its emphasis on the 'economy', this type of thought has been given the label 'economic Trinitarianism'. The description is apt and convenient so long as it is not assumed that Irenaeus's recognition of, and preoccupation with, the Trinity revealed in the 'economy' prevented him from recognizing also the mysterious three-in-oneness of the inner life of the Godhead. The whole point of the great illustrative image which he, like his predecessors, employed, that of a man with his intellectual and spiritual functions, was to bring out, however inadequately, the fact that there are real distinctions in the immanent being of the unique, indivisible Father, and that while these were only fully manifested in the 'economy', they were actually there from all eternity.

NOTE ON BOOKS

General. G. Bardy, 'Trinité' (art. in *Dict. Théol. Cath.*); J. Daniélou, *The Theology of Jewish Christianity* (Eng. trans.: London, 1964); G. Kretschmar, *Studien zur frühchristlichen Trinitätstheologie* (Tübingen, 1956); J. Lebreton, *Histoire du dogme de la Trinité* (Paris, 1928); F. Loofs, 'Christologie, Kirchenlehre' (art. in Hauck's *Realencyk.*); G. L. Prestige, *God in Patristic Thought* (London, 2 ed. 1952); A. E. J. Rawlinson (ed.), *Essays on the Trinity and the Incarnation* (London, 1928).

Special. N. Bonwetsch, *Die Theologie des Irenäus* (Gütersloh, 1925); L.W. Barnard, *Justin Martyr* (Cambridge, 1967); H. Chadwick, *Justin Martyr's Defence of Christianity* (Manchester, 1965); E. R. Goodenough, *The Theology of Justin Martyr* (Jena, 1923); R. M. Grant, 'Theophilus of Antioch to Autolycus' (art. in *Harv. Theol. Rev.*, 1947); J. Lawson, *The Biblical Theology of Irenaeus* (London, 1948); V. A. S. Little, *The Christology of the Apologists* (London, 1934); E. F. Osborn, *Justin Martyr* (Tübingen, 1973); M. Rackl, *Die Christologie des hl. Ignatius von Antiochien* (Freiburg i.B., 1914).

CHAPTER V

THIRD-CENTURY TRINITARIANISM

1. *Introduction*

THE third century saw the emergence of conflicting tendencies in Trinitarian thought which were to provide the material for later controversies. Hitherto the overriding preoccupation of Christian theism had been with the unity of God; the struggle with paganism and Gnosticism thrust this article well into the foreground. As a result, while theologians were obscurely aware of distinctions within the one indivisible Godhead, and Theophilus could even describe[1] the Father with His Word and His Wisdom as the Triad, they showed little disposition to explore the eternal relations of the Three, much less to construct a conceptual and linguistic apparatus capable of expressing them. Their most fruitful efforts, as we observed in the preceding chapter, were expended in considering the Triad as manifested in creation and redemption, and in attempting to show how the Son and the Spirit, revealed in the 'economy' as other than the Father, were at the same time inseparably one with Him in His eternal being.

Economic Trinitarianism of this type continued to find exponents in the late second and early third centuries; we shall give an account of the most noteworthy of them in the next section. Its very success, however, brought to the surface a powerful reaction in circles which fought shy of the Logos doctrine and suspected that the growing emphasis on the triplicity disclosed by revelation imperilled the divine unity. This current of thought was chiefly evident in the West; it was called monarchianism because its adherents, as Tertullian phrased it,[2] 'took fright at the economy' and sought refuge in 'the monarchy'

---

[1] See above, p. 102.   [2] *Adv. Prax.* 3

(μοναρχία), i.e. [the axiom that there was one divine source and principle of all things.] At the same time a diametrically opposite movement was under way in the East. This took the form of a frankly pluralistic conception of the Deity which tried, without sacrificing the basic tenet of monotheism, to do justice to the reality and distinction of the Three within God's eternal being—in other words, to Their subsistence as 'Persons'. Though associated in the first instance with Alexandria, this new approach was destined to leave a permanent impress on Greek Trinitarianism as a whole, and indeed on Christian thinking generally.

2. Hippolytus and Tertullian

Our first task is to consider two theologians who stood more or less directly in the line of the Apologists and Irenaeus, and reflected their influence at many points. These were the Roman anti-pope and martyr, Hippolytus († 235), and the North African Tertullian (c. 160–c. 225). Like their predecessors, both set great store by monotheism, devoting their energies to the refutation of Gnostic dualism, although ironically enough they were branded with the charge of polytheism in circles (we shall return to these later) where modalism flourished. While their ideas are in many respects similar, those of Hippolytus seem more archaic, less thoroughly worked out; Tertullian's brilliant mind was able to formulate a statement of more lasting value. The clue to their teaching, as to that of Irenaeus, is to approach it simultaneously from two opposite directions, considering God (a) as He exists in His eternal being, and (b) as He reveals Himself in the process of creation and redemption. The comprehensive term they borrowed from Irenaeus for the latter was 'economy' (οἰκονομία; dispensatio). From meaning[1] the divine plan, or God's secret purpose, the word became applied in Christian theology to the incarnation, the goal of the divine purpose. Among its original meanings, however, was that of distribution, organization, the arrangement of a number of

[1] Cf. Eph. 3, 9.

factors in a regular order or τάξις; and so it was extended to connote the distinction of Son and Spirit from the one Father as disclosed in the working out of God's redemptive plan.

First, then, they both had the conception of God existing in unique solitariness from all eternity, yet having immanent in and indivisibly one with Himself, on the analogy of the mental functions in a man, His reason or Word. This is the doctrine, familiar since the Apologists, of the *Logos endiathetos*, and Hippolytus actually uses[1] the technical term. For him, as for Tatian and Irenaeus, God's Word and His Wisdom are distinguished, being in fact the Son and the Spirit regarded as immanent; but Tertullian follows[2] the tradition which equates Wisdom with the Word. Thus Hippolytus affirms that there is always a plurality in the Godhead, stating,[3] 'Though alone, He was multiple (μόνος ὢν πολὺς ἦν), for He was not without His Word and His Wisdom, His Power and His Counsel'. Tertullian is rather more explicit, pointing out[4] that 'before all things God was alone, being His own universe, location, everything. He was alone, however, in the sense that there was nothing external to Himself. But even then He was not really alone, for He had with Him that Reason which He possessed within Himself, that is to say, His own Reason.' Moreover, he brings out, much more clearly than any of his predecessors, the otherness or individuality of this immanent reason or Word. The rationality, he explains,[5] by means of which a man cogitates and plans is somehow 'another' (*alius*), or 'a second' in himself (cf. *secundus quodammodo in te est sermo*); and so it is with the divine Word, with which God has been ratiocinating from everlasting and which constitutes 'a second in addition to Himself' (*secundum a se*).

Secondly, however, the threefoldness of God's intrinsic being is manifested in creation and redemption. According to Hippolytus,[6] when God willed, He engendered His Word, using Him to create the universe, and His Wisdom to adorn or order it. Later still, with the world's salvation in view, He

---

[1] *Ref.* 10, 33, 1.   [2] *Adv. Prax.* 6; *adv. Hermog.* 18; 20.
[3] *C. Noet.* 10.   [4] *Adv. Prax.* 5.   [5] *Ib.*   [6] *C. Noet.* 10 f.

rendered the Word, hitherto invisible, visible at the incarnation. Thereupon, alongside the Father (i.e. the Godhead Itself), there was 'another' (αὐτῷ παρίστατο ἕτερος), a second 'Person' (πρόσωπον), while the Spirit completed the Triad.[1] But if there are Three revealed in the economy, there is in fact only one God, since it is the Father Who commands, the Son Who obeys and the Spirit Who makes us understand. Hippolytus is most insistent on the essential unity, stating[2] that there is only one Power, and that 'when I speak of "another", I do not mean two Gods, but as it were light from light, water from its source, a ray from the sun. For there is only one Power, that which issues from the All. The All is the Father, and the Power issuing from the All is the Word. He is the Father's mind. . . . Thus all things are through Him, but He alone is from the Father'. Similarly, in stressing[3] that the Word's generation takes place as and when the Father wills, his intention is not to subordinate Him to the Father (judged by post-Nicene standards, his language has a subordinationist ring), but to emphasize the absolute unity of the Godhead, since that will of the Father is in fact none other than the Word Himself.

Hippolytus was reluctant[4] to designate the Word as Son in any other than a proleptic sense till the incarnation. Tertullian followed the Apologists in dating[5] His 'perfect generation' from His extrapolation for the work of creation; prior to that moment God could not strictly be said to have had a Son,[6] while after it the term 'Father', which for earlier theologians generally connoted God as author of reality, began to acquire the specialized meaning of Father of the Son.[7] As so generated, the Word or Son is a 'Person' (persona), 'a second in addition to the Father' (secundum a patre[8]). In the third place, however, there is the Spirit, the 'representative' or 'deputy' (vicaria vis[9]) of the Son; He issues from the Father by way of the Son (a patre per filium[10]), being 'third from the Father and the Son, just as

---

[1] C. Noet. 7; 11; 14.   [2] Ib. 10: cf. ib. 8.   [3] Ib. 10.
[4] Ib. 15.   [5] Adv. Prax. 7.   [6] Adv. Hermog. 3.
[7] Adv. Prax. 7.   [8] Ib. 5.   [9] De praescr. 13.
[10] Adv. Prax. 4.

the fruit derived from the shoot is third from the root, and as
the channel drawn off from the river is third from the spring,
and as the light-point in the beam is third from the sun'.[1] He,
too, is a 'Person',[2] so that the Godhead is a 'trinity' (trinitas:
Tertullian is the first to employ[3] the word). The three are indeed numerically distinct, being 'capable of being counted'
(numerum . . . patiuntur[4]). Thus Tertullian can state:[5] 'We
believe in one only God, yet subject to this dispensation, which
is our word for economy, that the one only God has also a Son,
His Word, Who has issued out of Himself . . . which Son then
sent, according to His promise, the Holy Spirit, the Paraclete,
out of the Father'; and later in the same context he can balance
the divine unity with 'the mystery of the economy, which
distributes the unity into Trinity, setting forth Father, Son and
Spirit as three'.

Tertullian exerted himself to show (the criticisms of the
modalists made him sensitive on the point) that the threeness
revealed in the economy was in no way incompatible with
God's essential unity. Like Hippolytus, he argued[6] that, though
three, the Persons were severally manifestations of a single
indivisible power, noting that on the analogy of the imperial
government one and the same sovereignty could be exercised
by coordinate agencies. Like the Apologists, he again and again
repudiated[7] the suggestion that the distinction between the
Three involved any division or separation; it was a distinctio or
dispositio (i.e. a distribution), not a separatio, and he quoted the
unity between the root and its shoot, the source and the river,
and the sun and its light as illustrations. His characteristic way
of expressing this was to state that Father, Son and Spirit are
one in 'substance'. Thus Father and Son are one identical substance which has been, not divided, but 'extended';[8] the
Saviour's claim, 'I and my Father are one' (unum), indicates
that the Three are 'one reality' (unum is neuter), not 'one
Person' (unus), pointing as it does to identity of substance and

---

[1] Ib. 8.   [2] Ib. 11.
[3] E.g. ib. 3 ; 11 ; 12 ; de pud. 21 (trinitas unius divinitatis).
[4] Adv. Prax. 2.   [5] Ib.   [6] Ib. 3.
[7] E.g. apol. 21, 11-13; adv. Prax. 8.   [8] Apol. 21, 12.

not mere numerical unity;[1] the Son is *unius substantiae* with the
Father,[2] and the Son and the Spirit are *consortes substantiae
patris*.[3] Using crudely materialistic language (his background
of ideas was Stoic,[4] and he regarded the divine spirit as a highly
rarefied species of matter), Tertullian can say[5] that 'the Father
is the whole substance, while the Son is a derivation from and
portion of the whole'—where the context makes it plain that
'portion' (*portio*) is not to be taken literally as implying any
division or severance. Thus, when he sums the matter up, he
dismisses[6] the idea that the Persons can be three in 'status' (i.e.
fundamental quality), substance or power; as regards these
the Godhead is indivisibly one, and the threeness applies only
to the 'grade' (*gradus*=Greek τάξις), or 'aspect' (*forma*), or
'manifestation' (*species*) in which the Persons are presented.

Hippolytus and Tertullian were at one with Irenaeus in regarding the Three revealed in the economy as manifestations of
the plurality which they apprehended, however obscurely, in
the immanent life of the Godhead. Where they were in advance
of him was (a) in their attempts to make explicit the oneness of
the divine power or substance of which the Three were expressions or forms, and (b) in their recognition of Them
(Hippolytus applied the word to Father and Son only) as Persons
(πρόσωπα; *personae*). This latter term, it should be noted, was
still reserved for Them as manifested in the order of revelation;
only later did it come to be applied to the Word and the Spirit
as immanent in God's eternal being. There has been much discussion about the precise meaning of their terminology, some
arguing that for Tertullian at any rate, with his legal upbringing, *substantia* signified a piece of property which several
people could jointly own. In fact, however, the metaphysical
sense was foremost in his mind, and the word connoted the
divine essence, that of which God is, with the emphasis on its
concrete reality. As he remarks,[7] 'God is the name for the substance, that is, the divinity'; and the Word, so far from being a
mere notional nonentity, is 'substantival', 'a substance composed

[1] *Adv. Prax.* 25.   [2] Ib. 2.   [3] Ib. 3.   [4] See above, pp. 17 f.
[5] *Adv. Prax.* 9.   [6] Ib. 2: cf. ib. 19.   [7] *Adv. Hermog.* 3.

of spirit and wisdom and reason'.[1] Hence, when he speaks of the Son as being 'of one substance' with the Father, he means that They share the same divine nature or essence, and in fact, since the Godhead is indivisible, are one identical being. On the other hand, the terms πρόσωπον and persona were admirably suited to express the otherness, or independent subsistence, of the Three. After originally meaning 'face', and so 'expression' and then 'role', the former came to signify 'individual', the stress being usually on the external aspect or objective presentation. The primary sense of persona was 'mask', from which the transition was easy to the actor who wore it and the character he played. In legal usage it could stand for the holder of the title to a property, but as employed by Tertullian it connoted the concrete presentation of an individual as such. In neither case, it should be noted, was the idea of self-consciousness nowadays associated with 'person' and 'personal' at all prominent.

3. Dynamic Monarchianism

The closing decades of the second century witnessed the emergence of two forms of teaching which, though fundamentally different, have been brought together by modern historians under the common name of monarchianism. 'Dynamic' monarchianism, more accurately called adoptionism, was the theory that Christ was a 'mere man' (ψιλὸς ἄνθρωπος: hence 'psilanthropism') upon whom God's Spirit had descended. It was essentially a Christological heresy, but the circumstances in which it arose justify its treatment here. Modalism, which was alone designated monarchianism by contemporaries, tended to blur the distinctions between Father, Son and Holy Spirit. The classification of both as forms of monarchianism stems from the assumption that, despite different starting-points and motives, they were united by a concern for the divine unity, or monarchia. This supposition goes back at least as far as Novatian (c. 250), who interpreted[2] adoptionism and modalism as misguided attempts to salvage the Bible dogma

[1] Adv. Prax. 7.   [2] De trin. 30.

that God is one. So far as the former is concerned, there is
nothing to show that this consideration carried much weight
with at any rate its original supporters. It may well have been
influencing their successors in Novatian's day, but they themselves seem to have been intellectuals inspired by current philosophical rationalism.

The originator of dynamic monarchianism is said to have
been a learned Byzantine leather-merchant, Theodotus, who
brought it to Rome about 190. Malicious critics explained[1] his
position as a makeshift device to cover up a previous act of
apostasy at Byzantium ('I have not denied God, but a man'),
but it was in fact carefully worked out and shows no signs of
improvisation. While in full agreement with orthodox views
about the creation of the world, the divine omnipotence and
even the virgin birth, Theodotus held[2] that until His baptism
Jesus lived the life of an ordinary man, with the difference that
He was supremely virtuous. The Spirit, or Christ, then descended
upon Him, and from that moment He worked miracles, without, however, becoming divine—others of the same school
admitted His deification after His resurrection. Theodotus and
his followers were much preoccupied[3] with Biblical exegesis
and textual criticism, and appealed[4] to such texts as *Deut.* 18, 15
and *Luke* 1, 35 (the latter amended to read 'Spirit of the Lord'),
to support their claim that Jesus was an ordinary man whom
the Spirit had inspired rather than indwelt. They also scandalized[5] the faithful by their interest in logic and geometry, and
the deference they paid to Aristotle, Euclid and, among contemporaries, the philosophical physician Galen. Theodotus was
himself excommunicated by Pope Victor (186–98), but his
ideas were immediately taken up[6] by another Theodotus, this
time a banker, an Asclepiodotus, and an Artemas, or Artemon,
who lived on at Rome beyond the middle of the third century.
Mixed up with the teaching of the second Theodotus were
bizarre speculations about Melchizedek, whom he regarded[7] as

---

[1] Cf. Epiphanius, *haer.* 54, 1, 7.   [2] Hippolytus, *ref.* 7, 35.
[3] Eusebius, *hist. eccl.* 5, 28, 13-17. [4] Epiphanius, *haer.* 54, 3, 1-6.
[5] Eusebius, op. cit. 5, 28, 13 f.   [6] Eusebius, op. cit. 5, 28, 1-3 and 9.
[7] Hippolytus, *ref.* 7, 36.

'the supreme Power', superior to Christ and mediator between God and man, 'spiritual and Son of God', and whom he may have equated with the Spirit which descended on Jesus.

These adoptionists were an isolated and unrepresentative movement in Gentile Christianity. It is an attractive guess[1] that Theodotus the leather-merchant and his coterie belonged to the circle of Galen, and were stimulated by his friendly, but critical, interest in the faith to work out a rationalizing version of it. Their scholarly sympathies and methods were certainly akin to his, and their chief object seems to have been to eliminate the idea, so uncongenial to people imbued with Greek philosophical culture, of an incarnation of the Deity. The second generation of the adoptionists may well have blended this rationalism with the suspicion that orthodoxy was virtually committed to ditheism, for Novatian puts[2] in their mouth the argument, 'If the Father is one and the Son another, and if the Father is God and Christ God, then there is not one God, but two Gods are simultaneously brought forward, the Father and the Son'. By Artemon's time they were claiming[3] to be the trustees of the true apostolic tradition, and seeking to show that their views about Christ had been accepted in the Church from the beginning down to the reign of Pope Zephyrinus (198–217), when the official teaching had been tampered with. In rejoinder Hippolytus had little difficulty in pointing[4] to the grand succession of teachers going back to the first century, 'by all of whom Christ is acknowledged as divine' (ἐν οἷς ἅπασι θεολογεῖται ὁ Χριστός), and whose works 'proclaim Christ as both God and man'.

Paul of Samosata, perhaps the most interesting exponent of this type of thought, flourished rather later in the century, being formally condemned[5] at the synod of Antioch held in 268. Further reference to his theory that Christ was an ordinary man inspired by the divine Wisdom will be made in the next chapter; here his attitude to the Godhead calls for remark.

---

[1] Made by R. Walzer (see Note on Books).   [2] *De trin.* 30.
[3] Hippolytus, *Little labyrinth* (in Eusebius, *hist. eccl.* 5, 28, 3 ff.).
[4] Loc. cit.   [5] Eusebius, op. cit. 7, 27-30.

According to a sixth-century writer,[1] 'Paul did not say that it was the self-subsistent Word Who was in Christ, but applied the title "Word" to God's commandment and ordinance, i.e. God ordered what He willed through the man, and so did it. . . . He did not say that Father, Son and Holy Spirit are one and the same, but gave the name of God to the Father Who created all things, that of Son to the mere man, and that of Spirit to the grace which indwelt the apostles'. If true, this suggests that he was prepared to use the officially accepted Trinitarian formula, but only as a veil to cover a theology which was in fact unitarian. This conclusion is supported by the fact, reported in a fourth-century homoeusian document,[2] that the bishops who outlawed him (they were Origenists committed to the belief in three eternal, subsistent Persons) thought it necessary to insist that the Word was an οὐσία, or substance. By this they meant that He was not simply a verbal utterance, without any subsistence of His own (this was presumably Paul's view), but a real Person distinct from the Father. There is further the report[3] that the synod rejected the idea that the Word was ὁμοούσιος, i.e. the same in ousia or substance, with the Father. If this report is correct, it is conceivable[4] that Paul, taking his cue from the language of his judges, may have used the term to protest against the sharp division between the Father and the Son which their assertion that they were distinct ousiai seemed to entail.

Paul's thought is notoriously difficult to evaluate, but the view that he was a strict unitarian, denying any subsistence or personality to the Word and teaching that the Son and the Spirit were merely the Church's names for the inspired man Jesus Christ and the grace which God poured upon the apostles, is probably accurate so far as it goes. It is possible, however, to represent[5] him as an 'economic Trinitarian', responsible for a doctrine resembling that of Irenaeus and Tertullian, and still more that of the fourth-century Marcellus of

[1] De sectis 3, 3 (PG 86, 1216).   [2] In Epiphanius, haer. 73, 12.
[3] Athanasius, de syn. 45; Hilary, de syn. 81; Basil, ep. 52, 1.
[4] So Hilary, loc. cit. See below, pp. 140; 234 f.
[5] Cf. F. Loofs, Paulus von Samosata, 1924, p. 257.

Ancyra.[1] The patristic tradition, we should note, tended increasingly to classify Paul with Sabellius and Marcellus, although at its earlier stages, as represented, for example, by the *Ecthesis macrostichos*[2] (345) and Athanasius,[3] it made no such juxtaposition, and depicted Paul exclusively in his character as an adoptionist. Further, in spite of certain ambiguous passages, all the evidence[4] goes to suggest that he was opposed to the idea that the Word became a subsistent Person as the economy unfolded. Points of contact there may have been between the theology of Paul and that of Marcellus; but while the focus of the latter was interest in the unfolding Trinity, that of the former was psilanthropism, with an exaggerated monarchianism as its premiss.

4. *Modalistic Monarchianism*

If dynamic monarchianism was a relatively isolated phenomenon with a predominantly rationalist appeal, the same cannot be said of monarchianism proper, otherwise called modalism. This was a fairly widespread, popular trend of thought which could reckon on, at any rate, a measure of sympathy in official circles; and the driving-force behind it was the twofold conviction, passionately held, of the oneness of God and the full deity of Christ. What forced it into the open was the mounting suspicion that the former of these truths was being endangered by the new Logos doctrine and by the efforts of theologians to represent the Godhead as having revealed Itself in the economy as tri-personal. Any suggestion that the Word or Son was other than, or a distinct Person from, the Father seemed to the modalists (we recall that the ancient view that 'Father' signified the Godhead Itself was still prevalent) to lead inescapably to the blasphemy of two Gods.

As early as Justin's time we read[5] of objections to his teaching that the Logos was 'something numerically other' ($\dot{\alpha}\rho\iota\theta\mu\hat{\omega}$ $\check{\epsilon}\tau\epsilon\rho\acute{o}\nu$ $\tau\iota$) than the Father; the critics argued that the Power

---

[1] See below, pp. 240 f.   [2] Cf. Athanasius, *de syn.* 26.
[3] E.g. *c. Ar.* 1, 25; 1, 38; 2, 13; 3, 26; 3, 51.
[4] Cf. H. de Riedmatten, *Les Actes du procès de Paul de Samosate*, 1952, chap. vi.   [5] *Dial.* 128, 3 f.

issuing from the Godhead was distinct only verbally or in
name, being a projection of the Father Himself. The first
theologian, however, formally to state the monarchian position
was Noetus of Smyrna, who was twice summoned before the
presbyters of that city in the closing years of the second century;
his contemporary, Hippolytus,[1] and the fourth-century Epiphanius[2] are our chief authorities for his teaching. Its pivot was
the vigorous affirmation that there was only one God, the
Father; patripassianism, or the idea that it was the Father Who
suffered and underwent Christ's other human experiences, was
a corollary which he seems to have embraced willingly enough.
If Christ was God, as Christian faith took for granted, then He
must be identical with the Father; otherwise He could not be
God. Consequently, if Christ suffered, the Father suffered, since
there could be no division in the Godhead. To his accusers he
retorted,[3] 'What wrong have I done, glorifying one only God,
Christ, Who was born, suffered and died?' For Scriptural support his followers appealed[4] to such texts as *Ex.* 3, 6 (taken
with 20, 3), and *Is.* 44, 6, which proclaimed the uniqueness of
God, *Is.* 45, 14 f. and *Bar.* 3, 36–8, which suggested that this
unique God had been present in Jesus Christ, and *John* 10, 30,
14, 8–10, and *Rom.* 9, 5, which seemed to point to the identity
of Father and Son. They rejected the Logos doctrine, arguing[5]
that the Prologue of the Fourth Gospel was to be taken
allegorically.

Noetus was condemned, the presbyters confronting[6] him
with the Church's rule of faith; but a disciple of his, Epigonus,
came to Rome, where he found an apt pupil in one Cleomenes
during Zephyrinus's pontificate (198–217). Summarizing the
position of the school, Hippolytus reports[7] that they believed in
one identical Godhead Which could be designated indifferently
Father or Son; the terms did not stand for real distinctions, but
were mere names applicable at different times. Indeed, the Godhead was like the universal monad postulated by the ancient

---

[1] Cf. *c. Noet.*: also *ref.* 9.   [2] *Haer.* 57.
[3] Hippolytus, *c. Noet.* 1: cf. Epiphanius, op. cit. 57, 1, 8.
[4] Hippolytus, op. cit. 2; 6 f.   [5] Id. 15.
[6] Id. 1.   [7] *Ref.* 9, 10.

philosopher Heracleitus (*c.* 502 B.C.), which comprised in itself
mutually contradictory qualities, being at once divisible and
indivisible, created and uncreated, mortal and immortal, etc.
It is precisely this position, supported apparently with the same
texts, that Tertullian combats in his *Adversus Praxeam*, written
about 213. Who Praxeas was remains a mystery; he is a
shadowy figure, and some have identified him ('Praxeas' could
be a nickname, meaning 'busybody') with Noetus or Epigonus,
or even (we shall see the point of this later) with Pope Callistus. Whoever he was, he seems to have taught[1] that Father
and Son were one identical Person (*duos unum volunt esse, ut idem
pater et filius habeatur*), the Word having no independent subsistence and being a mere *vox et sonus oris*,[2] and that consequently
it was the Father Himself Who entered the Virgin's womb, so
becoming, as it were, His own Son,[3] and Who suffered, died
and rose again.[4] Thus this unique Person united in Himself
mutually inconsistent attributes, being invisible and then
visible, impassible and then passible.[5] Yet Praxeas and his associates, it would seem,[6] were in the end obliged to recognize a
duality in the Lord, in the sense that the man Jesus was, strictly
speaking, the Son, while the Christ, i.e. the divine element
(*spiritum, id est deum*) was properly the Father. From this it was
an easy step to the formula[7] which excited both indignation and
derision, 'So, while it is the Son Who suffers, the Father co-
suffers' (*compatitur*). It is curious to observe how close at this
point modalism came to Theodotus's adoptionism. Although
starting from opposite poles, they reached rather similar conclusions about the Saviour as a man inspired by the Deity.

The naïveté of this earlier modalism stands out, but it was
very soon to be given a more systematic, philosophical shape.
The man responsible for this, it would appear, was Sabellius,[8]
who came to Rome towards the end of Zephyrinus's reign, was
fiercely attacked by Hippolytus and, after enjoying the confidence of Pope Callistus (217–22), was eventually excommunicated by him. This later, more sophisticated modalism,

---

[1] *Adv. Prax.* 5.   [2] Ib. 7.   [3] Ib. 10.   [4] Ib. 1; 2.
[5] Ib. 14.   [6] Ib. 27.   [7] Ib. 29.   [8] Cf. Hippolytus, *ref.* 9, 11 f.

known after its author as Sabellianism, tried to meet some of the objections to which the earlier brand was exposed. Sabellius, we are told,[1] regarded the Godhead as a monad (his name for it was υἱοπάτωρ[2]) which expressed itself in three operations. He used the analogy of the sun, a single object which radiates both warmth and light; the Father was, as it were, the form or essence, and the Son and the Spirit His modes of self-expression. He may also have exploited[3] the idea of the expansion or 'dilation' (πλατυσμός) of the divine monad, the Father by process of development projecting Himself first as Son and then as Spirit. Thus the one Godhead regarded as creator and law-giver was Father; for redemption It was projected like a ray of the sun, and was then withdrawn; then, thirdly, the same Godhead operated as Spirit to inspire and bestow grace.[4]

Ideas like these suggest that Sabellius was conscious of the difficulties inherent in the simple modalism of his predecessors, and was prepared to turn to account features borrowed from the economic Trinitarianism of their critics. Part of his motive may have been to explain the government of the universe when the Godhead appeared as the Son, and also to obviate the charge of patripassianism. Unfortunately we cannot be sure that all the details of the position just summarized can be attributed to Sabellius himself. Most of the surviving evidence dates from a century or more after his lifetime, when his theology and that of the much more familiar Marcellus of Ancyra[5] were hopelessly confused. One point which seems to be established is that the traditional belief that he spoke of Father, Son and Spirit as three prosopa, in the sense of masks or outward appearances, is erroneous. The term πρόσωπον, as we have already seen,[6] was used by Hippolytus to signify the otherness, or separate subsistence, of the Son, as revealed in the economy, from the Father, and it is most unlikely that Sabellius used it with a diametrically opposite meaning. Indeed, Hippolytus clearly implies[7] that for

[1] Epiphanius, haer. 62, 1, 4 ff.
[2] Arius, ep. ad Alex. (in Epiphanius, op. cit. 69, 7).
[3] Pseudo-Athanasius, c. Ar. 4, 25.   [4] Epiphanius, haer. 62, 1.
[5] See below, pp. 240 f.   [6] See above, p. 115.
[7] Ref. 10, 27, 4.

Callistus, whom he regarded as a Sabellian, the Godhead was but a single *prosopon*, i.e. individual or Person.

5. The Roman Theology

The theological activity we have been studying was largely concentrated in the West and at Rome. Yet none of the figures concerned in it had the standing of an official spokesman. Hippolytus and Tertullian might be described as free-lances, while most of the leading modalists were condemned as heretics. It might well be asked what was the attitude of official circles in the Roman church to the issues under discussion. The question is highly relevant, for it was in the first half of the third century that the standard pattern of Western Trinitarianism was taking shape. If one may anticipate, its starting-point was that profound conviction of the unity of God, the divine monarchy, which always dominated the minds of Western theologians, and of which modalism in all its forms was a well-intentioned distortion. In its formulation, however, it was greatly indebted, both for ideas and for terminology, to the classic statement of Tertullian.

At the initial stage the monarchian strain just mentioned was clearly in the ascendancy. This comes out in the attitude of Popes Zephyrinus (198–217) and Callistus (217–22), both of whom sympathized with the widespread popular reaction against the theories of Hippolytus and Tertullian, which they regarded as leading to ditheism. Hippolytus, for his part, considered[1] Zephyrinus an out-and-out modalist, the patron of Cleomenes and the school which collected round him. In proof of this he represents the pope, 'an ignorant and uncultured man', as declaring, 'I know only one God, Christ Jesus, and none other Who was born and suffered', and at the same time protesting, 'It was not the Father Who died, but the Son'. The former statement is practically identical with Noetus's profession of faith,[2] and many[3] have in consequence acquiesced in

---

[1] *Ref.* 9, 11.   [2] See above, p. 120.
[3] E.g. A. Harnack (*Sitzungsberichte Preuss. Akad.*, 1923, pp. 51–7).

the verdict of Hippolytus. Others[1] have drawn the conclusion
that he must somehow have misrepresented the pope. In view
of the second of the two statements cited these judgments seem
unduly hasty. There can be no doubt that Zephyrinus, like
other 'simple and uncultured' Christians,[2] viewed the new talk
of 'Persons' of the Godhead with unconcealed suspicion; the
former statement is evidence of his concern for the full deity of
the incarnate Lord. The second statement, however, suggests
that, however hostile he was to the ditheist-sounding language
of the learned theologians, he saw the necessity of recognizing
the reality of the distinction between Father and Son.

Hippolytus's estimate of Callistus was similar. He describes
him as the dupe of Sabellius, and summarizes his teaching in
two passages[3] which seem to combine authentic dicta of the
pope with possibly biased interpretations of his own. Bearing
in mind that Callistus excommunicated Sabellius, we can
fairly deduce the following points from them. First, he placed
the greatest possible emphasis on the divine unity. The Godhead in his eyes was the single, indivisible spirit which pervades the universe, and constituted one object of presentation
(if one may use such language of God), one being or 'Person'
(πρόσωπον). Secondly, he admitted the distinction of Father
and Word, the latter being the pre-temporal element which
became incarnate; the Son, strictly speaking, was the historical
figure, 'the man'. But he insisted that They were not separate
beings ('the Father is not one thing—ἄλλο—and the Son
another—ἄλλο—, but They are one and the same reality'), and
that the Word was not 'another alongside the Father' (ἕτερος
παρὰ τὸν πατέρα). Thirdly, since the Father was the unique
divine spirit, Callistus could speak of Him as being identical
with the Word, and even as becoming incarnate; but he was
careful to point out that the Father only 'co-suffered' with the
Son. Thoughts like these, though closely akin to the Praxeanism
combated by Tertullian and understandably anathema to Hippolytus, do not brand Callistus as a thoroughgoing modalist.

---

[1] E.g. B. Capelle (R. Bén. xxxviii, 1926, pp. 321-30).
[2] Cf. Tertullian, adv. Prax. 3.   [3] Ref. 9, 12, 16-19; 10, 27, 3 f.

They suggest, rather, that while his sympathies lay with modalism, he was conscious of its difficulties, and was struggling to develop a compromise approach to the problem which, while taking account of the real distinction between the Father and the Word, would stress the truth that even so They were manifestations of one divine spirit and thus avoid the dangers (as he conceived them) inherent in any doctrine of two or three 'Persons'.

Zephyrinus and Callistus were thus conservatives holding fast to a monarchian tradition which antedated the whole movement of thought inaugurated by the Apologists. Conservative, too, though at a more sophisticated and learned level, was the monarchian theology developed by the Roman presbyter Novatian (c. 250), which reflected the influence of Hippolytus and Tertullian but was at several points more archaic than their teaching. According to him,[1] the one and only Godhead is the Father, the author and sustainer of all reality. Nevertheless from Him, 'when He willed it, was born a Son, His Word'. This Word is no verbal nonentity (*non in sono percussi aeris . . . accipitur*), as modalism alleged, but has a subsistence of His own (*in substantia . . . agnoscitur*), being 'a second Person after the Father'. Three points in particular should be underlined. First, Novatian does not tie the generation of the Son to creation; since the Father is always Father, He must always have had a Son. Thus, while far from envisaging the idea of eternal generation, he is insistent that Christ 'existed substantially (*in substantia*, i.e. as a Person) before the foundation of the world'.[2] Secondly, while on occasion speaking of 'the power of Godhead' or 'the divine majesty' being transmitted by the Father to the Son, and even of the community of being (*substantiae . . . communionem*) between Them, he normally defines Their relationship (in marked contrast to Tertullian) in terms of moral unity. This comes out strikingly in his avoidance, when expounding texts like 'I and the Father are one' and 'He who has seen me has seen the Father', of any suggestion of unity of essence. But, thirdly, being greatly concerned to escape the

[1] *De trin.* 31.   [2] Ib. 16.

charge of teaching a duality of Gods brought against Hippolytus and Tertullian, he argues[1] on the one hand that the deity
bestowed by the Father on the Son for ever reverts to the Father,
and on the other that the divine attributes belong in the true
sense exclusively to Him.

Novatian c250

Thus, for all his emphatic assertion of the Son's distinct
subsistence as a Person, he succeeds in avoiding the ditheism he
dreads only by strongly subordinating Him to the Father, or
alternatively by making Him a passing moment in the divine
life of the Father. His doctrine of the Holy Spirit is, for his date,
rudimentary. While constantly speaking of the Father and the
Son as Persons, he nowhere describes the Spirit as one, in spite
of the clear teaching of Hippolytus and Tertullian on the point.
In fact, he conceived of Him only as a divine gift poured out
by the Father on the prophets, on the apostolic Church, on
Christ at His baptism, and on the faithful to sanctify them and
make them temples of God.[2] In discussing the statement that
God is spirit (*John* 4, 24) he even asserts that 'every spirit is a
creature', and one is left with the impression that he thought
of the Holy Spirit as such.[3] We are therefore not surprised to
note that, in contrast again to Hippolytus and Tertullian, the
term 'Trinity' is completely absent from his treatise. In this
respect, too, his theology represents a withdrawal to a position
which his predecessors had gone beyond, for unlike them he
seems to have had no inkling of the Trinitarian nature of the
Godhead. The view frequently encountered that his theology,
though primitive in formulation, anticipated the orthodoxy
of post-Nicene times represents a complete misreading of his
position.

6. *Clement and Origen*

Meanwhile an immensely significant development was
taking place in the East. This drew its initial inspiration from
the catechetical school at Alexandria, the two thinkers re-

---

[1] *De trin*. 31 ad fin.   [2] Ib. 29.
[3] Ib. 7: cf. 8.

sponsible for it being Clement (*fl.* 200) and Origen (*c.* 185–
c. 254). The latter a contemporary of Plotinus,[1] both were
profoundly influenced, in their attempts to understand and
expound the triune Godhead, by the revived, or 'middle',
Platonism[2] fashionable at this time at Alexandria.

*Clement
of
Alexandria*

We can deal briefly with Clement, who was a moralist rather
than a systematic theologian. For him[3] God is absolutely transcendent, ineffable and incomprehensible; He is 'unity, but
beyond unity, and transcending the monad', and yet somehow
embracing all reality. This is the Father (we note the pre-
Nicene connotation of the term); and He can be known only
through His Word, or Son, Who is His image and inseparable
from Him, His mind or rationality.[4] Like the Nous of middle
Platonism and of Neo-Platonism, the Word is at once unity
and plurality, comprising in Himself the Father's ideas, and
also the active forces by which He animates the world of
creatures.[5] His generation from the Father is without beginning   *Note*
('the Father is not without His Son; for along with being
Father, He is Father of the Son'[6]); and He is essentially one
with Him,[7] since the Father is in Him and He in the Father.[8]
The Spirit, thirdly, is the light issuing from the Word which,
divided without any real division, illuminates the faithful; He is
also the power of the Word which pervades the world and
attracts men to God.[9] Thus we have a Trinity which, though in
all its lineaments Platonic, Clement unhesitatingly identifies
with Christian theism. As he writes,[10] 'O wondrous mystery!
One is the Father of the universe, and one also the Word of
the universe; the Holy Spirit, again, is one and everywhere the
same.' He clearly distinguishes the Three, and the charge of
modalism, based on his lack of any technical term to designate
the Persons, is groundless; and if he appears to subordinate the
Son to the Father and the Spirit to the Son, this subordination

---

[1] See above, pp. 20–22.   [2] See above, pp. 19 f.
[3] *Paed.* 1, 71, 1; *strom.* 2, 6, 1; 5, 65, 2; 5, 78, 3; 5, 81, 3.
[4] *Prot.* 98, 3; *strom.* 5, 16, 3; 7, 5, 5.   [5] *Strom.* 4, 156, 1 f.; 5, 16, 3.
[6] Ib. 4, 162, 5; 5, 1, 3; 7, 2, 2.   [7] *Paed.* 1, 62, 4; 1, 71, 3; 3, 101, 1.
[8] Ib. 1, 24, 3; 1, 53, 1.   [9] *Strom.* 6, 138, 1 f.; 7, 9, 4; 7, 79, 4.
[10] *Paed.* 1, 42, 1: cf. ib. 3, 101, 2; *prot.* 118, 4; *quis div.* 34, 1; etc.

implies no inequality of being, but is the corollary of his Platonic conception of a graded hierarchy.

Origen

Origen's Trinitarianism was a brilliant reinterpretation of the traditional triadic rule of faith, to which as a churchman he was devoted, in terms of the same middle Platonism. At the apex of his system, as the source and goal of all existence, transcending mind and being itself, he placed God the Father, 'altogether Monad, and indeed, if I may so express it, Henad'.[1] He alone is God in the strict sense ($αὐτόθεος$), being alone 'ingenerate' ($ἀγέννητος$); and it is significant that Christ spoke of Him (*John* 17, 3) as 'the only true God'.[2] Being perfect goodness and power, He must always have had objects on which to exercise them; hence He has brought into existence a world of spiritual beings, or souls, coeternal with Himself.[3] To mediate, however, between His absolute unity and their multiplicity, He has His Son, His express image, the meeting-place of a plurality of 'aspects' ($ἐπίνοιαι$: these represent the ideas of Platonism proper) which explain His twofold relation to the Father and the world.[4] These 'aspects' stand for the manifold characters which the Word presents either in His eternal being (e.g. Wisdom, Truth, Life) or as incarnate (e.g. Healer, Door, Resurrection). Being outside time and immutable, the Father begets the Son by an eternal act ($ἀεὶ γεννᾷ$ $αὐτόν$), so that it cannot be said that 'there was when He was not[5]'; further, the Son is God, though His deity is derivative and He is thus a 'secondary God' ($δεύτερος θεός$[6]). The parallel with Albinus,[7] who believed in a supreme Father Who organized matter through a second God (Whom he, however, identified with the World-Soul), is striking; as is the fact that both thinkers envisaged[8] the generation of the Son as the result of His contemplation of the Father. But, thirdly (and here he realizes[9] that Christianity parts company with philosophy,

---

[1] *De princ.* 1, 1, 6; *c. Cels.* 7, 38.   [2] *In Ioh.* 2, 2, 16; 2, 10, 75.
[3] *De princ.* 1, 2, 10; 1, 4, 3; 2, 9, 1.
[4] *C. Cels.* 2, 64; *in Ioh.* 1, 20, 119.
[5] *De princ.* 1, 2, 4; *hom. in Ierem.* 9, 4: cf. Plotinus, *enn.* 5, 1, 6.
[6] *C. Cels.* 5, 39; *in Ioh.* 6, 39, 202.   [7] See above, p. 20.
[8] Cf. Origen, *in Ioh.* 2, 2, 18; Albinus, *didask.* 14, 3.
[9] *De princ.* 1, 3, 1-4.

relying on revelation alone), there is the Holy Spirit, 'the most honourable of all the beings brought into existence through the Word, the chief in rank of all the beings originated by the Father through Christ'.[1]

The Father, the Son and the Holy Spirit are, Origen states,[2] 'three Persons' (ὑποστάσεις). This affirmation that each of the Three is a distinct hypostasis from all eternity, not just (as for Tertullian and Hippolytus) as manifested in the 'economy', is one of the chief characteristics of his doctrine, and stems directly from the idea of eternal generation. *Hupostasis* and *ousia* were originally synonyms, the former Stoic and the latter Platonic, meaning real existence or essence, that which a thing is; but while *hupostasis* retains this connotation in Origen,[3] he more frequently gives it the sense of individual subsistence, and so individual existent. The error of modalism, he contends,[4] lies in treating the Three as numerically indistinguishable (μὴ διαφέρειν τῷ ἀριθμῷ), separable only in thought, 'one not only in essence but also in subsistence' (ἓν οὐ μόνον οὐσίᾳ ἀλλὰ καὶ ὑποκειμένῳ). The true teaching, on his view,[5] is that the Son is 'other in subsistence than the Father' (ἕτερος καθ' ὑποκείμενον), or even that the Father and the Son 'are two things in respect of Their Persons, but one in unanimity, harmony and identity of will' (ὄντα δύο τῇ ὑποστάσει πράγματα, ἓν δὲ τῇ ὁμονοίᾳ καὶ τῇ συμφωνίᾳ καὶ τῇ ταυτότητι τοῦ βουλήματος). Thus, while really distinct, the Three are from another point of view one; as he expresses it,[6] 'we are not afraid to speak in one sense of two Gods, in another sense of one God'.

For Origen the oneness of the Son with the Father is important, but His independence is theologically prior. Sometimes, as the passage quoted shows, he represents the unity as a moral one. Elsewhere[8] he appeals to Scripture, which declares that man and wife, though distinct beings, can be one flesh, and that, on a higher plane, the righteous man and Christ can be

---

[1] *In Ioh.* 2, 10, 75. [2] Ib. 2, 10, 75.
[3] E.g. ib. 20, 22, 182 f.; 32, 16, 192 f.
[4] Ib. 10, 37, 246: cf. ib. 2, 2, 16; *in Matt.* 17, 14.
[5] *De orat.* 15, 1; *c. Cels.* 8, 12. [6] *Dial. Heracl.* 2.
[7] *In Ioh.* 13, 36, 228 f. [8] *Dial. Heracl.* 3.

E.C.D.—5

one spirit. So on a higher plane still Father and Son, though distinct, are one God. The Son, moreover, is the Father's image, the reflection of His glory.[1] By themselves, however, thoughts like these hardly do justice to the whole of Origen's teaching, the pivot of which was that the Son had been begotten, not created, by the Father. Where he seems[2] to speak of Him as a creature, his language is a conscious concession to the usage of *Prov.* 8, 22 ('The Lord created me as a beginning', etc.) and *Col.* 1, 15 ('First-begotten of all creation'), and should not be pressed. As the Father's offspring, He participates in His Godhead; He is Son of God by nature, and His nature is united to the Father's.[3] He issues from Him as the will from the mind, which suffers no division in the process.[4] One must be careful, however, not to attribute to Origen any doctrine of consubstantiality between Father and Son. Appeal is often made to a famous passage in which, after deducing from *Wisdom* 7, 25 that the Son is 'a breath of the power of God, a pure effluence of the glory of the Almighty', he seems to point out[5] that 'both these illustrations suggest a community of substance between Father and Son. For an effluence would appear to be ὁμοούσιος, i.e. of one substance with, that body of which it is an effluence or vapour'. But this text, and several others expressing the same or similar ideas, remain open to grave suspicion because they survive only in Rufinus's white-washing Latin translation. In works which have been trans-mitted in the Greek original Origen always represents the union of Father and Son, as has been noted, as one of love, will and action.

Of the Spirit Origen states,[6] 'He supplies those who, because of Him and their participation in Him, are called sanctified with the matter, if I may so describe it, of their graces. This same matter of graces is effected by God, is ministered by Christ, and achieves individual subsistence (ὑφεστώσης) as the Holy Spirit.' Thus the ultimate ground of His being is the

---

[1] *De princ.* 1, 2, 6; 4, 4, 1.   [2] *In Ioh.* 1, 19, 115; c. *Cels.* 5, 37.
[3] *In Ioh.* 2, 2, 16; 2, 10, 76; 19, 2, 6.   [4] *De princ.* 1, 2, 6; 4, 4, 1.
[5] *Frag. in Hebr.* (PG 14, 1308).   [6] Ib. 2, 10, 77.

Father, but it is mediated to Him by the Son, from Whom also He derives all His distinctive attributes.[1]

It is not altogether fair to conclude, as many have done, that Origen teaches a triad of disparate beings rather than a Trinity; but the strongly pluralist strain in his Trinitarianism is its salient feature. The Three, on his analysis, are eternally and really distinct; They are separate hypostases or even, in his crude-sounding language, 'things'. No doubt he tries to meet the most stringent demands of monotheism by insisting that the fulness of unoriginate Godhead is concentrated in the Father, Who alone is 'the fountain-head of deity' (πηγὴ τῆς θεότητος[2]). 'But the Son and the Spirit are also in their degrees divine, possessing, though derivatively, all the characteristics of deity; distinct from the world of creatures, they cooperate with the Father and mediate the divine life flowing from Him.' This vision of 'the adorable, everlasting Triad',[3] of which he detected[4] an anticipation in the thrice-repeated 'holy' of Isaiah's seraphim, was to inspire generations of later Greek theologians. As it is formulated by Origen, however, the underlying structure of thought is unmistakably borrowed from contemporary Platonism. A striking illustration of this is the fact that, in addition to the Son or Word, he conceived of the whole world of spiritual beings (what he called *logikoi* or *noes*) as being co-eternal with the Father. Indeed, their relation to the Word is precisely parallel to that of the Word, at a higher level, to the Father; they are images of Him, as He is of the Father, and in their degree are equally entitled to be called gods. The reason for this is the axiom, which Origen picked up from middle Platonism, that the Father must always have had a world on which to exercise His power; but its effect is to undermine the Christian idea of a triune God Who transcends the contingent order.

In a more limited field the impact of Platonism reveals itself in the thoroughgoing subordinationism which is integral to Origen's Trinitarian scheme. The Father, as we have seen, is

[1] Ib. 2, 10, 76.   [2] Ib. 2, 3, 20.
[3] Ib. 6, 33, 166; 10, 39, 270.   [4] *Hom. in Is.* 4,1.

alone αὐτόθεος; so St. John, he points out,[1] accurately describes the Son simply as θεός, not ὁ θεός. In relation to the
God of the universe He merits a secondary degree of honour;[2]
for He is not absolute goodness and truth, but His goodness and
truth are a reflection and image of the Father's.[3] The same goes
for His activity; the Son is the Father's agent (ὑπηρέτης),
carrying out His commands, as in the case of creation.[4] For
this reason he concludes[5] that 'we should not pray to any
generate being, not even to Christ, but only to the God and
Father of the universe, to Whom our Saviour Himself prayed';
if prayer is offered to Christ, it is conveyed by Him to the
Father. Indeed, the Son and the Spirit are transcended by the
Father just as much as, if not more than, They Themselves
transcend the realm of inferior beings;[6] and if sometimes
Origen's language seems to contradict this, suggesting[7] that the
Son is God from the beginning, very Word, absolute Wisdom
and truth, the explanation is that He may appear such to
creatures, but from the viewpoint of the ineffable Godhead He
is the first in the chain of emanations. This conception of a
descending hierarchy, itself the product of his Platonizing
background, is epitomized in the statement[8] that, whereas the
Father's action extends to all reality, the Son's is limited to
rational beings, and the Spirit's to those who are being
sanctified.

7. The Influence of Origen

Such meagre evidence as survives of Greek Trinitarianism in
the latter half of the third century testifies to the extent of
Origen's influence. Some theologians gave prominence to his
emphasis on the Son's essential kinship to the Father, others to
his subordinationism. Among the former may be reckoned
Theognostus, head of the catechetical school at Alexandria
(fl. 250–80). While he called[9] the Son a creature and restricted

---

[1] Ib. 2, 2, 13 ff.   [2] C. Cels. 7, 57.
[3] De princ. 1, 2, 13; in Ioh. 13, 25, 151; 32, 28.   [4] C. Cels. 2, 9; 6, 60.
[5] De orat. 15, 1; 16 init.; c. Cels. 8, 13. [6] In Ioh. 13, 25, 151; in Matt. 15, 10.
[7] C. Cels. 3, 41; 6, 47; in Matt. 14, 7.   [8] De princ. 1, 3, 8.
[9] Cf. Photius, bibl. cod. 106.

His activity to rational beings, he also declared[1] that His substance (οὐσία) was derived, not out of nothingness, but out of the Father's substance, as brightness comes from light or steam from water. Just as the brightness and the steam were neither identical with the sun or with water nor alien (ἀλλότριον) from them, so the substance of the Son was neither identical with nor alien from the Father; He was an effluence (ἀπόρροια) of the Father's substance, which in the process suffered no division. His successor, Pierius (*fl.* 280–300), seems[2] to have spoken of the Father and the Son as two substances or natures (οὐσίαι; φύσεις), clearly using these terms as equivalents of Origen's 'hypostases'. Gregory Thaumaturgus († *c.* 270), the apostle of Pontus, was willing on occasion to speak[3] of the Son, in Origenist fashion, as 'a creature or a thing made' (κτίσμα; ποίημα). His formal teaching, however, as set out in his creed,[4] was to the effect that 'there is one God, Father of the living Word . . . perfect begetter of the perfect begotten. . . . There is one Lord, unique out of unique, God out of God, impress and image of Godhead, effective Word. . . . And there is one Holy Spirit, having His subsistence from God and being made manifest by the Son . . . in Whom is manifested God the Father, Who is above all and in all, and God the Son, Who is through all. So there is a perfect Triad . . . in the Triad there is nothing either created or servile, nor anything brought in, as if it formerly did not exist and was subsequently introduced. Thus neither was the Son ever wanting to the Father, nor the Spirit to the Son.'

The best-known exponent of Origen's subordinationist strain is his pupil Dionysius, bishop of Alexandria. In the late fifties of the century he was instigated[5] to set out what he considered to be the orthodox position by an outbreak of Sabellianism in the Libyan Pentapolis, which fell under his jurisdiction. Not unnaturally, since the rebuttal of modalism was his object, he thrust the personal distinction between Father and Son into the foreground; and the Sabellian group was able

---

[1] Cf. Athanasius, *de decret.* 25.   [2] Photius, *bibl.* cod. 119.
[3] Cf. Basil, *ep.* 210, 5.   [4] PG 10, 184-8.   [5] Cf. Athanasius, *de sent. Dion.* 5.

to find at any rate one[1] of his letters, addressed to bishops
Ammonius and Euphranor, full of indiscretions. They made a
formal complaint to the Roman pope, who was also named
Dionysius, and accused the Alexandrian bishop (a) of making
a sharp division, amounting to separation, between Father and
Son (διαιρεῖ καὶ μακρύνει καὶ μερίζει τὸν υἱὸν ἀπὸ τοῦ πατρός[2]);
(b) of denying the Son's eternity, and stating that the
Father had not always been Father and that 'the Son was not
before He came into existence';[3] (c) of naming the Father
without the Son and the Son without the Father, as if They
were not inseparable in Their very being;[4] (d) of failing to
describe the Son as ὁμοούσιος with the Father;[5] and (e) of
stating that the Son was a creature (ποίημα καὶ γενητόν), just
as much different from the Father in substance (ξένον κατ'
οὐσίαν) as a vine from its vinedresser, a boat from the ship-
wright who made it, etc.[6]

There is no doubt that Dionysius had used language unfortunate in itself and in its implications; in the following
century Athanasius tried[7] to whitewash him, but Basil's judgment was surer when he remarked[8] that Dionysius's anti-
Sabellian zeal had carried him to the opposite extreme.
Dionysius of Rome issued a brief[9] which, without mentioning
his name, in effect criticized Dionysius of Alexandria, and then
went on to expound a positive theology which shows how
powerful was the influence of Novatian at Rome. The pope
was clearly shocked by the Origen-inspired doctrine of three
hypostases, which seemed to him to undermine the divine
monarchy. Those Alexandrian theologians who taught it were,
he implied, virtual tritheists, splitting the indivisible oneness
of the Deity into 'three powers, three absolutely separate
hypostases, three divinities'. At all costs the indivisibility of
the holy Monad must be maintained; the Word and the Spirit
must therefore be regarded as inseparable from the God of the
universe, and must be summed up and gathered to Him. This

---

[1] Ib. 9; 10.　　[2] *De sent Dion.* 16.　　[3] Ib. 14.　　[4] Ib. 16.
[5] Ib. 18.　　[6] Ib. 4.　　[7] Cf. ib.　　[8] *Ep.* 9, 2.
[9] Cf. the fragments preserved by Athanasius, *de decret.* 26.

is the old idea that the almighty Father (in the old sense of the unique Godhead) can never have been without His Word and His Spirit since They belong to His very being. In harmony with this, the pope continued, if Christ is in the Father (cf. *John* 14, 11), if He is His Word, Wisdom and Power (cf. *1 Cor.* 1, 24), He must always have existed, and it is blasphemous to speak of Him as a creature or to say that there was when He was not. According to *Ps.* 109, 3 (LXX: 'Before the dawn I begat thee out of my belly'), and *Prov.* 8, 25 ('Before all the hills he begets me'), His origin was no act of creation, but 'a divine and ineffable generation'.

Dionysius of Alexandria made an elaborate rejoinder, in which he restated his position in less equivocal, more cautious terms, although without surrendering any of its essential features. He freely acknowledged[1] the impropriety of some of his expressions and analogies, but complained that his teaching had not been judged as a whole; and he skilfully adopted the pope's language in reformulating his own doctrine. First, he repudiated the charge of separating Father, Son and Spirit. The Three are obviously inseparable, as is demonstrated by Their very titles: a Father implies a Son, a Son implies a Father, and Spirit implies both the source from which and the medium by which it proceeds forth.[2] Even so, his definition of Them as 'three hypostases' must be retained, inasmuch as They are three, unless the Triad is to be dissolved.[3] Secondly, he affirmed unambiguously that the Son is eternal. God was always Father, and therefore Christ was always Son, just as if the sun were eternal the daylight would also be everlasting; the one cannot be conceived without the other.[4] Thirdly, dealing with the allegation that he had not employed ὁμοούσιος, he pointed out[5] that the term was non-Scriptural. Nevertheless he accepted its meaning, as the figures he had chosen proved. Parents and children, for example, are different people, but are 'homogeneous' (ὁμογενεῖς); the plant and its seed or root are

---

1 Cf. Athanasius, *de sent. Dion.* 14; 18.   2 Ib. 17.
3 Cf. Basil, *de spir. sanct.* 72.   4 Cf. Athanasius, op. cit. 15 f.
5 Ib. 18.

different, yet of the same nature (ὁμοφυῆ). So the river and its source are different in form and name, but consist of the self-same water. He evidently interpreted *homoousios* as meaning 'sharing the same nature', in the generic sense, as Origen himself may well have done. His whole object, it would appear, was to correct the false impression, as he judged it, that his doctrine of three hypostases excluded the essential unity of the Three. He summarized his position in the balanced formula,[1] 'We both expand the Monad into the Triad without dividing It'—thus he concedes to his Roman colleague that the Son and the Spirit are, as it were, projections of the indivisible divine essence—'and again we sum up the Triad in the Monad without subtracting from It'—that is, the oneness must be acknowledged, but not at the cost of failing to recognize the three Persons.

The incident supplies an instructive illustration of the very different lines along which Western and Eastern theologians were working. Scholars have often sought to explain the clash away as the result of a mere misunderstanding over terminology. To a certain extent it was that. For example, the pope may well have inferred, on sound etymological grounds, that ὑπόστασις was the Greek equivalent for *substantia*, which he had learned from Tertullian signified the indivisible concrete reality of the Godhead. Hence his shocked conclusion that his namesake's doctrine of three hypostases was tantamount to tritheism. But the matter went much deeper than words. Western Trinitarianism, as we noticed earlier, had long been marked by a monarchian bias. What was luminously clear to the theologians representing it was the divine unity; so mysterious did they find the distinctions within that unity that, though fully convinced of their reality, they were only beginning, haltingly and timidly, to think of them as 'Persons'. In the East, where the intellectual climate was impregnated with Neo-Platonic ideas about the hierarchy of being, an altogether different, confessedly pluralistic approach had established itself. The disagreement was thus theological at bottom, and was destined to manifest itself again in the following century.

[1] Cf. Athanasius, op. cit. 17.

NOTE ON BOOKS

General. G. Bardy, 'Trinité' (art. in *Dict. Théol. Cath.*); G. Kretschmar, *Studien zur frühchristlichen Trinitätstheologie* (Tübingen, 1956); J. Lebreton, *Histoire du dogme de la Trinité* (Paris, 1928); F. Loofs, 'Christologie-Kirchenlehre' (art. in Hauck's *Realencyk.*); R. A. Norris, *God and World in Early Christian Theology* (London, 1967); G. L. Prestige, *God in Patristic Thought* (London, 2 ed. 1952); A. E. J. Rawlinson (ed.), *Essays on the Trinity and the Incarnation* (London, 1928).

Special. É. Amann, 'Hippolyte' (art. in *Dict. Théol. Cath.*); A. d'Alès, *La Théologie de Tertullien* and *La Théologie d'Hippolyte* (Paris, 1905 and 1906); G. Bardy, 'Monarchianisme' (art. in *Dict. Théol. Cath.*); H. J. Carpenter, 'Popular Christianity and the Theologians in the Early Centuries' (art. in *Journ. Theol. Stud.*, 1963); H. Chadwick, *Early Christian Thought and the Classical Tradition* (Oxford, 1966); J. Daniélou, *Origen* (Eng. trans., London, 1955); E. Evans, *Tertullian's Treatise against Praxeas* (London, 1948); C. L. Feltoe, *The Letters of Dionysius of Alexandria* (Cambridge, 1904); J. Lebreton, 'Le Désaccord de la foi populaire et de la théologie savante dans l'eglise chrétienne du 3me siècle' (art. in *Rev. d'hist. eccl.*, 1923 and 1924); C. W. Lowry, 'Origen as Trinitarian' (art. in *Journ.Theol..Stud.*, 1936); R. A. Markus, 'Trinitarian Theology and the Economy' (art. in *Journ.Theol..Stud.*, 1958); P. Nautin, *Hippolyte contre les hérésies* (Paris, 1949); H. de Riedmatten, *Les Actes du procès de Paul de Samosate* (Fribourg en Suisse, 1952); M. Simonetti, 'Sul *De Trinitate* di Novaziano' (*Studi in onore di A. Monterverdi* 2: 1959); G. C. Stead, 'Divine Substance in Tertullian' (art. in *Journ. Theol. Stud.*, 1963); R. Walzer, *Galen on Jews and Christians* (Oxford, 1949); M. F. Wiles, 'Eternal Generation' (art. in *Journ.. Theol. Stud.*, 1961).

CHAPTER VI

THE BEGINNINGS OF CHRISTOLOGY

1. *One-sided Solutions*

THE problem of Christology, in the narrow sense of the word, is to define the relation of the divine and the human in Christ. For a full-dress attack on the issues involved we must wait until the fourth century; it was the decision, promulgated at Nicaea, that the Word shared the same divine nature as the Father, that focused attention upon them. Nevertheless the all but universal Christian conviction in the preceding centuries had been that Jesus Christ was divine as well as human. The most primitive confession had been 'Jesus is Lord'[1], and its import had been elaborated and deepened in the apostolic age. The New Testament writers generally regarded Christ as pre-existent; they tended[2] to attribute to Him a twofold order of being, 'according to the flesh' (κατὰ σάρκα), i.e. as man, and 'according to spirit' (κατὰ πνεῦμα), i.e. as God. So deeply was this formula embedded in their thinking that F. Loofs justly labelled[3] it 'the foundation datum of all later Christo-logical development'. As this contained all the elements of the Christological problem, thoughtful Christians could scarcely ignore it. We shall find that they did not do so, and that while most of the solutions proposed by the pre-Nicene Church were necessarily tentative, there were some which foreshadowed the mature discussion of later centuries.

In this book we are primarily concerned with the progress of doctrine within the central Christian tradition, i.e. in the Catholic Church. Here the double premiss of apostolic Christ-

---

[1] E.g. *Rom.* 10, 9; *Phil.* 2, 11.
[2] E.g. *Rom.* 1, 3 f.; 8, 9; *2 Cor.* 3, 17; *Hebr.* 9, 14; *1 Pet.* 1, 11; 3, 18.
[3] *Leitfaden zum Studium der Dogmengeschichte* (Halle, 5th ed. 1950), § 14, 5a.

ology, viz. that Christ as a Person was indivisibly one, and that He was simultaneously fully divine and fully human, was taken as the starting-point, the task of theology being to show how its two aspects could be held together in synthesis. In the first three centuries, however, the frontiers of orthodoxy were not so rigidly demarcated as they later became, and important currents of thought flowed outside the main channel. Certain of these 'heretical' trends have considerable Christological interest, and we shall glance briefly at a few of them before concentrating on the orthodox movement of thought.

First, then, we hear in the second century of a type of Christology, known as Ebionism, which solved the problem by denying the divinity altogether. The Ebionites were an offshoot of that specifically Jewish form of Christianity which was a potent force in the apostolic age, when it was only prevented with difficulty from saddling the Church with the full observance of the Jewish law. The rapid expansion of Gentile Christianity meant that its influence was bound to diminish, and the dispersal of the main community from Jerusalem to Transjordan on the outbreak of the Jewish war (A.D. 66) completed its isolation. After that date we only catch fleeting glimpses of Judaizing Christianity, and indeed it seems to have dissolved in splinter groups. Some of them, often called Nazaraeans, while strictly obeying the law and preferring a Judaizing gospel of their own, were perfectly orthodox in their belief that Jesus was the Son of God.[1] In distinction from these the Ebionites rejected[2] the virgin birth, regarding the Lord as a man normally born from Joseph and Mary; He was the predestined Messiah, and in this capacity would return to reign on earth. This at any rate was the core of their teaching, which in some quarters seems to have had a pronounced Gnostic colouring. Hippolytus[3] and Tertullian[4] connect their name with one Ebion, presumably the apocryphal founder of the sect; but in fact it derives from the Hebrew for 'poor', no doubt recalling

[1] Justin, *dial.* 47: cf. Hegesippus (in Eusebius, *hist. eccl.* 4, 22, 2 f.); Jerome, *ep.* 112, 13; Epiphanius, *haer.* 29, 7.
[2] Justin, ib.; Irenaeus, *haer.* 1, 26, 1; 3, 11, 7; 3, 21, 1.
[3] *Ref.* 7, 35, 1.   [4] *De praescr.* 33.

the humble title[1] by which the original Jewish-Christian community in Jerusalem liked to be known.

2 Secondly, Christologies of this type, attributing to Christ the status of a mere man ($\psi\iota\lambda\grave{o}s$ $\check{\alpha}\nu\theta\rho\omega\pi os$) pre-eminently endowed, were not wholly unexampled in non-Jewish circles. *non-Jewish ideas* In the previous chapter, when considering monarchianism, we examined[2] the adoptionism of the two Theodoti and Artemas, and noticed that Paul of Samosata was charged with disseminating similar teaching in the sixties of the third century. Reliable information about his position is in fact surprisingly meagre. Contemporary evidence, as represented by the synodal letter (268) condemning him reproduced by Eusebius,[3] alleges that in his doctrinal teaching Paul 'denied his Lord and God and repudiated the faith he himself had previously held', that 'he refused to acknowledge that the Son of God came down from heaven', declaring that 'Jesus Christ was from below', and finally that he 'revived the abominable heresy of Artemas', who was indeed his intellectual father. Jesus was, in fact, 'an ordinary man by nature'.[4] According to reports[5] circulating a century or so later, Paul contended that the divine Word which descended on the man Jesus and dwelt in Him was not a distinct hypostasis but was in God in the same way as a man's reason exists in him. Modern scholars, it is true, relying on fifth- and sixth-century fragments[6] purporting to record the debate at which his heresy was unmasked, present a very different picture. According to this, Paul was an early exponent of the 'Word-man' Christology (see below p. 281), understanding the incarnation as the indwelling of the Word in a man, while his critics supported a precociously mature 'Word-flesh' Christology. These fragments, however, are suspect, deriving apparently from an Apollinarian provenance, and the traditional view that Paul was a straightforward adoptionist is probably correct.

---

[1] E.g. *Rom.* 15, 26; *Gal.* 2, 10.   [2] See above, pp. 116–19.
[3] Eusebius, *hist. eccl.* 7, 30, 4; 11; 16.   [4] Ibid. 7, 27, 2.
[5] Epiphanius, *haer.* 65, 1, 5–8.
[6] For these fragments and a recent discussion accepting their authenticity, see H. de Riedmatten (op. cit. in Bibliography).

3. Thirdly, a diametrically opposite Christological tendency, effectively eliminating the Lord's humanity, was a factor to be reckoned with from apostolic times onwards. Known as Docetism, the distinctive thesis which gave it its name (δοκεῖν = 'to seem') was that Christ's manhood, and hence His sufferings, were unreal, phantasmal. Clearly its ultimate roots were Graeco-Oriental assumptions about divine impassibility and the inherent impurity of matter. The first expressly to mention 'Docetists' (δοκηταί) is Serapion of Antioch[1] (fl. 200). But Docetism was not a simple heresy on its own; it was an attitude which infected a number of heresies, particularly Marcionism[2] and Gnosticism.[3] This attitude is crystallized in a remark[4] of Justin's (?), 'There are some who declare that Jesus Christ did not come in flesh but only as spirit, and exhibited an appearance (φαντασίαν) of flesh'. Traces of teaching like this are visible in the New Testament itself, and very early in the second century we find Ignatius protesting[5] against 'godless' people who claimed that Christ had suffered in appearance only. By itself this might imply simply the theory, common enough at the time, that someone else was crucified in Christ's stead. But the vigour with which Ignatius defends[6] the actuality of all Christ's human experiences, as well as the hint[7] that his opponents declined to admit that He was genuinely 'flesh-bearing' (σαρκοφόρος), suggests that their Docetism went the whole way. Shortly afterwards Polycarp was anathematizing[8] the refusal to 'confess that Jesus Christ came in the flesh'; and the apocryphal *Gospel of Peter* was to state[9] that the Saviour on the cross had 'kept silence, as feeling no pain', implying that His bodily make-up was illusory.

The Christologies of Gnosticism transport us into a bizarre world of cosmic speculation. The burden of the myth of redemption, it will be recalled,[10] was the liberation of the divine element, the fragment of spirit, in fallen humanity, and this

---

[1] Cf. Eusebius, *hist. eccl.* 6, 12, 6. [2] See above, p. 57.
[3] See above, pp. 22-8. [4] *De res.* 2. [5] *Trall.* 10; *Smyrn.* 2.
[6] *Eph.* 7; 18-20; *Trall.* 9; *Smyrn.* 1-3; 7; *Magn.* 11. [7] *Smyrn.* 5.
[8] *Phil.* 7, 1. [9] 4, 11 (ed. M. R. James, p. 91).
[10] See above, pp. 23-7.

was accomplished by the bestowal of knowledge. There was a great variety of Gnostic systems, but a common pattern ran through them all. From the pleroma, or spiritual world of aeons, the divine Christ descended and united Himself for a time (according to Ptolemy,[1] between the baptism and the passion) to the historical personage, Jesus; and according to most accounts the latter's body was formed, not out of ordinary flesh, but of 'psychic' substance.[2] Thus the Gnostics' Christology tended to be pluralist; Christ Jesus on their view, as Irenaeus pointed out,[3] was compounded by two distinct substances ($ο\dot{υ}σίαι$), being at once the heavenly Christ and Jesus, the Son of the Demiurge, in a loose sort of liaison. It was also docetic, either as teaching that the heavenly Christ was invisible, impalpable and impassible, or as implying that the lower Christ himself, with whom the heavenly Christ joined Himself, was not real flesh and blood. Marcion's Christology, too, was docetic at any rate as regards the Lord's body; inconsistently, he treated His sufferings and death as real and as effecting the redemption.[4] Christ was not for him the Messiah foretold by the prophets, nor was He son of Mary; having neither birth nor growth, He suddenly appeared on earth as an adult man. Virtually modalist, Marcion conceived[5] of Jesus as manifesting in human form the invisible good God.

2. The Spirit Christology

These were tendencies on the fringe, yet Gnosticism at any rate came within an ace of swamping the central tradition. The fact that it did not do so was in large measure due (apart from an astonishing feat of pastoral care on the part of the ecclesiastical authorities) to the unwavering insistence in the rule of faith, as expressed in liturgy, catechetical teaching and preaching, that the Son of God had really become man. This fundamental datum ensured that the Christological scheme of the primitive

---

[1] Irenaeus, *haer.* 1, 7, 2.   [2] E.g. ib. 1, 6, 1.   [3] Ib. 3, 16, 5.
[4] Cf. Tertullian, *de carn. Chr.* 3–5; Origen, *frag. in Luc.* 1 (Rauer,[2] 227).
[5] Cf. Tertullian, *c. Marc.* 1, 19.

Church reproduced the pattern laid down in the New Testament—one Christ, at once human and divine, flesh and spirit. The most striking examples of it are provided by Ignatius, whose anti-heretical polemic prompted him to emphasize both the oneness of Christ and the reality of His twofold mode of existence. He delighted to proclaim these truths in such balanced antitheses as,[1] 'There is one physician, composed of flesh and of spirit, generate and ingenerate, God in man, authentic life in death, from Mary and from God, first passible and then impassible, Jesus Christ our Lord'. He was accustomed to drive home the fact that the subject of these seemingly contradictory experiences was indivisibly one by using expressions[2] like 'the blood of God', 'the suffering of my God', and 'God . . . was conceived by Mary', which anticipated the later doctrine of *communicatio idiomatum* (ἀντίδοσις ἰδιωμάτων), i.e. that in view of the unity of Christ's Person, His human and divine attributes, experiences, etc. might properly be interchanged.

This being the accepted formula, the suggestion once commonly advanced that the original type of Christology was naïvely adoptionist, i.e. envisaged Christ as a man promoted by divine favour to deity, has little to be said for it. In any case, as was shown in Chapter IV, the attribution of pre-existence to Christ was general among the Apostolic Fathers, and it is unlikely that even Hermas[3] was an adoptionist in the strict sense. The vast majority of Christians in the early second century probably shared the faith and practice of the simple Bithynian believers who, as they confessed to Pliny,[4] were in the habit of meeting together before dawn and singing a hymn 'to Christ as to God'. The Christological theory (if theory is an apt name for what was usually a pre-reflective supposition) which commanded most support, and which lingered on beyond the second century, may be described as a Spirit-Christology. By this is meant the view that in the historical Jesus Christ the pre-existent Son of God, Who is divine spirit, united Himself with human nature. This could take a variety of forms, according

[1] *Eph.* 7, 2.   [2] Ib. 1, 1; 18, 2; *Rom.* 6, 3.
[3] See above, pp. 94 f.   [4] *Ep. ad Traian. imp.* 96.

to the underlying conception. The idea seems sometimes to have been that the pre-existent Christ-Spirit indwelt the man Jesus, sometimes that He actually became man. 'Barnabas' provides an example of the former, with his statements[1] that the Son of God 'came' or 'manifested himself' in flesh, or in the form of flesh, and that the body which Christ offered in sacrifice was 'the receptacle of spirit'. An even more impressive illustration is Hermas's theory[2] that 'God caused the holy, pre-existent spirit which created the whole of creation to dwell in flesh that He desired', i.e. in the human Jesus, Who cooperated with it meritoriously.

On the other hand, the Christology of the Ignatian passage cited above clearly conforms to the second type. Belonging first to the supernatural order (cf. πνευματικός, ἀγέννητος, ἀπαθής, etc.), Jesus was fully and characteristically human. He was born 'of the seed of David, but also of holy spirit'[3]; He was 'of the seed of David as regards His flesh, but Son of God according to God's will and power'[4]. In agreement with this approach 2 Clement declares[5] that 'Christ the Lord, Who saved us, being first of all spirit, became flesh'; while in 1 Clement[6] we read that Christ addresses us in the Psalms 'through holy spirit'. To pass beyond the second century, the same theory, it is plain, lay behind Callistus's doctrine[7] that what became incarnate of the Blessed Virgin was 'holy spirit'. Both Hippolytus and Tertullian, as we shall see, were exponents of the Spirit-Christology; and Cyprian's statement[8] that at the incarnation God's Son 'descended into the Virgin and as holy spirit clothed Himself with flesh' illustrates its persistence. It is noteworthy that the all but unanimous exegetical tradition[9] of Luke 1, 35, equated 'the holy spirit' and 'the power of the Most High' which were to come upon Mary, not with the third Person of the Trinity, but with the Christ Who, pre-existing as spirit or Word, was to incarnate Himself in her

---

[1] 5, 6; 5, 10 f.; 12, 10; 7, 3.   [2] Sim. 5, 6, 5-7: see above, p. 94.
[3] Eph. 18, 2.   [4] Smyrn. 1, 1.   [5] 9, 5.   [6] 22, 1.
[7] Cf. Hippolytus, ref. 9, 12, 17: see above, p. 124.   [8] Quod idola 11.
[9] Cf. J. M. Creed, The Gospel according to St. Luke (London, 1930), ad loc.: see above p. 103.

womb. It is also highly probable that the ancient clause of the Old Roman Creed, WHO WAS BORN FROM HOLY SPIRIT AND THE VIRGIN MARY, reflects the same idea that Jesus Christ, the historic Son of God, was the product of the union of divine spirit with human nature in the womb of the Blessed Virgin.

3. The Apologists and Irenaeus

Little enough can be gleaned from the Apologists, Justin apart, about Christology. Preoccupied with the Logos, they evince surprisingly little interest in the Gospel Figure. Tatian, it is true, speaks[1] of Him as 'God in the form of a man'; while Aristides, using language coloured by the Spirit-Christology, states[2] that 'it is confessed that this Son of the most high God descended from heaven as holy spirit (ἐν πνεύματι ἁγίῳ) and took flesh from a virgin'. For Melito[3] He was 'by nature God and man'; He had 'clothed Himself with the man', His divine element being described as 'spirit'. Though sometimes coming close to it, Melito steered clear of modalism, clearly distinguishing the Word from the Father.[4] Justin himself was usually content to reproduce the familiar affirmations of the rule of faith. He is satisfied that the Word became man by being born from the Virgin. As he expresses[5] it, 'He Who was formerly Logos, and appeared now in the semblance of fire, now in incorporeal fashion, has finally by God's will become man for the human race'. He pre-existed as God, and was made flesh of the Virgin, being born as man.[6] His incarnation involved the assumption of flesh and blood,[7] and Justin insists,[8] in spite of the scandal thereby occasioned to Jewish critics, on the reality of the Messiah's physical sufferings. Yet He did not cease to exist as Word, being in fact at once 'God and man.'[9]

Passages like these emphasize the reality of the two natures, but throw no light on the manner of their co-existence in the

---

[1] Or. 21, 1.   [2] Apol. 15, 1.
[3] De pascha 8; 100; 66 f.   [4] Frgg. 2; 13; 15; de pascha 47.
[5] 1 apol. 63, 10.   [6] Dial. 87, 2: cf. 1 apol. 46, 5.
[7] 1 apol. 66, 2.   [8] Dial. 34, 2; 36, 1; 39, 7; 41, 1; 49, 2; etc.
[9] Ib. 71, 2: cf. ib. 100.

one Person of Christ. The only explanation Justin hints at is one suggested by his doctrine of the germinal Logos (λόγος σπερματικός [1]). Since we agree, he argues,[2] that the Logos manifested Himself in various forms to Abraham, Isaac and Moses (he is thinking of the Old Testament theophanies), why should we shrink from believing that He could be born as a man from the Virgin? The Logos, moreover, has been active in all men, imparting to them whatever goodness and knowledge they possessed.[3] The idea lurking in his mind seems to be that His presence in Jesus Christ should be understood as similar in kind to this universal presence, though much greater in degree. Yet he does not follow up or develop the idea, and in any case leaves the presence of the Word in other men in all ages itself unexplained. Sometimes he speaks of His dwelling in them or being implanted in them like a seed,[4] sometimes of them as living with the Logos,[5] sometimes of their having a share or portion of Him.[6]

There is, however, one crucial passage which has often been pointed to as providing an answer. This is Justin's statement[7] that Christianity is manifestly superior to all other human teaching 'for the reason that the rational principle in its entirety became the Christ Who appeared because of us, body and Logos and soul' (διὰ τοῦ τὸ λογικὸν τὸ ὅλον τὸν φανέντα δι᾽ ἡμᾶς Χριστὸν γεγονέναι, καὶ σῶμα καὶ λόγον καὶ ψυχήν). The implication of the final clause, it has been suggested, must be that on Justin's view the Logos took the place in the man Jesus of the human rational soul (νοῦς or πνεῦμα). If this interpretation is correct, Justin must have been a pioneer exponent of the 'Word-flesh' type of Christology which we shall later be studying; and it is certainly the case that, one or two passages excepted, he shows little or no interest in Christ's human soul. The Stoic influences in his environment must have prompted him to regard the Logos as the governing principle, or ἡγεμονικόν, in the God-man. On the other hand, the whole

---

[1] See above, p. 96.   [2] *Dial.* 75, 4.
[3] *1 apol.* 32, 8; 46, 3; *2 apol.* 8, 1; 10, 2; 13, 3.   [4] *1 apol.* 32, 8; *2 apol.* 8, 1.
[5] *1 apol.* 46, 3.   [6] *2 apol.* 10, 2; 13, 3.   [7] *Ib.* 10, 1-3.

point of the passage is that the difference between Christ and
ordinary men lies, not in any essential disparity of constitution,
but in the fact that, whereas the Logos works in them fragmentarily (κατὰ μέρος), or as a seed, He works in Christ as a
whole. Indeed, if that had been what he intended, nothing
could have been easier for Justin than to say quite frankly that
the Logos had substituted Himself for the kind of soul ordinary
men possessed. From this point of view it might be more
plausible to regard the text cited as bearing testimony to
Justin's belief that Christ's humanity was complete, including a
soul (ψυχή) animated and enlightened by the Word, as well as a
body. As a matter of fact, he has other passages,[1] e.g. where he
refers to the crucified Christ's surrendering His spirit (πνεῦμα),
or to His feelings when faced with His passion, which suggest
that he may have allowed for His possession of a human soul.
It is difficult, however, to feel any certainty where there is so
little evidence to go upon; and while speculation opens up
fascinating vistas, Justin's final conclusions on the matter must
remain a mystery.

Although influenced by the Apologists, Irenaeus owed much
more to the direct impact of St. Paul and St. John. In Christology his approach was conditioned negatively by his opposition to Gnosticism and Docetism, positively by his own
tremendous vision of Christ as the second Adam, Who summed
up in Himself the whole sequence of mankind, including the
first Adam, thereby sanctifying it and inaugurating a new, redeemed race of men. Thus he insists almost monotonously on
the unity of the God-man, repudiating[2] the Gnostic separation
of the heavenly Christ from the man Jesus. As he read the
Gospels and the rule of faith, it was the eternal Word Himself
Who became incarnate; and he never tires of applying the
formula[3] 'one and the same' to the Lord Jesus Christ. His
motive here was frankly soteriological; only if the divine Word
entered fully into human life could the redemption have been
accomplished. Similarly, as against Docetism, he argued for the

[1] *Dial.* 105, 5; 103, 7 f.   [2] E.g. *haer.* 3, 16, 8.
[3] E.g. ib. 1, 9, 2; 3, 16, 2 f.; 3, 16, 8; 3, 17, 4.

reality of Christ's corporeal nature. He was 'truly God' and 'truly man'[1]; if His flesh had differed in any respect (sinlessness excepted) from ordinary human flesh, the parallel between Him and the first Adam would not have been valid, and man's sinful nature could not have been reconciled to God.[2] The Word Himself fashioned His own humanity in the Virgin's womb; and if it be asked why He did this instead of creating some altogether novel substance, the answer[3] is that the humanity which was to be the instrument of salvation had to be identical with that which needed to be saved.

Thus Irenaeus, even more emphatically than Justin, is a representative of the view that at the incarnation the pre-existent Logos, Who revealed Himself in the creation of the world and in the Old Testament theophanies, actually became man. The difference between them is that, while Justin accentuates the distinction between the Logos and the Father, even calling the former a 'second God', for Irenaeus (here he is akin to Ignatius) He is the form in which the Godhead manifests Itself. A rather different Christology has been suspected to lie behind his habit of referring[4] to 'the God' and 'His man' (e.g. 'both confessing the God and firmly accepting His man'), as if the humanity were almost an independent person vis-à-vis the Word. But expressions like these do not betoken an incipient Nestorianism; they are simply examples of the vividly concrete language which Irenaeus was obliged to use because of his lack of abstract terms for 'divinity' and 'humanity'. Two further points of interest deserve to be noticed. First, while it is not absolutely clear whether he attributed a rational human soul to the incarnate Lord (the question had not been posed in his day), the probability is that he did in so far as he thought about the matter at all. At any rate he was satisfied[5] that human nature in its completeness includes such a soul, and that the Word became whatever human nature is. Secondly, there are passages in his writings which

---

[1] Ib. 4, 6, 7.   [2] Haer. 5, 14, 2 f.
[3] Ib. 3, 21 f.   [4] E.g. ib. 5, 14, 1; 5, 14, 4; 5, 21, 3.
[5] Ib. 3, 22, 1: cf. 5, 9, 1.

suggest that he was aware of some at any rate of the problems involved in the union of divinity and humanity. For example, he states[1] that when the Lord was tempted, suffered and died, the Word remained quiescent (ἡσυχάζοντος), but cooperated (συγγιγνομένου τῷ ἀνθρώπῳ) with the humanity in its victory, endurance and resurrection.

4. The Western Contribution

In the pre-Nicene era the West was quicker in formulating a mature Christology than the East. In part its success was due to its possessing theologians of the calibre of Hippolytus and Tertullian. If we concentrate on the latter in this section, the reason is that the pattern he shaped was to prove of lasting significance. Yet certain features of Hippolytus's Christology call for mention.

First, like his teacher Irenaeus, Hippolytus looked to the Johannine model, 'The Word was made flesh'. Some of his utterances seem at first sight to imply that the Logos simply assumed human flesh as an outward habiliment, as when he compares[2] Christ's humanity to a bridegroom's robe. Again, like Irenaeus, he sometimes speaks[3] of it as 'the man', as if it constituted an independent person. His true meaning, however, comes out in the statements[4] that 'the Logos became flesh and was made man', that entering into the Virgin He took flesh from her and 'became everything that a man is, sin excepted', and that (as against the Docetists) 'He became man really, not in appearance or in a manner of speaking'. Like St. John and Irenaeus, he used 'flesh' to connote human nature in its integrity, without raising the question of a rational soul, and referred to the divine element in Christ as 'spirit'. Secondly, he had a firmer grasp than most of his predecessors of the duality of natures in Christ as attested by the difference of operation and manifestation. More than once, in passages[5] packed with eloquent antitheses, he contrasts the weakness of the humanity

---

[1] Ib. 3, 19, 3.   [2] De antichr. 4.
[3] E.g. in Dan. 4, 39, 5.   [4] C. Noet. 4; 17.   [5] E.g. c. Noet. 18.

(what he calls τὰ ἀνθρώπινα) with the sublimity of the divine nature. Thirdly, he has an interesting text[1] in which he states, 'Neither the Logos without flesh and by Himself was Son in the full sense . . . nor could the flesh exist (ὑποστᾶναι) by itself apart from the Logos, since it has its support (σύστασιν) in the Logos'. Hippolytus is not here anticipating the much later doctrine that the human nature derived its subsistence from the Word. He is merely emphasizing his well-known view[2] that the Sonship, properly speaking, dated from the incarnation, and adding that the Word was the creator of His own flesh. But the introduction of the fateful term ὑποστᾶναι (cogn. ὑπόστασις) into Christological discussion deserves notice, as does the implied hint that the Person of the Word is the basis of the God-man.

  The central feature of Tertullian's Christology was its grasp of the two natures in Christ; to use the term which he preferred, the Saviour was composed of 'two substances'. The Word on his view, as we have already seen,[3] has existed alongside the Father from all eternity, a distinct Person at any rate from His generation, but one with Him in essence. He became man, however, for man's salvation, since only as man could He accomplish His work on our behalf. So He was born from the Virgin; as Son of God He needed no earthly father, but it was necessary for Him to derive His manhood from an earthly source.[4] Consequently, being divine spirit (here again we catch an echo of the Spirit-Christology), He entered into the Virgin, as the angel of the annunciation foretold, and received His flesh from her.[5] The birth was a real one; He was born *from* her and not, as the Gnostic Valentinus alleged, simply *through* her, as if she were a mere channel through which He passed.[6] Tertullian does not shrink from claiming[7] that in the process Mary, who had conceived as a virgin, lost her virginity. Christ's humanity was in every respect genuine,[8] and also complete; it included, as indispensable to man's constitution, a

---

[1] Ib. 15. [2] See above, p. 112. [3] See above, pp. 111 f.
[4] *De carn. Chr.* 17 f. [5] *Adv. Prax.* 26. [6] *De carn. Chr.* 20.
[7] Ib. 23. [8] Ib. 1; 5; 9.

soul as well as a body—indeed, the assumption of a soul was necessary if man was to be saved.[1] As a result, He was obliged to put up with the *passiones humanas*, such as hunger and thirst, tears, birth and death.[2] The governing principle in His make-up, however, was always the Word; Tertullian leaves one in no doubt that it was He, the divine spirit, Who 'took the man to Himself' (*suscepit hominem*), and 'mingled God and man in Himself'.[3]

If Jesus Christ, then, consists of 'two substances' (cf. *utramque substantiam Christi et carnis et spiritus non negas*[4]), what should we say about the relation between them? Tertullian has the distinction of being the first theologian frankly to tackle this issue. 'Thus the Word', he writes,[5] 'is in flesh. But this provokes the inquiry how the Word became flesh. Was He, so to speak, metamorphosed (*transfiguratus*) into flesh, or did He clothe Himself in it (*indutus carnem*)?' He has no hesitation in opting for the second alternative. A transformation is unthinkable, for the reason that God and His Logos are by definition immutable, and that the result of such a metamorphosis would be the destruction of both the Godhead and the manhood and the emergence of a monstrous *tertium quid*, a mixture or amalgam. The logical conclusion is that both 'substances' continue unaltered and unimpaired after the union. So, anticipating later definitions, Tertullian can say that each of them preserves its peculiar qualities (*salva est utriusque proprietas substantiae*) and activity (*substantiae ambo in statu suo quaeque distincte agebant*), the spirit performing the miracles and the humanity enduring the sufferings. Yet while the flesh remains flesh and the spirit spirit (he cites the Lord's remark to Nicodemus in *John* 3, 6 as Scriptural confirmation), they both belong to a single subject (*in uno plane esse possunt*); He Who was both Son of God and Son of man was one and the same Person.

He sums up:[6] 'We observe a twofold condition, not confused but conjoined, Jesus, in one Person at once God and man' (*videmus duplicem statum, non confusum sed coniunctum, in una*

---

[1] Ib. 10-13.   [2] *Adv. Prax.* 16.   [3] E.g. *c. Marc.* 2, 27.
[4] *De carn. Chr.* 18.   [5] *Adv. Prax.* 27.   [6] Loc. cit.

persona deum et hominem Iesum). Side by side in that indivisible
Person can be seen Godhead and manhood, divine spirit
and human flesh, immortality and mortality, strength and
weakness.[1] If it is said that Christ suffered and died, the reference
is to the human 'substance'. God does not suffer; the Christ-
spirit cannot even have 'suffered with' (*compassus*) the flesh, as
the modalists liked to plead.[2] The cry of dereliction on the cross
came from Christ's human flesh and soul, not from His divine
nature; and we should say that His death was in respect of His
human, not His divine, 'substance'.[3] So when the Saviour said
that His soul was troubled, He was referring to His human
soul.[4] Yet these careful distinctions did not prevent Tertullian
from using expressions like, 'God allows Himself to be born',
'the sufferings of God', 'God was truly crucified, truly died'[5]
—language which foreshadowed the 'interchange of characteristics' (*communicatio idiomatum*) which later counted as
orthodox. On the other hand he was convinced[6] that the man
Jesus had preserved intact the substance and form of human
flesh in heaven. In certain moods the sheer absurdity of these
paradoxes (*certum est quia impossibile*[7]) strikes him as the best
argument in their favour. His final position, with its recognition of the part played by the Lord's human soul, is one which
allows full scope to the humanity as an active principle, without,
however, thereby undermining the unity of the subject, viz.
the divine Word.

To a large extent Novatian, as we might expect, modelled his
ideas on those of Tertullian. Like his master, he declares[8] that
Christ is both God and man, combining 'both substances'
(*utramque substantiam*) in Himself. Like him, too, he stresses[9] the
reality of the human nature, picturing[10] the eternal Word as
putting it on like a garment or joining Himself to it as a bridegroom joins himself to his bride. Indeed, he carries Tertullian's
tendency to hold the two natures apart so far that he has been

---

[1] *De carn. Chr.* 5.   [2] *Adv. Prax.* 29.
[3] Ib. 30; 29.   [4] *De carn. Chr.* 13.
[5] Ib. 5; *de pat.* 3; *c. Marc.* 2, 27.   [6] *De resurr.* 51.
[7] *De carn. Chr.* 5: cf. *c. Marc.* 2, 16.   [8] *De trin.* 13.
[9] Ib. 10.   [10] Ib. 21; 13.

accused of being a Nestorian before Nestorius. For example, he speaks[1] of the man being joined with the God, and the God linked with the man. Again, commenting on *Luke* 1, 35, he distinguishes[2] between 'the holy thing' which was to be born from Mary, viz. the man Jesus, and the divine spirit which was to come upon her. Only the latter was in the strict sense the Son of God; He 'assumed' the Son of Man, and by attaching Him to Himself made Him Son of God. We should notice, however, that Tertullian's exegesis[3] of the Lucan text was similar, and Novatian's strong emphasis elsewhere[4] on the unity excludes the suspicion that he thought of two Sons yoked together in a purely moral union. On the other hand, it remains true that, in sharpest possible contrast to Tertullian, he apparently did not envisage the Lord's humanity as complete. Not only does he describe it exclusively as 'flesh' or 'body' (the concern, which he shared with Tertullian, to rebut the Gnostic disparagement of the body would account for this), but he nowhere refers unambiguously to Christ's human soul or mind. What is decisive, he regarded[5] His death as consisting simply in the laying aside of His body; and, drawing a parallel between His death and ours, he clearly suggests that, whereas ordinary men consist of body and soul, He was composed of flesh and the divine Word.[6]

5. The School of Alexandria

At Alexandria, under the influence of the speculative and ascetic ideas current there, an important new movement in Christology was under way in the third century. Though outwardly, and in intention too, loyal to the Church's rule of faith and doctrinal tradition, this took certain Hellenizing presuppositions for granted; its sympathies lay much more with Justin and the Apologists than with a theologian like Tertullian. We can observe this development at work in Clement. Much of his teaching conforms to the conventional pattern. The Logos, he states,[7] 'has come to us from heaven'; the Lord has

---

[1] Ib. 15.   [2] Ib. 24.   [3] *Adv. Prax.* 27.   [4] E.g. *de trin.* 11.   [5] Ib. 21.
[6] Ib. 25.   [7] *Protr.* 11, 111, 2; 11, 112, 1; *strom.* 5, 105, 4.

'entered into', or 'attached' Himself to, human flesh. In becoming incarnate and so making Himself visible, He has begotten Himself, i.e. created His own humanity.[1] So Christ is both human and divine—'alone both, God and man'.[2] He has 'clothed Himself with a man', being 'God in the form of a man, unsullied',[3] and as such has really suffered.[4] Though criticized[5] as such by Photius, Clement was no Docetist, and defended[6] the reality of the incarnation; but many of his statements, e.g. that Christ was no ordinary man with physical passions,[7] have a distinctly docetic ring. It seems certain, however, despite the questionings of many scholars, that he attributed[8] a human soul or mind to the God-man. The problematical element in his picture of Him springs from the way he allowed it to be coloured by the Greek ascetical ideal of apatheia, or emancipation from passion. Clement was convinced[9] that the Lord must have been exempt from all desires, both those necessary for maintaining the body and those peculiar to the soul, since His constitution was sustained by 'divine power'. His view seems to have been that the directive principle (in Stoic language, τὸ ἡγεμονικόν) which was the ground of His organic unity was the Logos.[10] He it was Who in effect was Christ's 'inner man'.[11] On this assumption, however, since Christ's human soul was a mere copy of the divine Word, it is difficult to see what practical part Clement can have envisaged it as playing. Soteriologically considered, the humanity of Jesus had little theological importance in his scheme.

Much more interesting was Origen's theory, and its central, most original feature can be stated at once. 'We believe', he lays it down,[12] 'that the very Logos of the Father, the Wisdom of God Himself, was enclosed within the limits of that man who appeared in Judaea; nay more, that God's Wisdom entered

---

[1] *Strom.* 5, 16, 5.　　[2] *Protr.* 1, 7, 1.　　[3] *Quis div.* 37, 3; *paed.* 1, 2, 4.
[4] *Strom.* 6, 127, 2.　　　　　　[5] *Bibl.* cod. 109.
[6] E.g. *protr.* 7, 2; *paed.* 3, 2, 2; *strom.* 3, 102, 1; 5, 341; 6, 127, 1.
[7] Ib. 3, 49, 3.
[8] E.g. *quis div.* 37, 4; *paed.* 1, 85, 2: cf. Socrates, *hist. eccl.* 3, 7.
[9] *Strom.* 6, 71.　　　　[10] Cf. ib. 6, 135, 1-4.　　　　[11] *Paed.* 3, 1, 2.
[12] *De princ.* 2, 6, 2.

a woman's womb, was born as an infant, and wailed like crying children.' The problem of how this came about he solved with brilliant simplicity. We recall[1] his belief that the world of spiritual beings (τὰ λογικά), including human souls, pre-existed from all eternity; he applied this as the key to the incarnation. One of these souls, the one destined to be the soul of the man Jesus, in every respect a human soul like the rest, was from the beginning attached to the Logos with mystical devotion; it burned with love and desire for justice.[2] All the other souls, by the misguided exercise of their free-will, fell away from the Logos, to Whom they ought to have adhered;[3] but this unique soul, as a result of its adoring contemplation, became inseparably united with Him.[4] The union is as complete as that of a lump of iron with the fire into which it has been plunged, becoming red-hot; and Origen quotes[5] *1 Cor.* 6, 17 as Scriptural proof that it formed 'one spirit' with Him. But since this soul, while thus cleaving to the Logos, properly belonged to a body, it formed the ideal meeting-point between the infinite Word and finite human nature. So when it was born from the Blessed Virgin with pure flesh created by the action of the Spirit, Godhead and manhood were inextricably united. Further, it was natural that, in union with the flesh with which it was conjoined, it should be designated God's Son, Power and Wisdom, being so fused with and penetrated by Him Who in very truth is God's Son, just as it is natural that He in His turn should be saluted as Son of Man and that we should speak of Him as being born as an infant and dying.[6]

With this theory of the mediating role of Christ's human soul as its basis, Origen expounds the doctrine of the incarnation (ἐνανθρώπησις:[7] the verb ἐνανθρωπεῖν occurs frequently). On the one hand, he insists on the duality of the natures, speaking[8] of Christ's manhood (ἀνθρωπότης) and divinity (θεότης), and of 'His divine and human nature' (φύσις), even of His 'hypostasis' (ὑπόστασις) as man and His

---

[1] See above, p. 128.   [2] *Ib.* 2, 6, 3-5.   [3] *Ib.* 2, 9, 2.
[4] *Ib.* 2, 6, 4.   [5] *Ib.* 2, 6, 6; 2, 6, 3; *c. Cels.* 2, 9.
[6] *Ib.* 2, 6, 1 f.   [7] E.g. *c. Cels.* 3, 14.
[8] *In Ioh.* 10, 6, 24; 32, 12, 192; *c. Cels.* 3, 28.

'hypostasis' as Only-begotten. Interpreting *Ps.* 72, 1, he explains[1] 'the king' and 'the king's son' as referring respectively to 'the nature (φύσιν) of the Word' and 'the man whom He assumed' and whom, because of His pre-eminence, He dominates. Both the natures retained their special characteristics. For example, 'the Logos, remaining Logos in essence, undergoes none of the experiences of the body or the soul';[2] whereas His human nature has to put up with the customary human lot.[3] The cries, 'My soul is exceedingly sorrowful' (*Matt.* 26, 38), and, 'Now is my soul troubled' (*John* 12, 27), refer to His human soul.[4] Similarly, we can say that the Son of God died, but only if we make clear that it was 'in respect of that nature which was in any case susceptible of death'.[5] On the other hand, the incarnate Lord is a unity—'a composite thing' (σύνθετον χρῆμα), as Origen forcefully describes[6] Him. The Gospel, he points out,[7] speaks of one, not of two; and he defines[8] the relationship of the two natures as an actual union (ἕνωσις) or commingling (ἀνάκρασις), resulting in the deification of the humanity, and not as a mere association (κοινωνία). The Logos and the humanity are really one (ἕν[9]), the reason being that He has united Himself substantially with Christ's human soul in a union more intimate than He ever effected with the souls of prophets or apostles by inspiration and grace.[10]

With the traditional teaching as his starting-point, Origen was thus able to explain the rationale of the incarnation in terms of his own philosophy. Two further points must be made in order to set his position in true perspective. First, while he clearly intends to represent the unity between the Logos and Christ's human soul as a real one, his theory as outlined above hardly succeeds in doing so. However intimate the relationship established by the soul's loving adhesion to the Word, it can in the end be no more than a special case, differing in degree but

---

[1] *In Ioh.* 1, 28, 195.
[2] *C. Cels.* 4, 15.   [3] *Ib.* 2, 23; *de princ.* 4, 4, 4; *in Ierem. hom.* 14, 6.
[4] *De princ.* 4, 4, 4 (31).   [5] *Ib.* 2, 6, 3.   [6] *C. Cels.* 1, 66.
[7] *In Ioh.* 1, 28, 196.   [8] *C. Cels.* 3, 41.   [9] *Ib.* 2, 9; 6, 47.
[10] *De princ.* 2, 6, 4; 4, 4, 4 (31).

Origen

not in kind, of that union of affection and will which the saints can attain with Him. In fact, however, his deepest thought seems to have been that the unity of the God-man (he was the first to use this description of the Incarnate) was located in the Logos Himself. While satisfied[1] that the Lord must have assumed a soul as well as a body if human nature was to be saved in its entirety, he regarded the soul as wholly subjected to the Logos. It was the nature of the Logos, as we saw above, which predominated (cf. προηγουμένη) in Christ; and his conception[2] is of the Logos indwelling and directing the manhood. The human soul was, on his view, totally suffused with, and caught up in, the divine wisdom, goodness, truth and life.[3] As Origen saw the matter, therefore, the Word had in effect taken over the role of the ἡγεμονικόν, or governing principle, in Christ.

The second point opens up larger issues. It must be recognized that the incarnation as such really stood outside the logic of Origen's system. While assigning it a place, out of loyalty to God's revealed word and the Church's tradition, he did not regard the Son's participation in human nature as either permanent or essential. It is the simple sort of Christians, he taught,[4] who are attached to Christ's manhood; the true gnostic, i.e. the man of real spiritual advancement and insight, strains upwards to the Logos, the soul's authentic life from which it originally fell away. The mediator between the only true God, i.e. the ineffable Father, and man is not, in the last analysis, the God-man Jesus Christ, but the Word Who bridges the gulf between the unoriginate Godhead and creatures.[5] So we are not surprised to learn[6] that Jesus was able to alter His body as and when He willed, and that it was 'more divine' than other bodies. Indeed, it shared in the Word's divinity, and while absolutely real (Origen had no wish to be a Docetist[7]) possessed a godlike, ethereal quality.[8] With the resurrection the deification of Christ's human nature really began, His body

---

[1] *Dial. Heracl.* 7.   [2] E.g. *c. Cels.* 2, 9; *in Ioh.* 6, 53, 275.
[3] *De princ.* 4, 4, 4 (31).   [4] *In Ioh.* 2, 3, 27-31: cf. ib. 1, 7, 43.
[5] E.g. *c. Cels.* 3, 34; *de orat.* 10, 2.   [6] *C. Cels.* 2, 64; 1, 69.
[7] E.g. ib. 2, 16.   [8] Ib. 3, 41.

becoming of a consistency midway between that of natural flesh and that of the soul freed from bodily ties;[1] and the Christian can say that, 'although the Saviour was a man, He is now no longer one'.[2] The exaltation of the Son of Man consists precisely in this, that He has ceased to be other than the Logos and has become identically one with Him.[3]

6. The East after Origen

Although we are largely in the dark about Christological development in the second half of the third century, such evidence as we possess suggests that, while Origen's general framework of ideas exerted a powerful influence, there was a widespread reaction against its most distinctive thesis, viz. that Christ's human soul was the point of union between the eternal Word and the humanity. We have already noticed that Novatian in the West, while usually a faithful disciple of Tertullian, refused to follow his master in including a rational soul in Christ's human make-up. His refusal, coming at about the same time as a similar reluctance was showing itself in the East, may well have resulted from the exchange of ideas between the two great sections of the Church. In the East at any rate the chief motive at work, apart from hostility to Origen's doctrine of the pre-existence of souls, seems to have been the growing suspicion that the recognition of a real human mind in the God-man must logically entail the disruption of His unity.

For an illustration of this reaction reference is often made to the views propounded by the bishops who excommunicated Paul of Samosata at Antioch in 268, and in particular by their able spokesman, the priest Malchion. These can be reconstructed, it is claimed, from the surviving fragments[4] of the acts of the synod, which represent them as putting forward, in opposition to Paul's 'divisive' Christology, a conception of the absolute unity of the Word with the man Jesus, a unity which is not one of participation or grace but of substance. If

---

[1] Ib. 2, 62.   [2] In Ierem. hom. 15, 6.
[3] In Ioh. 32, 25, 325.   [4] Text in H. de Riedmatten, op. cit.

we ask how this was brought about, the answer of the fragments is surprising and important. Although they were Origenists, there is no longer any suggestion of Origen's theory of the intimate adhesion of Christ's human soul to the Logos. On the contrary, the explanation seemingly advanced by Malchion and the bishops implies that Christ's humanity did not include a human soul at all, but that all the functions of one in His constitution were performed by the Word incarnate. This comes out very clearly in the statement[1] attributed to them that the God-man was a composite being (σύνθετον ζῷον) in the same way as an ordinary man is composite; just as the unity of the latter results from the concourse (σύνοδος) of flesh and 'something else' which inhabits the flesh (manifestly the higher soul or mind), so the unity of the Lord results from the coming together of the divine Word and the flesh He assumed from the Virgin. So they could say,[2] 'We recognize only one difference, admittedly a very important one, between His constitution and ours, viz. that the divine Logos is in Him what the interior man (ὁ ἔσω ἄνθρωπος) is in us'. By 'the interior man', apparently, they meant the higher soul or mind, and by substituting the Word for it in the structure of the Incarnate they intended, according to this account, to safeguard His unity against Paul's separation of the Word from 'the man'.

Unfortunately the trustworthiness of these fragments is open to serious question. The debate between Paul and Malchion, for example, only begins to make an appearance in Christological florilegia in the fifth century; and it seems scarcely credible that the ontological structure of the God-man was the subject of such mature and detailed discussion in the sixties of the third century. The views attributed to Malchion, moreover, bear a suspicious resemblance to those of Apollinarius, and on balance it seems likely that the fragments, like many other plausible forgeries, originated in fourth-century Apollinarian circles.

More reliable evidence that Origen's doctrine of Christ's human soul was coming under fire in the last decades of the

[1] S 36 (Riedmatten).   [2] S 30 (Riedmatten).

third century can be gleaned from the apology for the great teacher which Pamphilus of Caesarea prepared between 308 and 310. From this it emerges[1] that Origen was being charged with holding adoptionist views similar to those of Artemas and Paul of Samosata, and even with preaching two Christs. Evidently these alleged errors were taken by his critics to be the logical outcome of his thesis that the God-man possessed a human soul, for in defending him Pamphilus made the point[2] that there was nothing offensive in this suggestion of his, seeing that, on the evidence of Scripture, Christ Himself alluded to His soul on several occasions. But it is in Eusebius of Caesarea, an intense admirer of Origen if ever there was one, that the abandonment of his distinctive ideas can be most strikingly discerned. In broad outline his Christology reflects his master's, and like him he regarded the incarnation as the climax of the Word's function as mediator between God and creation. The whole notion, however, of the soul as the point of union between the Word and His Flesh has vanished without trace. Rather the role of the Word is to take the place of the soul in the constitution of the God-man. Thus Eusebius was quite explicit[3] that the Word indwelt the flesh of the Incarnate, 'moving it like a soul'; it was His 'corporeal instrument'. If he is prepared to make use of the Scriptural language referring to His human soul, he interprets it as signifying, not an actual human soul, but that which takes the place of one, viz. the eternal Word. So he explains[4] that, when the demons launched their attack 'against our Saviour's soul', the mistake they made lay in supposing that the soul inhabiting His body was an ordinary human one. Again, he understands[5] by Christ's death the departure of the Word from His flesh, which for its part is consigned to the grave. At the same time, while adopting a Word-flesh framework, he was careful, in order to preserve the Word's transcendence, to reduce His unity with the flesh to a

---

[1] Bk. 1 (PG 17, 578 f.: the Latin translation of Rufinus).
[2] Ib. (PG 17, 590).
[3] De eccl. theol. 1, 20, 90; theoph. 3, 39 (Gressmann, 142).
[4] Dem. ev. 10, 8, 503 f.
[5] Ib. 3, 4, 108: cf. ib. 4, 12, 166; theoph. 3, 41-4.

minimum, insisting that the experiences of the flesh (birth, suffering, death, etc.) had no effect on Him.

If ideas like these were to the fore in circles which were in other matters sympathetic to Origenism, it is not surprising that theologians less subservient to Origen's spell were disposed to dissociate themselves from his solution of the Christological problem. Methodius of Olympus († 311) is a good example; indeed, he is the only theologian falling into this category whose works have come down to us. Speaking of the incarnation, he states[1] that the Son of God 'truly became man', or even 'assumed the man'; he describes[2] the Incarnate as 'a man filled with deity unmixed and perfect, and a God contained in a man'. Phrases like these have an Origenist ring, as does his designation[3] of the Lord's humanity as an 'instrument' (ὄργανον). We should notice, however, that when he defines his meaning more precisely he affirms[4] that it was in virtue of His assumption of flesh that the heavenly Christ, not being man, became man. As a matter of fact, his major Christological passages[5] imply that there were only two elements compounded in the God-man, viz. the Word and His flesh. The effect of the incarnation, he states,[6] was that the body in a miraculous way became the receptacle of the Logos; and, identifying Christ's immaculate flesh with the bride of Solomon's Song, he represents[7] the Word as abandoning the Father for sheer love of it, descending to earth and cleaving to it in closest union. When we bear in mind that Methodius is a dichotomist[8] holding that human nature is composed of body and soul, and that on his view the soul is the immortal element in man and belongs to the order of intelligences of which the Word is the chief, the conclusion is inescapable that he too was an exponent of what we have called the 'Word-flesh' type of Christology, teaching that the Word took the place of the human mind or soul in the structure of the God-man.

---

[1] De res. 2, 18; symp. 7, 9.   [2] Symp. 3, 4.
[3] Ib. 3, 7.   [4] De res. 2, 18.   [5] De res. 2, 18; c. Porphyr.
[6] C. Porphyr. 1.   [7] Symp. 7, 8.   [8] Cf. de res. 1, 51; symp. 6, 4.

NOTE ON BOOKS

General. J. Daniélou, *The Theology of Jewish Christianity* (Eng. trans., London, 1964); J. A. Dorner, *History of the Development of the Doctrine of the Person of Christ* (Eng. trans., Edinburgh, 1878); C. Gore, *The Incarnation of the Son of God* (London, 1891); *Dissertations* (London, 1895); A. Grillmeier, *Christ in Christian Tradition* (2nd rev. ed.: Eng. trans., London, 1975); J. Liébaert, *Christologie: Von der apostolischen Zeit bis zum Konzil von Chalcedon* (*Handbuch der Dogmengeschichte* III, la: 1965); F. Loofs, 'Christologie' (art. in Hauck's *Realencyk.*); J. Michel, 'Incarnation' (art. in *Dict. Théol. Cath.*); R. L. Ottley, *The Doctrine of the Incarnation* (London, 1896); R. V. Sellers, *Two Ancient Christologies* (London, 1940).

Special. G. Bardy, 'Origène' (art. in *Dict. Théol. Cath.*); G. N. Bonwetsch, *Die Theologie des Methodius von Olympus* (Berlin, 1903); R. Cantalamessa, 'Méliton de Sardes: une christologie antignostique du 2me siècle' (art. in *Rev. sc. rel.*, 1963); *La Cristologia di Tertulliano* (*Paradosis* 18; Fribourg, 1962); H. J. Carpenter, 'The Birth from Holy Spirit and the Virgin in the Old Roman Creed' (art. in *Journ. Theol. Stud.*, 1939); H. Chadwick, 'Justin Martyr's Defence of Christianity' (art. in *Bull. J. Rylands Lib.*, 1965); J. Daniélou, *Origen* (Eng. trans., London, 1955); A. Houssiau, *La Christologie de saint Irénée* (Louvain, 1958); A. Lieske, *Die Theologie der Logos-Mystik bei Origenes* (Münster, 1938); H. de Riedmatten, *Les Actes du procès de Paul de Samosate* (Fribourg en Suisse, 1952).

CHAPTER VII

MAN AND HIS REDEMPTION

1. *The Sub-Apostolic Age*

THE development of the Church's ideas about the saving effects of the incarnation was a slow, long drawn-out process. Indeed, while the conviction of redemption through Christ has always been the motive force of Christian faith, no final and universally accepted definition of the manner of its achievement has been formulated to this day. Thus it is useless to look for any systematic treatment of the doctrine in the popular Christianity of the second century. It is true that the Apostolic Fathers make numerous references to Christ's work. For the most part, however, they are rehearsing the clichés of catechetical instruction, so that what they say smacks more of affirmation than explanation. While taking it for granted that men are sinful, ignorant and in need of true life, they never attempt to account for their wretched plight. Only once, in 'Barnabas's' remark,[1] 'Forasmuch as the transgression was wrought in Eve through the serpent', do we meet with what looks like an allusion to the Fall story in *Gen.* 3: although it should be noted that the same writer elsewhere[2] suggests that the souls of children are entirely sinless. Hermas, again, is a solitary witness[3] to the rabbinical theory of the origin of evil, viz. the presence of a wicked imagination or desire (what the Rabbis called the *yeçer ha-ra'*) in man's heart. Similarly, while enumerating all sorts of benefits bestowed by Christ, the Apostolic Fathers nowhere co-ordinate their main ideas or attempt to sketch a rationale of salvation.

When we analyse their utterances, we find that their chief emphasis is on what Christ has imparted to us—new knowledge,

[1] 12, 5.   [2] 6, 11.   [3] *Mand.* 12, 1 f.

fresh life, immortality, etc. The *Didache*, for example, con-
fines itself to thanking[1] God 'for the life and the knowledge', or 'for the knowledge, faith and immortality', which
God has disclosed 'through His servant Jesus' (the latter
formula, frequently repeated, hints at a fuller doctrine of the
mediatorial role of Christ's humanity). Through Christ, according to *1 Clement*,[2] we gaze up to heaven and 'taste immortal
knowledge'. Through Him God 'has called us from darkness
to light, from ignorance to knowledge of the glory of His
name'.[3] Christ has rescued us from the darkness of error;[4] it was
because of the enlightenment received from Him that those
who are now Christians abandoned idolatry.[5] In addition to
revealing the true God, states[6] Hermas, He makes God's law
known to us; indeed, 'this law is the Son of God, Who is
preached from end to end of the world'. In harmony with
this Christ's sufferings, and even His death, are set out chiefly
as models of obedience and self-effacing love.[7] Further, Christ
is 'the Saviour and prince of immortality, through Whom
God has revealed to us the truth and the heavenly life'.[8]
The object of His endurance, says[9] 'Barnabas', was to abolish
death and to demonstrate resurrection from the dead. For
Ignatius, with his intense Christ-mysticism, the essence
of salvation seems to consist in union with Christ, through
Whom new life and immortality flow into us. He dwells in
us, so that we become His temple.[10] Hence He is 'our true
life', 'our inseparable life';[11] by believing in His death we
escape death.[12]

Alongside thoughts like these, however, a rather different
strain is discernible in the Apostolic Fathers. This dwells on the
Lord's passion, death and resurrection, and affirms that He
suffered for our sakes. His blood, states[13] Clement, 'was given
on behalf of us'; again, it was because of His love that 'He gave
His blood for us, and His flesh for our flesh, and His soul for our

---

[1] 9, 3; 10, 2.   [2] 36, 2.   [3] 59, 2.
[4] *Barn.* 14, 5.   [5] *2 Clem.* 1, 4-7.   [6] *Sim.* 5, 5, 3; 8, 3, 2 f.
[7] E.g. *1 Clem.* 2, 1; 16 f.   [8] *2 Clem.* 20, 5.   [9] 5, 6.
[10] *Eph.* 15, 3: cf. *Magn.* 14; *Rom.* 6, 3.   [11] *Eph.* 3, 2; *Smyrn.* 4, 1.
[12] *Trall.* 2, 1.   [13] 21, 6; 49, 6.

souls'. He died and rose again on our behalf, declare[1] both
Ignatius and Polycarp. The former also claims[2] that 'we have
been restored to life through the blood of God', and the
latter[3] that 'He endured all His sufferings on account of us, that
we might live in Him'. Occasionally the remission of sins is
brought into the picture, so that 'Barnabas' can speak[4] of the
Lord as delivering His flesh to destruction 'so that we might be
cleansed by the remission of our sins, which cleansing is through
the blood of His sprinkling'. More often, however, the suggestion is that His sufferings should challenge us to repentance.
So the author of 2 Clement, after recalling them, exclaims,[5]
'What recompense shall we then give Him?' Clement himself,
after bidding his readers gaze on Christ's blood and observe
how precious it is to the Father, adds[6] that its shedding has
brought the grace of repentance to the world. Yet he is also
aware[7] that believers find redemption (λύτρωσις) through
the Lord's blood, and that His life was surrendered in sacrifice
for us. Only 'Barnabas', however, interprets Christ's passion in
expressly sacrificial terms, stating[8] that He offered His body as
a sacrifice for our sins and appealing to Isaac's sacrifice as a
prototype.

It must be admitted that, as compared with the New Testament, the Apostolic Fathers as a whole are not greatly preoccupied with sin, and that their writings exhibit a marked
weakening of the atonement idea. Although satisfied that
Christ died for us (often the repetition of the formula has a
conventional ring), they assign a relatively minor place to the
atoning value of His death. What looms much larger in their
imagination is the picture of Christ as the lawgiver, the be-
stower of knowledge, immortality and fellowship with God.
For 2 Clement,[9] for example, Christ's saving significance consists
in His role as the future righteous judge; what He accomplished
in His earthly sojourn was simply to summon men by His
preaching to that salvation. In view of this we need scarcely

---

[1] Rom. 6, 1; Phil. 9, 2.   [2] Eph. 1, 1.   [3] Phil. 8, 1.
[4] 5, 1: cf. 6, 11; 8, 3.   [5] 1, 2 f.   [6] 7, 4.
[7] 12, 7; 49, 6.   [8] 7, 3.   [9] E.g. 1, 1; 7, 16-18.

be surprised to miss that close logical connection between Christology and soteriology which was later to become characteristic of orthodox Christian thought. Ignatius is an exception, teaching[1] that Christ is 'the unique physician', that His cross bestows life and salvation, and that by taking human form He abolished sin and death. In none of the others, however, not even in Clement and 'Barnabas', do we meet with any real appreciation of the truth that through Christ's assumption of human nature the infusion of new life into fallen humanity has been made possible.

2. *The Apologists*

With the Apologists a marked change comes over the atmosphere, and the outlines of a definite anthropology, or doctrine of man, begin to take shape. Their general view of human nature is dichotomist, i.e. they consider it to be composed of two elements, body ($\sigma\hat{\omega}\mu\alpha$) and soul ($\psi\nu\chi\dot{\eta}$, or $\pi\nu\epsilon\hat{\nu}\mu\alpha$). And they are unanimous that man is endowed with free-will. We had no choice in being born, argues[2] Justin, but we have a choice, in virtue of the rational powers God has given us, whether to live in a fashion acceptable to Him or not. As a result, since we are reasonable beings, we are without excuse in God's eyes when we do wrong.[3] Athenagoras, Theophilus and Tatian agree[4] that it lies within the orbit of man's choice whether he is to do good or evil, with all the disastrous consequences which a decision for the latter entails. As against the Stoic doctrine[5] of fate ($\kappa\alpha\theta'$ $\epsilon\dot{\iota}\mu\alpha\rho\mu\dot{\epsilon}\nu\eta\varsigma$ $\dot{\alpha}\nu\dot{\alpha}\gamma\kappa\eta\nu$), Justin develops[6] the idea of human responsibility. The Christian belief in prophecy, with its premiss of divine foreknowledge, might seem to contradict free-will, but his rejoinder is that God does not so much predetermine men's actions as foresee how by their own volitions they are going to act, and so announces it beforehand through His prophets.[7] Sin on his

---

[1] *Eph.* 7, 2; 18–19. [2] *1 apol.* 10, 4. [3] *Ib.* 28, 3.
[4] *Supp.* 24, 4; *ad Autol.* 2, 27; *or.* 11, 2. [5] See above, p. 18.
[6] *1 apol.* 43; *2 apol.* 7. [7] *1 apol.* 44, 11; *dial.* 141, 2: cf. Tatian, *or.* 7, 2.

view consists in 'erroneous belief and ignorance of what is good' (ψευδοδοξία καὶ ἄγνοια τῶν καλῶν), and in the result-ant rebellion against God's commandments.[1]

How then do evil and sin arise? Quoting *Deut.* 27, 26 ('Cursed be everyone who does not abide in the injunctions of the book of the law, to do them'), Justin affirms[2] that the transgression of God's ordinances has placed the whole human race under a curse. The theory[3] which most consistently attracts him, as it attracts the Apologists generally, is that malign demons, them-selves the product of the union of fallen angels with the daughters of men, are to blame. Swarming everywhere, they have obsessed men's souls and bodies, infecting them with vice and corruption. In one passage,[4] it is true, he seems to posit a connection between the act of the serpent narrated in *Gen.* 3 and the present sinful condition of mankind, while in another[5] he speaks of '. . . the race of men, who from Adam's time have fallen under death and the deceit of the serpent'. The latter context, however, explicitly states that 'each man sinned by his own fault'. Elsewhere[6] he develops the theory, drawing a parallel between Eve and the Blessed Virgin, and arguing that Christ was made man of our Lady 'in order that, by the same way in which the disobedience proceeding from the serpent took its rise, it might also receive its abolition. For Eve, when a virgin undefiled, conceived the word of the serpent and brought forth disobedience and death.' The underlying sugges-tion, however, appears to be simply that the sin of Adam and Eve, consisting as it did in their yielding to the Devil's blandish-ments, is the prototype of our sin. So he interprets[7] *Ps.* 82, 7 ('Ye die like men, and fall like one of the princes') as signifying that men die in the same way as Adam and Eve, and fall in the same way as Satan. His nearest approach to a corporate con-ception of sin (and even here original sin in the later sense is excluded) is his assertion[8] that, having been born without our own knowledge and consent, we have been trained up in

---

[1] *2 apol.* 14, 1.   [2] *Dial.* 95, 1.
[3] E.g. *1 apol.* 5, 2; *2 apol.* 5, 3 f.; 17, 2 f.   [4] *Dial.* 94, 2.
[5] Ib. 88, 4.   [6] Ib. 100, 4-6.   [7] Ib. 124, 3.
[8] *1 apol.* 61, 10.

wicked ways by our environment, and in this sense perhaps may be called 'children of necessity'.

The treatment assigned to the subject in Tatian and Theophilus is fuller and more precise. Starting from the premiss that man was not created good but rather with a capacity for goodness, the former states[1] that he fell into sin through becoming attached to one of the angels who was 'more subtle than the rest' and venerating him as God. As a result, the guidance of the Spirit was withdrawn, and while the power of self-determination was not obliterated (Tatian is a firm believer in responsibility) he became henceforth the prey of demoniac assaults. According to Theophilus,[2] too, man as originally created was neither mortal nor immortal, but was capable of both; his destiny depended on how he exercised his free-will. As he expresses it, Adam was infantile and undeveloped, and indeed this was the reason why he was forbidden the acquisition of knowledge. Had he been content to remain obedient, he might have become immortal, but he disobeyed and so became mortal. All the physical woes of humanity can be traced to that act of disobedience and the expulsion from Paradise which it entailed. Like Justin, therefore, both of them seem to accept the Pauline teaching in so far as it links the entrance of sin and death into the world with Adam's act of disobedience; but neither of them, any more than Justin, sees that act as more than a type of the disobedience of the race, although its consequences persist in the subjection of Adam's descendants to labour, pain, death and, of course, the power of evil spirits.

When we inquire what effect the Apologists conceived Christ's coming to have had on fallen man, we find that only Justin provides anything resembling an answer, and that even his thought on the subject is shot through with ambiguity. Undoubtedly the principal purpose of the incarnation, when he views the matter as a philosopher, strikes him as having been didactic. Having forgotten the truth and having been inveigled into ignorance and positive error by the demons, men desperately need the restoration of the light they have lost. As 'the new

[1] *Or.* 7.   [2] *Ad Autol.* 2, 24 f.; 27.

law-giver',[1] or again, 'the eternal, final law, the faithful covenant which replaces all laws and commandments',[2] Christ imparts this saving knowledge. It was to bestow such illumination,
in particular the realization of the oneness of God and the
belief in the moral law, and to restore men by it, that the Logos
in fact became man.[3] We have already noticed the popularity
of the conception of redemption as enlightenment among the
Apostolic Fathers. It reappears in the Apologists, but is given a
firm, rational foundation in their doctrine of the Logos. Christ,
we should observe, does not merely impart fresh knowledge;
He at the same time breaks the spell of the devils who lead men
astray. God, states Justin,[4] has finally destroyed principalities
and powers by Him Who became passible according to His
will; the crucifixion has 'shattered the might of the serpent,
who instigated Adam's transgression'. The aim of the incarnation, he points out,[5] was the conquest of the serpent, who committed the initial sin, and of the fallen angels who imitated his
example. At the temptation in the wilderness,[6] or when He
hung on the cross,[7] and even at His birth,[8] Christ wielded
authority over the malefic spirits, and was proclaimed 'Lord of
the powers'.[9] So Justin thinks[10] that he can perceive a continua-
tion of the same victory in the power possessed by believing
Christians to rout by exorcism 'the demons who hold men
captive'.

If liberation from ignorance and error and from bondage to
demons is one side of Christ's work, Justin recognizes another
as well. He has a great deal to say about the cross, the presence
of which he notices everywhere in nature and in all forms of
life. It is 'the chief symbol of His might and rulership',[11] and
was foretold[12] in the Old Testament and even by Plato. 'The
Word of God', he declares,[13] 'became man for our sakes, so
that participating in our miseries He might heal them.' Jesus
Christ, our Saviour, assumed flesh and blood for our salvation;

---

[1] *Dial.* 18, 3.
[2] Ib. 11, 2: cf. ib. 43, 1; 51, 3.
[3] *1 apol.* 12-19; 23.
[4] *Dial.* 41, 1; 94, 2.
[5] Ib. 45, 4.
[6] Ib. 103, 6; 125, 4.
[7] Ib. 49, 8.
[8] Ib. 78, 9.
[9] Ib. 85, 1.
[10] *2 apol.* 6, 6; *dial.* 30, 3.
[11] *1 apol.* 55, 2.
[12] Ib. 60, 5; *dial.* 90 f.
[13] *2 apol.* 13, 4.

He suffered in order to purify with His blood those who believe in Him.[1] Thus we offer the eucharist in memory of the pains He endured on behalf of men; His death procures remission of sins and redemption from death.[2] How this was achieved, Justin does not fully explain. In one important passage[3] he argues that 'by His blood and the mystery of the cross' Christ has acquired possession of mankind; thus His death can be said to redeem men in the sense that He has earned them for Himself by what He has suffered. In another passage,[4] with a passing allusion to *Is. 53, 5*, he states that Christ suffered on our behalf so that by His stripes the human race might be healed. It was the Father's will that He should 'take upon Himself the curses of all, for He knew that, after He had been crucified and was dead, He would raise Him up'. In any case, because of what He endured, Christ has become the originator of a new humanity, regenerated by Him by water, faith and the cross. This last reference[5] would seem to contain an anticipation of the idea of recapitulation which will be discussed in the following section, and which Irenaeus actually attributes[6] to Justin. Thoughts like these indicate that, however ready he might be on occasion to avail himself of the idiom of Hellenistic speculation, he remained all the time a churchman, with his feet firmly planted in the Church's living liturgical and Scriptural tradition.

3. *The Theory of Recapitulation*

The conception, Pauline[7] in its ultimate derivation, of the inauguration of a new, restored humanity in Christ seems to have reached Justin from the theological tradition of Asia Minor. It was taken up and deepened by Irenaeus, who was also the first to work out comprehensive theories both of original sin and of redemption. Let us glance first at his anthropology, which recalls that of Tatian and Theophilus and again suggests the influence of Asia Minor.

---

[1] *1 apol.* 66, 2; 32, 7. [2] *Dial.* 41, 1; 111, 3. [3] Ib. 134, 5 f.
[4] Ib. 95, 2 f. [5] Ib. 138, 2. [6] *Haer.* 4, 6, 2.
[7] E.g. *Rom.* 5, 12–21; *1 Cor.* 15, 22; 15, 45.

In his original state, Irenaeus teaches, man was created 'in the image and likeness of God'. Although his usage is far from being consistent, he seems occasionally to have distinguished[1] between the 'image' and the 'likeness'. By the former he meant that Adam was a being possessed of reason and free-will, by the latter that he enjoyed a supernatural endowment through the action of the Spirit (*eam quam habui a Spiritu sanctitatis stolam*[2]). Yet there is no suggestion that this endowment amounted to what later theology was to call original righteousness. On the contrary, being a creature, Adam was necessarily far removed from the divine perfection and incorruptibility; an infinite distance divided him from God.[3] In Paradise, therefore, he was morally, spiritually and intellectually a child;[4] and Irenaeus makes the point[5] that, while God infused into the first man 'the breath of life' (*Gen.* 2, 7), He did not bestow upon him the Spirit of adoption which He gives to Christians. It was by a long process of response to grace and submission to God's will that Adam, equipped as he was with free choice, was intended to advance towards ever closer resemblance to his Maker.[6] Unfortunately, because of his very weakness and inexperience, the process was interrupted almost at the start; he fell an easy prey to Satan's wiles and disobeyed God.[7] Thus he lost the divine 'image and likeness'[8]—at any rate the likeness, since the image must have persisted in some degree—and fell into the clutches of the Devil.[9]

So much for Adam; Irenaeus regarded the story told in *Genesis* as authentic history. The essence of Adam's sin, it should be noted, consisted in disobedience. But that sin entailed consequences for the whole race; Irenaeus has no doubt that the first man's disobedience is the source of the general sinfulness and mortality of mankind, as also of their enslavement to the Devil. What Adam lost, all lost in him: '. . . through the disobedience of that one man who was first formed out of the untilled earth, the many were made sinners and lost life'.[10]

---

[1] *Haer.* 5, 6, 1; 5, 16, 2.   [2] Ib. 3, 23, 5.   [3] Ib. 4, 38, 1-3.
[4] *Dem.* 12.   [5] *Haer.* 5, 12, 2.   [6] Ib. 4, 37, 1; 4, 38, 3.
[7] *Dem.* 16.   [8] *Haer.* 3, 18, 1; 5, 2, 1.   [9] Ib. 5, 21, 3.
[10] Ib. 3, 18, 7.

More than that, all men participated in Adam's deed and therefore shared in his guilt. 'In the first Adam', he writes,[1] 'we
offended God, not fulfilling His commandment. . . . To Him
alone were we debtors, Whose ordinance we transgressed in
the beginning'; and again, 'In Adam disobedient man was
stricken'.[2] The theme, based on *Rom.* 5, that the human race
sinned 'in Adam' recurs so frequently that quotation is superfluous. Irenaeus nowhere formulates a specific account of the connexion between Adam's guilty act and the rest of mankind. He
clearly presupposes some kind of mystical solidarity, or rather
identity, between the father of the race and all his descendants.
At the time of the Fall they somehow already existed in him,
just as the author of *Hebrews* conceives[3] of Levi as having existed
seminally in Abraham, and the subsequent multiplication of the
race can be viewed as the subdivision of the original Adam into
myriads of individuals who were thus at once responsible for
the ancient act of transgression and the victims of its fatal
consequences.

What has been said so far gives the clue to the distinctively
Irenaean interpretation of the work of Christ. 'Because of His
measureless love,' he writes,[4] 'He became what we are in order
to enable us to become what He is.' The method he outlines in
the oft-repeated assertion that what we lost in Adam we recovered in Christ; its premiss is the idea that, if we fell through
our solidarity with the first man, we can be restored through
our solidarity with Christ. The key-conception which Irenaeus
employs to explain this is 'recapitulation' (ἀνακεφαλαίωσις),
which he borrows from St. Paul's description[5] of the divine
purpose as being 'to sum up all things in Christ'. He understands[6] the Pauline text as implying that the Redeemer gathers
together, includes or comprises the whole of reality in Himself,
the human race being included. In close conjunction with this
he exploits to the full the parallelism between Adam and
Christ which was so dear to St. Paul. Christ is indeed, in
his eyes, the 'second Adam' (ὁ δεύτερος 'Αδάμ[7]), and 're-

[1] *Haer.* 5, 16, 3.   [2] Ib. 5, 34, 2.   [3] 7, 9 f.   [4] *Haer.* 5, praef.
[5] *Eph.* 1, 10.   [6] *Haer.* 3, 16, 6.   [7] Ib. 5, 16, 3.

capitulated' or reproduced the first even in the manner of His birth, being generated from the Blessed Virgin as he was from virgin earth.[1] Further, just as Adam contained in himself all his descendants, so Christ (as the Lucan genealogy proves) 're-capitulated in Himself all the dispersed peoples dating back to Adam, all tongues and the whole race of mankind, along with Adam himself'[2] Thus, when He became incarnate, Christ 're-capitulated in Himself the long sequence of mankind', and passed through all the stages of human life, sanctifying each in turn.[3] As a result (and this is Irenaeus's main point), just as Adam was the originator of a race disobedient and doomed to death, so Christ can be regarded as inaugurating a new, redeemed humanity.[4]

Thus we see the outlines of Irenaeus's characteristic theory of redemption. The conclusion to which his argument leads is that humanity, which as we have seen was seminally present in Adam, has been given the opportunity of making a new start in Christ, the second Adam, through incorporation in His mystical body. The original Adam, by his disobedience, intro-duced the principle of sin and death, but Christ by His obedi-ence has reintroduced the principle of life and immortality. Because He is identified with the human race at every phase of its existence, He restores fellowship with God to all,[5] 'perfecting man according to God's image and likeness'.[6] And because He is a real man, born of a woman, He is able to vanquish the Devil, into whose power mankind had fallen.[7]

It is often stated that, in the light of this analysis (technically known as the 'physical' theory of the atonement), it is the incarnation itself which effects the redemption, but this is a dangerous half-truth. At most the incarnation, according to this account, is the presupposition of the redemption. In the first place, Irenaeus is quite clear that Christ redeemed us with His blood, and when using the imagery of our enslavement to the Devil he is prepared to speak[8] of the Saviour's blood as our

[1] Ib. 3, 21, 10.   [2] Ib. 3, 22, 3.   [3] Ib. 3, 18, 1; 2, 22, 4.
[4] E.g. ib. 3, 22, 4.   [5] Ib. 3, 18, 7.   [6] Ib. 5, 21, 2.
[7] Ib. 5, 21, 1; 5, 21, 3.   [8] Ib. 5, 1, 1.

Irenaeus

ransom. The theory of the Devil's rights over mankind, however, though present in his thought, is not fully integrated with it. Secondly, and more significantly, he emphasizes[1] that, since the essence of Adam's sin was disobedience, the obedience of Christ was indispensable; it is obedience that God requires, and in which man's glory consists.[2] Hence he stresses,[3] as an example of steadfast obedience, Christ's resistance to the temptations spread before Him by the Devil—a scene which was the exact counterpart of the original temptation in the garden. He further points out[4] that, in order to exhibit such obedience, the second Adam had to live His life through all its stages, not excluding death itself. Studied in this perspective, His passion and crucifixion fall perfectly into place, for 'in obliterating the disobedience of man originally enacted on the tree, He became obedient unto death, even the death on the cross, healing the disobedience enacted on the tree by obedience on a tree'.[5] There are passages in which, echoing traditional language, Irenaeus speaks[6] of Christ's dying for us or reconciling us to God by His passion, or of His 'propitiating for us the Father against Whom we had sinned', or of God's offering His Son as 'a sacrifice for our redemption', and these are commonly regarded as standing apart from his main theory of recapitulation. In fact, they cohere admirably with it, suggesting as they do that the Lord's passion and sacrificial death were the supreme and necessary expression of His obedience.

4. *The West in the Third Century*

In the third century a marked divergence between Eastern and Western thought on the subject of man and his redemption begins to manifest itself. So far as the West was concerned, the chief region of theological activity was North Africa, where a sombre picture of the Fall came to be developed anticipating at many points that of Augustine.

The figure of commanding influence here was Tertullian, the

[1] E.g. *haer.* 3, 21, 10.   [2] Ib. 4, 14, 1; 4, 17, 1-5.   [3] Ib. 5, 21, 2f.
[4] Ib. 2, 22, 4.   [5] b. 5, 16, 3.   [6] Ib. 3, 16, 9; 5, 17, 1; 4, 5, 4.

Tertullian

Material to traducianist view of the soul

salient feature of whose anthropology was the conception, borrowed from Stoicism,[1] of the soul as "material." Though simple and more subtle, he regards[2] it as a body intimately united with and occupying the same space as the physical body to which it belongs. Hence, when he speculates about its origin, he can reject current theories of pre-existence (cf. Origen). He has equally little use for the view that it was created by God simultaneously with the coming of the body into existence ('creationism'). In contrast he is a thoroughgoing 'traducianist', teaching[3] that each soul is derived along with the body with which it is united from the parent; the whole man, soul as well as body, is produced by one and the same generative act, and the paternal germ is not merely a portion of the father's body, but is charged with a definite quantity of his soul-stuff. There is a real sense, therefore, in which all souls, actual or potential, were contained in Adam, since they must all be ultimately detached portions of the original soul breathed into him by God. Every soul, as Tertullian expresses it,[4] is, as it were, a twig cut from the parent-stem of Adam and planted out as an independent tree.

It is a short step from this psychology to the doctrine of original sin. Tertullian is a firm believer in free-will; he defends[5] its existence against Marcion and Hermogenes, never ceasing to repeat[6] that a man is responsible for his acts. Yet free-will is not the only source of our misdeeds; account must be taken of the bias towards sin in which Adam's transgression has involved mankind.[7] 'We have borne the image of the earthy', he remarks,[8] 'through our participation in transgression, our fellowship in death, our expulsion from Paradise.' As the effect of this primeval sin human nature bears a stain, so that 'every soul is counted as being in Adam until it is re-counted as being in Christ, and remains unclean until it is so re-counted'.[9] The demons, he admits,[10] exert a baneful influence, but apart from that 'the evil that exists in the soul . . . is antecedent, being

[1] See above, p. 18. [2] *De an.* 9. [3] Ib. 27. [4] Ib. 19.
[5] *C. Marc.* 2, 5-7. [6] Ib. 2, 9 f.: cf. *de exhort. cast.* 2.
[7] *C. Marc.* 1, 22; *de carn. Chr.* 16. [8] *De res. carn.* 49.
[9] *De an.* 40. [10] Ib. 39; 41.

derived from the fault of our origin (*ex originis vitio*) and having become in a way natural to us. For, as I have stated, the corruption of nature is second nature (*alia natura*)'. Our whole substance has been transformed from its primitive integrity into rebellion against its Creator,[1] the causal connexion being provided by the quasi-physical identity of all souls with Adam. Deceived by Satan, the first man 'infected the whole race by his seed, making it the channel (*traducem*) of damnation'.[2] For this reason even the children of the faithful must be reckoned impure until they have been reborn by water and the Holy Spirit.[3]

Thus Tertullian takes the view that, while Adam received from God true human nature in its integrity, the nature he passed on to his descendants is vitiated by an inclination to sin; an 'irrational element' has settled in the soul (*irrationale autem . . . coadoleverit in anima ad instar iam naturalitatis*[4]). He is more explicit and outspoken about this sinful bias than previous theologians, in whose eyes corruption and death seem to have been the principal legacy of the Fall; but, although there has been much difference of opinion on the question, his language[5] about 'our participation in [Adam's] transgression', and about the 'impurity' (cf. *immundi*) of unbaptized infants, can hardly be read as implying our solidarity with the first man in his culpability (i.e. original guilt) as well as in the consequences of his act. Hints of a doctrine akin to his are to be found in Cyprian, who describes the effects of original sin, in language which was to become classical, as 'wounds' (*vulnera*). The Saviour came, he states,[6] in order to heal the wounds received by Adam and to cure the serpent's poison. Again, he speaks[7] of baptism as 'cleansing us from the stain of the primeval contagion'. Arguing for infant baptism, he states[8] that even a new-born child who has never committed actual sin has been 'born carnally after the pattern of Adam, and by his first nativity has contracted the contagion of the ancient death', although the sins involved here are 'not his own, but someone else's'. That

---

[1] *De spect.* 2.   [2] *De test. an.* 3.   [3] *De an.* 39.   [4] Ib. 16.
[5] *De res. carn.* 49; *de an.* 39.   [6] *De op. et eleem.* 1.
[7] *De hab. virg.* 23.   [8] *Ep.* 64, 5.

he linked the transmission of sinfulness with the process of generation is confirmed by his appeal[1] to *Ps.* 51, 5: 'Behold, I was conceived in iniquities, and in sins did my mother bear me'.

In contrast to the progress it had made in regard to original sin, Latin theology remained curiously backward and meagre in its treatment of the redemption. A fresh approach might have been expected from Tertullian, whose legal outlook led him to emphasize the necessity of reparation for offences committed, and who transferred the idea to theology. Thus he has the theory[2] that good deeds accumulate merit with God, while bad deeds demand 'satisfaction'—we observe the introduction of this important conception into Christian thought. Taken in conjunction with his doctrine of original sin, it might have enabled him to deal in a fresh way of his own with the problem of atonement. In fact, however, while using his ideas about satisfaction to explain the restoration of relations between the individual sinner and God, he altogether fails to apply them to the mediatorial role of Christ. He lays greater stress, indeed, on Christ's death than does Irenaeus, speaking[3] of it as 'the whole weight and fruit of the Christian name . . . the supreme foundation of the gospel'. Not only did Christ die for us, but He was sent for precisely this purpose.[4] Indeed, 'neither could our own death have been annulled except by the Lord's passion, nor our life have been restored without His resurrection'.[5] His death, further, was sacrificial; 'it was necessary for Him to be made a sacrifice for all nations',[6] and 'He delivered Himself up for our sins'.[7] These thoughts, however, while they may well contain the germ of a doctrine of substitution, are nowhere expanded or worked up into a synthesis, and there is a distinct tendency[8] in Tertullian to reduce Christ's achievement to 'the proclamation of a new law and a new promise of the kingdom of heaven', and to represent Him as 'the illuminator and instructor of mankind'.

Other Western theologians may be dealt with more cursorily.

---

[1] *Test.* 3, 54.   [2] E.g. *de poen.* 5 f.; *de exhort. cast.* 1; *scorp.* 6.
[3] *C. Marc.* 3, 8.   [4] *De carn. Chr.* 6.   [5] *De bapt.* 11.
[6] *Adv. Iud.* 13.   [7] *Scorp.* 7.   [8] *De praescr.* 13; *apol.* 21.

Hippolytus closely reproduces Irenaeus's doctrine of recapitulation, teaching[1] that the Word was born from the Virgin in order to restore and recapitulate in Himself the original Adam. Thus 'through His death He conquered death',[2] and mingled incorruptible with corruptible to make men sons of God;[3] as man he vanquished man's vanquisher on the cross.[4] His most characteristic thought, however, is one derived from the Apologists, viz. that the redemption chiefly consists in the knowledge of God mediated by the Word through nature and history, the law and the prophets, and finally the Gospel: 'appearing in the world as the truth, He has taught the truth'.[5] A generation or so later we find Cyprian teaching[6] that Christ suffered for our sins, healing our wounds and destroying death by His blood, and that we have been restored to life and our sins purged by it.[7] He spoke[8] of the Lord's passion as a sacrifice, and a hint of the doctrine of substitution appears in the statement,[9] 'Christ bore us all when He bore our sins'. At the same time he presents[10] Christ as the teacher of truth Who bestows 'a new law' and reinforces it through His own example. Those who are His servants must obey their Master's commandment, all the more so since not only has He set rewards and punishments before them, but it is their clear duty to make Him some recompense for His passion.[11] A similar conception of the process of redemption can be found in Lactantius;[12] it was the by-product of the growing Western tendency to think of God as the supreme lawgiver Whose relation to mankind must be conceived in almost juridical terms.

5. The Doctrine of Man in the East

The Alexandrian theologians drew an equally realistic picture of man's plight, but the chief premiss of the doctrine of original

[1] In Dan. 4, 11: cf. de antichr. 26; c. Noet. 17.   [2] De antichr. 26.
[3] De antichr. 3 f.   [4] In cant. magn. 1 (Achelis, 83).
[5] In Dan. 4, 41.   [6] De laps. 17; de op. et eleem. 1; ep. 55, 22; etc.
[7] Ad Fortun. 6; de op. et eleem. 2; 26.   [8] Ep. 63, 16 f.
[9] Ib. 63, 13.   [10] De op. et eleem. 1; 7; de laps. 21; de dom. or. 15; 28.
[11] De op. et eleem. 23.
[12] E.g. div. instit. 4, 10, 1; 4, 11, 14; 4, 13, 1; 4, 14, 15; 4, 24, 1; 4, 24, 6.

sin which we have seen emerging in the West, the conception of our physical solidarity with Adam and thus of our participation in his sinful act, was largely absent from their thinking.

In his primitive state, according to Clement,[1] man was childlike and innocent, destined to advance by stages towards perfection. Adam, he states,[2] 'was not created perfect in constitution, but suitable for acquiring virtue. . . . For God desires us to be saved by our own efforts.' Progress therefore depended upon free-will, on which Clement places great emphasis. The fault of Adam and Eve consisted in the fact that, using their volition wrongly, they indulged in the pleasures of sexual intercourse before God gave them leave.[3] Not that sex was wrong in itself (Clement strongly repudiates[4] the Gnostic suggestion that it is), but the violation of God's ordinance was. As a result they lost the immortal life of Paradise, their will and rationality were weakened, and they became a prey to sinful passions.[5] But while Clement accepts the historicity of Adam, he also regards him as symbolizing mankind as a whole. All men, he teaches,[6] have a spark of the divine in them and are free to obey or disobey God's law, but all except the incarnate Logos are sinners.[7] They are, as it were, sick, blind and gone astray; they are enslaved to the elements and the Devil; and their condition can be described as death.[8] He nowhere hints, however, that they are involved in Adam's guilt, and in one passage[9] vehemently denies that a new-born baby which has not performed any act of its own can have 'fallen under the curse of Adam'. In another[10] he explains *Job* 1, 21 ('Naked I came from my mother's womb') as implying that a child enters the world exempt from sin. On the whole, his insistence against the Gnostics that only the personal misdeeds that men have committed are imputable to them leaves no room for original sin in the full sense. On the

[1] *Protr.* II, III; *strom.* 2, 22, 131.   [2] *Strom.* 6, 12, 96.
[3] *Protr.* II, III; *strom.* 3, 17, 103.
[4] E.g. *strom.* 3, 12, 88 f.; 3, 17, 102.
[5] Ib. 2, 19, 98; *paed.* 1, 13, 101; *protr.* II, III.
[6] *Protr.* 6, 68; *strom.* 2, 15, 62; 3, 9, 63 ff.; 4, 24, 153.
[7] *Paed.* 1, 2, 4; 3, 12, 93.
[8] *Protr.* 1, 6 f.; 11, 114; *paed.* 1, 9, 83; *strom.* 1, 11, 53; etc.
[9] *Strom.* 3, 16, 100.   [10] Ib. 4, 25, 160.

other hand, although certain contexts[1] might seem to suggest that the connexion between the general human sinfulness and Adam's transgression amounts to no more than imitation, he in fact envisages it as much more intimate. His teaching[2] seems to be that, through our physical descent from Adam and Eve, we inherit, not indeed their guilt and curse, but a disordered sensuality which entails the dominance of the irrational element (τὸ ἄλογον) in our nature.

When we come to Origen, the whole atmosphere changes. He transforms the story recorded in *Genesis*, which Irenaeus, Tertullian and Clement had accepted as historical fact, into a cosmic myth, and lifts the origination of human sinfulness from the terrestrial to the transcendental plane. Unlike Tertullian, who believed that each soul is generated along with its body from the parent, Origen is a firm exponent of the theory (already mentioned in previous chapters[3]) of the pre-existence of all individual souls. In the beginning, he explains,[4] God out of His goodness created a fixed number of rational essences, all of them equal and alike (there was no reason for any diversity), and all of them endowed with free-will—thus he strives to defend the divine justice and the principle of liberty against the Gnostics. Since these souls were free, it rested with their own volition to advance by imitating God, or to fall away by neglecting Him, to depart from good being tantamount to settling down to evil. With the unique exception of Christ's pre-existent soul,[5] all these rational beings opted in varying degrees for the latter; the result was their fall, which gave rise to the manifold and unequal gradations of spiritual existence. 'Before the ages,' he writes,[6] 'they were all pure intelligences (νόες), whether demons or souls or angels. One of them, the Devil, since he possessed free-will, chose to resist God, and God rejected him. All the other powers fell away with him, becoming demons, angels and archangels according as their misdeeds were more, or less, or still less, heinous. Each obtained a lot

---

[1] Esp. *adumbr. in Iud.* 11.   [2] *Strom.* 3, 16, 100 f.: cf. ib. 3, 9, 63-5.
[3] See above, p. 128 and p. 155.   [4] *De princ.* 2, 9, 6.
[5] Ib. 2, 6, 3: cf. Jerome, *ep.* 124, 6.   [6] Ib. 1, 8, 1.

proportionate to his sin. There remained the souls; these had not sinned so grievously as to become demons or so venially as to become angels. God therefore made the present world, binding the soul to the body as a punishment. . . . Plainly He chastises each to suit his sin, making one a demon, another a soul, another an archangel.'

Such is Origen's theory of the pre-cosmic Fall. It explains to him the fact of universal sinfulness: 'all we men are clearly prone to sin by nature'.[1] It explains also the manifold disasters and tragedies of life: 'it is plain that the souls concerned were guilty of previous sins'.[2] Such Scriptural texts as *Ps.* 51, 5 ('I was conceived in iniquities, etc.') and *Ps.* 58, 3 ('The wicked are estranged from the womb'), implying as they do that children come into the world already stained with sin,[3] are in line with it, as is also, in Origen's opinion, the Church's practice of baptizing infants.[4] So, he suggests,[5] is David's cry (cf. *Ps.* 119, 67: in the LXX), 'Before I was humbled'—i.e. in my pre-natal life—'I went wrong.' He regards[6] the story of the Garden and Adam's expulsion from it as an allegory of this pre-cosmic Fall, pointing out that where Moses seems to be speaking of an individual he really has human nature as a whole in mind. The theory entails, of course, the abandonment of any doctrine of corporate sinfulness, for it suggests that if human beings are sinful from birth, their wickedness is the legacy of their own misguided choices in the transcendental world, and has nothing to do with the disobedience of any one first man. Interpreters of Origen have sometimes been reluctant to admit that this was his true teaching. There are passages in his writings, especially in his *Commentary on Romans*, where he appears to accept the doctrine that the whole race was present in Adam's loins and 'sinned in him'. It is difficult, however, to take them at their face value, for we know that in his translation Rufinus adjusted his teaching in the interests of orthodoxy. For example, he represented Origen as taking ἐφ' ᾧ in *Rom.* 5, 12 as meaning

---

[1] *C. Cels.* 3, 66: cf. ib. 3, 62. [2] *De princ.* 1, 8, 1.
[3] E.g. *c. Cels.* 7, 50. [4] *Hom. in Lev.* 8, 3; *hom. in Luc.* 14.
[5] *De princ.* 2, 8, 3. [6] *C. Cels.* 4, 37-40, esp. 4, 40.

'in whom', whereas he really understood it as meaning 'since'. Even in that commentary, however, in expounding[1] *Rom.* 5, 12-19, his whole emphasis is on the personal sins of individuals who have followed Adam's example, rather than on their solidarity with his guilt; and, while admitting the possibility that we may be in this vale of fears because we were in Adam's loins, he does not conceal his belief that each one of us was banished from Paradise for his personal transgression.

Thus men are pure intelligences fallen from their former splendour and united with bodies. Origen sees[2] these latter symbolized in the 'coats of skins' with which God clothed the nakedness of Adam and Eve after their transgression. Not that corporeity is on his view intrinsically bad; despite his language in certain contexts, he is opposed[3] to those who condemn the body as the principle of evil, and himself teaches that evil resides in the will alone. Rather, while corporeity can be regarded as the penalty of their fall, it is really an aspect of the diversity[4] belonging to the level of existence to which the spirits have been reduced. Even so, as he is never tired of emphasizing,[5] men retain their free-will; indeed, the idea of free-will provides the key to Origen's whole system. Nevertheless, in their struggle against the temptations of their nature and the world, men are exposed to the continuous assaults of malign demons;[6] the story of Adam and Eve mirrors the experience of every man and woman.[7] Origen agrees[8] with St. Paul that we have to do battle 'against principalities, against powers, against the rulers of darkness of this world, against spiritual forces of wickedness in heavenly places', and states[9] that if we have good angels to assist us, we have bad ones to prompt us to sin.

It is scarcely surprising that Origen's bold and original speculations excited a sharply critical reaction. Methodius of Olympus (†311), for example, brusquely repudiates[10] the whole conception of a multiplicity of pre-cosmic falls, proposing

---

[1] *In Rom.* 5 (PG 14, 1018 f.; 1024; 1029 f.).
[2] *C. Cels.* 4, 40.   [3] Ib. 3, 42; 4, 65 f.
[4] *De princ.* 2, 1, 4.   [5] E.g. ib. 3, 1, 2-4; *de orat. dom.* 6.
[6] *De princ.* 3, 2, 1-6.   [7] *C. Cels.* 4, 40.   [8] *De princ.* 3, 2, 1.
[9] *Hom. in Luc.* 13; 35.   [10] E.g. *de res.* 1, 55.

instead that the *Genesis* narrative should be taken literally. His views are important as representing the normal current of opinion in the late third century. The first man, he holds,[1] was created immortal, having had the breath of life breathed into him by God, and even prior to his sinning possessed a body like ours. He was also free, but when confronted with the divine prohibition he succumbed to desire. Methodius identifies Adam with the human race, stating[2] that from the day sin established itself in him we men were deprived of the divine breath and filled with troublesome thoughts and carnal yearnings. He approves[3] St. Paul's suggestion that sin actually dwells in us, identifying it with the sensual cravings which, arising out of our bodily nature, are fanned by the Devil and cause a man to be divided against himself. Death, which was the punishment prescribed for Adam's disobedience, is also God's remedy for sin, since by destroying the body it makes possible the restoration of incorruption.[4] His teaching thus reverts to the pre-Origenistic tradition, being marked by the optimistic colouring which was usually characteristic of Greek thought on the subject. This comes out both in the way he softens the Pauline antithesis (cf. *Rom.* 7, 9-25) between carnal desire and the spirit, and also in the way in which he combines a strong emphasis on man's free-will, apparently unimpeded by the effects of the Fall, with the affirmation that human nature inherits a bias towards sensuality from Adam.

OPTIMISTIC

6. *Eastern Views of the Work of Christ*

In expounding Christ's saving work Clement carries on the tradition we have already studied in the Apologists, though blending with it his own mysticism and shifting somewhat the emphasis. Thus he speaks[5] of Christ's laying down His life as a ransom (λύτρον) on our behalf, redeeming us by His blood, offering Himself as a sacrifice, conquering the Devil, and interceding for us with the Father. These are, however, conventional

Clement

---

[1] Ib. 1, 34-6; 52; 55.   [2] Ib. 2, 1.   [3] Ib. 2, 2-4.   [4] Ib. 1, 38 f.
[5] *Quis div.* 37, 4; *paed.* 1, 5, 23; 1, 11, 97; 3, 12, 98; *protr.* 11, 111; 12, 120.

phrases as used by him, and this is not the aspect of Christ's achievement which makes the chief appeal to him. His most frequent and characteristic thought is that Christ is the teacher Who endows men with true knowledge, leading them to a love exempt from desires and a righteousness whose prime fruit is contemplation. He is their guide at the different levels of life, 'instructing the gnostic by mysteries, the believer by good hopes, and the hard-hearted by corrective chastisement'.[1] It is as teacher that He is 'the all-healing physician of mankind',[2] Who bestows immortality as well as knowledge.[3] 'God's will', he remarks,[4] 'is the knowledge of God, and this is participation in immortality.' So man is deified: 'the Word . . . became man so that you might learn from man how man may become God'.[5] As God Christ forgives us our sins, while the function of His humanity is to serve as a model so as to prevent us from sinning further.[6] It is clear that Clement's soteriology issues in a Christ-mysticism in which the Lord's passion and death have little or no redemptive part to play.

A mysticism closely akin to this permeates Origen's thought about the redemption. As we saw in the preceding chapter,[7] he conceives of Jesus's human nature as having been progressively deified through its union with the Logos; after the resurrection its materiality disappears and His human soul becomes fused ineffably with the Logos. This illustrates the way in which Origen visualizes the restoration of rational beings in general and men in particular. The Logos is our teacher, law-giver and model;[8] by associating with Him we lose our deadness and irrationality, becoming 'divinely possessed and rational'.[9] He is 'the pattern of the perfect life',[10] the exemplar of true virtue into Whose likeness Christians are transformed,[11] thereby being enabled to participate in the divine nature.[12] As he puts it,[13] 'Discoursing in bodily form and giving Himself out as flesh, He

---

[1] Strom. 7, 2, 6.　　[2] Paed. 1, 2, 6.　　[3] Protr. 12, 120, 3.
[4] Strom. 4, 6, 27.　　[5] Protr. 1, 8, 4.　　[6] Paed. 1, 3, 7.
[7] See above, pp. 157 f.
[8] De princ. 4, 1, 2; 4, 3, 12; c. Cels. 2, 52; 3, 7; etc.
[9] In Ioh. 1, 37, 268.　　[10] C. Cels. 1, 68.　　[11] Ib. 8, 17.
[12] De princ. 4, 4, 4.　　[13] C. Cels. 6, 68.

summons to Himself those who are flesh, in order that He may first of all transform them into the likeness of the Word Who has been made flesh, and after that may exalt them so as to behold Him as He was before He became flesh'; and again,[1] 'With Jesus human and divine nature began to be woven together, so that by fellowship with divinity human nature might become divine, not only in Jesus Himself, but also in all those who believe and embrace the life which Jesus taught, the life which leads everyone who lives according to His commandments to friendship with God and fellowship with Him'.

Mystical Exaltation

Illumination and mystical exaltation, however, do not, according to Origen, exhaust the work of the Redeemer. His death, he declares,[2] 'not only has been set forth as an example of dying for religion, but has effected a beginning and an advance in the overthrow of the evil one, the Devil, who dominated the whole earth'. From the moment of His birth His life was a conflict with the powers of darkness.[3] His passion and resurrection signified their final defeat, and Origen appeals[4] to *Col.* 2, 15 as proving that the Saviour's death has a twofold aspect, being both an example and also the trophy of His victory over the Devil, who in effect was nailed to the cross with his principalities and powers. This conception of Christ's work as consisting in a struggle with, and ultimate triumph over, the demoniac forces which hold sway over the world went back, as we have seen,[5] at least as far as Justin among the fathers, and it undoubtedly plays a big part in Origen's soteriology. The underlying idea seems to be that the Devil, with whom death is identified, deluded himself into imagining that he had triumphed over Christ, but his seeming victory was turned to defeat when the Saviour rose from the grave.[6] Elsewhere Origen, like Irenaeus[7] before him, varies his imagery and makes use of the Gospel metaphor of a ransom. He speaks[8] of Jesus delivering up His soul, or life, not indeed to God, but to the Devil in

Aulén's Motif

Ransom

[1] Ib. 3, 28.   [2] Ib. 7, 17.
[3] Ib. 1, 60; 6, 45; *hom. in Luc.* 30; 31.
[4] *Hom. in Ios.* 8, 3; *in Matt.* 12, 40.   [5] See above, p. 169.
[6] *In Matt.* 13, 9.   [7] See above, pp. 173 f.
[8] *In Matt.* 16, 8 : cf. ib. 12, 28; *in Ioh.* 6, 53, 274; *hom. in Exod.* 6, 9; etc.

exchange for the souls of men which the Devil had claimed as his due because of their sinfulness. The Devil accepted the exchange, but could not hold Jesus, Who proved stronger than death, in his clutches and was thus cheated of his victim. We should note, however, that, while exploiting to the full the idea of a ransom, Origen thinks much more in terms of Christ's conquest of the Devil than of any actual transaction with him.

More Conquest than Ranson

Thirdly, however, Origen was prepared to interpret Christ's death as an act of vicarious substitution or propitiatory sacrifice. He is indeed the first of the fathers to treat this aspect of the Lord's work in full detail, and he conceives of His death, not simply as an obedient surrender to God's will, but as an offering which has positive influence on the Father. Thus he argues[1] that, as leader of the Church, Jesus is the head of a body of which we are members; He has taken our sins upon Himself, has borne them and has suffered freely for us. As a true priest, He has offered the Father a true sacrifice in which He is Himself the victim, thereby propitiating the Father.[2] Sin called for a propitiation, and Christ stepped forward as 'a victim spotless and innocent', propitiating the Father to men by His generous self-oblation.[3] In this mood Origen applies[4] *Is.* 53, 4 f. to Christ's passion, stating that 'He too has borne our sins and has been bruised because of our iniquities, and the punishment which was owing to us, in order that we might be chastised and might obtain peace, has fallen on Him'.

SUBSTITUTIO N

Scholars have often found Origen's thoughts on the redemption complex to the point of being mutually irreconcilable, and have been hard put to it to discover a unifying theme in them. But if we bear his system as a whole in mind, we should not find it impossible to grasp the relation of at any rate the first two of the theories discussed above. For a complete and final salvation such as Origen envisages, the restoration of the fallen spirits, angels and demons, as well as of men, to their pristine transcendental status is required. Hence the role of the Logos as illuminating men's souls, purifying and deifying

---

[1] *Hom. in Lev.* 1, 3.   [2] *In Rom.* 3, 8.   [3] *Hom. in Num.* 24, 1.
[4] *In Ioh.* 28, 19, 165.

them by His transforming contact, must obviously be primary. But Origen, as we have seen, was also acutely conscious of the malefic efforts of the Devil and his coadjutors to enslave men and hold them back from any return. Hence the destruction of their power was to his mind an indispensable preliminary to the purgative process worked by the Logos. Admittedly his sacrificial views, if taken in their literal sense, cannot logically be harmonized with the rest of his system, not least because it excludes the idea of original sin as a corporate infection and the whole conception of human solidarity. It was natural, of course, that he should make use of this sacrificial imagery, since the Bible was full of it, when he was expounding Holy Scripture. He made it quite plain, however, that whatever value it might have for simpler Christians, the more advanced would be bound to leave it behind. 'Happy are they', he wrote,[1] 'who no longer need the Son of God as a physician Who heals the sick, nor as shepherd, nor as redemption, but as wisdom, and as word, and as righteousness.' Like St. Paul (2 *Cor.* 5, 16), the mature Christian does not need the historical Jesus.[2] This being his view, he is able to acquiesce in the factual narrative of the Gospels, and the theological interpretation of the Passion which goes with it, while holding all the time that the ultimate truth of the matter transcends the categories of history and sacrifice.

Origen's severe critic, Methodius, takes up Irenaeus's doctrine of recapitulation in a somewhat weakened form, and we shall bring this chapter to a close with a cursory reference to his ideas. Christ on his view[3] is the new Adam because He assumed human nature and, just as all died in the first Adam, so they are made alive in the second. It was fitting that the Devil should be defeated and the judgment of death which he had brought on the human race annulled through the very man he had originally deceived. We observe that in this account Christ is virtually identified with Adam, and Methodius actually remarks[4] how appropriate it was that the only-begotten Logos

---

[1] *In Ioh.* 1, 20, 124. [2] *Hom. in Ierem.* 15, 6.
[3] *Symp.* 3, 6, 65. [4] *Ib.* 3, 4, 60.

should unite Himself with the first-born of men. Yet, while Irenaeus saw a positive, almost dynamic significance in Christ's death as the supreme instance of His obedience, Methodius almost completely overlooks this aspect. Rather he views[1] the Lord's humanity as the instrument by means of which He disclosed the resurrection of the flesh. More important in his eyes than the conquest of sin and death on the cross[2] is the fact that the Logos 'took to Himself this suffering body in order that ... what was mortal might be transformed into immortality and what was passible into impassibility'.[3] It is clear that, while the outward forms of Irenaeus's physical theory of redemption have been retained, it has lost much of its original emphasis on the atoning death, and has been shot through with mysticism.

[1] *Symp.* 3, 7, 69.   [2] *Frg. c. Porphyr.* 1, 3.   [3] *De res.* 3, 23, 4.

NOTE ON BOOKS

General. G. Aulén, *Christus Victor* (English trans., London, 1931); J. K. Mozley, *The Doctrine of the Atonement* (London, 1915); J. Rivière, *Le Dogme de la rédemption* (Paris, 1905); A. Slomkowski, *L'État primitif de l'homme dans la tradition de l'Église avant saint Augustin* (Paris, 1928); H. E. W. Turner, *The Patristic Doctrine of Redemption* (London, 1952); N. P. Williams, *The Ideas of the Fall and Original Sin* (London, 1927).
Special. A. d'Alès, 'La Doctrine de la récapitulation en saint Irénée' (art. in *Rech. de science relig.* 6, 1916); A. Benoit, *Saint Irénée: Introduction* (Paris, 1960); J. Daniélou, *Origen* (Eng. trans., London, 1955); H. Koch, 'Zur Lehre vom Urstand und der Erlösung bei Irenäus' (*Theol. und Kritik.*, 1925); T. Rüther, *Die Lehre von der Erbsünde bei Clemens von Alexandrien* (Freiburg im Breisgau, 1902); F. Stoll, 'Die Lehre des hl. Irenäus von der Erlösung und Heiligung' (art. in *Der Katholik*, 1905); A. Wintersig, *Die Heilsbedeutung der Menscheit Iesu in der vornicänischen Theologie* (Tübingen, 1932).

CHAPTER VIII

THE CHRISTIAN COMMUNITY

1. *The Beginnings of Ecclesiology*

LOOKED at from the outside, primitive Christianity has the appearance of a vast diffusion of local congregations, each leading its separate life with its own constitutional structure and officers and each called a 'church'. In a deeper sense, however, all these communities are conscious of being parts of one universal Church, which Ignatius implies[1] is related to Christ as the body is to its head. It extends, we are informed,[2] to the ends of the earth, and God gathers it together from the four winds. So the church of Smyrna sends[3] its report of Polycarp's martyrdom not only to the church at Philomelium, but to all the communities (παροικίαις) composing 'the holy and Catholic Church'. As he faces death, Polycarp himself prays[4] 'for the entire Catholic Church throughout the world'. Ignatius suggests[5] that Christ's standard rallies His followers everywhere, whether Jews or Gentiles, 'in one body of His Church'. He adds[6] that the Catholic Church is to be found wherever Christ is present, in contrast to the local church, which is confined to the district presided over by the bishop. So for Hermas[7] the Church collects its members from the whole world, forming them into one body in unity of understanding, mind, faith and love. Justin speaks[8] of all those who believe in Christ as being united 'in one soul, one synagogue, one Church, which is brought into being through His name and shares in His name; for we are all called Christians'.

Because of its unity and universality Christians liked to think of the Church as a special grouping of mankind. According to

---

[1] *Eph.* 17, 1.   [2] *Did.* 9, 4; 10, 5.   [3] *Mart. Polyc.* inscr.
[4] *Ib.* 8, 1.   [5] *Smyrn.* 1, 2.   [6] *Ib.* 8, 2.
[7] *Sim.* 9, 17.   [8] *Dial.* 63, 5.

'Barnabas',[1] it is 'the new people' which God has called into existence; while Aristides explains[2] that there are three sorts of men—pagans, Jews and Christians. So both *The Preaching of Peter*[3] and *Ad Diognetum*[4] refer to Christians as 'a third race' or 'this new race'. Alternatively (and this conception harks back to the New Testament) the Church is regarded as the new, authentic Israel which has inherited the promises which God made to the old. So Clement of Rome sees[5] in its election the fulfilment of the prophecies that Jacob should become the Lord's portion and Israel the lot of His inheritance. Justin puts[6] the claim forcibly to the Jew Trypho, and of course it is the presupposition underlying the Christian appropriation[7] of the Hebrew Scriptures. The term 'holy', the stock epithet of the Church, expresses the conviction that it is God's chosen people and is indwelt by His Spirit. As regards 'Catholic', its original meaning was 'universal' or 'general', and in this sense Justin can speak[8] of 'the catholic resurrection'. As applied to the Church, its primary significance was to underline its universality as opposed to the local character of the individual congregations. Very quickly, however, in the latter half of the second century at latest, we find[9] it conveying the suggestion that the Catholic is the true Church as distinct from the heretical congregations.

In all this there is implied a distinctive, if far from consciously formulated, ecclesiology. If the Church is one, it is so in virtue of the divine life pulsing through it. Called into existence by God, it is no more a mere man-made agglomerate than was God's ancient people Israel. It is in fact the body of Christ, forming a spiritual unity with Him as close as is His unity with the Father, so that Christians can be called[10] His 'members'. As the incarnation is the union of seen with unseen, flesh with spirit, so Ignatius teaches[11] that the Church is at once flesh and

[1] 3, 6; 5, 7.   [2] *Apol.* 2.
[3] In Clement Alex., *strom.* 6, 5, 41.   [4] 1.   [5] 29, 1-3.
[6] E.g. *dial.* 11, 5; 123.   [7] See above, p. 52.
[8] Ib. 81, 4.   [9] Cf., e.g. Muratorian Canon.
[10] E.g. Ignatius, *Eph.* 5, 1; *Trall.* 11, 2.
[11] *Eph.* 10, 3; *Magn.* 13; *Smyrn* 12, 2.

Spirit, its unity being the union of both. And it is a holy community within which the divine Spirit lives and operates. Among the multiplicity of local bodies making up this community, he seems to suggest[1] that the Roman church occupies a special position; he speaks of the church 'which has the primacy (προκάθηται) in the place of the region of the Romans'. This may be merely an elaborate way of defining the area of the authority of the congregation addressed, but something more appears to be implied since he goes on to salute the Roman church as possessing 'a primacy of love' (προκαθημένη τῆς ἀγάπης—an expression which some have translated, rather forcedly, 'presiding over the love-community', i.e. over the Church universal).

What these early fathers were envisaging was almost always the empirical, visible society; they had little or no inkling of the distinction which was later to become important between a visible and an invisible Church. Yet speculation about the Church as a pre-existent, spiritual reality was already at work, and traces of it appear in 2 Clement and Hermas. The former, perhaps taking his cue from St. Paul (Eph. 1, 3-5), represents[2] the Church as having been created before sun and moon and as being the mother of Christians. Like Christ, Whose bride she is, she is spiritual (πνευματική), and has been manifested in these latter days in His flesh for our salvation. Only those who have scrupulously observed the law of purity may belong to her. Hermas describes[3] the Church under the figure of an old woman; she is aged because she was created before everything else, and indeed the universe was made because of her. These are passing hints, however; Hermas at any rate is much more concerned with the visible Christian society, with its ministers and its more or less perfect members. For the fuller development of the theory of the invisible, pre-existent Church we have to look to Valentinian Gnosticism. In its cosmology, as expounded by Irenaeus,[4] the Church was a mysterious aeon, a member of the primitive ogdoad from which all things are derived.

---

[1] Rom. inscr.   [2] 14, 1-4; 2, 1.
[3] Vis. 2, 4, 1; 3, 5, 1.   [4] Haer. 1, 2, 2; 1, 11, 1; 1, 12, 3.

Irenaeus

Irenaeus gathers together the main second-century ideas about the Church and, in conscious reaction against Gnosticism, imposes a sharper outline on them. Like his predecessors, he regards[1] the Church as the new Israel; it is Christ's glorious body, the mother of Christians.[2] It is endowed with mysterious powers which it exercises without charge, and bestows graces which cannot be counted.[3] And it is the unique sphere of the Spirit, Who has indeed been especially entrusted to it, so that we can only attain communion with Christ in the Church. 'Where the Church is,' he writes,[4] 'there is the Spirit of God; and where the Spirit of God is, there is the Church and all grace; and the Spirit is the truth. Those, therefore, who do not participate in the Spirit neither feed at their mother's breasts nor drink the bright fountain issuing from Christ's body.' His most characteristic thought, however, is that the Church is the sole repository of the truth, and is such because it has a mono-poly of the apostolic writings, the apostolic oral tradition and the apostolic faith. Because of its proclamation of this one faith inherited from the apostles the Church, scattered as it is throughout the entire world, can claim to be one.[5] Hence his emphasis[6] on 'the canon of the truth', i.e. the framework of doctrine which is handed down in the Church and which, in contrast to the variegated teachings of the Gnostics, is identical and self-consistent everywhere. In a previous chapter[7] we noticed his theory that the unbroken succession of bishops in the great sees going back to the apostles themselves provides a guarantee that this faith is identical with the message which they originally proclaimed.

To illustrate his argument Irenaeus singled out, in a famous and much debated passage,[8] the Roman church; its greatness, its antiquity, its foundation by the apostles Peter and Paul, the fact too that it was universally known, made it an apt example. *Ad hanc enim ecclesiam*, so the surviving Latin translation runs, *propter potentiorem principalitatem necesse est omnem convenire*

---

[1] E.g. *haer.* 5, 32, 2; 5, 34, 1.   [2] Ib. 4, 33, 7; 3, 24, 1; 5, 20, 2
[3] Ib. 2, 31, 3; 2, 32, 4.   [4] Ib. 3, 24, 1.   [5] Ib. 1, 10, 2.
[6] E.g. ib. 1, 9, 4; 1, 10, 1 f; 1, 22, 1.
[7] See above, p. 37.   [8] Ib. 3, 3, 2.

ecclesiam, hoc est eos qui sunt undique fideles, in qua semper ab his qui sunt undique conservata est ea quae est ab apostolis traditio. If *convenire* here means 'agree with' and *principalitas* refers to the Roman primacy (in whatever sense), the gist of the sentence may be taken to be that Christians of every other church are required, in view of its special position of leadership, to fall into line with the Roman church, inasmuch as the authentic apostolic tradition is always preserved by the faithful who are everywhere. This interpretation, or some variant of it, has been accepted by many, but it is awkward to refer *in qua* to *hanc . . . ecclesiam*, and anachronistic to attribute such thinking to Irenaeus. Hence it seems more plausible to take *in qua* with *omnem . . . ecclesiam*, and to understand Irenaeus as suggesting that the Roman church supplies an ideal illustration because, 'in view of its preeminent authority' based on its foundation by both Peter and Paul, its antiquity, and so on, every church— or perhaps the whole church—in which the apostolic tradition has been preserved must as a matter of course agree with it. There is therefore no allusion to the later Petrine claims of the Roman see.

2. *Early Views of the Sacraments*

The Church's sacraments are those external rites, more precisely signs, which Christians believe convey, by Christ's appointment, an unseen sanctifying grace. Their number has been reckoned differently at different times; in this section we shall glance at three—baptism, the eucharist and penance—for which some circumstantial evidence survives from the second century. We should note that, while the technical terms for sacrament were to be μυστήριον in Greek and *sacramentum* in Latin, there are no absolutely certain instances of their use before the Alexandrian fathers and Tertullian respectively.

From the beginning baptism was the universally accepted rite of admission to the Church; only 'those who have been baptized in the Lord's name' may partake of the eucharist.[1]

---

[1] *Did.* 9, 5.

Whether or not administered originally in Christ's name only, as numerous New Testament texts appear to suggest, in the second century it was administered in water in the threefold name.[1] As regards its significance, it was always held to convey the remission of sins, but the earlier Pauline conception of it as the application of Christ's atoning death to the believer seems to have faded. On the other hand, the theory that it mediated the Holy Spirit was fairly general. Clement appears to have had this in mind in his reference[2] to 'one Spirit of grace poured out upon us', and this is clearly what lies behind the description of baptism as 'the seal' (σφραγίς) or 'the seal of the Son of God', which the baptized must keep unsullied, in 2 Clement[3] and Hermas.[4] According to the latter, we descend into the water 'dead' and come out again 'alive'; we receive a white robe which symbolizes the Spirit. In 'Barnabas'[5] it is the remission of sins which is emphasized; we enter the water weighed down and defiled by our transgressions, only to emerge 'bearing fruit in our hearts, having fear and hope in Jesus in the Spirit'. The Spirit is God Himself dwelling in the believer, and the resulting life is a re-creation. Prior to baptism, he remarks, our heart was the abode of demons; and Ignatius develops this idea, suggesting[6] that baptism supplies us with the weapons for our spiritual warfare.

Justin has left a description[7] of baptism which has become famous. He finds authority for its use in Is. 1, 16-20 ('Wash, make yourselves clean, etc.') as well as John 3, 5 ('Unless you are born again, etc.'), and the chief points he brings out are that it is a washing with water in the Triune name which has as its effects regeneration, illumination and remission of sins. Elsewhere[8] he calls it 'the bath of repentance and knowledge of God', the living water which alone can cleanse penitents and which, being a baptism with the Holy Spirit, is to be contrasted with Jewish washings. It is a spiritual rite replacing circumcision, the unique doorway to the remission of sins

---

[1] Did. 7, 1-3.   [2] 46, 6.   [3] 7, 6; 8, 6.
[4] Sim. 8, 2, 2 f.; 8, 6, 3; 9, 16, 3 f.   [5] 11, 11; 16, 7 f.
[6] Polyc. 6, 2.   [7] 1 apol. 61.   [8] Dial. 14, 1; 29, 1.

prophesied by Isaiah.[1] Theophilus of Antioch represents[2] it as imparting remissions of sins and rebirth (παλιγγενεσία); it was prefigured, he thinks, in the production of living being from the waters on the fifth day of creation. For Irenaeus[3] it is 'the seal of eternal life and our rebirth in God, so that we are no longer the sons of mortal men only, but also children of the immortal and indefectible God'. It cleanses the soul as well as the body, bestowing the Spirit as an earnest of resurrection. 'We have received baptism', he writes,[4] 'for the remission of sins in the name of God the Father, and in the name of Jesus Christ the Son of God, Who was incarnate and died and rose again, and in the Holy Spirit of God. And thus baptism is the seal of eternal life and new birth unto God.' Through it we are washed, have the Spirit imparted to us, and obtain 'the image of the heavenly'.

The early view, therefore, like the Pauline, would seem to be that baptism itself is the vehicle for conveying the Spirit to believers; in all this period we nowhere come across any clear pointers to the existence of a separate rite, such as unction or the laying on of hands, appropriated to this purpose. It is true that in one passage,[5] making an obvious allusion to *Acts* 8, 17, Irenaeus betrays his recognition that the Spirit had been bestowed by the imposition of the apostles' hands, but even here there is no hint that the contemporary Church was familiar with any such practice. Again, it is far-fetched to seek to extract a reference to physical anointing out of his statement[6] that Christians are to be saved 'by partaking of His unction'. The unction of Christ here mentioned is the descent of the Spirit upon Him at His baptism, and the anointing of Christians, so far from being a literal one, consists in their reception of the Spirit similarly in baptism. As a matter of fact, whether or not the second-century Church employed unction, the clearest evidence[7] for its use at this period is in the initiation ceremonies of certain Gnostic sects.

---

[1] Ib. 44, 4.   [2] *Ad Autol.* 2, 16.   [3] *Dem.* 3.
[4] Ib. 41 f.; *haer.* 5, 11, 2.   [5] *Haer.* 4, 38, 2.
[6] Ib. 3, 9, 3: cf. ib. 3, 17, 1-3.   [7] Ib. 1, 21, 3.

If such was the Church's understanding of baptism, the eucharist was regarded as the distinctively Christian sacrifice from the closing decade of the first century, if not earlier. Malachi's prediction (1, 10 f.) that the Lord would reject the Jewish sacrifices and instead would have 'a pure offering' made to Him by the Gentiles in every place was early seized[1] upon by Christians as a prophecy of the eucharist. The *Didache* indeed actually applies[2] the term $\theta v\sigma i\alpha$, or sacrifice, to the eucharist, and the idea is presupposed by Clement in the parallel he discovers[3] between the Church's ministers and the Old Testament priests and levites, as in his description[4] of the function of the former as the offering of gifts (cf. $\tau o\dot{v}s \ldots \pi\rho o\sigma\epsilon\nu\epsilon\gamma\kappa\acute{o}\nu\tau\alpha s \tau\grave{\alpha} \delta\hat{\omega}\rho\alpha$). Ignatius's reference[5] to 'one altar, just as there is one bishop', reveals that he too thought in sacrificial terms. Justin speaks[6] of 'all the sacrifices in this name which Jesus appointed to be performed, viz. in the eucharist of the bread and the cup, and which are celebrated in every place by Christians'. Not only here but elsewhere[7] too, he identifies 'the bread of the eucharist, and the cup likewise of the eucharist', with the sacrifice foretold by Malachi. For Irenaeus[8] the eucharist is 'the new oblation of the new covenant', which the Church has received from the apostles and offers to God throughout the whole world.

It was natural for early Christians to think of the eucharist as a sacrifice. The fulfilment of prophecy demanded a solemn Christian offering, and the rite itself was wrapped in the sacrificial atmosphere with which our Lord invested the Last Supper. The words of institution, 'Do this' ($\tau o\hat{v}\tau o \pi o\iota\epsilon\hat{\iota}\tau\epsilon$), must have been charged with sacrifical overtones for second-century ears; Justin at any rate understood[9] them to mean, 'Offer this'. If we inquire what the sacrifice was supposed to consist in, the *Didache* for its part provides no clear answer. Justin, however, makes it plain[10] that the bread and the wine themselves were the 'pure offering' foretold by Malachi. Even

[1] E.g. *did.* 14, 3; Justin, *dial.* 41, 2 f.; Irenaeus, *haer.* 4, 17, 5.
[2] 14, 1.   [3] 40-4.   [4] 44, 4.   [5] *Philad.* 4.
[6] *Dial.* 117, 1.   [7] Ib. 41, 3.   [8] *Haer.* 4, 17, 5.
[9] *1 apol.* 66, 3: cf. *dial.* 41, 1.   [10] *Dial.* 41, 3.

if he holds[1] that 'prayers and thanksgivings' (εὐχαριστίαι) are the only God-pleasing sacrifices, we must remember that he uses[2] the term 'thanksgiving' as technically equivalent to 'the eucharistized bread and wine'. The bread and wine, moreover, are offered 'for a memorial (εἰς ἀνάμνησιν) of the passion', a phrase which in view of his identification of them with the Lord's body and blood implies much more than an act of purely spiritual recollection. Altogether it would seem that, while his language is not fully explicit, Justin is feeling his way to the conception of the eucharist as the offering of the Saviour's passion. Irenaeus's thought[3] moves along rather different lines and does not link the eucharist so closely with Christ's atoning death. When the bread and wine are offered to God, he thinks of them primarily as first-fruits of the earth which Christ has instructed us to offer, not because the Father needs them, but that we may not be found unfruitful or ungrateful. This is 'the oblation of the Church', and is well-pleasing to God as the expression of a sincere and faithful disposition. But the idea of the passion pervades this approach too, for Irenaeus identifies the gifts with Christ's body and blood and describes them, in language reminiscent of the Lord's words at the Last Supper, as 'the oblation of the new covenant'.

This leads us to consider the significance attached to the elements themselves in this period. From the *Didache*[4] we gather that the bread and wine are 'holy'; they are spiritual food and drink communicating immortal life. Ignatius roundly declares[5] that 'the eucharist is the flesh of our Saviour Jesus Christ, which suffered for our sins and which the Father in His goodness raised'. The bread is the flesh of Jesus, the cup His blood.[6] Clearly he intends this realism to be taken strictly, for he makes[7] it the basis of his argument against the Docetists' denial of the reality of Christ's body. Because the eucharist brings Christians into union with their Lord, it is the great bond between them;[8] and since it mediates communion with

---

[1] Ib. 117, 2.   [2] *1 apol.* 65, 3-5.
[3] Cf. esp. *haer.* 4, 17, 4-6; 4, 18, 1-6; 4, 33, 2; 5, 2, 2 f.
[4] 9, 5; 10, 3.   [5] *Smyrn.* 6, 2.   [6] *Rom.* 7, 3.
[7] *Smyrn.* 6 f.   [8] *Eph.* 13, 1; *Philad.* 4.

Christ, it is a medicine which procures immortality (φάρμακον
ἀθανασίας), an antidote against death which enables us to live
in the Lord forever.[1] Justin actually refers to the change. 'We
do not receive these', he writes,[2] 'as common bread or common
drink. But just as our Saviour Jesus Christ was made flesh
through the Word of God and had both flesh and blood for our
salvation, so also we have been taught that the food which has
been eucharistized by the word of prayer from Him (that food
which by process of assimilation nourishes our flesh and blood)
is the flesh and blood of the incarnate Jesus.' So Irenaeus
teaches[3] that the bread and wine are really the Lord's body and
blood. His witness is, indeed, all the more impressive because
he produces it quite incidentally while refuting the Gnostic
and Docetic rejection of the Lord's real humanity. Like Justin,
too, he seems to postulate a change, for he remarks:[4] 'Just as the
bread, which comes from the earth, when it receives the invoca-
tion of God, is no longer common bread but eucharist, being
composed of two elements, a terrestrial one and a celestial, so
our bodies are no longer commonplace when they receive the
eucharist, since they have the hope of resurrection to eternity'.

In contrast to baptism and the eucharist, our knowledge
about the Church's theology of penance in this early period
remains bafflingly meagre. Essentially the problem was that of
dealing with sins committed after baptism; sins committed
prior to baptism were of course remitted at the font. A powerful current of thought in the second-century Church favoured
the view that no remission was possible for sins deliberately
committed after baptism. The author of *Hebrews*,[5] it will
be recalled, had represented this standpoint, as had the author
of *1 John* when he forbade[6] prayer for what he called 'the
sin unto death'. So Hermas reports with[7] approval the opinion
of 'certain teachers' (he uses the technical term διδασκάλων)
that the only penance available to Christians is the one undergone in baptism, and Justin puts forward[8] the ideal of living

---

[1] *Eph.* 20, 2.   [2] *1 apol.* 66, 2.
[3] *Haer.* 4, 17, 5: cf. ib. 4, 18, 4; 5, 2, 3.   [4] Ib. 4, 18, 5: cf. ib. 5, 2, 3.
[5] 6, 4-6; 10, 26-31.   [6] 5, 16 f.
[7] *Mand.* 4, 3, 1.   [8] *Dial.* 44, 4.

sinless!

without sin once one has been baptized. On the other hand, there is abundant evidence in contemporary literature that a more lenient attitude was widely adopted in practice. Clement emphasizes[1] God's mercy and the desirability of repentance and confession. In the *Didache*[2] public, possibly corporate, confession of sin is prescribed, while Ignatius envisages[3] the reconciliation of schismatics after due repentance. Polycarp prays[4] that God may grant repentance to the fallen priest Valens and his wife, and expects the Philippian church to receive them back into fellowship. An unknown preacher urges[5] his auditors not to postpone their penitence until they are dead, 'when we can no longer confess and repent'. We are completely in the dark about the practical arrangements, if any, connected with this embryonic anticipation of penitential discipline. Its emergence, however, provoked a vigorous reaction, exemplified in the repudiation[6] by the Montanists of the power of the Church's ministers to forgive post-baptismal sin. Yet it is plain that pastoral considerations were making the old rigorism difficult to maintain. A striking illustration is provided by Hermas, who, while approving (as we have seen) the traditional attitude, proclaimed,[7] on the basis of revelation, a special second opportunity for repentance for older Christians. It was, we should note, limited to them, not being available either to the recently baptized or to future converts;[8] and even in their case it was a once-for-all indulgence which could not be repeated.[9] An important feature of it was that it apparently did not exclude those heinous sins (apostasy, adultery and murder) which were later to be treated as reserved, for Hermas explicitly states[10] that the adulterous wife should be taken back by her husband, if she is really sorry for her sin, and that apostates who have denied Christ with the mouth, if not the heart, can take advantage of the concession.

STRICT

Repentance Possible

---

[1] 7, 3-7; 18; 48, 1; 51, 3.   [2] 4, 14; 14, 1.
[3] *Philad.* 3, 2; 8, 1.   [4] *Phil.* 11, 4.
[5] 2 *Clem.* 8, 1-3.   [6] Cf. Tertullian, *de pud.* 21.
[7] *Vis.* 2, 2, 4 f.; 3, 5, 5; *mand.* 4, 3, 3-5; *sim.* 8, 9.   [8] *Mand.* 4, 3, 3.
[9] Ib. 4, 3, 6.   [10] Ib. 4, 1, 7 f.; *sim.* 9, 26, 5.

early Tertullian

church the mother

3. Developments in the Doctrine of the Church

While the third century was to see significant advances in the
theology of the Church, old-fashioned views were still to the
fore at the outset. Tertullian's conception, for example, at any
rate during his Catholic phase, hardly differed from that of
Irenaeus. 'We are a body', he writes,[1] 'knit together by the
bond of piety, by unity of discipline and by the contract of
hope.' There can only be one Church spread throughout the
world, just as there is one God, one Christ, one hope, one
baptism;[2] and this is the bride of Christ mentioned in Solomon's
Song,[3] the mother of Christians (*domina mater ecclesia*[4]). In this
latter thought can be discerned more than the germ of the later
axiom that only he who has the Church for his mother can
have God for his Father. Like Irenaeus again, as we have already
seen,[5] Tertullian insists that the Church is the unique home of
the Spirit, the sole repository of the apostolic revelation, with
its teaching guaranteed by the unbroken succession of bishops.
But these ideas underwent a radical transformation when, about
207, he joined the Montanists, and for the visible, hierarchically
constituted Church we find[6] him substituting a charismatic
society. He is even prepared at this stage to define the Church's
essential nature as Spirit. Such being its nature, he claims, it
must be pure and undefiled, composed exclusively of spiritual
men. The rigorist strain in him, which had always been present,
was thus given full rein, and he could argue that there can be no
difference between clergy and laity, since authority belongs to
those who possess the Spirit, and not to bishops as such.

Tertullian was not the only churchman to be attracted by
rigorism. Indeed, as we shall see in a later section, the prevailing
view at this time was that the graver sins were incapable of remission, and it is obvious that the conception of the Church's
nature and function corresponding to this must have been
equally strict. We find a strong expression of it in Hippolytus,

[1] *Apol.* 39, 1.   [2] *De virg. vel.* 2, 2.   [3] *C. Marc.* 4, 11.
[4] *Ad mart.* 1: cf. *de orat.* 2; *c. Marc.* 5, 4, 8.   [5] See above, p. 192.
[6] E.g. *de exhort. cast.* 7; *de pud.* 21.

Hippolytus

who, while picturing[1] the Church as Christ's bride, or again as a
ship sailing East through the billows of the world, envisages[2] it
as 'the holy society of those who live in righteousness'. There
is no place in it for heretics or sinners, as is demonstrated by its
Old Testament type, Susannah, who preferred death to defile-
ment. Rather the Church is the earthly Eden from which the
backslider who plunges into sin is extruded.[3] But other and
perhaps more characteristically Christian ideas were now gaining currency, their acceptance being commended by pastoral
necessity and the need of coping with the ever-growing swarm
of converts. With the enlargement of the penitential discipline,
which we shall shortly examine, a wider appreciation of the
Church's role was beginning to make headway; instead of regarding it as a community of saints, the new school of theologians looked upon it as a training-ground for sinners. There is
reason to suppose that Pope Callistus, when introducing his
reforms in penance, was fully conscious of the implications of
his more liberal attitude for ecclesiology. According to Hippolytus,[4] he appealed to the parable of the tares as suggesting
that sinners should be permitted to remain in the Church.
Further, he cited Noah's ark as a type of the Church, pointing
out that unclean as well as clean beasts found lodgment in it.

Meanwhile at Alexandria, as we might expect, while the
visible Church received its meed of recognition, the real focus
of interest tended to be the invisible Church of the true gnostic;
the treatment accorded to the earthly hierarchy was generally
perfunctory. Clement, for example, is ready enough to use
empirical categories and to distinguish[5] 'the ancient and Catholic
Church' from heretical conventicles. This is the Church in
which the apostolic tradition is enshrined, and to which those
whom God predestines to righteousness belong. Like God Himself, it is one;[6] it is also the virgin mother of Christians, feeding
them on the Logos as holy milk.[7] Imperceptibly, however, the
conception is spiritualized. The Church becomes 'the gathering

---

[1] *In cant.* 16; 19 (Achelis, 355 f.; 364; 369); *de antichr.* 59.
[2] *In Dan.* 1, 17.   [3] *Ib.* 1, 15 ff.   [4] *Ref.* 9, 12, 22 f.
[5] *Strom.* 7, 17, 107.   [6] *Paed.* 1, 4, 10.
[7] *Ib.* 1, 6, 42: cf. *ib.* 1, 5, 21.

of the elect',[1] an impregnable city ruled by the Logos;[2] and
he states[3] that the pious and righteous gnostics who teach and
do God's will are its true priests and deacons, even if they have
never been promoted to such office on earth. The earthly
Church, moreover, is a copy of the heavenly; that is why we
pray that God's will may be accomplished on earth as it is in
heaven.[4] The perfect gnostics, he writes,[5] 'will rest on God's
holy mountain, the Church on high ($\tau\hat{\eta}$ $\dot{a}\nu\omega\tau\dot{a}\tau\omega$ $\dot{\epsilon}\kappa\kappa\lambda\eta\sigma\dot{\iota}a$),
in which are assembled the philosophers of God, the authentic
Israelites who are pure in heart ... giving themselves over to the
pure intuition of unending contemplation'. It is this 'spiritual
Church' which is Christ's mystical body; such of its members
as still live like the heathen are, as it were, its flesh, while those
who truly cleave to the Lord and become one spirit with Him
form the holy Church in the real sense of the word.[6]

Platonizing influences[7] were clearly at work in Clement's
distinction between the visible but imperfect Church and the
perfect spiritual one, and we may expect to find Origen succumbing to them too. He has a firmer grasp than Clement of
the Church as an organized community, describing[8] it as 'the
congregation of Christian people' or 'the assembly of believers';
and he has a high opinion[9] of the office and responsibilities of
its ministers, and deplores[10] their all too frequent unworthiness.
The Church seems[11] to him a sort of world-wide republic, with
its own laws and constitution; it is, in fact, 'the city of God'
($\dot{\eta}$ $\pi\dot{o}\lambda\iota s$ $\tau o\hat{v}$ $\theta\epsilon o\hat{v}$[12]). It is also (he develops this idea more fully
than anyone before him) the body of Christ, being animated
by Him exactly as an ordinary body is animated by the soul,
and the faithful who belong to it are His members.[13] In this
mystical sense Christ's body comprises the whole of humanity,
indeed the whole of creation;[14] for according to Origen's teaching all creatures will ultimately be saved, and for that they

---

[1] Strom. 7, 5, 29.   [2] Ib. 4, 26, 172.   [3] Ib. 6, 13, 106 f.
[4] Ib. 4, 8, 66.   [5] Ib. 6, 14, 108.   [6] Ib. 7, 11, 68; 7, 14, 87 f.
[7] See above, pp. 15 f.   [8] Hom. in Ezech. 1, 11; in Exod. 9, 3.
[9] E.g. c. Cels. 8, 75; hom. in Ierem. 11, 3.
[10] E.g. hom. in Num. 2, 1.   [11] C. Cels. 4, 22.
[12] Hom. in Ierem. 9, 2; in Ios. 8, 7.
[13] C. Cels. 6, 48: cf. in Matt. 14, 17.   [14] Hom. in 36 ps. 2, 1.

must belong to the Church. Hence he can affirm[1] that on the last day, when death has been vanquished, the resurrection of Christ's veritable body will take place, and all those who are united to Him, after suffering crucifixion and death here, will be raised up so as to constitute a perfect man, according to the measure of the fulness of Christ's body.

All the time, however, there is an acute tension in his mind between the empirical Church here on earth and the ideal Church. In the former, he recognizes,[2] there are many merely apparent members, just as there were many Jebusites in Zion; but the true Church (ἡ κυρίως ἐκκλησία), in contrast, is as St. Paul described it, 'without spot or wrinkle', holy and blameless.[3] To it belong all who attain perfection here on earth, i.e. the τέλειοι who, according to Origen's mystical theology, become united to the Logos. This elect portion of the terrestrial Church is identified with 'the heavenly Church' (ἡ οὐράνιος ἐκκλησία), which Origen regards[4] as having existed since before creation. In this sense the Church is 'the assembly of all the saints', and its body is constituted by 'all those souls which have attained perfection'.[5] Many have inferred from his preoccupation with this spiritual Church that Origen did not in the last resort regard the true devotees of the Logos as belonging to the visible, hierarchical Church, but this is a perversion of his teaching. Despite the distinction he draws between the spiritual Church, the immaculate bride of Christ, and the earthly Church with all its defects, it remains his clear belief[6] that the two somehow coincide, and in several passages[7] he indicates that the spiritually advanced are the teachers or, as it were, 'the eyes' of the visible, empirical body. As the body of Christ, with the Logos animating it as its life-principle, the latter is 'an imitation of the coming kingdom',[8] and the true gnostics form its spiritual core.

From the mystical, sometimes elusive, theorizing of Alexandria we turn to Cyprian, whose conception of the Church

the ideal & the visible coincide some

[1] *In Ioh.* 10, 35 f., 229-38.   [2] *In Matt.* 12, 12; *hom. in Ios.* 21, 1.
[3] *De orat.* 20, 1.   [4] *In Cant.* 2 (Baehrens, 157).
[5] Ib. 1; 3 (Baehrens, 90; 232).   [6] E.g. ib. 3 (Baehrens, 176 f.).
[7] E.g. ib. 2 (Baehrens, 154 f.).   [8] *De princ.* 1, 6, 2.

Cyprian

and ministry was to dominate the West until Augustine's time, and at once find ourselves breathing a different atmosphere. For all his profound sense of the Church as a spiritual entity, his approach was practical and even legalistic, owing much to analogies borrowed from Roman law and conditioned by the problems created by the Novatianist schism. This was a rigorist, doctrinally orthodox movement, representing the party which advocated severity towards those who had lapsed in the Decian persecution and now wished to resume Church membership, and so Cyprian was obliged to find some other basis for unity than strict orthodoxy of teaching.

In all his discussions his unquestioned premiss is the assumption that the Catholic Church not only ought to be, but in fact is, one. The 'unity handed down by the Lord through the apostles'[1] was prefigured, he holds,[2] in the Old Testament, was implied by Christ's seamless robe, was proclaimed by the apostle Paul, and was the object of the Saviour's high-priestly prayer. It was grounded in the very nature and being of God.[3] The question before Cyprian, faced as he was with seceders whose creed was unexceptionable, was how this unity was expressed and where its guarantee was to be discerned. For an *episcopate* answer he points to the episcopate, arguing that, considered as a whole and in its individual members, this is the God-given principle of unity in the Church. The bishops stand in the place of the apostles, not only in the sense that they are their lineal successors, but that like them they have been chosen and established in their offices by the Lord's special decree.[4] Moreover, the bishops, each presiding in a diocese which is the whole Church in microcosm, form a college, for the episcopate itself is one and indivisible, and the several bishops enjoy the plenitude of it exactly as shareholders do of a joint property (*episcopatus unus est, cuius a singulis in solidum pars tenetur*[5]). Hence the Church is founded on the bishops;[6] it is 'united and held together by the glue of the mutual cohesion of the

---

[1] *Ep.* 45, 3. [2] E.g. *de unit. eccl.* 4; 7 f.; *ep.* 75, 3.
[3] *De unit. eccl.* 23. [4] E.g. *ep.* 8, 1; 59, 5; 69, 5.
[5] *De unit. eccl.* 5: cf. *ep.* 55, 24. [6] *Ep.* 33, 1.

bishops';[1] but the theory implies, as Cyprian made plain,[2] that
each bishop is entitled to hold his own views and to administer
his own diocese accordingly, and that the principle of charitable
respect for each other's opinions must be maintained.

In proof of the unity Cyprian appeals[3] to Christ's commission to St. Peter recorded in *Matt.* 16, 18 f. and His words
to the apostles generally reported in *John* 20, 21 f. His argument seems to be that, although the Lord was founding a col-
legiate episcopate, He deliberately gave His mandate to St.
Peter alone in the first instance so as to establish conclusively
the principle of unity in the Church from the start. In view of
its importance the passage must be quoted: 'The Lord said to
Peter, "I tell you, you are Peter ...". Thus He built His Church
upon a single man; and although after His resurrection He
assigned equal authority to all the apostles, saying, "As the
Father sent me, so send I you ...", nevertheless in order to
bring out the Church's unity vividly, He so ordered the origin
of that unity as to make it begin with a single man. Assuredly
the other apostles were all exactly what Peter was, equipped
with an equal share of honour and authority; but a beginning
was made from unity, so that the oneness of Christ's Church
might be manifested.' If this is the true text, it supports the col-
legiate conception of the episcopate which Cyprian advocates
elsewhere, only adding that St. Peter was the starting-point
and symbol of unity. There is no suggestion that he possessed
any superiority to, much less jurisdiction over, the other
apostles, any more than in the numerous other contexts[4] in
which the Church's unity is traced to him. There exists, however, another (the so-called 'Papal') version of the passage
which (a) speaks of the setting up of 'one chair' (*unam cathe-
dram*) and of the giving of a primacy to Peter (*primatus Petro
datur*), and (b) omits the mention of the other apostles' being
armed with the same authority as he. It seems likely that this
too comes from Cyprian's pen, being earlier than the *textus*

---

[1] Ib. 66, 8.
[2] Ib. 72, 3: cf. *sent. episcop.* praef. in Augustine, *de bapt.* 6, 9.
[3] *De unit. eccl.* 4.
[4] E.g. *ep.* 33, 1; 43, 5; 66, 8; 73, 7: cf. 75, 17 (by Firmilian).

receptus and representing his attitude prior to his dispute with Pope Stephen on the necessity of rebaptizing heretics and schismatics. The use made of it by Stephen's supporters in order to assert the authority of Rome over other sees may well have induced him to modify it in favour of a less awkward version. Even the 'Papal text', however, does not necessarily conflict with his general teaching, viz. that the Church's unity is to be found in the consensus of the collective episcopate. While he is prepared, in a well-known passage,[1] to speak of Rome as 'the leading church', the primacy he has in mind seems to be one of honour. At any rate he lays it down, a few lines later, that 'each of the shepherds (i.e. bishops) has had a portion of the flock assigned to him to rule and govern, and will have to render an account of his charge to the Lord'.

Cyprian does not hesitate to draw the logical corollaries from his theory. The criterion of Church membership is no longer, as for Irenaeus, acceptance of the teaching guaranteed by the episcopate as apostolic, but submission to the bishop himself.[2] Rebellion against him is rebellion against God,[3] and the schismatic, however correct his doctrine or virtuous his life, renounces Christ, bears arms against His Church and resists God's ordinances.[4] In effect he is a heretic, so that Cyprian can write[5] of Novatian himself: 'We are not interested in what he teaches, since he teaches outside the Church. Whatever and whatsoever kind of man he is, he is not a Christian who is not in Christ's Church.' And, since 'he cannot have God for his Father who has not the Church for his mother',[6] there is no salvation outside the Church (*salus extra ecclesiam non est*[7]). It goes without saying that outside the Church sacraments are impossible (e.g. 'the oblation cannot be consecrated where the Spirit is not present'[8]), and in particular that baptism by schismatics or heretics is invalid. On this last point, as is well known, Cyprian met with strong opposition at Rome, where Pope Stephen argued[9] on the basis of tradition that baptized

---

[1] *Ep.* 59, 14. [2] Ib. 49, 2. [3] Ib. 66, 1. [4] *De unit. eccl.* 17.
[5] *Ep.* 55, 24. [6] *De unit. eccl.* 6. [7] *Ep.* 73, 21.
[8] Ib. 65, 4: cf. ib. 67, 3; 72, 2. [9] Ib. 74, 1 (quoting Stephen).

heretics entering the Church needed only the imposition of
hands. If his doctrine seems harsh and legalist, it was only the
obverse of his passionate conviction that the Church was the
body of Christ, pulsing with the life of the Spirit, and that to
claim the grace of Christ and His Spirit outside its frontiers
was at once presumptuous and illogical. Further, schism in his
eyes[1] was the mark of pride, selfishness and partisan feeling,
just as the unity which he saw expressed in the episcopal hierarchy was the outcome and manifestation of charity.

4. Baptism in the Third Century

Speculation about baptism in the third century revolves
around its function, universally admitted hitherto, as the
medium of the bestowal of the Spirit. Infant baptism was now
common, and this fact, together with the rapid expansion of
the Church's numbers, caused the administration of the sacrament to be increasingly delegated by bishops to presbyters.
The existence of schismatics, as we have seen, raised the problem of their rebaptism on joining the Church. Ever-growing
importance, consequently, was coming to be attached to the
subsidiary rites associated with baptism—chrismation, or
anointing with the sign of the cross, and the laying on of
hands. We observe a tendency to limit the effect of baptism
itself to the remission of sins and regeneration, and to link the
gift of the Spirit with these other rites.

Let us look first at the East, where conservative ideas persisted longer. Clement of Alexandria speaks[2] of baptism as
imparting regeneration, enlightenment, divine sonship, immortality, remission of sins; the sonship, he explains,[3] is the
result of the regeneration worked by the Spirit. Baptism im-
prints a seal, or stamp, which is in fact the Spirit, the image of
God;[4] the indwelling Spirit is a 'shining impress' ($\chi\alpha\rho\alpha\kappa\tau\acute{\eta}\rho$)
of the Christian's membership of Christ.[5] As he nowhere hints
at any liturgical rite of unction or the imposition of hands, we

---

[1] De zel. et liv. 6.   [2] Paed. 1, 6, 26.   [3] Ib. 1, 5, 21.
[4] Excerpta Theod. 86, 2.   [5] Strom. 4, 18, 116.

may reasonably infer that he regards baptism itself as mediating the Spirit. Origen lays much greater stress on the inward significance and spiritual efficacy of baptism, and has a firmer hold on the biblical doctrine. For example, he insists[1] on penitence, sincere faith and humility as its prerequisites, as well as on the gradualness with which it transforms the soul. In it, he believes,[2] the Christian is united with Christ in His death and resurrection. It is the unique means of obtaining remission of sins;[3] it frees us from the power of the Devil and makes us members of the Church as Christ's body.[4] Even little children, he assumes,[5] being defiled with sin, must be baptized. His normal teaching[6] is that the Spirit is received in baptism, the convert being 'baptized in Christ, in the water and the Holy Spirit'. The Spirit descends upon the Christian at his baptism as upon Christ at His, and he becomes 'pneumatic'.[7] It is plain, however, that he finds such passages as *Acts* 8, 17 puzzling, and is sometimes led to distinguish[8] between 'the grace and regeneration of baptism' and the gift of the Spirit mediated by apostolic hands. But it would be a mistake to regard him, even in these moods, as dividing Christian initiation into two separate rites. Rather he stresses its unity, placing all the emphasis on the inward effects, and treating such features as the imposition of hands and chrismation as subordinate aspects of a single rite.

When we turn to the West, we discover a growing readiness to focus the gift of the Spirit on the later rites. Hippolytus, it is true, generally preserves the traditional theology, associating[9] both remission of sins and the reception of the Spirit with baptism. He provides valuable evidence, however, of the importance which other ceremonies, e.g. the laying on of the bishop's hand with prayer, and unction with oil, were now assuming, and on occasion links[10] the reception of the Spirit

---

[1] *Hom. in Lev.* 6, 2; *in Luc.* 21; *in Exod.* 10, 4.
[2] *Hom. in Ierem.* 19, 14.   [3] *Exhort. ad mart.* 30.
[4] *Hom. in Exod.* 5, 5; *in Rom.* 8, 5.   [5] *In Rom.* 5, 9; *hom. in Luc.* 14.
[6] *De princ.* 2, 10, 7; *hom. in Exod.* 5, 5.   [7] *Hom. in Luc.* 22; 27.
[8] E.g. *de princ.* 1, 3, 7.   [9] E.g. *trad. apost.* 22, 1 f. (Latin version).
[10] E.g. *in Dan.* 1, 16.

with the latter. Tertullian carries us a stage further. Baptism, he holds,[1] is necessary to salvation; following Christ's example, we are born in the water, and can only be saved by remaining in it. It is administered to children, although he personally prefers[2] that it should be postponed until they reach years of discretion. It cannot be repeated, the only exception being the case of the baptism of heretics, who have never received true baptism anyway.[3] Its effects include remission of sins, liberation from death, rebirth and the gift of the Spirit.[4] The view that the Spirit is received in baptism comes out strongly in the opening chapters of his treatise on the sacrament, but he later changes his mind, remarking,[5] 'Not that we receive the Holy Spirit in the water, but after being restored in the water we are prepared under an angel for the Holy Spirit'. Later still he speaks[6] of the bishop's hand, when imposed in blessing, 'summoning and invoking the Holy Spirit', and supports his theory by the implied typology of *Gen.* 48, 14 (where Jacob lays his hands in blessing on Ephraim's and Manasseh's heads) and by the episode of the Ephesian disciples in *Acts* 19. Similar teaching is to be found elsewhere[7] in his writings, and his theology seems to have remained confused.

By Cyprian's time the development had reached its logical term. The conservative viewpoint still had important advocates at Rome, such as the theologian Novatian. The Spirit, he taught,[8] is the active force we experience in baptism, regenerating and dwelling in us with His personal presence, giving us a foretaste of eternal life and preparing us for immortality; and he altogether ignored confirmation. The more general Roman teaching, however, was now in advance of this and was tending to identify the gift of the Spirit with the rites which followed the baptism in water. Pope Cornelius (251-3), we note, criticized[9] Novatian, who had been baptized by affusion on what was thought to be his death-bed, for not supplementing this by being 'sealed' at the hands of a bishop:

---

[1] *De bapt.* 1; 12-15. [2] Ib. 18. [3] *De pud.* 19.
[4] *De bapt.* 1; 18; *c. Marc.* 1, 28. [5] *De bapt.* 6. [6] Ib. 8; 10.
[7] E.g. *de res. carn.* 8. [8] *De trin.* 29.
[9] Cf. Eusebius, *hist. eccl.* 6, 43, 15.

'since he failed to obtain this, how could he have obtained the Holy Spirit?' Much the same theology may be assumed to lie behind Pope Stephen's (254–7) willingness, as against Cyprian, to recognize the validity of schismatical baptism; with the weakening of the significance of baptism itself, the result in part of its delegation to presbyters, the importance of the imposition of hands or of sealing with chrism, which were reserved to the bishop, became enhanced. The unknown author of the anti-Cyprianic tract *De rebaptismate*, written in N. Africa about 256, makes[1] the demarcation between baptism (*baptisma aquae*) and the laying on of hands (*baptisma Spiritus*, or *spiritale*) complete, designating them as 'the less' and 'the greater' respectively. Appealing to *Acts* 8, 17; 9, 17; 19, 6, he describes water-baptism as 'a maimed, incomplete mystery of faith', and suggests[2] that confirmation (if we may so term it) is what bestows the Spirit and, apparently, remission of sins as well, and that salvation is bound up with it. The cheapening of baptism proper could go no further, and we can understand why he did not think it necessary to rebaptize schismatics so long as they accepted the episcopal laying on of hands.

Cyprian's own position is not without ambiguity. Through the washing with water, he holds,[3] the convert is reborn to newness of life, and this is the result of the Spirit's descent. He explicitly affirms[4] that 'the Spirit is received in baptism, and when they have been baptized and have obtained the Holy Spirit converts draw near to drink the Lord's cup'. Even infants, according to their capacity, receive the Spirit in baptism;[5] and as against Cornelius he contends[6] strongly that those who have been only clinically baptized in sickness (thereby missing, presumably, the bishop's laying on of hands and anointing) have received the Holy Spirit no less than their fellows who have undergone the full public rite. All this is old-fashioned doctrine, and it coheres with his insistence on the rebaptism of heretics and schismatics. At times, however, influenced no doubt by the

---

[1] *De rebapt.* 11; 6 ad fin.   [2] Ib. 5.   [3] *Ad Donat.* 3 f.
[4] *Ep.* 63, 8.   [5] Ib. 64, 3.   [6] Ib. 69, 13 f.

current custom of getting the bishop to lay his hand on the newly baptized as well as by his reading of the notorious texts in *Acts*, he wavers and attributes[1] the gift of the Spirit to the imposition of hands and the signing with the cross. He even interprets[2] *John* 3, 5, with its reference to being born again by water and the Spirit, as if it implied two sacraments. As compared with his contemporaries, however, Cyprian must count as a conservative who resisted the fashionable tendency to recognize two entirely distinct rites, and endeavoured rather to hold them together as two different aspects of Christian initiation.

5. Progress in Eucharistic Doctrine

In the third century the early Christian identification of the eucharistic bread and wine with the Lord's body and blood continued unchanged, although a difference of approach can be detected in East and West. The outline, too, of a more considered theology of the eucharistic sacrifice begins to appear.

In the West the equation of the consecrated elements with the body and blood was quite straightforward, although the fact that the presence is sacramental was never forgotten. Hippolytus speaks[3] of 'the body and the blood' through which the Church is saved, and Tertullian regularly describes[4] the bread as 'the Lord's body'. The converted pagan, he remarks,[5] 'feeds on the richness of the Lord's body, that is, on the eucharist'. The realism of his theology comes to light in the argument,[6] based on the intimate relation of body and soul, that just as in baptism the body is washed with water so that the soul may be cleansed, so in the eucharist 'the flesh feeds on Christ's body and blood so that the soul may be filled with God'. Clearly his assumption is that the Saviour's body and blood are as real as the baptismal water. Cyprian's attitude is similar. Lapsed Christians who claim communion without doing penance, he declares,[7] 'do violence to His body and blood,

---

[1] Ib. 73, 9.   [2] Ib. 72, 1.
[3] Frag. arab. *in Gen.* 38, 19 (Achelis, 96).
[4] E.g. *de orat.* 19; *de idol.* 7.   [5] *De pud.* 9.
[6] *De res. carn.* 8.   [7] *De laps.* 16: cf. *ep.* 15, 1.

and sin more heinously against the Lord with their hands and mouths than when they denied Him'. Later he expatiates[1] on the terrifying consequences of profaning the sacrament, and the stories he tells confirm that he took the real presence literally. So, when he comments on the Lord's Prayer, he states[2] that Christ is our bread 'because He is the bread of us who touch His body'; and elsewhere he argues[3] that prospective martyrs should be fortified 'with the protection of Christ's body and blood. . . . For how can we teach or incite them to shed their own blood in confessing the Name if, as they set out on their service, we refuse them the blood of Christ?'

Occasionally these writers use language which has been held to imply that, for all its realist sound, their use of the terms 'body' and 'blood' may after all be merely symbolical. Tertullian, for example, refers[4] to the bread as 'a figure' (*figura*) of Christ's body, and once speaks[5] of 'the bread by which He represents (*repraesentat*) His very body'. Yet we should be cautious about interpreting such expressions in a modern fashion. According to ancient modes of thought a mysterious relationship existed between the thing symbolized and its symbol, figure or type; the symbol in some sense *was* the thing symbolized. Again, the verb *repraesentare*, in Tertullian's vocabulary,[6] retained its original significance of 'to make present'. All that his language really suggests is that, while accepting the equation of the elements with the body and blood, he remains conscious of the sacramental distinction between them. In fact, he is trying, with the aid of the concept of *figura*, to rationalize to himself the apparent contradiction between (a) the dogma that the elements are now Christ's body and blood, and (b) the empirical fact that for sensation they remain bread and wine. Similarly, when Cyprian states[7] that 'in the wine Christ's blood is shown' (*in vino vero ostendi sanguinem Christi*), we should recall that in the context he is arguing against heretics who wilfully use water instead of wine at the eucharist. In choosing

---

[1] *De laps.* 25 f.   [2] *De orat. dom.* 18.   [3] *Ep.* 57, 2.
[4] E.g. *c. Marc.* 3, 19; 4, 40.   [5] Ib. 1, 14: cf. Hippolytus, *apost. trad.* 32, 3.
[6] Cf. ib. 4, 22; *de monog.* 10.   [7] *Ep.* 63, 13: cf. ib. 63, 2.

the term 'is shown', therefore, he is not hinting that the wine merely symbolizes the sacred blood. His point is simply that wine is an essential ingredient of the eucharist, since numerous Old Testament texts point to it as a type of the precious blood. It is significant that only a few lines above[1] he had spoken of 'drinking the Lord's blood'.

A different situation confronts us when we turn to the Alexandrian fathers, for, while they verbally reproduce the conventional realism, their bias to allegory and their Platonizing absorption in the spiritual world behind phenomena alter their perspective. Clement frequently writes in terms of the equivalence of the elements with Christ's body and blood, in one passage[2] representing Him as identifying them with Himself. To drink Jesus's blood, he states,[3] is to participate in His incorruptibility; the eucharistic wine is a mingling ($\kappa\rho\hat{a}\sigma\iota s$) of the Logos with material substance, and those who drink it are sanctified in body and soul. More often than not, however, what seems a firm reference to the eucharist dissolves into an allegory of the true gnostic's knowledge; feeding on the flesh and blood of the Logos means apprehending the divine power and essence.[4] Origen's teaching is of a piece with this, only clearer. He is prepared to speak[5] of Christ giving His body and blood to Christians, and informs[6] Celsus that 'we consume bread which by virtue of the prayer has become body, a holy thing which sanctifies those who use it with a sound purpose'. He commends[7] the reverence shown to the consecrated elements, and emphasizes[8] the wrongness of approaching the body and blood with traitorous feelings towards one's brethren or thoughts otherwise impure. In the sacrament he seems[9] to distinguish two aspects, the corruptible matter which passes through the communicant and the incorruptible reality which sanctifies him. Much more important in his eyes, however, than this 'typical and symbolical body', as he designates[10] the consecrated bread, is the Logos Himself, Who became flesh and is

---

[1] Ib. 63, 11.   [2] Quis div. 23, 4.   [3] Paed. 2, 2, 20.

[4] Strom. 5, 10, 66.   [5] Hom. in Ierem. 19, 13.   [6] C. Cels. 8, 33.

[7] Hom. in Exod. 13, 3.   [8] In Matt. comm. ser. 82; hom. in 37 ps. 2, 6.

[9] In Matt. 11, 14.   [10] Ib.

Origen on eucharist

Eucharist for the dead

our authentic food. A host of passages[1] suggest that for him Christ's body and blood signify, in a deeper and more spiritual sense, His teaching, the ineffable truth which He reveals and which nourishes and sustains the soul. The outward rite, he implies,[2] which imparts the sacramental body and blood, is for the simpler grade of Christians, while the more advanced, with their profounder insight, find nourishment in the Logos Himself.

The eucharist was also, of course, the great act of worship of Christians, their sacrifice. The writers and liturgies of the period are unanimous in recognizing it as such. Clement applies[3] the term 'sacrifice' ($\pi\rho\sigma\phi\rho\alpha$) to it, citing Melchizedek's offering as its type. Tertullian defines[4] the priestly function as one of 'offering' (*offerre*); the 'offering of the sacrifice'[5] is as much a Christian occasion to him as the preaching of the Word. Though the first to mention[6] it, he treats the offering of the eucharist for the dead (*oblationes pro defunctis*) as one of the established customs which tradition has hallowed. What the sacrifice consists in, he does not specify. No doubt he views[7] it primarily as an offering of prayer and worship, but worship in the context of the Saviour's passion and of the elements which 'represent' His sacrificed body and blood. Hippolytus is a little more definite, speaking[8] of it as the new sacrifice foretold by Malachi, 'the sacrifice and libation which are now offered'. In his eyes it commemorates the Last Supper and the passion; the bread and the cup are offered in it, but only after the celebrant has recalled the Lord's words and actions at the Supper. The whole is 'the oblation of the holy Church', its object being that Christians may praise and glorify God through His incarnate Son.[9] Origen presupposes[10] the idea of the eucharist as a sacrifice of first-fruits and prayers to the Creator; but at the same time he argues[11] that the Christian rite

[1] E.g. *hom. in Lev.* 7, 5; *hom. in Num.* 16, 9; 23, 6; *in Matt. comm. ser.* 85; *de orat.* 27, 1-5. [2] *In Ioh.* 32, 24, 310.
[3] *Strom.* 1, 19, 96; 4, 25, 161. [4] *De virg. vel.* 9.
[5] *De cult. fem.* 2, 11. [6] *De cor.* 3; *de monog.* 10; *de exhort. cast.* 11.
[7] Cf. *apol.* 30; *de orat. dom.* 28; *ad Scap.* 2.
[8] *In Cant.* 3, 4; *in Dan.* 4, 35. [9] *Trad. apost.* (Latin version), 4.
[10] *C. Cels.* 8, 33 f. [11] *Hom. in Lev.* 9, 10.

replaces the propitiatory sacrifices of Israel. The shew-bread of Israel, for example, was a type of Christ and the eucharistic bread; and it is the commemoration of His sacrifice in the eucharist which alone makes God propitious to men.[1] What he says, however, must be read with discernment, for the deeper meaning which he himself perceives[2] behind the Church's sacrificial system is the surrender of the heart to God.

Cyprian was the first to expound something like a theory of the eucharistic sacrifice. While he regularly uses the terms 'sacrifice' and 'oblation', and even refers[3] once to 'the dominical victim' (*dominica hostia*), his views receive fullest expression in *Ep.* 63, in which he sets out to refute certain heretics (Aquarians) who celebrated with water instead of wine. Running through this is the key-thought[4] that the eucharist should exactly reproduce Christ's action and intention at the Last Supper. Hence the Aquarians must be wrong since, apart from violating ancient prophecy, 'they do not do what Jesus Christ, our Lord and God, the institutor and teacher of this sacrifice, did and taught'. In harmony with this idea Cyprian implies[5] that the priest acts as the representative of Christ, our high-priest, so that 'he fulfils the role of Christ when he imitates what He did, and only then does he offer a true, complete sacrifice in the Church to the Father when he begins to offer it after the pattern of Christ's offering'. Since Christ's offering consisted in the surrender of Himself in His passion, it is clear that His passion must be the object of our sacrificial offering too. As Cyprian expresses[6] it, 'As to our mentioning His passion in all our sacrifices—for it is in the Lord's passion that our sacrifice consists (*passio est enim domini sacrificium quod offerimus*)—we ought to do nothing other than He Himself did'. The priest, it would appear, sacramentally re-enacts the oblation of His passion which the Saviour originally presented to the Father. Further, it is clear from what he says elsewhere about offering it on behalf of people in need,[7] and especially on behalf of the

Cyprian

---

[1] Ib. 13, 3.   [2] E.g. ib. 4 f.   [3] *De unit. eccl.* 17.
[4] *Ep.* 63, 1.   [5] Ib. 14.   [6] Ib. 17.   [7] Ib. 15, 1; 17, 2.

dead,[1] that Cyprian conceived of the eucharistic sacrifice as possessing objective efficacy.

A further point Cyprian makes[2] is that, when Christ suffered for us and thus offered His sacrifice, we were in Him inasmuch as He was bearing our sins. Thus in His physical body and blood the people of God were being offered to the Father. In the eucharist there is a parallel union between Christ and His people, so that the rite is in effect the offering of the whole Church, both its Head and the faithful who in it have been made one with Him.

6. *The Penitential Discipline*

No Private Penance

With the dawn of the third century the rough outlines of a recognized penitential discipline were beginning to take shape. In spite of the ingenious arguments of certain scholars,[3] there are still no signs of a sacrament of private penance (i.e. confession to a priest, followed by absolution and the imposition of a penance) such as Catholic Christendom knows to-day. The system which seems to have existed in the Church at this time, and for centuries afterwards, was wholly public, involving confession, a period of penance and exclusion from communion, and formal absolution and restoration—the whole process being called *exomologesis*. The last of these was normally bestowed by the bishop, as Hippolytus's prayer[4] of episcopal consecration implies, but in his absence might be delegated to a priest. There is plenty of evidence[5] that sinners were encouraged to open their hearts privately to a priest, but nothing to show that this led up to anything more than ghostly counsel. Indeed, for the lesser sins which even good Christians daily commit and can scarcely avoid, no ecclesiastical censure seems to have been thought necessary; individuals were expected to deal with them themselves by prayer, almsgiving and mutual forgiveness.[6] Public penance was for graver sins; it was, as far as we

[1] *Ep.* 1, 2; 12, 2; 39, 3.   [2] Ib. 63, 13.
[3] E.g. P. Galtier, *L'Église et la rémission des péchés* (Paris, 1932).
[4] *Trad. apost.* 3, 5.
[5] E.g. Origen, *hom. in Num.* 10, 1; *hom. in 37 ps.* 2, 6.
[6] Cf. Origen, *hom. in Lev.* 2, 4.

know, universal, and was an extremely solemn affair, capable
of being undergone only once in a lifetime. So Tertullian,
when still a Catholic, speaks[1] of a second penance (second, that
is, after the original one involved in baptism) available to all
once (*iam semel . . . sed amplius nusquam*), but which it would be
hazardous to presume upon; and Clement, after quoting what
Hermas had said[2] about the one and only penance possible
after baptism, does his best to show[3] that this ought to be
sufficient and that to permit more than one such penance would
spell disaster. Origen characterizes[4] this public penance as 'the
hard and laborious remission of sins through penance when the
sinner is not ashamed to reveal his sins to the priest of the Lord
and ask for a cure'.

The most noteworthy advance in the theology of penance
in the third century was in connexion with the Church's attitude to certain sins esteemed particularly heinous. In the last
decades of the second century adultery, homicide and idolatry
(or apostasy) seem to have been treated in practice, if not
in theory, as irremissible, even by means of the once-for-all
exomologesis described above. Some have doubted whether this
was in fact the case, but even allowing for a good deal of local
variation it is difficult to resist the impression that it was, at any
rate in many important centres. Certainly Hippolytus, protesting[5] against Callistus's innovations, and Tertullian[6] in his later
Montanist phase took it for granted that it had been the
Church's practice to reserve such sins hitherto. Origen supplies[7]
confirmatory evidence for the East, explaining that, under the
guidance of the Holy Spirit, the good bishop 'forgives whatever sins God forgives, but reserves others which are incurable'
(ἀνίατα). He quotes 1 *Sam.* 2, 25 ('If a man sin against the
Lord, who shall intreat for him?'), a classic text in discussions
about penance, and adds that idolatry, adultery and fornication
figure among these sins for which there is no remedy. Cyprian
is an important witness, for he shows[8] (a) that, while sexual sins

---

[1] *De paen.* 7, 10.   [2] See above, p. 199.   [3] *Strom.* 2, 13, 56–9.
[4] Loc. cit.   [5] *Ref.* 9, 12, 20–26.   [6] *De pud.* passim.
[7] *De orat.* 28, 8 f.   [8] *Ep.* 55, 20 f.

were remissible at Carthage in his day, there had previously been disputes on the subject; and (b) that idolatry, irremissible in the past, only came to be included among sins capable of forgiveness as a result of the Decian persecution.

We can only obtain spasmodic glimpses of the steps by which this severity came to be relaxed. Pope Callistus, it appears, took an important initiative. From a highly prejudiced report[1] left by Hippolytus we gather that he was the first to adopt, as a matter of Church policy, a more generous attitude towards the sins of the flesh. For authority he appealed to the parable of the tares (*Matt.* 13, 24-30), the Apostle's sharp question (*Rom.* 14, 4), 'Who are you to judge another man's servant?', and the mixed assortment of animals in Noah's ark; all these, he argued, suggested that there should be room for sinners in the Church. Shortly after this we find Tertullian indignantly upbraiding[2] a bishop who had published a 'peremptory edict' to the effect that he was prepared to grant absolution, due penance having been done, to persons guilty of adultery or fornication. Although a case has been made out for his being Agrippinus, the local bishop of Carthage, the more usual assumption that Tertullian was hitting at Callistus is probably correct. This more indulgent practice soon established itself, for as we have indicated Cyprian frankly admits,[3] 'We allow adulterers an opportunity of penance and grant them absolution'. As regards idolatry, his *Testimonia*, compiled before the outbreak of the Decian persecution, clearly shows[4] that at that date it was still considered an irremissible sin. In 251, however, at a council held when the persecution had died down, the policy approved was more merciful,[5] viz. that *libellatici*, i.e. people who had satisfied the State by merely producing certificates that they had fulfilled its requirements, should be readmitted at once, while *sacrificati*, i.e. people who had actually offered the sacrifices prescribed by the imperial edict, should undergo lifelong penance and be readmitted on their deathbed.

[1] Loc. cit.   [2] *De pud.* 1, 6: also passim.
[3] *Ep.* 55, 20.   [4] 3, 28.   [5] *Ep.* 55, 6 and 17.

The days of rigorism were far from being over. An apt illustration of the persistence of old-fashioned severity is provided by the Spanish council of Elvira (303), which is chiefly memorable for the large number of canons[1] it promulgated, ordering lifelong excommunication without hope of reconciliation even at death. Nevertheless a more compassionate attitude, more appreciative of human frailty and more in tune with the spirit of the Gospels, was steadily gaining ground. It received a fine expression in the *Didascalia Apostolorum*, a Syrian document dating from the middle of the third century. Here the Christian ideal that baptism ought to be the one and only penance is amply recognized:[2] 'it is known to all that whosoever does evil after baptism, the same is condemned to the Gehenna of fire'. At the same time the bishop is exhorted[3] to reconcile all repentant sinners—idolaters, murderers and adulterers included. He is depicted[4] as sitting in the Church as a judge appointed by God and charged by Him with the power of binding and loosing. His authority is from on high, and he should be loved like a father, feared like a king and honoured as God.

[1] Mansi II, pp. 6 ff.   [2] 2, 7.   [3] 2, 23.   [4] 2, 18 f.

NOTE ON BOOKS

The Church. G. Bardy, *La Théologie de l'Église*, Vols. I and II (Paris, 1945 and 1947); P. Batiffol, *L'Église naissante* (Paris, 9 ed. 1927); M. Bévenot, 'Saint Cyprian's *De unitate*, Chap. IV, in the Light of the Manuscripts' (in *Analecta Gregoriana*, 1938); 'St. Cyprian on the Papacy' (art. in *Journ. Theol. Stud.*, 1954); E. W. Benson, *Saint Cyprian* (London, 1897); J. Chapman, 'Les Interpolations dans le traité de s. Cyprien sur l'unité de l'Église' (art. in *Rev. Bén.*, 1902-3); J. Daniélou, *The Theology of Jewish Christianity*, chap. 10 (Eng. trans., London, 1964); R. P. C. Hanson, '*Potentiorem principalitatem* in Irenaeus iii, 3, 1' (*Studia Patristica* III: Berlin, 1961); W. L. Knox, 'Irenaeus, *Adv. Haer.* 3, 3, 2' (art. in *Journ. Theol. Stud.*, 1946); H. Koch, 'Cyprian und der römische Primat' (in *Texte und Untersuchungen*, XXXV, 1910); A. Lieske, *Die Theologie der Logosmystik des Origenes*, pp. 74-98 (Münster i. W., 1938); C. H. Marrou, 'Le témoignage de saint Irénée sur l'église de Rome' (*Studi in onore di A. Pincherle*: Rome, 1967); Ch. Mohrmann,

'A propos de Irenaeus, *Adv. haer.* 3, 3, 1' (*Vig. Christ.* 3, 1949); J. C. Plumpe, *Mater Ecclesia* (Washington, 1943); D. Stone, *The Christian Church* (London, 1905); H. B. Swete (ed.), *Essays on the Early History of the Church and Ministry* (London, 1918).

Baptism. J. G. Davies, 'The Disintegration of the Christian Initiation Rite' (art. in *Theology,* 1947); G. Dix, *The Theology of Confirmation in Relation to Baptism* (London, 1946); G. W. H. Lampe, *The Seal of the Spirit* (London, 2 ed. 1967); P. Lundberg, *La Typologie baptismale dans l'ancienne Église* (Uppsala, 1942); A. J. Mason, *The Relation of Confirmation to Baptism* (London, 2 ed. 1893); P. B. Neunheuser, *Taufe und Firmung* (*Handbuch der Dogmengeschichte* IV, 2, 1956).

Eucharist. P. Batiffol, *L'Eucharistie: la présence réelle* (Paris, rev. ed. 1913); J. Betz, *Die Eucharistie in der Zeit der Griechischen Väter* (Freiburg, 1958); A. Gaudel, 'Messe' (art. in *Dict. Théol. Cath.*); C. Gore, *The Body of Christ* (London, 3 ed. 1903); F. Kattenbusch, 'Messe' (art. in Hauck's *Realencyk.*); F. Loofs, 'Abendmahl' (art. in Hauck's *Realencyk.*); J. H. Srawley, 'Eucharist (to the end of the Middle Ages)' (art. in Hastings' *Encyc. Relig. Eth.*); D. Stone, *A History of the Doctrine of the Holy Eucharist* (London, 1909).

Penance. É. Amann, 'Pénitence' (art. in *Dict. Théol. Cath.*); P. Galtier, *L'Église et la rémission des péchés* (Paris, 1932); R. C. Mortimer, *The Origins of Private Penance in the Western Church* (Oxford, 1939); B. Poschmann, *Die abendländische Kirchenbusse* (Munich, 1928); *Paenitentia Secunda* (1940); W. Telfer, *The Forgiveness of Sins* (London, 1959); O. D. Watkins, *A History of Penance* (London, 1920).

PART III

FROM NICAEA TO CHALCEDON

CHAPTER IX

THE NICENE CRISIS

1. *The Eve of the Conflict*

THE end of the third century marked the close of the first great phase of doctrinal development. With the opening of the second phase we resume consideration of the central dogma of the Godhead, and can plunge without more ado into a controversy which, in retrospect, we can see to have been uniquely *Decisive* decisive for the Christian faith. This was the embittered debate which, touched off by the flaring up of Arianism, was to culminate, as the next chapter will show, in the formulation of Trinitarian orthodoxy. At its outbreak the problem of the Trinity as such might not seem to have been directly involved. The theological issue at stake was, or seemed to be, a much narrower one, viz. the status of the Word and His relation to the Godhead. Was He fully divine, in the precise sense of the term, and therefore really akin to the Father? Or was He after all a creature, superior no doubt to the rest of creation, even by courtesy designated divine, but all the same separated by an unbridgeable chasm from the Godhead? Once these questions had been raised, however, as the course of the controversy was to reveal, the further question of what Christians meant by the divine Triad could not be evaded.

The villain in the piece (to use the language of orthodoxy) was the arch-heretic Arius, but before his theology is explained a brief sketch must be given of the theories about the position of the Word in the Godhead which held the field in the first decades of the fourth century. Here we must largely confine ourselves to the Greek-speaking section of the Church. Little or no evidence survives to show what Western theologians were thinking, although it is a safe conjecture that, like Pope

Dionysius[1] a few generations earlier, they were chiefly concerned for the divine unity and found the distinctions within the Godhead mysterious. More information is available for the East, where the dominant influence remained that of Origen. So far as the Word was concerned, two types of Origenism seem to have been in vogue, one cautious and middle-of-the-road, the other more radical. As an exponent of the former we can cite Alexander, bishop of Alexandria 313–28, who was to have the responsibility of calling Arius to order. A typical exponent of the more radical approach is Eusebius of Caesarea, the church historian, whose opinions, at any rate in their more moderate form, reflected the attitude of great numbers of Eastern clergy.

An outline of Alexander's position can be recovered from certain letters[2] which he wrote in criticism of Arius. Having been drafted after the latter had shown his hand, they probably make Alexander's theology out to be more definite on the disputed points than it may earlier have been. However that may be, although accused by Arius of Sabellianism because he insisted on the unity of the Triad (ἐν τριάδι μονάδα εἶναι[3]), it is manifest that he conceived of the Word as a 'Person' (ὑπόστασις) or 'nature' (φύσις: we notice his use of this word in a sense virtually identical with that of ὑπόστασις, i.e. 'individual being') distinguishable from the Father. In true Origenistic fashion he describes[4] Him as the unique nature which mediates (μεσιτεύουσα φύσις μονογενής) between God and creation; but He is not Himself a creature, being derived from the Father's being. The Father alone is 'ingenerate' (ἀγέννητος), i.e. unoriginate or self-existent; on this point he is firm, although charged by his opponents with teaching that the Son is unoriginate too. What he actually teaches[5] is that the Son, as Son, is co-eternal with the Father, since God can never have been without His Word, His Wisdom, His Power, His Image, and the Father must always have been Father. Further,

[1] See above, pp. 134–6.
[2] Ep. encyc. (in Socrates, hist. eccl. 1, 6); ep. ad Alex. Byz. (or possibly Thessal.: in Theodoret, hist. eccl. 1, 4).   [3] Cf. Socrates, hist. eccl. 1, 5.
[4] Ep. ad Alex. 45.   [5] Ib. 26 f.; ep. encyc. 13.

the Sonship of the Word is a real, metaphysical one, natural as opposed to adoptive (cf. the LXX wording of *Ps.* 110, 3: 'Before the dawn I begat thee out of my belly'[1]): which implies, although Alexander does not explicitly say so, that He shares the Father's nature. To explain His co-eternity he makes full use of Origen's conception[2] of eternal generation, speaking[3] of the Son's ἄναρχος γέννησις from the Father. The Two are indeed, as *John* 1, 18 indicates, 'two realities inseparable from one another' (ἀλλήλων ἀχώριστα πράγματα δύο[4]), the Son being the Father's express image and likeness. But we must not, he warns[5] us, interpret *John* 10, 30 as implying that the Son is identical with the Father, or that these 'natures which are two in hypostasis are in fact one'. All that the text should be taken to convey is that there is a perfect likeness (κατὰ πάντα ὁμοιότης) between Them.

Alexander thus reproduces elements in Origen's teaching (e.g. the idea of eternal generation) which suggest the Son's divine status; he has also picked up some hints (cf. his insistence on the inseparability of the Persons) from Pope Dionysius's letter to his predecessor. Eusebius, on the other hand, reflects Origen in his most subordinationist mood, and his overriding interest is cosmological rather than soteriological. The keystone of his system, which was already fixed before the emergence of Arianism, is the thought of the unique, transcendent Father, the indivisible Monad Who is 'above and beyond reality' (ὁ ἐπέκεινα τῶν ὅλων), Who is the cause of all things, and Who is alone self-existent and without beginning (ἄναρχος καὶ ἀγέννητος[6]). The Word, a distinct hypostasis begotten from Him before all ages, is His intermediary for creating and governing the universe, for the contingent order could not bear direct contact with absolute being.[7] He is 'perfect and only-begotten Son . . . the reflection of everlasting light'[8]; being the Father's offspring, He differs from all creatures,[9]

---

[1] *Ep. ad Alex.* 32-5.   [2] See above, p. 128.   [3] Ib. 52.
[4] Ib. 15.   [5] Ib. 38.
[6] E.g. *de eccl. theol.* 2, 6 f.; *dem. ev.* 4, 1, 145; *c. Marc.* 1, 1, 11.
[7] *De eccl. theol.* 1, 13, 1; *dem. ev.* 4, 6, 1-6.
[8] *Dem. ev.* 4, 3, 1 and 4.   [9] Ib. 5, 1, 14-17.

and because He carries in Himself the image of the ineffable
Godhead He is entitled to be called God.[1] At this point,
however, we come across features which reveal Eusebius's
radical bias. First, while freely recognizing[2] that the Son exists
'before all ages', 'before eternal times', etc., he consistently
refuses to concede that He is co-eternal with the Father. On the
contrary,[3] since the Father is alone ἀγέννητος, 'everyone must
admit that the Father is prior to and pre-exists the Son'. So
he corrects the time-honoured analogy of the light and its
brightness, pointing out[4] that the brightness exists simultaneously with the light, whereas the Father precedes the
Son. Secondly, in his earlier phase at any rate (after signing the
Nicene creed he became more discreet), he teaches[5] that the
Son's existence depends on a specific act of the Father's will. It
should further be mentioned that, not content with appropriating Origen's subordinationism in all its detail (e.g. the
idea that the Son, though God, is not 'true God'; He is only
God as the image of the one true God[6]), Eusebius stresses the
unbridgeable gulf between the Father as alone unoriginate and
the Son as originate.[7] Nor has the Son been derived from the
Father's being. That would involve a quasi-corporeal division
of the indivisible Monad and lead to the absurd doctrine of two
unoriginate beings. The unity of the Son with the Father, on
his exegesis[9] of *John* 10, 30, consists simply in His sharing an
identical glory; and he is not afraid to add that the saints also
can enjoy precisely the same kind of fellowship with the
Father.

2. The Teaching of Arius

Such was the theological climate in which Arius's controversial conclusions about the Word (he was presbyter of the
church district of Baucalis in Alexandria) were being hotly debated in the decade before 324. He had a handful of resolute co-

---

[1] *Dem. ev.* 4, 2, 1 f. [2] E.g. ib. 4, 3, 13; 5, 1, 18.
[3] Ib. 5, 1, 20. [4] Ib 4, 3, 5. [5] Ib. 4, 3, 7.
[6] *De eccl. theol.* 2, 23; *ep. ad Euphrat.* (Mansi XII, 176).
[7] E.g. *Dem. ev.* 5, 6, 2–4. [8] *Ep. ad Caes.* 12; *dem. ev.* 5, 1, 20.
[9] *De eccl. theol.* 3, 19.

adjutors, Eusebius of Nicomedia being the political tactician of the group. Our chief sources of information about his ideas are certain letters by himself, his allies and his critics, and such fragments of his *Thalia*, or 'Banquet', a popular medley of prose and verse, as Athanasius has preserved in his polemical writings.

The fundamental premiss of his system is the affirmation of the absolute uniqueness and transcendence of God, the unoriginate source ($\dot{\alpha}\gamma\acute{\epsilon}\nu\nu\eta\tau os$ $\dot{\alpha}\rho\chi\acute{\eta}$) of all reality. So the authoritative, though diplomatically worded, profession of faith[1] which, along with his close partners, he sent to Bishop Alexander opens with the uncompromising statement, 'We acknowledge one God, Who is alone ingenerate ($\dot{\alpha}\gamma\acute{\epsilon}\nu\nu\eta\tau o\nu$, i.e. self-existent), alone eternal, alone without beginning ($\ddot{\alpha}\nu\alpha\rho\chi o\nu$), alone true, alone possessing immortality, alone wise, alone good, alone sovereign, alone judge of all, etc.' Since it is unique, transcendent and indivisible, the being or essence ($o\dot{v}\sigma\acute{\iota}\alpha$) of the Godhead cannot be shared or communicated. For God to impart His substance to some other being, however exalted, would imply that He is divisible ($\delta\iota\alpha\acute{\iota}\rho\epsilon\tau os$) and subject to change ($\tau\rho\epsilon\pi\tau\acute{os}$), which is inconceivable. Moreover, if any other being were to participate in the divine nature in any valid sense, there would result a duality of divine beings, whereas the Godhead is by definition unique. Therefore whatever else exists must have come into existence, not by any communication of God's being, but by an act of creation on His part, i.e. must have been called into existence out of nothing.

By God he means, of course, God the Father. What then of the Son or 'Word' (an inaccurate title, according to Arius), whom the Arians agreed[2] that the Father, because the contingent world could not bear His direct impact, used as His organ of creation and cosmic activity? The attitude of Arius and his colleagues can be summarized in four propositions which follow logically from the preceding premiss. First, the Son must be a creature, a $\kappa\tau\acute{\iota}\sigma\mu\alpha$ or $\pi o\acute{\iota}\eta\mu\alpha$, Whom the Father has formed out of nothing by His mere fiat. The term 'beget'

---

[1] In Athanasius, *de syn.* 16.   [2] Cf. Athanasius, *c. Ar.* 2, 24; *de decret.* 8.

(γεννᾶν) applied to the Son's generation must therefore bear
the purely figurative sense of 'make' (ποιεῖν[1]). To suggest that
the Son is an emanation from (προβολή), or a consubstantial
portion of (μέρος ὁμοούσιον), the Father is to reduce the
Godhead to physical categories.[2] True, He is a perfect creature,
and not to be compared with the rest of creation;[3] but that He
is a creature, owing His being wholly to the Father's will,
follows from the primary fact that He is not self-existent. We
should observe that the Arians exploited the systematic ambiguity of the term ἀγέννητος, deducing from the self-evident
truth that the Son is not ingenerate the more questionable
conclusion that He must belong to the contingent order.

Secondly, as a creature the Son must have had a beginning.
'We are persecuted', Arius protests,[4] 'because we say the Son
has a beginning whereas God is without beginning.' 'He came
into existence', he writes in the same letter, 'before the times
and the ages'—inevitably so, because He is the creator of
time itself, no less than of everything else belonging to the world
of contingency. Nevertheless, although 'born outside time
(ἀχρόνως γεννηθείς) . . . prior to His generation He did not
exist'.[5] Hence the familiar, monotonously repeated Arian
slogan, 'There was when He was not' (ἦν ποτε ὅτε οὐκ ἦν).
The orthodox suggestion that He was in the strict sense
eternal, i.e. co-eternal with the Father, seemed to Arius to entail presupposing 'two self-existent principles' (δύο ἀγεννήτους
ἀρχάς[6]), which spelt the destruction of monotheism.

Thirdly, the Son can have no communion with, and indeed
no direct knowledge of, His Father. Although He is God's
Word and Wisdom, He is distinct from that Word and that
Wisdom which belong to God's very essence; He is a creature
pure and simple, and only bears these titles because He participates in the essential Word and Wisdom.[7] In Himself He is,
like all other creatures, 'alien from and utterly dissimilar to the
Father's essence and individual being' (ἀλλότριος καὶ ἀνόμοιος
κατὰ πάντα τῆς τοῦ πατρὸς οὐσίας καὶ ἰδιότητος[8]). Being

---

[1] C. Ar. 1, 5; 1, 9.   [2] Ep. ad Alex. (in Athanasius, de syn. 16).   [3] Ib.
[4] Ep. ad Euseb. Nicom. (in Epiphanius, haer. 69, 6).   [5] Ep. ad Alex.
[6] Ib.   [7] Cf. Athanasius, c. Ar. 1, 5; 2, 37.   [8] Ib. 1, 6.

finite, therefore, and of a different order of existence, He
cannot comprehend the infinite God. 'The Father', Arius
remarks,[1] 'remains ineffable to the Son, and the Word can
neither see nor know the Father perfectly and accurately . . .
but what He knows and sees, He knows and sees proportionately
to His capacity, just as our knowledge is adapted to our powers.'
Fourthly, the Son must be liable to change and even sin (τρεπτός;
ἀλλοιωτός). At a conference one of the Arians, surprised by a
sudden question, admitted[2] that He might have fallen as the
Devil fell, and this was what they in their heart of hearts
believed. Their official teaching,[3] however, was a tactful modi-
fication of this to the effect that, while the Son's nature was in
principle peccable, God in His providence foresaw that He
would remain virtuous by His own steadfast resolution, and
therefore bestowed this grace on Him in advance.

It might be asked in what sense, according to the Arians, the
Son could be called God, or was indeed Son of God. Their
answer was that these were in fact courtesy titles. 'Even if He
is called God', wrote[4] Arius, 'He is not God truly, but by
participation in grace (μετοχῇ χάριτος). . . . He too is called
God in name only.' Similarly it is by grace that He is designated
Son.[5] Arius could speak of the holy Triad, in speciously
Origenistic language, as consisting of three Persons (τρεῖς
ὑποστάσεις). But the Three he envisages are entirely different
beings, not sharing in any way the same nature or essence.[6]
This was the conclusion he deduced, by the exercise of his
ruthless dialectic, from his analysis of the concept of agennetos,
which literally meant 'ingenerate' (being generate, the Son
was admittedly not agennetos in this sense), but which in current
philosophical parlance had come to mean the same as agenetos,
i.e. 'unoriginated', or 'self-existent', the attribute of transcendent deity. In addition, however, the Arians amassed a formidable array of Scriptural texts[7] in support of their theses.

---

[1] Cf. Athanasius, *ep. ad episc. Aeg. et Lib.* 12: cf. *de syn.* 15.
[2] Cf. Alexander, *ep. encyc.* 10.   [3] Athanasius, *c. Ar.* 1, 5.
[4] Ib. 1, 6.   [5] Ib. 1, 5; 1, 9.   [6] *Ep. ad Alex.*; Athanasius, *c. Ar.* 1, 6.
[7] A full treatment of disputed texts will be found in Athanasius, *c. Ar.*
passim, and Epiphanius, *haer.* 69, 12–79.

Chief among these were passages suggesting that the Son was a creature, such as *Prov.* 8, 22 (LXX: 'The Lord created me etc.'), *Acts* 2, 36 ('God has made Him Lord and Christ'), *Rom.* 8, 29 ('the first-born among many'), *Col.* 1, 15 ('the first-born of all creation'), *Hebr.* 3, 2 ('Who was faithful to Him Who made him'), etc. Others were texts representing God the Father as the sole veritable God, the classic example being *John* 17, 3 ('this is life eternal, that they should know Thee the only true God, and Him Whom Thou didst send, Jesus Christ'). A third category comprised texts which seemed to imply Christ's inferiority to the Father, notably *John* 14, 28 ('the Father is greater than I'). Lastly, there was a host of passages which attributed ignorance, weakness, suffering or development to the Son of God.

The net result of this teaching was to reduce the Son to a demigod; if He infinitely transcended all other creatures, He Himself was no more than a creature in relation to the Father. Arius did not claim originality for his views; he and Eusebius of Nicomedia, he implied,[1] were 'fellow-Lucianists', and Eusebius is elsewhere[2] described as a disciple of Lucian. This is the martyr Lucian (†312), who is said to have founded the catechetical school at Antioch, having been a pupil of Paul of Samosata. Because of this some scholars point to Antioch, with its literalist exegesis and exaggerated monarchianism, as the probable source of Arius's ideas. But the assumptions that there was a homogeneous Antiochene theology in the third century, and that Arius was indebted to Paul through Lucian, are open to grave objection. Lucian himself remains a complete enigma; there is no evidence that Arius's exegesis was particularly literalist; and there was a vast difference between his conception of the Son as a distinct hypostasis and Paul's view of the Word as a *dunamis* immanent in the Father. The Arians themselves claimed to be simply continuing the Alexandrine tradition as exemplified, for example, by bishops Dionysius and Alexander. This would set them firmly in an Origenistic milieu, and in fact

[1] *Ep. ad Euseb. Nicom.*: cf. Alexander, *ep. ad Alex.* 35 f.
[2] Philostorgius, *hist. eccl.* 1 (cf. Nicetas Choniata, *thes.* 5, 7: PG 139, 1368).

all the distinctive features of their system can be satisfactorily explained in terms of one. Arius had, of course, discarded certain of Origen's ideas, notably his doctrine of eternal generation, and he had carried his subordinationism to radical lengths, reducing the Son to creaturely status. In doing so he was following, despite his consciously Biblical starting-point, a path inevitably traced for him by the Middle Platonist preconceptions he had inherited.

3. The Theology of Nicaea

Teaching like this, going far beyond Dionysius of Alexandria's most unguarded statements and verging, as Athanasius was quick to note,[1] on polytheism, stood little chance of proving acceptable in the East, much less in the West. Nevertheless Arius was able to hold his own for a few years. His bishop, Alexander, as we should expect, came out strongly against him at once, suspending him from office after a public inquiry. He had powerful friends, however, and was a master of propaganda. He even won over Eusebius of Caesarea, who was not really an Arian at heart, probably by representing[2] Alexander's teaching in the worst possible light and his own in the best. But after the capitulation of Licinius in 324 Constantine turned his attention to the affair, determined to re-establish doctrinal unity in the Church. By this time the uneasiness of the Eastern episcopate as a whole was becoming obvious, and the sympathies of Ossius, the emperor's ecclesiastical confidant, whose standpoint was thoroughly Western, were not likely to lie with Arius. His tenets were anathematized at a synod held under Ossius's chairmanship at Antioch early in 325, and Eusebius of Caesarea (so the surviving synodal letter indicates[3]) was placed under provisional excommunication at the same time. A few months later, in June, the ecumenical council which Constantine had planned met at Nicaea, and Arianism was soon officially

---

[1] C. Ar. 3,15 f.
[2] Cf. ep. ad Euseb. Nicom.; also the profession of faith in ep. ad Alex., which impressed Eusebius (cf. the latter's ep. ad Alex.: H. Opitz, Urk. 7).
[3] See J. N. D. Kelly, Early Christian Creeds (London, 3 ed. 1972), 208; 220 ff.

condemned. The following is a translation of the creed[1] which
the council drafted and required all the bishops present to sign:

> We believe in one God, the Father almighty, maker of all
> things, visible and invisible;
> And in one Lord Jesus Christ, the Son of God, begotten
> from the Father, only-begotten, that is, from the substance
> of the Father, God from God, light from light, true God from
> true God, begotten not made, of one substance with the
> Father, through Whom all things came into being, things in
> heaven and things on earth, Who because of us men and
> because of our salvation came down and became incarnate,
> becoming man, suffered and rose again on the third day,
> ascended to the heavens, and will come to judge the living
> and the dead;
> And in the Holy Spirit.
> But as for those who say, There was when He was not,
> and, Before being born He was not, and that He came into
> existence out of nothing, or who assert that the Son of God
> is from a different hypostasis or substance, or is created, or is
> subject to alteration or change—these the Catholic Church
> anathematizes.

Our immediate task is to investigate the theological attitude
of the council, as expressed principally in this creed. From the
negative point of view there can be no doubt what that
attitude was. Arianism, it is clear, at any rate in its original form

outlined in the previous section, was placed under a decisive
ban. The Son, the creed states emphatically, is begotten, not
made (γεννηθέντα, οὐ ποιηθέντα); He is also 'true God', i.e. not
God in a secondary degree. Anyone who affirms that the
Father pre-existed the Son, or that the Son is a creature produced out of nothingness, or is subject to moral change or
development, is formally declared a heretic. In thus repudiating
Arianism we may reasonably conjecture that the fathers of
Nicaea shared Alexander's conviction[2] that Scripture and

---

[1] For Greek text, see J. N. D. Kelly, op. cit. 215 f.
[2] *Ep. ad Alex.* 4; 9; passim.

tradition alike attested the divinity and immutability of the Word. Later, in his anti-Arian treatises, Athanasius was to deploy a triple onslaught based on the Church's living faith and experience. First, he argued[1] that Arianism undermined the Christian doctrine of God by presupposing that the divine Triad is not eternal and by virtually reintroducing polytheism. Secondly,[2] it made nonsense of the established liturgical customs of baptizing in the Son's name as well as the Father's, and of addressing prayers to the Son. Thirdly,[3] and perhaps most importantly, it undermined the Christian idea of redemption in Christ, since only if the Mediator was Himself divine could man hope to re-establish fellowship with God. Considerations like these may well have carried weight with the council.

Much more difficult to determine is its positive teaching. The creed supplies some hints, stating that as begotten the Son is 'out of the Father's substance' (ἐκ τῆς οὐσίας τοῦ πατρός), and that He is 'of the same substance as the Father' (ὁμοούσιον τῷ πατρί). We know that these phrases (the latter owed its insertion to Constantine's express wish) caused embarrassment at the council to the Origenistic majority represented by Eusebius, and in his letter to the Caesarean church he records the interpretation he was prepared to put upon them. The former, he explains,[4] simply means that the Son is 'from the Father' (by itself, we note, a meaningless phrase, since all things come from God), not that He is 'a portion of His substance' (a question-begging alternative, which the orthodox were bound to dissociate themselves from because of its implication that the divine essence is divisible). The latter, he says, is not to be taken in any corporeal sense (the emperor himself had been reassuring on that point—as well he might), nor as suggesting that the Father's substance had undergone any change or division; rather it indicated that the Son bore no resemblance to creatures, but was in every respect like the Father, and that He came from Him and 'not from any other hypostasis or *ousia*'. The

---

[1] E.g. *c. Ar.* 1, 17 f.; 1, 20; 3, 15 f.
[2] Ib. 2, 41 f.; *ep. ad episc. Aeg. et Lib.* 4.   [3] E.g. *c. Ar.* 2, 67; 2, 70.
[4] *Ep. ad Caes.* 5; 7.

question is whether this interpretation adequately represents the intention of the creed. As regards 'out of the Father's substance' we can be fairly confident that it does not. Whereas the Arians (e.g. Eusebius of Nicomedia writing to Paulinus) objected to the expression as suggesting a quasi-physical division in the Godhead, for the orthodox it signified that the sonship was a real one, and that the Word shared the same divine nature as the Father from Whose being He was derived. In support they liked to appeal to certain texts which Alexander had cited,[1] long before the council, in 319, e.g. *Ps.* 45, 1 ('My heart has delivered itself of a goodly word'), and *Ps.* 110, 3 in the LXX version ('Before the morning star I have begotten thee out of my belly'). It is reasonable to suppose, *pace* Eusebius, that a similar meaning, viz. 'of the same nature', was read into the homoousion. But if this is granted, a further question at once arises: are we to understand 'of the same nature' in the 'generic' sense in which Origen was alleged to have employed[2] ὁμοούσιος, or are we to take it as having the meaning accepted by later Catholic theology, viz. numerical identity of substance? The root word οὐσία could signify[3] the kind of substance or stuff common to several individuals of a class, or it could connote an individual thing as such.

There can be no doubt that, as applied to the Godhead, *homoousios* is susceptible of, and in the last resort requires, the latter meaning. As later theologians perceived, since the divine nature is immaterial and indivisible, it follows that the Persons of the Godhead Who share it must have, or rather be, one identical substance. But the question is whether this idea was prominent in the minds of the Nicene fathers, or rather of that group among them whose influence may be presumed to lie behind the creed. The great majority of scholars have answered unhesitatingly in the affirmative. Indeed, the doctrine of numerical identity of substance has been widely assumed to have been the specific teaching of the Nicene council. Nevertheless there are the strongest possible reasons for doubting this. The chief of these is the history of the term ὁμοούσιος

[1] *Ep. encyc.* 12.   [2] See above, p. 130.   [3] See above, pp. 16 f.

itself, for in both its secular and its theological usage prior to
Nicaea it always conveyed,[1] primarily at any rate, the 'generic'
sense. Christian writers seem to have borrowed it from the
Gnostics, for whom it signified the relationship between beings
compounded of kindred substance (e.g. Achamoth, who is
spiritual, and the spiritual part of the world; the 'psychic'
Demiurge and 'psychic' objects; aeons and the higher aeons
from which they emanated; etc.). This is understandable enough
where creatures are concerned, for while finite beings can be
of the same kind of substance, they cannot actually be the same
identical substance; and so we find Origen,[2] Methodius,[3]
Eusebius[4] and other Christians employing it in secular contexts
with a similar connotation. But it was with this 'generic' sense
that the word was first applied in Christian theology, too, to
express the Son's relation to the Father. Origen, if Rufinus's
translation can be trusted, had used it so when he spoke[5] of a
'community of substance between Father and Son', citing steam
and the water from which it is generated as an analogy.
Dionysius of Alexandria, similarly, understood[6] ὁμοούσιος as
synonymous with ὁμογενής or ὁμοφυής, i.e. 'homogeneous',
'of the same nature'; and Dionysius of Rome seems to have
been content with his interpretation. The use of the term at the
council of Antioch (268) remains something of a mystery,[7] but
on balance it appears likely that it was given the meaning
generally accepted in the third century.

In view of all this it is paradoxical to suppose that the
Nicene fathers suddenly began employing what was after all a
familiar enough word in an entirely novel and unexpected
sense. The only reasonable inference is that in selecting it for
insertion in their creed they intended it to underline, formally
and explicitly at any rate, their conviction that the Son was
fully God, in the sense of sharing the same divine nature as His
Father. Several other considerations lend support to this. First,
we know that Arius himself, on the eve of the council, more

---

[1] For the evidence, see G. L. Prestige, *God in Patristic Thought*, ch. 10.
[2] *In Ioh.* 20, 20, 170.   [3] *De res.* 2, 30, 8.   [4] *Dem. ev.* 1, 10, 13.
[5] See above, p. 130.   [6] See above, p. 135.   [7] See above, p. 118.

than once used[1] ὁμοούσιος, or expressions equivalent to it, in passages denying that the Son was of the same nature as the Father; but it is transparently clear that it was His alleged divinity, not His substantial unity with the Father, that he was repudiating. Secondly, the great issue before the council, as all our sources agree, was not the unity of the Godhead as such; it was the Son's co-eternity with the Father, which the Arians denied, His full divinity in contrast to the creaturely status they ascribed to Him. Thirdly, we may be sure that, if Eusebius and his allies had had the slightest suspicion that numerical identity of substance was being foisted on them in ὁμοούσιος, they would have loudly objected to it as Sabellian. In fact, as we know from his apologia to the Caesarean church, it was its materialistic flavour that he found awkward. Lastly, we know that afterwards, when the identity of substance of the three Persons was fully acknowledged, the most orthodox theologians continued to use ὁμοούσιος, in the appropriate contexts, with the sense of generic unity.

The theology of the council, therefore, if this argument is sound, had a more limited objective than is sometimes supposed. If negatively it unequivocally outlawed Arianism, positively it was content to affirm the Son's full divinity and equality with the Father, out of Whose being He was derived and Whose nature He consequently shared. It did not attempt to tackle the closely related problem of the divine unity, although the discussion of it was inevitably brought nearer. The deeper implications of ὁμοούσιος, as applied to the unique and indivisible Godhead, may already have been apparent to some, for quite soon after the council we find[2] Eusebius of Caesarea accusing Eustathius of Antioch (one of its ardent champions) of reading a Sabellian meaning into the word. It is highly probable that the handful of Western bishops at any rate, led by Ossius of Cordoba, took it for granted that unity of substance was entailed. Athanasius indeed, years later, was to claim[3] that the deliberate object of the term's insertion

---

[1] E.g. ep. ad Alex.; Athanasius, c. Ar. 1, 6.
[2] Cf. Socrates, hist. eccl. 1, 23.   [3] De decret. 20 (350/51).

was to emphasize that the Son was not merely like the Father but, in virtue of His unique generation, 'identical in His likeness . . . inseparable from His essence'. But this was a politically misleading reconstruction of events. The ancient tradition that it was Ossius who suggested ὁμοούσιος to Constantine may well be correct, but, if he did, he did not also succeed in persuading the emperor to accept his interpretation of it. Whatever the theology of the council was, Constantine's own overriding motive was to secure the widest possible measure of agreement. For this reason he was not prepared to bar the door to anyone who was willing to append his signature to the creed. There is thus a sense in which it is unrealistic to speak of the theology of the council. While different groups might read their own theologies into the creed and its key-word, Constantine himself was willing to tolerate them all on condition that they acquiesced in his creed and tolerated each other.

4. *The Aftermath of Nicaea*

The Nicene crisis did not come to an end with the closing of the council. Arianism proper had, for the moment, been driven underground, but the conflict only served to throw into relief the deep-seated theological divisions in the ranks of its adversaries. The Church's new relation to the State, which meant that the success or failure of a doctrine might hinge upon the favour of the reigning emperor, tended to sharpen these divisions. In fact, the dispersal of the council marked the commencement of a protracted period of controversy lasting at least until Constantius's death in 361. Even then two further decades had to elapse before the Nicene faith was securely and finally established.

Though the detail belongs to Church history, the student of doctrine ought to be given at least a bird's-eye view of the chief phases in the fluctuating debate. The first, lasting until Constantine's death in 337, saw a widespread reaction against Nicaea. The Arian leaders, who had been exiled, returned, and Eusebius of Nicomedia became head of an anti-Nicene

325
-337

Niceans
exiled

coalition. While the emperor was alive, his creed was sacrosanct, but the Eusebians (as we may conveniently call them after their leader) were able to engineer the deposition and exile of their principal opponents, Athanasius (since 328 patriarch of Alexandria), Eustathius of Antioch and Marcellus of Ancyra. From 337 to 350, although the 'Arianizing' Constantius ruled the East, the Western emperor, Constans, backed the Nicene cause and protected its leaders. So, while the Eusebians were now openly campaigning to get behind the Nicene creed, the formulae[1] they produced at Antioch (341), Philippopolis (342) and Antioch again (344: the *Ecthesis macrostichos*), were on the whole moderate, omitting the homoousion, it is true, but usually critical of Arianism proper and sometimes even conciliatory to the Nicenes. From 350 to 361 Constantius reigned as sole emperor and made a determined effort to bypass the Nicene doctrine. The genuinely Arian elements in the great anti-Nicene party now took the initiative and succeeded in getting a thoroughly subordinationist creed omitting the ban on Arianism accepted at the third council of Sirmium (357), and Homoean creeds at the synods of Nicé (359) and Constantinople (360).[2] This was the situation which instigated Jerome to write,[3] 'The whole world groaned and marvelled to find itself Arian'. At the same time, however, as a result of the very triumph of extremism, the moderates in the vast amorphous party began to rally under Basil of Ancyra around the compromise formula 'of like substance' (ὁμοιούσιος). The final phase, from 361 to 381, witnessed the overthrow of Arianism and the gradual conversion of the now dominant 'Homoeousians' to acceptance of the homoousion. At the council of Constantinople (381) the Nicene faith was reaffirmed, and the various Arian and Arianizing deviations were placed under a ban.

A superficial glance at the polemical literature of the period leaves the impression of a battle-royal between Sabellians and

---

[1] For the texts of these creeds, see J. N. D. Kelly, op. cit. 268 ff.; 275 ff.; 279 f.

[2] Cf. J. N. D. Kelly, op. cit. 285 ff.; 291 ff.   [3] *Dial. c. Lucif.* 19.

Homoousion vs. homoeousian
Athanasius
Arians Origenists

Arians. While the two parties hurled these epithets at each other, it would be a mistake to take them at their face-value. On one side stood the group headed by Athanasius, small in numbers but strong in the consciousness that the Western church was solidly behind them. They were devoted advocates of the homoousion, and had come to perceive that identity of substance must follow from the doctrine that Father and Son share the same Godhead. With one or two exceptions, they were very far from being Sabellians; it was their reluctance to accept the formula 'three hypostases', which they thought was being exploited in a way prejudicial to the divine unity, which caused them to be suspected of ignoring the personal distinctions in the Godhead. Ranged against them was a much larger, more variegated group comprising by far the greater portion of Greek-speaking churchmen. Held together by dissatisfaction with Nicaea, it included representatives of markedly different standpoints. A small, determined minority were definitely Arian, although they deemed it politic at first to veil their intentions. The great majority, however, were as far removed from Arianism as their opponents from Sabellianism; the typical Arian theses were, in fact, anathema to them. Origenist in outlook, they thought naturally in terms of three hypostases, and were easily induced to believe that the homoousion imperilled them. The teaching of its more extreme advocates, especially Marcellus, satisfied them that it was a cloak for Sabellianism. Most of them were not theologians at all; they were conservatives who preferred the traditional lack of definition and objected to the Nicene key-word as a departure from pure Biblical standards.

The historian Socrates (c. 380–c. 450), writing some generations later, has left a vivid description of the astonishing failure of the two sides to comprehend each other. 'The situation', he remarked,[1] 'was exactly like a battle by night, for both parties seemed to be in the dark about the grounds on which they were hurling abuse at each other. Those who objected to the word *homoousios* imagined that its adherents were bringing in the

[1] *Hist. eccl.* I, 23.

doctrine of Sabellius and Montanus. So they called them blasphemers on the ground that they were undermining the personal subsistence of the Son of God. On the other hand, the protagonists of *homoousios* concluded that their opponents were introducing polytheism, and steered clear of them as importers of paganism. . . . Thus, while both affirmed the personality and subsistence of the Son of God, and confessed that there was one God in three hypostases, they were somehow incapable of reaching agreement, and for this reason could not bear to lay down arms.'

5. *The Nicene Party and Athanasius*

It is time to look more closely at these rival theologies. Both had extremist as well as more moderate spokesmen, the chief example of the former in the Nicene group being Marcellus, bishop of Ancyra († *c.* 374). An enthusiastic supporter of the homoousion, he wrote a treatise (*c.* 335) in its defence, giving it what the Eusebians considered a Sabellian interpretation. As a result of this, although he lost his see, he remained their bogy for the rest of his active life.

His theology he tried to ground[1] on the Bible and the apostolic tradition, and would have nothing to do with merely human opinions, or even with the authority of the fathers. From Scripture he deduced[2] that God is spirit, 'an indivisible Monad', 'a single *prosopon*'. Before all ages the Logos was in God as His immanent reason,[3] identical with Him (ἐν καὶ ταὐτὸν . . . τῷ θεῷ) as a man's reason is with himself[4]. So he condemns[5] the Origenist conception that the Logos is a distinct hypostasis or *ousia* as threatening to disrupt this unity and lead to polytheism. All that can be said about the pre-existent Logos is that He was Logos;[6] there can be no talk of His generation, and Marcellus restricts[7] the title 'Son' to the Incarnate. But if the Logos was thus immanent in God as 'potency' (δυνάμει), He was also externalized as God's 'active energy' (ἐνέργεια

---

[1] Frg. 121; 98; 86; 88 (ed. E. Klostermann, G.C.S. 14).
[2] Frg. 54; 71; 76; 77.   [3] Frg. 52; 54; 60.   [4] Frg. 61; 71; 73.
[5] Frg. 76; 82; 83.   [6] Frg. 42; 43; 91; 103.   [7] Frg. 3-6; 43; 48.

δραστική) for creation and revelation, since everything that
the Father says or does is accomplished through His Word.[1]
Indeed, it is precisely His function as God's self-activization
and self-revelation which, Marcellus claims,[2] distinguishes
the Logos from His possessor, and it is the recognition of this,
he holds,[3] that differentiates his own position from Sabellianism.
This externalization of the Logos does not, of course, result in
His becoming a second hypostasis; His coming forth or procession (he uses[4] terms like ἐξῆλθεν, ἐκπορεύεται, etc.) is
described[5] as an extension or expansion (cf. the verb πλατύ-
νεσθαι) of the Monad, which at creation and the incarnation
becomes, without undergoing any division, a dyad, and with
the outpouring of the Spirit a triad. Eventually, after the judgment, the process will be reversed;[6] the Logos will be reabsorbed
in the Monad, and the reign, or kingdom, of Christ—not, we
observe, of the Logos as such—will come to an end.

It is clear that Marcellus was not strictly a Sabellian. Several
of his ideas are reminiscent of Irenaeus, Hippolytus and Tertullian and the 'economic Trinitarianism' associated with them.
His conception, for example, of the expansion of the Monad
recalls Tertullian's description[7] of the Son's generation as extending the divine substance without dividing it, as well as
Dionysius of Rome's statement,[8] 'We expand (πλατύνομεν)
the indivisible Monad into the Triad'. Further, although he
lacked language and even concepts to express the distinction,
he envisaged the pre-existent Logos as somehow other than the
indivisible spirit with Whom He was nevertheless 'one and the
same'. His position was distinctive in that it rejected the now
fashionable Origenist, basically Middle Platonist conception of
three hypostases and viewed the Trinity as immanent in God.
We need not be surprised that it scandalized the Eusebians.
The frequent appearance of the clause 'Of Whose reign there
will be no end' in the creeds they manufactured testifies to
their dread of it. His pupil Photinus, bishop of Sirmium, taught

---

[1] Frg. 52; 61; 121.   [2] Frg. 61.   [3] Frg. 44.
[4] Frg. 68; 121.   [5] Frg. 67; 71.   [6] Frg. 117; 121.
[7] Apo.. 21.   [8] In Athanasius, de sent. Dion. 17.

a more provocative form of the same doctrine, possibly combined with an adoptionist Christology, and was even more suspect in their eyes. The Nicene party at first espoused his cause, and a Roman council held in 341 under Pope Julius I cleared him of the charge of heresy. When they realized the embarrassment he was causing them, their attitude became cooler, and although they never formally condemned him they gradually dissociated themselves from him and his standpoint.

Marcellus was an extremist; the attitude of the average, particularly Western, adherent of the Nicene theology is better represented by the so-called creed of Serdica,[1] which the Western members of the council held there (343) drafted after the Easterners had withdrawn. Negatively it repudiates the 'Arian' theory that there are 'different, quite separate hypostases of Father, Son and Holy Spirit'. On the contrary, the Catholic and apostolic tradition, it affirms, is that the Three have one identical hypostasis or substance (*hupostasis* and *ousia*, we note, are treated as synonyms, as in the anathemas to the Nicene creed), viz. the hypostasis of the Father. It is clear (a) that hypostasis here means the being of God, and (b) that actual identity of essence is insisted upon. On the other hand, as against Marcellus, the creed admits that the Word was generated for the purpose of creation, and it adds that it is false to suppose that He ever had a beginning (the Arian thesis) or will have an end (against Marcellus). Further, the substantial identity of Father and Son, it states, does not entail that the Son actually is the Father; on the contrary, the Father is Father, and the Son is Son of the Father, His Word, Wisdom and Power. He is a true, not adoptive, Son because His substance (*hupostasis*) is identical with the Father's. The Godhead of both is one and the same (μίαν πατρὸς καὶ υἱοῦ θεότητα), and if the Father is greater than the Son, that is 'because the very name of father is greater than that of son'. Thus Their unity is based, not on mutual harmony and concord (συμφωνία; ὁμόνοια), as the Origenists claimed,[2] but on 'oneness of hypostasis' (ἡ τῆς ὑποστάσεως

---

[1] Cf. Theodoret, *hist. eccl.* 2, 8, 37-52; J. N. D. Kelly, op. cit. 277 f.
[2] Cf. Origen, *c. Cels.* 8, 12.

ἑνότης). The Son's reign will never end. The term ὁμοούσιος, it is noteworthy, nowhere occurs in the creed, and its favourite formula is 'identity of hypostasis'.

Writing[1] almost twenty years later, in 362, Athanasius might find it convenient to disown the Serdican manifesto; in fact its main theses, though expressed in old-fashioned terminology, coincided very closely with his own. His theology, of course, represents the classic exposition of the Nicene standpoint. As a Christian thinker he stood in complete contrast to Arius and even to Eusebius of Caesarea. Rationalists at heart, they started from *à priori* ideas of divine transcendence and creation. The Word, they held, could not be divine because His being originated from the Father; since the divine nature was incommunicable, He must be a creature, and any special status He enjoyed must be due to His role as the Father's agent in creation. In Athanasius's approach philosophical and cosmological considerations played a very minor part, and his guiding thought was the conviction of redemption. Admittedly the Father used the Word as His organ of creation, but to suppose that He needed an intermediary was absurd.[2] On the other hand, by his fellowship with Christ man has been made divine and has become the child of God. Hence the Word Himself must be intrinsically divine, since otherwise He could never have imparted the divine life to men. As he put the matter,[3] 'the Word could never have divinized us if He were merely divine by participation and were not Himself the essential Godhead, the Father's veritable image'.

Let us examine first his conception of the divine Sonship. God, he holds,[4] can never be without His Word, any more than the light can cease to shine or the river source to flow. Hence the Son must exist eternally alongside the Father. The explanation of this is that His generation is an eternal process; 'just as the Father is always good by nature, so He is by nature always generative' (ἀεὶ γεννητικός[5]). 'It is entirely correct', he writes,[6] 'to call Him the Father's eternal offspring. For the

---

[1] *Tom. ad Antioch.* 5.   [2] *C. Ar.* 2, 24-6; 2, 29 f.   [3] *De syn.* 51.
[4] E.g. *c. Ar.* 2, 32.   [5] *Ib.* 3, 66.   [6] *Ib.* 1, 14.

Father's being was never incomplete, needing an essential feature to be added to it; nor is the Son's generation like a man's from his parent, involving His coming into existence after the Father. Rather He is God's offspring, and since God is eternal and He belongs to God as Son, He exists from all eternity. It is characteristic of men, because of the imperfection of their nature, to beget in time; but God's offspring is eternal, His nature being always perfect.' Like Irenaeus, Athanasius regards[1] the Son's generation as mysterious, but he interprets[2] it as implying that, so far from being a creature, He must, like a human offspring, be derived from and share His Father's nature. Not that we should press the analogy of human generation so far as to conclude that the Son is, as it were, a portion of divine substance separated out of the Father; this is impossible, the divine nature being immaterial and without parts.[3] Nor is the Son's generation, as the Arians claimed, the result of a definite act of the Father's will, which would reduce the Son's status to that of a creature. It certainly happens according to the Father's will, but it is misleading to speak of a specific act of volition in regard to what is an eternal process inherent in God's very nature.[4] We should also reject the suggestion that the Son is not, like the Father, *agennetos*, if the connotation put upon this ambiguous term is 'eternally existing' or 'increate', although He is of course not *agennetos* if the word retains its etymological sense of 'ingenerate'.[5]

Athanasius is satisfied that, as the Father's offspring (γέννημα), the Son must be really distinct (ἕτερον) from Him;[6] and since the generation is eternal, it follows that the distinction too is eternal and does not belong simply to the 'economy'. It also follows, however, that, as a Son derived from His Father's being, He must share the same nature. As he puts it,[7] 'The Son is other in kind and nature (ἑτερογενὴς καὶ ἑτεροφυής) than the creatures, or rather belongs to the Father's substance (τῆς τοῦ πατρὸς οὐσίας ἴδιος) and is of the same nature as He'.

---

[1] *C. Ar.* 2, 36; 3, 66 f. [2] *Ib.* 1, 26–8; 2, 59 f. [3] *De decret.* 11.
[4] *C. Ar.* 3, 59–66. [5] *Ib.* 1, 31; *de decret.* 28–30. [6] *C. Ar.* 3, 4.
[7] *Ib.* 1, 58: cf. *de decret.* 23; *de syn.* 53; *ad Serap.* 2, 6.

Considered as two Persons, therefore, Father and Son are 'alike' (ὅμοιοι). The Son is the Father's image;[1] He is the stream and the Father the source, He the brightness and the Father the light.[2] Hence anyone who sees Christ sees the Father, 'because of the Son's belonging to the Father's substance and because of His complete likeness (κατὰ πάντα ὁμοιό-τητα) to the Father'.[3] This likeness is no external resemblance, however, such as exists between man and man,[4] but extends to His very substance or nature. 'He is the offspring',[5] says Athanasius, 'of His Father's substance, so that none may doubt that in virtue of His likeness to His immutable Father the Word also is immutable.' So he repudiates[6] the Arian proposal that the likeness is one of will, comparable with a human being's voluntary imitation of a teacher whom he reveres: 'this likeness and unity must be in respect of the Son's essence' (οὐσία).

From this it was only a short step to oneness (ἑνότης), even identity (ταυτότης), of being, and Athanasius did not hesitate to take it. Perhaps, as some students have suggested, he and his associates may have had their eyes opened to the full implications of the homoousion in the West; but it is more likely that his own theological instinct lighted upon them. Thus he declares[7] that 'the divinity of the Father is identical with that of the Son', and even[8] that 'the Son's divinity is the Father's divinity'. Again,[9] 'the fulness of the Father's divinity is the being (τὸ εἶναι) of the Son'. In illustration of this he endlessly exploits[10] his favourite analogy of the light and its brightness, which while distinguishable as two are one and the same substance. 'The Son', he argues,[11] 'is of course other than the Father as offspring, but as God He is one and the same; He and the Father are one in the intimate union of Their nature and the identity of Their Godhead. . . . Thus They are one, and Their Godhead is one, so that whatever is predicated of the Son is predicated of the Father.' Human beings can, of course, be

[1] E.g. c. Ar. 2, 29. [2] E.g. ib. 2, 41; 3, 4. [3] Ib. 2, 22.
[4] De syn. 53. [5] C. Ar. 1, 39: cf. de decret. 12.
[6] C. Ar. 3, 10 f. [7] Ib. 1, 61. [8] Ib. 3, 41. [9] Ib. 3, 6.
[10] E.g. ib. 3, 11; de decret. 23 f. [11] C. Ar. 3, 4.

described as ὁμοούσιοι.[1] But whereas the human nature they share is necessarily apportioned out among individuals, so that they cannot possess one and the same identical substance, the divine nature is indivisible.[2] In his earlier works Athanasius does not make much use of *homoousios* to express this numerical identity, but contents himself with such expressions as 'impropriate to the Father's essence' (ἴδιος τῆς τοῦ πατρὸς οὐσίας), 'like in substance' (ὅμοιος κατ' οὐσίαν), etc. Later, however, faced with the Eusebians speaking of the Son as 'like the Father' in their own defective sense of 'like', and with the Homoeousians defining Him with similar reservations as 'like in substance', he came increasingly to employ[3] the Nicene key-word as the term uniquely adapted to bring out what he believed to be the truth of the matter.

So Athanasius's thought has two sides which must be held together in tension. Just as much as Arius, he believes that the Godhead is a unique, indivisible Monad; there is only one monarchy, one supreme principle (μίαν ἀρχὴν οἴδαμεν[4]). It is his firm grasp of this truth, as of the parallel truth that the analogy between finite and infinite breaks down because of the pure spirituality of the latter, that enables him to draw the inference that Father and Son must be one identical substance, the same indivisible reality existing in two forms of presentation. At the same time he is no less firmly convinced of the truth of the distinction between Them. As against Sabellianism he affirms,[5] 'Two They are, because the Father is Father and not Son, and the Son is Son and not Father'. The Scriptural revelation, no less than the relation of offspring to parent, of image to original, etc., demands a real duality. It is because They are really two that he is able to speak of Them as 'alike' (ὅμοιοι), while in the next breath affirming identity of substance. He sums the matter up simply in the sentence,[6] 'If the Son as offspring is other than the Father, He is identical with Him as God'.

He had no term of his own, we should note, to express Their subsistence as Persons, and seems to have discerned little or no

[1] *Ad Serap.* 2, 3.   [2] *De decret.* 11; 24; *c. Ar.* 1, 26; 1, 28.
[3] *De syn.* 53.   [4] *C. Ar.* 3, 15.   [5] Ib. 3, 4.   [6] Ib.

difference between οὐσία and ὑπόστασις. In a later work,[1] written in 369, he could still say, 'Hupostasis is the same as ousia, signifying nothing other than being itself' (αὐτὸ τὸ ὄν). His fundamental position is that the divine ousia, simple and indivisible, is shared at once by Father and Son. The distinction between Them is real, and lies in the distinction between the Godhead considered as eternally activating, expressing and begetting Itself, and the selfsame Godhead considered as eternally activated, expressed and begotten. The Son is the self-same Godhead as the Father, but that Godhead manifested rather than immanent. So He is 'the Father's very own self-illuminative and creative activity, without Whom He neither creates anything nor is known'.[2] Again, 'Whatever works the Son accomplishes are the Father's works, for the Son is the manifestation (εἶδος) of the Father's divinity, which accomplished the works'.[3] Indeed, the Father achieves nothing except through the Son,[4] Who is the Godhead regarded as active in the work of divinizing and illuminating.[5]

6. The Anti-Nicenes

If such was the teaching of Athanasius and his allies, at least three types of theology found shelter at different times in the anti-Nicene camp. The first, indefinite, on occasion ambiguous on the crucial issues, but on the whole conciliatory, reflects the attitude of the great conservative 'middle party'. The earlier creeds of the period provide samples of it. The creed[6] of the Dedication Council of 341 (the 'Second Creed of Antioch') reveals both its left- and its right-wing strains. Strongly anti-Sabellian in tone, it brands Arian tenets in terms which leave a loop-hole for the more sophisticated forms of the heresy. These could easily get round such statements as that the Son is 'unalterable and unchangeable', and that He is 'not a creature as the creatures'. Its positive doctrine is that there are three divine

---

[1] Ep. ad Afr. 4: cf. de decret. 27; de syn. 41. [2] De syn. 52.
[3] C. Ar. 3, 6.   [4] Ib. 3, 12.   [5] De syn. 51.
[6] Cf. J. N. D. Kelly, op. cit. 268 ff.

hypostases, separate in rank and glory but united in harmony of will. The creed[1] drafted at Philippopolis in 343, when hopes of agreement with the West ran high, is more eirenical. There is no mention of the homoousion, of course, but equally none of 'three hypostases'; and by anathematizing the suggestion of 'three Gods', it goes out of its way to still the anxieties of many anti-Origenists. Of greater importance is the *Ecthesis macro-stichos*,[2] or 'Long-lined Creed', which was despatched to Milan in 345 in an attempt to explain the Eastern viewpoint to the West. It scrupulously avoids contentious terms like *ousia* and *hupostasis*, and rejects the idea of the Son's generation out of nothingness, as also the formula 'There was when He was not'. The Son, it declares, is 'from God alone'. The Father alone is 'ingenerate' and 'unoriginate', and He begets the Son 'outside time'. The Son is 'perfect and true God in nature'; His coming to be ($\H{v}\pi\alpha\rho\xi\iota\varsigma$) is 'before the ages'. The Three are 'three objects and three Persons' ($\pi\rho\acute{\alpha}\gamma\mu\alpha\tau\alpha \ldots \pi\rho\acute{o}\sigma\omega\pi\alpha$: the latter word is no doubt chosen as translating the Western *persona*), but Their inseparability is forcefully emphasized. 'They are united with each other without mediation or distance', and possess 'one dignity of Godhead'. Though by-passing the homoousion, the document leans a little towards Homoeous-ianism, and goes some way to meet the Western standpoint.

Secondly, we have the specifically Arian theology which, always lurking beneath the surface, emerged into the open in the fifties. A by-product of this was the notorious Second Creed, or 'Blasphemy', of Sirmium[3] (357), for which the politically-minded prelates Ursacius and Valens were mainly responsible. Though not explicitly inculcating Arianism, it has an unmistakable Arian bias, since it studiously abstains from criticizing any Arian tenet while prohibiting both the slogans 'of the same substance' and 'of like substance'. 'The Catholic doctrine', it states, 'is that there are two Persons of the Father and the Son, the Father greater and the Son subordinated (*subiectum*) to the Father . . . the Father having no beginning . . .

---

[1] Cf. J. N. D. Kelly, op. cit. 275 ff.   [2] Ib. 279 f.
[3] Cf. Hilary, *de syn.* 11 (J. N. D. Kelly, op. cit. 285 f.).

but the Son having been begotten.' More significant, however, both intellectually and historically, was a new radical Arianism, known as Anomoeism (ἀνόμοιος = 'unlike'), which emerged in the 350s. Its promoters were Aetius and Eunomius,[1] who argued with a relentless dialectic which their critics derided as 'technology' or logic-chopping.[2] In fact they were presenting a restatement of fundamental Christian dogma in terms of a Neo-Platonic metaphysic of three hierarchically ordered, mutually exclusive οὐσίαι. They used a theory of language according to which names express the essence of the things they denote. Thus God, the supreme οὐσία, was 'ingenerate' (ἀγέννητος), and 'ingenerateness' exhaustively defined His being. 'Father' designated the activity (ἐνέργεια) by which the second οὐσία, or Son, was created, and since He was by nature 'generate' (γεννητός), He was utterly unlike the ingenerate God. In His turn the Son brought into existence the third, or Holy Spirit, and subordinate to Him the entire creation. It was because of this creative activity that St. Paul had described Him as 'the image' of the Father.[3] Unlike Arius the Anomoeans conceded that, in virtue of His creative role, the Son possessed a relative divinity. Unlike both Arius and their orthodox contemporaries, they deduced that, since God's essence was ἀγεννησία and nothing more, it was completely comprehensible by men.[4]

The third type of theology was the Homoeousianism (unfairly called Semi-Arianism by Epiphanius[5]) to which an ever-growing number of moderates of the middle party rallied after the out-and-out Arians in the anti-Nicene camp had thrown off the mask. Some of its adherents, like Meletius of Antioch and Cyril of Jerusalem, held a high doctrine of the Son, but objected to the un-Biblical homoousion, suspected some of its advocates, and preferred reverent reticence as regards the manner of the Son's generation. Thus Cyril taught that He was 'like the Father in all things', sharing His divinity,[6] but as a

---

[1] See esp. Aetius, *syntagmation* (in Epiphanius, *haer.* 76, 12); Eunomius, *First Apology* (PG 30, 835–68).   [2] Cf. Theodoret, *haer. fab.* 4, 3.
[3] Eunomius, *apol.* 24 (on Col. 1, 15–17).
[4] Cf. Socrates, *hist. eccl.* 4, 7.   [5] *Haer.* 73.   [6] *Cat.* 4, 7; 6, 6; 11, 16.

distinct hypostasis from all eternity.[1] Others, while admitting the deity of the Word and the likeness of substance, even the perfect resemblance, between Him and the Father, retained a subordinationist strain and felt obliged to think of His generation as depending on an unfettered act of the Father's will. A party was formed under the leadership of Basil of Ancyra, and at the synod of Ancyra (358) published the first Homoeousian manifesto.[2] This pronounced that Christ was not a creature but Son of the Father, for 'creator and creature are one thing, Father and Son quite another'; and it condemned other typical Arian theses. On the other hand, the Son was not simply an 'energy' of the Father, as Marcellus was presumed to have taught, but 'a substance (οὐσία) like the Father'—we observe that in their terminology ousia approximated to the sense of 'Person'. In distinction from all creatures He is really Son. But the likeness between Father and Son is not to be conceived of as identity (ταυτότης); being another ousia, the Son can be like the Father, but not identical with Him. So the statement speaks of 'the likeness of ousia to ousia', and condemns anyone who defines the Son as ὁμοούσιος or ταὐτούσιος with the Father. Thus the formula ὁμοιούσιος, put under a ban at Sirmium in 357, was deliberately taken up. Only a year later, in 359, a Homoeousian memorandum was drafted[3] which reveals how rapidly the gap between the new party and the Nicenes was narrowing. First, after explaining that Eastern theologians simply used ὑπόστασις to express 'the subsistent characteristics of the Persons', this lays it down that Father and Son are two hypostases, and that from this point of view 'a likeness in respect of substance' (κατ' οὐσίαν ὁμοιότης) exists between Them. But, secondly, it adds that the Son, having been begotten from the Father, is spirit like Him, and from this point of view is 'one and the same' (τὸ αὐτό) as He. Although the identity here presupposed is qualitative rather than numerical, the memorandum clearly marks an approximation to the Athanasian point of view.

---

[1] E.g. cat. 11, 10.   [2] Text in Epiphanius, *haer.* 73, 3-11.
[3] By George of Laodicea: text in Epiphanius, *haer.* 73, 12-22.

The Homoeans, the party of compromise headed by Acacius, whose formula 'like (ὅμοιος) the Father' was incorporated in the creeds[1] of Nicé (359) and Constantinople (360), can hardly lay claim to a separate theological position. Although their intention was to facilitate unity by avoiding contentious issues, they inevitably left the door open to Arianism;[2] support for them collapsed with the advent of the Nicene-minded emperors Gratian and Theodosius I.

[1] Texts in Theodoret, *hist. eccl.* 2, 21, 3-7; Athanasius, *de syn.* 30: see J. N. D. Kelly, op. cit. 291; 293-5.   [2] Cf. Epiphanius, *haer.* 73, 23.

NOTE ON BOOKS

General. G. Bardy, 'Trinité' (art. in *Dict. Théol. Cath.*); É. Boularand, *L'hérésie d'Arius et la 'foi' de Nicée* (Paris, 1972); A. E. Burn, *The Council of Nicaea* (London, 1925); J. Gummerus, *Die Homöusianische Partei bis zum Tode des Konstantius* (Leipzig, 1900); H. M. Gwatkin, *Studies of Arianism* (Cambridge, 2 ed. 1900); J. N. D. Kelly, *Early Christian Creeds* (London, 3 ed. 1972); F. Loofs, 'Arianismus' and 'Christologie' (arts. in Hauck's *Realencyk*); G. L. Prestige, *God in Patristic Thought* (London, 2 ed. 1952); E. Schwartz, *Kaiser Constantin und die christliche Kirche* (Berlin, 2 ed. 1938).

Special. P. Arnou, 'Arius et les relations trinitaires' (art. in *Gregorianum* xiv, 1933); G. Bardy, *Recherches sur Lucien d'Antioche et son école* (Paris, 1936); H. Berkhof, *Die Theologie des Eusebius von Caesarea* (Amsterdam, 1939); W. Gericke, *Marcell von Ancyra* (Halle, 1940); E. P. Meijering, *Orthodoxy and Platonism in Athanasius* (Leiden, 1968); H. G. Opitz, *Urkunden zur Geschichte des arianischen Streites* (in Vol. III of Berlin edition of Athanasius); I. Ortiz de Urbina, *El símbolo niceno* (Madrid, 1947); T. E. Pollard, 'The Origins of Arianism' (art. in *Journ. Theol. Stud.*, 1958); M. Simonetti, *Studi sull' Arianesimo* (Rome, 1965); G. C. Stead, 'The Platonism of Arius' (art. in *Journ. Theol. Stud.*, 1964); 'Homoousios dans la pensée de saint Athanase' (in *Politique et théologie chez Athanase d'Alexandrie:* ed. Ch. Kannengiesser, Paris, 1974); A. A. Stephenson, *The Works of Saint Cyril of Jerusalem*, Vol. 1, Introduction (Washington D.C., 1969); M. Wiles, 'In Defence of Arius' (art. in *Journ. Theol. Stud.*, 1962).

Get this!

CHAPTER X

THE DOCTRINE OF THE TRINITY

1. *The Return to the Homoousion*

IN the Arian struggle, as we have seen, the question agitating
men's minds was the full deity of the Son, and although this
was an essential constituent in the doctrine of the Trinity the
latter was at first kept in the background. The Nicene creed,
indeed, merely affirmed belief 'in the Holy Spirit', and many
years had to elapse before there was any public controversy
about His position in the Godhead. Nevertheless, a discussion of
the deeper issues could not be postponed indefinitely, and in
this chapter we shall trace the formulation of Trinitarian orthodoxy. The theologians chiefly responsible for this were, in the
East, the Cappadocian fathers, Basil the Great (†379), Gregory
of Nazianzus (†*c.* 390) and Basil's younger brother, Gregory of
Nyssa (†394), and, in the West, Augustine of Hippo (†430).
Before examining their syntheses, however, we must glance at
two important lines of development without which their contribution cannot be understood. The first is the conversion of
the great body of Homoeousian churchmen to the acceptance
of the homoousion. The second is the emergence of interest in
the status of the Holy Spirit, culminating in His recognition as
fully personal and consubstantial with the Father and the Son.

The figures largely instrumental in the first of these developments were Athanasius and Hilary of Poitiers; the latter spent
356–9 in exile in Asia Minor and for the first time found himself in direct contact with the Eastern theological debate. Both
of them realized that, as regards the fundamental issues, the gap
between the Homoeousians and the Nicene party was extremely
narrow, and that the final success of the latter could be ensured
by establishing a rapprochement between them. So in his *De*

synodis (359) Athanasius made a conciliatory gesture, saluting[1] the Homoeousians as brothers (ὡς ἀδελφοὶ πρὸς ἀδελφοὺς διαλεγόμεθα) who in essentials were at one with himself. Since they recognized that the Son was 'out of the Father's *ousia* and not from another hypostasis', His authentic offspring and coeternal with Him, they were near enough to admitting the homoousion, which alone expressed with precision the truth which they evidently accepted. Hilary went even further in a work with a similar title published in the same year. He conceded[2] that the homoousion, unless safeguarded by a proper stress on the distinction between the Persons of the ingenerate Father and the generate Son, lent itself to Sabellian interpretations. He even allowed[3] the propriety of ὁμοιούσιος, especially in view of its anti-Sabellian emphasis on the three Persons, since it had to be understood in the sense of perfect equality, and that strictly entailed unity of nature. His conclusion[4] was that, since they acknowledged the distinction of Persons, the Catholics, *i.e.* the Nicenes, could not deny the homoeousion, while the Homoeousians for their part were bound to allow unity of substance if they believed seriously in the perfect likeness of substance.

A further practical step of great importance was taken in 362 at the council of Alexandria, which met under Athanasius's chairmanship during the *détente* caused by the death of Constantius (361) and the accession of Julian the Apostate. Every alert reader must have noticed, and been astonished by, the extent to which theological divisions at this time were created and kept alive by the use of different and mutually confusing theological terms. At the council it was formally recognized that what mattered was not the language used but the meaning underlying it. Thus the formula 'three hypostases', hitherto suspect to the Nicenes because it sounded in their ears painfully like 'three *ousiai*', i.e. three divine beings, was pronounced[5] legitimate provided it did not carry the Arian connotation of 'utterly distinct, alien hypostases, different in substance from each other', in other words 'three principles or three Gods', but

---

[1] *De syn.* 41.   [2] *De syn.* 67-71.   [3] *Ib.* 72-6.
[4] *Ib.* 84-9: cf. *ib.* 91.   [5] *Tom. ad Antioch.* 5.

merely expressed the separate subsistence of the three Persons in the consubstantial Triad. The opposite formula, 'one hypostasis', so disturbing to anti-Nicenes of every school, was equally approved,[1] its adherents having explained that they had no Sabellian intent but, equating *hupostasis* with *ousia*, were merely trying to bring out the unity of nature between Father and Son. By this statesmanlike decision, which incidentally shocked many[2] in the West who saw in 'three hypostases' a confession of tritheism, the union between the two parties was virtually sealed, and we can see foreshadowed in it the formula which became the badge of orthodoxy, 'one *ousia*, three *hupostaseis*'.

The theory has been advanced (e.g. by F. Loofs, R. Seeberg and J. Gummerus) that in making these overtures Athanasius and Hilary were, consciously or unconsciously, sanctioning the use of the homoousion in a homoeousian sense, i.e. as implying generic unity rather than numerical identity of substance, and were thus tacitly introducing a 'Neo-Nicene' theology. The premiss on which it rests, however, is misconceived, for we have seen that, whatever the deeper implications of ὁμοούσιος, the original Nicene teaching was, not that Father and Son are numerically one in substance, but that They share the same divine nature. There is, further, no real antithesis between generic and numerical oneness so long as the Son's essential deity is acknowledged, for Godhead (as these fathers were never tired of pointing out) is *ex hypothesi* simple and indivisible. Both of them, it should be noted, in making concessions to the Homoeousians, take for granted[3] their admission that the Son is a real offspring, deriving His substance from the Father's substance. Athanasius, indeed, for all his friendliness to the Homoeousians, still insists[4] that, in regard to the divine substance, 'identity' is a more appropriate term than 'likeness', and that Father and Son must be 'one (ἕν) in substance'. Hilary, admittedly, has learned from the Homoeousians the value of the idea of resemblance as a protection against the

---

[1] *Tom. ad Antioch.* 6.   [2] E.g. Jerome, *ep.* 15, 4 (dated 376).
[3] Athanasius, *de syn.* 41; Hilary, *de syn.* 51; 71-4; 84.
[4] *De syn.* 53; 48.

exploitation of the homoousion in a Sabellian sense; and in his *De synodis* he explains[1] the latter as meaning that the Son is perfectly like, or equal to, the Father in virtue of His generation from the Father's substance. Elsewhere,[2] however, both before and after 359, he makes his belief in identity of substance clear beyond any manner of doubt. If considered as Father and Son the Persons are two and can properly be designated as 'like', the substance which They both possess, and are, is one and indivisible.

This statesmanlike attitude of Athanasius and Hilary was not without effect. Coming at a time when the great body of the Homoeousians were growing increasingly apprehensive of the menace of unmitigated Arianism, it quietened their suspicions that the orthodox party was inveterately Sabellian, and made the homoousian theology more palatable to them.

2. *The Homoousion of the Spirit: Athanasius*

The second line of development, viz. the recognition of the full deity of the Spirit, demands a lengthier discussion, including an account of the pioneer contribution of Athanasius.

Since Origen's day theological reflection about the Spirit had lagged noticeably behind devotional practice. Alexander merely repeated[3] the old affirmation that He inspired the prophets and apostles. Arius considered[4] Him a hypostasis, but regarded[5] His essence as utterly unlike that of the Son, just as the Son's was utterly unlike that of the Father. Although the problem of the Spirit was not raised at Nicaea, a heightening of interest becomes discernible from now on. On the one hand, a radical like Eusebius of Caesarea, while clear that the Spirit is a hypostasis, reckons[6] He is 'in the third rank', 'a third power' and 'third from the Supreme Cause', and uses[7] Origen's exegesis of *John* 1, 3 to argue that He is 'one of the things which have come into existence through the Son'. If it is asked why,

[1] E.g. 67; 84; 88.
[2] *In Matt.* 8, 8; 16, 4; 31, 3; *de trin.* 4, 33; 7, 13; 11, 1; *c. Aux.* 7 f.; 11.
[3] *Ep. ad Alex.* 53.   [4] *Ep. ad Alex.*   [5] Cf. Athanasius, *c. Ar.* 1, 6.
[6] *Praep. ev.* 11, 20.   [7] *De eccl. theol.* 3, 6, 3.

Good argued by orthodox

unlike other created rational and spiritual beings, He is 'included in the holy and thrice blessed Triad', his embarrassed answer[1] is that He transcends them in honour and glory. The later Arians, Aetius and Eunomius, true to the logic of their position, regard[2] Him merely as the noblest of the creatures produced by the Son at the Father's bidding, the source of illumination and sanctification. On the other hand, a conservative churchman like Cyril of Jerusalem, while discouraging inquiry into His Person and origin, has a doctrine which shows later orthodoxy in the making. The Spirit, he claims,[3] belongs to the Trinity, and 'we do not divide the holy Triad as some do, nor do we work confusion in It as Sabellius does'. It is in union with the Spirit that the Son participates in the Father's Godhead,[4] and the Spirit is 'the universal sanctifier and deifier', 'a being divine and ineffable'.[5] Hence, like the Son, He is far removed from creatures, even the most exalted,[6] and enjoys a perfect knowledge of the Father.[7] His relation to the other Two is defined in the formulae,[8] 'The Father gives to the Son, and the Son communicates to the Holy Spirit', and, 'The Father bestows all graces through the Son with the Holy Spirit'. There is no hint of consubstantiality, but He is 'subsistent' (ὑφεστώς), 'ever-present with the Father and the Son',[9] and is glorified inseparably with Them.[10]

Cyril delivered his *Catechetical Lectures* about 348. It was in 359 or 360 that Athanasius was instigated to expound his own theology of the Spirit. Serapion, bishop of Thmuis, had called his attention to a group of Egyptian Christians who combined a recognition of the Son's deity with disparaging views of the Spirit. Called 'Tropici' by Athanasius[11] because of their figurative exegesis of Scripture (τρόπος = 'figure'), they argued that the Spirit was a creature brought into existence out of nothingness.[12] To be more precise, He was an angel, superior to other

the Tropici

---

[1] *De eccl. theol.* 3, 5, 17.
[2] Cf. Eunomius, *apol.* 25; 28; Basil, *c. Eunom.* 2, 33.   [3] *Cat.* 16, 4.
[4] Ib. 6, 6.   [5] Ib. 4, 16; 16, 3.   [6] Ib. 8, 5; 16, 23.
[7] Ib. 7, 11; 11, 12.   [8] Ib. 16, 24.   [9] Ib. 17, 5.
[10] Ib. 16, 4; 17, 38.   [11] E.g. *ad Serap.* I, 21; I, 30.
[12] Ib. I, 1; 1, 17; 1, 26; etc.

angels in rank, but to be classified among the 'ministering spirits' mentioned in *Hebr.* 1, 14,[1] and consequently was 'other in substance' (ἑτεροούσιον) from Father and Son.[2] They appealed[3] to three proof-texts in particular, viz. *Am.* 4, 13 ('Lo, I who establish thunder and create spirit . . .'), *Zech.* 1, 9 ('These things says the angel that speaks within me'), and *1 Tim.* 5, 21 ('I adjure you in the sight of God and Christ Jesus and the elect angels'). It seems probable that the Tropici, while anticipating the later Pneumatomachians and Macedonians, were not connected with them, but were a purely local sect.

Athanasius's teaching, set out in rejoinder to these theses, is that the Spirit is fully divine, consubstantial with the Father and the Son. First, after exposing the mistaken exegesis of the Tropici, he demonstrates that Scripture as a whole is unanimous that, so far from having anything in common with creatures, the Spirit 'belongs to and is one with the Godhead Which is in the Triad'.[4] Thus, while creatures come from nothingness, are the recipients of sanctification and life, and are mutable, circumscribed and multiple, the Spirit comes from God, bestows sanctification and life, and is immutable, omnipresent and unique.[5] Secondly, he makes much of the argument that the Triad is eternal, homogeneous and indivisible, and that since the Spirit is a member of it He must therefore be consubstantial with Father and Son.[6] Thirdly, he dwells on the close relation between the Spirit and the Son, deducing from it that He belongs in essence to the Son exactly as the Son does to the Father.[7] He is, for example, the Spirit of the Son, 'the vital activity and gift whereby He sanctifies and enlightens', and He is bestowed by the Son;[8] whatever He possesses is the Son's.[9] He joins with the Son in His work of creation, as *Pss.* 104, 29 f. and 33, 6 indicate;[10] and Their indivisibility is also illustrated by Their co-activity in the inspiration of the prophets and in the incarnation.[11] Lastly, he infers[12] the Spirit's divinity from the fact that He makes us all 'partakers of God [cf. *1 Cor.* 3, 16 f.]. . . .

---

[1] E.g. ib. 1, 1.	[2] Ib. 1, 2.	[3] Ib. 1, 3; 1, 11; 1, 10.
[4] Ib. 1, 21.	[5] Ib. 1, 22-7.	[6] Ib. 1, 2; 1, 20; 3, 7.
[7] E.g. ib. 1, 25; 3, 2.	[8] Ib. 1, 20.	[9] Ib. 3, 1.
[10] Ib. 3, 4 f.	[11] Ib. 3, 5 f.	[12] Ib. 1, 24.

If the Holy Spirit were a creature, we should have no participation in God through Him; we should be united to a creature and alien from the divine nature. . . . If He makes men divine, His nature must undoubtedly be that of God.' In deference to current convention Athanasius abstains from calling Him God directly. But his doctrine is that He belongs to the Word and the Father, and shares one and the same substance (ὁμοούσιος) with Them.[1]

What Athanasius says about the Spirit, we should observe, rounds off his teaching about the Trinity. The Godhead, according to this conception, exists eternally as a Triad of Persons (we recall that he had no term of his own for this) sharing one identical and indivisible substance or essence. All three Persons, moreover, are possessed of one and the same activity (ἐνέργεια), so that 'the Father accomplishes all things through the Word in the Holy Spirit'.[2] Whatever the Father effects in the way of creation, or government of the universe, or redemption, He effects through His Word; and whatever the Word carries out, He carries out through the Spirit. Hence he can write,[3] 'The holy and blessed Triad is indivisible and one in Itself. When mention is made of the Father, the Word is also included, as also the Spirit Who is in the Son. If the Son is named, the Father is in the Son, and the Spirit is not outside the Word. For there is a single grace which is fulfilled from the Father through the Son in the Holy Spirit.'

3. The Homoousion of the Spirit: the Cappadocians

If Athanasius took the lead in defending the homoousion of the Spirit, the task was completed, cautiously and circumspectly, by the Cappadocian fathers. We have already seen that the moderate section of the great central party, of which Cyril of Jerusalem was a typical representative, possessed a doctrine in effect acknowledging the divine status of the Spirit while declining to employ the homoousion to express it; but the old Eusebian subordinationism was still tenaciously upheld

---

[1] *Ad Serap.* 1, 27.   [2] Ib. 1, 28 : cf. ib. 1, 30 f.   [3] Ib. 1, 14.

by the left wing. As a result the manifesto[1] circulated by Basil of Ancyra and his friends after the synod of 358 contented itself with vague formulae stating[2] that the Spirit 'is given to the faithful from the Father through the Son', and 'has His being (ὑφεστώς) from the Father through the Son'. In 362, however, at the council of Alexandria, Athanasius secured acceptance of the proposition[3] that the Spirit is not a creature but belongs to, and is inseparable from, the substance of the Father and the Son. From now onwards the question of the Spirit's status becomes an urgent issue, and the underlying divergences of opinion are brought out into the light of day. In a sermon[4] preached in 380 Gregory of Nazianzus gives an illuminating picture of the wide variety of views which still held the field. Some, he reports, consider the Holy Spirit to be a force (ἐνέργεια), others a creature, others God. Others, making the vagueness of Scripture their excuse, decline to commit themselves. Of those who acknowledge His deity, some keep it as a pious opinion to themselves, others proclaim it openly, and yet others seem to postulate three Persons possessing deity in different degrees.

The two main divisions of opinion merit closer scrutiny. The opponents of the full deity of the Spirit were known as Macedonians or Pneumatomachians ('Spirit-fighters'). The former name, which only came into use after 380, recalls Macedonius, the Homoeousian bishop of Constantinople, who was deposed by the Arians in 360, but there is nothing to show that he had anything in fact to do with 'Macedonianism'. The Pneumatomachians, as they are more suitably named, harked back to the left-wing Homoeousians whom Athanasius must have had in mind when insisting on the homoousion of the Spirit at Alexandria. The moderate among them accepted[5] the consubstantiality of the Son, but the more radical (led by Eustathius of Sebaste after his rupture with Basil in 373—'the leader of the sect of the Spirit-fighters'[6]) preferred[7] 'like in

---

[1] See above, p. 250. [2] Cf. Epiphanius, *haer.* 73, 16.
[3] *Tom. ad Antioch.* 3; 5 f. [4] *Or.* 31, 5.
[5] Cf., e.g., Gregory Naz., *or.* 41, 8. [6] Basil, *ep.* 263, 3.
[7] Cf. Basil, *ep.* 244, 9; Sozomen, *hist. eccl.* 7, 2; Pseudo-Athanasius, *dial. c. Maced.* 1, 15.

substance' or 'like in all things'. The position of both groups is aptly summarized in the statement[1] attributed to Eustathius that he did 'not choose to call the Spirit God nor presume to call Him a creature'; as others expressed[2] it, 'He occupies a middle position, being neither God nor one of the others [i.e. the creatures]'. Their case was partly Scriptural; they cited[3] a multitude of texts suggestive of the Spirit's inferiority and pointed,[4] in particular, to the silence of the Bible respecting His divinity. They also argued[5] that, since no relationship was conceivable within the Godhead except that of Father and Son, the Spirit, if God, must be either a coordinate unoriginate principle with the Father or else the brother of the Son; since neither alternative was acceptable, He could no more be God than the other spirits.

In the opposite camp, because of the wide variety of opinion which had to be placated, progress towards the full Athanasian position was necessarily gradual. Gregory of Nazianzus describes[6] how Basil, when preaching in 372, studiously abstained from speaking openly of the Spirit's deity. At this stage he preferred to win over the wavering by tactful 'reserve' (οἰκονομία), contenting himself with the negative criterion of denial or acceptance of the creatureliness of the Spirit.[7] After his break with Eustathius and the increasing activity of the Pneumatomachians, he became progressively more definite. So, in the following year, in the profession of faith submitted to Eustathius, he advanced[8] a new test: the Spirit must be recognized as intrinsically holy, one with 'the divine and blessed nature', inseparable (as the baptismal formula implied) from Father and Son. In his De Spiritu sancto (375) he took a further step, urging that the Spirit must be accorded the same glory, honour and worship as Father and Son; He must be 'reckoned with' (συναριθμεῖσθαι), not 'reckoned below' (ὑπαριθμεῖσθαι) Them. This was as far as he was to go. He nowhere calls the

---

[1] Socrates, hist. eccl. 2, 45. [2] Didymus, de trin. 2, 8 (PG 39, 617).
[3] Ib. 3, 30-40. [4] Ib. 2, 10; Gregory Naz., or. 31, 23-8.
[5] Cf. Gregory Naz., or. 31, 7 f.; Didymus, de trin. 2, 5; Pseudo-Athanasius, dial. c. Maced. 1, 1. [6] Ep. 58.
[7] Epp. 113; 114 (dated 372). [8] Ep. 125, 3.

Spirit God or affirms His consubstantiality in so many words, although he makes it plain[1] that 'we glorify the Spirit with the Father and the Son because we believe that He is not alien to the divine nature'. The high-lights of his argument are (a) the testimony of Scripture to the Spirit's greatness and dignity, and to the power and vastness of His operation; (b) His association with the Father and Son in whatever They accomplish, especially in the work of sanctification and deification; and (c) His personal relation to both Father and Son.

The other Cappadocians repeat and extend Basil's teaching. Gregory of Nyssa, for example, emphasizes[2] the 'oneness of nature' shared by the three Persons, and quotes *Ps.* 33, 6 ('By the word of the Lord were the heavens established, and all the power of them by the Spirit [lit. 'breath'] of His mouth') to prove that the Word and the Spirit are coordinate realities. According to his version of *Lk.* 11, 2, the Lord's Prayer read, 'Thy Holy Spirit come upon us and purify us'. From this he concluded[3] that the activity of the Spirit was identical with that of the Father; and since the Son also was indistinguishable, there could be no difference of nature between the Persons. Gregory Nazianzen throws off all inhibitions. 'Is the Spirit God?' he inquires,[4] 'Yes, indeed. Then is He consubstantial? Of course, since He is God.' He, too, finds[5] support for his doctrine in the testimony of Scripture (e.g. *John* 4, 24; *Rom.* 8, 26; *1 Cor.* 14, 15), and also in the Spirit's character as the Spirit of God and of Christ, His association with Christ in the work of redemption, and the Church's devotional practice. To explain the lateness of His recognition as God he produces[6] a highly original theory of doctrinal development. Just as the acknowledgment of the Father's Godhead had to precede the recognition of the Son's, so the latter had to be established before the divinity of the Spirit could be admitted. The Old Testament revealed the Father, and the New the Son; the latter only hinted at the Spirit, but He dwells in us and discloses His nature more clearly.

---

[1] *Ep.* 159, 2.   [2] *Or. cat.* 3 f.   [3] *De orat. dom.* 3 (PG 44, 1157-61).
[4] *Or.* 31, 10: cf. ib. 34, 11.   [5] Cf. esp. *or.* 31.   [6] Ib. 31, 26.

A problem which the Cappadocians had to face, if they were to counter the Arian jibe that the homoousion of the Spirit seemed to involve the Father in having two Sons, was to differentiate between the mode of origin of the Son and that of the Spirit. All that Basil can say[1] on the subject is that the Spirit issues from God, not by way of generation, but 'as the breath of His mouth'; thus His 'manner of coming to be' (τρόπος τῆς ὑπάρξεως) remains 'ineffable'. He further teaches[2] that the one Spirit 'is linked with the one Father through the one Son'; it is 'through the Only-begotten' that the divine qualities reach the Spirit from the Father. Gregory Nazianzen is satisfied[3] with the Johannine statement (*John* 15, 26) that He 'proceeds' (ἐκπορεύεται) from the Father; what 'procession' means he can no more explain than can his adversaries what the Father's *agennesia* or the Son's generation means, but it distinguishes the Spirit from both. It was Gregory of Nyssa, however, who provided what was to prove the definitive statement. The Spirit, he teaches,[4] is out of God and is of Christ; He proceeds out of the Father and receives from the Son; He cannot be separated from the Word. From this it is a short step to the idea of the twofold procession of the Spirit. According to him,[5] the three Persons are to be distinguished by Their origin, the Father being cause (τὸ αἴτιον) and the other two caused (cf. τὸ αἰτιατόν). The two Persons Who are caused may be further distinguished, for one of Them is directly (προσεχῶς) produced by the Father, while the other proceeds from the Father through an intermediary. Viewed in this light, the Son alone can claim the title Only-begotten, and the Spirit's relation to the Father is in no way prejudiced by the fact that He derives His being from Him through the Son. Elsewhere Gregory speaks[6] of the Son as related to the Spirit as cause to effect, and uses[7] the analogy of a torch imparting its light first to another torch and then through it to a third in order to illustrate the relation of the three Persons.

---

[1] *De spir. sanct.* 46. [2] Ib. 45; 47. [3] *Or.* 31, 7 f.
[4] *C. Maced.* 2; 10; 12; 24. [5] *Quod non sint* ad fin.
[6] *C. Eunom.* 1, 42 (PG 45, 464). [7] *C. Maced.* 6.

It is clearly Gregory's doctrine that the Son acts as an agent, no doubt in subordination to the Father Who is the fountainhead of the Trinity, in the production of the Spirit. After him the regular teaching of the Eastern Church is that the procession of the Holy Spirit is '*out of the Father through the Son*'. Epiphanius, after describing the Holy Spirit as 'proceeding from the Father and receiving of the Son', takes a further step, influenced perhaps by his Western contacts, and omits the crucial preposition 'through'. In his view[1] the Holy Spirit is 'not begotten, not created, not fellow-brother nor brother to the Father, not forefather nor offspring, but out of the same substance of Father and Son'. He is 'Spirit of the Father' and 'Spirit of the Son', not through any composition analogous to that of body and soul in a man, but 'centrally to Father and Son, out of the Father and the Son'. He is 'from both, a Spirit derived from spirit, for God is spirit'.[2] Origen more than a century before, we recall, basing himself on *John* 1, 3, had taught[3] that the Spirit must be included among the things brought into existence through the Word. The same theory, with a strongly subordinationist flavour, reappears in his radical successors, such as Eusebius of Caesarea.[4] As stated by the Cappadocians, however, the idea of the twofold procession from Father through Son lacks all trace of subordinationism, for its setting is a wholehearted recognition of the homoousion of the Spirit.

4. *The Cappadocians and the Trinity*

The climax of the developments we have been studying was the reaffirmation of the Nicene faith at the council of Constantinople in 381. At this the consubstantiality of the Spirit as well as of the Son was formally endorsed. The theology which prevailed, as exemplified by the great Cappadocians themselves and by teachers like Didymus the Blind († c. 398) and Evagrius Ponticus († 399), may be fairly described as in substance that of

---

[1] *Ancor.* 7, 7 f.   [2] Ib. 70.   [3] E.g. *in Ioh.* 2, 10, 75 f.
[4] See above, p. 255.

Athanasius. It is true that their angle of approach was somewhat different from his. Emerging from the Homoeousian
tradition, it was natural that they should make the three
hypostases, rather than the one divine substance, their starting-
point. Hence, while the formula which expresses their position
is 'one *ousia* in three *hupostaseis*', their emphasis often seems to be
on the latter term, connoting the separate subsistence of Father,
Son and Holy Spirit, rather than on the former, which stood
for the one indivisible Godhead common to Them. Like
Athanasius, however, they were champions of the homoousion
both of the Son and (as we have just seen) of the Spirit. We
have already glanced at the kind of arguments they employed
to prove the deity of the latter. As regards the Son, they pressed
home the time-honoured considerations of His generation out
of the Father's being and of His functions as creator and redeemer, and in particular of the worship offered to Him in the
Church.

The essence of their doctrine is that the one Godhead exists
simultaneously in three modes of being, or hypostases. So Basil
remarks,[1] 'Everything that the Father is is seen in the Son, and
everything that the Son is belongs to the Father. The Son in
His entirety abides in the Father, and in return possesses the
Father in entirety in Himself. Thus the hypostasis of the Son is,
so to speak, the form and presentation by which the Father is
known, and the Father's hypostasis is recognized in the form
of the Son'. Here we have the doctrine of the co-inherence, or
as it was later called 'perichoresis', of the divine Persons. The
Godhead can be said to exist 'undivided . . . in divided Persons'
(ἀμέριστος ἐν μεμερισμένοις . . . ἡ θεότης[2]), and there is an
'identity of nature' (ταὐτότης φύσεως) in the three hypostases.[3]
'We confess', writes[4] Evagrius Ponticus, 'identity of nature
and so accept the homoousion. . . . For He Who is God in
respect of substance is consubstantial with Him Who is God
in respect of substance.' Gregory of Nazianzus explains[5] the

---

[1] *Ep.* 38, 8 (possibly Gregory of Nyssa is the author).
[2] Gregory Nazianzen, *or.* 31, 14.
[3] Didymus, *de trin.* 1, 16 (PG 39, 336).
[4] Cf. Basil, *ep.* 8, 3 (probably by Evagrius).   [5] *Or.* 42, 15.

position by stating, 'The Three have one nature, viz. God, the ground of unity being the Father, out of Whom and towards Whom the subsequent Persons are reckoned'. While all sub-ordinationism is excluded, the Father remains in the eyes of the Cappadocians the source, fountain-head or principle of the Godhead. Their thought is (as we have already seen when discussing the Holy Spirit) that He imparts His being to the two other Persons, and so can be said to cause Them. So Gregory of Nyssa speaks[1] of 'one and the same Person (πρόσ-ωπον) of the Father, out of Whom the Son is begotten and the Spirit proceeds', adding that 'in the strict sense (κυρίως) we describe the unique cause of Those caused by Him one God'.

To explain how the one substance can be simultaneously present in three Persons they appeal to the analogy of a universal and its particulars. 'Ousia and hupostasis', writes[2] Basil, 'are differentiated exactly as universal (κοινόν) and particular (τὸ καθ' ἔκαστον) are, e.g. animal and particular man.' From this point of view each of the divine hypostases is the ousia or essence of Godhead determined by its appropriate particularizing characteristic (ἰδιότης; ἰδίωμα), or identifying peculiarity (cf. γνωριστικαὶ ἰδιότητες[3]), just as each indi-vidual man represents the universal 'man' determined by certain characteristics which mark him off from other men.[4] For Basil[5] these particularizing characteristics are respectively 'paternity' (πατρότης), 'sonship' (υἱότης), and 'sanctifying power' or 'sanctification' (ἁγιαστικὴ δύναμις; ἁγιασμός). The other Cappadocians define[6] them more precisely as 'ingener-ateness' (ἀγεννησία), 'generateness' (γέννησις), and 'mission' or 'procession' (ἔκπεμψις; ἐκπόρευσις), although Gregory of Nazianzus has to confess[7] his inability to indicate wherein the Spirit's procession differs from the generation of the Son. Thus the distinction of the Persons is grounded in Their origin and mutual relation. They are, we should observe,

---

[1] Ex commun. not. (Jaeg. III, i, 25).   [2] Ep. 236, 6.
[3] Basil, ep. 38, 5.   [4] Ib. 2 f.   [5] Ep. 214, 4; 236, 6.
[6] Cf. Gregory Nazianzen, or. 25, 16; 26, 19; 29, 2.
[7] E.g. or. 31, 8.

so many ways in which the one indivisible divine substance distributes and presents Itself, and hence They come to be termed 'modes of coming to be' (τρόποι ὑπάρξεως). So Basil's friend Amphilochius of Iconium, after stating his belief in 'one God made known in three forms of presentation' (προσώποις), suggests[1] that the names Father, Son and Holy Spirit do not stand for essence or being ('God' does), but for 'a mode of existence or relation' (τρόπος ὑπάρξεως ἤτουν σχέσεως); and Pseudo-Basil argues[2] that the term ἀγέννητος does not represent God's essence but simply the Father's 'mode of existence'. A modern theologian[3] has aptly summarized their thought in the sentence, 'The whole unvaried substance, being incomposite, is identical with the whole unvaried being of each Person . . . the individuality is only the manner in which the identical substance is objectively presented in each several Person'.

The Cappadocians had thus analysed the conception of hypostasis much more thoroughly than Athanasius. As we have seen, they were emphatic that the three hypostases share one and the same nature. In the Triad the Monad is adored, just as the Triad is adored in the Monad;[4] and the distinction of hypostases in no way rends the oneness of nature asunder.[5] Their theory is that the unity of the *ousia*, or Godhead, follows from the unity of the divine action (ἐνέργεια) which is disclosed in revelation. 'If we observe', writes[6] Gregory of Nyssa, 'a single activity of Father, Son and Holy Spirit, in no respect different in the case of any, we are obliged to infer unity of nature (τὸ ἡνωμένον τῆς φύσεως) from the identity of activity; for Father, Son and Holy Spirit cooperate in sanctifying, quickening, consoling and so on.' Basil similarly finds[7] proof of the deity of the Spirit in the fact that His energy is coordinate with that of Father and Son. As Pseudo-Basil (possibly Didymus) remarks,[8] 'Those whose operations are identical have a single substance. Now

---

[1] Frg. 15 (PG 39, 112).   [2] C. Eunom. 4 (PG 29, 681).
[3] G. L. Prestige, *God in Patristic Thought* (2nd ed. 1952), 244.
[4] Gregory Nazianzen, *or.* 25, 17.   [5] Basil, *ep.* 38, 4.
[6] Cf. Basil, *ep.* 189, 6 f. (by Gregory).   [7] C. Eunom. 3, 4.
[8] C. Eunom. 4 (PG 29, 676).

there is a single operation of the Father and the Son, as is shown by "Let us make man in our image etc.", or, "Whatsoever the Father does, the Son does likewise"; and therefore there is a single substance of Father and Son.' Along similar lines Gregory of Nyssa argues[1] that, whereas men must be regarded as many because each of them acts independently, the Godhead is one because the Father never acts independently of the Son, nor the Son of the Spirit. The divine action begins from the Father, proceeds through the Son, and is completed in the Holy Spirit; none of the Persons possesses a separate operation of His own, but one identical energy passes through all Three.

The Cappadocians have often been charged with accepting the homoousion while interpreting it in a merely specific or generic sense, and the designation of 'Neo-Nicenes' has consequently been applied to them. The accusation, however, rests on a misconception, for we have seen[2] that it is exceedingly doubtful whether the fathers of Nicaea themselves used the term ὁμοούσιος to suggest anything more than the truth that the Son shares the same divine nature as the Father. Much more to the point is the related suggestion, which was advanced as much in their own day as in ours, that their doctrine, despite its sincere intention of maintaining the divine unity, was inescapably tritheistic. Admittedly certain features of their thought seem to lend colour to the charge, not least their unfortunate comparison of the *ousia* of Godhead to a universal manifesting itself in particulars. In his anxiety to evade the tritheistic implications of likening the Triad to three men sharing the same *ousia* of manhood, Gregory of Nyssa is forced to conclude[3] that in strictness of language we should not speak of a multiplicity of men but of one man. Yet the fathers themselves were fully conscious of the deficiencies of the analogy. Gregory of Nyssa, as we have noted, expressly draws attention to the unity of operation between Father, Son and Spirit; and Gregory of Nazianzus emphasizes[4] that the unity of the divine Persons is

---

[1] *Quod non sint tres* (Jaeg. III, i, 47).   [2] See above, pp. 235 f.
[3] Ib. (Jaeg. III, i, 41).   [4] *Or.* 31, 15.

real as opposed to the purely 'notional' (μόνον ἐπινοίᾳ θεωρητόν) unity of several men. Thus if Father, Son and Spirit are distinguishable numerically as Persons, They are indistinguishable as essence.[1] Vis-à-vis the Father, the Son is identical in substance (ταὐτὸν κατ' οὐσίαν[2]); and the analogy between the Trinity and Adam, Eve (made out of his rib) and Seth (the product of both) breaks down because the divine essence is indivisible.[3] In the very letter[4] which expounds the universal-particular analogy most fully, Basil (or whoever was its author) argues eloquently for the inseparability of the Persons and the ineffable oneness of Their being. The fundamental point which should be remembered is that for these writers the ousia of Godhead was not an abstract essence but a concrete reality.

This brings us to an element in the Cappadocians' thought which their critics often ignore, viz. their belief in the simplicity and indivisibility of the divine essence. In certain moods they seem reluctant to apply the category of number to the Godhead at all, taking up the old Aristotelian doctrine[5] that only what is material is quantitatively divisible. How can we be accused of tritheism, exclaims[6] Evagrius, seeing we exclude number entirely from the spiritual nature of deity? According to Gregory of Nyssa,[7] number is indicative merely of the quantity of things, giving no clue as to their real nature; and Basil insists[8] that if we use number of deity at all we must use it 'reverently' (εὐσεβῶς), pointing out that while each of the Persons is designated one, They cannot be added together. The reason for this is that the divine nature which They share is simple and indivisible. As Gregory of Nazianzus remarks,[9] it is 'absolutely simple and indivisible substance', 'indivisible and uniform and without parts' (ἀδιαίρετός ἐστι καὶ μονοειδὴς καὶ ἀμερής). In other words, they have transferred their emphasis from mere numerical unity to unity of nature.

---

[1] Or. 29, 2.   [2] Ib. 30, 20.   [3] Ib. 31, 11.   [4] Ep. Basil. 38, 4.
[5] Cf. Aristotle, met. 12, 8, 1074a; 14, 2, 1098 b.   [6] Ep. Basil. 8, 2.
[7] C. Eunom i (Jaeg. I, 85).   [8] De spir. sanct. 44.
[9] Ep. 243 (ad Evag. Pont., PG 46, 1104 f.: sometimes attributed to Gregory of Nyssa).

Evagrius says as much when he writes,[1] 'In answer to those who upbraid us with tritheism, let it be said that we worship one God, one not in number but in nature. Whatever is described as one in a merely numerical sense is not one really, and is not simple in nature; but everyone recognizes that God is simple and incomposite.' But the corollary of this simplicity is that tritheism is unthinkable.

5. The Trinity in the West

In the meantime Western theological reflection about the Trinity, virtually quiescent since Novatian, had begun to bestir itself. We have seen how Hilary, as a result of his sojourn in the East, was able to collaborate with Athanasius in winning over the Homoeousians, himself teaching a doctrine which, while absolutely clear as against Sabellianism on the distinction of the Persons, insisted on Their consubstantiality. A characteristic formula of his was,[2] Unum sunt, non unione personae sed substantiae unitate, and he cited[3] Is. 45, 14 f. (Old Latin) as proving that 'the Godhead of Father and Son is indivisible and inseparable'. A little later we find Ambrose conceiving[4] of three Persons Who are one (unum sunt) through Their having one substance, one divinity, one will, one operation; the idea of a universal with its particulars does not suffice to explain Their unity. A more conservative approach, reflecting the still powerful influence of Tertullian, comes to light in writers such as Phoebadius of Agen († after 392). 'We must hold fast the rule', he wrote,[5] 'which confesses the Father in the Son and the Son in the Father. This rule, preserving unity of substance in the two Persons, recognizes the economy (dispositionem) of the Godhead.' The Spirit, he added, is from God, so that if God has a second Person in the Son, He has a third in the Spirit. 'Yet all in all They are one God; the Three are a unity (unum).' Far the most original and interesting figure, however, in the

---

[1] Ep. Bas. 8, 2.   [2] De trin. 4, 42.   [3] Ib. 5, 38.
[4] Cf. de fid. 1, 2, 17-19; 4, 34; 5, 42; de incarn. dom. sacr. 8, 81-8.
[5] C. Ar. 22.

middle decades of the fourth century was Victorinus, the Neo-Platonic philosopher who after his conversion *c.* 355 set himself to defend the homoousion against Arian criticisms. Important for their own sake, his ideas are also noteworthy for the impact they had on Augustine.

Victorinus draws his inspiration from Plotinus, although his devotion to Scripture and the Christian revelation obliges him to make drastic modifications in the Neo-Platonic scheme. In harmony with the Biblical idea of a living God, he thinks of the Deity as essentially concrete and active; God is eternally in motion, and in fact His *esse* is equivalent to *moveri*.[1] In relation to the contingent order this movement takes the form of creation, while in relation to the Word it is generation.[2] He is thus able to develop a doctrine of eternal generation which evades the Arian objection that generation implies change. At the same time he holds[3] that the immanent dialectical process within the Godhead is intrinsically triadic; God is τριδύναμος, 'possessing three powers—being, living, understanding' (*esse, vivere, intelligere*). From this point of view the Father is the divine essence considered as absolute and unconditioned; He is entirely without attributes or determination, invisible and unknowable; strictly, He is 'prior to being' (προόν[4]). The Son is the 'form' by which the Godhead determines or limits Itself, thereby coming into relation with the finite and making Itself knowable.[5] He is, as it were, the eternal object of the Father's will, or again the object of His knowledge, the image by which He knows Himself.[6] He is related to the Father as act to potency,[7] or as Word to eternal silence.[8] The Spirit, about Whom Victorinus has less to say, is distinguishable from the Son as intelligence is from life, as the voice from the mouth which utters it. So Victorinus can write that[9] 'the Father is silence eloquent, Christ is His voice, and the Paraclete is the voice of the voice'; and again[10] that, 'if Christ is life, the Spirit is understanding'.

---

[1] *Adv. Ar.* 1, 43.   [2] *De gen. verb.* 29 f.   [3] *Adv. Ar.* 4, 21.
[4] E.g. ib. 4, 20; *de gen. verb.* 2.   [5] E.g. *adv. Ar.* 3, 7; 4, 20.
[6] Ib. 1, 31.   [7] Ib. 1, 41.   [8] Ib. 1, 13; 1, 41.
[9] Ib. 3, 16.   [10] Ib. 1, 13.

In one of his hymns[1] he sums up the characters of the Persons as 'Existence, Life, Knowledge—O blessed Trinity!'; and affirms, 'God is substance, the Son form, the Spirit concept'. Yet these three dynamic characters are shared alike by all three Persons; each with the others is only one substance, one will and life, one knowledge.[2] Again and again he insists on the circuminsession, or mutual indwelling, of the Persons (e.g. *omnes in alternis existentes*[3]). They are one with the unity which transcends number;[4] yet there is a distinction between Them which Victorinus would prefer to express by *tres subsistentiae* rather than by *tres personae*, or else by saying that the absolute Godhead subsists *tripliciter*.[5] He seems to envisage the being of God as in a continuous process of unfolding and re-folding (cf. *status, progressio, regressus*).[6] If the Son, as the form and image of the Godhead, reveals the unknowable, in the Spirit the same Godhead knows Itself, and so returns back to Itself. The Spirit is thus the link, or *copula*, between the Father and the Son, completing the perfect circle of the divine being.[7] Victorinus finds[8] the best analogy to, or expression of, the Triune Godhead in the soul, which on his view exists in man as a part, as it were, of God. In it can be seen the triad *esse, vivere* and *intelligere*, determinations or distinctions which are related to each other as the Persons of the Trinity of which it is the image, and which, like Them, are consubstantial.

6. *The Contribution of Augustine*

It was Augustine, however, who gave the Western tradition its mature and final expression. All his life as a Christian he was meditating the problem of the Trinity, explaining the Church's doctrine to inquirers and defending it against attack, and perhaps his greatest work is the long and elaborate discussion known as the *De trinitate*, which he put together at different dates between 399 and 419. He accepts[9] without question the

---

[1] *Hymn* 3.   [2] *Adv. Ar.* 3, 4; 3, 17.   [3] Ib. 1, 15 f.
[4] Ib. 3, 1.   [5] Ib. 2, 4; 3, 4.   [6] *Hymn* 3.
[7] *Adv. Ar.* 1, 60; hymn 1.   [8] *Adv. Ar.* 1, 32; 1, 62-4.
[9] E.g. *de fid. et symb.* 16; *de doct. christ.* 1, 5; *de trin.* 1, 7.

truth that there is one God Who is Trinity, and that Father, Son and Holy Spirit are at once distinct and co-essential, numerically one in substance; and his writings abound in detailed statements of it. Characteristically, he nowhere attempts to prove it; it is a datum of revelation which, on his view, Scripture proclaims on almost every page[1] and which 'the Catholic faith' (*fides catholica*[2]) hands on to believers. His immense theological effort is an attempt at comprehension, the supreme example of his principle[3] that faith must precede understanding (e.g. *praecedit fides, sequitur intellectus*). Here there is only space to single out the salient features of his exposition.

(1) While Augustine's exposition of Trinitarian orthodoxy is Scriptural throughout, his conception of God as absolute being, simple and indivisible, transcending the categories, forms its ever-present background. So in contrast to the tradition which made the Father its starting-point, he begins with the divine nature Itself. It is this simple, immutable nature or essence (he prefers 'essence' to 'substance', for the latter suggests a subject with attributes, whereas God for Augustine is identical with His attributes[4]) which is Trinity: cf. *et haec trinitas unus est deus*, and, *trinitatem quae deus est*.[5] The unity of the Trinity is thus set squarely in the foreground, subordinationism of every kind being rigorously excluded. Whatever is affirmed of God is affirmed equally of each of the three Persons.[6] Since it is one and the same substance which constitutes each of Them, 'not only is the Father not greater than the Son in respect of divinity, but Father and Son together are not greater than the Holy Spirit, and no single Person of the Three is less than the Trinity Itself'.[7]

Several corollaries follow from this emphasis on the oneness of the divine nature. First, Father, Son and Spirit are not three separate individuals in the same way as three human beings who belong to one genus.[8] Rather, each of the divine Persons, from the point of view of substance, is identical with the others

---

[1] Cf. *de trin*. Bks. 1-4.   [2] E.g. *serm*. 7, 4; *ep*. 120, 17; *Ioh. tract*. 74, 1.
[3] E.g. *serm*. 118, 1; *de trin*. 15, 2.   [4] *De trin*. 5, 3; 7, 10.
[5] *De civ. dei* 11, 10; *ep*. 120, 17.   [6] *De trin*. 5, 9.
[7] Ib. 8, 1: cf. ib. 6, 9.   [8] *Ioh. tract*. 39, 2-4.

or with the divine substance itself.[1] In this way God is not correctly described, as Victorinus had described Him, as 'threefold'
(*triplex*: a word which suggested to Augustine the conjunction
of three individuals), but as a Trinity,[2] and the Persons can be
said severally to indwell or coinhere with each other.[3] Secondly,
whatever belongs to the divine nature as such should, in strictness of language, be expressed in the singular, since that nature
is unique.[4] As the later Athanasian creed, which is Augustinian
through and through, puts it, while each of the Persons is increate, infinite, omnipotent, eternal, etc., there are not three in-
creates, infinites, omnipotents, eternals, etc., but one. Thirdly,
the Trinity possesses a single, indivisible action and a single will;
Its operation is 'inseparable'.[5] In relation to the contingent order
the three Persons act as 'one principle' (*unum principium*[6]), and,
'as They are inseparable, so They operate inseparably'.[7] In his
own words,[8] 'where there is no difference of natures, there is
none of wills either'. In illustration of this Augustine argues[9]
that the theophanies recorded in the Old Testament should not
be regarded, as the earlier patristic tradition had tended to
regard them, as appearances exclusively of the Son. Sometimes
they can be attributed to the Son or to the Spirit, sometimes to
the Father, and sometimes to all Three; on occasion it is impossible to decide to which of the Three to ascribe them.
Lastly, Augustine faces the obvious difficulty which his theory
suggests, viz. that it seems to obliterate the several roles of the
three Persons. His answer[10] is that, while it is true that the Son,
as distinct from the Father, was born, suffered and rose again,
it remains equally true that the Father cooperated with the Son
in bringing about the incarnation, passion and resurrection; it
was fitting for the Son, however, in virtue of His relation to
the Father, to be manifested and made visible. In other words,
since each of the Persons possesses the divine nature in a
particular manner, it is proper to attribute to each of Them, in

---

[1] *De trin.* 6, 9; 7, 11; 8, 1.   [2] Ib. 6, 9.   [3] Ib.; *Ioh. tract.* 20, 13.
[4] *De trin.* 5, 10 f.; 8, 1.   [5] Ib. 2, 9; *c. serm. Ar.* 4; *enchir.* 38.
[6] *De trin.* 5, 15.   [7] Ib. 1, 7: cf. ib. 2, 3.   [8] *C. Maxim.* 2, 10, 2.
[9] *De trin.* 2, 12-34: cf. ib. 3, 4-27.
[10] *Serm.* 52 passim: cf. *de trin.* 2, 9; 2, 18; *ep.* 11, 2-4.

the external operation of the Godhead, the role which is appropriate to Him in virtue of His origin. It is a case of what later Western theologians were to describe as appropriation.

(2) This leads us to the distinction of the Persons, which Augustine sees is grounded in Their mutual relations within the Godhead. While They are identical considered as the divine substance, the Father is distinguished as Father because He begets the Son, and the Son is distinguished as Son because He is begotten.[1] The Spirit, similarly, is distinguished from Father and Son inasmuch as He is 'bestowed' by Them; He is Their 'common gift' (*donum*), being a kind of communion of Father and Son (*quaedam patris et filii communio*), or else the love which They together pour into our hearts.[2] The question then arises what in fact the Three are. Augustine recognizes that they are traditionally designated Persons, but is clearly unhappy about the term; probably it conveyed the suggestion of separate individuals to him. If in the end he consents to adopt the current usage, it is because of the necessity of affirming the distinction of the Three against Modalism ('the formula "three Persons" was employed, not so that that might be said, but so as to avoid having to say nothing at all'), and with a deep sense of the inadequacy of human language.[3] His own positive theory was the original and, for the history of Western Trinitarianism, highly important one that the Three are real or subsistent relations. His motive[4] in formulating it was to escape a cunning dilemma (*callidissimum machinamentum*) posed by Arian critics. Basing themselves on the Aristotelian scheme of categories,[5] they contended that the distinctions within the Godhead, if they existed, must be classified under the category either of substance or of accident. The latter was out of the question, God having no accidents; the former led to the conclusion that the Three are independent substances. Augustine rejects both alternatives, pointing out that the concept of relation (*ad aliquid relatio*) still remains. The Three, he goes on to claim, are

---

[1] *Ep.* 170, 7; *de trin.* 5, 6; 5, 8; 5, 15.
[2] *De trin.* 5, 12; 5, 15-17; 8, 1; *Ioh. tract.* 74, 1-4.
[3] *De trin.* 5, 10; 7, 7-9; *de civ. dei* 11, 10; *c. serm. Ar.* 32.
[4] *De trin.* 5, 4.   [5] See above, p. 16.

relations, as real and eternal as the factors of begetting, being begotten and proceeding (or being bestowed) within the Godhead which give rise to them. Father, Son and Spirit are thus relations in the sense that whatever each of Them is, He is in relation to one or both of the others.[1] To modern people, unless schooled in technical philosophy, the notion of relations (e.g. 'above', 'to the right of', 'greater than') as having a real subsistence sounds strange, although they are usually prepared to concede their objectivity, i.e. that they exist in their own right independent of the observer. To Augustine it was more familiar, for both Plotinus and Porphyry had taught it.[2] The advantage of the theory from his point of view was that, by enabling him to talk meaningfully about God at a new language level, it made it possible simultaneously to affirm unity and plurality of the Deity without lapsing into paradox.

(3) Augustine was always puzzled[3] to explain what the procession of the Spirit is, or wherein it differs from the Son's generation. He was certain,[4] however, that the Spirit is the mutual love of Father and Son (*communem qua invicem se diligunt pater et filius caritatem*), the consubstantial bond which unites Them. His consistent teaching, therefore, was that He is the Spirit of both alike; as he put it,[5] 'The Holy Spirit is not the Spirit of one of Them, but of both'. This he believed to be the clear deliverance of Scripture. Thus in relation to the Holy Spirit the Father and the Son form a single principle: inevitably so, since the relation of both to Him is identical, and where there is no difference of relation Their operation is inseparable.[6] Hence Augustine, more unequivocally than any of the Western fathers before him, taught[7] the doctrine of the double procession of the Spirit from the Father and the Son (*filioque*). Answering the objection that since both the Son and the Spirit derive from the Father there should be two Sons, he stated,[8]

---

[1] For the theory of relations see *Ioh. tract.* 39; *enarr. in ps. 68*, 1, 5; *ep. 170*; 238-41; *de civ. dei* 11, 10; *de trin.* Bks. 5-7.
[2] E.g. Plotinus, *enn.* 6, 1, 6-8.   [3] E.g. *de trin.* 9, 17; 15, 45.
[4] Ib. 15, 27: cf. ib. 5, 12 (*ineffabilis quaedam patris filiique communio*).
[5] *Ioh. tract.* 99, 6; *de trin.* 1, 7.   [6] *De trin.* 5, 15.
[7] E.g. *ep. 170*, 4; *de trin.* 5, 12; 15, 29; 15, 45.   [8] *C. Maxim.* 2, 14, 1.

'The Son is from the Father, the Spirit also is from the Father. But the former is begotten, the latter proceeds. So the former is Son of the Father from Whom He is begotten, but the latter is the Spirit of both since He proceeds from both. . . . The Father is the author of the Spirit's procession because He begot such a Son, and in begetting Him made Him also the source from which the Spirit proceeds.' The point is that, since the Father has given all He has to the Son, He has given Him the power to bestow the Spirit.[1] It should not be inferred, he warns us,[2] that the Spirit has therefore two sources or principles; on the contrary, the action of the Father and Son in bestowing the Spirit is common, as is the action of all three Persons in creation. Further, despite the double procession, the Father remains the primordial source (cf. *de patre principaliter . . . communiter de utroque procedit*), inasmuch as it is He from Whom the Son derives His capacity to bestow the Spirit.[3]

(4) We come lastly to what is probably Augustine's most original contribution to Trinitarian theology, his use of analogies drawn from the structure of the human soul. The function of these, it should be noted, is not so much to demonstrate that God is Trinity (on his view revelation provides ample assurance of that), as to deepen our understanding of the mystery of the absolute oneness and yet real distinction of the Three. Strictly speaking, according to Augustine,[4] there are 'vestiges' of the Trinity everywhere, for in so far as creatures exist at all they exist by participating in the ideas of God; hence everything must reflect, however faintly, the Trinity Which created it. For Its veritable image, however, a man should look primarily into himself, for Scripture represents God as saying, 'Let *us* [i.e. the Three] make man in *our* image and *our* likeness'.[5] Even the outer man, i.e. man considered in his sensible nature, offers 'a kind of resemblance to the Trinity' (*quandam trinitatis effigiem*[6]). The process of perception, for example, yields[7] three distinct elements which are at the same

---

[1] *C. Maxim.* 2, 14, 7-9; *Ioh. tract.* 99, 9; *de trin.* 15, 47.
[2] *De trin.* 5, 15.   [3] Ib. 15, 47.   [4] E.g. *de ver. relig.* 13.
[5] E.g. *serm.* 52, 17-19.   [6] *De trin.* 11, 1.   [7] Ib. 11, 2-5.

time closely united, and of which the first in a sense begets the second while the third binds the other two together, viz. the external object (*res quam videmus*), the mind's sensible representation of it (*visio*), and the intention or act of focussing the mind (*intentio*; *voluntas*; *intentio voluntatis*). Again,[1] when the external object is removed, we have a second trinity, much superior because located entirely within the mind and therefore 'of one and the same substance', viz. the memory impression (*memoria*), the internal memory image (*visio interna*), and the intention or setting of the will. For the actual image, however, of the Triune Godhead we should look to the inner man, or soul, and in the inner man to his rational nature, or *mens*, which is the loftiest and most God-like part of him.[2]

It has often been assumed that Augustine's principal Trinitarian analogy in the *De trinitate* is that disclosed by his analysis[3] of the idea of love (his starting-point is the Johannine dictum that God is love) into the lover (*amans*), the object loved (*quod amatur*), and the love (*amor*) which unites, or strives to unite, them. Yet, while expounding this analogy, he himself reckons[4] that it affords only an initial step towards our understanding of the Trinity (*coepit utcumque . . . apparere*), at best a momentary glimpse of It (*eluxit paullulum*). His discussion of it is quite brief, and forms no more than a transition to what he considers his all-important analogy, based on the inner man, viz. the mind's activity as directed upon itself or, better still, upon God. This analogy fascinated him all his life, so that in such an early work as the *Confessions*[5] (397–8) we find him pondering the triad of being, knowing and willing (*esse, nosse, velle*). In the *De trinitate* he elaborates it at length in three successive stages, the resulting trinities being (a)[6] the mind, its knowledge of itself, and its love of itself; (b)[7] memory or, more properly, the mind's latent knowledge of itself, understanding, i.e. its apprehension of itself in the light of the eternal reasons, and the will, or love of itself, by which this process of

<hr />

[1] Ib. 11, 6 f. [2] E.g. *enarr. in ps. 42*, 6; *serm. de symb.* 1, 2.
[3] *De trin.* 8, 12–9, 2. [4] Ib. 15, 5; 15, 10. [5] 13, 11.
[6] *De trin.* 9, 2–8. [7] Ib. 10, 17–19.

self-knowledge is set in motion; and (c)[1] the mind as remembering, knowing and loving God Himself. Each of these, in different degrees, reveals three real elements which, according to Augustine's metaphysic of personality, are coordinate and therefore equal, and at the same time essentially one; each of them throws light on the mutual relations of the divine Persons. It is the last of the three analogies, however, which Augustine deems most satisfactory. The three factors disclosed in the second 'are not three lives but one life, not three minds but one mind, and consequently are not three substances but one substance'[2]; but he reasons that it is only when the mind has focussed itself with all its powers of remembering, understanding and loving on its Creator, that the image it bears of Him, corrupted as it is by sin, can be fully restored.

While dwelling at length on these analogies and drawing out their illustrative significance, Augustine has no illusions about their immense limitations. In the first place, the image of God in man's mind is in any case a remote and imperfect one: 'a likeness indeed, but a far distant image. . . . The image is one thing in the Son, another in the mirror.'[3] Secondly, while man's rational nature exhibits the trinities mentioned above, they are by no means identical with his being in the way in which the divine Trinity constitutes the essence of the Godhead;[4] they represent faculties or attributes which the human being possesses, whereas the divine nature is perfectly simple. Thirdly, as a corollary from this, while memory, understanding and will operate separately, the three Persons mutually coinhere and Their action is one and indivisible.[5] Lastly, whereas in the Godhead the three members of the Trinity are Persons, they are not so in the mind of man. 'The image of the Trinity is one person, but the supreme Trinity Itself is three Persons': which is a paradox when one reflects that nevertheless the Three are more inseparably one than is the trinity in the mind.[6] This discrepancy between the image and the Trinity Itself merely reminds

---

[1] *De trin.* 14, 11-end.
[2] Ib. 10, 18.
[3] *Serm.* 52, 17: cf. *de trin.* 9, 17; 10, 19.
[4] Ib. 15, 7 f.; 15, 11-13.
[5] Ib. 15, 43.
[6] Ib.

us of the fact, of which the Apostle has told us, that here on earth we see 'in a mirror, darkly'; afterwards we shall see 'face to face'.

NOTE ON BOOKS

General. G. Bardy, 'Trinité' (art. in *Dict. Théol. Cath.*); J. Gummerus, *Die homöusianische Parteibis zum Tode des Konstantius* (Leipzig, 1900); J. N. D. Kelly, *Early Christian Creeds* (London, 3 ed. 1972); J. C. Murray, *The Problem of God* (New Haven, 1964); G. L. Prestige, *God in Patristic Thought* (London, 2 ed. 1952); R. Seeberg, *Lehrbuch der Dogmengeschichte* II (Basel, 4 ed. 1953).

Special. R. Arnou, 'Unité numérique et unité de nature chez les pères après le concile de Nicée' (art. in *Gregorianum*, 1934); G. Bardy, *Didyme l'Aveugle* (Paris, 1910); 'Macédonius et les Macédoniens' (art. in *Dict. Théol. Cath.*); J. Chevalier, *La Théorie augustinienne des relations trinitaires* (Fribourg en Suisse, 1940); A. Gardeil, *La Structure de l'âme et l'expérience mystique* (Paris, 2 ed. 1927); J. Gribomont and P. Smulders, 'Esprit saint chez les pères' (art. in *Dict. Spirit.* IV); K. Holl, *Amphilochius von Ikonium und seine Verhältnisse zu den grossen Kappadoziern* (Tübingen, 1904); J. N. D. Kelly, *The Athanasian Creed* (London, 1964); J. Lebon, 'La Position de saint Cyrille de Jérusalem' (art. in *Rev. d'hist. ecclés.*, 1924); F. Loofs, *Eustathius von Sebaste* (Halle, 1898); 'Makedonius und die Makedonier' (art. in Hauck's *Realencyk.*); M. Schmaus, *Die psychologische Trinitätslehre des hl. Augustins* (Münster i.W., 1927); C. R. B. Shapland, *The Letters of Saint Athanasius concerning the Holy Spirit* (London, 1951); M. Simonetti, *Studi sull' Arianesimo* (Rome, 1965); 'Alcune considerazioni sul contributo di Atanasio alla lotta contro gli Ariani' (in *Studi e Materiali di Storia delle Religioni*, 1967); 'La processione dello Spirito santo nei padri latini' (art. in *Maia*, 1955); H. B. Swete, *The Holy Spirit in the Ancient Church* (London, 1912).

CHAPTER XI

FOURTH-CENTURY CHRISTOLOGY

1. *Introduction*

A CASUAL glance might suggest that during the greater part of the Trinitarian controversy the specifically Christological issue was left on one side. The council of Nicaea certainly ignored it, although producing a creed embellished with the emphatic statement that the Son WAS MADE FLESH, BECOMING MAN. These words were later interpreted[1] as designed to correct the Arian attribution of a defective humanity to the Redeemer, but it is much more likely that the intention behind them was to stress the reality of His incarnation against Gnosticism and Docetism. Since all were agreed, however, that the Word was in Christ, any conclusions about His status in relation to the Godhead were bound to react upon the view taken of the structure (if we may so call it) of the Incarnate. The Arians' denial of His divinity, for example, was closely connected with, and may have been a corollary of, their preconceived ideas about the union of the Word with the human element in Christ. The Nicenes, for their part, in affirming the homoousion, inevitably confronted themselves with the problem of combining deity and manhood in the Saviour. Hence, although matters were only brought to a head with the outbreak of Apollinarianism shortly after the middle of the century, the Christological implications of the Nicene debate had been lurking not far below the surface right from the start.

Our concern in this chapter will be with the Eastern Church. It was in the East that the issues were constructively fought out; and while theologians like Hilary had interesting ideas, the West generally lacked originality in Christology, and its

---

[1] E.g. Theodore of Mopsuestia, *hom. cat.* 5, 17.

contribution can be relegated to the next chapter. This means that Apollinarianism must occupy the centre of the stage here. Account must also be taken, however, of the Christological theories which held the field in the earlier half of the century, and of the emergence of rather different, anti-Apollinarian trends in the second half. For a large part of the period the prevalent bias was towards what has been called the 'Word-flesh' type of Christology, of which the theologians who reacted against Origen's special teaching in the third century were exponents.[1] Making no allowance for a human soul in Christ, this viewed the incarnation as the union of the Word with human flesh, and took as its premiss the Platonic conception of man as a body animated by a soul or spirit which was essentially alien from it. In rivalry with this, however, we can trace the growing influence of a 'Word-man' type of Christology, based on the idea that the Word united Himself with a complete humanity, including a soul as well as a body. Behind this lay the Aristotelian theory of man as a psycho-physical unity, and also the determination to do justice to the genuinely human character of the Figure delineated in the Gospels. These two types have been designated 'Alexandrian' and 'Antiochene' respectively, and although these labels are not always strictly accurate, they have a certain practical convenience.

2. *The Arians and Eustathius*

The clash between these two approaches to Christology can be usefully studied, decades before Apollinarianism entered upon the scene, by contrasting left-wing Alexandrianism, as represented by the Arians, with the teaching put forward in opposition to it by Eustathius of Antioch († 336), one of the keenest champions of the Nicene settlement.

All our authorities[2] agree that the Arians taught that in Christ the Word had united Himself to a human body lacking a rational soul, Himself taking the place of one. As a result they

[1] See above, pp. 158-60.
[2] E.g. Epiphanius, *ancor.* 33, 4; *haer.* 69, 19, 7; Theodore Mops., *hom. cat.* 5, 7-19.

had a straightforward, naturalistic conception of the unity in
Christ, as comes to light in the creed[1] ascribed to Eudoxius,
successively bishop of Antioch and Constantinople: 'We
believe . . . in one Lord . . . Who was made flesh but not man.
For He did not take a human soul, but became flesh so that God
might have dealings with us men through flesh as through a
veil. [He was] not two natures (οὐ δύο φύσεις), for He was not
complete man, but God in place of a soul in flesh. The whole
is one nature resulting from composition (μία . . . κατὰ
σύνθεσιν φύσις).' So far there was nothing singular about their
position, which closely reproduced that outlined by Malchion[2]
at Antioch in 268, especially in its insistence on the metaphysical
unity formed by the Word and the flesh. What apparently
shocked the earlier critics of the Arians was not so much their
'Word-flesh' Christology as the fact that they exploited it in
the interests of their general theology. Thus we gather from
Athanasius[3] that it was to the Logos that they referred the
difficult texts *John* 12, 27 ('Now is my soul troubled'), *John* 13,
21 ('Jesus was troubled in *spirit*'), etc., as well as the Gospel
passages attributing to the Lord ignorance, growth in wisdom,
and the need for help in temptation. This they could do without
inconsistency or embarrassment since His status on their theory
was that of a creature, superior to all others but none the less
passible and susceptible of change—as one Who was God by
nature manifestly could not be. Further, one of the points they
pressed home[4] against the orthodox was the difficulty of explaining His relation to the flesh on the assumption that He was
divine. That concrete metaphysical unity which the facts of
the case demanded could not, they insinuated, be established
between a Logos Who was truly transcendent and human flesh.

On the premises of the Word-flesh Christology these considerations were not without force; it was the realization of this
that prompted the reaction of which Eustathius was one of the
pioneers. Although tradition reckoned him an out-and-out
Antiochene, his thought prior to the Nicene struggle exhibited

---

[1] Holl, *Bibliothek der Symbole*, § 191.   [2] See above, p. 159.
[3] *C. Ar* 3, 26.   [4] Cf. Athanasius, ib. 3, 27.

some markedly un-Antiochene traits. Thus, while always admitting a human soul in the God-man, he regarded[1] it as having been in some measure deified by its association with the divine Logos. Christ's body, too, was 'holy', so that His divinity was reflected in His countenance.[2] At this stage he was even prepared to accept the typically Alexandrian *communicatio idiomatum*, speaking[3] of John the Baptist embracing the Word and the Jews crucifying Him, and of the Blessed Virgin as 'God-bearing' (θεοτόκος[4]). He was one of the first, however, to detect the real drift of the Arian Christology. 'Why are they so set', he inquired,[5] 'on demonstrating that Christ took a body without a soul, grossly deceiving their followers? In order that, if only they can induce some to believe this false theory, they may then attribute the changes due to the passions to the divine Spirit, and thus easily persuade them that what is so changeable could not have been begotten from the unchanging nature' (i.e. from the Father). Hence we find him insisting[6] not only that Christ had a rational soul or mind as well as a body, but that this was the subject of His sufferings. In this mood he rejected the *communicatio idiomatum*, declaring[7] it misleading to say that God was led like a lamb to the slaughter or that the Word died on the cross.

The Christology implied in his developed doctrine was clearly of the Word-man type. In expounding it Eustathius was led to distinguish a duality of natures in the God-man, and this has often been pointed to as an anticipation of Nestorianism. Thus he speaks of 'the man' and 'the God', writing[8] in Antiochene vein, 'The sentence, "I have not yet ascended to my Father", was not uttered by the Logos, the God Who comes down from heaven and abides in the Father's bosom, nor by the Wisdom which embraces all created things. It was spoken by the man made up of diverse limbs, Who had risen from the dead but had not yet ascended after His death to the

---

[1] *De engast.* 17 f. (Klostermann, 45).
[2] Ib. 10 (Klostermann, 31); frg. 74 (Spanneut, 121).
[3] Frgg. 64; 70; 68 (Spanneut, 114; 118; 116).   [4] See below, p. 322.
[5] Frg. 15 (Spanneut, 100).   [6] Frg. 41 (Spanneut, 108).
[7] Frgg. 37; 48 (Spanneut, 107; 109 f.).   [8] Frg. 24 (Spanneut, 102 f.).

Father.' Theories of this type are always faced with the problem of explaining how the Word and 'the man' formed a real unity, and Eustathius's was no exception. His most frequent suggestion[1] was that the Word 'dwelt in' the humanity, which served as His temple, His house, His tent. This indwelling was analogous, we may infer, to the Word's indwelling in prophets and inspired men, but differed, it would seem, in being continuous.[2] The meeting-point was the Lord's human soul, which according to Eustathius[3] 'cohabits with ($\sigma\upsilon\nu\delta\iota\alpha\iota\tau\omega\mu\acute{\epsilon}\nu\eta$) God the Word', so that the Incarnate can be described[4] as 'a God-bearing man' ($\check{\alpha}\nu\theta\rho\omega\pi\sigma\varsigma$ $\theta\epsilon\sigma\phi\acute{\sigma}\rho\sigma\varsigma$). Language like this lent itself to misinterpretation, but it is clear that, although he could give no satisfactory account of it, Eustathius was deeply concerned for the unity.

3. The Christology of Athanasius

If the Arian Christology, with its premiss that the Word was a creature in status, stood at the extreme left wing of the Alexandrian approach, Athanasius was its classic representative. His starting-point is *John* 1, 14, which he interprets[5] as meaning that 'the Logos has become man, and has not entered into a man'. With his strongly soteriological interest he claims that only God can save the fallen race, and for him the Word is of course fully divine. 'We ourselves', he states,[6] 'were the motive of His incarnation; it was for our salvation that He loved man to the point of being born and of appearing in a human body.' The incarnation, it should be noted, did not seem to Athanasius to have altered His transcendent status in any way, for 'in taking flesh He does not become different, but remains the same'.[7] Indeed, while encompassed in a human body, He continued to exercise sovereignty over the universe ($\kappa\alpha\grave{\iota}$ $\check{\epsilon}\xi\omega$ $\tau\hat{\omega}\nu$ $\check{\sigma}\lambda\omega\nu$ $\check{\eta}\nu$[8]). To describe what happened in His becoming man, Athanasius says that He took flesh or a body,[9] or that He

---

[1] E.g. frgg. 19; 41; 44; 45; 47 (Spanneut, 101; 108; 109).
[2] Frg. 9 (Spanneut, 98).   [3] Frg. 17 (Spanneut, 100).
[4] Frgg. 42; 43; 59 (Spanneut, 108; 109; 112).
[5] C. Ar. 3, 30.   [6] De incarn. 4.   [7] C. Ar. 2, 8.
[8] De incarn. 17.   [9] Ib. 8; 9; 10; etc.

fashioned a body for Himself in the Virgin's womb.[1] In this body He dwells as in a temple[2] (the use of this image, suggested by *John* 2, 19 f., was not confined to the Antiochenes), making use of it as His instrument (ὄργανον[3]). But His relation to it is no casual or accidental one, for He 'appropriates' (ἰδιοποιεῖται) it to Himself;[4] it is not another's body, but His very own[5]—if it were another's, His redemptive purpose could not have been accomplished. Hence it is a true incarnation, or 'becoming man' (ἐνανθρώπησις), of the Logos,[6] and it can be said that 'He became flesh, not that He has been changed into flesh, but that He has taken living flesh on our behalf and has become man'.[7]

Athanasius has therefore no use for Christologies of the Word-man type. How can they be called Christians, he inquires,[8] who say that the Word entered into a holy man, just as He entered into the prophets, and not that He became man, taking His body from Mary, and who dare to assert that Christ is 'one' and the divine Logos 'another'? The Stoics had conceived[9] of the Logos as the soul of the universe, and Athanasius borrows this idea, with the difference that for him the Logos is of course personal. On his view[10] the Logos is the animating, governing principle of the cosmos, and the rational soul of man, which fulfils an identical role in relation to its body, is a close copy of Him, in fact a Logos in miniature. Christ's human nature was, as it were, a part of the vast body of the cosmos, and there was no incongruity in the Logos, Who animates the whole, animating this special portion of it. The paradox was rather that, while present in the body of the Incarnate, animating and moving it, He was simultaneously present everywhere else in the universe, vivifying and directing it with His life-giving power.[11]

From this account it follows that the Word for Athanasius was the governing principle, or ἡγεμονικόν, in Jesus Christ, the subject of all the sayings, experiences and actions attributed to

---

[1] Ib. 18. [2] Ib. 8; 9; 20; *ep. ad Adelph.* 7. [3] *C. Ar.* 3, 35.
[4] *De incarn.* 8. [5] Ib. 18. [6] Ib. 4; 16; 54.
[7] *Ep. ad Epict.* 8. [8] Ib. 2: cf. ib. 11; 12; *ep. ad Adelph.* 3.
[9] See above, p. 18. [10] *C. gent.* 44; 30-4. [11] *De incarn.* 17.

the Gospel Figure.[1] It was, for example, one and the same Word
Who performed the miracles and Who wept and was hungry,
prayed in Gethsemane and uttered the cry from the cross, and
admitted ignorance of the date of the last day.[2] Experiences like
these might be thought hard to reconcile with His deity and
impassibility, and indeed the Arians argued that they were. But
Athanasius draws a careful distinction between what belonged
to the Word in His eternal being and what belonged to Him as
incarnate. The Apostle Peter himself (cf. *1 Pet.* 4, 1), he reminds
us,[3] made the point that Christ 'suffered for us in the flesh', the
innuendo being that it is to His fleshly nature that we should
attribute these human weaknesses and sufferings. 'These things',
he explains,[4] 'were not proper to the nature of the Word as
Word, but the Word . . . was subject of the flesh which
suffered them.' His treatment of the Lord's emotional experiences and apparent mental limitations (e.g. His distress of spirit,
His prayer for the removal of the cup, His cry of abandonment, His confession of ignorance) is in line with this principle.
As far as possible, for example, he gives[5] a purely physical explanation of His distress, fear, etc.; these traits were παθήματα
τῆς σαρκός. If Scripture says that Jesus advanced in wisdom and
grace, its real meaning[6] is that there was a parallel and progressive development of His body and disclosure of His deity.
When He is reported to have professed ignorance, it was a case
of feigned, not genuine, ignorance. Being Word, He knew all
things; but since He had become flesh, and flesh is naturally
ignorant, it was fitting that He should make a show of
ignorance.[7]

Athanasius sums up his position by saying[8] that we are correct
in our theology if, while distinguishing two sets of actions
which Christ performs as God and as God-made-man respectively, we also perceive that both sets issue from one and
the same Person (ἀμφότερα ἐξ ἑνὸς πραττόμενα). This brings
us face to face with the central problem of His Christology,

---

[1] E.g. *c. Ar.* 3, 35.   [2] Ib. 3, 43; 3, 54.   [3] Ib. 3, 34.
[4] Ib. 3, 55.   [5] Ib. 3, 54-8.   [6] Ib. 3, 51-3.
[7] Ib. 3, 42-6.   [8] Ib. 3, 35.

viz. whether he envisaged Christ's humanity as including a human rational soul, or regarded the Logos as taking the place of one. His anthropology, it should be pointed out, which was thoroughly Platonic and treated the soul as having no necessary connexion with the body, was perfectly consistent with the latter hypothesis. And indeed the alternative view, natural enough while the two pseudonymous treatises C. Apollinarium were assumed to come from his pen, is exposed to serious objections, at any rate so far as his attitude down to 362 is concerned. In the first place, his regular description of Christ's human nature as 'flesh' or 'body' seems to point in this direction, as does his failure to make any unambiguously clear mention of a soul. In reply it has been urged that such language was traditional, reflecting New Testament usage,[1] and that Athanasius himself drew attention[2] to the Biblical equation of 'man' with 'flesh'. Even if the linguistic argument, however, is inconclusive, the fact must be faced that his thought simply allowed no room for a human mind. As we have noticed, he represented the Word as the unique subject of all Christ's experiences, human as well as divine. So much was this the case that he regarded[3] His death as the separation of the Word from His body, and spoke[4] of the descent of the Word to hell. His attitude was revealed in a very striking way when he came to deal with the Arians' contention that the Saviour's ignorance, sufferings, etc., should properly be attributed to the Word, Who on their hypothesis was a creature. Had Athanasius admitted a human soul, here surely was a golden opportunity for him to point to it, rather than the divine, impassible Word, as the true subject of these experiences. But this obvious solution, as we have seen, never apparently occurred to him; instead he strained every nerve to attribute them to the flesh.

Athanasius's Christology, therefore, just as much as that of the Arians, conformed to the Word-flesh scheme; he differed from them only in his estimate of the status of the Word. Some scholars, while conceding his lack of overt interest in Christ's

[1] E.g. John 1, 14; Rom. 8, 3; Hebr. 5, 7; 1 Pet. 4, 1.
[2] C. Ar. 3, 30.   [3] Ib. 3, 57.   [4] Ep. ad Epict. 5 f.

human mind, have pointed to the fact that he nowhere expressly denies the existence of one, and have concluded that he may well have tacitly presupposed it. In view of what we know of the Alexandrian tradition, this seems an improbable theory. It remains a question, however, whether his attitude underwent a change about 362. At the synod of Alexandria held in that year agreement[1] was reached to the effect that 'the Saviour did not have a body lacking soul, sensibility or intelligence (οὐ σῶμα ἄψυχον οὐδ' ἀναίσθητον οὐδ' ἀνόητον εἶχεν). For it was impossible that, the Lord having become man on our behalf, His body should have been without intelligence (ἀνόητον), and the salvation not only of the body but of the soul as well was accomplished through the Word Himself.' Athanasius was chairman of the synod and, since he endorsed this formula, it has usually been inferred that from 362 at any rate he recognized a normal human psychology in Christ. Among the delegates present were representatives of Paulinus of Antioch, devoted to the memory of Eustathius and his belief in Christ's human soul; their argument that, if the Redeemer was to save men's souls as well as their bodies, He must have assumed a created soul Himself may have impressed Athanasius. Shortly afterwards we find him making precisely the same soteriological point,[2] viz. that our salvation embraces 'the whole man, body and soul', in as much as 'the Saviour really and in very truth became man'.

This conclusion may well be justified: although those who accept it are obliged to allow that, on the evidence of his later writings, Athanasius's acknowledgement of a human soul must have been purely formal, for he never succeeded in assigning it any theological importance. In view of this, however, serious doubts have been raised whether in fact he underwent the conversion suggested. It is possible that he may have understood the crucial words οὐ σῶμα ἄψυχον οὐδ' ἀναίσθητον οὐδ' ἀνόητον as meaning, not that the Lord possessed a created mind, but that the Logos Himself was the vivifying principle of His body and served as the intelligence or soul of the God-man. The

---

[1] *Tom. ad Antioch.* 7.   [2] *Ep. ad Epict.* 7.

formula was evidently put forward at Alexandria by adherents of the Word-flesh Christology in order to counter objections to it, presumably along the lines that it presupposed a maimed humanity. Their natural rejoinder was that it was misleading to represent Christ's humanity as being on their theory incomplete, since the Word, the archetype of the mind or soul, had united Himself with His flesh. This surely was the true import of the sentence which followed, 'It was impossible that His body should have been without an intelligence, seeing that it was the Lord Who became man on our behalf', where the accent should be placed on 'the Lord' rather than, as it is commonly placed, on 'man'. Apollinarius, we should observe, understood[1] these words in this sense; and this interpretation of the whole difficult passage accords much better than the conventional one both with the Alexandrian Christology in general and with the Alexandrian conception of the mind or νοῦς as the image of the divine Word. On the whole, the case for the view that Athanasius did not modify his Christology about the time of the synod of 362 must be reckoned the more weighty.

4. Apollinarianism

We come now to the heresy associated with the name of Athanasius's friend and coadjutor, Apollinarius of Laodicea (c. 310–c. 390). It was in fact the most subtle and thoroughgoing attempt to work out a theory of Christ's Person in the fourth century, and carried tendencies long accepted in the Alexandrian school to their logical limit. Because the rejection of a human mind in Jesus was its salient feature, scholars have sometimes been tempted to trace its ancestry to Arianism. Apollinarius himself, they have pointed out, had served as a reader under Theodotus, the Arian bishop of Laodicea, so that the intellectual atmosphere he breathed as a young man may well have been impregnated with Arian ideas. Yet it is paradoxical that so stout an antagonist of the Arians in the matter

[1] *Ep. ad Diocaes.* 2 (Lietzmann, *Apollinaris von Laodicea und seine Schule*, 1904, 256).

of the Godhead should have succumbed to their influence in Christology, and the hypothesis is in fact unnecessary. We have seen that the refusal to admit, or at any rate to take practical account of, a human mind or soul in the God-man was a permanent feature in the Alexandrian tradition and the Word-flesh Christology generally. Apollinarius himself, as reported by Gregory of Nyssa,[1] regarded his teaching as a restatement of the position of the fathers who condemned Paul of Samosata in 268, and we shall find that this self-diagnosis was not very wide of the mark.

According to Gregory of Nazianzus,[2] the beginnings of the Apollinarian heresy can be dated as early as c. 352. It was not until the council of Alexandria (362), however, that its teaching became a public issue, and not until a decade later that serious controversy flared up. An enthusiast for the homoousion of the Son, Apollinarius was a life-long opponent of the dualist, later to be called 'dyophysite', strain in the Antiochene approach to Christology. This reflected, he thought, the baneful influence of Paul of Samosata, whose doctrines were, he believed, being revived by the followers of Eustathius and Paulinus, and by Flavian and Diodore of Tarsus. 'I am astonished', he writes,[3] to find people confessing the Lord as God incarnate, and yet falling into the separation (τῇ διαιρέσει) wickedly introduced by the Paul-imitators. For they slavishly follow Paul of Samosata, differentiating between Him from heaven, Whom they declare to be God, and the man derived from the earth.' He protests against those who 'confess, not God incarnate, but a man con-joined (ἄνθρωπον θεῷ συναφθέντα) with God', i.e. in a merely external union,[4] and against the misleading distinction between 'two Sons', the Son of God and the son of Mary.[5] Such dis-tinctions imply that Christ is 'two',[6] whereas Scripture is emphatic that He is a unity (ἕν; μία φύσις[7]); and in any case, Scripture apart, such a duality is inconceivable.[8] That Apol-linarius was deeply influenced by soteriological motives is

---

[1] Antirrh. 9. [2] Ep. 102, 2. [3] Ep. ad Dion. 1, 1 (Lietz., 256 f.).
[4] K.M.P. 30 (Lietz., 178). [5] E.g. ad Iov. 3 (Lietz., 253).
[6] Frg. 81 (Lietz., 224). [7] Ep. ad Dion. 1, 1-9 (Lietz., 257-60).
[8] Frg. 2; 9 (Lietz., 204; 206 f.).

apparent. He was convinced that, if the divine is separated
from the human in the Saviour, our redemption is imperilled.
Considered merely as man, Christ had no saving life to bestow;[1]
He could not redeem us from our sins, revivify us, or raise us
from the dead.[2] How could we worship Him, or be baptized
into His death, if He was only an ordinary man indwelt by the
Godhead?[3] As such He must have been fallible, a prey like the
rest of mankind to corrupt imaginings, and consequently unable to save us.[4]

In order to eliminate the dualism which he considered so
disastrous, Apollinarius put forward an extreme version of the
Word-flesh Christology. He delighted to speak[5] of Christ as
'God incarnate' ($\theta\epsilon\grave{o}s$ $\check{\epsilon}\nu\sigma\alpha\rho\kappa\sigma s$), 'flesh-bearing God' ($\theta\epsilon\grave{o}s$
$\sigma\alpha\rho\kappa\sigma\phi\acute{o}\rho\sigma s$), or 'God born of a woman'. By such descriptions
he did not mean that the flesh was, as it were, simply an out-
ward covering which the Word had donned, but rather that it
was joined in absolute oneness of being with the Godhead
($\pi\rho\grave{o}s$ $\acute{\epsilon}\nu\acute{o}\tau\eta\tau\alpha$ $\theta\epsilon\hat{\omega}$ $\sigma\upsilon\nu\hat{\eta}\pi\tau\alpha\iota$) from the moment of its conception.[6] 'The flesh', he states,[7] 'is not something superadded
to the Godhead for well-doing, but constitutes one reality or
nature ($\sigma\upsilon\nu\sigma\upsilon\sigma\iota\omega\mu\acute{\epsilon}\nu\eta$ $\kappa\alpha\grave{\iota}$ $\sigma\acute{\upsilon}\mu\phi\upsilon\tau\sigma s$) with It.' The Incarnate
is, in effect, 'a compound unity in human form' ($\sigma\acute{\upsilon}\nu\theta\epsilon\sigma\iota s$
$\mathring{\alpha}\nu\theta\rho\omega\pi\sigma\epsilon\iota\delta\acute{\eta}s$[8]), and there is 'one nature ($\mu\acute{\iota}\alpha\nu$ . . . $\phi\acute{\upsilon}\sigma\iota\nu$)
composed of impassible divinity and passible flesh'.[9] Apolli-
narius interprets[10] the text 'I sanctify myself' (*John* 17, 19) as
implying precisely this: it 'reveals the indivisibility of a single
living entity', i.e. the substantial oneness of the Word with His
flesh (='myself'). The reason for this was that, as he viewed
the matter, the body of Christ could not by itself exist as an
independent 'nature'; to exist as such it needed to be conjoined
with, and animated by, spirit.[11] He brings out the full significance of his teaching in the statement,[12] 'The flesh, being

---

[1] *De fid. et incarn.* 9 (Lietz., 202).   [2] *Anaceph.* 9; 13; 20 (Lietz., 243 f.).
[3] Ib. 28 (Lietz., 245).   [4] Frg. 76; *ep. ad Diocaes.* 2 (Lietz., 222; 256).
[5] Frg. 108; 109; 49; 52 (Lietz., 232; 233; 216).
[6] *De un.* 2 (Lietz., 186).   [7] Frg. 36 (Lietz., 212).
[8] *Ep. ad Dion.* 1, 9 (Lietz., 260).   [9] Ib. 6 (Lietz., 258 f.).
[10] *De un.* 10 (Lietz., 189).   [11] *Ep. ad Dion.* 1, 8 (Lietz., 259).
[12] Frg. 107 (Lietz., 232).

dependent for its motions on some other principle of movement and action (whatever that principle may be), is not of
itself a complete living entity, but in order to become one
enters into fusion with something else. So it united itself with
the heavenly governing principle [i.e. the Logos] and was
fused with it. . . . Thus out of the moved and the mover was
compounded a single living entity—not two, nor one composed
of two complete, self-moving principles.'

The frankly acknowledged presupposition of this argument
is that the divine Word was substituted for the normal human
psychology in Christ. According to Apollinarius's anthropology,[1] man was 'spirit united with flesh'. So in the God-man,
as he expressed it,[2] 'the divine energy fulfils the role of the
animating spirit ($\psi\nu\chi\hat{\eta}s$) and of the human mind' ($\nu o\acute{o}s$).
Linked with this is the problem whether he was a dicho-
tomist (i.e. believed that human nature consists of body and
soul) or a trichotomist (i.e. believed it to consist of body,
animal soul or $\psi\nu\chi\acute{\eta}$, and rational soul or $\nu o\hat{\nu}s$). What is important, however, is that on his interpretation the Word was both
the directive, intelligent principle in Jesus Christ, and also the
vivifying principle of His flesh. The common account of his
Christology, viz. that it represented the Word as performing
the functions usually exercised by the will and intellect, does
not do justice to what was in fact its most distinctive feature.
This was his theory[3] that the Word was the sole life of the God-
man, infusing vital energy and movement into Him even at the
purely physical and biological levels. If it is objected that this
makes Him different from ordinary men, Apollinarius had no
hesitation in agreeing. He found[4] confirmation of the difference
in the wording of such texts as 'Found _as_ a man', and, 'In the
likeness of men'; and he suggested[5] that the theological significance of the virgin birth lay precisely in the fact that divine
spirit replaced the spermatic matter which gives life to ordinary
men. From his point of view the elimination of a human

---

[1] _Anaceph._ 16; _tom. syn._ (Lietz., 244; 263).   [2] Frg. 2 (Lietz., 204).
[3] E.g. _de un._ 11-13 (Lietz., 190 f.).   [4] E.g. frg. 45 (Lietz., 214).
[5] _De un._ 13; frg. 142 (Lietz., 191; 241).

psychology had the advantage of excluding the possibility of there being two contradictory wills and intelligences in Christ.[1] It also ensured the Saviour's sinlessness. A human mind, he explained,[2] is 'fallible and enslaved to filthy thoughts', whereas the Word is immutable. But, further, having the divine life pulsing through Him, the Incarnate was made immune from psychic and fleshly passions, and became not only Himself invincible to death, but also able to destroy death.[3] It was because the Word was, biologically and physically, the vital force and energy in Him that He was able to raise the dead and bestow life.[4]

Thus Christ, on this theory, is an organic, vital unity, just as a man compounded of soul and body is a unity; there is a 'unity of nature' (ἕνωσις φυσική) between the Word and His body.[5] As Apollinarius expresses it,[6] 'He is one nature (μία φύσις) since He is a simple, undivided Person (πρόσωπον); for His body is not a nature by itself, nor is the divinity in virtue of the incarnation a nature by Itself; but just as a man is one nature, so is Christ Who has come in the likeness of men'. We observe that his term for the God-man considered as a Person is *prosopon*. He also on occasion uses[7] *hupostasis*, being the first to introduce it into the vocabulary of Christology; it connotes for him a self-determining reality. His regular description of the Incarnate is 'one nature' (μία φύσις), and he never ceases to protest against the doctrine of 'two natures' taught by the Antiochenes. In a phrase which was to become famous he declared[8] that there was 'one incarnate nature of the divine Word' (μίαν φύσιν τοῦ θεοῦ λόγου σεσαρκωμένην). It is tempting, especially in view of his use[9] of the two terms in the same context, to regard 'nature' and 'Person' as synonymous in his vocabulary. If we do so, however, we shall be in danger of missing the special significance of his theology and of attributing to it ideas which were really alien from it. If the Person of the

[1] Frg. 2 (Lietz., 204). [2] Ep. ad Diocaes. 2 (Lietz., 256).
[3] K.M.P. 30 (Lietz., 176). [4] Anaceph. 20; 23 (Lietz., 244 f.).
[5] Frg. 129; 148 (Lietz., 239; 247). [6] Ep. ad Dion. 1, 2 (Lietz., 257).
[7] E.g. de fid. et incarn. 6 (Lietz., 199). [8] Ad Iov. 1 (Lietz., 251).
[9] Cf. de fid. et incarn. 6 (Lietz., 199).

Apollinarianism

Incarnate is constituted by the Word, the description of Him as 'one incarnate nature' connotes the organic unity, on the biological, physical and spiritual levels, constituted by the fusion of divine and human in Him. He explains his position clearly in an important passage:[1] 'The body is not of itself a nature, because it is neither vivifying in itself nor capable of being singled out from that which vivifies it. Nor is the Word, on the other hand, to be distinguished as a separate nature apart from His incarnate state, since it was in the flesh, and not apart from the flesh, that the Lord dwelt on earth.'

This close connexion of the flesh with the Godhead, their fusion 'into a single life and hypostasis' (to quote one of his disciples[2]), represents the distinctive core of Apollinarius's thought. Certain important features of his Christology flow logically from it, and can only be appreciated in the light of it. First, as a result of its fusion with the Word, he regarded Christ's flesh as being glorified. It has become 'divine flesh', or 'the flesh of God'.[3] Christ Himself can be properly described as 'the heavenly man' because of the union in Him of flesh with heavenly spirit.[4] Doctrines like these caused Apollinarius to be accused[5] of teaching that the Lord's flesh was heavenly in origin and pre-existent. His authentic doctrine, however, is that the body was derived from the Blessed Virgin; if it is a divine body, that is because it has never existed apart from the Word. So he remarks,[6] 'It is plain from all we have written that we do not say that the Saviour's flesh has come down from heaven, nor that His flesh is consubstantial with God, inasmuch as it is flesh and not God; but it is God in so far as it is united with the Godhead so as to form one Person'.

Secondly, as a corollary of this, he affirms[7] that Christ's flesh is a proper object of worship. The reason for this is, of course, that it cannot be separated from the adorable Word, to Whom

---

[1] *Ep. ad Dion.* 1, 8 (Lietz., 259).
[2] Timothy of Berytus, *ep. ad Hom.* (Lietz., 278).
[3] Frg. 116; 153; 160; *anaceph.* 29 (Lietz., 235; 248; 254; 246).
[4] *Tom. syn.*; frg. 25; *anaceph.* 12 (Lietz., 263; 210; 243).
[5] E.g. Gregory of Nazianzus, *ep.* 101, 6; Gregory of Nyssa, *antirrh.* 13; 15; 25.
[6] Frg. 164: cf. *ad Iov.* 3 (Lietz., 262; 253).
[7] Frg. 85; *de fid. et incarn.* 6; *ad Iov.* 3 (Lietz., 225; 197; 253).

it belongs and in Whose divine qualities it consequently shares.[1]
Thirdly, like all Alexandrian thinkers, he accepts and exploits
the *communicatio idiomatum*, stating[2] that 'the flesh of the Lord,
while remaining flesh even in the union (its nature being
neither changed nor lost) shares in the names and properties of
the Word; and the Word, while remaining Word and God, in
the incarnation shares in the names and properties of the
flesh'. As employed by Apollinarius, however, this is not
merely an external interchange of words and titles made possible by the fact that only one Person is subject. As the fact that
worship may be offered to the flesh reveals, it involves a real
exchange of attributes since both flesh and Word, while remaining distinct, are conceived of as being fused in 'one nature'.
Lastly, inasmuch as the flesh actually participates in the properties of the Word, Apollinarius draws the inference that the
divine nature is imparted to the faithful when they consume
the Lord's body at the eucharist. 'The holy flesh', he remarks,[3]
'is one nature (συμφυής) with the Godhead, and infuses
divinity into those who partake of it'; and as a result 'we are
saved by partaking of it as food'.[4] In other words, the believer
is deified by assimilating the deified flesh of the Redeemer,
and so Apollinarius's Christology is logically linked with his
soteriology.

5. *The Orthodox Reaction*

The brilliance and thoroughgoing logic of Apollinarius's
synthesis are undeniable. Nevertheless certain of its features
were bound to arouse disquiet. Opposition first manifested
itself at Antioch, where his disciple Vitalis had established the
heresy. After discussion with him Epiphanius insisted[5] that to
achieve man's salvation the Only-begotten must have assumed
a complete manhood. But the storm broke in 377. Pope
Damasus had become alive to the implications of Apollinarius's
position, and held a council at Rome which condemned him
outright. Its sentence was confirmed by synods at Alexandria

---

[1] Frg. 9 (Lietz., 206 f.).
[2] Cf. Timothy of Berytus, *ep. ad Hom.* (Lietz., 278).
[3] Frg. 155 (Lietz., 249).   [4] Frg. 116 (Lietz., 235).   [5] *Ancor.* 119.

and Antioch in 378 and 379 respectively, and by the council
of Constantinople in 381. The Cappadocian fathers, led by
Basil, had marshalled the case against Apollinarianism, and by
a series of decrees issued in 383, 384 and 388 Theodosius brought
it under the censure of the State and outlawed its adherents.

The chief objections advanced against Apollinarianism may
be shortly summarized. One of the most damaging and lasting,
based on the divinization of Christ's flesh which Apollinarius
taught, was that it was virtually docetic, implying that the
Saviour was not a real man but only 'appeared as a man'.[1] The
libellous, but none the less effective, suggestion that He had
brought His flesh from heaven was, as we have seen, a mis-
representation which was closely connected with this. Secondly,
the underlying assumptions of the whole theory were queried.
Was it necessarily the case, it was asked,[2] that two complete
entities, divinity and humanity, could not coalesce so as to form
a real unity? Or that the coexistence of two distinct volitional
principles in one individual was inconceivable?[3] Or that the
presence of human free-will in the God-man must have resulted
in His being sinful?[4] Thirdly, if it is assumed that Christ lacked
the most characteristic element in man's make-up, a rational
mind and will, His alleged manhood was not in the strict sense
human, but must have been something monstrous;[5] it is absurd
to call Him a man at all, since He was not a man according to
the accepted definition.[6] Fourthly, the rejection of a normal
human psychology clashes with the Gospel picture of a Saviour
Who developed, exhibited signs of ignorance, suffered and
underwent all sorts of human experiences.[7] Lastly (this was the
most important, most frequently recurring argument), for all
its concern for soteriology, the Apollinarian Christology, in the
opinion of its critics, failed to meet the essential conditions of redemption. It was man's rational soul, with its power of choice,
which was the seat of sin; and if the Word did not unite such
a soul with Himself, the salvation of mankind could not have

---

[1] Ps. Athanasius, *c. Apoll.* 2, 4.   [2] Gregory Nyss., *antirrh.* 39.
[3] Ib. 45.   [4] Ps. Athanasius, *c. Apoll.* 1, 15: cf. ib. 1, 19.
[5] Gregory Nyss., *antirrh.* 29; 45.   [6] Ib. 23; 33.
[7] E.g. ib. 24; 26; 34; Ps. Athanasius, *c. Apoll.* 1, 4 f.

been achieved. In a famous phrase[1] of Gregory Nazianzen, 'What has not been assumed cannot be restored; it is what is united with God that is saved'. It was Adam's νοῦς, he recalled,[2] which originally violated the commandment, so that it became imperative that the Redeemer should possess one too. According to Gregory of Nyssa,[3] 'By becoming exactly what we are, He united the human race through Himself to God'; while according to an unknown critic,[4] He used His incorruptible body to save men's corruptible bodies, His immortal soul to save souls doomed to death. It was necessary for Him to have both, for 'it was impossible for Him to give one in exchange for the other; and so He gave His body for men's bodies, and His soul for men's souls'. As the new Adam enabling us to participate in His divinity, Christ necessarily possessed human nature in its completeness.[5]

Opposition to Apollinarianism obliged churchmen to ponder the Christological problem. We may select the two Gregories as instructive examples. Gregory of Nazianzus teaches[6] that the Logos 'comes to His own image, and bears flesh for the sake of my flesh, and conjoins Himself with an intelligent soul for my soul's sake, cleansing like by like, and in all points, sin excepted, becomes man'. Thus there are 'two natures (δύο φύσεις) concurring in unity' in the God-man, and He is 'twofold' (διπλοῦς), 'not two, but one from two'; and of course there are not 'two Sons'.[7] His two natures are distinguishable in thought,[8] and can be referred to as 'the one' (ἄλλο) and 'the other' (ἄλλο), but there are not two Persons (ἄλλος καὶ ἄλλος); rather, 'they both form a unity (ἕν) by their commingling, God having become man and man God'.[9] So far from conceiving of this union as a moral one, or as a union of 'grace' like that between God and His prophets and saints, Gregory states[10] that the two natures 'have been substantially (κατ' οὐσίαν) conjoined and knit together'. To explain this union he propounds[11] the theory,

---

[1] Ep. 101, 7.
[2] Ib. 101, 11: cf. or. 30, 21.
[3] C. Eunom. 3, 10 (Jaeg. II, 294).
[4] C. Apoll. 1, 17.
[5] Gregory Naz., or. 30, 5 f.
[6] Or. 38, 13.
[7] Ib. 37, 2.
[8] Ib. 30, 8.
[9] Ep. 101, 4.
[10] Ep. 101, 5.
[11] Ep. 101, 10: cf. or. 38, 13.

reminiscent of Origen's,[1] that the Lord's rational soul provides a meeting-place for them; because of His natural affinity to the soul, the Word can 'mingle' with it. We notice his predilection for terms like 'fusion' or 'mixture' which later generations were to eschew as savouring of Eutychianism. His conception of the union, however, permitted him to exploit the *communicatio idiomatum* to the full, and to speak,[2] for example, of the birth of God from the Virgin and of 'God crucified', as well as to insist[3] on the propriety of calling Mary 'the mother of God' (θεοτόκος). A marked weakness of his theory, however, was its failure, despite its recognition of a human mind in Christ, to make adequate use of it in understanding such experiences as His growth in knowledge, His ignorance of the last day, His agony in Gethsemane and His cry of dereliction. The first he interpreted[4] as the gradual disclosure of the omniscience of the Logos, while in explanation of the second he suggested[5] either that Christ as man posed as being ignorant or that, strictly speaking, the Son could be said to be ignorant since He derived His knowledge from the Father. The other experiences he explained away,[6] clearly regarding the Logos and not the human mind as their subject.

The Saviour's human experiences received a much more realistic treatment from Gregory of Nyssa, whose Christology owed much both to Origen and to the Antiochene school. In contrast to Nazianzen, who thought of divinity and humanity as substantially united in the God-man, he conceived of the Godhead entering into and controlling the manhood, so that Jesus could be called[7] 'the God-receiving man' (θεοδόχος ἄνθρωπος), 'the man in whom He tabernacled'. According to his account,[8] the Holy Spirit at the incarnation first prepared the human body and soul as a special receptacle (οἰκεῖον σκεῦος) for the divinity, and the heavenly Son then 'mingled Himself' with them, the divine nature thereby becoming 'present in

---

[1] See above, p. 155.   [2] *Carm. dogm.* 10, 49; *or.* 45, 29.
[3] *Ep.* 101, 4.   [4] *Or.* 43, 38.
[5] Ib. 30, 15 f.   [6] Ib. 30, 12; 30, 5.
[7] *In cant. hom.* 13; *c. Eunom.* 3, 3 (Jaeg. VI, 311; II, 126).
[8] *Antirrh.* 9; 55; *de trid. spat.* (Jaeg. IX, 292).

them both'. Thus 'God came to be in human nature', but the manner of the union is as mysterious and inexplicable as the union between body and soul in man.[1] In this 'mingling' (ἀνάκρασις was his favourite term) the flesh was the passive, the Logos the active, element,[2] and a transformation (cf. μετα- στοιχειοῦν; μεταπεποιῆσθαι) of the human nature into the divine was initiated. In the historical Jesus, however, the characteristics of the two natures remained distinguishable.[3] Consequently, when Christ endured suffering or other human experiences, it was not His divinity which endured them, but 'the man attached by the union to the divinity'; they belonged 'to the human part of Christ'.[4] The Godhead, being impassible, remained unaffected, although through its concrete oneness with the humanity it indirectly participated in its limitations and weaknesses. In the same way Gregory could recognize[5] in Christ a real human will distinct from, and on occasion contrary to, His divine will, although the divine will always prevailed. Similarly he took[6] the meaning of *Luke* 2, 52 to be that Christ's human soul, through its union with the divine Wisdom, itself gradually developed in wisdom and knowledge, in much the same way as His body grew as a result of the nourishment it consumed from day to day.

Gregory of Nyssa thus tended to hold the two natures apart, regarding the Logos as the active principle and the manhood as the passive one, and strongly emphasizing the independent character of the latter. Yet the union between them, effected at Christ's conception, was, on his view,[7] unbreakable, designed to last for ever. The God-man was 'one Person' (ἓν πρόσ- ωπον[8]); and because of the close conjunction and fusion (διὰ τὴν συνάφειάν τε καὶ συμφυίαν) between the Lord and 'the servant in whom the Lord is', the attributes and experiences properly belonging to the one could correctly be ascribed to the other.[9]

---

[1] Or. cat. 11.   [2] C. Eunom. 3, 3; 3, 4 (Jaeg. II, 130; 136); antirrh. 40.
[3] C. Eunom. 3, 4 (Jaeg. II, 135 f.).
[4] Antirrh. 21; 24; c. Eunom. 3, 4 (Jaeg. II, 136 f.).
[5] Antirrh. 32: cf. de trid. spat. (Jaeg. IX, 292).
[6] Antirrh. 28   [7] Or. cat. 16.
[8] C. Eunom. 3, 3 (Jaeg. II, 122).   [9] Ib. 3, 3 (Jaeg. II, 131).

Even so, when Gregory called[1] the Virgin 'Theotokos', he seems to have been making a concession to popular usage, and the customary language of the *communicatio idiomatum* about God's suffering, dying, etc., clearly did not come naturally to his lips. On the other hand, if he allows full play to the human nature during Christ's earthly life, the situation changes with His resurrection and glorification. Then begins 'the transformation of the lowly into the lofty'.[2] The immaterial essence of the Logos 'transelements' the material body born of the Virgin into the divine, immutable nature;[3] the flesh which suffered becomes then, as a result of the union, identical with the nature which assumed it.[4] Like a drop of vinegar which falls into the sea and is wholly absorbed, the humanity loses all its proper qualities and is changed into divinity.[5]

change after the Resurrection

We may glance briefly at some features in the Christologies of leading contemporary teachers. Epiphanius taught[6] that the Word 'became man, that is, took a complete man comprising animal soul, body and rational mind . . . He became man completely'. His divinity was not affected by His sufferings, which could nevertheless be predicated of it.[7] Unlike the other Cappadocians, Basil had nothing fresh to contribute. He stressed, however, the reality of Christ's human soul, fully accepted[8] that it was the subject of the affections (weariness, grief, etc.) necessary to a living being, but refused to attribute to it 'the affections which sully the purity of our life'. He also declined[9] to admit that Jesus could have been ignorant, explaining *Mk.* 13, 32 as meaning, not that the Son did not really know 'that day or that hour', but that although He possessed this knowledge, He derived it from the Father. His friend Amphilochius of Iconium used to be acclaimed as the originator of the 'one hypostasis' or 'one prosopon' formula, but the texts suggesting this have been shown to be spurious. In fact his

---

[1] Cf. *ep.* 3 (PG 46, 1024).
[2] *C. Eunom.* 3, 3 (Jaeg. II, 123).
[3] *Antirrh.* 25: cf. ib. 53.
[4] *C. Eunom.* 3, 3 (Jaeg. II, 119).
[5] *Antirrh.* 42.
[6] *Ancor.* 119, 5 f.
[7] *Ancor.* 92, 2 f.; *haer.* 77, 33.
[8] *Ep.* 261, 3.
[9] *Ep.* 236, 1 f.

Christology was relatively unsophisticated and fluid, betraying no influence from the great Cappadocians. While he sometimes distinguished[1] sharply between 'the Godhead' and 'the man', he could equally readily emphasize the *communicatio idiomatum*, speaking[2] of the Maker of the universe being born of a virgin, and of 'the Lord's passion'. One of his most interesting statements,[3] directed perhaps against the Apollinarians, is that Christ had complete freedom of will (αὐτεξούσιος), acting 'without any compulsion in respect of the two elements out of which He was according to His nature composed.' If we exclude the *De trinitate* formerly attributed to him, Didymus the Blind had relatively undeveloped Christological views. He repeatedly emphasized[4] the Incarnate's possession of a complete humanity, adding[5] however that His human soul 'did not commit or know sin'. A fuller recognition, however, of the theological importance of Christ's human soul may be discerned in the *Commentary on Psalms* found at Toura in 1941. The unknown author (the case for his being Didymus cannot be dismissed) affirmed that it was of the same nature (ὁμοούσιος) as other human souls, and thus was susceptible to at least the initial stirrings of passion (προπάθεια).[6] These did not involve it in sin, but were the essential precondition of the reality and merit of the Saviour's struggle against evil.[7] Christ was at once God and man, having 'two modes of manifestation' (δύο πρόσωπα), the unity of His person being assured by the recognition that he was 'God become man' (θεὸς ἐνανθρωπήσας).[8]

6. The Antiochene Christology

While alive to the dangers of Apollinarianism, the theologians discussed in the last section worked for the most part within the same 'Word-flesh' framework of ideas and (the commentary of Toura excepted) had little positive contribution to make to the solution of the Christological problem. What was called for, if dogma was to renew contact with the Gospel

[1] E.g. frgg. 1, 12 (PG 39, 100A; 109A).   [2] Frg. 3 (PG 39, 100C and 101A).
[3] Frg. 16 (PG 39, 116A).   [4] E.g. *in Zach.* 4, 92; 235.   [5] Ib. 1, 177; 281.
[6] Text xviii, 10, 2–7.   [7] Text xiv, 14, 7–14.   [8] Texts x, 7, 22; 5, 20.

revelation, was a thoroughly realistic acknowledgement of the human life and experiences of the Incarnate and of the theological significance of His human soul. It was the achievement of the Antiochene School, in the last decades of the fourth and first half of the fifth centuries, to supply this. Whatever the defects of its own doctrine as sometimes expounded, it deserves credit for bringing back the historical Jesus. The 'Word-man' Christology of Eustathius of Antioch has already been noticed. After his deposition c. 330 his supporters grouped themselves around the priest Paulinus, loyally maintaining his teaching, and succeeded at Alexandria in 362 in carrying the point, although in what we have seen was an ambiguous formula, that the Lord's humanity must have included an animating principle and a normal human mind. The decisive impulses, however, towards what is conventionally called the Antiochene Christology seem to have come from thinkers connected with the anti-Paulinian party of bishop Meletius of Antioch. We have now to consider briefly the two most famous of these, both great exegetes as well as bishops, Diodore of Tarsus († c. 394) and Theodore of Mopsuestia († 428).

Although branded as a Nestorian by a synod held at Constantinople in 499, Diodore was reckoned a pillar of orthodoxy in his own day. When Julian the Apostate was residing at Antioch in 362–3, he stoutly defended the full divinity of 'the Galilaean' against the emperor's sceptical jibes, and Theodosius eulogized him as a champion of the faith in his decree ratifying the decisions of the council of Constantinople of 381. The sparseness of the surviving fragments[1] of his writings, and the uncertainty of the provenance of some of them, make it difficult to reconstruct his Christology with precision. One surprising fact which they reveal is that, despite its 'Antiochene' pattern and tendency, it did not conform to the 'Word-man' type, and in fact started from and remained marked by 'Word-flesh' presuppositions. This 'Alexandrian' strain is brought out by such facts[2] as (a) that, while recognizing the existence of a

[1] Collected by R. Abramowski, Z.N.T.W. 42 (1949), and by M. Brière, Revue de l'orient chrétien 10 (30), 1946.　　[2] E.g. frg. 36; 16; 39 (Brière).

human soul in Christ, Diodore assigned it no practical role in His growth in wisdom (*Lk.* 2, 52) or in His descent to hell, and (b) that he regularly contrasted 'the Word' and 'the flesh' (not 'the man') in the God-man. In harmony with this his polemic against Apollinarianism seems to have been aimed less at its mutilation of the Lord's humanity than at its monophysite tendency. In particular, the proposition that the Incarnate was a single hypostasis aroused his criticism.[1] The divinity, he argued, must be compromised if the Word and the flesh form a substantial unity analogous to that formed by body and soul in man. In reaction to this his own theory strove to hold them apart, and thus he was led to distinguish[2] the Son of God and the son of David. Scripture, he pleaded,[3] draws a sharp line of demarcation between the activities of the 'two Sons'. The union was not the result of any fusion ('mixture') of the Word with the flesh; if it had been, why should those who blaspheme against the Son of Man receive forgiveness, while those who blaspheme against the Spirit do not?[4] Rather it came about through the Word dwelling in the flesh as in a temple.[5] The relationship, though similar in kind, differed from that of God with His prophets, for whereas they enjoyed the fragmentary, very occasional inspiration of the Spirit, the son of David was permanently and completely filled with the glory and wisdom of the Word.[6] Yet both were united in worship, since the son of David shared in the devotion offered to the Son of God, just as the purple robe of the monarch can be said to share in the reverence paid to his person.

If we depend on fragments for our knowledge of Diodore, we have much richer and fuller materials available for understanding the thought of his pupil Theodore. Some of these (e.g. the fragments of his *De incarnatione*) consist of collections of extracts from his writings deliberately compiled in order to discredit him at the Fifth General Council (553), and consequently must be treated with caution, though not necessarily

---

[1] Frg. 26 (Brière). [2] E.g. frg. 42 (Abram.).
[3] Frg. 19: cf. frg. 42 (Abram.). [4] Frg. 20 (Abram.).
[5] Frg. 20; 35 (Abram.). [6] Frg. 35; 38 (Abram.).

with the extreme scepticism which has become fashionable in
some quarters. Unlike Diodore, Theodore made opposition to
the Alexandrian truncation of Christ's humanity his starting-
point, fastening particularly on the Arian and Apollinarian
versions of it. Thus he repeats[1] the familiar plea that, since sin
originates in acts of will, Christ must of necessity have assumed
a human soul. But he carries his criticism of the Word-flesh
Christology much deeper than any of the theologians studied
so far. The premiss of that theory in its developed form had
been that the Word was the unique directive principle in Christ,
being His rationality and also the vital force animating His
whole physical structure. Theodore undermines this by pointing out[2] that, if it were true, the Lord's humanity must have
been immune from all the weaknesses and defects (e.g. hunger,
thirst, weariness) of human nature, since these are not intrinsic
to it but spring from the imperfections of the soul normally
presiding over it. He concludes[3] that 'He took not only a body
but a complete man, composed of a body and an immortal
soul', indicating elsewhere[4] that he considered soul and body
distinct natures. Thus the Lord's created soul had real significance in his eyes; it was the principle of life and activity in Him,
and equally of the saving acts which secure our redemption.
He was aware, of course, of the Apollinarian argument that
the soul is naturally sinful, but cited[5] *1 Tim.* 3, 16 ('He was
justified in the Spirit') and *Hebr.* 9, 14 ('Who in the Spirit
offered Himself without spot to God') as demonstrating
that divine grace kept Christ's mind and will immune from
sin.

Positively considered, Theodore's Christology conforms to
the 'Word-man' scheme. He presupposes a human nature
which is complete and independent, which undergoes real
growth in knowledge and the discernment of good and evil as
well as in physical development,[6] and which has to struggle
with temptation.[7] He dwells at length on the details of the

---

[1] *Hom. cat.* 5, 10-14.   [2] Ib. 5, 9.   [3] Ib. 5, 19.
[4] *C. Apoll.* 4 (in H. B. Swete, *Theodore of Mopsuestia on the Minor Epistles
of S. Paul,* 2, 318 f.).   [5] Ib. 5, 19.
[6] *De incarn.* 7 (Swete, 297 f.).   [7] Ib. 15 (Swete, 311).

Lord's earthly career.[1] It is characteristic of him to describe[2] the humanity as 'the man assumed', and occasionally his language[3] seems almost to suggest that the Word adopted a human being who was already in existence. A typical sentence runs,[4] 'Let us apply our minds to the distinction of natures; He Who assumed is God and only-begotten Son, but the form of a slave, he who was assumed, is man'. He thus gives the impression of pre-supposing a real duality. Yet he dismisses[5] Diodore's theory of two Sons as 'naive', arguing that 'the distinction of natures does not prevent their being one'. How then does he conceive of the union between the *homo assumptus* and the Word Who assumed him? The metaphor of <u>indwelling</u> (ἐνοίκησις) provides him with his most satisfying explanation. 'He applies the term "garment"', he remarks[6] on *Ps.* 45, 8, 'to His body, which was wrapped about Him, the divinity being within in virtue of His indwelling'. Again, he teaches[7] that the human nature is, as it were, a temple or shrine in which the Godhead dwells, finding authority for this line of thought in the Lord's identification of His body with the Temple in *John* 2, 19. In a well-known passage[8] preserved by his critics, he argued that the Word cannot have pervaded the humanity either sub-stantially (κατ' οὐσίαν) or by direct activity (κατ' ἐνέργειαν), since the Godhead is necessarily present everywhere in both these ways, whereas the presence of the Word in the *homo assumptus* must presumably be special. His conclusion is that the union is κατ' εὐδοκίαν, i.e. by favour or grace. By this he suggests that God does not simply approve of the men in whom He dwells, but that He actively cooperates with and assists them by His loving disposition. In contrast to the Apostles and just men, however, He dwelt in the *homo assumptus* 'as in a son'. This meant[9] that 'He united the whole man assumed with Himself, causing Him to share with Him in all the honour which He, the Son by nature indwelling him, enjoys'. Thus He accom-plishes all things in him.

---

[1] *Hom. cat.* passim. [2] E.g. ib. 8, 5; *in ps.* 2, 6 (Devreesse, 11).
[3] E.g. *hom. cat.* 16, 2 ('one from among us'). [4] Ib. 8, 13.
[5] Ib. 8, 14: cf. *de incarn.* 12 (Swete, 303). [6] *In ps.* 44, 9 (Devreesse, 11).
[7] *Hom. cat.* 8, 5. [8] *De incarn.* 7 (Swete, 293). [9] *De incarn.* 7 (Swete, 296).

Thus the God-man is a unity, and Theodore points out[1] that, although St. Paul (*Rom.* 9, 5) might properly have said of Christ 'in Whom God is over all', he preferred to apply the formula 'Who is God over all' to Him 'by reason of the perfect conjunction of the two natures'. He draws attention[2] to the fact that, while Scripture distinguishes the natures, it at the same time stresses the unity between them in such a way as to attribute 'as to one' what properly belongs either to the humanity or the divinity. 'The Son is unique', he affirms,[3] 'because of the perfect conjunction of natures operated by the divine will.' Again,[4] 'we point to difference of natures, but to unity of Person'; and,[5] 'the two natures are, through their connexion, apprehended to be one reality' (*unum . . . quiddam connexione intelliguntur*). Theodore's doctrine is therefore that a single Person (πρόσωπον) results from the coming together of the Word and the humanity, or more precisely that 'the natures have in virtue of the union brought about (ἀπετέλεσαν) one *prosopon*'.[6] As some fragments[7] preserved by Facundus of Hermiane express it, 'one Person has been effected' by the union. The Syriac translation, it should be noticed, of an important fragment[8] represents him as saying that the two natures, distinct in their hypostases if considered separately, 'are one *prosopon* and hypostasis' as a result of the conjunction; but in view (a) of the fact that the same fragment as quoted by Leontius[9] simply says, 'When we look to the connexion, we say there is then one *prosopon*', and (b) of the fact that the formula 'one *prosopon* and one hypostasis' is unparalleled elsewhere in Theodore's writings and has no support in his general teaching and usage, we are bound to regard the Syriac version with considerable suspicion. His true teaching, it would seem, is that the Incarnate is 'one *prosopon*', and by this he means that He is the 'one subject' Who can be addressed now as God and now as man. This comes out in the fact that, while he was constantly alert to distinguish in his exegesis between the two natures, he

---

[1] *Hom. cat.* 5, 7.   [2] Ib. 8, 10 f.   [3] Ib. 3, 10.
[4] *De incarn.* 11 (Swete, 302).   [5] Frg. *in ep. ad Rom.* (PL 67, 601).
[6] *De incarn.* 8 (Swete, 299).   [7] PL 67, 587; 753: cf. hom. cat. 3, 10; 6, 3.
[8] *De incarn.* 8, 62 (Sachau, 69).   [9] Cf. Swete, 299.

was also aware that Scripture spoke of the two natures together. The Bible, as he points out, predicates what belongs both to the divinity and to the humanity 'as of one alone'; [1] it applies different titles to Christ 'as to a single *prosopon*'.[2] By *prosopon* he did not mean Person in the full Chalcedonian sense, but rather the external presentation of a reality which might be twofold (e.g. soul and body).[3] His doctrine was, not that Christ was a third *prosopon* effected by the union of the *prosopa* of the Word and the man, but that the indwelling Word imparted His own *prosopon* to the man in indissoluble, ineffable union.

This brings us to the central problem of Theodore's Christology. Cyril of Alexandria singled him out for attack, and ever since the Fifth General Council (Constantinople) in 553 he has been branded as a Nestorian before Nestorius, i.e. as guilty of the heresy of concentrating to such an extent on the completeness and independence of 'the man' and the Word as to have lost sight of the unity of the Person. In modern times, especially since the rediscovery of the relatively innocuous *Catechetical Homilies*, there has been a decided reaction against this verdict. It has been emphasized, for example, that he was deeply concerned, so far as his categories of thought allowed, to establish the oneness of subject in the God-man. Some of the evidence for this has been set out in the preceding paragraph. Further, attention has been drawn to the fact that certain of the formulae he employed strikingly anticipated those canonized at Chalcedon. He can write,[4] for example, 'Thus there results neither any confusion of the natures nor any untenable division of the Person; for our account of the natures must remain unconfused, and the Person must be recognized as indivisible'; and again, 'We display a distinctio of natures, but unity of Person'. For these and similar reasons the traditional estimate has been replaced by a more appreciative one which views him primarily as a theologian who championed the reality of the Lord's manhood against Apollinarianism and strove to do justice to His human experiences. At the very worst he was only a Nestorian

T. accused of down-playing the unity of Christ's person

★ Good

---

[1] *Hom. cat.* 6, 6; 8, 10; 8, 11 f.   [2] Ib. 3, 10.
[3] *C. Apoll.* 4 (Swete, 318).   [4] *De incarn.* 5; 11 (Swete, 292; 302).

in the sense that there were certain tendencies in his Christological thinking which, harmless enough in themselves and in
their context, lent themselves to dangerous exploitation at the
hands of his less cautious disciples.

This reaction has on the whole been healthy; Theodore was
no Nestorian, and the doctrine of 'two Sons' repelled him.
Nevertheless the desire to be fair to him, and to give due recognition to his undoubted excellences, should not blind one
to the weaknesses of his position. In the first place, even his
most benevolent critic must admit that there were dangers in
his habitual use of the contrast between the Word and 'the
man', the God and His shrine, the 'assumer' and the 'assumed',
Him Who indwells, or puts on, and him who is indwelt, or put
on. These dangers are glaringly illustrated by the way in which
he represents[1] the man Jesus as thanking the Father for counting
him worthy of adoption, or discoursing with the Word as if
they were separate Persons. Secondly, for all his insistence on
the unity of the natures, his conception of it as a 'conjunction'
(συνάφεια) rather than a 'union' (ἕνωσις) was ultimately
unsatisfactory. It is not really surprising to discover that he
sometimes thought[2] of the Holy Spirit as the medium of this
conjunction, thereby veering perilously close to adoptionism.
Thirdly, it is apparent that, while he was alive to the necessity
of a unique subject in the God-man and regularly spoke of 'one
prosopon', he had not clearly worked out all the implications
of this. On his theory the Godhead and the manhood were
juxtaposed, finding their unity in a 'common Person'. Thus he
could say[3] that 'when our Lord spoke of His humanity and of
His divinity, He applied the pronoun "I" to the common
Person'. This 'common Person', however, does not seem,
strictly speaking, to be the Person of the Word, but rather the
external unity of presentation resulting from the 'indwelling'
of the man by the Word. What was lacking to his thought, as
to Antiochene theology generally at this time, was a clearly
worked out metaphysic of personality; in particular, the differ-

[1] *Comm. in Ioh.* 17, 10; 10, 15 (Vosté, 224; 145).
[2] Ib. 16, 14; 17, 11 (Vosté, 212; 226).   [3] Ib. 8, 16 (Vosté, 119).

ence between 'nature' and 'Person' had not been properly appreciated. When all is said and done, however, it would be anachronistic to label Theodore a heretic on these grounds, for it was precisely towards the apprehension of this distinction that Christology in this epoch was feeling its way, and it would be unfair to expect him to provide definitive solutions which the Alexandrian school itself was still unable to furnish.

NOTES ON BOOKS

General. A. Grillmeier, *Christ in Christian Tradition* (Eng. trans., London, 2 ed. 1975); F. Loofs, 'Christologie' (art. in Hauck's *Realencyk.*); A. Michel, 'Incarnation' (art. in *Dict. Théol. Cath.*); R. L. Ottley, *The Doctrine of the Incarnation* (London, 1896); G. L. Prestige, *Fathers and Heretics* (London, 1940); R. V. Sellers, *Two Ancient Christologies* (London, 1940); E. Weigl, *Die Christologie vom Tode des Athanasius bis zum Ausbruch des nestorianischen Streites* (Munich, 1925).

Special. É. Amann, 'Théodore de Mopsueste' (art. in *Dict. Théol. Cath.*); P. T. Camelot, 'De Nestorius à Eutychès' (art. in *Das Konzil von Chalkedon* I); R. Devreesse, *Essai sur Théodore de Mopsueste* (Vatican City, 1948); V. Ermoni, 'Diodore de Tarse et son rôle doctrinal' (art. in *Le Muséon,* NS 2, 1901); A. Gesché, *La christologie du Commentaire sur les Psaumes découvert à Toura* (Gembloux, 1962); 'L'âme humaine de Jésus dans la christologie du ivme siècle' (art. in *Rev. hist. ecclés.* 54, 1959); R. A. Greer, 'The Antiochene Christology of Diodore of Tarsus' (art. in *Journ. Theol. Stud.,* 1966); A. Michel, 'Hypostase' (art. in *Dict. Théol. Cath.*); J. Montalverne, *Theodoreti Cyrensis doctrina antiquior de Verbo 'inhumanato'* (Rome, 1948); R. A. Norris, *Manhood and Christ* (Oxford, 1963); M. Richard, 'Saint Athanase et la psychologie du Christ selon les Ariens' (art. in *Mélanges de sc. relig.* 4, 1947); 'Hypostase' (arts in. *Mélanges de sc. relig.* 2, 1945); H. de Riedmatten, 'Some Neglected Aspects of Apollinarist Christology' (art. in *Dominican Studies* I, 1948); 'La Christologie d'Apollinaire de Laodicée' (essay in *Studia Patristica,* Vol. II, TU LXIV): R. V. Sellers, *Eustathius of Antioch* (Cambridge, 1928); F. A. Sullivan, *The Christology of Theodore of Mopsuestia* (Rome, 1956); M. F. Wiles, 'The Nature of the Early Debate about Christ's Human Soul' (art. in *Journ. Theol. Stud.,* 1963).

CHAPTER XII

THE CHRISTOLOGICAL SETTLEMENT

1. *Nestorianism* 428-451

WE have now reached the decisive period for Christology, viz. the short span between the outbreak of the Nestorian controversy in 428 and the council of Chalcedon in 451. We have studied the emergence and development of two main types of Christology in the fourth century: the so-called 'Word-flesh' type, with its concentration on the Word as the subject in the God-man and its lack of interest in the human soul, and the 'Word-man' type, alive to the reality and completeness of the humanity, but more hesitant about the position of the Word as the metaphysical subject. Each had its strong points, but also its counter-balancing defects, and it must have been obvious that, if a solution was to be found, they would both have to make their contribution. As things turned out, it was their head-on collision in these critical decades which precipitated the required synthesis. In a book like this there is only space to plot the salient features in the acrimonious debate. The reader should be warned, however, that at no phase in the evolution of the Church's theology have the fundamental issues been so mixed up with in the clash of politics and personalities. For this reason, if he desires to appreciate the doctrinal evolution, he should equip himself with at least an outline account of the historical situation.

It is first of all necessary to describe the teaching of Nestorius, who was enthroned as patriarch of Constantinople on 10 April 428. He was an Antiochene in Christology, deeply influenced by the ideas of Theodore of Mopsuestia, and it was his maladroit, crudely expressed exposition of the implications of the Antiochene position that set the spark to the controversy.

Quite early in his reign, it would appear, he was called upon[1] to pronounce on the suitability of θεοτόκος ('God-bearing') as a title of the Blessed Virgin, and ruled[2] that it was of doubtful propriety unless ἀνθρωποτόκος ('man-bearing') was added to balance it. In any case, he held, χριστοτόκος ('Christ-bearing') was preferable as begging no questions. The disputed title, we recall, was widely accepted in the Alexandrian school; it followed from the *communicatio idiomatum*, and expressed the truth that, since His Person was constituted by the Word, the Incarnate was appropriately designated God. Even Antiochene theologians like Theodore[3] had admitted it with the same qualifications as Nestorius prescribed. But in delivering himself on the subject Nestorius used intemperate language which was calculated to inflame people whose approach differed from his own. God cannot have a mother, he argued,[4] and no creature could have engendered the Godhead; Mary bore a man, the vehicle of divinity but not God. The Godhead cannot have been carried for nine months in a woman's womb, or have been wrapped in baby-clothes, or have suffered, died and been buried.[5] Behind the description of Mary as *Theotokos*, he professed[6] to detect the Arian tenet that the Son was a creature, or the Apollinarian idea that the manhood was incomplete.

The provocative flavour of these outbursts is apparent. They played into the hands of Nestorius's bitter rival, Cyril of Alexandria, who claimed[7] to see in them a revival of the theory, rejected in the fourth century, of two Sons linked by a purely moral union. By exploiting this interpretation he was able, as we shall see, to secure their author's condemnation and downfall. Others (e.g. Eusebius, later bishop of Dorylaeum), alarmed by the assertion that Mary bore a mere man, jumped to the conclusion[8] that Nestorius was restoring the adoptionism of Paul of Samosata. On the basis of these judgments the traditional picture of Nestorianism as the heresy which split the God-man

---

[1] *Ep. ad Ioh. Antioch.* (F. Loofs, *Nestoriana*, 185).
[2] E.g. *ep. ad Caelest.* 1; 3; *ad schol. eunuch.* (Loofs, 167; 181 f.; 191).
[3] Cf. *de incarn.* 15 (Swete, 310).   [4] *Serm.* 1 (Loofs, 252).
[5] *Nulla deterior* (Loofs, 245 f.).   [6] Loofs, 273.
[7] E.g. *epp.* 3; 10.   [8] Cf. A.C.O. I, 1, 1 (p. 101 f.).

into two distinct Persons rapidly formed itself. Nestorius himself indignantly repudiated[1] this account of his teaching, and
in recent times the whole question what in fact it amounted
to has been opened up afresh. The discovery early this century
of the *Book of Heracleides*, a prolix apologia which he wrote
some twenty years after the main controversy and in which he
avowed[2] himself satisfied with the Christology of Leo canonized
at Chalcedon, has seemed to make a reassessment necessary.
Modern students are sharply divided, some regarding him as
essentially orthodox but the victim of ecclesiastical politics,
others concurring in differing degrees in the traditional verdict. In reconstructing his views we may fairly use the *Book of
Heracleides*, for while he formulated them more temperately in
it, and in a more mature form, there is no reason to suspect that
he had altered his fundamental position.

His guiding principles are at any rate clear. A thoroughgoing Antiochene, he insisted that the two natures of the incarnate Christ remained unaltered and distinct in the union. 'I
hold the natures apart ($\chi\omega\rho\iota\zeta\omega$ $\tau\grave{\alpha}\varsigma$ $\phi\acute{\upsilon}\sigma\epsilon\iota\varsigma$), but unite the
worship' was his watchword;[3] and he envisaged[4] the Godhead
as existing in 'the man' and 'the man' in the Godhead without
mixture or confusion. His reasons are not far to seek. First, he
was much concerned to maintain[5] that the incarnation cannot
have involved the impassible Word in any change or suffering.
On Cyril's theory of 'hypostatic union', he thought, the Word
inevitably became the subject of the God-man's sufferings. So
he objected to the Alexandrian habit of speaking of God being
born and dying, and Mary bearing the divine Word—expressions which he considered[6] contrary to the practice of Scripture
and the creed. Secondly, he thought[7] it vitally important that
Christ should have lived a genuinely human life of growth,
temptation and suffering; if the redemption was to be effected,
the second Adam must have been a real man. Yet an authentic-

[1] E.g. *serm.* 1; 2; 4 (Loofs, 259; 275; 299).
[2] *Heracl.* (ed. Nau) 514; 519.   [3] E.g. *serm.* 1 (Loofs, 262).
[4] E.g. *nulla deterior* (Loofs, 249).   [5] *Heracl.* 59 f.; 133-5; etc.
[6] Cyril, *c. Nest.* frg. 35; 40 (Loofs, 278; 295-7).
[7] E.g. *Heracl.* 132-7; 91; *serm.* 1 (Loofs, 254 f.).

ally human experience would have been impossible if the Lord's humanity had been fused with, or dominated by, His divinity. Hence the two, divinity and humanity, must have existed side by side, each retaining its peculiar properties and operation unimpaired. Each was a 'nature' (φύσις), a term which in his vocabulary connoted, not simply a collection of qualities in the abstract, but the concrete character of a thing. As he explained,[1] he could not think of two natures except as each having its *prosopon* (i.e. its external aspect, or form, as an individual) and its *hupostasis* (i.e. concrete subsistence). By this he meant to convey, not that each nature was an actually subsistent entity, but that it was objectively real.

It should be observed that the Alexandrian school, as represented by Nestorius's antagonist Cyril, was ready to recognize the distinction of the divinity and the humanity. Cyril, for example, could write,[2] 'The natures which are brought together into this true union are different, but out of the two there is one Christ, one Son, the difference of natures not being destroyed as a result of the union'. His conception of the union, however, as 'hypostatic', analogous to the union of soul and body[3] (to Antiochenes soul and body, in contrast to the Word and the man, were incomplete natures united necessarily, not voluntarily[4]), and his description of the God-man as 'one nature', suggested to Nestorius that confusion of natures which he held in horror. Yet the latter's doctrine, as he initially expressed it, left the converse impression of two Persons artificially linked together. In fact, there could be no more misleading travesty of his teaching. He was outspoken in his criticism of the Samosatene heresy of two Sons, which he considered[5] incompatible with the Prologue of St. John's Gospel. For himself he was absolutely certain that the Incarnate was a unity, a single *prosopon*. 'God the Word', he remarked,[6] 'and the man in whom He came to be are not numerically two; for the Person (πρόσωπον) of both was one in dignity and honour, worshipped by all creation, in no way and at no time divided by

---

[1] *Heracl.* 304 f.; 442 f.   [2] *Ep.* 4.   [3] Cf. *Heracl.* 236 f.
[4] E.g. ib. 415–8.   [5] Ib. 67–71.   [6] Frg. 198 (Loofs, 224).

difference of purpose or will'. Again,[1] 'Christ is indivisible in
His being Christ, but He is twofold in His being God and man.
. . . We know not two Christs or two Sons or Only-begottens
or Lords, not one and another Son, not a first and a second
Christ, but one and the same, Who is seen in His created and
His increate natures'. Statements like these recur with monot-
onous regularity in his writings. They make it plain that what
he was striving to convey was the idea, not of two Persons
juxtaposed in a loose connexion, but of one Person, or *prosopon*,
Who combined in Himself two distinct elements, or *ousiai*,
Godhead and manhood, with all the characteristics proper to the
Word and a man, complete and intact though united in Him.

This unity calls for closer examination. In the first place,
Nestorius had no use, as we have seen, for the 'natural'
($\phi v \sigma \iota \kappa \acute{\eta}$; $\kappa a \tau \grave{a} \phi \acute{v} \sigma \iota v$) or 'hypostatic' union envisaged by Cyril,
which seemed to him to extinguish the separateness of the
natures. It was all-important in his eyes that the impassibility of
'the God' should be preserved, and that 'the man' for his part
should retain his spontaneity and freedom of action. Hence,
though speaking on occasion of a 'union' ($\emph{ἕνωσις}$), the term
he preferred was 'conjunction' ($\sigma v v \acute{a} \phi \epsilon \iota a$), which seemed to
avoid all suspicion of a confusion or mixing of the natures.
Cyril objected[2] to it as scarcely implying a real union, but
Nestorius was careful to add such safeguarding predicates as 'per-
fect' ($\emph{ἄκρα}$[3]), 'exact' ($\emph{ἀκριβής}$[4]), and 'continuous' ($\delta \iota \eta v \epsilon \kappa \acute{\eta} s$[5]).
'The man', he liked to say,[6] with a pointed reference to *John* 2,
19, was the temple in which 'the God' dwelt. Like Theodore,
he explained[7] the manner of this indwelling as being $\kappa a \tau'$
$\emph{εὐδοκίαν}$, i.e. by good-pleasure, insisting[8] however that it
utterly transcended His mode of dwelling in prophets, apostles,
even angels. 'The union of God the Word with them (i.e. the
body and human soul)', he wrote,[9] 'is neither "hypostatic" nor
"natural", but voluntary.' By this he meant,[10] not that the two

---

[1] Cyril, *c. Nest.* frg. 49 (Loofs, 280).   [2] *Ep.* 11 (Appendix 1).
[3] E.g. *ep. ad Cyrill.* 2; *serm.* 2 (Loofs, 178; 275).
[4] E.g. Cyril, *c. Nest.* frg. 71 (Loofs, 357).   [5] *Serm.* 2 (Loofs, 275).
[6] E.g. frg. 261 (Loofs, 242).   [7] E.g. frg. 102 (Loofs, 220).
[8] Cyril, *c. Nest.* frg. 47 (Loofs, 289).   [9] *Heracl.* 262.   [10] Ib. 432; 289 f.

natures adhered together by love (as his critics alleged), but that they mutually interpenetrated each other as the Persons of the Trinity do. As a result, Christ was a single being, with a single will and intelligence, inseparable and indivisible.[1]

The second point brings us to the most original feature of Nestorius's Christology. His way of describing this unity was to say that there was but one (ἕν, or μοναδικόν) *prosopon* in the God-man, using the word in its ordinary sense of an individual considered from the point of view of his outward aspect or form. 'It is Christ', he stated,[2] 'Who is the *prosopon* of union'; and he criticized[3] Cyril for beginning his analysis with 'the creator of the natures', i.e. the eternal Word, instead of with 'the *prosopon* of union', i.e. the historical Figure of the Gospels. The latter was his own primary datum; He was 'the common *prosopon* of the divinity and the humanity'.[4] Since he assumed[5] that each of the natures continued to subsist in its own *prosopon* as well as in the '*prosopon* of union', the question arises of the relation of the latter to the former. The answer[6] he seems to suggest is that the '*prosopon* of union' or 'common *prosopon*' is not identical with either the *prosopon* of the Word or the *prosopon* of the humanity, but that it results from the coalescence, coming together or union of the two natures or *ousiai*. ' We do not speak', he wrote,[7] 'of a union of *prosopa*, but of natures'; and again, 'the two natures were united by their union in a single *prosopon*'. The natures, he explained,[8] made reciprocal use of their *prosopa*, so that 'the incarnation is conceived of as the mutual use of the *prosopa*, by taking and giving'. Again, he stated,[9] 'The union took place in the *prosopon* in such wise that the one is the other, and the other the one'. The idea he was thus trying to bring out would seem to be that, just as the Word assumed the form of a servant, manifesting Himself as man,[10] so the humanity had the form of Godhead bestowed upon it, the result of the exchange being the unique *prosopon* of Jesus Christ. Neither the Godhead was changed into

[1] Ib. 102: cf. frgg. 201 f. (Loofs, 219 f.).   [2] Ib. 212: cf. ib. 250; 307.
[3] Ib. 225.   [4] Ib. 219: cf. ib. 250; 331; 439.   [5] Ib. 305.
[6] E.g. ib. 211 f.   [7] Ib. 252; 210.   [8] Ib. 289; 307; 334; 362.
[9] Ib. 331.   [10] Ib. 216; 267.

human nature, nor was the manhood deified, but each took the form of the other. Hence the incarnate Lord is indivisibly one in *prosopon*, while remaining twofold in nature.[1]

The corollary of this teaching was Nestorius's special treatment of the *communicatio idiomatum*. Strictly speaking, he contended,[2] since the natures remained quite separate and neither was identical with the '*prosopon* of union', the human attributes, actions and experiences attributed to Jesus Christ should be predicated of the human nature, and *vice versa* the divine attributes, actions and experiences should be predicated of the divinity; but in virtue of the union both could be predicated indifferently of the '*prosopon* of the economy', i.e. the God-man Who united both natures in His single *prosopon*. It was even possible, he thought,[3] in harmony with the usage of Scripture, to allow a certain interchange of predicates, describing 'the man' as God, and God the Word as man, so long as it was clearly understood that this was done ὁμωνύμως, i.e. as a mere matter of words. We have already noticed the qualification with which he hedged around the description of the Blessed Virgin as *Theotokos*. He was prepared[4] to allow simple folk to use the title, provided they did not regard the Virgin as divine personally; his own preference was for χριστοτόκος, or even θεοδόχος ('God-receiving'[5]). As regards the passion, he stated[6] similarly that 'God incarnate did not die, but He raised up him in whom He became incarnate'. But he allowed[7] that there was some sense in which the Word could properly be said to have suffered, viz. the sense in which a monarch suffers when, for example, his statue is dishonoured.

Crucial When we try to assess the character of Nestorius's teaching, one thing which is absolutely clear is that he was not a Nestorian in the classic sense of the word. As we have seen, the doctrine of 'two Sons' was abhorrent to him, and he flung back the charge of adoptionism by pointing out[8] that no one ever saw

---

[1] Cyril, *c. Nest.* frg. 49 (Loofs, 281).   [2] *Heracl.* 229-34.
[3] Frg. 78 (Loofs, 217 f.); *Heracl.* 343 f.
[4] Cyril, *c. Nest.* frg. 43 (Loofs, 353).   [5] *Serm.* 2 (Loofs, 276).
[6] *Serm.* 1 (Loofs, 252).
[7] Cf. Severus Antioch., *philalethes* (Sanda, 271).   [8] *Heracl.* 76.

an inspired man making use in his own *prosopon* of the *prosopon* of God. His repeated assertion that Christ's manhood was a hypostasis or *prosopon* was not meant to imply that it was a distinct Person, but merely that it was objectively real; and his insistence on this latter point should count to his credit, his motive being to do justice to the Lord's human experiences. Indeed, there is no reason to question the sincerity of his protestations that the Incarnate was a unity. When all this has been granted, however, grave doubts must still remain whether the special solution he propounded, viz. the idea that the unity was to be found in the 'common *prosopon*', was really adequate. All that it in fact amounted to was the truism that Jesus Christ, the historical Figure, was a single object of presentation, a concrete psychological unity. The real problem, however, especially for one who set the independence and completeness of the natures so much in the foreground, was to explain what constituted His Person, the metaphysical subject of His being, and this Nestorius's theory hardly touched. He was reluctant to recognize the Word as the subject, fearing that either His impassibility or the reality of the human nature would be imperilled, but he had no alternative to propose except his largely external concept of the 'common *prosopon*'. It is little wonder that contemporaries, approaching Christology from the oneness of the Person rather than the distinction of the natures, jumped to the conclusion that this was a doctrine of an ordinary man, the human Jesus, linked to the Word by harmony of will and by divine favour. This was a travesty of what Nestorius intended to teach, but the fault lay with his inability to provide a deeper analysis of the substantial unity of the Lord's Person of which he was convinced. As a result, despite his good intentions, the connexion which his theory established between the Lord's divinity and humanity was bound to be interpreted, undeservedly, as an artificial device.

2. *Cyril of Alexandria*

The opposition to Nestorius found a brilliant, if far from scrupulous, mouthpiece in Cyril, patriarch of Alexandria.

While jealousy of the upstart see of Constantinople sometimes made him adopt an uncharitable tone, he was basically inspired by concern for theological truth. As he understood it, Nestorius's teaching, epitomized in his attack on *Theotokos*, presupposed a merely external association between the Word and an ordinary man. From this point of view the incarnation became an illusion, a matter of 'appearance' and 'empty words'.[1] The redemption was undermined, since Christ's sufferings and saving acts were, presumably, not those of God incarnate but of one who was a mere man.[2] Similarly the conception of Christ as the second Adam inaugurating a new, regenerated race of mankind demanded, he thought,[3] a much more intimate union of the Word with the flesh than Nestorius postulated. Above all, in his opinion[4] Nestorius had deprived the eucharist of life-giving force and reduced it to cannibalism, since on his premisses only the body of a man lay on the altar and the flesh consumed by the faithful was not truly vivified by the Logos. A deep Christological cleavage lay behind these criticisms, but it was reinforced by a difference of terminology. In Antiochene circles the key-word φύσις, or 'nature', connoted the humanity or the divinity conceived of as a concrete assemblage of characteristics or attributes. Cyril himself accepted this sense of the word, especially when adapting himself to the language of his opponents. In his normal usage, however, he preferred to give *phusis* the meaning which it had borne at Alexandria at least as early as bishop Alexander's day,[5] viz. concrete individual, or independent existent. In this sense *phusis* approximated to, without being actually synonymous with, *hupostasis*. For what the Antiochenes called the natures he preferred[6] such circumlocutions as 'natural property' (ἡ ἰδιότης ἡ κατὰ φύσιν), 'manner of being' (ὁ τοῦ πῶς εἶναι λόγος), or 'natural quality' (ἡ ποιότης φυσική).

The clue to Cyril's own teaching is the realization that he

---

[1] *Apol. c. Orient.* (PG 76, 324).   [2] E.g. *c. Nest.* 3, 2; 4, 4; 5, 1.
[3] Ib. 1, 1: cf. *adv. anthrop.* 10; ep. 45 (PG 77, 236).
[4] *C. Nest.* 4, 5; 4, 6; *ep. ad Nest.* 3, 7: cf. *ep.* 17 (PG 77, 113).
[5] See above, p. 224.
[6] Cf. *ep.* 46; *c. Nest.* 2, 6; *ep.* 40 (PG 77, 241; 76, 85; 77, 193).

was an Alexandrian, nurtured in the school of Athanasius and Didymus the Blind. With this background the Christological problem did not present itself to him as that of explaining the union of two disparate natures. An exponent of the 'Word-flesh' scheme, he thought rather in terms of two phases or stages in the existence of the Logos, one prior to and the other after the incarnation. The Logos, as he liked to say, 'remains what He was'; what happened was that at the incarnation, while continuing to exist eternally in the form of God, He added to that by taking the form of a servant.[1] Both before and after the incarnation He was the same Person, unchanged in His essential deity. The only difference was that He Who had existed 'outside flesh' (ἄσαρκος) now became 'embodied' (ἐνσώματος[2]). The nature or hypostasis which was the Word became 'enfleshed' (σεσαρκωμένη); henceforth the Word was 'incarnate'. Thus the clearest, most succinct epitome of Cyril's doctrine is the famous formula[3] which he took over, in the sincere but mistaken belief that it had the authority of the great Athanasius behind it, from certain treatises of Apollinarian provenance, 'one nature, and that incarnate, of the divine Word' (μία φύσις τοῦ θεοῦ λόγου σεσαρκωμένη). 'Nature' here has the sense of 'concrete individual'; as Cyril himself put the matter,[4] 'after the union one nature is understood, viz. the enfleshed nature of the Word'.

Such being Cyril's guiding principle, he could admit of no division in the Incarnate. By 'flesh' he meant[5] human nature in its fulness, including a rational soul; he took the refutation of Apollinarianism for granted. This humanity was real and concrete. He spoke[6] of the two aspects of Christ's being as two 'natures' or 'hypostases', or even 'things' (πράγματα). The humanity was as real as the divinity, and the modern allegation that he regarded it as a collection of purely abstract qualities conflicts with his express language. So, if Christ was one, He

---

[1] *Quod unus* (PG 75, 1301); *c. Nest.* 5, 2.   [2] *Explic. 12 capp.* 2.
[3] E.g. *c. Nest.* 2, prooem.; *ep.* 40; *ep. ad Succens.* 2, 3: cf. *apol. c. Orient.* (PG 76, 349).   [4] *C. Nest.* 2, prooem.
[5] *Ad regin.* 1, 13; *de incarn. unigen.*; *quod unus* (PG 76, 1221; 75, 1220; 1289).
[6] E.g. *apol. c. Theodor.* (PG 76, 396); *ad Theodos.* 44.

Cyril

was 'one out of two' (εἶς ἐκ δύο): 'the single, unique Christ
out of two different natures'.[1] 'There has been', he remarked,[2]
'a coming together (σύνοδος) of things and hypostases', and
Christ is 'one out of both'.[3] But since the Incarnate was none
other than the eternal Word in a new state, His unity was
presupposed from the start. Hence Cyril could[4] have nothing
to do with the Antiochene conception of a 'conjunction'
(συνάφεια) based upon a harmony of wills or upon 'good
pleasure'; such an association seemed to him artificial and external. Even the analogy of indwelling, which (like Athanasius)
he had used before the controversy, became suspect[5] in his eyes
unless it was carefully hedged around. On his view the union
was absolutely real, and he liked to describe it as 'natural'
(φυσική; κατὰ φύσιν) or 'hypostatic' (καθ' ὑπόστασιν). This
formula, he explained[6], 'simply conveyed that the nature or
hypostasis of the Word, that is, the concrete being of the Word,
being truly united to human nature, without any change or confusion, is understood to be, and is, one Christ'. In other words,
the Lord's humanity became a 'nature' or 'hypostasis', i.e. a
concrete existent reality (this was the sense in which 'nature'
was here used) in the nature or hypostasis of the Word. It
never existed on its own (ἰδικῶς), as the Antiochene position
seemed to suggest, still less could be described at any stage of its
existence as 'the man', but from the moment of its conception in
Mary's womb it belonged to the Word, Who made it His very
own. The body was the body of the Word, not of some man,[7]
and in the union the two constituted a single concrete being.

So Immanuel was one, not 'bi-personal' (διπρόσωπος[8]). This
did not entail, however, that there was any confusion or mixing
together of the two natures, hypostases or 'things' which
coalesced in Him. Although opposition to Nestorius made him
concentrate on the unity, Cyril was insistent that there was no

[1] *Ep. 45 ad Succens.* I (PG 77, 233).
[2] *Apol. c. Theodor.* (PG 76, 396).   [3] *Schol. de incarn.* 25.
[4] *C. Nest.* 2, prooem.; *quod B.M. sit deip.* (PG 76, 60; 265).
[5] E.g. *ep.* I (PG 77, 24); *schol. de incarn.* 17.
[6] *Apol. c. Theodor.* (PG 76, 401).
[7] E.g. *ep.* 17 (*ad Nest.* 3), anath. 11.
[8] *De incarn. unigen.; ep.* 46 (PG 75, 1221; 77, 241).

alteration in, much less intermingling of, the Word and the humanity. 'He is a babbler', he wrote,[1] 'who says that there was any confusion or mixture' (φυρμὸν καὶ σύγκρασιν); the union was indissoluble, but involved no confusion or change (ἀσυγχύτως καὶ ἀτρέπτως). The divinity and the humanity, he pointed out,[2] were utterly different in essence, and while the union excluded all division it could not eliminate that difference. On the contrary, despite the fact that the God-man is 'one nature', each of the elements in His being 'remains and is perceived in its natural property'[3]. Any suggestion that 'the difference of natures was abolished by the union' was to be rejected.[4] Rather, the two continued to subsist each in its 'natural quality' (ποιότης φυσική[5]). For an illustration he appealed[6] to the live coal of Isaiah's vision. When the charcoal was penetrated by the fire, each retained its distinct identity; and in the same way the Word remained very Word while appropriating what was human, and the humanity continued unchanged while having the operation of the Word's nature conferred upon it. His favourite analogy,[7] however, was that of the union of soul and body; although according to Platonic ways of thinking these were two wholly disparate essences, they were nevertheless indivisibly conjoined in the human person. Thus, while the unity was absolute, the distinction of natures was always there to be perceived. But it was a distinction which involved no separation, and which could only be apprehended 'with the eyes of the mind', i.e. by an act of intellectual insight or analysis.[8]

Cyril thus envisaged the Incarnate as the divine Word living on earth as very man. Here lay the strength of his position from the religious and soteriological standpoints; the Jesus of history was God Himself in human flesh, living and dying and rising again for men. Understood in this light, his horror of Nestorius's rejection of *Theotokos* is comprehensible. As he saw the matter,

---

[1] *Quod unus; ep.* 45 (PG 75, 1292; 77, 232). [2] *C. Nest.* 2, 6.
[3] *Ep.* 46 (*ad Succens.* 2) (PG 77, 241). [4] *Ep.* 4 (*ad Nest.* 2).
[5] *Ep.* 40 (PG 77, 193). [7] *Schol. de incarn.* 9.
[6] E.g. *ep.* 46 (*ad Succens.* 2); *quod unus* (PG 77, 241; 75, 1292).
[8] E.g. *ep.* 45 (PG 77, 232).

the Word was Son of God by nature, but He was also naturally
Mary's son too, since the humanity conceived in Mary's womb
was exclusively and inalienably His. By the same token he
spurned the Antiochene suggestion that 'the man' might
properly be 'co-adored' along with the divine Word; Immanuel, he argued,[1] that is, the Lord made flesh, was to be
worshipped with a single, indivisible adoration. It goes without
saying that he expoited the 'communion of idioms' in the
fullest sense, stating[2] that it was correct to say that 'the Word
of God suffered in flesh, and became first-begotten from the
dead'. Indeed, so close and real was the union that Cyril conceived[3] of each of the natures as participating in the properties
of the other. 'We must therefore confess that the Word has
imparted the glory of the divine operation to His own flesh,
while at the same time taking to Himself what belongs to the
flesh.'[4] Thus the humanity was infused with the life-giving
energy of the Word, and itself became life-giving. Yet there
were limits to this principle. As he explained,[5] the Word did
not actually suffer in His own nature; He suffered as incarnate
(cf. ἦν γὰρ ὁ ἀπαθὴς ἐν τῷ πάσχοντι σώματι), i.e. in respect of
the human nature which was truly His, while remaining Himself as immune as the fire into which a red-hot bar which is
being hammered is plunged.

At a first glance Cyril's Christology might seem poles apart
from that of the Antiochene theologians. His adoption of the
Word-flesh scheme and the formula 'one nature' certainly
aligned him much more with Apollinarius, and a wide chasm
yawned between his doctrine of 'hypostatic union' and the
Antiochene axiom that the natures must be held apart. Further,
in his earlier phase, before Nestorius began preaching, although
he formally acknowledged the presence of a human soul in the
God-man, he assigned it no practical functions. Like his master
Athanasius,[6] he attributed[7] the Lord's trials and sufferings to His

---

[1] C. Nest. 2, 10.   [2] Anath. 12.
[3] De incarn. unigen. (PG 75, 1244).
[4] Ib. (PG 75, 1241): cf. schol. de incarn. 9.
[5] Ep. 4; 45 (PG 77, 48; 236); c. Nest. 5, 4.
[6] See above, p. 286.   [7] In Ioh. ev. 6, 38 f.

flesh; and the only growth in knowledge he would admit[1] was the gradual disclosure of the omniscience of the Word. It is important, however, to assess his position in the light of its development. As a result of study and reflection induced by the controversy, he came to realize[2] that the rational soul was the principle of suffering in the Redeemer. In particular, it was this soul which played the decisive part in His act of obedience and self-oblation.[3] The reality of the human nature after the union was thus soteriologically vital to him; if there was 'one nature' after the union, i.e. the nature of the Word, as he delighted to say,[4] that nature was 'enfleshed' (μία φύσις μετὰ τὴν ἔνωσιν, ἡ αὐτοῦ τοῦ λόγου σεσαρκωμένη). Having gone so far, it might have been expected that he would abandon the 'one nature' categories of thought which he had borrowed, under a misapprehension, from Apollinarius and which created so much misunderstanding in the opposite camp. There is evidence[5] that he did in fact come to see that the recognition of Christ's human soul as an active principle was tantamount to confessing that the humanity was a second nature. In any case we can understand, in the light of this development, why he found a compromise with moderate Antiochenism possible. It is clear that, if he rejected the 'two natures' formula, it was not for its own sake, but because it seemed to lead logically to a 'separation' of the natures. Once he was satisfied that there was no danger of this, such a compromise became a matter of practical politics.

3. From Ephesus Towards Unity

The clash between the points of view outlined in the preceding sections was at first violent. Cyril was quick to intervene when he heard of Nestorius's caricature of *Theotokos*, devoting his pastoral[6] for Easter 429 as well as a special letter[7] destined for the Egyptian monks to the refutation of what he deemed gross

---

[1] Ib. 1, 15; *thesaur.* 28.   [2] *Ep.* 46; *ad regin.* (PG 77, 240; 76, 1413).
[3] *Schol. de incarn.* 8.   [4] *C. Nest.* 2; *ep.* 40 (PG 76, 60; 77, 192 f.).
[5] E.g. *ep.* 46, 2.   [6] I.e. *hom.* 17.   [7] *Ep.* 1.

heresy. A sharp exchange of letters[1] took place between the two patriarchs without either making much headway. Cyril saw that he must detach the emperor, Theodosius II (408–50), along with his wife and sisters, from the Nestorian cause, and composed his treatises *De recta fide* for their benefit. About the middle of 430 he made contact[2] with Pope Celestine, sending him a dossier of extracts from Nestorius's sermons and from the pronouncements of revered fathers of past generations on the incarnation. Nestorius had also written[3] to the Pope, somewhat spoiling the effect of his letters by tactless inquiries about certain Pelagians who had sought refuge in Constantinople. Celestine did not take long to make up his mind, and held a synod at Rome (August 430) which came down in favour of the title *Theotokos* and against Nestorius, 'the denier of the birth of God'. These decisions were embodied in letters sent out to all the parties concerned on 11 August, and Nestorius was warned[4] that, unless he abjured his teaching within ten days of receiving this notification and adopted that 'of Rome, Alexandria and the whole Catholic Church', he must be treated as excommunicate. Cyril was charged with the execution of the sentence, and his manner of carrying out the task was perhaps characteristic. After holding a synod at Alexandria, he despatched a third, more lengthy epistle[5] to Nestorius appending twelve anathemas which he required him to subscribe.

Deliberately provocative, these anathemas summarize the Cyrilline Christology in uncompromising terms. The first asserts that Mary is *Theotokos*, 'for she bore after the manner of flesh the God-Logos made flesh'. According to the second, the Word is united 'hypostatically' (καθ' ὑπόστασιν) to the flesh. The third rejects any separation of hypostases after the union or any attempt to link them by a mere association (μόνη . . . συναφείᾳ) based on dignity, authority or power; they are brought together in 'a natural union' (ἕνωσιν φυσικήν). The fourth denies the propriety of distinguishing the

---

[1] Cyril, *epp.* 2 and 4; for Nestorius, see Loofs, *Nestoriana*, 168 f.; 173–80.
[2] *Ep.* 11.
[3] Loofs, 165–8; 169–72.
[4] *Ep. Caelest.* 13, 11 (PL 50, 483).
[5] *Ep.* 17 (*cum salvator*).

statements made about Christ, as if some properly applied to the Word and others to the man. The description 'God-inspired man' (θεόφορος ἄνθρωπος) is repudiated in the fifth on the ground that Christ is very God, the Word having become flesh and sharing our flesh and blood. It is wrong, states the sixth, to say that the divine Word is Christ's God or Lord, and not rather that after the incarnation He is simultaneously God and man. The seventh denies that Jesus as man was moved by the Word or clothed in His glory, as if there were a distinction between Him and the Word. The eighth condemns those who speak of 'the man assumed' as deserving to be worshipped along with the Word (this was the formula Nestorius favoured) and designated God along with Him, for that suggests a separation; Immanuel is the Word incarnate, and one indivisible worship is owing to Him. The ninth lays it down that, so far from being a power alien to Jesus which enabled Him to work miracles, the Holy Spirit is His very own. According to the tenth, our high-priest is not a man distinct from the Word, but the incarnate Word Himself. The eleventh declares that the Lord's flesh is the very (ἰδίαν) flesh of the Word, possessing in consequence quickening power. The twelfth insists on the fact that the Word really suffered, was crucified and died in His flesh.

Cyril's action in promulgating these was most ill-judged. The Pope had never asked for a fresh definition to be drafted, and the form he gave them could not fail to shock and alienate moderate Antiochenes. These included such figures as John of Antioch, Andrew of Samosata and Theodoret of Cyrus. The last-mentioned may be taken as illustrating their Christological attitude, which followed traditional Antiochene lines while avoiding Nestorius's more extreme affirmations. His guiding principles, we should note, were the completeness and distinction of the natures (cf. ἡ λαβοῦσα and ἡ ληφθεῖσα φύσις[1]), and their union in one Person (πρόσωπον). Though in his earlier days he was ready enough, like other Antiochenes, to speak[2] of

[1] *Eran.* 2 (PG 83, 109).
[2] *Expos. rect. confess.* 10; *de incarn.* 11; 18; 30 (PG 6, 1224; 75, 1433; 1452; 1472).

'the Word' and 'the man', contrasting 'Him Who assumes' with 'him who is assumed', he avoided such language once the controversy had made the issues clear; in particular, he pro-tested[1] against the accusation of preaching 'two Sons'. Because of his insistence on the reality of the human nature, he was able[2] to make full allowance for Christ's human ignorance, growth in knowledge, feelings of fear, etc. The union between the Word and the humanity He assumed was the result of His free decision and loving favour towards men, and for this reason among others Theodoret objected[3] to Cyril's description of it as 'natural' or 'hypostatic'; these terms seemed to imply some kind of necessity. This union, or ἕνωσις, he maintained, was absolutely real, and he rejected Nestorius's conception of two natural *prosopa*; the correct teaching[4] was that there was one *prosopon*, one Christ and Son. It is true that he left the precise significance of *prosopon*, for most of his life at any rate, vague and unexplained, and failed to bring out that the hypostasis of the Word was the unique metaphysical subject in Christ. It is true also that he rejected[5] the thoroughgoing use of the *communicatio idiomatum* advocated in the Alexandrian school; in his opinion it suggested a confusion or intermingling of the natures. But not even his worst enemies could with justice interpret his teaching as what has been traditionally designated 'Nesto-rianism'. There is even evidence[6] that at a late stage (449) he was prepared to affirm clearly and unambiguously that the *prosopon* of the God-man was none other than the Only-begotten Himself.

Not unnaturally Cyril's anathemas, which in Antiochene ears had an unmistakably Apollinarian ring, gravely disturbed people of this way of thinking. His subsequent behaviour was at least equally exasperating. On 19 November 430, yielding to Nestorius's persuasions, Theodosius issued letters summoning a general council to meet at Ephesus at Pentecost (7 June) the

---

[1] *Ep.* 104; 109.
[2] *De incarn.* 20; *rep. anathem.* 4 (PG 75, 1453; 76, 411).
[3] *Rep. anathem.* 3 (PG 76, 401-4).   [4] E.g. *eran.* 3 (PG 83, 280).
[5] E.g. *rep. anathem.* 4 (PG 76, 413).
[6] *Epp.* 145; 146 (PG 83, 1389; 1393).

following year. There is no space here to describe the astonishing medley of rival meetings that in the event took place. It is sufficient to recall that, taking advantage of the delayed arrival of the Oriental (i.e. Antiochene) bishops, Cyril held a synod of some sixty like-minded bishops under his own presidency on 22 June in face of the protests of the imperial commissioner, the count Candidianus. Nestorius, who was already at Ephesus, naturally declined to participate. This assembly then proceeded to anathematize and depose him ('the new Judas') in his absence, after having had the correspondence between him and Cyril read out as well as a dossier of patristic authorities. It is true that, when John of Antioch and the Oriental bishops eventually arrived on 26 June, they too held a session of their own at which they deposed both Cyril and the local prelate, Memnon, and repudiated the Twelve Anathemas. It was Cyril's gathering, however, which the Papal legates endorsed when they reached Ephesus on 10 July, and which has gone down to history as the Third General Council. From its own point of view it was effective, for Nestorius was never rehabilitated. After languishing at Antioch for some years, he was finally exiled to the Great Oasis, and died c. 451. Its more positive achievement was to canonize the Nicene creed as enshrining the core of Christological orthodoxy, and Cyril's Second Letter to Nestorius as its authoritative interpretation.

It might seem that an unbridgeable chasm now yawned between Alexandrians and Antiochenes. Yet there were already pointers indicating the possibility of a *rapprochement*. Cyril's Twelve Anathemas, we should note, were formally read out at the session on 22 June, but there was no move to canonize them along with his second letter. Similarly, although the Oriental bishops under John condemned Cyril and Memnon, Nestorius's name was passed over by them in discreet silence. At a deeper theological level, too, the parties were moving towards a measure of understanding. On receiving, on 30 November 430, Cyril's letter demanding subscription to the Anathemas, Nestorius had passed them on to John of Antioch. In the latter's eyes they bore the stamp of Apollinarianism, and he charged Theodoret of Cyrus and Andrew of Samosata to refute them. The ensuing debate[1] was fierce, but there is reason to suppose that in the course of it Cyril began to understand his critics' point of view. On the other hand, Theodoret, who had at first been hostile[2] to Cyril's use of 'hypostatic union', came himself to use[3] *hupostasis* as synonymous with *prosopon*. In the same way Andrew of Samosata came, it would seem,[4] near to sanctioning the formula 'one hypostasis' in his rejoinder to Cyril.

In the two years following Ephesus strenuous efforts were made to heal the divisions in the Church. The way was made clear by the death of Pope Celestine on 16 July 432, for the new Pope, Xystus III, was inclined to favour a reconciliation provided the Ephesine decisions were recognized. The chief obstacles were, on the one hand, Cyril's Anathemas, which the Antiochenes viewed with intense suspicion, and the condemnation of Nestorius, which Cyril insisted on and which they were loth to concede. Eventually, after negotiations in which the venerable Acacius of Beroea played a leading part, an accord was reached. Cyril, who was still suspected of Apollinarian leanings, furnished[5] explanations of his teaching, especially in substantiation of his denial of any change or confusion of the two natures. These were deemed acceptable, and the leading Antiochenes were induced, though with considerable reluctance, to abandon Nestorius. The instrument of agreement (known as the Symbol of Union) was contained in a letter[6] sent by John to Cyril; in fact it consisted, apart from the closing sentence, of a formula, undoubtedly drafted by Theodoret, which the Oriental bishops had approved at Ephesus in August 431 and had despatched to Theodosius. It ran as follows:[7]

We confess, therefore, our Lord Jesus Christ, the only-begotten Son of God, perfect God and perfect man com-

---

[1] The argument of Theodoret and Andrew can be reconstructed from Cyril's *apol. c. Theodor.* and *apol. c. Orient.*
[2] *Rep. anathem.* 2 (PG 76, 400).   [3] *Eran.* 3 (PG 83, 252).
[4] Cyril, *apol. c. Orient.* (PG 76, 333).   [5] *Ep.* 33 (to Acacius).
[6] Cyril, *ep.* 38.   [7] For the Greek text see A.C.O. I, 1, 4, pp. 8 f.

posed of a rational soul and a body, begotten before the ages from His Father in respect of His divinity, but likewise (τὸν αὐτόν) in these last days for us and our salvation from the Virgin Mary in respect of His manhood, consubstantial with the Father in respect of His divinity and at the same time (τὸν αὐτόν) consubstantial with us in respect of His manhood. For a union (ἕνωσις) of two natures has been accomplished. Hence we confess one Christ, one Son, one Lord. In virtue of this conception of a union without confusion we confess the holy Virgin as *Theotokos* because the divine Word became flesh and was made man and from the very conception united to Himself the temple taken from her. As for the evangelical and apostolic statements about the Lord, we recognize that theologians employ some indifferently in view of the unity of person (ὡς ἐφ' ἑνὸς προσώπου) but distinguish others in view of the duality of natures (ὡς ἐπὶ δύο φύσεων), applying the God-befitting ones to Christ's divinity and the humble ones to His humanity.

Cyril greeted this formulary with enthusiasm in his letter *Laetentur coeli*.[1] Yet at first sight it seemed to make large concessions to the Antiochene point of view. Clearly, the Anathemas which he had made so much of had dropped into the background, and even his favourite expressions, 'one nature' and 'hypostatic union', had disappeared. Instead he found himself accepting the Antiochene language of 'one *prosopon*' and 'union of two natures', while one phrase (ὡς ἐπὶ δύο φύσεων) emphasized the duality of the natures after the union. *Theotokos* was admitted, but only with safeguards which satisfied the Antiochenes, and it was balanced by the admission of their traditional description of the humanity as the Word's 'temple'. A form of *communicatio* was sanctioned, but a much less thoroughgoing form than the one for which he had contended. On the other hand, he had gains as well as losses to count. The condemnation of Nestorius had been accepted, and *Theotokos*, even though with safeguards, had been pronounced orthodox;

[1] *Ep.* 39.

and the bogy of 'Nestorianism', with its doctrine of 'two Sons', was no more. Moreover, the identification of the subject in the God-man with the eternal Word had been clearly recognized in the repeated, emphatic use of τὸν αὐτόν. All talk of 'conjunction', etc., had vanished, and the union was now described as ἕνωσις. When we look beneath the terminology in which he clothed it to what was really important in his Christology, and recall the victory he had won in the political field, we can well understand how Cyril could afford to survey the accord reached with a reasonable measure of satisfaction.

4. The Case of Eutyches

A brief paragraph must suffice for the fifteen years between the agreement patched up in 433 and the outbreak of the next crisis in 448. Neither of the great parties was as a whole content with the terms of the Union Symbol. On the one hand, Cyril's right-wing allies viewed his acceptance of the Two Natures doctrine with unconcealed dismay. In self-defence he was obliged to muster arguments[1] to show that, for all the at first sight objectionable language in which it was expressed, it was essentially the teaching he had always supported. On the Antiochene side there was an extremist Cilician group which persisted in declaring Cyril a heretic. More important, the sentence passed on Nestorius rankled in the consciences of even those moderate Antiochenes who had come to recognize Cyril's orthodoxy. Theodoret of Cyrus, for example, absolutely refused to endorse it. The Tome which Proclus, the new patriarch of Constantinople, published in 435 and which listed a series of excerpts from Theodore's writings as heretical, affords a good illustration of the rising tension. Cyril himself, however, stood for moderation, and while he was alive he restrained his hot-headed partisans. With his death in 444 the reaction against the Two Natures doctrine gathered force and is reflected in attacks launched on the teaching of Theodoret,[2] now the leading theologian of the Antiochene school. Cyril's successor, Dios-

---

[1] E.g. ep. 40 (to Acacius); 44 (to Eulogius).   [2] Cf. epp. 83; 85; 86.

corus, an energetic and ruthless prelate, put himself at the head
of it. He was determined, cost what it might, to reassert the
One Nature doctrine which, he sincerely believed, had the
authority of the fathers behind it and which had only been
compromised by Cyril in a moment of weakness.

Matters were brought to a head by the case of Eutyches,
the aged and muddle-headed archimandrite who, because of
the favour and influence he enjoyed at court, found himself the
rallying-point of all who disliked the accord of 433. On 8
November 448, at a meeting of the Standing Synod of Constantinople, he was denounced as heretical by Eusebius of
Dorylaeum. Formal discussions began on 12 November, the
chairman being Flavian, the local patriarch, and we should note
that he seized the opportunity to read out a profession of faith
containing the important formulary,[1] 'We confess that Christ
is of two natures (ἐκ δύο φύσεων) after the incarnation, confessing one Christ, one Son, one Lord, in one *hupostasis* and one
prosopon'. Although 'out of two natures' was to become the
battle-cry of monophysitism, it is clear that Flavian was using
it to imply that the Incarnate had two natures. His identification
of *hupostasis* and *prosopon* marked an important step towards
Chalcedon. Eutyches refused to appear at this session, and when
he did appear, on 22 November, it was to hear sentence passed
on himself. The verdict of those present, all supporters of the
Union Symbol, was that he was a follower of Valentinus and
Apollinarius, and he was accordingly deposed. Historically he
counts as the founder of an extreme and virtually Docetic form
of monophysitism, teaching that the Lord's humanity was
totally absorbed by His divinity. That such ideas were current
at this time is clear. Theodoret had aimed his *Eranistes* the year
before against people who, holding that Christ's humanity and
divinity formed 'one nature', taught that the former had not
really been derived from the Virgin, and that it was the latter
which had suffered.[2] Their theory was, apparently, that 'the
divine nature remains while the humanity is swallowed up

---

[1] For the text, see A.C.O. II, 1, 1, p. 114.
[2] *Eran.* praef. (PG 83, 28 f.).

($\kappa\alpha\tau\alpha\pi\omega\theta\hat{\eta}\nu\alpha\iota$) by it'.[1] The nature assumed was not annihilated, but rather transformed into the substance ($o\dot{v}\sigma\iota\alpha$) of the divinity. Though he named no names, it is fairly certain that Theodoret had Eutyches in view.

What Eutyches's actual doctrine was has never been easy to determine. At a preliminary examination, before the envoys of the synod, he declared[2] that 'after the birth of our Lord Jesus Christ I worship one nature, viz. that of God made flesh and become man'. He vigorously repudiated[3] the suggestion of two natures in the Incarnate as un-Scriptural and contrary to the teaching of the fathers. Yet he expressly allowed[4] that He was born from the Virgin and was at once perfect God and perfect man. He denied[5] ever having said that His flesh came from heaven, but refused[6] to concede that it was consubstantial with us. At his interrogation before the synod he yielded[7] the point that Christ was 'of two natures' ($\dot{\epsilon}\kappa$ $\delta\dot{v}o$ $\phi\dot{v}\sigma\epsilon\omega\nu$), but argued that that was only before the union; 'after the union I confess one nature'. He repeated[8] that Christ took flesh of the Virgin, and added[9] that it was a complete incarnation ($\dot{\epsilon}\nu\alpha\nu\theta\rho\omega\pi\hat{\eta}\sigma\alpha\iota$ ... $\tau\epsilon\lambda\epsilon\iota\omega\varsigma$) and that the Virgin was consubstantial with us. Flavian then pressed[10] him to admit that the Lord was consubstantial with us. Eutyches consented[11] to do so if the synod insisted. His reluctance hitherto, he explained,[12] had been due to the fact that he regarded Christ's body as the body of God; he had been shy of calling the body of God 'the body of a man', (evidently he took 'consubstantial with us' as implying an individual man), but had preferred to speak of it as 'a human body', and to say that the Lord became incarnate of the Virgin. This, however, was a passing remark; he soon returned to his monotonous affirmation of two natures before the incarnation, one after.

The traditional picture of Eutyches, it is clear, has been formed by picking out certain of his statements and pressing

---

[1] *Eran.* 2 (PG 83, 153; 157).
[2] E. Schwartz, *Der Prozess des Eutyches* (*Sitzb. Bay. Akad. Wiss.*, Phil. hist. 1929, 5), 14. [3] Ib. 15; 17; 19. [4] Ib. 15. [5] Ib. 15.
[6] Ib. 15. [7] Ib. 25: cf. ib. 26. [8] Ib. 23. [9] Ib. 23; 24.
[10] Ib. 24. [11] Ib. 24: cf. ib. 25. [12] Ib. 25.

them to their logical conclusion. From his rejection of 'consubstantial with us' it has been inferred that Christ's humanity was in his eyes mere appearance; hence he must have been a Docetist. From his affirmation of two natures before and only one after the union the conclusion has been drawn that either the two must have been fused into a *tertium quid* or the humanity must have been swallowed up by the divinity. In fact he seems to have been a confused and unskilled thinker (*multum imprudens et nimis imperitus*, said[1] Leo), blindly rushing forward to defend the unity of Christ against all attempts to divide Him. He was no Docetist or Apollinarian; nothing could have been more explicit than his affirmation of the reality and completeness of the manhood. His hesitations about 'consubstantial with us' were due to his exaggerated suspicion that it might be twisted to imply the Nestorian conception of the humanity as being an individual man whom the Godhead assumed. If he had a horror of 'two natures', it sprang from the fact that, like so many of the Alexandrian way of thinking, he took *phusis*, or 'nature', to mean a concrete existence. Even more than Cyril himself, whose depth of insight and grasp of essentials he lacked, he had been nurtured on literature of Apollinarian provenance which he pathetically believed to be fully orthodox, and he was devoted to Cyril's formula 'one nature', although he omitted to add his saving qualification 'made flesh'. If his condemnation is to be justified, it must be in the light of more far-reaching considerations. The Church at this epoch was feeling its way towards a balanced Christology. The type of thought which Eutyches represented was one-sided to a degree. While possibly susceptible, if strained in that direction, of an orthodox interpretation, it upset the required balance; without the emphasis on the other side which the Two Natures doctrine supplied, Christology might well have drifted into the errors his opponents attributed to him.

Although Eutyches was excommunicated and deposed, his disgrace did not last long. He wrote[2] to the Pope, but his letter did not bear the wished-for fruit. Flavian had already informed

---

[1] *Ep.* 28, 1: cf. *ep.* 29 (*imperite et imprudenter*).   [2] *Ep. Leon.* 21.

Leo of his condemnation, and now wrote[1] in greater detail
defining his heresy. As a result, on 13 June 449, Leo despatched
his famous Dogmatic Letter, or *Tome*,[2] to Flavian, and made his
hostility to the One Nature doctrine clear. Eutyches had greater
success with Dioscorus, who from the start refused to recognize
his excommunication, and with his aid induced Theodosius II
to summon a general council. This met at Ephesus in August
449. It was dominated with brutal efficiency by Dioscorus, and
although the Pope sent three legates they were not given an
opportunity of reading out his *Tome*. Eutyches was immediately rehabilitated and his orthodoxy vindicated. The
Union Symbol was formally set aside as going beyond the
decisions of the council of Ephesus of 431, and the confession
of two natures after the union was anathematized. Flavian and
Eusebius of Dorylaeum, and along with them Theodoret and
all the dyophysite leaders, were condemned and deposed. So
ended the council which became known as the Robber Synod,
or 'Brigandage' (*Latrocinium*[3]), of Ephesus.

5. *The West and Leo*

So far, Tertullian excepted, the West had made little or no
contribution to Christological theory, but the importance
which Leo's *Tome* was to assume makes it desirable to glance
at the Latin fathers. In general they reproduce the framework
of ideas, and even the formulae, inherited from Tertullian. If
they seem to lack the speculative interest of the East, this is to
some extent explained by the remarkable success with which
Tertullian's theory held both the aspects which reflection was
showing to be necessary to a sound Christology in balance.

For Hilary, for example, the two natures of Christ (he
regularly uses the term *natura*) are united in one Person.[4] Christ
is true man and true God, one but comprising two natures in
His unity.[5] Each nature is complete, the humanity possessing

---

[1] *Ep. Leon.* 22.   [2] *Ep.* 28.
[3] The phrase was Leo's: cf. *ep.* 95, 2 (to Pulcheria: 20 July 451).
[4] *De trin.* 9, 14.   [5] Ib. 9, 3.

a rational soul[1]—this is insisted upon in reply to the Arian habit of referring the Lord's experiences of emotion and suffering to the Logos[2]—and the union entails no change or confusion.[3] Further, while Hilary does not hesitate to speak[4] of the humanity as 'the man assumed', he regards[5] the Person of the Incarnate as identical with the Person of the Word: 'He Who is in the form of a servant is none other than He Who is in the form of God'. This Pauline imagery suggested to him the self-emptying (*evacuatio* or *exinanitio*) which the Incarnation must have involved. This does not consist, as he sees it,[6] in the Word's surrendering any of His powers or ceasing to be what He essentially is (*evacuatio formae non est abolitio naturae*), but rather in His contracting or limiting Himself to human conditions. In other words, he relinquishes, during His earthly career, the glory appropriate to 'the form of God'. Alongside this, however, should be set Hilary's treatment of the Lord's experiences of pain, weakness, human emotion, etc. These experiences, he teaches,[7] were perfectly genuine, but they were strictly unnatural to Him: 'He had a body susceptible of suffering, and so suffered, but His nature was not capable of pain'. The point is that, Christ's body having been conceived by the Holy Spirit, it was not really earthly but heavenly (*corpus coeleste*[8]), and was raised above human weaknesses; hence if He consented to succumb to them, He was making a concession, by the free act of His will, to what was expected of Him.[9] Similarly the glory of the Transfiguration and the walking on the sea were not strictly miraculous, but were natural to such a body as His.[10] Thus, side by side with his conviction of the reality of the human nature, there was a strain in Hilary's thought which veered close to Docetism.

Ambrose stood even nearer than Hilary to the Latin Christological tradition. 'It is one Son of God', he stated,[11] 'Who speaks in both, for both natures are in one and the same

---

[1] Ib. 10, 19.   [2] Cf. ib. 10, 50-60.   [3] *Tract. in ps.* 138, 2.
[4] E.g. ib. 68, 25.   [5] *De trin.* 9, 14: cf. ib. 10, 22.
[6] Ib. 9, 4; 9, 14; 11, 48; 12, 6.   [7] Ib. 10, 23-32; 10, 35.
[8] Ib. 10, 18.   [9] Ib. 10, 24; 10, 35.   [10] Ib. 10, 23.
[11] *De fide* 2, 77.

subject' (*in eodem*). He refers[1] to 'the twin substances . . . of divinity and flesh'. The human nature of course includes a rational soul,[2] and the distinction between the two natures is sharply maintained.[3] The Person being indivisibly one, he can make use of the 'communication of idioms', remarking,[4] for example, 'The Lord of majesty is said to have been crucified because, participating in both natures, the human and the divine, He endured His passion in the human nature'.

Along similar lines Augustine taught[5] that 'Christ is one Person of twofold substance (*una persona geminae substantiae*), being both God and man'. Mediator between God and man, He 'conjoins both natures in oneness of Person';[6] 'in Christ there are two substances, but one Person'.[7] The humanity was absolutely real,[8] and of course complete: 'there was a human soul in Christ, not just the non-rational part of it, but the rational part we call the mind'.[9] It was the rational soul, indeed, which provided the point of union between the Word and the flesh.[10] Yet, while the human nature was real, the fact that it was born from a pure virgin preserved it from original sin;[11] nor was it susceptible, despite the Gospel statements which seem to suggest the contrary, to human ignorance.[12] It was characteristic of Augustine to speak of it as 'the man', referring[13] to 'the man' whom the Son of God carried or assumed. While this usage, however, indicates that he assigned the humanity a relative independence, he makes it plain[14] that it never existed apart from the Word. Thus the two natures are united in one Person, the Person of the Word. 'Into unity with His Person', he wrote,[15] 'the form of God remaining invisible, Christ took the visible form of a man', and in so doing He 'neither lost nor diminished the form of God'.[16] Because of this union, he affirmed,[17] both sets of predicates can be freely applied

---

[1] De fide 3, 65.   [2] De incarn. dom. sacram. 64 ff.; 76.
[3] De fide 2, 77; de incarn. dom. sacram. 23.   [4] De fide 2, 58.
[5] C. Maxim. Ar. 2, 10, 2.   [6] Ep. 137, 9.   [7] Serm. 130, 3.
[8] De agon. Chr. 20; 24.   [9] Tract. in ev. Ioh. 23, 6: cf. ib. 47, 9.
[10] Ep. 137, 8; 140, 12.   [11] Enchir. 34; 41.
[12] De trin. 1, 23; enarr. in ps. 6, 1.
[13] De agon. Chr. 12; 20; 21; 22; 25.   [14] De trin. 13, 22.
[15] C. Maxim. Ar. 1, 19.   [16] Enchir. 35.   [17] C. serm. Ar. 8.

to Christ however described, so that the Son of God can correctly be said to have been crucified and buried, and the son of man to have come down from heaven. To illustrate the unity he often invoked[1] the comparison of soul and body, which together constitute a single man.

The Christology which appears in Leo's *Tome* has no special originality; it reflects and codifies with masterly precision the ideas of his predecessors. The following are the chief points he was concerned to bring out. First, the Person of the God-man is identical with that of the divine Word. As he expressed it,[2] 'He Who became man in the form of a servant is He Who in the form of God created man'. Though describing the incarnation as a 'self-emptying' (*exinanitio*), he claimed[3] that it involved no diminution of the Word's omnipotence; He descended from His throne in heaven, but did not surrender His Father's glory. Secondly, the divine and human natures co-exist in this one Person without mixture or confusion. Rather, in uniting to form one Person each retains its natural properties unimpaired (*salva . . . proprietate utriusque naturae et substantiae*), so that, just as the form of God does not do away with the form of a servant, so the form of a servant does not diminish the form of God.[4] Indeed, the redemption required that 'one and the same mediator between God and men, the man Jesus Christ, should be able both to die in respect of the one and not to die in respect of the other'. Thirdly, the natures are separate principles of operation, although they always act in concert with each other. So we have the famous sentence, 'Each form accomplishes in concert with the other what is appropriate to it, the Word performing what belongs to the Word, and the flesh carrying out what belongs to the flesh'.[5] Lastly, the oneness of the Person postulates the legitimacy of the 'communication of idioms'. We can affirm, for example, that the Son of God was crucified and buried, and also that the Son of Man came down from heaven.

These four theses may not have probed the Christological

---

[1] E.g. *serm.* 186, 1; *tract. in ev. Ioh.* 19, 15.
[2] *Ep.* 28, 3 (Leo's 'Tome').   [3] Ib. 4.   [4] Ib. 3.   [5] Ib. 4.

problem very deeply; it is obvious that they left the issues
which puzzled Greek theologians largely untouched. They had
the merit, however, of setting out the factors demanding recognition fairly and squarely. Moreover, they went a long way
towards meeting the points of view of both the schools of
thought struggling for supremacy in the East. Antiochenes
could recognize their own theology in Leo's vigorous affirmation of the duality in Christ, and of the reality and independence of the two natures. Some of his sentences, indeed, particularly the one cited above, were to prove stones of stumbling
to Alexandrian Christologians. Nevertheless these latter, too,
could see the essentials of their standpoint vindicated in the
Pope's unerring grasp of the identity of the Person of the
Incarnate with that of the eternal Word. As he expressed it in a
Christmas sermon,[1] 'It is one and the same Son of God Who
exists in both natures, taking what is ours to Himself without
losing what is His own'.

6. The Chalcedonian Settlement

The Robber Synod had been held under imperial auspices,
and Theodosius was resolved[2] to maintain its decisions despite
all Leo's manœuvres to get the doctrinal question reopened. An
extremely awkward situation looked like developing when,
contrary to all expectation (the orthodox not unnaturally interpreted it as an act of Providence), the deadlock was broken by
the Emperor's death by falling from his horse (28 July 450). A
professional soldier, Marcian, succeeded to the throne, cement-
ing his position by marrying the late emperor's sister, Pulcheria.
Both sympathized with the Two Natures doctrine, and this,
combined with the manifest desirability of securing Church
unity in the empire, caused them to fall in readily with pro-
posals for a general council. The Pope had striven[3] to persuade
Theodosius to summon one, preferably in Italy, being anxious
to reassert his position vis-à-vis Alexandria as well as to annul
the theological work of the Robber Synod; and now Theodoret,

[1] Serm. 27, 1.   [2] Cf. epp. Leon. 62-4.   [3] Ep. 44; 45; 54; 70.

Oct. 8, 451

back from exile, was reviving[1] the demand. Originally planned
for Nicaea (not Italy, as the Pope wanted[2]), the council was
transferred to Chalcedon, as being nearer the capital and thus
more convenient for Marcian. More than five hundred bishops
took part, the Pope as usual being represented by legates; the
proceedings opened on 8 October 451.

The whole object of the council, from the imperial point of
view, was to establish a single faith throughout the empire.
The majority of bishops present, it is true, objected to the
formulation of a new creed; they considered[3] it sufficient to
uphold the Nicene faith and recognize the binding force of
Cyril's Dogmatic Letters and Leo's *Tome*. If the council was to
succeed, however, the imperial commissioners knew that it
must produce a formulary which everyone could be required to
sign, and they made their intentions clear.[4] Hence the Definition which was finally agreed took the following form.[5] First,
after a preamble, it solemnly reaffirmed the Nicene Creed as the
standard of orthodoxy, setting the creed of the council of Constantinople (the creed now recited at the eucharist) beside it as
refuting heresies which had sprung up since Nicaea. Secondly,
it canonized Cyril's two Letters and Leo's *Tome*, the former as
disposing of Nestorianism and as a sound interpretation of the
creed, and the latter as overthrowing Eutychianism and confirming the true faith. Thirdly, it set out a formal confession of
faith in the following terms:

> In agreement, therefore, with the holy fathers, we all
> unanimously teach that we should confess that our Lord
> Jesus Christ is one and the same Son, the same perfect in God-
> head and the same perfect in manhood, truly God and truly
> man, the same of a rational soul and body, consubstantial
> with the Father in Godhead, and the same consubstantial
> with us in manhood, like us in all things except sin; begotten
> from the Father before the ages as regards His Godhead, and
> in the last days, the same, because of us and because of our

---

[1] *Epp.* 138-40.   [2] *Epp.* 76 f. (Marcian and Pulcheria).
[3] A.C.O. II, 1, 2, pp. 78-81.   [4] A.C.O. II, 1, 2, p. 78.
[5] For the text, see A.C.O. II, 1, 2, pp. 126-30.

salvation begotten from the Virgin Mary, the *Theotokos*, as regards His manhood; one and the same Christ, Son, Lord, only-begotten, made known in two natures without confusion, without change, without division, without separation, the difference of the natures being by no means removed because of the union, but the property of each nature being preserved and coalescing in one *prosopon* and one *hupostasis*— not parted or divided into two *prosopa*, but one and the same Son, only-begotten, divine Word, the Lord Jesus Christ, as the prophets of old and Jesus Christ Himself have taught us about Him and the creed of our fathers has handed down.

It should be noted that the imperial commissioners, in their desire to avoid a split, had to exert considerable pressure before agreement could be reached. In the first place, apart from the widespread objection to framing a new creed, three passages in Leo's *Tome* (*c.* 3: *ut . . . et mori posset ex uno et mori non posset ex altero*; *c.* 4: *agit enim utraque forma . . .* ; and *c.* 4: *quamvis . . . una persona sit, aliud tamen est unde . . . contumelia, aliud unde . . . gloria . . .*) excited grave disquiet in the Illyrian and Palestinian delegations.[1] It required the special explanations of the Roman legates, as well as a dossier of citations from Cyril, to satisfy them that the Pope was not dividing Christ as Nestorius had done, but was only recognizing and drawing the practical implications of the distinction of natures. Secondly, the first draft of the formal confession, produced at the Fifth Session on 22 October, seems to have lacked the extracts from the *Tome* which stand in the final version, and also to have read 'from two natures' (ἐκ δύο φύσεων) instead of 'in two natures' (ἐν δύο φύσεσιν[2]). Although this echoes Flavian's declaration of faith[3] at the Constantinopolitan Standing Synod, it did not clearly affirm the subsistence of two natures after the union, and indeed, in the light of Eutyches's position, was consistent with a denial of it. Only by dint of consummate skill and diplomacy was the assembly induced to accept the necessary amendments.[4]

In its final shape the Definition is a mosaic of excerpts from

[1] A.C.O. II, 1, 2, pp. 81 f.   [2] A.C.O. II, 1, 2, pp. 123 f.
[3] See above, p. 331.   [4] A.C.O. II, 1, 2, pp. 123-5.

Cyril's two Letters, Leo's *Tome*, the Union Symbol and Flavian's profession of faith at the Standing Synod. Its distinctive theology is to be seen in the equal recognition it accords both to the unity and to the duality in the God-man. We notice, in addition to the formula 'one *prosopon* and one *hupostasis*', which came straight from Flavian's profession, the monotonous repetition of the words 'the same', and the insistence that, in spite of the two natures, Christ remains 'without division, without separation'. To exclude all further possibility of doubt, we read that He is 'not parted or divided into two *prosopa*'. Clearly the divine Word, even if Cyril's favourite slogan 'hypostatic union' is discarded, is regarded as the unique subject of the Incarnate, and this is reinforced by the sanction given to the controverted title *Theotokos*. This is the essential truth which the Alexandrian theology had grasped, for which Cyril had struggled, and which the council of Ephesus canonized. On the other hand, the long debate had proved that this truth could not be allowed to stand alone. Without an explicit acknowledgement of the reality of Christ's human life, the Antiochene tradition would remain unsatisfied at the point where its theological intuition was soundest, and a door would be left open, as the emergence of Eutychianism had demonstrated, for dangerous forms of monophysitism. So, side by side with the unity, the Definition states that, as incarnate, the Word exists 'in two natures', each complete and each retaining its distinctive properties and operation unimpaired in the union. Rejecting 'natural union' with its monophysite implications, it singles out *hupostasis*, along with *prosopon*, to express the oneness of the Person, thereby distinguishing it once for all from *phusis*, which it reserved for the natures.

Chalcedon is often described as the triumph of the Western, and with it of the Antiochene, Christology. It is true, of course, that the balanced position attained long since in the West and given expression in Leo's *Tome*, gave the fathers a model of which they made good use. It is true, also, that without Rome's powerful support the Antiochene formula 'two natures' would never have been given such prominence. Further, large sections

of the Eastern church, regarding the council's endorsement of
that formula and of Leo's *Tome*, as well as its rejection of 'hypostatic union', as a betrayal of Cyril and of the Alexandrian
tradition generally, were prepared to drift off into schism as
monophysites. These are some of the points that underline the
substantial truth of the verdict. It does less than justice, however,
to the essential features of Cyril's teaching enshrined, as has
been shown, in the council's confession, especially the recognition, in language of a clarity unheard of in Antiochene circles,
of the oneness of Christ and of the identity of the Person of the
God-man with that of the Logos. It also overlooks the fact that
Cyril's Synodical Letters were given just as honourable a position as the *Tome*, and greatly exaggerates the theological difference between the two. To take but one point, Cyril himself
admitted, as his correspondence[1] after the act of union reveals,
that it was possible to speak of two natures without dividing
the one Christ. His predilection for 'one nature' was based, not
on any objection to the Two Natures doctrine properly interpreted, but on his belief that it bore the stamp of Athanasian
authority and provided a uniquely useful safeguard against
Nestorianism. As this heresy was unambiguously denounced
in the Definition, it is reasonable to suppose, in the light of his
attitude to the Union Symbol, that he too would have acquiesced in the Chalcedonian settlement and would have been
embarrassed by the intransigence of his over-enthusiastic allies.
Thus, if the Antiochene Christology was victorious at Chalcedon, it was so only after absorbing, and being itself modified by,
the fundamental truths contained in the Alexandrian position.

In spite of all, however, Chalcedon failed to bring permanent
peace. The story really lies outside this book, but we may note
that, if the West remained loyal to the council, there was an
immediate hostile reaction in the East which was to last for
centuries. Nestorianism proper had been driven beyond the
frontiers of the empire, but monophysitism in its various forms
waged incessant war against the Definition. The chief an-
tagonists were its strict dyophysite supporters, branded as

[1] E.g. *ep.* 40.

Nestorians by their critics, and monophysites who as often as not (cf. Severus of Antioch: †538) were substantially orthodox except for their refusal to speak of 'two natures'. The struggle, as embittered as it was long and closely entangled with politics, resulted in the emergence in the East in the sixth century (cf. the second council of Constantinople, 553) of a 'Neo-Chalcedonianism' which subtly shifted the bias of the council, interpreting its teaching in a positive Cyrilline sense. The affirmation at the third council of Constantinople (680) of the existence of two wills in Christ, which settled the monothelite controversy, represented an attempt to restore the Chalcedonian balance.

NOTE ON BOOKS

General. T. H. Bindley, *The Oecumenical Documents of the Faith* (rev. by F. W. Green, London, 4 ed. 1950); P. T. Camelot, 'De Nestorius à Eutychès' (art. in *Das Konzil von Chalkedon* I); A. Grillmeier, *Christ in Christian Tradition* (Eng. trans., London, 2 ed. 1975); F. Loofs, 'Christologie'(art. in Hauck's *Realencyk.*); G. L. Prestige, *Fathers and Heretics* (London, 1940); R. V. Sellers, *Two Ancient Christologies* (London, 1940); *The Council of Chalcedon* (London, 1953).

Special. É. Amann, 'Nestorius' (art. in *Dict. Théol. Cath.*); J. F. Bethune-Baker, *Nestorius and His Teaching* (Cambridge, 1908); H. Chadwick, 'Eucharist and Christology in the Nestorian Controversy' (art. in *Journ. Theol. Stud.*, 1951); R. Draguet, 'La Christologie d'Eutychès' (art. in *Byzantion*, 6, 1931); G. R. Driver and L. Hodgson, *Nestorius: The Bazaar of Heracleides*, Appendix IV (Oxford, 1925); P. Lamarche, *Christologie von der apostolischen Zeit bis zum Konzil von Chalcedon* (451) (HDG III, Freiburg etc., 1965); J. Liébaert, *La Doctrine christologique de saint Cyrille d'Alexandrie avant la querelle nestorienne* (Lille, 1951); F. Loofs, *Nestorius and His Place in the History of Christian Doctrine* (Cambridge, 1914); A. Michel, 'Hypostase' (art. in *Dict. Théol. Cath.*); J. Montalverne, *Theodoreti Cyrensis doctrina antiquior de Verbo 'inhumanato'* (Rome, 1948); M. Richard, 'L'Introduction du mot "hypostase" dans la théologie de l'incarnation' (art. in *Mélanges de science relig.* 2, 1945); L. I. Scipioni, *Ricerche sulla cristologia del 'Libro di Eraclide' di Nestorio* (*Paradosis* XI, Fribourg, 1956).

CHAPTER XIII

FALLEN MAN AND GOD'S GRACE

1. *The Soul's Origin*

It was in the fourth and fifth centuries that the doctrine of human nature became an issue of prime importance in the Church. For the fathers, with their Biblical presuppositions, the problem was one of history rather than analysis. They sought to explain man's present situation, and also to throw light on his hope of redemption, by expounding the story (whether taken literally or allegorically) of his creation and fall. During the larger portion of our period, when Greek writers are being passed in review, we shall find that the estimate formed of man's plight is relatively optimistic. This was partly due to the Hellenic temperament, but partly also to the fact that the rival philosophy was Manichaeism[1], with its fatalism and its dogma that matter, including the body, was intrinsically evil. When we turn to the West and approach the Pelagian controversy, the shadows deepen, and the picture of man passed on to the middle ages by Augustine is sombre, even pessimistic. Before we start our study, however, a brief note on a question which greatly exercised thought at this time will be useful.

In both East and West alike it was taken for granted that man is a composite being made up out of body and soul. He is a 'rational animal' ($\lambda o\gamma\iota\kappa\grave{o}\nu$ $\zeta\hat{\omega}o\nu$), with a foot in the higher, or intellectual, as well as the lower, or sensible, world. We have seen how frequently the union of body and soul, two disparate substances, was quoted by Alexandrian teachers as an illustration of the union of divinity and humanity in Christ.[2] But where did the soul come from? A few thinkers maintained the Origenist theory that, created by God, the soul pre-existed

[1] See above pp. 13 f.   [2] See above, pp. 293; 321.

Origen's idea prevalent

the body to which it was assigned as a penalty for its sins. Didymus the Blind,[1] for example, taught along these lines, as did the followers[2] of the Spanish heretic Priscillian (✝ 385). Victorinus seems to have held[3] a variation of the same doctrine. Most of the Greek fathers,[4] however, rejected this view, which was to be formally condemned in the sixth century. Augustine, too, reacted[5] against the pessimistic valuation of the material order and the suggestion that the body serves as a prison for the soul which it implies. The prevalent Greek theory[6] was creationism, i.e. that each individual soul was created independently by God at the moment of its infusion into the body. Western writers like Hilary, Ambrose and Jerome shared it, teaching that the soul was spiritual and immortal, being extended throughout the whole body, although existing particularly in a special part of it. Pelagius and his disciples, it need hardly be said, accepted[7] creationism, which harmonized well with their general position.

Creationism

The explanation to which Augustine on the whole leaned, although with many hesitations, was the traducianist one associated with Tertullian, viz. that each soul is somehow generated from the parent's soul. Among the Greeks there are hints of it in Gregory of Nyssa. Arguing against the Origenists, he urged[8] that the soul came into existence simultaneously with the body and was inseparable from it, the power of God working mysteriously on the human sperm to change it into a precious living being. Augustine himself was critical[9] of the materialist strain in Tertullian's brand of traducianism, but observed[10] that a spiritual version of the same theory fitted in best with his teaching about original sin. The danger, as he saw it,[11] was how on this hypothesis the integrity of the personality could be assured. At the same time, while conscious of diffi-

Traducianism

---

[1] E.g. *comm. in Iob* 3, 3–5 (Henrichs 1, 172 ff.).
[2] Cf., e.g., Leo, *ep.* 15, 10.   [3] *In Eph.* 1, 4.
[4] E.g. Cyril Hieros., *cat.* 4, 19; Gregory Nazianzen, *or.* 37, 15; Gregory Nyss., *de anim. et res.* (PG 46, 125; 128).   [5] *De civ. dei* 11, 23; *ep.* 166, 27.
[6] E.g. Cyril Hieros., *cat.* 4, 18 f.; Epiphanius, *ancor.* 55; Cyril Alex., *in Ioh.* 1, 9.   [7] E.g. Pelagius, *libellus fidei* 9 (PL 45, 1718).
[8] *De hom. opif.* 28; 29.   [9] E.g. *ep.* 190, 14.
[10] E.g. *de Gen. ad litt.* 10, 23-end.   [11] E.g. *ep.* 190, 15.

culties in each case, he remained alive[1] to the attractions of
various forms of the creationist theory. The truth is that, despite
his bias to traducianism, he could never make up his mind
about the matter, and in his later writings frankly confessed[2]
that he was baffled.

2. Athanasius and the Fall

A sketch of Athanasius's teaching makes the best introduction to a discussion of Greek views about the wider problem
of man's condition.

As we might expect, the account he gives is a blend of
Platonizing metaphysics and the *Genesis* story. Its most interesting feature is the contrast presupposed throughout between
man considered as a creature, i.e. in his natural state, and as the
recipient of God's bountiful favour. As a creature, man has
been called, like all other finite beings, out of nothingness by
the Word. Like them, he is liable to change and decay, ever
tending to slip back to nothingness, and being contingent is
incapable of knowing the transcendent God.[3] But if this is his
natural state, it is in a sense a theoretical one. As a matter of fact
God showed Himself more generous to man than to the rest of
creation. He enabled him to participate in His Word, thereby
making him in His image. This communion with the Word
bestowed supernatural knowledge upon him, made him
rational, and placed incorruption and immortality within his
grasp. But to preserve this resemblance or likeness to God, it
was necessary for him to contemplate the Word without remission, and so God placed him in Paradise, giving him a special
law to steady his will.[4] All these gifts, we observe, do not in
Athanasius's opinion belong to man's constitution as such, but
come to him from outside.[5]

Man's primitive state was thus one of supernatural blessedness; here we see the idea of original righteousness and perfection in embryo. What the Bible imagery describes as the

[1] *De lib. arbit.* 3, 56–9; *ep.* 166, 6–12.
[2] *De anim. et eius orig.* 1, 26; 4, 2; *retract.* 1, 1, 3; *c. Iul. op. imperf.* 2, 178.
[3] Cf. *c. gent.* 35; *de incarn.* 3; 4; 11.   [4] *C. gent.* 3; *de incarn.* 3; 4.
[5] *C. Ar.* 2, 68.

free intercourse of man with God in the garden, [Athanasius's
mysticism easily allegorizes as contemplation mixed with desire
which ever renews the divine likeness in the soul.] Instead of
keeping their gaze fixed on God, however, the first human
beings, Adam and Eve, allowed themselves to be distracted by
the material world which was closer to them, particularly by
their bodies.[1] They turned away, in other words, from Him
Who alone is being in the true sense to things which have no
real being of their own. So they fell. Deprived of the grace of
the divine image, they were reduced to the corruption which,
after all, was their nature,[2] lapsing into ignorance and idolatry.
'Thus death wielded its power more and more, and corruption
gathered force against men; the human race went to destruction, and man, rational and made in the image of the Word,
began to perish.'[3]

Athanasius therefore teaches that the wretchedness of mankind is directly traceable to our first parents' lapse. It was
through the fault committed by their free volition that the dis-
integrating forces in any case latent in our nature were released.
His argument presupposes the unity, or solidarity, of the race
with the first man, an idea with a long history, as we have seen,[4]
going back through Irenaeus to St. Paul. The disintegration, we
should notice, was not total. If man has lost the immortality of
his body, he retains that of the soul, and his will remains free.[5]
The obliteration of the image, too, seems to have been progressive; it is always open to men, Athanasius seems to think,[6]
using their free will, to throw off the entanglements of sensuality and recover their vision of the Word. The image is not so
much annihilated as lost to sight, like a picture overlaid with
dirt.[7] But, as one of the consequences of Adam's trespass, 'sin
has passed to all men;[8] indeed, that is implicit in the debacle of
human nature which Adam caused. But Athanasius never hints
that we participate in Adam's actual guilt, i.e. his moral culpability, nor does he exclude the possibility of men living entirely

NOT A TOTAL

---

[1] *C. gent.* 3.   [2] *De incarn.* 4; 7.   [3] Ib. 6.
[4] See above, pp. 167 f.; 170-2.   [5] *C. gent.* 4; 31-3.
[6] Ib. 34; *de incarn.* 12.   [7] *De incarn.* 14.   [8] *C. Ar.* I, 51.

without sin. In one passage,[1] for example, he claims that Jeremiah and John the Baptist actually did so.

3. *The Greek Fathers*

Athanasius's ideas about the perfection and blessedness of man in his primeval state had a far-reaching influence on the Eastern church of the fourth century. The Cappadocian fathers, for example, depict Adam as leading an idyllic, godlike existence in Eden. Stamped with the divine image, he was free from all the now normal disabilities, such as death, and he was endowed with freedom of will, filled with love for his creator and blest with the most intimate intercourse with Him.[2] Like Athanasius, they call in philosophizing allegory to aid them in interpreting the Biblical story. For Gregory Nazianzen[3] the Garden is clearly the Platonists' intelligible world of ideas,[4] its plants being 'divine concepts'. Gregory of Nyssa carried speculation to the point of proposing,[5] on the basis of *Gen.* 1, 26 f., a double creation. The first consisted in the production of the ideal or archetypal man, in the Platonic sense, perfect and without sexual differentiation, comprising in himself all possible men and women. It was because God foresaw that, being creaturely and therefore mutable, he would sin, that He subdivided him, by a second creative act, into male and female, thus inaugurating the actual race of men. The infiltration of philosophy is much less evident in theologians of the Antiochene tradition, with their attachment to the literal sense of Scripture. By the image of God in man Chrysostom understands[6] Adam's sovereignty over the rest of creation, including woman; and he interprets[7] the reduplication, 'and in our likeness', in the *Genesis* passage as meaning that man can, by his own efforts, attain the likeness of God by mastering his passions. As created he was neither corruptible nor mortal,[8] and Adam and Eve lived an angelic

---

[1] *C. Ar.* 3, 33.
[2] Cf. Basil, *hom.* 9 (*quod deus non est*), 6 f.; Gregory Nazianzen, *or.* 45, 8; Gregory Nyss., *or. cat.* 6.　　　[3] Loc. cit.　　　[4] See above, pp. 15 f.
[5] *De hom. opif.* 16.　　　[6] *In Gen. hom.* 3, 2; 9, 4.
[7] *Ib.* 9, 3.　　　[8] *Ad pop. Antioch. hom.* 11, 12.

life free from care.[1] Adam's wisdom and knowledge were perfect; he knew the meaning of the divine command and the penalties attached to its violation, and he enjoyed perfect freedom.[2]

From this beatitude our first parents fell, not (these writers all emphasize the point) through any necessity, and still less through any action of God's, but by the misuse of their own free will;[3] and to that fatal lapse of theirs are to be attributed all the evils to which man is heir. 'Having been deceived, we were destroyed', writes[4] Cyril of Jerusalem, '. . . we fell . . . we were blinded.' Hence man's mortality, his subjection to pain and sickness, his ignorance, his weakness of will and enslavement to desire; hence idolatry in religion, and violence, poverty and slavery in the social sphere.[5] The image of God has been defaced. In arguing thus these thinkers are trying to refute Manichaeism by removing the blame for evil from God. But do they hold that, along with its tragic after-effects, Adam has transmitted his actual sinfulness, i.e. his guilt, to posterity? The answer usually given is negative, and much of the evidence seems at first sight to support this. The Greek fathers, with their insistence that man's free will remains intact and is the root of actual sinning,[6] have a much more optimistic outlook than the West. It is easy to collect passages from their works which, at any rate in the light of later orthodoxy, appear to rule out any doctrine of original sin. Both the Gregories, for example, as well as Chrysostom, teach[7] that newly born children are exempt from sin. The latter, further, interprets[8] St. Paul's statement (*Rom.* 5, 19) that the many were made sinners by one man's disobedience as meaning only that they were made liable to punishment and death. It is hardly surprising that the

---

[1] *In Gen. hom.* 16, 5; 18, 4.   [2] *Ib.* 16, 5 f.
[3] E.g. Basil, *hom.* 9 (*quod deus non est*), 7.   [4] *Cat.* 2, 5.
[5] Cf. Gregory Nazianzen, *or.* 19, 13 f.; 14, 25; 22, 13; 45, 8; 45, 12; Gregory Nyss., *or. cat.* 6; 8; J. Chrysostom, *ad pop. Antioch. hom.* 11, 2; *in Gen. hom.* 16, 5 f.; 17, 2.
[6] E.g. Basil, *hom.* 8, 3; 8, 5; Gregory Nyss., *or. cat.* 7; Chrysostom, *in Gen. hom.* 19, 1; 20, 3.
[7] Gregory Nazianzen, *or.* 40, 23; Gregory Nyss., *de infant. qui praemat. mor.* (PG 46, 177–80); Chrysostom, *in Matt. hom.* 28, 3.
[8] *In Rom. hom.* 10, 2 f.

Pelagian Julian of Eclanum later claimed[1] that their teaching had foreshadowed his own position.

The customary verdict, however, seems unjust to the Greek fathers, perhaps because it depends on the assumption that no theory of original sin holds water except the full-blown Latin one. It is imperative to get rid of this prejudice. Admittedly there is hardly a hint in the Greek fathers that mankind as a whole shares in Adam's guilt, i.e. his culpability. This partly explains their reluctance to speak of his legacy to us as sin, and of course makes their indulgent attitude to children dying unbaptized understandable. But they have the greatest possible feeling for the mystical unity of mankind with its first ancestor. This is the ancient doctrine of recapitulation, and in virtue of it they assume without question that our fall was involved in Adam's. Again, their tendency is to view original sin as a wound inflicted on our nature. If we bear these points in mind, and also the fact that their treatment of the subject is almost always incidental, we can perhaps define their position. First, they take it for granted that all men were involved in Adam's rebellious act. For Basil, for example, the purpose of the tree of knowledge in Paradise was that '*our* obedience might be tested';[2] Gregory of Nazianzus envisages[3] the whole race as participating in Adam's sin and fall, and expressly claims[4] as his own the weakness which the primal man displayed in the garden; and Gregory of Nyssa, after saying that we wear skins 'as if Adam lived in us', adds[5] that men ought to ask for forgiveness daily since they share in Adam's fall. Secondly, alongside their assumption of free will, they clearly hold that the Fall affected our moral nature. Their lists of evils flowing from it include disorders attributable to the unleashing of lust and greed.[6] Gregory of Nazianzus traces[7] his own congenital weakness of will to it, and Gregory of Nyssa states[8] that 'human nature is weak in regard to doing good, having been once for

---

[1] Cf. Augustine, *in Iul. op. imperf.* 1, 21; 1, 22; 1, 26.
[2] *Hom.* 9, 9.   [3] *Or.* 33, 9.   [4] Ib. 45, 8.
[5] *De orat. dom.* or. 5 (PG 44, 1184).
[6] E.g. Gregory Nazianzen, *or.* 14, 25; 19, 13 f.
[7] *Carm.* 2, 1, 45 (vv. 95-107).   [8] *De orat. dom.* or. 4 (PG 44, 1164).

all hamstrung through weakness'. According to Chrysostom,[1] the death imposed as a penalty on the human race entails concupiscence.

Thirdly, however, there are not wanting passages which suggest that certain fathers envisaged also the transmission of sin itself. Basil actually uses the phrase, bidding[2] the rich give food to the poor so as to wipe out the sin which Adam 'transmitted' (παρέπεμψεν) when he ate the forbidden fruit. Chrysostom seems to have spoken[3] of an 'ancestral obligation' written out by Adam amounting to 'the first portion of a debt which we have increased by our subsequent sins'. But Gregory of Nyssa is much more outspoken. Not only does he describe[4] the humanity assumed by Christ as 'prone to sin' (ἁμαρτητικήν), and sin as 'congenital to our nature', but he can write:[5] 'Evil was mixed with our nature from the beginning . . . through those who by their disobedience introduced the disease. Just as in the natural propagation of the species each animal engenders its like, so man is born from man, a being subject to passions from a being subject to passions, a sinner from a sinner. Thus sin takes its rise in us as we are born; it grows with us and keeps us company till life's term.' Such thoughts are more frequent in Ps.-Didymus, who speaks of 'the ancient sin'[6] of Adam in virtue of which all men are held under sin (ὑπὸ ἁμαρτίαν εἰσίν[7]). They contract it 'by transmission' (κατὰ διαδοχήν), the sexual union of their parents being apparently the means.[8] But this sin which we inherit from Adam, and which as such is not voluntary, seems to him[9] to call for purification rather than for punishment.

Though falling short of Augustinianism, there was here the outline of a real theory of original sin. The fathers might well have filled it in and given it greater sharpness of definition had the subject been directly canvassed in their day. A point on

[1] *In Rom. hom.* 13, 1.   [2] *Hom.* 8, 7.
[3] Cf. Augustine, *c. Iul.* 1, 26.
[4] *De vit. Moys.; in ps.* 6 (PG 44, 336; 609).
[5] *De beat.* or. 6 (PG 44, 1273).
[6] *De trin.* 2, 12; 3, 12; 3, 17; 3, 21 (PG 39, 684; 860; 876; 916).
[7] *In 2 Cor.* 4, 17 (PG 39, 1692).   [8] *C. Manich.* 8 (PG 39, 1096).
[9] *In Iob* 10, 15 (PG 39, 1145).

which they were all agreed was that man's will remains free; we are responsible for our acts.[1] This was a vital article in their anti-Manichaean propaganda, but it raised the question of man's need of divine grace. The issue is usually posed in the terms which the later Augustinian discussion has made familiar, and so viewed their position was that grace and free will co-operate. Our salvation comes, stated[2] Gregory Nazianzen, both from ourselves and from God. If God's help is necessary for doing good and if the good will itself comes from Him, it is equally true that the initiative rests with man's free will. Chrysostom similarly teaches[3] that without God's aid we should be unable to accomplish good works; nevertheless, even if grace takes the lead, it co-operates ($\sigma\upsilon\mu\pi\rho\acute{\alpha}\tau\tau\epsilon\iota$) with free will. We first of all begin to desire the good and to incline ourselves towards it, and then God steps in to strengthen that desire and render it effective. But these were superficial answers; Augustine's starting-point was not theirs, and they could not be expected to have thought the problem through. The orbit within which they worked was quite different, being marked out by the ideas of participation in the divine nature, rebirth through the power of the Spirit, adoption as sons, new creation through Christ—all leading to the concept of deification ($\theta\epsilon o\pi o\acute{\iota}\eta\sigma\iota\varsigma$). Their attitude is illustrated by the statement[4] attributed to Athanasius, 'The Son of God became son of man so that the sons of men, that is, of Adam, might become sons of God ... partakers of the life of God. . . . Thus He is Son of God by nature, and we by grace.' Cyril of Alexandria made the same point:[5] 'We are made partakers of the divine nature and are said to be sons of God, nay we are actually called divine, not only because we are exalted by grace to supernatural glory, but also because we have God dwelling in us'. Grace thus conceived is a state of communion with God, and if a man must use his free will to attain it, there can be no question but that the blessedness in which it consists is wholly the gift of God.

---

[1] E.g. Cyril Hieros., *cat.* 4, 18-21; Epiphanius, *haer.* 64, 49; Gregory Nazianzen, 37, 21; Gregory Nyss., *or. cat.* 30 f.   [2] *Or.* 37, 13-15.
[3] *In Gen. hom.* 25, 7; 58, 5; *in Rom. hom.* 14, 7; 19, 1; *in Hebr. hom.* 12, 3.
[4] *De incarn. et c. Ar.* 8.   [5] *In Ioh.* 1, 9 (PG 73, 157).

4. *The West before Augustine*

For our knowledge of fourth-century Latin theories of human nature we shall draw mainly, though not exclusively, on Ambrose and his anonymous contemporary, the Roman exegete whom Erasmus designated Ambrosiaster. Both must have influenced Augustine, and Ambrosiaster anticipated his teaching at a number of points.

In the first place, the general Western view was that man's primitive state had been one of supernatural blessedness. According to Hilary,[1] he was created immortal, destined to share the blessedness of God Himself. Ambrosiaster argued[2] that, although Adam's body was not intrinsically immortal, he halted its tendency to decay by eating of the Tree of Life. It was Ambrose, however, perhaps inspired by his acquaintance with the Cappadocians, who painted the picture in the most glowing colours. Adam had been a 'heavenly being', breathing etherial air and immune from life's cares and boredoms.[3] Accustomed to conversing with God face to face,[4] he held his carnal appetites in sovereign control.[5] Along with Eve he radiated perfect innocence and virtue,[6] and was even exempt from the need of food.[7] From this happy state, however, he fell, being condemned to concupiscence and death. The root cause of his lapse, according to Ambrose,[8] was pride: 'he wanted to claim for himself something which had not been assigned to him, equality with his Creator'. In Ambrosiaster's view[9] his sin was akin to idolatry, since he fondly imagined he could become God. By treating the Devil as God, Adam placed himself in his power.[10] It was his soul, of course, which sinned, but the act corrupted his flesh, and sin established its abode there. Thus the Devil took possession of it, so that henceforth it could be designated a 'flesh of sin'.[11]

Secondly, the solidarity of the race with Adam, with all that

---

[1] *In ps.* 2, 15 f. ; 59, 4 ; 118, litt. 10, 1.   [2] *Quaest. vet. et novi test.* 19.
[3] *Ps.* 118 *expos.* 15, 36; 4, 5.   [4] *Enarr. in ps.* 43, 75.
[5] *Expos. ev. Luc.* 7, 142.   [6] *De parad.* 24; 63; *ep.* 58, 12.
[7] *De parad.* 42.   [8] *Ps.* 118 *expos.* 7, 8; *ep.* 73, 5.
[9] *In Rom.* 5, 14.   [10] *Ib.* 7, 14.   [11] *Ib.* 7, 18.

that notion entails, received much fuller recognition in the West than the East. An unknown author writes,[1] 'Assuredly we all sinned in the first man, and by the inheritance of his nature an inheritance of guilt (*culpae*) has been transmitted from one man to all. . . . Adam is therefore in each of us, for in him human nature itself sinned.' To return to Ambrose,[2] 'Adam existed, and in him we all existed; Adam perished, and in him all perished'; and again, even more forcibly,[3] 'In Adam I fell, in Adam I was cast out of Paradise, in Adam I died. How should God restore me, unless He find in me Adam, justified in Christ, exactly as in that first Adam I was subject to guilt (*culpae obnoxium*) and destined to death?' Ambrosiaster's teaching is particularly noteworthy because it relies on an exegesis of *Rom.* 5, 12 which, though mistaken and based on a false reading, was to become the pivot of the doctrine of original sin. In the Greek St. Paul's text runs, '. . . so death passed to all men inasmuch as (ἐφ' ᾧ) all sinned'; but the Old Latin version which Ambrosiaster used had the faulty translation '. . . in whom (*in quo*) all sinned'. Hence we find him commenting,[4] ' "In whom", that is, in Adam, "all sinned." He said, "In whom", in the masculine, although speaking about the woman, because his reference was to the race, not the sex. It is therefore plain that all men sinned in Adam as in a lump (*quasi in massa*). For Adam himself was corrupted by sin, and all whom he begat were born under sin. Thus we are all sinners from him, since we all derive from him.'

What are the practical implications of this solidarity? The second of Ambrose's texts cited above suggests that the race is infected with Adam's actual guilt. His more general doctrine, however, is that, while the corrupting force of sin is transmitted, the guilt attaches to Adam himself, not to us. Certainly no one can be without sin (i.e., presumably, the sinful tendency), not even a day-old child;[5] the corruption actually increases, in the individual as he grows older[6] and in the race as generation succeeds generation.[7] But our personal (*propria*) sins are to be

[1] Pseudo-Ambrose, *apol. proph. David* 2, 71.
[2] *Expos. ev. Luc.* 7, 234.　　[3] *De excess. Satur.* 2, 6.
[4] *In Rom.* 5, 12.　　[5] *De Noe* 9; 81; *de poenit.* 1, 4.
[6] *De Noe* 81.　　[7] *Ep.* 45, 13-15.

contrasted with those we inherit (*haereditaria*); baptism removes the former, but the rite of the washing of feet the latter.[1] In the *De sacramentis* (if he is the author of this work) he makes the same curious distinction, stating[2] that 'the serpent's poison' is done away by the washing of feet. This hereditary sin, he argues elsewhere,[3] is a wound which makes us stumble, but need cause us no anxiety at the day of judgment; we shall only be punished then for our personal sins. Baptism is of course necessary for infants, but because it opens the kingdom of heaven to them.[4] It is clear that he envisages the inherited corruption as a congenital propensity to sin (the phrase he uses is *lubricum delinquendi*) rather than as positive guilt. The moment of transmission he identifies,[5] in reliance on *Ps.* 51, 5 ('I was conceived in iniquities, and in sins my mother bore me'), with the act of physical generation. Thus he can claim that Christ escaped the taint of hereditary sin by His virginal conception.

In Ambrosiaster's view man's body, as a result of the fatal legacy, is a prey to sin; Satan holds him captive, and can compel him to do his will.[6] The reason is that, as we saw above, Adam's sin corrupted the flesh, and the corruption is passed on by physical descent (*per traducem fit omnis caro peccati*[7]). Man cannot plead that he is not responsible for the resulting sins; even if he commits them unwillingly in a sense, it was nevertheless he who originally, presumably in Adam, enslaved himself to the Devil.[8] At the same time Ambrosiaster distinguishes degrees in men's subjection to sin. The majority, no doubt, sin after the model of Adam, despising God; but there are others, the good, who acknowledge the moral law and, when they sin, do so while retaining their respect for the divine majesty.[9] It is only the former who are destined for the second death and for the lower, or real, hell; the latter remain in an upper hell, which for the just is really a place of refreshment (*refrigerium*[10]). The point is that for Ambrosiaster, as for Ambrose, we are not punished for Adam's sin, but only for our own sins. As he

---

[1] *De myst.* 32; *enarr. in ps.* 48, 8.   [2] 3, 5-7.
[3] *Enarr. in ps.* 48, 9.   [4] *De Abrah.* 2, 79.
[5] *Apol. proph. Dav.* 56 f.   [6] *In Rom.* 7, 14.   [7] Ib. 7, 22.
[8] Ib. 7, 20.   [9] Ib. 5, 14.   [10] Ib. 5, 12; 5, 14.

says,[1] 'You perceive that men are not made guilty by the fact of their birth, but by their evil behaviour'. Baptism is therefore necessary, not as abolishing inherited guilt, but as delivering us from death and opening the gates of the kingdom of heaven.[2]

Although we have only cited these two, there is little doubt that their views were representative. On the related question of grace, the parallel truths of man's free will and his need of God's help were maintained, although we can discern increasing emphasis being laid on the latter. 'We must be assisted and directed', wrote[3] Hilary, 'by His grace'; but he makes it plain that the initial move in God's direction lies at our own disposition. God's mercy, he points out elsewhere,[4] does not exclude man's desert, and a man's own will must take the lead in lifting him from sin. 'It is for God to call', remarks[5] Jerome, 'and for us to believe.' The part of grace, it would seem, is to perfect that which the will has freely determined; yet our will is only ours by God's mercy.[6] So Ambrose states,[7] 'In everything the Lord's power cooperates with man's efforts'; but he can also say,[8] 'Our free will gives us either a propensity to virtue or an inclination to sin'. In numerous passages[9] he lays it down that the grace of salvation will only come to those who make the effort to bestir themselves. Yet in other moods, with a lack of consistency which is understandable, these writers evince a deeper sense of man's dependence upon God. Ambrose, for example, states[10] that grace is not bestowed as a reward for merit, but 'simply according to the will of the Giver'. A man's decision to become a Christian, he explains,[11] has really been prepared in advance by God; and indeed every holy thought we have is God's gift to us.[12] Ambrosiaster agrees[13] with him that grace is granted freely, not in reward for any merits of ours; and

---

[1] *Quaest. vet. et novi test.* 21 f.　　　　[2] Ib. 81.
[3] *Tract. in ps.* 118, litt. 1, 2; ib., litt. 16, 10.
[4] *Tract. in ps.* 142, 3; 118, litt. 14, 20.　　[5] *In Is.* 49, 4.
[6] *C. Pelag.* 1, 5; 3, 1; *ep.* 130, 12.　　　[7] *Expos. ev. Luc.* 2, 84.
[8] *De Iac.* 1, 1.
[9] E.g. *tract. in ps.* 43, 7; 118, litt. 12, 13; *de interpell. Iob* 4, 4; *de Abrah.* 2, 74.
[10] *Exhort. virg.* 43.　　　　　　　[11] *Expos. ev. Luc.* 1, 10.
[12] *De Cain et Ab.* 1, 45.　　　　　[13] *In Rom.* 11, 6.

Victorinus insists[1] most plainly that the very will to do good is the work of God and owes its existence to the operation of His grace.

5. The Doctrine of Pelagius

The preceding pages, while revealing the firm hold which fourth-century Christians had on the truth of man's fallen condition and consequent need of divine help, have also brought to light the persistence, side by side with it, of a dogged belief in free will and responsibility. These two sets of ideas were not necessarily irreconcilable, but a conflict was unavoidable unless their relations were set down very subtly. This was the situation which emerged quite early in the fifth century. By 396, as his *Ad Simplicianum*, finished in that year, proves, Augustine was already putting before contemporary Christians his conception of mankind as a 'lump of sin', unable to make any move to save itself and wholly dependent on God's grace. About the same time, between 384 and 409, the austere British monk (he belonged to no religious order, but *monachus* connoted a dedicated 'servant of God') Pelagius, now a fashionable teacher at Rome, was disseminating a diametrically opposite doctrine of human nature. A clash was inevitable, and it came when he and his disciple Celestius left Italy in 409 in face of Alaric's invasion and crossed over to Africa, where the latter settled at Carthage.

Pelagius was primarily a moralist, concerned for right conduct and shocked by what he considered demoralizingly pessimistic views of what could be expected of human nature. The assumption that man could not help sinning seemed[2] to him an insult to his Creator. Augustine's prayer,[3] 'Give what Thou commandest, and command what Thou wilt' (*da quod iubes et iube quod vis*), particularly distressed him,[4] for it seemed to suggest that men were puppets wholly determined by the movements of divine grace. In reaction to this the keystone of his whole system is the idea of unconditional free will and responsibility. In creating man God did not subject him, like

---

[1] *In Phil.* 2, 12 f.   [2] *Ad Demet.* 16 f. (PL 30, 30 f.).
[3] *Confess.* 10, 40.   [4] Cf. Augustine, *de dono persev.* 53.

other creatures, to the law of nature, but gave him the unique privilege of being able to accomplish the divine will by his own choice. He set life and death before him, bidding him choose life (*Deut.* 30, 19), but leaving the final decision to his free will. Thus it depends on the man himself whether he acts rightly or wrongly; the possibility of freely choosing the good entails the possibility of choosing evil.[1] There are, he argues,[2] three features in action—the power (*posse*), the will (*velle*) and the realization (*esse*). The first of these comes exclusively from God, but the other two belong to us; hence, according as we act, we merit praise or blame. It would be wrong to infer, however, that he regarded this autonomy as somehow withdrawing man from the purview of God's sovereignty. Whatever his followers may have said, Pelagius himself made no such claim. On the contrary, along with his belief in free will he has the conception of a divine law proclaiming to men what they ought to do and setting the prospect of supernatural rewards and pains before them.[3] If a man enjoys freedom of choice, it is by the express bounty of his Creator, and he ought to use it for the ends which He prescribes.

The rest of Pelagius's system coheres logically with this central thought. First, he rejects the idea that man's will has any intrinsic bias in favour of wrong-doing as a result of the Fall. Since each soul is, as he believes, created immediately by God, it cannot come into the world soiled by original sin transmitted from Adam. To suppose that it does savours of the traducian theory that souls, like bodies, are generated from the parents, and is tantamount to Manichaeism.[4] Even if true, however, would not the theory entail that the offspring of baptized parents are not only free from Adam's taint but inherit their sanctification?[5] In any case God, Who forgives human beings their own sins, surely cannot blame them for someone else's.[6] Adam's trespass certainly had disastrous consequences; it intro-

---

[1] *Ad Demet.* 2 (PL 30, 16 f.).
[2] Cf. Augustine, *de grat. Chr. et pecc. orig.* 1, 5.
[3] *Ad Celant.* 13-15; *ad Demet.* 16 (PL 22, 1210 f.; 30, 30 f.).
[4] Augustine, *op. imperf. c. Iul.* 6, 8; 6, 21.
[5] *In Rom.* 5, 15.   [6] Ib.

duced death, physical and spiritual, and set going a habit of disobedience. But this latter is propagated, not by physical descent,
but by custom and example.[1] Hence there is no congenital fault
in man as he is born: 'before he begins exercising his will, there
is only in him what God has created'.[2] Pelagius's baptismal
teaching naturally fitted in with this. For adults the sacrament
was medicinal and regenerative, but its effect on infants was
purely benedictory; what they received at the font was not
eternal life (like Ambrose and Ambrosiaster, he believed they
were eligible for that already), but 'spiritual illumination,
adoption as children of God, citizenship of the heavenly
Jerusalem, sanctification and membership of Christ, with inheritance in the kingdom of heaven'.[3]

Secondly, he equally resists the suggestion that there can be
any special pressure on man's will to choose the good. In effect
this means the limitation of grace to such purely external aids
as God has provided; no room is left for any special, interior
action of God upon the soul, much less any predestination to
holiness. Pelagius stated,[4] it is true, that grace is necessary 'not
only every hour and every moment, but in every act'. He also
admitted[5] that grace is bestowed 'to make the fulfilment of
God's commands easier'. By grace, however, he really meant
(a) free will itself, or the possibility of not sinning with which
God endowed us at our creation;[6] (b) the revelation, through
reason, of God's law, instructing us what we should do and
holding out eternal sanctions;[7] and (c), since this has become
obscured through evil custom, the law of Moses and the teaching and example of Christ.[8] Thus grace on his view is in the
main *ab extra*; it is 'a grace of knowledge'[9] or, as Augustine put
it,[10] a grace consisting in 'law and teaching'. The only exception
he allows is the bestowal of the forgiveness of sins (to adults, of

[1] Ib. 5, 12; 5, 16; *ad Demet.* 8; 17.
[2] Augustine, *de grat. Chr. et pecc. orig.* 2, 14.
[3] Augustine, *op. imperf. c. Iul.* 1, 53; *de grat. Chr. et pecc. orig.* 2, 20-3.
[4] Augustine, *de grat. Chr. et pecc. orig.* 1, 2; 1, 8; 1, 36.
[5] Ib. 1, 27-30.   [6] Augustine, *de gest. Pelag.* 22; *ep.* 186, 1.
[7] *Ad Demet.* 2 (PL 30, 16 f.).
[8] Ib. 4 ff.; 8; Augustine, *de grat. Chr. et pecc. orig.* 1, 45.
[9] *In Phil.* 1, 6.   [10] *De grat. Chr. et pecc. orig.* 1, 45.

course) in baptism and penance.[1] Grace is, further, offered equally to all, and Pelagius will have nothing to do with the idea that God bestows special favour upon some; He is no 'acceptor of persons'.[2] By merit alone men advance in holiness, and God's predestination operates strictly in accordance with the quality of the lives He foresees they will lead.[3]

With these as his presuppositions Pelagius does not shrink from the corollary logically implied in them that 'a man can, if he will, observe God's commandments without sinning'.[4] Was it not written in the Bible, 'Ye shall be holy, for I am holy' (Lev. 19, 2), and, 'Ye shall be perfect, as your heavenly Father is perfect' (Matt. 5, 48[5])? It would be impious to suggest that God, the Father of all justice, enjoins what He knows to be impossible.[6] As a matter of fact, he argued,[7] Scripture can point to many examples of blameless lives. So Pelagius's austere doctrine of impeccantia takes shape. It is the whole law which must be fulfilled, for 'a Christian is he who is one not in word but in deed, who imitates and follows Christ in everything, who is holy, innocent, unsoiled, blameless, in whose heart there is no malice but only piety and goodness, who refuses to injure or hurt anyone, but brings succour to all. . . . He is a Christian who can justly say, "I have injured no one, I have lived righteously with all".'[8] He does not imagine, of course, that anyone will live such a life from childhood to death. What he envisages is not a state of perfection acquired once for all, but rather one which is attained by strenuous efforts of the will and which only steadily increasing application will be able to maintain.[9]

Pelagius's teaching is often described as a species of naturalism, but this label scarcely does justice to its profoundly religious spirit. Defective though it is in its recognition of man's weakness, it radiates an intense awareness of God's majesty, of the wonderful privileges and high destiny He has vouchsafed to

---

[1] Augustine, de nat. et grat. 20; 31; 60-4.   [2] De cast. 13.
[3] In Rom. 9, 10: cf. ib. 8, 29 f.   [4] Augustine, de gest. Pelag. 16.
[5] Qualiter 4 (in Caspari, Briefe, etc. 119).   [6] Ib. 2.
[7] Augustine, de nat. et grat. 42-4.   [8] De vita christ. 6 (PL 40, 1037).
[9] Ad Demet. 27 (PL 30, 42); cf. Augustine, de gest. Pelag. 20.

men, and of the claims of the moral law and of Christ's
example. Yet its one-sidedness made it grievously inadequate
as an interpretation of Christianity, and this inadequacy was
heightened by Pelagius's disciples. Celestius, for example, who
became the practical leader of the movement, made it his
policy to stress the irritating tenets which the more conciliatory
Pelagius himself tried to soften down. Thus he pushed the
denial of original sin into the foreground, teaching that Adam
was created mortal and would have died anyhow, whether he
sinned or not. He proclaimed that children were eligible for
eternal life even without baptism (later he adopted more
cautious formulae), and enlarged on the incompatibility of
grace and free will.[1] This rationalizing strain was further intensified by Julian of Eclanum, probably the ablest thinker in
the Pelagian group. According to him, man's free will placed
him in a position of complete independence *vis-à-vis* God (*a deo
emancipatus homo est*[2]). Making God's goodness his major premiss, he dismissed[3] Augustine's teaching as pure Manichaeism,
and, as against his gloomy estimate of the sex instinct, urged[4]
that its moderate indulgence was natural and innocent. Even
apart from such provocative sallies, however, Pelagianism, with
its excessively rosy view of human nature and its insufficient
acknowledgement of man's dependence on God, invited
criticism. Celestius was condemned at Carthage early in 412.
Other condemnations followed at Carthage and Milevum in
416, and at the great African council held at Carthage in 418.
The doctrine was finally anathematized at the council of
Ephesus on 22 July 431.

6. *Augustine and Original Sin*

Augustine had worked out his own theory of man and his
condition long before the outbreak of the Pelagian controversy.
His starting-point is a glowing picture of human nature as it

---

[1] Augustine, ib. 23 f.; *de perfect. justit. hom.* passim.
[2] Augustine, *op. imperf. c. Iul.* 1, 78.
[3] E.g. Augustine, op. cit. 6, 10.
[4] E.g. Augustine, op. cit. 1, 71; 3, 142; 5, 5 f.

comes from the Creator's hands; he carries to its highest pitch
the growing tendency to attribute original righteousness and
perfection to the first man. Adam, he holds,[1] was immune from
physical ills and had surpassing intellectual gifts; he was in a
state of justification, illumination and beatitude. Immortality
lay within his grasp if only he continued to feed upon the Tree
of Life.[2] Freedom he possessed, not in the sense of the inability
to sin (the *non posse peccare* which Augustine regards as the true
liberty enjoyed in heaven by the blessed), but of the ability not
to sin (*posse non peccare*[3]). And his will was good, that is,
devoted to carrying out God's commands, for God endowed it
with a settled inclination to virtue.[4] So his body was subject to
his soul, his carnal desires to his will, and his will to God.[5]
Already he was wrapped around with divine grace (*indu-
mentum gratiae*[6]), and he was further granted the special gift
of perseverance, i.e. the possibility of persisting in the right
exercise of his will.[7]

Nevertheless, as the Bible records, he fell. It is clear from
Augustine's account that the fault was entirely his own. God
could not be blamed, for He had given him every advantage;
the one prohibition He imposed, not to eat the forbidden fruit,
was the reverse of burdensome, and his desires did not conflict
with it.[8] His only weakness was his creatureliness, which meant
that he was changeable by nature and so liable to turn away
from the transcendent good.[9] Any blame must lie exclusively
with his own will, which, though inclined towards goodness,
had the possibility, being free, of choosing wrongfully. When
it did so, the latent ground of the act was pride, the desire to
break away from his natural master, God, and be his own
master. If there had not been this proud satisfaction with self in
his soul, this craving to substitute self for God as the goal of his
being, he would never have listened to the Tempter.[10] And from

---

[1] Op. cit. 5, 1; *de Gen. ad litt.* 8, 25.
[2] *De Gen. ad litt.* 6, 36; *de civ. dei* 13, 20.
[3] *De corrept. et grat.* 33.   [4] *De civ. dei* 14, 11.
[5] *De pecc. mer. et remiss.* 2, 36; *de nupt. et concup.* 2, 30.
[6] *De civ. dei* 14, 17; *de Gen. ad litt.* 11, 42.
[7] *De corrept. et grat.* 34.   [8] *De civ. dei* 14, 12.
[9] Ib. 12, 8.   [10] Ib. 14, 13: cf. *de lib. arbit.* 3, 2.

this character of the first sin flows its heinousness. Trivial though it might appear, it can be seen on analysis to have involved sacrilege (through disbelieving God's word), murder, spiritual fornication, theft and avarice.[1] It was worse than any other conceivable sin in proportion as Adam was nobler than any other man and as the will which produced it was uniquely free.[2] In fact, such was its gravity that it resulted in the ruin of the entire race, which became a *massa damnata*, sinful itself and propagating sinners.[3]

So Augustine has no doubt of the reality of original sin. *Genesis* apart, he finds Scriptural proof of it in *Ps. 51, Job* and *Eph. 2, 3,*[4] but above all in *Rom. 5, 12* (where, like Ambrosiaster, he reads[5] 'in whom') and *John 3, 3-5.*[6] The Church's tradition, too, he is satisfied, is unanimously in favour of it, and he marshals[7] an array of patristic evidence to convince Julian of Eclanum of this. The practice of baptizing infants with exorcisms and a solemn renunciation of the Devil was in his eyes proof positive that even they were infected with sin.[8] Finally, the general wretchedness of man's lot and his enslavement to his desires seemed to clinch the matter.[9] Like others before him, he believed that the taint was propagated from parent to child by the physical act of generation, or rather as the result of the carnal excitement which accompanied it and was present, he noticed, in the sexual intercourse even of baptized persons.[10] As we have seen,[11] Augustine was divided in mind between the traducianist and various forms of the creationist theory of the soul's origin. If the former is right, original sin passes to us directly from our parents; if the latter, the freshly created soul becomes soiled as it enters the body.[12]

Nothing is more difficult to understand, Augustine once wrote,[13] than the nature of 'the ancient sin'. His account has two aspects which it is desirable to treat separately. In the first

---

[1] *Enchir. 45.*   [2] *Op. imperf. c. Iul. 6, 22; 3, 57.*

[3] Ib.; *de nupt. et concup.* 2, 57; *enchir.* 27.

[4] *Enarr. in ps.* 50, 10; *serm.* 170, 2.   [5] *De pecc. mer. et remiss.* I, 11.

[6] Ib. 1, 26.   [7] *C. Iul.* 1, 6-35.   [8] E.g. *de nupt. et concup.* 1, 22.

[9] *Op. imperf. c. Iul.* 5, 64; 6, 27; 6, 14.

[10] Ib. 2, 42; *de nupt. et concup.* 2, 36; *de pecc. mer. et remiss.* 2, 11.

[11] See above, p. 345.   [12] *C. Iul.* 5, 17.   [13] *De mor. eccl. cath.* I, 40.

place, as he sees it, the essence of original sin consists in our participation in, and co-responsibility for, Adam's perverse choice. We were one with him when he made it, and thus willed in and with him. As he expresses it,[1] 'In the misdirected choice of that one man all sinned in him, since all were that one man, from whom on that account they all severally derive original sin'. Sin is a matter of the will (*nusquam nisi in voluntate esse peccatum*[2]), and 'all sinned in Adam on that occasion, for all were already identical with him in that nature of his which was endowed with the capacity to generate them'.[3] Others before Augustine had stressed our solidarity with Adam, but none had depicted so vividly our complicity with him in his evil willing. His attitude is very clearly indicated when he faces the objection that, if sin lies in the will, infants must be exempt from original sin since they cannot will freely. His rejoinder[4] is that there is nothing absurd in speaking of their original sin as voluntary, derived as it is from the free act of their first parent. As a result, while drawing a distinction between the guilt (*reatus*) of original sin and the evil it inflicts on our nature, he sees nothing incongruous in saddling us with both. Indeed, it is precisely this guilt, he argues,[5] that baptism was designed to remove.

Secondly, as a consequence of Adam's rebellion which, as we have seen, is ours too, human nature has been terribly scarred and vitiated. Augustine does not inculcate a doctrine of 'total depravity', according to which the image of God has been utterly obliterated in us. Even though grievously altered, fallen man remains noble:[6] 'the spark, as it were, of reason in virtue of which he was made in God's likeness has not been completely extinguished'.[7] Nevertheless the corruption has gone far enough. The most obvious symptom of it, apart from the general misery of man's existence, is his enslavement to ignorance, concupiscence and death.[8] In Augustine's vocabulary concupiscence stands, in a general way, for every inclination making

[1] *De nupt. et concup.* 2, 15.   [2] E.g. *retract.* 1, 15, 2.
[3] *De pecc. mer. et remiss.* 3, 14.   [4] *Retract.* 1, 13, 5.
[5] *C. Iul.* 6, 49 f.   [6] *De trin.* 14, 6.   [7] *De civ. dei* 22, 24, 2.
[8] E.g. ib. 13, 3; 13, 14; *op. imperf. c. Iul.* 4, 104; 6, 17; 6, 22.

man turn from God to find satisfaction in material things which are intrinsically evanescent. Far the most violent, persistent and widespread of these, however, is in his opinion sexual desire, and for practical purposes he identifies concupiscence with it. It is misleading to interpret him, as many have done, as in effect equating original sin with sexual passion. This disorder in our physical nature, which he describes as both sinful and the fruit of sin, is itself the product of our primeval wilful rebellion. That it is not identical with original sin comes out, for example, in the fact that, although baptism removes the guilt (*reatus*) attaching to it, it cannot do away with its actuality (*actus*) in our members.[1] Yet the equation is easy to make, for Augustine seems obsessed with the ravages which unbridled sexuality produces in human beings. Even chaste people, he remarks,[2] married or single, are conscious of a tragic war within themselves which did not exist in Paradise. Not that marriage, instituted as it was by God, is sinful in itself; but marriage as mankind now knows it seems inseparable from sexual pleasures of which man in his innocence was ignorant.[3] It was in view of this, to avoid the taint of concupiscence, that the Saviour chose to be born of a pure virgin.[4]

Further, as a by-product of our fall in Adam, we have lost that liberty (*libertas*) which he enjoyed, viz. of being able to avoid sin and do good. Henceforth we cannot avoid sin without God's grace, and without an even more special grace we cannot accomplish the good. Not that Augustine intends to convey by this that we have been deprived of free will (*liberum arbitrium*) itself. His language[5] occasionally appears to suggest this, but his normal doctrine[6] is that, while we retain our free will intact, the sole use to which in our unregenerate state we put it is to do wrong. In this sense he can speak[7] of 'a cruel necessity of sinning' resting upon the human race. By this he means, not

[1] *De nupt. et concup.* 1, 28 f.: cf. *c. duas epp. Pelag.* 1, 27.
[2] *C. Iul.* 3, 57.
[3] *De grat. Chr. et pecc. orig.* 2, 38; *de nupt. et concup.* 1, 20; 2, 25; 2, 36; etc.
[4] *De nupt. et concup.* 1, 27; *enchir.* 34; *serm.* 151, 5.
[5] E.g. *enchir.* 30; *ep.* 145, 2.
[6] *C. duas epp. Pelag.* 1, 5; 3, 24; *serm.* 156, 12; *in ev. Ioh. tract.* 5, 1.
[7] *De perfect. iustit. hom.* 9; *op. imperf. c. Iul.* 1, 106; 5, 61.

that our wills are in the grip of any physical or metaphysical determinism, but rather that, our choice remaining free, we spontaneously, as a matter of psychological fact, opt for perverse courses. In his latest phase he is, in consequence, driven to repudiate the Pelagian thesis that certain saints of the Old and New Testaments managed to live without sin; it is disproved, he suggests,[1] by the fact that all are bound to say in the Lord's Prayer, 'Forgive us our debts'. Little wonder that on his view the whole of humanity constitutes 'a kind of mass (massa= "lump") of sin', or 'a universal mass of perdition',[2] being destined to everlasting damnation were it not for the grace of Christ. Even helpless children dying without the benefit of baptism must pass to eternal fire with the Devil,[3] although their sufferings will be relatively mild as compared with those of adults who have added sins of their own to their inherited guilt.[4]

7. Grace and Predestination

With this sombrely pessimistic vision of man's plight we can readily understand Augustine's opposition to Pelagianism. For him grace was an absolute necessity: 'without God's help we cannot by free will overcome the temptations of this life'.[5] The letter of the law can only kill unless we have the life-giving Spirit to enable us to carry out its prescriptions.[6] And grace cannot be restricted to the purely external aids which the Pelagians were prepared to allow. Before we can even begin to aspire to what is good, God's grace must be at work within us. It is, therefore, 'an internal and secret power, wonderful and ineffable', by which God operates in men's hearts.[7] For Augustine this power of grace is in effect the presence of the Holy Spirit, for Whom his favourite description is 'Gift' (donum[8]). It is the Spirit, he states,[9] Who assists our infirmity.

---

[1] C. duas epp. Pelag. 4, 27.
[2] Ad Simplic. 1, 2, 16; 1, 2, 20; de grat. Chr. et pecc. orig. 2, 34.
[3] Op. imperf. c. Iul. 3, 199; serm. 294, 2-4; de pecc. mer. et remiss. 1, 55.
[4] Enchir. 93.　　[5] Enarr. in ps. 89, 4.　　[6] Ep. 188, 11 f.
[7] De grat. Chr. et pecc. orig. 1, 25.　　[8] Enchir. 37; de trin. 15, 37.
[9] Ep. 194, 16 f.

He envisaged grace under several aspects. There is, first, 'prevenient grace' (from *Ps*. 59, 10: 'His mercy will go before—in Latin, *praeveniet*—me'), by which God initiates in our souls whatever good we think or aspire to or will.[1] Again, there is 'cooperating grace', by which He assists and co-operates with our will once it has been bestirred.[2] There is also 'sufficient grace' (or the *adiutorium sine quo*) and 'efficient grace' (the *adiutorium quo*). The former is the grace which Adam possessed in Paradise and which placed him in the position, subject to his using his free will to that end, to practise and persevere in virtue. The latter is granted to the saints predestined to God's kingdom to enable them both to will and to do what He expects of them.[3] But grace of whatever kind is God's free gift: *gratia dei gratuita*.[4] The divine favour cannot be earned by the good deeds men do for the simple reason that those deeds are themselves the effect of grace: 'grace bestows merits, and is not bestowed in reward for them'.[5] No worth-while act can be performed without God's help,[6] and even the initial motions of faith are inspired in our hearts by Him.[7]

Viewing God's saving activity in this light, Augustine is brought face to face with the wider problems of free will and predestination. The former arises because grace (a) anticipates and indeed inaugurates every stirring of man's will in the direction of the good, and (b), being the expression of God's almighty will, must carry all before it. We cannot evade the question what room is left, on this theory, for free will as ordinarily understood. Augustine's solution can be set down in stages. First, in the strict sense of free choice (*liberum arbitrium*), he holds that man is always free, that is, he can choose freely the course he will pursue; but since his will acts on motives and certain motives may press irresistibly on it, the range of choices which are 'live options' for him is limited by the sort of man he is. Fallen man, for example, breathing the atmosphere of concupiscence, though theoretically free, as a matter of fact only

---

[1] *Enchir.* 32; *de nat. et grat.* 35.   [2] *De grat. et lib. arbit.* 33.
[3] *De corrept. et grat.* 29-34.   [4] *Ep.* 186, 26; 194, 7.
[5] *De pat.* 17.   [6] Ib. 21 f.; *op. imperf. c. Iul.* 6, 15.
[7] *Ad Simplic.* 1, 2, 10; *de grat. et lib. arbit.* 29.

opts for sinful objects. From this point of view grace heals and restores his free will, not so much enlarging his area of choice as substituting a system of good choices for evil ones.[1] Secondly, Augustine acknowledges that God's omnipotent will, operating on our wills by grace, is irresistible. But he points out[2] that He works through our wills, the effect being that they freely and spontaneously will what is good. To be more explicit,[3] God knows in advance under the influence of what motives this or that particular will will freely consent to what He proposes for it, and arranges things accordingly. Thus grace accommodates itself to each individual's situation and character, and Augustine can claim[4] that, for all the power of grace, it rests with the recipient's will to accept or reject it. Thirdly, however, we should recall his distinction between free will (*liberum arbitrium*) and freedom (*libertas*). Freedom is free will put to a good use, and that man is free in the full sense who is emancipated from sin and temptation; he is free to live the life God desires him to live.[5] Its first stage, which Adam enjoyed, is the ability not to sin; its culminating stage, to be enjoyed in heaven, is the inability to sin.[6] In this sense not only could there be no opposition between grace and freedom, but it is grace which confers freedom. Man's free will is most completely itself when it is in most complete subjection to God, for true liberty consists in Christ's service.[7]

The problem of predestination has so far only been hinted at. Since grace takes the initiative and apart from it all men form a *massa damnata*, it is for God to determine which shall receive grace and which shall not. This He has done, Augustine believes[8] on the basis of Scripture, from all eternity. The number of the elect is strictly limited, being neither more nor less than is required to replace the fallen angels.[9] Hence he has to twist[10] the text 'God wills all men to be saved' (*1 Tim.* 2, 4), making it

---

[1] *De grat. et lib. arbit.* 31; *de spir. et litt.* 52; *ep.* 157, 10; 177, 4; *enchir.* 105.
[2] *De corrept. et grat.* 45.   [3] *Ad Simplic.* 1, 2, 13.
[4] E.g. *de spir. et litt.* 60.   [5] E.g. *enchir.* 32; *op. imperf. c. Iul.* 6, 11.
[6] *De corrept. et grat.* 33
[7] *De mor. eccl. cath.* 1, 21; *tract. in ev. Ioh.* 41, 8; *de grat. et lib. arbit.* 31.
[8] *De corrept. et grat.* 12–16; *enchir.* 98 f.; etc.
[9] *De civ. dei* 22, 1, 2; *enchir.* 29; 62.
[10] *De corrept. et grat.* 44; *enchir.* 103.

mean that He wills the salvation of all the elect, among whom men of every race and type are represented. God's choice of those to whom grace is to be given in no way depends on His foreknowledge of their future merits, for whatever good deeds they will do will themselves be the fruit of grace. In so far as His foreknowledge is involved, what He foreknows is what He Himself is going to do.[1] Then how does God decide to justify this man rather than that? There can in the end be no answer to this agonizing question. God has mercy on those whom He wishes to save, and justifies them; He hardens those upon whom He does not wish to have mercy, not offering them grace in conditions in which they are likely to accept it. If this looks like favouritism, we should remember that all are in any case justly condemned, and that if God decides to save any it is an act of ineffable compassion. Certainly there is a deep mystery here, but we must believe that God makes His decision in the light of 'a secret and, to human calculation, inscrutable justice'.[2] Augustine is therefore prepared to speak[3] of certain people as being predestined to eternal death and damnation; they may include, apparently, decent Christians who have been called and baptized, but to whom the grace of perseverance has not been given.[4] More often, however, he speaks of the predestination of the saints which consists in 'God's foreknowledge and preparation of the benefits by which those who are to be delivered are most assuredly delivered'.[5] These alone have the grace of perseverance, and even before they are born they are sons of God and cannot perish.[6]

8. The Western Settlement

The council of Carthage (418), as confirmed by Pope Zosimus in his *Epistula tractoria*,[7] outlawed Pelagianism in unambiguous terms. The main points insisted upon were (a) that

---

[1] *De dono persev.* 35; 47; 48; *de praedest. sanct.* 19; *ep.* 149, 20.
[2] *Ad. Simplic.* 1, 2, 14–16.
[3] E.g. *tract. in ev. Ioh.* 43, 13, 110, 2; 111, 5; *de civ. dei* 15, 1, 1; 21, 24, 1.
[4] *De dono persev.* 21.   [5] Ib. 35.
[6] *De corrept. et grat.* 23.   [7] Cf. PL 20, 693–5.

death was not an evil necessarily attaching to human nature, but was a penalty imposed on it in view of Adam's sin; (b) that original sin inherited from Adam is present in every man, and even newly born children need baptism if they are to be cleansed from this taint of sin; and (c) that grace is not simply given us so that we can do more easily what we can in any case do by our own free will, but is absolutely indispensable since the Lord said, 'Without Me you can do nothing'. Men like Julian of Eclanum might strive to prolong the debate, but the widespread acceptance of these propositions spelt failure for their efforts. On the other hand, Augustine could not fairly claim that the Church had ratified his distinctive teaching in its fulness. So far as the East was concerned, his ideas, as we shall see, had no noticeable impact. In the West, especially in South Gaul, there were many, including enthusiastic supporters of the council, who found some of them wholly unpalatable. Chief among these were the suggestion that, though free, the will is incapable in its fallen state of choosing the good, and the fatalism which seemed inherent in his theory of predestination.

The standpoint of these Semi-Pelagians, as they have been rather unkindly called since the seventeenth century, can be glimpsed in Augustine's correspondence. From Hadrumetum (Susa) came the plea[1] that grace should be regarded as aiding, rather than replacing, free will. From South Gaul complaints poured in[2] from men who were otherwise his admirers, Prosper of Aquitaine and a fellow-layman Hilary, to the effect that his doctrine of predestination paralysed moral effort and verged on fatalism, not to say Manichaeism. Pelagius could surely have been refuted without going so far.[3] Admittedly all sinned in Adam, and no one can rescue himself,[4] but the initial movement of faith (*credulitas*) is the sinner's own.[5] Grace surely assists the man who has begun to will his salvation, but does not implant that will.[6] The Augustinian theory scarcely does justice to the Biblical datum that God wills *all* men (surely *omnes omnino, ut*

---

[1] *Ep.* 214, 1.   [2] Ib. 225, 3; 226, 2–6.
[3] Ib. 226, 8.   [4] Ib. 225, 3; 226, 2.
[5] Ib. 225, 6.   [6] Ib. 226, 2: cf. ib. 225, 5.

nullus habeatur exceptus) to be saved.[1] The ablest representative of this school of thought was the famous monk of Marseilles, John Cassian. Though inflexible in his opposition to Pelagianism, he urges the following points against Augustine. First, while sometimes (e.g. the cases of St. Matthew and St. Paul) the first beginnings of a good will clearly come from God, sometimes (e.g. the case of Zacchaeus) they originate in the man's own volition, and God confirms and strengthens them.[2] Secondly, despite the disastrous effects of the Fall, Adam retained his knowledge of the good.[3] Thirdly, the human will is therefore not so much dead as sick;[4] the function of grace is to restore and assist it, and may be defined as 'cooperation'.[5] Without God's help it cannot bring virtuous acts to completion,[6] although He sometimes withholds His grace so as to prevent a man from becoming slack.[7] Fourthly, since God wills all men to be saved, those who perish must perish against His will, and therefore God's predestination must be in the light of what He foresees is going to be the quality of our behaviour (i.e. *post praevisa merita*[8]).

Despite obvious attractions, and the support of men like Vincent of Lérins, Semi-Pelagianism was doomed. It suffered, inevitably, but unjustly, from a suspected bias to Pelagianism, but what chiefly sealed its fate was the powerful and increasing influence of Augustine in the West. It is true that some of his theses, notably his belief in the irresistibility of grace and his severe interpretation of predestination, were tacitly dropped, but by and large it was his doctrine which prevailed. It is outside the scope of this book to trace the stages of its triumph. It is sufficient to note that at the council of Arausiacum (Orange: 529) the following propositions were established:[9] (a) As a result of Adam's transgression both death and sin have passed to all his descendants; (b) man's free will has consequently been so distorted and weakened that he cannot now believe in, much less love, God unless prompted and assisted

---

[1] Ib. 226, 7: cf. ib. 225, 4. [2] *Coll.* 13, 8, 4; 13, 11, 1 f.
[3] Ib. 13, 12, 2.   [4] Ib. 3, 12, 3-5.   [5] Ib. 13, 13, 1.
[6] Ib. 13, 9, 5.   [7] Ib. 13, 13-14.   [8] Ib. 13, 7.
[9] For the acts of the council of Orange, see Mansi, VIII, 711-19.

thereto by grace; (c) the saints of the Old Testament owed their merits solely to grace and not to the possession of any natural good; (d) the grace of baptism enables all Christians, with the help and co-operation of Christ, to accomplish the duties necessary for salvation, provided they make the appropriate efforts; (e) predestination to evil is to be anathematized with detestation; and (f) in every good action the first impulse comes from God, and it is this impulse which instigates us to seek baptism and, still aided by Him, to fulfil our duties.

9. The East in the Fifth Century

The development of ideas in the East in the meantime followed traditional lines, almost unaffected by what was happening in the West. Cyril of Alexandria provides a good illustration of the more optimistic outlook that prevailed there. According to him, Adam by his trespass lost the incorruptibility which, along with his rational nature, constituted the image of God in him,[1] and so fell a prey to concupiscence.[2] Death and corruption thus entered the world, and Adam's descendants found themselves sinning, victims like him of carnal passions.[3] In the first place, however, Cyril seems to distinguish[4] 'Adam's transgression' from 'the sin which dominates us', i.e. the concupiscence which is the consequence of the former. He carefully explains[5] that the reason why we are sinful, i.e. prone to sin, is not that we actually sinned in Adam (that is out of the question, since we were not even born then), but that Adam's sin caused the nature which we inherit to be corrupted. Secondly, he assumes[6] that the image of God in us is very far from being completely destroyed. In particular, our free will, notwithstanding the force of the passions, has not been suppressed.[7] Nevertheless we cannot recover the divine image in its fulness (viz. incorruptibility) without the saving help of the Word Himself.[8]

---

[1] In Ioh. 14, 20 (PG 74, 276); c. anthropomorph. 8.
[2] In Rom. 5, 3-12; 18 f.   [3] In Ioh. 19, 19; in Rom. 5, 18.
[4] Cf. de ador. in spir. et verit. 10 (PG 68, 657; 672).
[5] In Rom. 5, 18 f.   [6] De trin. dial. 1 (PG 75, 673 ff.).
[7] E.g. in Rom. 7, 15.   [8] E.g. in Luc. 5, 19.

To judge by its leading representatives, Theodore and Theodoret, variants of such teaching were current in the Antiochene school too, though crossed with an intensified emphasis on individualism. Tradition has branded the former as an Eastern Pelagius, the author of a treatise denying the reality of original sin;[1] but there are few, if any, traces of the alleged Pelagianizing strain in his authentic works, unless the Eastern attitude generally is to be dismissed as Pelagian. We may suspect that the evidence marshalled in support of the charge by his detractors has been tampered with. Actually he seems to have shared the widespread view that, as a result of Adam's rebellion, death and sin passed to all mankind.[2] Theodoret also states[3] that, having become mortal through his trespass, Adam engendered children who were subject like himself to death, concupiscence and sin. Both of them make the point,[4] in almost exactly the same words, that the vitiation of human nature consists in a powerful bias (ῥοπή) towards sin, the implication being that men's actual sins are not inevitable and therefore deserve blame. Theodore is satisfied[5] that, though inheriting the consequences of our first parents' sin, we do not participate in their guilt; and Theodoret, correctly interpreting ἐφ' ᾧ in *Rom.* 5, 12 as meaning 'because', not 'in whom', argues[6] that 'each of us undergoes the sentence of death because of his own sin, not because of the sin of our first parent'. If infants are baptized, the reason is not that they have actually 'tasted of sin', but in order that they may secure the future blessings of which baptism is the pledge.[7] He also holds[8] that, just as many lead sinful lives in this era of grace, so there were Old Testament heroes, like Abel, Enoch and Noah, who were 'superior to the greater sins'.

Theodore lays great stress[9] on the existence in men of free will, an attribute belonging to rational beings as such. Consequently, while we all have a definite propensity to sin, the

[1] Cf. Photius, *bibl.* cod. 177.   [2] *Hom. cat.* 1, 5; *in Rom.* 5, 18 f.; 7, 4.
[3] *In ps.* 50, 7.
[4] Theodore, *in Rom.* 5, 12; 5, 21; *hom. cat.* 1; Theodoret, *in ps.* 50, 7.
[5] *In ps.* 50, 7.   [6] *In Rom.* 5, 12.   [7] *Haer. fab. comp.* 5, 18.
[8] *In Rom.* 5, 19.   [9] *In ps.* 38, 6; *in Gal.* 2, 15 f.

soul retains all the time a clear knowledge of the good, and has the power to choose it. But if we are to pass from our present condition to the blessed life which God has in store for us, we shall have to receive it as a gift from Him.[1] Theodoret's view[2] is that, while all men need grace and it is impossible to take a step on the road to virtue without it, the human will must collaborate with it. 'There is need', he writes,[3] 'of both our efforts and the divine succour. The grace of the Spirit is not vouchsafed to those who make no effort, and without that grace our efforts cannot collect the prize of virtue.' But in the same context he acknowledges that our exertions as well as our believing are gifts of God, and that this recognition does not nullify free will but merely emphasizes that the will deprived of grace is unable to accomplish any good.

[1] *In Rom.* 11, 15.   [2] *In ps.* 31, 10 f.; 36, 23 f.   [3] *In Phil.* 1, 29 f.

NOTES ON BOOKS

General.   A. Slomkowski, *L'État primitif de l'homme dans la tradition de l'Église avant saint Augustin* (Paris-Strasbourg, 1928); F. R. Tennant, *The Sources of the Doctrine of the Fall and Original Sin* (Cambridge, 1903); N. P. Williams, *The Ideas of the Fall and of Original Sin* (London, 1927).

Special.   É. Amman, 'Semi-Pélagiens' (art. in *Dict. Théol. Cath.*); J. de Blic, 'Le Péché originel selon saint Augustin' (art. in *Rech. de science relig.*, 1926); T. Bohlin, *Die Theologie des Pelagius und ihre Genesis* (Uppsala, 1957); G. Bonner, *St. Augustine of Hippo* (London, 1963); O. Chadwick, *John Cassian* (Cambridge, 2 ed. 1968); J. Chéné, *La Théologie de saint Augustin: grâce et prédestination* (Lyon, 1962); R. Devreesse, *Essai sur Théodore de Mopsueste* (*Studi e Testi* 141, Rome, 1948); R. F. Evans, *Pelagius: Inquiries and Reappraisals* (London, 1968); É. Gilson, *Introduction a l'étude de saint Augustin* (Paris, 3 ed, 1949); J. B. Mozley, *A Treatise on the Augustinian Doctrine of Predestination* (London, 3 ed. 1883); R. A. Norris, *Manhood and Christ*, Pt. III (Oxford, 1963); G. de Plinval, *Pélage* (Lausanne, 1943); J. M. Rist, 'Augustine on Free Will and Predestination' (art. in *Journ. Theol. Stud.*, 1969); H. Rondet, 'La liberté et la grâce dans la théologie augustinienne' (in *Saint Augustin parmi nous*, 1954).

CHAPTER XIV

CHRIST'S SAVING WORK

1. *The Clue to Soteriology*

THE student who seeks to understand the soteriology of the fourth and early fifth centuries will be sharply disappointed if he expects to find anything corresponding to the elaborately worked out syntheses which the contemporary theology of the Trinity and the Incarnation presents. In both these latter departments controversy forced fairly exact definition on the Church, whereas the redemption did not become a battle-ground for rival schools until the twelfth century, when Anselm's *Cur deus homo* (*c.* 1097) focussed attention on it. Instead he must be prepared to pick his way through a variety of theories, to all appearance unrelated and even mutually incompatible, existing side by side and sometimes sponsored by the same theologian.

Three of these are particularly significant, and it will make for clarity if we set them down at the threshold of our discussion. First, there was the so-called 'physical' or 'mystical' theory (we have already come across[1] it in Irenaeus) which linked the redemption with the incarnation. According to this, human nature was sanctified, transformed and elevated by the very act of Christ's becoming man. Often, though not quite correctly, described as the characteristically Greek theory, it cohered well with the Greek tendency to regard corruption and death as the chief effects of the Fall. In its strict form it tended to be combined with the Platonic doctrine[2] of real universals, in the light of which it was able to treat human nature as a generic whole. Secondly, there was the explanation of the redemption in terms of a ransom offered to, or a forfeit imposed on, the Devil. The former version goes back[3] to

---

[1] See above, pp. 172 f.   [2] See above, pp. 15 f.
[3] See above, pp. 173 f.; 185 f.

Irenaeus and Origen; the latter began to emerge in our period
with the growing realization of the incongruity of attributing
any rights to the Devil in the matter. Thirdly, there was the
theory, often designated 'realist', which directed attention to
the Saviour's sufferings. Making more of sin and the punishment due for it than of its tragic legacy, this placed the cross
in the foreground, and pictured Christ as substituting Himself
for sinful men, shouldering the penalty which justice required
them to pay, and reconciling them to God by His sacrificial
death.

Faced with this diversity, scholars have often despaired of
discovering any single unifying thought in the patristic teaching about the redemption. These various theories, however,
despite appearances, should not be regarded as in fact mutually
incompatible. They were all of them attempts to elucidate the
same great truth from different angles; their superficial divergences are often due to the different Biblical images from which
they started, and there is no logical reason why, carefully
stated, they should not be regarded as complementary. In most
forms of the physical theory, for example, the emphasis on the
incarnation was not intended to exclude the saving value of
Christ's death. The emphasis was simply the offshoot of the
special interest which the theologians concerned had in the
restoration in which, however conceived, the redemption
culminates. Similarly, the essential truth concealed behind the
popular, often crudely expressed imagery of a deal with
Satan was the wholly Scriptural one (cf. *Acts* 26, 18) that fallen
man lies in the Devil's power and salvation necessarily includes
rescue from it.

There is a further point, however, which is not always accorded the attention it deserves. Running through almost all
the patristic attempts to explain the redemption there is one
grand theme which, we suggest, provides the clue to the
fathers' understanding of the work of Christ. This is none other
than the ancient idea of recapitulation[1] which Irenaeus derived
from St. Paul, and which envisages Christ as the representative

---

[1] See above, pp. 170-72.

of the entire race. Just as all men were somehow present in Adam, so they are, or can be, present in the second Adam, the man from heaven. Just as they were involved in the former's sin, with all its appalling consequences, so they can participate in the latter's death and ultimate triumph over sin, the forces of evil and death itself. Because, very God as He is, He has identified Himself with the human race, Christ has been able to act on its behalf and in its stead; and the victory He has obtained is the victory of all who belong to Him. All the fathers, of whatever school, reproduce this motif. The physical theory, it is clear, is an elaboration of it, only parting company with it when, under the influence of Platonic realism, it represents human nature as being automatically deified by the incarnation. The various forms of the sacrificial theory frankly presuppose it, using it to explain how Christ can act for us in the ways of substitution and reconciliation. The theory of the Devil's rights might seem to move on a rather different plane, but it too assumes that, as the representative man, Christ is a fitting exchange for mankind held in the Devil's grasp.

2. *Athanasius*

The dominant strain in Athanasius's soteriology is the physical theory that Christ, by becoming man, restored the divine image in us; but blended with this is the conviction that His death was necessary to release us from the curse of sin, and that He offered Himself in sacrifice for us. Both aspects are sometimes combined in a single context, as when he writes,[1] 'It is just that the Word of God . . ., in offering His body as a ransom for us, should discharge our debt by His death. So, united to all mankind by a body like theirs, the incorruptible Son of God can justly clothe all men with incorruptibility.' Again,[2] 'The Word became flesh in order both to offer this sacrifice and that we, participating in His Spirit, might be deified'.

Let us look more closely at the former aspect. The effect of

[1] *De incarn.* 9.   [2] *De decret.* 14.

the Fall was that man lost the image of God and languished in corruption. Hence the prime object of the incarnation was his restoration. 'None other',[1] says Athanasius, 'could restore a corruptible being to incorruption but the Saviour Who in the beginning made everything out of nothing. None other could re-create man according to the image, but He Who is the Father's image. None other could make a mortal being immortal, but He Who is life itself, our Lord Jesus Christ.' The restoration of the image means, first of all, that men recover the true knowledge of God which is life eternal. Adam enjoyed this in Paradise, but when he lost the image through sin his descendants were reduced to ignorance and idolatry.[2] Secondly, they become partakers of the divine nature (cf. *2 Pet.* 1, 4), since fellowship with Christ is fellowship with God.[3] Again and again we come across formulae like, 'The Word became man so that we might be deified',[4] or, 'The Son of God became man so as to deify us in Himself'.[5] As an alternative to the idea of divinization ($\theta\epsilon o\pi o i\eta\sigma\iota s$), Athanasius often uses that of adoption as sons ($\upsilon i o\pi o i\eta\sigma\iota s$), saying,[6] for example, 'By becoming man He made us sons to the Father, and He deified men by Himself becoming man', and, 'Because of the Word in us we are sons and gods'. Thirdly, the Word being the principle of life, the principle of death is reversed in us and the precious gift of incorruptibility ($\dot\alpha\phi\theta\alpha\rho\sigma i\alpha$) lost at the Fall is restored.[7] Hence the redemption can be described as a re-creation carried out by the Word, the original author of creation.[8]

Athanasius's language often suggests that he conceived of human nature, after the manner of Platonic realism, as a concrete idea or universal in which all individual men participate. From this point of view, when the Word assumed it and suffused it with His divinity, the divinizing force would be communicated to all mankind, and the incarnation would in effect be the redemption. Such is the clear implication of numerous passages, such as, 'Forasmuch as the Word became

---

[1] *De incarn.* 20.   [2] Ib. 11–16.   [3] *C. Ar.* 1, 16.
[4] *De incarn.* 54.   [5] *Ad Adelph.* 4.   [6] *C. Ar.* 1, 38; 3, 25.
[7] E.g. *de incarn.* 8; *c. Ar.* 3, 33.   [8] *Ad Adelph.* 8.

man and appropriated what belongs to the flesh, these affections no longer attach to the body because of the Word Who assumed it, but have been destroyed by Him',[1] and, 'Seeing that all men were perishing as a result of Adam's transgression, His flesh was saved and delivered before all the others because it had become the body of the Word Himself, and henceforth we are saved, being of one body with Him in virtue of it'.[2] The stress laid on the kinship of His body with ours, and on the consubstantiality[3] which exists between all men, points in the same direction. There is little doubt that Athanasius's Platonism tended at times to lose touch with his Christianity. His more considered teaching,[4] however, is that divinization through the Word does not come naturally to all men, but only to those who are in a special relation to Him. To be more precise, we are divinized by intimate union with the Holy Spirit Who unites us to the Son of God, and through Him to the Father. As he says,[5] 'This is God's loving-kindness to men, that by grace He becomes the Father of those whose Creator He already is. This comes about when created men, as the Apostle says, receive the Spirit of His Son crying, "Abba, Father", in their hearts. It is these who, receiving the Spirit, have obtained power from Him to become God's children. Being creatures by nature, they would never have become sons if they had not received the Spirit from Him Who is true Son by nature.'

Nothing so far has suggested that Athanasius appreciated the part played by Christ's human life, in particular by His passion, in the redemption. Actually he took the view[6] that 'Christ's death on the cross for us was fitting and congruous. Its cause was entirely reasonable, and there are just considerations which show that only through the cross could the salvation of all have been properly achieved'. This brings us to the second aspect of his teaching, which is summarized in the passage,[7] 'It still remained to pay the debt which all owed, since all, as I have explained, were doomed to death, and this was the

---

[1] C. Ar. 3, 33. [2] Ib. 2, 61. [3] E.g. ad Serap. 2, 6.
[4] Cf. de incarn. 27-32. [5] C. Ar. 2, 59: cf. ad Serap. 1, 23 f.
[6] De incarn. 26. [7] Ib. 20.

chief cause of His coming among us. That is why, after revealing His Godhead by His works, it remained for Him to offer
the sacrifice for all (ὑπὲρ πάντων τὴν θυσίαν), handing over the
temple of His body to death for all, so that He might rescue and
deliver them from their liability for the ancient transgression,
and might show Himself superior to death, revealing His own
body as immortal as a foretaste of the incorruption of all. . . .
Because both the death of all was fulfilled in the Lord's body,
and death and corruption were annihilated because of the Logos
Who indwelt it. For there was need of death, and a death had to
be undergone for all, so that the debt of all might be discharged.'
His underlying thought is that the curse of sin, i.e. death, lay
heavy on all mankind; it was a debt which had to be paid
before restoration could begin. On the cross Christ, the representative man, accepted the penalty in His own body, and died.
Thus He released us from the curse, procured salvation, and
became our Lord and king.[1] To describe this the traditional
language came readily to Athanasius's pen. Christ's death, he
wrote,[2] was a sacrifice which He offered to the Father on our
behalf. It was 'the ransom (λύτρον) for men's sins';[3] and Christ
not only heals us, but bears the heavy burden of our weaknesses
and sins.[4] On the surface the doctrine is one of substitution, but
what Athanasius was seeking to bring out was not so much
that one victim was substituted for another, as that 'the death
of all was accomplished in the Lord's body'.[5] In other words,
because of the union between His flesh and ours, His death and
victory were in effect ours. Just as through our kinship with
the first Adam we inherit death, so by our kinship with 'the
man from heaven' we conquer death and inherit life.[6]

3. Fourth-century Greek Fathers

Next to Athanasius the chief exponent of the physical theory
in the fourth century was Gregory of Nyssa. Here and there,

[1] C. Ar. 2, 76: cf. ib. 1, 60; 3, 33.   [2] Ib. 1, 41; 2, 7; de decret. 14.
[3] C. Ar. 1, 45.   [4] Ib. 3, 31.   [5] De incarn. 20.
[6] C. Ar. 1, 44; 2, 61; 2, 67.

admittedly, hints of it appear in other writers. Basil, for example, emphasizes[1] that if the Lord had possessed a nature different from ours, 'we who were dead in Adam should never have been restored in Christ . . . that which was broken would never have been mended, that which was estranged from God by the serpent's wiles would never have been brought back to Him'. Through becoming incarnate, writes[2] Gregory Nazianzen, 'He takes me wholly, with all my infirmities, to Himself, so that as man He may destroy what is evil, as fire destroys wax or the sun's rays the vapours of the earth, and so that as a result of this conjunction I may participate in His blessings'. John Chrysostom explains[3] that it is precisely because the Word has become flesh and the Master has assumed the form of a servant that men have been made sons of God. But their most characteristic ideas move, as we shall see, in a different orbit. For Gregory of Nyssa, however, the incarnation, culminating in the resurrection, is the sovereign means for restoring man to his primitive state. His theory[4] is that the effect of the Fall has been the fragmentation of human nature, body and soul being separated by death. By becoming man, and by dying and rising again in the human nature which He assumed, Christ has for ever reunited the separated fragments. Thus, just as death entered the world by one man, so by one man's resurrection the principle of life has been given back to us.[5] His argument, we observe, depends on the classic antithesis between the first and second Adams. Like Athanasius, too, he translates the Biblical idea of solidarity into the language of Platonic realism. The whole of human nature, he claims,[6] constitutes as it were a single living being (καθάπερ τινὸς ὄντος ζῴου πάσης τῆς φύσεως), so that the experience of a part becomes the experience of the whole. In this way all mankind is seen to share in what Christ achieves by His resurrection.[7]

Thus the Lord 'conjoined Himself with our nature in order that by its conjunction with the Godhead it might become

[1] Ep. 261, 2.
[2] Or. 30, 6: cf. ib. 2, 23-5.
[3] In Ioh. hom. 11, 1.
[4] Or. cat. 16; antirrh. 55.
[5] Or. cat. 16.   [6] Ib. 32.
[7] Cf. antirrh. 16; 55.

divine, being exempted from death and rescued from the adverse tyranny. For His triumphal return from death inaugurated the triumphal return of the human race to life immortal.'[1] Christ's death, we notice, was integral to the scheme, and so Gregory had no difficulty in applying the Biblical language of sacrifice to it. Christ is the good shepherd who gives his life for the sheep, at once priest and victim.[2] He is the paschal lamb Who offered Himself on our behalf,[3] the great high-priest Who sacrificed His own body for the world's sin.[4] If the underlying idea in this is expiation, Is. 53, 4 suggested that of substitution, and Gregory was able to speak[5] of Christ making our sufferings His own and submitting to the stripes due to us. At the same time, since the Fall placed man in the power of the Devil, he liked to envisage the redemption as our emancipation from him. As Gregory developed this aspect, his chief concern was for God's justice; hence his reiteration that it was through his own free choice that man fell into the Devil's clutches. The Devil, therefore, had a right to adequate compensation if he were to surrender him, and for God to have exercised *force majeure* would have been unfair and tyrannical. So He offered him the man Jesus as a ransom. When Satan saw Him, born as He was of a virgin and renowned as a worker of miracles, he decided that the exchange was to his advantage. What he failed to realize was that the outward covering of human flesh concealed the immortal Godhead. Hence, when he accepted Jesus in exchange for mankind, he could not hold Him; he was outwitted and caught, as a fish is by the bait which conceals the hook.[6] There was no injustice in this, Gregory tried to show,[7] for the Devil was only getting his deserts, and in any case God's action was going to contribute to his own ultimate benefit (Gregory shared[8] the doctrine of his master, Origen, that in the final restoration the pains of the damned, Satan included, would come to an end).

Precisely the same theory of the Devil's right to keep man-

---

[1] *Or. cat.* 25.
[3] *De perf. chr. form.* (PG 46, 264).
[5] *Antirrh.* 21. [6] *Or. cat.* 22–4.
[8] Ib. 26; 35: see below, pp. 473 f.; 483 f.

[2] *Antirrh.* 16 f.
[4] *C. Eunom.* 6 (PG 45, 717).
[7] Ib. 26.

kind in bondage until given adequate compensation found
support with his elder brother Basil. All men, he taught,[1] are
subject to the authority of the prince of this world, and only
Christ can claim (cf. *John* 14, 30) that 'he hath nothing in me'.
Hence a ransom is necessary if their deliverance is to be effected,
and it cannot consist in any ordinary human being. The Devil
could hardly be induced to hand over his captives by receiving
a mere man; in any case such a man would require redemption
himself. What is needed is someone who transcends human
nature—in fact, the God-man Jesus Christ.[2] Gregory's grotesque
imagery of the bait and hook, we observe, is absent here, and
Basil does not seem to press the theory. In the same context he
oscillates between interpreting Christ's death as a ransom paid
to the Devil and as a sacrifice offered to God. On the other hand,
the whole conception of rights belonging to the Devil and of
the Son of God being handed over to him was subjected to
an important, extremely damaging critique by Gregory of
Nazianzus. 'It is worth our while', he remarked,[3] 'to examine a
point of doctrine which is overlooked by many but seems to me
deserving of examination. For whom, and with what object,
was the blood shed for us, the great and famous blood of God,
our high-priest and sacrifice, outpoured? Admittedly we were
held in captivity by the Devil, having been sold under sin and
having abdicated our happiness in exchange for wickedness.
But if the ransom belongs exclusively to him who holds the
prisoner, I ask to whom it was paid, and why. If to the Devil,
how shameful that that robber should receive not only a ransom
from God, but a ransom consisting of God Himself, and that so
extravagant a price should be paid to his tyranny before he
could justly spare us!' Gregory went on to show that Christ's
blood was not, strictly speaking, a ransom paid to God the
Father either, since it is inconceivable that He should have
found pleasure in the blood of His only Son. The truth rather
is that the Father accepted it, not because He demanded or
needed it, but because in the economy of redemption it was
fitting that sanctification should be restored to human nature

---

[1] *Hom. in ps.* 7, 2.   [2] Ib. 48, 3 f.   [3] *Or.* 45, 22.

through the humanity which God had assumed. As for the Devil, he was vanquished by force.

The cogency of objections like these must have been felt, and it is not surprising that John Chrysostom's account of the transaction was less vulnerable to attack. According to this,[1] the Devil was strictly within his rights in dealing despitefully with men; they had sinned, thereby placing themselves under his jurisdiction. But in sowing the seed of conspiracy in Judas's heart and in lifting his hand against the sinless Christ, he exceeded his rights. In fact, he brought down well-merited sanctions on his own head, and being thrust forth from his empire he lost his hold over those whom he kept in bondage. So the bizarre conception of just claims which could only be circumvented by a palpable ruse practised on the Devil by God Himself faded into the background, and attention was focussed on his scandalous abuse of his powers.

Neither the physical theory, however, nor the mythology of man's deliverance from the Devil represents the main stream of Greek soteriology in the fourth century. For this we have to look to doctrines which interpreted Christ's work in terms of a sacrifice offered to the Father. We saw that both Athanasius and Gregory of Nyssa, while viewing man's restoration as essentially the effect of the incarnation, were able to find a logical place for the Lord's death conceived as a sacrifice. This aspect is forcibly presented by Athanasius's contemporary, Eusebius of Caesarea. Christ appropriated our sins, he argues,[2] and accepted the punishment we deserved; His death is a substitutionary sacrifice. And He was able to identify Himself with our sins and the penalties attached to them because, as very man, He shared our nature. But teaching like this fits awkwardly into Eusebius's system, according to which the function of the Word is to reveal eternal truths rather than to accomplish saving acts. A much more representative witness to the soteriology of the period is Cyril of Jerusalem. Writing for a popular audience, he stresses the unique importance of the passion. It is the cross which brings

[1] *In Ioh. hom.* 67, 2 f.; *in Rom. hom.* 13, 5.   [2] *Dem. ev.* 1, 10; 10, 1.

light to the ignorant, deliverance to those bound by sin, and redemption to all.[1] By offering Himself as a ransom Christ has appeased God's wrath towards sinful men.[2] Innocent himself, He has given His life for our sins.[3] Again the idea is that of substitution based on the Saviour's kinship with us; as the new Adam He can take responsibility for our misdeeds. Cyril's freshest contribution is the suggestion that the universal efficacy of His sacrifice is explained by the measureless value attaching to His Person. 'It was not someone of no significance', he states,[4] 'who died for us. It was no irrational beast, no ordinary man, not even an angel. It was God incarnate. The iniquity of our sins was not so great as the righteousness of Him Who died for us. Our transgressions did not equal the goodness of Him Who laid down His life on our behalf.'

Similar teaching appears in Basil, Gregory of Nazianzus and John Chrysostom. The first of these speaks[5] of the Son of God giving His life to the world 'when He offered Himself as a sacrifice and oblation to God on account of our sins'. No mere man, he explains,[6] can offer expiation ($\dot{\epsilon}\xi\iota\lambda\hat{\alpha}\sigma\theta\alpha\iota$) for sinners, being himself guilty of sin. It is only the God-man Who can offer to God adequate expiation for us all. According to Gregory,[7] Christ is our redemption 'because He releases us from the power of sin, and offers Himself as a ransom in our place to cleanse the whole world'. The explanation he gives is that, as the second Adam, Christ is head of the body, and so can appropriate our rebellion and make it His own. As our representative He identifies Himself with us ($\dot{\epsilon}\nu$ $\dot{\epsilon}\alpha\upsilon\tau\hat{\omega}$ ... $\tau\upsilon\pi o\hat{\iota}$ $\tau\dot{o}$ $\dot{\eta}\mu\dot{\epsilon}\tau\epsilon\rho o\nu$[8]). As a result He has been able, not merely to assume the form of a servant, but to ascend the cross, taking our sins with Him in order that they may perish there.[9] When He was crucified, He crucified our sins at the same time.[10] Chrysostom teaches[11] that mankind stood condemned to death by God, and was indeed virtually dead; but Christ has delivered us by handing Himself over to death. Whereas the sacrifices of the

---

[1] *Cat.* 13, 1.
[4] Ib. 13, 33: cf. ib. 13, 2.
[7] *Or.* 30, 20.
[10] Ib. 38, 16.
[2] Ib. 13, 2.
[5] *Hom. in ps.* 28, 5.
[8] Ib. 30, 5.
[11] *In Gal. comm.* 2, 8.
[3] Ib. 13, 3–6; 13, 21–3.
[6] Ib. 48, 3 f.
[9] Ib. 4, 78.

old Law were incapable of achieving this, Christ has saved us
by His unique sacrifice.[1] He has done this, Chrysostom makes
it clear, by substituting Himself in our place. Though He was
righteousness itself, God allowed Him to be condemned as a
sinner and to die as one under a curse, transferring to Him not
only the death which we owed but our guilt as well.[2] And the
sacrifice of such a victim was of surpassing efficacy, being
sufficient to save the entire race.[3] 'He died for all men, to save
all, so far as He was concerned; for that death was a fair equivalent (ἀντίρροπος) in exchange for the destruction of all.'[4] In dying
His object was to save all; and if in fact not all have achieved
salvation, the reason lies in their refusal to accept Him.

4. The West in the Fourth Century

Western thought on the redemption conformed broadly to
the pattern we have observed in the East, with even greater
emphasis on the Lord's death as a sacrifice. The physical theory
found support chiefly among thinkers who were subject to
Greek influences. Hilary, for example, can write,[5] 'It was we
who needed that God should become flesh and dwell in us,
that is, by taking a single flesh to Himself should inhabit flesh
in its entirety'. The Platonic conception of human nature as a
universal clearly lies in the background here. We can see it
again in his statement,[6] 'For the sake of the human race the Son
of God was born from the Virgin and Holy Spirit . . . so that
by becoming man He might take the nature of flesh to Himself
from the Virgin, and so the body of the human race as a whole
might be sanctified in Him through association with this
mixture'. The same Platonic realism inspires Victorinus when
he writes,[7] 'When He took flesh, He took the universal idea of
flesh (universalem λόγον carnis); for as a result the whole power
of flesh triumphed in His flesh. . . . Similarly He took the
universal idea of soul. . . . Therefore man as a whole was

[1] In Hebr. hom. 15, 2. [2] In 2 Cor. hom. 11, 3 f.; in Eph. hom. 17, 1.
[3] In Gal. comm. 2, 8. [4] In Hebr. hom. 17, 2.
[5] De trin. 2, 25. [6] Ib. 2, 24: cf. tract. in ps. 51, 16.
[7] C. Ar. 3, 3.

assumed, and having been assumed was liberated. For human nature as a whole was in Him, flesh as a whole and soul as a whole, and they were lifted to the cross and purged through God the Word, the universal of all universals.' Elsewhere[1] he argues that, since Christ's body is 'catholic', i.e. universal as opposed to particular, all individual human bodies were crucified in it, and His sufferings have a universal quality.

The theory of a transaction with Satan enjoyed considerable currency. In the hands of Ambrose the emphasis is generally on the Devil's rights and the compensation justly owing to him in requital for surrendering mankind. The Devil, he states,[2] held us in possession, our sins being the purchase money by which he had bought us, and required a price if he was to release us; the price was Christ's blood, which had to be paid to our previous purchaser. Sometimes he suggests[3] that, when Christ paid over what was owing to the Devil, He transferred the debt to Himself, with the result that we changed our creditor, although He has in fact most generously forgiven the debt. Ambrose is not afraid[4] to dwell on, and elaborate the details of, the deception worked on the Devil, who would of course never have accepted Christ's blood had he known Who He really was. On the other hand, we find examples of the milder version of the theory, according to which the transaction consisted not so much in the satisfaction of the Devil's supposed rights as in his proper punishment for going beyond them. Hilary, for example, points out[5] that Satan condemned himself when he inflicted death, the punishment for sin, on the sinless author of life. Quite apart from that, so far from resting on justice, the sovereignty exercised by the powers of evil over the human race was only established by their wicked usurpation.[6] Ambrosiaster develops the same theme, teaching[7] that the Devil sinned when he slew the innocent One Who knew no sin. When Christ was crucified, he overreached himself, and lost the authority by which he held men captive on account of Adam's

---

[1] In Gal. 2, 6, 14.
[2] Ep. 72, 8: cf. de Iac. et vit. beat. 1, 12; expos. ev. Luc. 7, 117.
[3] Ep. 41, 7 f. [4] E.g. expos. ev. Luc. 2, 3; 4, 12; 4, 16.
[5] Tract. in ps. 68, 8. [6] Ib. 2, 31. [7] In Rom. 7, 4.

sin.[1] When the principalities and powers who seduced the first man laid hands on the Saviour, they put themselves in the wrong, and were justly penalized by being deprived of the souls they kept in prison.[2]

It is Christ's passion and death, however, which particularly interest these writers. Hilary, for example, states[3] that 'the Lord was smitten, taking our sins upon Himself and suffering in our stead . . . so that in Him, smitten even unto the weakness of crucifixion and death, health might be restored to us through His resurrection from the dead'. Being 'the second Adam from heaven', He has assumed the nature of the first Adam, and so can identify Himself with us and save us. If this is the language of recapitulation, Hilary passes easily to that of sacrifice, stressing the voluntary character of what Christ accomplished. 'He offered Himself to the death of the accursed in order to abolish the curse of the Law by offering Himself of His own free will to God the Father as a sacrifice. . . . To God the Father, Who spurned the sacrifices of the Law, He offered the acceptable sacrifice of the body He had assumed . . . procuring the complete salvation of the human race by the oblation of his holy and perfect sacrifice.'[4] It was by His blood, he emphasizes,[5] and by His passion, death and resurrection that Christ redeemed us. The effect of His death was to destroy the sentence of death passed on us,[6] to expiate our sins,[7] and to reconcile us to God.[8] Though these are incidental remarks, they give substance to the claim that Hilary must be regarded as one of the pioneers of the theology of satisfaction. We come across similar ideas, expressed in terms of redemption and substitution rather than sacrifice, in his contemporary Victorinus. He speaks[9] of Christ redeeming (*mercaretur*) man by His passion and death, pointing out[10] that these only avail to procure remission of sins because the victim is the Son of God. He gave Himself, he states,[11] to death and the cross in our stead, thereby delivering us from our sins.

---

[1] *In. Rom.* 8, 4.   [2] *In Col.* 2, 15.   [3] *Tract. in ps.* 68, 23.
[4] Ib. 53, 13.   [5] Ib. 135, 15.   [6] *De trin.* 1, 13.
[7] *Tract. in ps.* 64, 4.   [8] Ib. 129, 9.   [9] *C. Ar.* 1, 45.
[10] Ib. 1, 35.   [11] *In Gal.* 1, 2, 20.

Ambrose elaborates a theory of Christ's death as a sacrifice offered to satisfy the claims of divine justice. He sees it prefigured in the slaughter of Abel,[1] as also in the oblations prescribed by the Jewish Law.[2] It is a sacrifice performed once for all,[3] its effect being that through Christ's blood our sins are washed away.[4] Christ has destroyed the sentence of death which was against us, and death itself as well.[5] Ambrose explains[6] how this was accomplished: 'Jesus took flesh so as to abolish the curse of sinful flesh, and was made a curse in our stead so that the curse might be swallowed up in blessing. . . . He took death, too, upon Himself that the sentence might be carried out, so that He might satisfy the judgment that sinful flesh should be cursed even unto death. So nothing was done contrary to God's sentence, since its terms were implemented.' The second Adam died, he adds,[7] in order that, 'since the divine decrees cannot be broken, the person punished might be changed, not the sentence of punishment' (*persona magis quam sententia mutaretur*). Here the idea of recapitulation is combined with that of substitution; because He shares human nature, Christ can substitute Himself for sinful men and endure their punishment in their place. 'What', he exclaims,[8] 'was the purpose of the incarnation but this, that the flesh which had sinned should be redeemed by itself?' Ambrose describes[9] Christ's sacrifice as propitiatory, but recognizes[10] both the love of the Son Who gave Himself and the love of the Father Who gave Him. He also brings out the unique fitness of Christ to be our redeemer, both because of His sinlessness and because of the excellence of His Person.[11]

The sacrificial interpretation of the Lord's death is regular in the other Latin writers of the period. Ambrosiaster often recalls[12] that Christ died for us and our sins, offering thereby a sweet-smelling sacrifice. The whole value of this oblation, he indicates, lay in the love and obedience displayed in it. According

[1] *De incarn. dom. sacram.* 4.
[2] *De spir. sanct.* 1, 4.
[3] *Expos. ev. Luc.* 10, 8.
[4] E.g. *enarr. in ps.* 39, 2; 14; 17.
[5] *De fid.* 3, 13; 3, 84.
[6] *De fuga saec.* 44.
[7] *Expos. ev. Luc.* 4, 7.
[8] *De incarn. dom. sacram.* 56.
[9] *De Abrah.* 1, 16; *de offic.* 3, 102.
[10] *De Is. et an.* 46; *de Iac.* 1, 25; *de spir. sanct.* 1, 129.
[11] *In ps.* 118, 6, 22.
[12] *In Rom.* 5, 6-10; *in Eph.* 5, 2.

to Pelagius,[1] Jesus Christ 'was alone found fit to be offered as a spotless sacrifice on behalf of all who were dead in sins'. God had decreed death to sinners, and by dying Christ was able at once to maintain that decree and to exempt mankind from its effects.[2] A point which Pelagius tries to bring out[3] is that Christ's life could reasonably be offered in place of ours because, being innocent, He did not already deserve death on His own account. Jerome, too, although his ideas were unsystematic to a degree, recognized[4] that Christ 'endured in our stead the penalty we ought to have suffered for our crimes'. No one, he claimed,[5] can draw near to God apart from the blood of Christ.

5. *Augustine*

All these thoughts, with some fresh ones of his own, were woven together into a loose but effective unity by Augustine. It was his special role, in this as in other aspects of the faith, to sum up the theological insights of the West, and pass them on, with the impress of his genius and authority, to the Middle Ages. For this reason it is fitting that his doctrine should be set out in rather greater detail than was necessary in the case of his predecessors.

First, then, Augustine makes much of Christ's function as mediator between God and man. 'He is the one true mediator', he writes,[6] 'reconciling us to God by the sacrifice of peace, remaining one with Him to Whom He made the offering, making one in Himself those for whom He offered it, Himself one as offerer and sacrifice offered.' This is indeed Christ's specific activity, and Augustine claims on the authority of *1 Tim.* 2, 5 ('there is . . . one mediator between God and men, Himself man, Christ Jesus') that He exercises it exclusively in His human capacity. 'In so far as He is man,' he states,[7] 'He is mediator, but not in so far as He is Word, for as such He is co-equal with God.' The whole object of the Word's incarnation

---

[1] *In 2 Cor.* 5, 15.   [2] *In Rom.* 3, 25.   [3] Ib. 3, 24; *in Gal.* 3, 13.
[4] *In Is.* 53, 5-7.   [5] *In Eph.* 2, 14.   [6] *De trin.* 4, 19.
[7] *Confess.* 10, 68: cf. *tract. in ev. Ioh.* 82, 4.

was that He might be head of the Church[1] and might act as
mediator.[2] It is through His humanity that Christ exalts us to
God and brings God down to us.[3] In taking this line Augustine
does not intend to eliminate the role of the Word, Who is of
course the subject of the God-man's Person, but rather to bring
home that Christ's humanity, as opposed to His divine nature, is
the medium of our restoration. While he can say,[4] 'Christ is
mediator between God and man as man, not as God', he has
also to admit,[5] 'We could never have been delivered by the one
mediator . . . were He not also God'. What this doctrine seeks
to establish is that in Christ's humanity fallen man and his
Creator have a common meeting-ground where the work of
reconciliation and restoration can take effect.

Secondly, in expounding what the Mediator actually accomplishes, Augustine adopts several avenues of approach. He occasionally hints at the physical theory, as when he says,[6] 'We are
reconciled to God through our Head, since in Him the Godhead of the Only-begotten participated in our mortality so that
we might participate in His immortality'; or when he remarks[7]
that Christ 'has delivered our nature from temporal things,
exalting it to the Father's right hand', and that 'He Who was
God became man so as to make those who were men gods'.
This is at best a secondary motif, however, for the deification
spoken of is presumably a corollary of the saving work, not
the direct effect of the incarnation as such. Much more frequent
and characteristic is his description of the redemption as
·our release from Satan's bondage. Augustine is inclined to
dramatize the transaction by using colourful language which
gives a misleading impression of his true thought. He speaks,
for example, of Christ's blood as the price which was paid over
for us and which the Devil accepted, only to find himself
enchained,[8] and again of His body as a bait by which Satan was
caught like a mouse in a trap (cf. *tanquam in muscipula escam
accepit*[9]). But his authentic teaching was more in line with that

[1] *Enarr. in ps.* 148, 8.   [2] *Serm.* 361, 16.   [3] Ib. 81, 6; 189, 4.
[4] Ib. 293, 7.   [5] *Enchir.* 108: cf. *de civ. dei* 9, 15, 1.
[6] *Ep.* 187, 20.   [7] *De doct. christ.* 1, 38; *serm.* 192, 1.
[8] *De trin.* 13, 19.   [9] E.g. *serm.* 263, 1.

of Chrysostom, Hilary and Ambrosiaster, and may be summarized as follows.[1] (a) The Devil owned no rights, in the strict
sense, over mankind; what happened was that, when men
sinned, they passed inevitably into his power, and God permitted rather than enjoined this. (b) No ransom as such was
therefore due to Satan, but on the contrary, when the remission of sins was procured by Christ's sacrifice, God's favour
was restored and the human race might well have been freed.
(c) God preferred, however, as a course more consonant with
His justice, that the Devil should not be deprived of his
dominion by force, but as the penalty for abusing his position.
(d) Hence Christ's passion, the primary object of which was of
course quite different, placed the Son of God in Satan's hands,
and when the latter overreached himself by seizing the divine
prey, with the arrogance and greed which were characteristic
of him, he was justly constrained, as a penalty, to deliver up
mankind.

There have been scholars who have fastened upon man's
release in this way from the Devil as the pivot of Augustine's
soteriology. But such a thesis cannot be sustained. Augustine
clearly represents our release as consequent upon and as pre-
supposing our reconciliation; the Devil is conquered precisely
because God has received satisfaction and has bestowed pardon.[2]
This brings us to what is in fact his central thought, viz. that the
essence of the redemption lies in the expiatory sacrifice offered
for us by Christ in His passion. This, it seems, is the principal
act which He performs as mediator: 'Him Who knew no sin,
Christ, God made sin, i.e. a sacrifice for sins, on our behalf so
that we might be reconciled'.[3] According to Augustine,[4] all the
Old Testament sacrifices looked forward to this sacrifice, and
he emphasizes[5] that Christ gave Himself to it entirely of His
own free choice (*non necessitatis sed arbitrii*), being at once priest
and victim (*ipse offerens, ipse et oblatio*). In its effect it is expiatory
and propitiatory: 'By His death, that one most true sacrifice

---

[1] Cf. *de trin.* 13, 16–19.   [2] Cf. *de civ. dei* 10, 22; *de trin.* 4, 17.
[3] *Enchir.* 41.   [4] *Enarr. in ps.* 39, 12.
[5] *Serm.* 152, 9; *de civ. dei* 10, 20.

offered on our behalf, He purged, abolished and extinguished
. . . whatever guilt we had'.[1] By it God's wrath was appeased,
and we were reconciled to Him: 'He offered this holocaust to
God; He extended his hands on the cross . . . and our wickednesses were propitiated. . . . Our sins and wickednesses having
been propitiated through this evening sacrifice, we passed to the
Lord, and the veil was taken away.'[2] Its fundamental rationale,
as we might expect, is that Christ is substituted for us, and being
Himself innocent discharges the penalty we owe. 'Though
without guilt,' Augustine writes,[3] 'Christ took our punishment
upon Himself, destroying our guilt and putting an end to our
punishment.' Again, 'You must confess that without our sin He
took the penalty owing to our sin upon Himself';[4] and, 'He
made our trespasses His trespasses, so as to make His righteousness ours'.[5] It was precisely His innocence which gave atoning
value to His death, for 'We were brought to death by sin, He
by righteousness; and so, since death was our penalty for sin,
His death became a sacrifice for sin'.[6]

Thirdly, Augustine's teaching stresses the exemplary aspect
of Christ's work in a way that is without precedent. He has
sharp words,[7] it is true, for those who imagine that the cross
provides no more than an ideal for us to model ourselves upon,
but the subjective side of the incarnation and atonement has
immense value in his eyes. Both in His Person and in what He
has done, Christ, our mediator, has demonstrated God's wisdom
and love.[8] The spectacle of such love should have the effect
of inciting us to love Him in return: *nulla est enim maior ad
amorem invitatio quam praevenire amando*.[9] More particularly, it
should bestir our hearts to adore the humility of God which, as
revealed in the incarnation, breaks our pride. So for Augustine
the humility of the Word revealed in His amazing self-abasement forms a vital part of His saving work. 'This we do well to
believe,' he writes,[10] 'nay, to hold fixed and immovable in our
hearts, that the humility which God displayed in being born of

[1] *De trin.* 4, 17.   [2] *Enarr. in ps.* 64, 6.   [3] *C. Faust. Manich.* 14, 4.
[4] Ib. 14, 7.   [5] *Enarr. 2 in ps.* 21, 3.   [6] *De trin.* 4, 15.
[7] *In ev. Ioh. tract.* 98, 3.   [8] Ib. 110, 6.   [9] *De cat. rud.* 7 f.
[10] *De trin.* 8, 7.

a woman and in being haled so ignominiously by mortal men to death, is the sovereign medicine for healing our swollen pride, the profound mystery (*sacramentum*) by which the bond of sin is broken.' Pride, we recall, was the cause of Adam's lapse, and so Augustine exclaims,[1] 'Only by humility could we return, since it was by pride that we fell. So in His own Person the Redeemer has deigned to hold out an example of this humility, which is the way by which we must return.' But in case this should appear an unduly subjective account of the redemption, we should remember (a) that, while the Christian must reproduce Christ's humility, it is that objective humility showing itself in the incarnation and passion which first makes our reconciliation possible, and (b) that for Augustine the imitation of Christ by us is itself the effect in our hearts of the divine grace released by the sacrifice on the cross.

As historians have often pointed out, Augustine brings together the various strands of his soteriology in a famous passage[2] of his *Enchiridion*, and this may fittingly be reproduced. It runs: 'We could never have been delivered even by the one mediator between God and men, the man Jesus Christ, had He not been God as well. When Adam was created, he was of course righteous, and a mediator was not needed. But when sin placed a wide gulf between mankind and God, a mediator was called for Who was unique in being born, in living and in being slain without sin, in order that we might be reconciled to God and brought by the resurrection of the flesh to eternal life. Thus through God's humility human pride was rebuked and healed, and man was shown how far he had departed from God, since the incarnation of God was required for his restoration. Moreover, an example of obedience was given by the God-man; and the Only-begotten having taken the form of a servant, which previously had done nothing to deserve it, a fountain of grace was opened, and in the Redeemer Himself the resurrection of the flesh promised to the redeemed was enacted by anticipation. The Devil was vanquished in that selfsame nature which he gleefully supposed he had deceived.' This text brings out

---

[1] *De fid. et symb.* 6.   [2] *Enchir.* 108.

that for Augustine reconciliation and restoration are the primary features of the incarnation. A few chapters before,[1] going into more detail, he recalled that God made Christ sin for us, that is, 'a sacrifice for sins by which our reconciliation is made possible'. The passage shows, too, that while Christ's humility is an example to us, its essential function is to be the inward side of that act of self-abasement and self-surrender which constitutes the sacrifice. Finally, it sets our emancipation from the Devil in the true perspective, regarding it as consequent upon, and thus subordinate to, the reconciliation itself.

6. *The East in the Fifth Century*

Greek soteriology in the earlier decades of the fifth century cannot point to any figure comparable with Augustine. The general tendency was for theories of the realist type to come to the fore, the idea of recapitulation often providing the setting. A good example is Theodore of Mopsuestia, who sets out[2] the ancient doctrine of the substitution of the first Adam by the second in classic form. Through the latter's death and resurrection the link between God and man, shattered as a result of the first man's sin, has been indissolubly renewed;[3] by His fellowship with us 'the man assumed' has enabled us to participate in His triumph.[4] Theodore's disciple, Theodoret, teaches that Christ's death was a ransom, or rather 'a sort of ransom' ($o\mathring{\iota}\acute{o}\nu\ \tau\iota$ $\lambda\acute{\upsilon}\tau\rho o\nu$), paid on our behalf by One Who Himself owed nothing,[5] a voluntary and freely chosen sacrifice for expiating our sins and reconciling us to God.[6] The precondition of this reconciliation is that in shedding His blood He has discharged our debt for us.[7] As Isaiah prophesied, we merited and had been sentenced to punishment on account of our transgressions, but He, Who was free from sin and spotless, consented to be chastised in our stead.[8]

The other types of theory, however, were far from being

---

[1] Ib. 41.   [2] *In Rom.* 5, 13 f.   [3] Ib. 8, 19.
[4] *In 1 Tim.* 2, 5.   [5] *In Rom.* 3, 24; *in 1 Tim.* 2, 6.
[6] *In Dan.* 9, 24.   [7] *In Col.* 1, 20-2.   [8] *In Is.* 53, 4-8.

obsolete, although the desirability of bringing them into a correct relation to the Lord's atoning sacrifice seems to have been appreciated. In particular, the dramatic picture of mankind being rescued from the Devil continued in favour as a popular account of the redemption. But the transaction was no longer represented as consisting in the satisfaction of the Devil's supposed rights by the payment of a ransom presumed to be his due. In the interpretation which was now in vogue with writers like Cyril (often, we may suspect, they exploited the idea as a piece of consciously rhetorical imagery), the tendency was to thrust Satan's rights into the background, or even to deny them, and to stress rather his abuse of his powers and his consequent amply deserved punishment.[1] Pseudo-Cyril (he is probably none other than Theodoret) writes as follows:[2] 'Death being the penalty of sinners, He Who was without sin had a right to enjoy life rather than undergo death. Sin [i.e. the Devil] was therefore conquered when he condemned his conqueror to death. He passed on Him precisely the same sentence as he always passed on us, his subjects, and was therefore convicted of usurpation. So long as Sin only inflicted death on his own subjects, his action was fair enough and God sanctioned it. But when he subjected the innocent and blameless One . . . to the same penalties, he acted outrageously, and had to be expelled from his dominion.'

We may fittingly close this study with a sketch of Cyril's teaching as a whole. It was he who, working on the soteriological insights of his predecessors, produced a synthesis which remained influential until John of Damascus published his classic reformulation of Greek theology in the eighth century. As we have noted, the theory of the conquest of Satan had its place in his scheme; so had the physical theory which, as an Alexandrian, he inherited from Athanasius. 'Is it not most manifest', he wrote,[3] '. . . that the Only-begotten made Himself like us, that is, complete man, so as to deliver our earthly

---

[1] Cf. Cyril Alex. *ad regin.* 2, 31; Theodoret, *de provid.* 10 (PG 83, 757-60); Maximus Confessor, *cap. quinq. cent.* cent. 1, 11.

[2] *De incarn. dom.* 11 (PG 75, 1433 ff.).

[3] *De incarn. unigen.* (PG 75, 1213).

body from the corruption which had invaded it? This is why He condescended to become identical with us by the mystery of the union and took a human soul, thereby making it able to prevail against sin and, as it were, colouring it with the tincture of His own immortality. . . . He is thus the root, so to speak, and the first-fruits of those who are restored in the Spirit to newness of life and to immortality of body and to the firm security of divinity. . . . So we say the Word in His entirety united Himself with man in his entirety.' The purpose of the incarnation, he proclaimed,[1] was that the life-giving Word, by assuming human nature in all its corruption and decay, might infuse His own incorruptibility into it, just as fire impregnates with its nature the iron with which it is brought into contact. His argument, we observe, was influenced by the Platonic realism which affected the thought of Athanasius and Gregory of Nyssa. Human nature was treated as a generic whole, so that when the divine Word assumed it at the incarnation it could reasonably be said,[2] 'By virtue of the flesh united to Him, He has us all in Himself', and, 'We were all in Christ; the common person of humanity comes again to life in Him'.

This doctrine that by the incarnation human nature is deified and made to participate in the divine nature was a favourite theme of Cyril's; it was, we recall,[3] an over-riding motif in his Christology. But it did not lead him to overlook, or in any way to under-estimate, the peculiar saving efficacy attaching to the Lord's death. If He had merely lived on earth as man for several years, he argued, He could have been no more than our teacher and example. More positively, he was prepared to state[4] that 'Christ's death is, as it were, the root of life. It eliminated corruption, abolished sin and put an end to the divine wrath.' Again he could say,[5] 'When He shed His blood for us, Jesus Christ destroyed death and corruptibility. . . . For if He had not died for us, we should not have been saved; and if He had not

---

[1] *Hom. pasch.* 17 (PG 77, 785-7).
[2] *C. Nest.* 1; *in Ioh.* 1, 14; 16, 6 f. (PG 76, 17; 73, 161; 74, 432).
[3] See above, p. 322. [4] *In Hebr.* 2, 14.
[5] *Glaph. in Exod.* 2 (PG 69, 437).

gone down among the dead, death's cruel empire would never
have been shattered.' Thoughts like these link Cyril with
Athanasius, who also held[1] that, although the incarnation exalts
human nature, the death of the God-man was a necessary step
in the process, seeing that men already lie under a sentence of
death. In addition, however, Cyril saw[2] that the Saviour's
death was a sacrifice, the spotless offering obscurely foreshadowed in the Old Testament sacrificial system. Not only
death, but sin which was the cause of death, was the obstacle to
man's restoration. This point of view comes out forcibly in
such a text as the following:[3] 'Now that Lamb, foreshadowed of
old in types, is led to the slaughter as a spotless sacrifice for all
in order to do away with the sin of the world, to overthrow the
destroyer of mankind, to annihilate death by dying for all, to
rid us of the curse which lay upon us. . . . For when we were
guilty of many sins, and for that reason were liable to death and
corruption, the Father gave His Son as a ransom ($\dot{a}\nu\tau\dot{\iota}\lambda\upsilon\tau\rho\sigma\nu$),
one for all. . . . For we were all in Christ, Who died on our
account and in our stead and rose again. But sin being destroyed, how could it be that death, which springs from sin,
should not be destroyed as well?'

In this passage the several strains in Cyril's doctrine, including
the thought of Christ as the second Adam inaugurating a new
humanity, are held together in synthesis. Two further features
of it need to be mentioned if its true character is to be grasped.
First, his guiding idea is the familiar one of penal substitution.
Like almost all the patristic writers we have mentioned, he draws
his inspiration from *Is.* 53, 4. Christ did not suffer for His
own sins, he states,[4] 'but He was stricken because of our transgressions. . . . From of old we had been at enmity with God. . . .
It was necessary that we should be chastised for our contumacy.
. . . But this chastisement, which was due to fall on sinners so
that they might cease warring with God, descended upon
Him. . . . God delivered Him up because of our sins so that He

---

[1] See above, pp. 379 f.
[2] E.g. *in Hebr.* 2, 18; 3, 1; 7, 27; 9, 12; 10, 14.
[3] *In Ioh.* 1, 29 (PG 73,192).   [4] *In Is.* 53, 4-6.

might release us from the penalty.' In another context he writes,[1] 'The Only-begotten became man . . . in order that, submitting to the death which threatened us as the punishment for our sins, He might thereby destroy sin and put an end to Satan's incriminations, inasmuch as in the Person of Christ we had paid the penalty owing for our sins'. Secondly, Cyril grasped the fact, more clearly than any of his predecessors, that what enabled Christ to achieve this was not only His identification of Himself with sinful human nature, but the infinite worth of His Person. 'It was no ordinary man', he reminds us[2] (with a pointed reference to Nestorianism), 'that God the Father delivered over on our behalf, promoted to the rank of mediator, enjoying the glory of an adoptive Son and honoured with lasting association with Himself . . . but it was He Who transcends all creation, the Word begotten from His own substance, so that He might be seen to be amply equivalent for the life of all.' As he points out,[3] the deaths of even such holy people as Abraham, Jacob, Moses and Samuel could do nothing to help the human race in its plight. If in the Person of Christ one did prove able, by His death, to offer satisfaction on behalf of all, that was because His dignity and status (i.e. the fact that He was very God) so far exceeded the dignity and status of all those whom He was saving taken together. Since He was God incarnate, precious beyond all human valuing, the offering made with His blood was abundantly sufficient (ἀξιόχρεως ἡ λύτρωσις τοῦ κόσμου παντός) to redeem the whole world.[4]

[1] De ador. in spir. et verit. 3 (PG 68, 293 ff.).
[2] Quod unus (PG 75, 1341): cf. ad regin. 2, 7; ep. 50 (PG 76, 1344; 77, 264).
[3] De recta fide ad regin. 7 (PG 76, 1208).   [4] Ib. (PG 76, 1292).

NOTE ON BOOKS

General. G. Aulén, Christus Victor (English trans., London, 1934); R. S. Franks, A History of the Doctrine of the Work of Christ (London, 1918); J. K. Mozley, The Doctrine of the Atonement (London, 1915); J. Rivière, Le Dogme de la rédemption: essai d'étude historique (Paris, 1905; Eng.

trans., London, 1909); H. E. W. Turner, *The Patristic Doctrine of Redemption* (London, 1952).

Special.   G. A. Pell, *Die Lehre des hl. Athanasius von der Sünde und Erlösung* (Passau, 1888); J. Rivière, *Le Dogme de la rédemption chez saint Augustin* (Paris, 1928); O. Scheel, *Die Anschauung Augustins über Christi Person und Werk* (Leipzig, 1901); D. Unger, 'A Special Aspect of Athanasian Soteriology' (*Franciscan Studies,* 1946).

CHAPTER XV

CHRIST'S MYSTICAL BODY

1. Ecclesiology in the East

IT is customarily said that, as contrasted with that of the West, Eastern teaching about the Church remained immature, not to say archaic, in the post-Nicene period. In the main this is a fair enough verdict, at any rate so far as concerns deliberate statements of ecclesiological theory. An instructive sample of it, popular in form and dating from the middle of the fourth century, can be studied in Cyril of Jerusalem's *Catechetical Lectures*.[1] The Church, he explains, is a spiritual society which God called into existence to replace the Jewish church, which conspired against the Saviour. By His famous words to St. Peter (*Matt.* 16, 18), Christ has given it the promise of indefectibility. According to St. Paul (*1 Tim.* 3, 15), it is 'the pillar and ground of the truth', the Holy Spirit being its supreme teacher and protector.[2] It is also the fold within which Christ's sheep are safe from the wolves.[3] Its function is to gather together the faithful everywhere, of every rank, type and temperament, and it is called 'Catholic' (i.e. universal) because it does so. This title also draws attention to its capacity to teach every doctrine needful for man and to cure every kind of sin. Further, the Church is one and holy, the home of wisdom and knowledge as well as manifold virtues, and it extends throughout the entire world. As such Cyril contrasts it with particular sects, like those of the Marcionites and Manichees, which falsely usurp the name of churches. Finally, it is the bride of Christ and mother of us all, once sterile but now numerous in her offspring. It is in the holy Catholic Church that men

---

[1] *Cat.* 18, 22-8.   [2] Ib. 16, 19.   [3] Ib. 6, 36.

receive saving instruction, and are admitted to the kingdom of God and eternal life.

These are time-honoured commonplaces; it is plain that Cyril had scarcely pondered the problems involved in the Church's existence. We note in particular the absence of any discussion either of its hierarchical structure, so prominent in Cyprian[1] a full century before, or of the relation between the outward, empirical society and the invisible community of the elect—a theme which was later to absorb Augustine. Meagre and superficial though it was, however, it is Cyril's theology, with minor embellishments, which the other Greek fathers reproduce. Chrysostom, for example, states[2] that the Church is the bride which Christ has won for Himself at the price of His own blood. Unity is its outstanding characteristic, the bond which holds it together being mutual charity, and the schisms which split it asunder are just as pernicious and blameworthy as the heresies which distort its faith. The Church, he holds, is Catholic, that is to say, spread throughout the whole world; it is indestructible and eternal, the pillar and ground of the truth. After the canonization of the Constantinopolitan creed in 381, the predicates 'one', 'holy', 'Catholic' and 'apostolic' came to be regularly applied to the Church. For Cyril of Alexandria[3] this unity derived from 'the harmony of true doctrine' which united the various particular churches composing it, and also from the fact that there was no division of belief among the faithful, and that there is but one baptism; and Theodoret argued[4] that, while there might be a plurality of churches geographically, they were all one Church spiritually, dependent on the Lord, Who adorned it with beauty and sweetness as His bride. According to the seventh-century Maximus,[5] the Church was established by the Saviour as 'the orthodox, saving confession of belief'; while earlier Isidore of Pelusium († c. 435) had defined[6] it as 'the assembly of saints knit together

---

[1] See above, pp. 203-7.
[2] E.g. in Eph. hom. 11, 5; in 1 Cor. argum.; in Matt. hom. 54, 2; in illud 'Vidi dom.' hom. 4, 2; in 1 Tim. hom. 11, 1.
[3] In ps. 44, 10.
[4] In Cant. Cant. 3, 6, 1-4.
[5] Vita ac cert. 24 (PG 90, 93).
[6] Ep. 2, 246: cf. ib. 4, 5.

by correct faith and excellent manner of life', adding that it should abound in spiritual gifts. Cyril of Alexandria was voicing universally held assumptions when he wrote[1] that 'mercy is not obtainable outside the holy city', and claimed[2] that the Church was a visible society, plain for all to see, and that it was spotless and without the slightest blemish.

It would be a mistake to infer that conventional clichés like these represent the sum-total of the Greek fathers' understanding of the nature of the Church. Admittedly their expressly stated ecclesiology was neither original nor profound, the reason being that the subject was not a vital issue in the East and nothing therefore instigated them to explore it in so thorough a way as to reach solid conclusions. That they had deeper, more positive ideas about the Church as a spiritual society is apparent, although the evidence has for the most part to be gleaned from contexts which at first sight seem to have little to do with the Church as such. The clue to these ideas is the conviction, shared by fathers of every school and of course stemming from St. Paul's teaching, that Christians form a mystical unity with one another through their fellowship with, and incorporation into, Christ. Not infrequently, of course, this doctrine is expounded with direct reference to the Church, as when Gregory of Nazianzus[3] and Chrysostom[4] designate it the body of Christ, or when Theodore of Mopsuestia defines[5] Christ's body as that union of believers which is brought into existence through baptism and the operation of the Holy Spirit. More often than not, however, the conception of the mystical body is expounded for its own sake, without allusion to the doctrine of the Church and in the setting, say, of Trinitarian or Christological argument. To make this a pretext for neglecting it would be unfortunate, for as a matter of fact it constitutes the core of the patristic notion of the Church and its most fruitful element.

In Athanasius, for example, the idea of the mystical body lies

---

[1] *In ps.* 30, 22.   [2] *In Is. or.* 2 (PG 70 68).
[3] *Or.* 2, 3; 32, 11.   [4] *In 1 Cor. hom.* 32, 1.
[5] *In Ioh.* 16, 14 (Vosté, 212); *hom. cat.* 10, 16-19.

behind the whole of his polemic against the Arians. The nerve
of this was his doctrine of the deification of the Christian in
Christ, and this implies the mystical body. We are in Christ and
have been made sons of God by adoption, for we have been
united with God.[1] It is because we have been conjoined
mystically with the Word that we are able to participate in His
death, His resurrection, His immortality.[2] Regenerated by water
and the Spirit, Christians are quickened in Christ, and their very
flesh is charged with the Word (λογωθείσης τῆς σαρκός[3]). Most
illuminating is Athanasius's explanation of the text *John* 17, 21
('that they all may be one, as Thou, Father, art in Me, and I in
Thee . . .'). The Arians used this to support their case, deducing
from the analogy that the union between Father and Son could
only be one of resemblance. Not so, replied[4] Athanasius; men
are not only united, as the Arians suggested, by similarity of
nature, but 'through participation in the same Christ we all
become one body, possessing the one Lord in ourselves'.

The Cappadocians echo the same teaching, and Gregory of
Nazianzus explains[5] the 'novel mystery' into which Christians
are admitted as consisting in the fact 'that we are all made one
in Christ, Who becomes completely all that He is in us'. The
deification of the Christian is a persistent theme with Gregory
of Nyssa; his polemic against Apollinarianism, for example,
relies[6] largely on the plea that man's restoration can only be
effected if human nature in its entirety is united to God in the
Saviour. His point of view comes out forcibly in his exposition
of *1 Cor.* 15, 28, which the Arians regarded as a gift text. He
argues[7] that, when St. Paul speaks of the Son's being subjected
to the Father, he is really thinking of us human beings in our
capacity of adopted sons of God. 'Since we are all by participation conjoined with Christ's unique body, we become one
single body, viz. His. When we are all perfect and united with
God, the whole body of Christ will then be subjected to the
quickening power. The subjection of this body is called the sub-

---

[1] E.g. *c. Ar.* 1, 39; 2, 69 f.　　　[2] Ib. 2, 69.　　　[3] Ib. 3, 33.
[4] Ib. 3, 22.　　　[5] *Or.* 7, 23: cf. ib. 39, 13.　　　[6] E.g. *antirrh.* 16.
[7] *In illud 'Tunc ipse'* (PG 44, 1317).

jection of the Son Himself for the reason that He is identified
with His body, which is the Church.' In what follows he explains that, since Christ is present in all the faithful, He receives
into Himself all who are united with Him by communion with
His body, with the result that the multiplicity of His members
can be said to comprise one single body. Chrysostom, too,
without explicitly alluding to the Church, emphasizes[1] the
closeness of the union formed between Christians and Christ in
baptism. He sees the eucharist as the mainspring of this unity
stating[2] that 'We are mingled with this body, we become one
body of Christ, one single flesh'. Those who communicate at
the altar become 'the body of Christ: not a multiplicity of
bodies, but one body. . . . Thus we are united with Christ and
with one another.'[3]

As we might expect, these thoughts reached their fullest
flowering in Cyril of Alexandria. His exegesis[4] of *John* 1, 14
('The Word . . . dwelt in us'—$\dot{\epsilon}\nu$ $\dot{\eta}\mu\hat{\iota}\nu$) was that by His incarnation the Word identified Himself with human nature. A
mystical unity was established between men, the servants of sin,
and Him Who voluntarily took the form of a servant; thus
they were all reconciled to God in one body. Like Athanasius
before him, Cyril interprets[5] Christ's petition that His followers
may be one as Father and Son are one as implying, not simply a
moral union of the kind postulated by the Arians, but a real or
'physical' union ($\phi\upsilon\sigma\iota\kappa\hat{\eta}s$ $\dot{\epsilon}\nu\dot{\omega}\sigma\epsilon\omega s$). As he expresses it, 'If we
are all one body with one another in Christ—not only with one
another, but with Him Who comes to us in His flesh—, how
can we help being one, all of us, both with one another and in
Christ? Christ is the bond of unity inasmuch as He is one and
the same, God and man.' In this passage he stresses the role of
the Holy Spirit in bringing this unity about: 'We all receive
the same unique Spirit into ourselves, the Holy Spirit, and we
are all thereby conjoined with one another and with God.
Although we are distinct from one another and the Spirit of the

[1] E.g. *in Gal. comm.* 3, 5.   [2] *In Matt. hom.* 82, 5.
[3] *In 1 Cor. hom.* 24, 2.   [4] Cf. *in Ioh.* 1, 14 (PG 73, 161-4).
[5] Ib. 17, 21 f. (PG 74, 557-61).

Father and the Son dwells in each, nevertheless this Spirit is one
and indivisible. Thus by His power He joins together the many
distinct spirits in unity, making them as it were a single spirit in
Himself.' He also connects this unity with the eucharist in a
way which is characteristic of his teaching throughout. It is by
receiving Christ's sacramental body, he contends,[1] that we have
His life and power communicated to us, and that we maintain
and intensify our fellowship with Him. So he declares[2] that
'the body of Christ in us binds us in unity . . . we are brought
into unity both with Him and with one another.'

2. The East and the Roman See

Although the question belongs rather to Church history than
doctrine, something must now be said about the Eastern attitude
towards the Church's constitutional structure. The fourth and
fifth centuries were the epoch of the self-conscious emergence
of the great patriarchates; the position of Rome, Alexandria and
Antioch was recognized at Nicaea (325), while Constantinople
and Jerusalem were later accorded the rank of patriarchates at
the councils of Constantinople (381) and Chalcedon (451) respectively. Everywhere, in the East no less than the West, Rome
enjoyed a special prestige, as is indicated by the precedence
accorded without question to it. The only possible rival was the
new, rapidly expanding see of Constantinople, but the highest
claim that the second Ecumenical Council (381) could put in
for it (even that claim was ignored by Alexandria, and was to
be rejected by the papal legates at Chalcedon and declared null
by Pope Leo I) was to the effect[3] that 'the bishop of Constantinople shall hold the first rank after the bishop of Rome,
because Constantinople is new Rome'. Thus Rome's pre-
eminence remained undisputed in the patristic period. For
evidence of it the student need only recall the leading position
claimed as a matter of course by the popes, and freely conceded to them, at the councils of Ephesus (431) and Chalcedon

[1] E.g. *in Ioh.* 6, 54 ff. (PG 73, 577-84).
[2] *C. Nest.* 4, 5 (PG 76, 193).   [3] Canon 3.

(451). We even find the fifth-century historians Socrates[1] and Sozomen[2] concluding, on the basis of a misreading of the famous letter[3] of Julius I to the Eastern bishops (340) protesting against the deposition of Athanasius and Marcellus, that it was unconstitutional for synods to be held without the Roman pontiff being invited or for decisions to be taken without his concurrence. At the outbreak of the Christological controversy, it will be remembered,[4] both Nestorius and Cyril hastened to bring their cases to Rome, the latter declaring[5] that the ancient custom of the churches constrained him to communicate matters of such weight to the Pope and to seek his advice before acting. In one of his sermons[6] he goes so far as to salute Celestine as 'the archbishop of the whole world' (πάσης τῆς οἰκουμένης ἀρχιεπίσκοπος).

The crucial question, however, is whether or not this undoubted primacy of honour was held to exist by divine right and so to involve an over-riding jurisdiction. So far as the East is concerned, the answer must be, by and large, in the negative. While showing it immense deference and setting great store by its pronouncements, the Eastern churches never treated Rome as the constitutional centre and head of the Church, much less as an infallible oracle of faith and morals, and on occasion had not the least compunction about resisting its express will. It is instructive to notice their estimate of the Apostle Peter, for it was the promises and charges made to him (see especially *Matt.* 16, 18 f.; *Luke* 22, 32; *John* 21, 15-17) that were to provide the theological substructure of the later Papacy. On the one hand, St. Peter's position as prince of the apostles was acknowledged without the smallest reservation. Didymus, for example, hails[7] him as the coryphaeus (κορυφαῖος), the leader (πρόκριτος) who held the chief rank (τὰ πρωτεῖα) among the apostles; the power of reconciling penitents was given to him directly, and only through him to the other apostles.[8] Chrysostom describes[9] him

[1] *Hist. eccl.* 2, 17.
[2] *Hist. eccl.* 3, 10.
[3] Cf. Athanasius, *apol. c. Ar.* 21-35.
[4] See above, p. 324.
[5] *Ep.* 11, 1; 11, 7.
[6] *Hom. div.* 11 (PG 77, 1040).
[7] *De trin.* 1, 27; 2, 18; 2, 10 (PG 39, 408; 725; 640).
[8] Ib. 1, 30 (PG 39, 417).
[9] *Hom. in illud* 'Hoc scitote' 4.

as 'the coryphaeus of the choir, the mouthpiece of the apostolic company, the head of that band, the leader of the whole world, the foundation of the Church, the ardent lover of Christ'. Later writers, like Cyril of Alexandria[1] and Theodoret,[2] reflect the same point of view in almost identical language. In harmony with this one school of interpretation equated the rock mentioned in *Matt.* 16, 18 with the actual person of Peter. So Cyril explains[3] that Simon was named Peter 'because Jesus Christ proposed to found His Church upon him' (ἐπ' αὐτῷ). Epiphanius[4] and Maximus[5] the Confessor can be cited as witnesses to the same exegesis. On the other hand, there is no suggestion in the Greek fathers that St. Peter's position as leader carried with it a status different in kind from that of the other apostles. The current exegesis of the Petrine texts on the whole ran strongly counter to such an inference. Cyril of Alexandria, for example, is equally ready[6] to refer the rock of *Matt.* 16, 18 to Christ Himself as apprehended by faith, while Epiphanius,[7] Chrysostom[8] and Theodoret[9] (cf. σημαίνει δὲ ἡ πέτρα τῆς πίστεως τὸ στερρὸν καὶ ἀκράδαντον) see it as the symbol of St. Peter's faith. The charge 'Feed my sheep, etc.' (*John* 21, 15-17), so far from being taken as indicating any special authority or rank, denotes for Cyril[10] no more than the formal confirmation of his pastoral functions as apostle after his denial of the Lord. Similarly the admonition to establish his brethren (*Luke* 22, 32) is usually interpreted[11] as simply illustrating a general truth of God's dealings with men, viz. that restoration after sin is possible on condition of repentance. What is perhaps more significant, there are only very occasional hints (e.g. in the shout, 'Peter has spoken through Leo', with which the bishops at Chalcedon greeted Leo's *Tome*) that St. Peter's authority was mystically transmitted to, and as a result present in, his successors in the Roman see.

---

[1] *In Ioh.* 19, 25; *de trin. dial.* 4 (PG 74, 661; 75, 865).
[2] *Quaest. in Gen. interr.* 110; *in ps.* 2 (PG 80, 220; 873).
[3] *In Ioh.* 1, 42 (PG 73, 220): cf. *in Luc.* 22, 32 (PG 72, 916).
[4] *Ancor.* 9.   [5] *Vita ac cert.* 24 (PG 90, 93).
[6] *In Is.* 4, or. 2 (PG 70, 940).   [7] *Haer.* 59, 7.
[8] *In Matt. hom.* 54, 2; *in Gal. comm.* 1, 1.
[9] *Quaest. in Exod. interr.* 68.   [10] *In Ioh.* 21, 15-17 (PG 74, 749).
[11] E.g. Chrysostom, *in Matt. hom.* 82, 3; Basil, *hom. de humil.* 4.

3. Western Doctrines: Hilary and Optatus

If Western theology was able to grapple with the problem of the Church at a deeper level, this was because the struggle with Donatism focussed attention on it. Where Donatism made little or no impact, as in Italy and Gaul, ideas about the Church's nature did not differ materially from those fashionable about the same time in the East. For Ambrose, for example, the Church was the city of God, Christ's immaculate body;[1] those who rent it asunder and severed themselves from it were guilty of the unforgivable sin.[2] Hilary teaches that, externally considered, the Church is 'the harmonious fellowship of the faithful';[3] from a more spiritual angle it is the bride of Christ, His mystical body, the mouth by which He speaks to men.[4] Founded by Christ and established by the apostles, it is one, and teaches the truth with authority; its unity is that of a single integrated body, not that of a congeries of assorted bodies, and is based on its common faith, the bond of charity and unanimity of will and action.[5] As these passages disclose, the idea of the Church as mystically one with Christ was vividly alive in the West; indeed Hilary, who may have been influenced by his Eastern contacts, had a particularly strong sense of it. Through baptism, he argues, believers undergo a spiritual transformation of their bodies and 'enter into fellowship with Christ's flesh';[6] 'He is Himself the Church, comprehending it all in Himself through the mystery of His body', and so they are incorporated into Him.[7] The heretics, he points out,[8] claim (again the reference is to *John* 17, 21) that the unity which exists between Christians is merely one of concord and mutual charity, and take their stand on *Acts* 4, 32 ('the multitude of them that believed were of one heart and soul'). Actually it is a real unity (*unitas naturalis*), founded on the new life imparted at baptism and consisting in the fact that they have all put on the one, indivisible Christ. The reality of this union is guaranteed by the eucharistic mystery,

---

[1] *In ps.* 118, 15, 35.   [2] *De poen.* 2, 24.   [3] *Tract. in ps.* 131, 23.
[4] Ib. 127, 8; 128, 9; 138, 29.   [5] *De trin.* 6, 9 f.; 7, 4; *tract. in ps.* 121, 5.
[6] *In ps.* 91, 9.   [7] Ib. 125, 6.   [8] Cf. *de trin.* 8, 6–13.

by which the Christian's incorporation into Christ's body is maintained and intensified.[1]

Hints of the doctrine of the communion of saints appear in Hilary's writings, as when he refers[2] to the Church 'whether in the sense of that which exists now or of that consisting of saints which will be hereafter'. His contemporary, Niceta of Remesiana, expressly defines[3] the Church as 'the congregation of all the saints', stating that one of the benefits believers enjoy in it is 'communion with the saints', i.e. with the apostles, prophets, martyrs and just persons of all ages. But Hilary was also acutely conscious[4] that, as at present constituted, the Church is a mixed society containing sinners (*in ecclesia quidem manentes, sed ecclesiae disciplinam non tenentes*) as well as good men.

This was precisely the issue which Donatism raised. For more than a hundred years this schism split the African church, spreading bitter discord and violence. While a variety of non-theological factors (e.g. nationalist feeling, economic stringency) complicated the issue, its ostensible origin was the alleged irregularity of the consecration of Caecilian as bishop of Carthage in 311. One of the consecrators, Felix of Aptunga, was accused (falsely, according to the Catholics) of being a *traditor*, i.e. of having surrendered copies of the Scriptures to the civil authorities during Diocletian's persecution (303). The Donatists took the lines of rigorism; the validity of the sacraments, they taught, depended on the worthiness of the minister, and the Church ceased to be holy and forfeited its claim to be Christ's body when it tolerated unworthy bishops and other officers, particularly people who had been *traditores*, in its ranks. In this case the resulting contamination, they held,[5] infected not only Caecilian and his successors, but everyone in Africa and throughout the whole world who maintained communion with them. Presupposed in this attitude is the puritan conception of the Church as a society which is *de facto* holy, consisting exclusively of actually good men and women. With this as their premiss the Donatists argued that they alone could be the

---

[1] *De trin.* 8, 15 f.   [2] *Tract. in ps.* 132, 6.   [3] *De symb.* 10.
[4] *Tract. in ps.* 1, 4; 52, 13; *in Matt.* 33, 8.   [5] Cf. Augustine, *ep.* 129.

ecclesia catholica, which Scripture attested to be the immaculate
bride of Christ, without spot or wrinkle, since they required
positive holiness from laity and clergy alike. The so-called
Catholics, they urged, could not with justice make out their
claim to be the true Church.

The Catholic reaction to this fanatical brand of puritanism is
well illustrated in the six (later expanded to seven) books which
Optatus, bishop of Milevis, wrote in 366 or 367 to refute the
Donatist leader and publicist, Parmenianus. First, he points out[1]
that sacraments derive their validity from God, not from the
priest who administers them. In baptism, for example, it is
the Triune Godhead invoked in the trinitarian formula Who
bestows the gift. Whoever it is that plants and whoever that
waters, it is always God Who gives the increase; the person of
the officiant is of necessity continually changing, but the Trinity
is always present in the rite. For this reason he is ready enough[2]
to acknowledge the Donatists as brethren (after all, both they
and he have had 'one and the same spiritual nativity'), and to
recognize the efficacy of their sacraments. Secondly, he criticizes
the Donatists' definition of the Church's holiness and their insistence that membership must be confined to people who are
in a *de facto* state of goodness. The Church is holy, he contends,[3]
not because of the character of those who belong to it, but
because it possesses the symbol of the Trinity, the chair of Peter,
the faith of believers, Christ's saving precepts, and, above all,
the sacraments themselves. The petition, 'Forgive us our trespasses', which our Lord enjoined, and such texts as *1 John* 1, 8
('If we say that we have no sin, we deceive ourselves'), as well
as the Parable of the Tares, abundantly prove that Christ is prepared to tolerate sinners in His Church until the day of judgment.[4] It is wrong, not to say impossible, for us to attempt what
the apostles themselves never presumed to do, viz. to dis-
criminate between the good and bad in Christ's flock. Thirdly,
he suggests that catholicity and unity are at least as decisive
tokens of the true Church as holiness. The former connotes

---

[1] *De schism. Donat.* 5, 4; 5, 7.   [2] Ib. 1, 3 f.; 4, 2; 5, 1.
[3] Ib. 2, 1; 2, 9; 2, 10; 7, 2.   [4] Ib. 2, 20; 7, 2.

world-wide extension, in accordance with the Saviour's promise, so that the Donatists are ruled out as a sect confined to 'a fragment of Africa, a mere corner of a minute region'.[1] The unity of the Church, foretold in Scripture in such passages as *Cant.* 6, 8 ('One is my dove'), was willed by our Lord, and its visible manifestation consists in communion with the see of Peter.[2] In Optatus's eyes, as in Cyprian's,[3] schism is tantamount to apostasy, being a negation of the spirit of charity (*catholicum facit . . . unitas animorum, schisma vero . . . livore nutritur*[4]). Since the Church is indivisibly one, schismatics like the Donatists do not so much rend it asunder as sever themselves from it, like branches which are broken off from the parent tree.[5] Like Cyprian, too, he condemns them in Jeremiah's words for leaving the fountains of living water and digging cisterns for themselves which cannot hold water.[6]

4. *Western Doctrines: Augustine*

It was another African, Augustine, who developed and deepened these thoughts of Optatus's during his prolonged controversy with the Donatists. According to him, the Church is the realm of Christ, His mystical body and His bride, the mother of Christians.[7] There is no salvation apart from it; schismatics can have the faith and sacraments (in this he differs from his admired master, Cyprian,[8] preferring the traditional Western doctrine that the sacraments are valid even if administered outside the Church), but cannot put them to a profitable use since the Holy Spirit is only bestowed in the Church.[9] In appropriate circumstances grace can certainly be had outside it by means of God's direct, invisible action, as the case of the centurion Cornelius recorded in *Acts* demonstrates; but the strict condition is that the recipient must not attempt to by-pass the visible means of grace (*contemptor sacramenti visibilis invisibiliter sanctificari nullo modo potest*[10]). It goes without

---

[1] *De schism. Donat.* 2, 1; 2, 5; 2, 11; 3, 2 f.   [2] *Ib.* 1, 10; 2, 2 f.
[3] See above, p. 206.   [4] *Ib.* 1, 11.   [5] *Ib.* 2, 9.
[6] *Ib.* 4, 9.   [7] *Ep.* 34, 3; *serm.* 22, 9.   [8] See above, p. 206.
[9] *De bapt.* 4, 24; 7, 87; *serm. ad Caes.* 6.   [10] *Quaest. in hept.* 3, 84.

saying that Augustine identifies the Church with the universal
Catholic Church of his day, with its hierarchy and sacraments,
and with its centre at Rome. In fact, its catholicity consists
partly in its claim to teach the whole truth and not selected
fragments of it,[1] but even more, it would seem,[2] in its world-
wide extension. The latter characteristic marks it off from the
sects, each of which flourishes in a particular locality.[3] Not that
the Church, on Augustine's view, is to be confined to the
universal, empirical society visible at any one time. It includes
in its ranks not only present-day Christians, but all who have
believed in Christ in the past and will do so in the future. It is,
moreover, as against the Donatists' conception, 'a mixed community' (corpus permixtum[4]) comprising bad men as well as good,
and the Bible texts which dwell on its absolute perfection and
spotless purity should be balanced by others (e.g. the Parable
of the Tares) pointing to its mixed character, and should be
interpreted as referring to its condition, not here and now, but
at the final consummation.[5]

Most of these points are commonplaces of fourth-century
Latin Catholicism. We must elaborate some of them if we are
to appreciate Augustine's special contribution to the doctrine of
the Church. First, the heart of his teaching is his conception of
the Christian society as Christ's mystical body. Christ has, he
holds,[6] a triple mode of existence. He exists as the eternal Word,
and also as the God-man or Mediator; but, in the third place,
He exists as the Church, of which He is the head and the faithful the members. The whole constitutes a single spiritual entity
or person. 'There are many Christians', he writes,[7] 'but only
one Christ. The Christians themselves along with their Head,
because He has ascended to heaven, form one Christ. It is not a
case of His being one and our being many, but we who are
many are a unity in Him. There is therefore one man, Christ,
consisting of head and body.' Christ and His members are 'one
person' (una quaedam persona[8]), an organic unity in which all

[1] Ep. 93, 23.   [2] Ib. 49, 3; 185, 5; serm. 46, 32 f.
[3] Serm. 46, 18.   [4] Cf. de doct. christ. 3, 45.
[5] E.g. c. litt. Pet. 3, 4; brevic. coll. 3, 15-19.   [6] Serm. 341.
[7] Enarr. in ps. 127, 3.   [8] Enarr. 1 in ps. 30, 4.

have their several functions, and which is figuratively represented in the one bread of the eucharist.[1] And just as an ordinary body is permeated, quickened and held together by the soul or spirit, so the life-principle of the mystical body is the Holy Spirit, Who cannot be received outside the Church.[2] But since the Holy Spirit is love personified, the product of the mutual love of the Father and the Son, the life-principle of the Church can be equally well described as love.[3] It is precisely this unifying, quickening love or charity which is the Church's essence; it welds the multiplicity of members together and unites the body with its Head, the result being 'one single Christ Who loves Himself'.[4] Faith and hope are naturally combined with love, for only through faith in the incarnation and cross are men brought into fellowship with the Mediator,[5] and the Church looks forward with hope to the fulness of the redemption.[6] Thus in its inward being the Church is the communion of all those who are united together, along with Christ their Lord, in faith, hope and love.

Secondly, Augustine's idea of the Church's unity follows logically from his conception of it as a fellowship of love. Its members must be united since they are members of one body; just as Adam and Eve engendered us for death, so Christ and the Church, His bride and our spiritual mother, have engendered us for eternal life.[7] This unity, of course, involves unity of belief,[8] and any breach of this leads to heresy.[9] But, deeper and more important than this, it is also a union of love; it is absurd to suppose that anyone can belong to the Church who does not love God and his fellow-Christians.[10] The antithesis of love is the spirit which promotes schism, rending Christ's seamless robe and tearing His body apart by an act of 'criminal severance' (*nefaria separatio*[11]). It is therefore their abandonment of the principle of love which in Augustine's

---

[1] *Ep.* 187, 20 and 40; *tract. ev. Ioh.* 13, 17; *serm.* 354, 4.
[2] *Serm.* 267, 4; 268, 2.   [3] *Enarr.* 2 *in ps.* 32, 21; *de trin.* 15, 33-7.
[4] *Tract. in ep. Ioh.* 10, 3.
[5] *De civ. dei* 18, 47: cf. *de nat. et grat.* 2; *c. Iul.* 4, 17.
[6] *Enarr. in ps.* 103; *serm.* 4, 17; *ep.* 55, 25 f.
[7] *Serm.* 22, 10; 121, 4; 216, 8.   [8] *De civ. dei* 18, 50, 1.
[9] *Ep.* 118, 32.   [10] *C. Cresc.* 1, 34.   [11] *Serm.* 265, 7; *ep.* 43, 21.

eyes puts the Donatists outside the Church: 'who can truthfully say that he has the charity of Christ when he does not embrace His unity?'[1] They may be orthodox in belief, their baptisms and ordinations may be technically correct, and their austerities may be beyond all praise; but all these things are made of none effect by the lack of charity which plunges them into schism. For Cyprian, as we have seen,[2] schism was in effect spiritual suicide; it meant cutting oneself off from Christ's body, which remained in itself as united as ever. On Augustine's view it was positive sacrilege, since schismatics really rend the Church asunder by their lack of charity.

Thirdly, while insisting on the basis of Scripture that the Church as a historical institution must include sinners as well as just men and that the two groups will only be separated at the final consummation,[3] Augustine came to make a significant admission in order to meet the Donatists' point that Christ's bride must be 'without spot or wrinkle' here and now. This consisted in drawing a careful distinction between the essential Church, composed of those who genuinely belong to Christ, and the outward or empirical Church. With his Platonic background of thought this distinction came easily to him, for the contrast[4] between the perfect essence, eternal and transcending sensation, and its imperfect phenomenal embodiment was always hovering before his mind. From this point of view only those who are ablaze with charity and sincerely devoted to Christ's cause belong to the essential Church;[5] the good alone 'are in the proper sense Christ's body' (cf. *boni, qui proprie sunt corpus Christi*[6]). The rest, that is to say sinners, may seem to be within the Church, but they have no part in 'the invisible union of love' (*invisibilis caritatis compages*[7]). They are inside the house, but remain alien to its intimate fabric.[8] They belong to the *catholicae ecclesiae communio*[9] and enjoy the *communio sacramentorum*;[10] but it is the just who constitute 'the congregation

---

[1] *Ep.* 61, 2. [2] See above, p. 206. [3] E.g. *serm.* 88, 22 f.
[4] See above, pp. 15 f. [5] *De bapt.* 5, 38; 6, 3; 7, 99.
[6] *C. Faust.* 13, 16. [7] *De bapt.* 3, 26.
[8] Ib. 7, 99. [9] *Ep.* 93, 3; 112, 3.
[10] *De unic. bapt. c. Petil.* 24; *c. Cresc.* 3, 35; *de bapt.* 7, 100.

and society of saints',[1] the 'holy Church' in the strict sense of the words.

Thus Augustine's solution of the age-old problem was to argue that the authentic bride of Christ really does consist, as the Donatists claimed, exclusively of good and pious men, but that this 'invisible fellowship of love' is only to be found in the historical Catholic Church, within whose frontiers good men and sinners meanwhile consort together in a 'mixed communion'. The error of the Donatists, on this hypothesis, was to make a crude institutional division between them, whereas the precedent of Israel showed that the division was a spiritual one and that God intended the two types of men to exist side by side in this world. As he worked out his doctrine of predestination,[2] however, he was led to introduce a refinement on this distinction between the visible and the invisible Church. In the last resort, he came to see, the only true members of the Church (the 'enclosed garden . . . spring shut up, fountain sealed . . . the paradise with the fruit of apples', spoken of so eloquently in *Cant.* 4, 12 f.) could be 'the fixed number of the elect'. But 'in God's ineffable foreknowledge many who seem to be within are without, and many who seem to be without are within'. In other words, many even of those who to all appearances belong to 'the invisible fellowship of love' may not possess the grace of perseverance, and are therefore destined to fall away; while many others who at present may be heretics or schismatics, or lead disordered lives or even are unconverted pagans, may be predestined to the fulness of grace.[3] It is obvious that this line of thought transferred the whole problem of the Church's nature to an altogether different plane. Augustine never attempted to harmonize his two conceptions, that distinguishing the Church as a historical institution from the true Church of those really devoted to Christ and manifesting His spirit, and that identifying Christ's body with the fixed number of the elect known to God alone. Indeed, it may be doubted whether any synthesis was ultimately possible, for if the latter

---

[1] *De civ. dei* 10, 6.   [2] See above, pp. 368 f.
[3] Cf. *de bapt.* 5, 38 f.; *de corrept. et grat.* 39-42.

doctrine is taken seriously the notion of the institutional Church ceases to have any validity.

5. *The West and the Roman Primacy*

By the middle of the fifth century the Roman church had established, *de jure* as well as *de facto*, a position of primacy in the West, and the papal claims to supremacy over all bishops of Christendom had been formulated in precise terms. The detailed narrative of the stages by which this process was accomplished belongs properly to the field of Church history rather than to that of doctrine. Here we need only remark that, strictly theological factors apart, the position of Rome as the revered ancient capital and sole apostolic see of the West, the all-embracing influence it exercised liturgically and theologically in the Western empire, and the special role the popes were called upon to fulfil in the era of barbarian invasions, all contributed to the development. The student tracing the history of the times, particularly of the Arian, Donatist, Pelagian and Christo-logical controversies, cannot fail to be impressed by the skill and persistence with which the Holy See was continually advancing and consolidating its claims. Since its occupant was accepted as the successor of St. Peter, the prince of the apostles, it was easy to draw the inference that the unique authority which Rome in fact enjoyed, and which the popes saw con-centrated in their persons and their office, was no more than the fulfilment of the divine plan.

In this section our concern is with the function of the Roman primacy in the theology of the Church. There is little to be gleaned on the subject from Hilary, who agrees[1] that St. Peter was the first to believe, the captain of the apostolic band (*apostolatus princeps*), the foundation upon which the Church was built and the janitor of the celestial gates, but does not appear to connect these facts with the contemporary Roman see. Ambrose's teaching is much fuller, and there can be no doubt of the extraordinary veneration in which he held the Roman

[1] *In Matt.* 7, 6; 16, 7.

church. From the earliest times, he taught,[1] it had been the un-swerving exponent of the Church's creed in its integrity and purity; to be in communion with Rome was a guarantee of correct belief. Hence he advises[2] that matters touching on faith and order and the mutual relations of orthodox churches should be referred for settlement to the Roman pontiff. Yet he no-where recognizes the latter as the final interpreter of the laws of ecclesiastical discipline, much less ascribes supreme jurisdiction over the Church to him. It is clear that Ambrose's exegesis of the great Petrine texts which were to supply that jurisdiction with its theological substructure was inconsistent, and in any case fell short of identifying the apostle with the later popes. If, for example, he sometimes[3] interprets *Matt.* 16, 18 as implying that the Church was erected upon St. Peter, even adding that 'where Peter is, there is the Church', his fuller discussion of the text suggests that the rock mentioned in it was not the apostle's person so much as his faith in Christ's Messiahship or divinity,[4] or even the Saviour Himself, the object of his faith.[5] Similarly, while sometimes[6] attributing special authority over the Church to St. Peter himself, he also states[7] that the gift of the keys was not bestowed on St. Peter personally or exclusively, but as the representative of the apostles and of all Catholic bishops descending from them.

In Africa meanwhile, the prevailing doctrine was an ex-tension of Cyprian's.[8] Optatus of Milevis, as we have seen,[9] in his controversy with the Donatist Parmenianus, reckoned 'the chair of Peter' as one of the indispensable possessions of the true Church: *claves . . . solus Petrus accepit.*[10] By this he seems to have meant, as indeed he proceeds to explain, that the episcopal commission was first and uniquely conferred upon St. Peter, and that the other apostles and their successors participate equally in the selfsame commission. In this way the possibility

---

[1] *Ep.* 42, 5; 11, 4; *de excess. Sat.* 1, 47.   [2] *Ep.* 56, 7: cf. ib. 13, 7.
[3] *De fid.* 4, 56; *enarr. in ps.* 40, 30.
[4] E.g. *de incarn. dom. sacram.* 33 f.; *expos. ev. Luc.* 6, 98.
[5] *Expos. ev. Luc.* 6, 97; *ep.* 43, 9.   [6] *Enarr. in ps.* 43, 40.
[7] Ib. 38, 37; *de poen.* 2, 12.   [8] See above, pp. 205 f.
[9] See above, p. 411: cf. *de schism. Donat.* 2, 2.   [10] Ib. 1, 10.

of there being several 'chairs', with the disunity which would inevitably result, was effectively ruled out. For Optatus, therefore, communion with the see of Peter was a vital necessity, although we should note that he laid almost equal stress[1] on the desirability of communion with the Oriental churches and what he called the *septiformis ecclesia Asiae*. Augustine's attitude was not dissimilar. Following Cyprian, he regarded St. Peter as the representative or symbol of the unity of the Church and of the apostolic college, and also as the apostle upon whom the primacy was bestowed (even so, he was a type of the Church as a whole[2]). Thus the Roman church, the seat of St. Peter, 'to whom the Lord after His resurrection entrusted the feeding of His sheep',[3] was for him the church 'in which the primacy (*principatus*) of the apostolic chair has ever flourished'.[4] The three letters[5] relating to Pelagianism which the African church sent to Innocent I in 416, and of which Augustine was the draughtsman, suggest that he attributed to the Pope a pastoral and teaching authority extending over the whole Church, and found a basis for it in Scripture. At the same time there is no evidence that he was prepared to ascribe to the bishop of Rome, in his capacity as successor of St. Peter, a sovereign and infallible doctrinal magisterium. For example, when in his controversy with Julian of Eclanum he appealed to Innocent, his view[6] was that the Pope was only the mouthpiece of truths which the Roman church had held from ancient times in harmony with other Catholic churches. Nor was he willing, in practical matters, to surrender one jot of the disciplinary independence of the African church which Cyprian had defended so stoutly in his day. The truth is that the doctrine of the Roman primacy played only a minor role in his ecclesiology, as also in his personal religious thinking.

The real framers and promotors of the theory of the Roman primacy were the popes themselves. Men like Damasus (366–384), Siricius (384–99), Innocent (402–17) and their successors

---

[1] Ib. 2, 6; 6, 3.   [2] *Enarr. in ps.* 108, 1; *serm.* 46, 30; 295, 2.
[3] *C. ep. fund.* 5 (PL 42, 175).   [4] *Ep.* 43, 7.
[5] Augustine, *epp.* 175-7.   [6] *C. Iul.* 1, 13.

not only strove to advance it on the practical plane, but sketched out the theology on which it was based, viz. the doctrine that the unique position and authority assigned by Christ to St. Peter belonged equally to the popes who followed him as bishop of Rome. Leo the Great (440–61) was responsible for gathering together and giving final shape to the various elements composing this thesis. His conception of the primacy is admirably set out in the letter[1] which he sent to Anastasius, bishop of Thessalonica, in 446. 'Bishops indeed', he declared, 'have a common dignity, but they have not uniform rank, inasmuch as even among the blessed apostles, notwithstanding the similarity of their honourable estate, there was a certain distinction of power. While the election of all of them was equal, yet it was given to one [i.e. St. Peter] to take the lead of the rest. From this model has arisen a distinction of bishops also, and by an important ordinance it has been provided that everyone should not arrogate everything to himself, but that there should be in each province one whose opinion should have precedence among the brethren; and again that certain whose appointment is in the greater cities should undertake a fuller responsibility, and that through them the care of the universal Church should converge towards Peter's one chair, and nothing anywhere should be separate from its head.' His teaching, as expounded in many contexts, involves the following ideas. First, the famous Gospel texts referring to St. Peter should be taken to imply that supreme authority was conferred by our Lord upon the apostle. Secondly, St. Peter was actually bishop of Rome, and his magisterium was perpetuated in his successors in that see. Thirdly, St. Peter being in this way, as it were, mystically present in the Roman see, the authority of other bishops throughout Christendom does not derive immediately from Christ, but (as in the case of the apostles) is mediated to them through St. Peter, i.e. through the Roman pontiff who in this way represents him, or, to be more precise, is a kind of *Petrus redivivus*. Fourthly, while their mandate is of course limited to their own dioceses, St. Peter's magisterium,

[1] *Ep.* 14, 11.

and with it that of his successors, the popes of Rome, is a *plenitudo potestatis* extending over the entire Church, so that its government rests ultimately with them, and they are its divinely appointed mouthpiece.

NOTE ON BOOKS

P. Batiffol, *Le Catholicisme de saint Augustin* (Paris, 1920); G. Bonner, *St. Augustine of Hippo* (London, 1963); L. Bouyer, *L'Incarnation et l'église-corps du Christ dans la théologie de s. Athanase* (Paris, 1943); W. Bright, *The Roman See in the Early Church* (London, 1896); P. T. Camelot, *Die Lehre von der Kirche: Väterzeit bis ausschliesslich Augustinus* (HDB III, 3b: Freiburg-Basel-Wien, 1970); W. H. C. Frend, *The Donatist Church* (Oxford, 1952); S. L. Greenslade, *Schism in the Early Church* (London, 1953); F. Hofmann, *Der Kirchenbegriff des hl. Augustinus* (Munich, 1933); T. G. Jalland, *The Church and the Papacy* (London, 1944); B. J. Kidd, *The Roman Papacy to* A.D. 461 (London, 1936); É. Mersch, *Le Corps mystique du Christ* (Brussels and Paris, 3 ed. 1951: Eng. trans., *The Whole Christ*, London, 1956); A. Robertson, *Regnum Dei* (London, 1901); T. Specht, *Die Lehre von der Kirche nach dem hl. Augustin* (Paderborn, 1892); H. B. Swete (ed.), *The Early History of the Church and Ministry* (London, 1918); G. G. Willis, *Saint Augustine and the Donatist Controversy* (London, 1950).

CHAPTER XVI

THE LATER DOCTRINE OF THE SACRAMENTS

1. General Theory

IN the fourth and fifth centuries little or no attempt was made, in East or West, to work out a systematic sacramental theology. The universal, if somewhat vague, assumption was that the sacraments were outward and visible signs marking the presence of an invisible, but none the less genuine, grace. Chrysostom, for example, pointed out[1] that, in order to understand the mysteries (by these he meant baptism and the eucharist), we must study them with the intellectual eye, attending to what the Lord promised rather than what sense perceives. According to Theodore of Mopsuestia,[2] 'every sacrament is the indication, by means of signs and symbols, of invisible and ineffable realities'; while the late fifth-century Pseudo-Dionysius stated[3] that 'the sensible rites (τὰ αἰσθητὰ ἱερά) are representations of intelligible things, and conduct and guide us to them'. Ambrose similarly distinguished[4] the external ritual from the unseen grace or presence. The former, he pointed out, carries with it a symbolism which corresponds to man's twofold nature, and this explains its efficacy. So in baptism water washes the body, while the soul is cleansed by the Spirit;[5] in the eucharist what is perceived after the consecration is only a sign of what is actually there.[6] Augustine lays particular stress on this contrast. 'The sacrament itself', he declares,[7] 'is one thing, and the power (virtus) of the sacrament another.' Elsewhere he writes[8] of the eucharistic bread and wine, 'So they are called sacraments

---

[1] In Matt. hom. 82, 4.   [2] Hom. cat. 12, 2.
[3] De eccl. hierarch. 2, 3, 2 (PG 3, 397).
[4] De myst. 8; de sacram. 1, 10.
[5] Expos. ev. Luc. 2, 79.   [6] De myst. 50; 52; 54; de sacram. 4, 14-16.
[7] Tract. in ev. Ioh. 26, 11.   [8] Serm. 272.

because one thing is seen in them, another understood. What is seen has a bodily appearance, but what is understood has spiritual fruit.' In baptism the water serves as the sacrament of the grace imparted, but the grace itself is invisibly operated by the Holy Spirit.[1]

While this was the prevalent idea of sacraments, their number was not yet definitely fixed. To a certain extent this was due to the vagueness which still attached to the terms μυστήριον and *sacramentum*. Chrysostom could apply the former in one and the same context[2] both to Christ's humiliation and crucifixion and to holy baptism. In Hilary's vocabulary the latter stood on occasion for the mystery of the divine unity,[3] or of the Lord's divinity,[4] or of the incarnation.[5] There was a growing tendency, however, to recognize a specialized sense of the words in which they denoted the efficacious signs of the Gospel, and to classify these together. For Cyril of Jerusalem[6] and Ambrose,[7] interested as they were primarily in the training of catechumens, there were three sacraments in this sense—baptism, confirmation or chrism, and the eucharist. Cyril of Alexandria also enumerated[8] these three. This list was generally accepted, but since the conception of a sacrament was still elastic it should not be regarded as exhaustive. The language of Gregory of Nyssa[9] about ordination and of Chrysostom[10] about penance suggests that these, too, qualified for the title in their eyes. Augustine illustrates both the wider and the narrower meanings of *sacramentum*. 'Signs are called sacraments', he explains,[11] 'when they have reference to divine things.' On this definition anything might be a sacrament which is a token, natural or conventional, of a divine reality. So he can include under the term such rites as the blessed salt handed to catechumens,[12] the baptismal exorcisms,[13] and the formal tradition of the creed and the Lord's Prayer to catechumens,[14] as well as the Old Testament

[1] *Ep.* 98, 2.   [2] *In 1 Cor. hom.* 7, 1.   [3] *De trin.* 7, 23; 9, 19.
[4] Ib. 10, 48.   [5] Ib. 9, 25 f.   [6] *Cat.* 19-23.
[7] *De myst.; de sacram.*   [8] *In Ioel* 32.
[9] *In bapt. Chr.* (PG 46, 581-4).   [10] *De sacerdot.* 3, 6.
[11] *Ep.* 138, 7.   [12] *De cat. rud.* 50.   [13] *Serm.* 227.
[14] Ib. 228, 3.

events and personages mysteriously foreshadowing Christ and
His salvation.[1] On the other hand, he speaks[2] of 'the few most
salutary sacraments of the Gospel', and contrasts[3] the manifold
rites of the old Law with 'the sacraments, very few in number,
very easy to take note of, and most glorious in their significance', by means of which Christ has united His people together. The instances he gives are baptism and the eucharist;
and these are the two he cites elsewhere[4] when stating that 'the
Lord Himself and the apostolic discipline have handed down a
few signs, easy to enact and august in their meaning'.

It should not be inferred, however, that thought about the
sacraments was entirely lacking in definiteness of outline. We
should notice the emergence in this period of certain ideas
which, though not yet fully worked out, were to pave the way
for the mature medieval doctrine. In the first place, it is now
taken as axiomatic that in the administration of the sacraments
God or Jesus Christ is the principal agent, the priest being merely
His instrument. 'God's gifts', protests[5] Chrysostom, 'are not
such as to be the result of any virtue of the priest's; they are
wholly the work of grace. The priest's function is simply to
open his mouth, and it is God Who accomplishes what is
done. . . . The eucharistic oblation remains the same, whether
Paul or Peter offers it. The oblation which Christ gave to His
disciples is identical with the one now offered by the priests.
The latter is no whit inferior to the former, for it is not men
who consecrate it, but He Who consecrated the original oblation.' So 'when the priest baptizes, it is not he who baptizes, but
God Who compasses your head with His invisible power'.[6] In
the West, as we saw[7] in the preceding chapter, these principles
received forceful acknowledgement as a result of the Church's
clash with Donatism. Baptism, Optatus argues,[8] is the gift of
God, not of any human minister; it is the Holy Trinity Who
sanctifies the catechumen, so that while the minister may be
changed the Trinitarian formula must remain inviolate. So

---

[1] Enarr. in ps. 83, 2. [2] De ver. rel. 33. [3] Ep. 54, 1.
[4] De doct. christ. 3, 13. [5] In 2 Tim. hom. 2, 4.
[6] In Matt. hom. 50, 3. [7] See above, p. 411.
[8] De schism. Donat. 5, 7.

Augustine teaches[1] that the truth of a sacrament is not impugned by the unsuitability of its minister, for its actual author is God Himself. For example, in spite of the diversity of those who administer it, baptism remains one and the same sacrament since it is Christ Who in fact bestows it.[2]

Secondly, it is clear that much thought was given in this period to the efficient cause linking the spiritual gift with the outward, perceptible sign. According to Cyril of Jerusalem,[3] once the Trinity has been invoked (he uses the term ἐπίκλησις), the baptismal water possesses sanctifying power in view of the fact that it is no longer mere water, but water united with the Holy Spirit, Who acts in and through it. So Gregory Nazianzen bases[4] the efficacy of baptism on the Spirit, and Basil declares[5] that 'if the baptismal waters have any grace, they derive it, not from their own nature, but from the presence of the Holy Spirit'. Ambrose follows Basil in teaching[6] that the efficacy of the sacrament springs from the presence of the Holy Spirit in the water. The Trinitarian formula, however, is also indispensable: 'unless the catechumen is baptized in the name of the Father and of the Son and of the Holy Spirit, he cannot receive the remission of sins or imbibe the gift of spiritual grace'.[7] For Augustine the operative factor seems to have been the candidate's belief in the Trinity as expressed in his answers to the threefold baptismal interrogations. 'Take away the word', he remarks,[8] 'and what is the water but water? When the word is added to the element, it becomes a sacrament.' He goes on to explain that it is not merely the uttering of the word, but the word considered as a vehicle of faith, that endows the water with saving power; and the context, with its references to *Rom.* 10, 8-10 and *1 Pet.* 3, 21, makes it plain that he is thinking of the triple questionnaire and the confession of faith made in response to it.

As regards the Holy Communion, the eucharistic prayer had previously been conceived as effecting the consecration, but

---

[1] *C. litt. Pet.* 2, 69.   [2] *De unit. eccles.* 58.   [3] *Cat.* 3, 3 f.
[4] *Or.* 39, 17.   [5] *De spir. sanct.* 35.
[6] *De spir. sanct.* 1, 77; *de myst.* 8.
[7] *De myst.* 20; *de spir. sanct.* 2, 104 f.   [8] *Tract. in ev. Ioh.* 80, 3.

attempts were now made to define the causal efficacy more precisely. One widespread theory was that consecratory power lay in the repetition by the priest, acting in Christ's stead, of the words used by Christ at the Last Supper. Chrysostom, for example, states[1] that the priest, standing in the Lord's place, repeats the sentence, 'This is my body', and its effect is to transform the elements on the altar. Gregory of Nyssa reflects[2] the same strain of thought; and in the West it established itself with Ambrose[3] as one of its most noteworthy exponents. On the other hand, such a document as Serapion's liturgy exhibits[4] traces of the idea that what consecrates the gifts is the descent of the divine Word upon them. At the same time we see emerging the theory, already adumbrated in the *Didascalia*,[5] that their transformation is the work of the Holy Spirit. Cyril of Jerusalem, for example, envisages[6] a liturgy in which 'we entreat God . . . to send forth the Holy Spirit upon the offerings that He may make the bread the body of Christ and the wine the blood of Christ; for whatsoever comes into contact with the Holy Spirit is hallowed and changed'. Chrysostom himself on occasion depicts[7] the priest as calling upon the Spirit to descend and touch the elements, making no pretence of harmonizing this doctrine with the theory of consecration by means of the words of institution. Theodore of Mopsuestia seems to combine the two conceptions, stating[8] that 'when the priest declares them [i.e. the bread and wine] to be Christ's body and blood, he clearly reveals that they have become such by the descent of the Holy Spirit', although his general teaching[9] is that the eucharistic mystery is accomplished by the descent of the Spirit. In a similar way, as regards penance, the doctrine[10] takes shape that when the Church's minister absolves sinners with the power of the keys bestowed by Christ, it is really God Himself Who acts.

---

[1] *De prod. Iud. hom.* 1, 6: cf. *in 2 Tim. hom.* 2, 4.   [2] *Or. cat.* 37.
[3] *De myst.* 50; 52; 54; *de sacram.* 4, 14-23.
[4] 13, 15 (Funk, II, 174-6): cf. Pseudo-Athanasius, *ad nuper baptiz.* (PG 26, 1325).   [5] 6, 22, 2: cf. 6, 21, 2 (Funk, I, 376; 370).
[6] *Cat.* 23, 7.   [7] *Hom. in coem. app.* 3: cf. *de sacerdot.* 3, 4.
[8] *Hom. cat.* 16, 12.   [9] Cf. *in Ioh.* 6, 63 (Vosté, 109).
[10] Cf. Pacian, *ep. ad Symp.* 1, 6; Ambrose, *de poenit.* 1, 34-9; Cyril Alex., *in Luc.* 5, 24; 7, 28.

These two ideas, that the grace contained in sacraments is God's gift and has nothing to do with the officiant as such, and that its production is tied to the divinely prescribed formula rehearsed by the minister, go a long way towards the so-called *ex opere operato* doctrine of sacraments, i.e. that they are signs which actually and automatically realize the grace they signify. A closely related point which deserves notice is the attitude of the Church in the fourth and fifth centuries to sacraments celebrated by heretics and schismatics. A wide variety of opinion prevailed in the East. Athanasius roundly states[1] that the baptism of Arians, Manichaeans, Montanists and Paulianists is utterly void; they may carry out the rite, but since their faith is defective they gave the words another meaning. Ps.-Didymus insists[2] on rebaptizing Eunomians and Montanists, the former because they baptize only into the Lord's death, and the latter because they do not baptize into three divine Persons but confuse Father, Son and Spirit. At Jerusalem Cyril rejected[3] the baptism of all heretics alike, but Eusebius of Caesarea treated[4] the Roman tradition[5] about rebaptism as more ancient. Basil distinguishes[6] between heretics, whose baptism he regards as worthless, and schismatics, about whom he is not prepared to dogmatize. In the West, as we have seen,[7] the controversy with Donatism resulted in the conclusion that sacraments administered at any rate by schismatics must be held to be valid. In this debate the particular sacraments which interested Augustine were baptism and ordination. The man who has received either, he states,[8] retains even as a schismatic the power to transmit its grace to others, so that rebaptism and reordination are out of the question. The reason for this is that both sacraments impart a permanent character (*dominicus character*) which is no more lost if its bearer goes astray in schism than in the stamp branded on sheep.[9] But if constrained in this way to admit the validity of Donatist sacraments, Augustine was sufficiently the heir of Cyprian and the African tradition to feel it necessary to

---

[1] *C. Ar.* 2, 42 f.   [2] *De trin.* 2, 15.   [3] *Procat.* 7.
[4] *Hist. eccl.* 7, 2.   [5] See above, p. 206.   [6] *Ep.* 188, 1.
[7] See above, pp. 411; 412; 424.   [8] *C. ep. Parm.* 2, 28.
[9] *Ep.* 185, 23; 173, 3: cf. *c. ep. Parm.* 2, 29.

emphasize their defects at the same time. Hence he distinguishes between the validity of a sacrament and its efficaciousness, and points out[1] that Cyprian's mistake lay precisely in his failure to draw this distinction. A sacrament, on this view, can exist and possess technical validity without its recipient's obtaining the grace properly associated with it; this grace can only be enjoyed within the Church. So he explains[2] that 'the Church's baptism can exist outside the Church, but the gift of blessed life is only found inside the Church'. Schismatical baptism is thus perfectly valid, but it altogether fails to produce its appropriate effects unless and until its recipient is a full member of the Catholic Church.[3]

2. Baptism

From these general considerations we turn to the particular sacraments. Cyril of Jerusalem provides a full, if not always coherent, account of the conception of baptism which commended itself to a fourth-centuary theologian in Palestine. The name he applies to the rite is 'baptism'[4] or 'bath' ($\lambda ov\tau\rho\acute{o}v$[5]). It is 'the bath of regeneration[6]' in which we are washed both with water and with the Holy Spirit.[7] Its effects can be summarized under three main heads. First, the baptized person receives the remission of sins, i.e. all sins committed prior to baptism.[8] He passes from sin to righteousness, from filth to cleanliness;[9] his restoration is total, and can be likened to a cure which causes not only the patient's wounds but the very scars to disappear.[10] In elaborating this transformation Cyril fully exploits the traditional images of the purification of the soul, the putting off of the old man, deliverance from slavery, etc. Secondly, baptism conveys the positive blessing of sanctification, which Cyril describes[11] as the illumination and deification of the believer's soul, the indwelling of the Holy Spirit, the putting on of the new man, spiritual rebirth and salvation, adoption as God's son by grace, union with Christ in His resurrection as in His

---

[1] De bapt. 6, 1.   [2] Ib. 4, 1.   [3] Ib. 1, 18; 5, 9; 6, 7.
[4] Procat. 16; cat. 3, 15.   [5] Procat. 7; 11; cat. 3, 3; etc.
[6] Procat. 11.   [7] Cat. 3, 3 f.   [8] Ib. 3, 15.   [9] Ib. 1, 4.
[10] Ib. 18, 20.   [11] Procat. 2; 6; cat. 1, 2; 3, 2; 3, 13-15; 20, passim.

suffering and death, the right to a heavenly inheritance. If the remission of sins is granted equally to all, he points out,[1] the infusion of the Holy Spirit is made proportionate to the recipient's faith. Thirdly, and closely connected with this, baptism impresses a seal (τὴν δι' ὕδατος σφραγῖδα) on the believer's soul. Just as the water cleanses the body, the Holy Spirit seals (σφραγίζει) the soul.[2] This sealing takes place at the very moment of baptism[3] (the passages cited link it directly with the immersion), and as a result of it the baptized person enjoys the presence of the Holy Spirit.

These ideas are fairly representative of Greek and Latin teaching about baptism in the fourth and fifth centuries. There is no need to dwell at length on the aspect of the remission of sins. Ps.-Didymus, for example, declares[4] that the authentic baptism, as contrasted with the Pool of Bethesda which prefigured it, delivers us from all our sins, working the cure of all spiritual ailments; while according to Cyril of Alexandria[5] 'baptism cleanses us from all defilements, making us God's holy temple'. In the West Optatus, taking the Flood as the type of baptism, suggests[6] that the sinner who is plunged in the baptismal water is washed of the filth of sin and restored to his pristine purity; and Jerome acknowledges[7] that sins, impurities and blasphemies of every sort are purged in Christ's laver, the effect being the creation of an entirely new man. As Augustine expresses it,[8] 'Baptism washes away all, absolutely all, our sins, whether of deed, word or thought, whether sins original or added, whether knowingly or unknowingly contracted'. Not that it should be supposed that baptism safeguards the baptized Christian from sinning in the future. Towards the end of the fourth century the heretic Jovinian argued this thesis, contending[9] that once baptized a man could no longer be tempted by the Devil to sin. It fell to Jerome to refute him,[10] adducing numerous Scriptural passages to show that the baptized are not only

---

[1] Ib. 1, 5.   [2] Ib. 3, 4.   [3] Ib. 4, 16; 16, 24.
[4] De trin. 2, 14 (PG 39, 708).   [5] In Luc. 22, 8.
[6] De schism. Donat. 5, 1.   [7] Ep. 69, 2 f.
[8] C. duas epp. Pelag. 3, 3, 5.   [9] Augustine, de haer. 82.
[10] Adv. Iov. 2, 1-4.

exposed to temptation but are quite capable of succumbing to it.

The widespread diffusion of infant baptism inevitably called for a rationale. As we have seen,[1] the Greek fathers were reluctant to attribute sin, at any rate in the sense of guilt, to newly born children. Gregory of Nazianzus, who discussed the problem, gave[2] as a good reason for their being baptized the desirability of their being sanctified and dedicated to the Spirit from earliest infancy; he stressed the importance of their being initiated and receiving the 'seal'. In the West Ambrose judged[3] baptism necessary for infants, not as relieving them of inherited guilt, but as opening the kingdom of heaven to them; and Pelagius, as we saw,[4] adopted a similar line. With the establishment of the strict Latin doctrine of original sin such explanations became obsolete. Thus for Augustine[5] any child born into the world was polluted with sin, and baptism was the indispensable means to its abolition. Jerome echoed his ideas, teaching[6] that once children have been baptized they are free from sin, but until then they bear the guilt of Adam.

As regards the positive effects of baptism, it is important to notice the place which continued to be assigned, in spite of the increasing prestige of confirmation, to the gift of the Holy Spirit. The fathers, it would seem, were greatly confused about the manner in which Christians received the Spirit, and echoes of the older doctrine are to be found side by side with the new. Athanasius, for example, maintains[7] that the Spirit is granted to those who believe and are reborn in the bath of regeneration; Hilary, too, teaches[8] that the presence of the Spirit within the soul begins when the convert is regenerated by baptism, and that through Him we are renewed in body and soul. Jerome is a convinced exponent[9] of the view that baptism and the Spirit are inseparable, while Chrysostom explains[10] that only through the power of the Spirit can the baptismal water produce its effect. According to Theodore,[11] we obtain the gift of the Holy

---

[1] See above, p. 349.   [2] Or. 40, 17; 40, 28.
[3] De Abrah. 2, 79.   [4] See above, p. 359.
[5] E.g. de peccat. mer. et remiss. 1, 34.   [6] Dial. adv. Pelag. 3, 17 f.
[7] Ad Serap. 1, 4.   [8] Tract. in ps. 64, 15; in Matt. 11, 24.
[9] Dial. c. Lucif. 6; 9.   [10] In Act. hom. 1, 5.   [11] In Gal. 2, 16.

Spirit at the same time as we receive baptism, for it is He Who regenerates us and is the first-fruits of our perfection. Augustine similarly states[1] that 'the Holy Spirit dwells, without their knowledge, in baptized infants'. Not infrequently the fathers describe the bestowal of the Spirit in terms of the New Testament image of the seal. Didymus, for example, states[2] that we are conformed to the primal image as a result of our reception of the seal of the Spirit in baptism, and elsewhere[3] associates sealing with regeneration as part of the activity of the Spirit which the Christian experiences. Chrysostom similarly speaks[4] of the seal of the Spirit in baptism as a distinctive sign like the badge worn by soldiers. The Christian's sealing with the Spirit, he claims,[5] corresponds to the sealing of the Jew with the rite of circumcision.

More frequently, however, the positive effects of baptism are delineated in other ways. Through baptism, according to Athanasius, man is united with the Godhead;[6] it is the sacrament of regeneration by which the divine image is renewed.[7] The participant becomes an heir of eternal life,[8] and the Father's adoptive son.[9] For Gregory of Nyssa similarly the baptized person receives God and is in Him; united with Christ by spiritual rebirth, he becomes God's son by adoption and puts on the divine nature.[10] Chrysostom speaks[11] of the Christian's having Christ in himself as a result of baptism and so being assimilated to Him; stepping out of the sacred bath, the catechumen is clothed with light and, fully regenerated, enjoys possession of justice and holiness.[12] Cyril of Alexandria states[13] that perfect knowledge of Christ and complete participation in Him are only obtained by the grace of baptism and the illumination of the Holy Spirit. The baptismal initiation makes us the image of the archetype, i.e. of Him Who is Son of God by nature, and so sons of God by adoption.[14] According to Theodore,[15] baptism

[1] Ep. 187, 26.
[2] De trin. 2, 15 (PG 39, 717).
[3] Ib. 2, 12 (PG 39, 680).
[4] In 2 Cor. hom. 3, 7.
[5] In Eph. hom. 2, 2.
[6] C. Ar. 2, 41.
[7] De incarn. 14.
[8] Ad Serap. 1, 22.
[9] C. Ar. 1, 34.
[10] Or. cat. 40; c. Eunom. 3 (PG 45, 609).
[11] In Gal. comm. 3, 5.
[12] Ad illumin. cat. 1, 3.
[13] Glaph. in Exod. 2 (PG 69, 432).
[14] In Rom. 1, 3.
[15] In Ioh. 3, 3–5; 17, 20 f.; in Gal. 3, 21.

is our second birth, as a result of which we belong to Christ
and are associated with the privileges of His glorious life, being
His body and His members. Having received it, we can call
God our Father, for we have been adopted as sons and have
been promised immortality. The language of the Latin fathers
is not dissimilar, although it lacks the emphasis on deification
which is characteristic of the Greek. For Hilary,[1] for example,
in addition to obliterating our sins baptism is the sacrament of
divine birth, making the recipient God's temple and immune
from death, as well as His adoptive son. According to Ambrose,[2]
it imparts rebirth, in the sense of resurrection, renewing us
through the impact of the Holy Spirit and making us God's
sons by adoption; dying with Christ in the font, we become
partakers of His grace. Ambrosiaster makes the point[3] that,
whereas those who were baptized before Christ's passion received only remission of sins, those baptized after His resurrection are justified by virtue of the Trinitarian formula and,
having received the Spirit, are admitted to divine sonship.
Augustine emphasizes[4] that the baptized, even infants, are endowed with the graces of illumination and justification, and are
grafted into Christ's body; released from death, they are reconciled to God unto eternal life, and from being sons of men
receive the status of sons of God.

3. Confirmation or Chrism

In the fourth and fifth centuries confirmation, or consignation, while still closely associated with baptism, was also clearly
distinguished from it. Cyril of Jerusalem, for example, devoted
his twenty-first catechectical lecture to it, and Ps.-Didymus
treated[5] it as different from baptism; Ambrose's account[6] of it
followed his description of the major rite, while for Augustine[7]

---

[1] De trin. 1, 21; 6, 44; tract. in ps. 65, 11.
[2] De sacram. 3, 3; de spir. sanct. 3, 63-8; de excess. Sat. 2, 43.
[3] In Rom. 4, 23-5.
[4] De peccat. mer. et remiss. 1, 10; 1, 39; c. duas epp. Pelag. 2, 11.
[5] De trin. 2, 14; 2, 15 (PG 39, 712; 720).   [6] De myst. 29 f.; 42.
[7] C. litt. Pet. 2, 239.

too it was a *sacramentum* distinct from the latter. The general procedure was that, on coming up from the baptismal water, the newly baptized Christian was anointed with scented oil, at the same time receiving the laying on of hands. In the East the anointing was always the essential feature, and if Athanasius[1] and Cyril of Jerusalem[2] speak of the bestowal of the Spirit by the apostles' hands, they do not connect this with chrismation as they know it. The laying on of hands retains some importance in the *Apostolical Constitutions*,[3] although here it is fused with episcopal consignation; and where writers like Cyril of Alexandria[4] and Theodoret[5] mention it, they are probably simply referring to the bishop's action in consignation. In the West, however, the laying on of hands continued, side by side with chrism, to be an important element in the process of initiation. Optatus saw it[6] as normal and regular, finding its prototype in the blessing pronounced by God the Father on Jesus at His baptism. Jerome, it is true, played down[7] its importance, ascribing the gift of the Spirit in His fulness to baptism, but Augustine taught[8] that in practising it the bishops were merely following the precedent of the apostles.

The general theory was that through chrismation, with or without the laying on of hands, the Holy Spirit was bestowed. According to Cyril of Jerusalem,[9] just as Christ after His baptism received the Spirit in the form of a dove, so the oil with which the newly baptized Christian is anointed symbolizes the Spirit Who sanctifies him. Through the words of blessing it has become 'the chrism of Christ, capable of producing the Holy Spirit through the presence of His divinity'. Hilary describes[10] how, after passing through the baptismal waters, the Spirit descends upon us (again he recalls the descent of the dove on Jesus), and we are suffused with the unction of celestial glory. In his liturgy Serapion[11] has a special prayer beseeching God to grant divine and heavenly power to the oil of chrism, so that

---

[1] *Ad Serap.* 1, 6.   [2] *Cat.* 14, 25.   [3] 3, 16, 3 f. (Funk, I, 211).
[4] *De ador. in spir. et litt.* 11 (PG 68, 772).
[5] *In Hebr.* 6, 1; *quaest. in Num.* 47.   [6] *De schism. Donat.* 4, 7.
[7] *Dial. c. Lucifer.* 9.   [8] *De trin.* 15, 46.   [9] *Cat.* 21, 1-3.
[10] *In Matt.* 2, 6.   [11] *Euchol.* 25, 2 (Funk, II, 187).

those who have already taken the bath of regeneration may also receive the Spirit. Ps.-Didymus takes up[2] Cyril's idea that the anointing with oil corresponds to Christ's reception of the Spirit, but also identifies the outward unction with the anointing mentioned in *2 Cor.* 1, 21 and *1 John* 2, 20. Gregory of Nyssa goes so far as to insist[2] that, if the Christian is to lay hold on Christ and possess the Spirit, he must first be anointed with myrrh. For Cyril of Alexandria[3] the rite is the symbol of our participation in the Holy Spirit, and Theodoret speaks[4] of the anointed receiving the invisible grace of the Spirit in the myrrh 'as in a type'. In the West, where the imposition of hands loomed larger, Scriptural authority was found for the practice in the passages in *Acts* referring to the laying on of the apostles' hands, and the effect was naturally taken to be the bestowal of the Spirit. Innocent I, for example, writing to Decentius of Gubbio, argued[5] that consignation, as distinct from the unction administered by presbyters after baptism, belongs properly to the bishop, being the medium by which he bestows the Paraclete.

While this was the main idea associated with chrismation, other interpretations of the rite continued side by side with it. In general it was regarded as an edifying symbol of the Christian's membership of Christ and fellowship with His death and resurrection. So Basil, commenting on *Matt.* 6, 17, exclaims,[6] 'Wash thy soul for sins [i.e. be baptized]; anoint thy head with holy chrism so that thou mayest become a partaker of Christ'. Before him Cyril of Jerusalem had recognized[7] chrismation as the act which confers the status of Christian on us. An unknown fifth-century writer explains[8] that unction after baptism is a token of the Christian's participation in the sufferings and glory of his Lord, while Augustine declares[9] that it signifies our membership of Christ's body. The forty-eighth canon of Laodicea states[10] that it is unction with chrism which makes us sharers of Christ's

---

[1] *De trin.* 2, 6 (PG 39, 557; 560).   [2] *Adv. Maced.* 16.
[3] *In Is.* 25, 6 f. (PG 70, 561).   [4] *In Cant.* 1, 2 (PG 81, 60).
[5] *Cod. can. eccl. et const. s. sed. apost.* 23, 3.   [6] *Hom. de ieiun.* 1, 2.
[7] *Cat.* 21, 5.   [8] *Quaest. et resp. ad orthodox.* 137 (PG 6, 1389).
[9] *Enarr. in 26 ps.* 2, 2.   [10] Mansi, II, 571.

kingdom; and it is a commonplace of patristic teaching[1] that it betokens the baptized convert's admission to the kingship and priesthood of the Messiah.

From what has been said so far it should be clear that there was considerable confusion between the theology of consignation, or chrismation, and that of baptism. Both rites, it would appear, were regarded as conferring the gift of the Spirit and as uniting the believer to Christ. So long as the great sacrament of initiation remained an unbroken whole, there was no serious disadvantage in this, and the confusion created no difficulty. Once unction and the laying on of hands, however, were detached, the problem of the precise relation of the two rites became increasingly urgent. Hints of the solution which later theology was to provide are found in Serapion, who suggests[2] that one effect of the gift of the Spirit in chrismation is the 'strengthening' (cf. ἀσφαλισθέντες τῇ σφραγῖδι ταύτῃ) of the candidate, and also in Ps.-Didymus's idea[3] that the Spirit's function when bestowed is to 'fortify' (ῥώσῃ) us. Parallel to this is the line of thought, found in Cyril of Alexandria,[4] that it signifies the 'perfecting' (τελείωσις) of those who have been justified through Christ in baptism. In the same sense Dionysius the Areopagite describes[5] chrismation as 'an anointing which perfects' (τελειωτικὴ χρῖσις), while for Augustine[6] it is the unction which 'will make us spiritually perfect in that life which will be ours hereafter'. Ambrose attempts[7] to distinguish the regenerative activity of the Spirit in baptism from the bestowal of His sevenfold gifts in the consignation which follows. Because of this growing emphasis on strengthening, the name confirmation (confirmatio) came to be generally substituted in the West for consignation, appearing first in the second canon[8] of the first council of Orange (441). The fully developed theology is set out in an influential homily[9] on Pentecost ascribed to

[1] E.g. apost. const. 3, 16, 4; Chrysostom, in 2 Cor. hom. 3, 5; Augustine, serm. 351, 12; enarr. in 26 ps. 2, 2.   [2] Euchol. 25, 2 (Funk, II, 186).
[3] De trin. 2, 14 (PG 39, 712).   [4] In Ioel 32.
[5] De eccl. hierarch. 4, 3, 11 (PG, 3, 484).   [6] Enarr. in 26 ps. 2, 2.
[7] De sacram. 3, 8-10; 6, 6 f.   [8] Mansi, VI, 435.
[9] Hom. in Pentecost. (ed. J. Gagnaeus, Paris, 1547, pp. 77-9).

Faustus of Riez. According to its author, the blessings of regeneration (i.e. baptism) are sufficient for those who are going
to die straightaway, but the help provided by confirmation is
desirable for those whose life lies before them. The Holy Spirit,
already given in baptism, strengthens the faithful in confirmation for the perils and combats of this life. Confirmation is thus
a kind of blessing (*benedictio*) which equips Christ's soldiers with
the weapons they need, imparting an increase of grace. 'In
baptism we are regenerated for life, but after baptism we are
confirmed for the struggle; in baptism we are nourished, but
after baptism we are strengthened.'

4. *Penance*

The documents of the fourth and fifth centuries abound in
references to the Church's practice of remitting sins committed
after baptism; many of these were prompted by the desire to
refute Novatianist rigorism. In the East both Basil and Gregory
of Nyssa give detailed accounts of the penitential system
familiar to them. The former describes[1] the length of penance
imposed (from one to four years for bigamy or trigamy, ten
years for abortion, eleven for murder, etc.), and establishes the
principle, known to Western canonists as *non bis in idem*, that
persons in holy orders convicted of fornication should be reduced to lay status but not excluded from communion. The
latter lays bare[2] the roots of sins in the soul, endeavouring to
bring them all under the heads of the three capital sins of
apostasy, adultery and murder. Gregory Nazianzen joins issue[3]
with the Novatianists in justifying the efficacy of repentance
and the possibility of post-baptismal pardon; while Epiphanius,
although agreeing that there is only one 'perfect repentance',
viz. that of baptism, and that *Hebr.* 6, 4-6 precludes any second
restoration in this sense, argues[4] that the sequel (6, 9 f.) proves
that God is ready to welcome the guilty back in consideration
of their good works, i.e. repentance. In *Apostolical Constitutions*,
2, 10-16, the duties of bishops, their obligations and rights in

---

[1] *Ep.* 188.   [2] *Ep. can.*   [3] *Or.* 39, 17-19.   [4] *Haer.* 59, 1 f.

regard to sinners, and the procedure for the reconciliation of the latter, are succinctly sketched. At Constantinople, according to Socrates,[1] the bishop for a time delegated his functions in this matter to a penitentiary priest, who imposed penances on people after they had confessed their sins, and the office was only suppressed in the episcopate of Nectarius (381–97) as a result of a scandal.

In the West we find Ambrose criticizing[2] the severity of the Novatianists in refusing to remit post-baptismal sins. The Church's power to do so, he contends, rests on precisely the same authority as its power to baptize. He carefully examines[3] the Scriptural passages (e.g. 1 Sam. 2, 25; Hebr. 6, 4-6; 1 John 5, 16) commonly cited as proof of the irremissibility of sins, and puts forward what he considers their true interpretation. For example, St. Paul's harsh language in Hebr. 6, 4-6 must be harmonized, he argues, with the leniency he exhibits elsewhere. Thus one should take him as meaning either that baptism as such cannot be repeated, or that the restitution of sinners is impossible with men, but not necessarily with God. Ambrose's contemporary, Pacian of Barcelona, provides much valuable material in his letters to Symphronianus. The latter had summarized the essentials of the Novatianist position in three points: (a) after baptism there can be no place for penitence; (b) the Church cannot remit mortal sins; and (c) it undergoes irreparable injury in receiving sinners back after reconciliation. In reply[4] Pacian examines the relevant Bible texts and, pointing to the power of the keys committed to the Church, claims that a constructive attitude to sinners accords best with the spirit of the Gospel, and that in principle all sins can be remitted. Augustine, whose allusions to penance are countless, divides[5] it into three categories. First, there is the penitence which precedes baptism, as a result of which sins of every sort and degree are remitted to the sacrament; secondly, there is the remission which Christians obtain daily for their venial sins by

[1] Hist. eccl. 5, 19: cf. Sozomen, hist. eccl. 7, 16.   [2] De poen. 1, 33–9.
[3] Ib. 1, 40–96; 2, 6–19.   [4] Ep. 3, 8 ad fin.
[5] E.g. serm. 352, 2–8; serm. ad catech. 15 f.

means of prayer, fasting, etc.; and, thirdly, for really serious sins after baptism there is the formal penitential discipline, in which the Church raises the sinner from the moribund state in which he lies just as Christ raised Lazarus. These 'grave and mortal sins', as he expresses it,[1] 'are remitted by means of the keys of the Church', for 'the Church, founded as it is on Christ, received from Him in the person of Peter the keys of the kingdom of heaven, that is, the power of binding and loosing sins'.[2]

Certain features of the sacrament of penance as it existed in this period should be noticed. First, it retained the character which it possessed in earlier centuries of being a discipline which could only be undergone once and could not be repeated. 'Just as there is one baptism', observes[3] Ambrose, 'so there is but one public penance'; and Augustine alludes[4] to 'the prudent and salutary provision' whereby one, and only one, exercise of penance has been permitted in the Church. The malicious allegations[5] brought against John Chrysostom that he encouraged its frequent reiteration at least serve to confirm that Eastern practice was in line with Western on this point.

Secondly, penance, in the strict sense of the Church's official reconciliation of sinners, continued to be a formal and public act. The formidable process involved (a) the sinner's exclusion from communion and admission by the imposition of hands, after confession, to the order of penitents, and, where necessary, his being taken to task by the bishop; (b) his performance of a prescribed course of self-humiliation and prostration known technically as *exomologesis*, the period depending on the gravity of his sins and varying at different times and places; and (c) his formal absolution and restoration. Attempts have been made[6] to trace at any rate the beginnings of private penance and absolution to this period. Yet there is no clear evidence in favour of this, and much that tells against it. What the fathers describe seems always to be public penance, and such a writer

---

[1] *Serm.* 278, 12.   [2] *Tract. in ev. Ioh.* 124, 5.   [3] *De poen.* 2, 95.
[4] *Ep.* 153, 7.   [5] Cf. Socrates, *hist. eccl.* 6, 21.

as Augustine, as we have seen, is quite positive that the only form of penance apart from this is that which sinners practise daily for their more venial sins by prayer, almsgiving, etc. It is true that he not infrequently mentions[1] 'certain medicines of rebukes' (*correptionum medicamenta*), and cites[2] *Matt.* 18, 15 as authorizing private remonstrance with the offender. But these are references to exhortations intended to bring him to a right frame of mind and to submit himself to public penance. It rests with the bishop, of course, to whom the penitent opens his heart to determine what treatment his guilt requires,[3] and he may sometimes decide, even in the case of a sin like adultery, that public penance is for one reason or another impracticable or inexpedient, and that the sinner must be dealt with in private.[4] But nothing goes to show that this *correptio secreta*, or private taking to task of the guilty party by the ecclesiastical authority, culminated in sacramental absolution. The first reliable evidence for private penance as a sacrament is found in canon 2[5] of the third council of Toledo (589), which castigates it as an *execrabilis praesumptio*.

Thirdly, while the broad distinction between graver and lesser sins was recognized, there seem to have been different opinions as to which sins fell into the former category and so called for public penance. Basil's list[6] of such sins is fairly comprehensive, including abortion, murder, sexual offences, bigamy, etc.; but Gregory of Nyssa, as we have seen,[7] makes an attempt to reduce serious misdeeds to the three capital sins of apostasy, adultery and murder. Pacian, too, states[8] that, while other crimes may be atoned for by good works, these three demand a more serious remedy. Augustine on occasion cites[9] the traditional list, but elsewhere defines[10] the *peccata mortifera* as 'those which the Decalogue of the Law contains, and with regard to which the Apostle says (*Gal.* 5, 21), "Those who do such things shall not possess the kingdom of God" '. In practice, it would seem, the severity of penance and the fact that it could

---

[1] E.g. *de fid. et op.* 48.   [2] Loc. cit.; *serm.* 82.   [3] Cf. *serm.* 351, 9.
[4] E.g. *serm.* 82, 11.   [5] Mansi, IX, 995.   [6] *Ep.* 188.
[7] See above, p. 436.   [8] *Paraen.* 4.
[9] *Serm.* 352, 8; *de fid. et op.* 34.   [10] *Serm.* 351, 7.

only be undergone once meant that many deferred it until their death-bed, thereby reducing the publicity to a minimum. In Africa, too, if Augustine[1] can be taken as a guide, the *correptio secreta* of the bishop provided a practical method, albeit non-sacramental, of dealing pastorally with sins which, though falling short of extreme heinousness, were sufficiently grave to trouble tender consciences.

5. *The Eucharistic Presence*

In examining the later doctrine of the eucharist it will be convenient, as in Chapter VIII, to begin with the ideas currently entertained about the Lord's presence in the sacrament. Eucharistic teaching, it should be understood at the outset, was in general unquestioningly realist, i.e. the consecrated bread and wine were taken to be, and were treated and designated as, the Saviour's body and blood. Among theologians, however, this identity was interpreted in our period in at least two different ways, and these interpretations, mutually exclusive though they were in strict logic, were often allowed to overlap. In the first place, the figurative or symbolical view, which stressed the distinction between the visible elements and the reality they represented, still claimed a measure of support. It harked back, as we have seen,[2] to Tertullian and Cyprian, and was to be given a renewed lease of life through the powerful influence of Augustine. Secondly, however, a new and increasingly potent tendency becomes observable to explain the identity as being the result of an actual change or conversion in the bread and wine. The connexion between these theories and the different ideas about consecration referred to in the first section of this chapter hardly needs to be pointed out.

As an example of the former tendency we may cite the *Apostolical Constitutions*, which describes[3] the mysteries as 'antitypes (ἀντίτυπα) of His precious body and His blood', and speaks of commemorating Christ's death 'by virtue of the

---

[1] E.g. *de fid. et op.* 48.　　[2] See above, pp. 212 f.
[3] 5, 14, 7; 6, 23, 5; 7, 25, 4 (Funk, I, 273; 361; 412).

symbols (συμβόλων χάριν) of His body and blood'. In the liturgy we give thanks for the precious blood and for the body, 'of which we celebrate these antitypes' (ἀντίτυπα). Yet at the same time the formula at communion is 'the body of Christ' and 'the blood of Christ'. Serapion, while referring to the elements as 'the body and the blood', speaks[1] of 'offering this bread' as 'a likeness (ὁμοίωμα) of the body of the Only-begotten', and 'offering the cup' as 'a likeness (ὁμοίωμα) of the blood'. The theologians use the same language as the liturgies. So Eusebius of Caesarea, while declaring[2] that 'we are continually fed with the Saviour's body, we continually participate in the lamb's blood', states[3] that Christians daily commemorate Jesus's sacrifice 'with the symbols (διὰ συμβόλων) of His body and saving blood', and that He instructed His disciples to make 'the image (τὴν εἰκόνα) of His own body', and to employ bread as its symbol. His contemporary, Eustathius of Antioch, commenting on *Prov.* 9, 5, says[4] that 'by bread and wine he [i.e. the author] refers prophetically to the antitypes of Christ's bodily members'. Even the pioneer of the conversion doctrine, Cyril of Jerusalem, is careful to indicate[5] that the elements remain bread and wine to sensible perception, and to call them 'the antitype' of Christ's body and blood: 'the body is given to you in the figure (τύπῳ) of bread, and the blood is given to you in the figure of wine'.[6] Gregory of Nazianzus, who of course accepts the current realism, exhorting[7] his hearers to 'eat the body, drink the blood', similarly describes[8] his sister as mingling her tears with the 'antitypes' of Christ's precious body and blood treasured in her hands; while Macarius of Egypt († c. 390) speaks[9] of bread and wine as being offered in the Church as 'a symbol of His flesh and blood'. Athanasius, too, while not employing such terms as 'symbol' or 'antitype', clearly distinguishes[10] the visible bread and wine from the spiritual nourishment they convey.

It must not be supposed, of course, that this 'symbolical'

---

[1] *Euchol.* 13, 12-14 (Funk, II, 174).
[2] *De solemn. pasch.* 7.
[3] *Dem. ev.* I, 10, 39; 8, 1, 380.
[4] Frg. 2 (PG 18, 685).
[5] *Cat.* 22, 9; 23, 20.   [6] Ib. 22, 3.
[7] *Or.* 45, 19.
[8] Ib. 8, 18.   [9] *Hom.* 27, 17.
[10] *Ad Serap.* 4, 19.

language implied that the bread and wine were regarded as mere pointers to, or tokens of, absent realities. Rather were they accepted as signs of realities which were somehow actually present though apprehended by faith alone. For a truly spiritualizing interpretation we must look to the heirs of the Origenist tradition. Eusebius of Caesarea, for example, while usually content with the 'symbolical' doctrine, is also prepared to deduce[1] from *John* 6 that what our Lord said about eating His flesh and drinking His blood must be understood in a spiritual sense. The flesh and blood which He required His disciples to eat and drink were not His physical flesh and blood, but rather His teaching. Evagrius Ponticus echoes this approach when he writes,[2] 'We eat His flesh and drink His blood, becoming partakers through the incarnation both of the sensible life of the Word and of His wisdom. For by the terms "flesh" and "blood" He both denoted the whole of His mystic sojourning on earth, and pointed to His teaching, consisting as it did of practical, natural and theological insights.'

Almost everywhere, however, this conception of the sacrament was yielding ground to the more popular, vividly materialist theory which regarded the elements as being converted into the Lord's body and blood. A good example is furnished by a fragment[3] attributed to Athanasius: 'You will see the levites bringing loaves and a cup of wine, and placing them on the table. So long as the prayers and invocations have not yet been made, it is mere bread and a mere cup. But when the great and wondrous prayers have been recited, then the bread becomes the body and the cup the blood of our Lord Jesus Christ. . . . When the great prayers and holy supplications are sent up, the Word descends on the bread and the cup, and it becomes His body.' Cyril of Jerusalem argues[4] that we become 'of one body and one blood with Christ', citing *1 Cor.* 11, 23-5 to prove his point; for since He Himself has said, 'This is my body, this is my blood', who can doubt that the bread and the wine are truly His body and blood? But he goes further,

---

[1] *Eccl. theol.* 3, 12.   [2] Basil, *ep.* 8, 4.
[3] Frg. *ex serm. ad baptiz.* (PG 26, 1325).   [4] *Cat.* 22, 1.

attempting to explain the nature of the effect of the consecrating words on the elements. He uses[1] the verb 'change' or 'convert' (μεταβάλλειν), pointing out that, since Christ transformed water into wine, which after all is akin to blood, at Cana, there can be no reason to doubt a similar miracle on the more august occasion of the eucharistic banquet. The explanation he gives[2] is that, in response to the celebrant's prayer, God sends the Holy Spirit on the oblations so as to make them Christ's body and blood, for whatever the Spirit touches is sanctified and transformed (μεταβέβληται). The idea of conversion was taken up by Gregory of Nyssa, who expounds[3] it in a striking way of his own in an attempt to solve the problem how Christ's unique body, which is distributed daily to thousands of the faithful, can be received in its entirety by each communicant while remaining entire in itself. His theory is to the effect that, when the Word incarnate nourished Himself with bread and wine, He assimilated them to His flesh and blood. Thus they were transformed into the nature of His body. What happens now in the eucharist is analogous, although with a characteristic difference. Whereas in the days of Christ's earthly sojourning bread and wine were transformed by the digestive process, now they are metamorphosed instantaneously into the body of the Word. We should observe that he describes 'the nature of the visible objects' as being 'transelemented' (μετασοιχειώσας). What he envisages would seem to be an alteration in the relation of the constituent elements (στοιχεῖα) of the bread and wine, as a result of which they acquire the 'form' (εἶδος) of the Lord's body and blood, and corresponding properties.

Other writers did not follow Gregory in his speculative attempts to elucidate the manner of the change, but from this time onwards the language of conversion became regular in the East. Gregory Nazianzen speaks[4] of the priest calling down the divine Word and, using his voice as a knife, cleaving asunder the Saviour's body and blood. While admitting[5] that the

---

[1] Ib. 22, 2.   [2] Ib. 23, 7.   [3] Or. cat. 37.
[4] Ep. 171.   [5] In Matt. hom. 82, 4.

spiritual gift can be apprehended only by the eyes of the mind and not by sense, Chrysostom exploits the materialist implications of the conversion theory to the full. He speaks[1] of eating Christ, even of burying one's teeth in His flesh. The wine in the chalice is identically that which flowed from His pierced side, the body which the communicant receives is identically that which was scourged and nailed to the cross.[2] Thus the elements have undergone a change, and Chrysostom describes[3] them as being refashioned (μεταρρυθμίζειν) or transformed (μετασκευάζειν). In the fifth century conversionist views were taken for granted by Alexandrians and Antiochenes alike. According to Cyril,[4] Christ's words at the Last Supper, 'This is my body, this is my blood', indicate that the visible objects are not types or symbols (evidently he understands these words in a negative sense), but have been transformed (μεταποιεῖσθαι) through God's ineffable power into His body and blood. Elsewhere[5] he remarks that God 'infuses life-giving power into the oblations and transmutes them (μεθίστησιν αὐτά) into the virtue of His own flesh'. Theodore of Mopsuestia argued[6] very similarly that 'He did not say, "This is the symbol of my body", and, "This is the symbol of my blood", but, "This is my body and my blood", thereby instructing us not to look to the nature of the oblations, for that has been changed, by the eucharistic prayer, into flesh and blood'. Nestorius, too, contended[7] that what we receive in the eucharist is Christ's body and blood, which are of one substance with our own. Both Nestorius and Cyril were thus agreed that there is a real conversion; what divided them, as we have seen,[8] was the latter's insistence that on Nestorius's principles the eucharistic flesh could not be life-giving, suffused with the energy of the Word, but could only be the flesh of an individual man. Obviously, however, the conversion theory lent itself to exploitation at the hands of monophysites, some of whom concluded[9] that the

---

[1] *In Ioh. hom.* 46, 3.   [2] *In 1 Cor. hom.* 24, 1-4.
[3] *In prod. Iud. hom.* 1, 6; *in Matt. hom.* 82, 5.   [4] *In Matt.* 26, 27.
[5] *In Luc.* 22, 19.   [6] *In Matt.* 26, 26 (PG 66, 713): cf. *cat.* 6.
[7] *Heracl.* 39 (Nau).   [8] See above, p. 318.
[9] Cf. Theodoret, *eran.* 2 (PG 83, 168).

bread and wine were changed into a different substance after the epiclesis just as the Lord's body was transformed into His divinity after His ascension. Hence we are not surprised to find the moderate Antiochene, Theodoret, leading a reaction against it. It is not the case, he urged,[1] that after the consecration the oblations lose their proper nature: 'they remain in their former substance, appearance and form, visible and tangible as before'. Since he admitted, however, that the bread was now called body and habitually used realistic language of the sacrament, he was faced with the problem of explaining what the consecration effected. His explanation[2] was that, while a change (μεταβολή) certainly took place, it did not consist in the transformation of the substance of bread and wine into that of Christ's body and blood, but rather in their being made the vehicles of divine grace. As he put it, in designating them His body and blood Christ did not change their nature, but added grace to their nature. This was in effect a dyophysite theory of the eucharist parallel to his Christological theory, since the bread and wine were thought of both as remaining in their own nature and as being able to mediate the nature of the Lord's body and blood.

In the West the conception of the eucharistic gifts as symbols continued in vogue in this period. The canon of the mass in the Ambrosian *De sacramentis*, which dates from the fourth century, may be taken as an illustration. This is an imitation of the Last Supper, in word and act, solemnly performed before God, and the repetition of the Lord's words is regarded as establishing the sacramental association of the bread and wine with the divine realities they represent. So the oblation is 'a figure (*figura*) of the body and blood of our Lord Jesus Christ'.[3] According to Jerome, the wine in the chalice is 'the type (*typus*) of His blood',[4] and the eucharistic mystery is 'the type of His passion' (*in typum suae passionis*[5]). In the consecrated bread the Saviour's body 'is shown forth' (*ostenditur*); by means of the elements He 'represents' (*repraesentat*) His body

---

[1] Loc. cit.   [2] Op. cit. 1 (PG 83, 53-6).
[3] Cf. *de sacram.* 4, 21.   [4] *In Ierem.* 3, 10.   [5] *Adv. Iovin.* 2, 17.

and blood.[1] Ambrosiaster similarly states[2] that 'we receive the mystic chalice as a type' (*in typum*) of the divine blood, and Hilary[3] that 'we veritably consume the flesh of His body under a mystery'. About this time, however, through the agency of Ambrose, the idea of the conversion of the elements was being introduced into the West. Thus he remarks[4] that 'through the mystery of the sacred prayer they are transformed into flesh and blood'. The word he employs (*transfigurantur*), as Tertullian had pointed out[5] long before, connotes the actual change of something from what it previously was to a fresh mode of being. Ambrose does not discard, it should be noted, older forms of expression, and can speak of Christ's body as being 'signified' (*corpus significatur*) by the bread and of the wine being 'called' (*nuncupatur*) His blood after the consecration.[6] The sacrament is received 'in a likeness' (*in similitudinem*), but conveys the virtue of the reality it represents.[7] It is the conversion idea, however, which is most characteristic of his teaching. The consecration, he argues,[8] is a miracle of divine power analogous to the miracles recorded in the Bible; it effects an actual change in the elements (*species mutet elementorum*), being a quasi-creative act which alters their natures (cf. *mutare naturas*) into something which they were not before.

If Ambrose's influence helped to mediate the doctrine of a physical change to the West, that of Augustine was exerted in a rather different direction. His thought about the eucharist, unsystematic and many-sided as it is, is tantalizingly difficult to assess. Some, like F. Loofs, have classified him as the exponent of a purely symbolical doctrine; while A. Harnack seized upon the Christian's incorporation into Christ's mystical body, the Church, as the core of his sacramental teaching. Others have attributed receptionist views to him. There are certainly passages in his writings which give a superficial justification to all these interpretations, but a balanced verdict must agree that he accepted the current realism. Thus, preaching on 'the sacra-

---

[1] *Ep.* 98, 13; *in Marc.* 14, 17 f.; *in Matt.* 26, 26.   [2] *In 1 Cor.* 11, 26.
[3] *De trin.* 8, 13.   [4] *De fid.* 4, 124.   [5] *C. Prax.* 27, 7.
[6] *De myst.* 54.   [7] *De sacram.* 6, 3.   [8] *De myst.* 51-3.

ment of the Lord's table' to newly baptized persons, he remarked,[1] 'That bread which you see on the altar, sanctified by
the Word of God, is Christ's body. That cup, or rather the
contents of that cup, sanctified by the word of God, is Christ's
blood. By these elements the Lord Christ willed to convey His
body and His blood, which He shed for us.' 'You know', he
said in another sermon,[2] 'what you are eating and what you are
drinking, or rather, Whom you are eating and Whom you are
drinking.' Commenting on the Psalmist's bidding that we
should adore the footstool of His feet, he pointed out[3] that this
must be the earth. But since to adore the earth would be
blasphemous, he concluded that the word must mysteriously
signify the flesh which Christ took from the earth and which
He gave to us to eat. Thus it was the eucharistic body which
demanded adoration. Again, he explained[4] the sentence, 'He
was carried in his hands' (LXX of 1 Sam. 21, 13), which in the
original describes David's attempt to allay Achish's suspicions,
as referring to the sacrament: 'Christ was carried in His
hands when He offered His very body and said, "This is my
body"'.

One could multiply texts like these which show Augustine
taking for granted the traditional identification of the elements
with the sacred body and blood. There can be no doubt that he
shared the realism held by almost all his contemporaries and
predecessors. It is true that his thought passes easily from
Christ's sacramental to His mystical body. It does so, first,
because the consecrated bread and wine themselves, composed
as they are of a multitude of once separated grains of wheat and
grapes, are a manifest' symbol of unity;[5] and, secondly, in a
more profound sense, because the fact that the faithful participate in the eucharist is a sign of their membership of the
Church.[6] His controversy with the Donatists led him to emphasize this aspect, but it does not represent either the whole,
or even the most important part, of his teaching; in any case,

[1] *Serm.* 227.   [2] Ib. 9, 14.   [3] *Enarr. in ps.* 98, 9.
[4] Ib. 33, 1, 10.   [5] *Serm.* 272.
[6] Cf. ib.; *de civ. dei* 22, 10; *tract. in ev. Ioh.* 26, 13.

the two bodies, the mystical and the sacramental, remained distinct in his thought.[1] It is true, also, that he occasionally used language which, taken by itself, might suggest that he regarded the bread and wine as mere symbols of the body and blood. Thus, when the African bishop Boniface inquired how baptized children can be said to have faith, Augustine's reply[2] was to the effect that baptism itself was called faith (*fides*), and that current usage allowed one to designate the sign by the name of the thing signified. For example, although Christ was of course only slain once, it is proper to speak of Him as being slain daily in a sacramental sense. 'For if sacraments did not bear a certain resemblance to the things of which they are sacraments, they would not be sacraments. In most cases this resemblance results in their receiving the names of those things. So, just as the sacrament of Christ's body is after a certain fashion Christ's body, and the sacrament of His blood is after a certain fashion His blood, so the sacrament of faith is faith.' The argument here, however, presupposes Augustine's distinction between a sacrament as a sign and the reality, or *res*, of the sacrament to which reference has been made above.[3] Considered as physical, phenomenal objects, the bread and wine are properly *signs* of Christ's body and blood; if conventionally they are designated His body and blood, it must be admitted that they are not such straightforwardly but 'after a fashion'. On the other hand, in the eucharist there is both what one sees and what one believes; there is the physical object of perception, and the spiritual object apprehended by faith,[4] and it is the latter which feeds the soul. Even in the passage cited, Augustine's language is fully consistent with his recognition of its reality and actual presence.

This leads us to the vital question how he conceives of the eucharistic body. There is no suggestion in his writings of the conversion theory sponsored by Gregory of Nyssa and Ambrose; there is indeed no reason to suppose that he was acquainted with either the *Oratio catechetica* or the *De mysteriis*.

---

[1] See above, p. 413.   [2] *Ep.* 98, 9.   [3] See pp. 422 f.
[4] Cf. *serm.* 112, 5; *de doct. christ.* 3, 13.

His thought moves, as we should expect, much more along the lines laid down by Tertullian and Cyprian. For example, he can speak[1] of 'the banquet in which He presented and handed down to His disciples the figure (*figuram*) of His body and blood'. But he goes further than his predecessors in formulating a doctrine which, while realist through and through, is also frankly spiritualizing. In the first place, he makes it clear that the body consumed in the eucharist is not strictly identical with Christ's historical body, and represents[2] Him as saying, 'You must understand what I have said in a spiritual sense. You are not going to eat this body which you see or drink that blood which those who will crucify me are going to shed.' The historical body ascended in its integrity to heaven.[3] In any case, the eucharistic flesh is not like 'flesh rent asunder in a corpse or sold in the meat-market'.[4] This crude idea was characteristic of the Capharnaites. Secondly, and more positively, the gift which the eucharist conveys is a gift of life. This is a spiritual gift, and the eating and drinking are spiritual processes.[5] The eucharistic body is not the sensible flesh; rather we receive the essence of this flesh, viz. the spirit which quickens it.[6] Sometimes he carries this spiritualizing tendency to its limits, as when he says,[7] 'Why make ready your teeth and your belly? Believe, and you have eaten'; or again,[8] 'To believe in Him is to eat living bread. He Who believes eats, and is invisibly filled, because he is reborn invisibly.' His real point, however, is that Christ's body and blood are not consumed physically and materially; what is consumed in this way is the bread and wine. The body and blood are veritably received by the communicant, but are received sacramentally or, as one might express it, *in figura*.

6. *The Eucharistic Sacrifice*

During this period, as we might expect, the eucharist was regarded without question as the Christian sacrifice. But before

---

[1] *Enarr. in ps.* 3, 1. [2] *Ib.* 98, 9.
[3] *Serm.* 131, 1; *tract. in ev. Ioh.* 27, 5. [4] *Tract. in ev. Ioh.* 27, 5.
[5] *Serm.* 131, 1. [6] *Tract. in ev. Ioh.* 27, 5. [7] *Ib.* 25, 12.
[8] *Ib.* 26, 1.

we probe the ideas involved in this, we must glance at the
effects which communion was supposed to have on individual
communicants. The general belief may be summed up by saying that anyone who partook by faith was held to be united and
assimilated to Christ, and so to God. Hilary, for example,
argues[1] that, since he receives Christ's veritable flesh, the
Saviour must be reckoned to abide in him; hence he becomes
one with Christ, and through Him with the Father. He is thus
enabled to live here below the divine life which Christ came
from heaven to give to men.[2] Ambrose writes[3] similarly, 'Forasmuch as one and the same Lord Jesus Christ possesses Godhead
and a human body, you who receive His flesh are made to
participate through that nourishment in His divine substance'.
Both these theologians teach[4] that among the fruits of communion are the gift of eternal life, the remission of sins, and
the imparting of heavenly joy. We have already examined[5] the
place occupied by incorporation in Christ's mystical body in
Augustine's eucharistic thought. According to Cyril of Jerusalem,[6] 'We become Christ-bearers, since His body and blood
are distributed throughout our limbs. So, as blessed Peter expressed it, we are made partakers of the divine nature.' The
essence of communion, states[7] John Chrysostom, is the uniting
of the communicants with Christ, and so with one another:
'the union is complete, and eliminates all separation'.[8] Thus
'we feed on Him at Whom angels gaze with trembling. . . .
We are mingled with Him, and become one body and one
flesh with Christ.'[9] In Theodore's view[10] the consecrated bread
and wine have the power of conveying immortality.

In short, the eucharist for the fathers was the chief instrument of the Christian's divinization; through it Christ's
mystical body was built up and sustained. We must now consider how they understood 'the bloodless sacrifice' celebrated
by means of the 'symbols' of Christ's body and blood in com-

---

[1] *De trin.* 8, 13.   [2] Ib. 8, 15-17.   [3] *De sacram.* 6, 4.
[4] E.g. Hilary, *tract. in ps.* 127, 10; Ambrose, *de ben. patriarch.* 39; *in Luc.* 10,
49; *de sacram.* 5, 14-17.   [5] See above, p. 447.   [6] *Cat.* 22, 3.
[7] *In 1 Cor. hom.* 24, 2.   [8] *In 1 Tim. hom.* 15, 4.
[9] *In Matt. hom.* 82, 5.   [10] *Hom. cat.* 18, passim.

memoration of His death.[1] While much of the language they use is conventional, we find an elaborate statement of the sacrificial aspect in Cyril of Jerusalem. In agreement with tradition he speaks[2] of it as 'the spiritual sacrifice' and 'the unbloody service', but he also describes[3] it as 'the holy and most awful sacrifice' and 'the sacrifice of propitiation' ($\tau\hat{\eta}s$ $\theta\upsilon\sigma\acute{\iota}as$ ... $\tau o\hat{\upsilon}$ $\acute{\iota}\lambda a\sigma\mu o\hat{\upsilon}$), in the presence of which God is entreated for the peace of the churches and our earthly needs generally. Indeed, intercession may be offered for the dead as well as the living while the dread victim lies before us, for what we offer is 'Christ slain on behalf of our sins, propitiating the merciful God on behalf both of them and of ourselves'. Later in the century Chrysostom develops Cyril's teaching, referring[4] to 'the most awesome sacrifice' ($\tau\grave{\eta}\nu$ $\phi\rho\iota\kappa\omega\delta\epsilon\sigma\tau\acute{a}\tau\eta\nu$ ... $\theta\upsilon\sigma\acute{\iota}a\nu$), and to 'the Lord sacrificed and lying there, and the priest bending over the sacrifice and interceding'.[5] He makes the important point[6] that the sacrifice now offered on the altar is identical with the one which the Lord Himself offered at the Last Supper. He emphasizes this doctrine of the uniqueness of the sacrifice in commenting[7] on the statement in *Hebrews* that Christ offered Himself once: 'Do we not offer sacrifice daily? We do indeed, but as a memorial of His death, and this oblation is single, not manifold. But how can it be one and not many? Because it has been offered once for all, as was the ancient sacrifice in the holy of holies. This is the figure of that ancient sacrifice, as indeed it was of this one; for it is the same Jesus Christ we offer always, not now one victim and later another. The victim is always the same, so that the sacrifice is one. Are we going to say that, because Christ is offered in many places, there are many Christs? Of course not. It is one and the same Christ everywhere; He is here in His entirety and there in His entirety, one unique body. Just as He is one body, not many bodies, although offered in many places, so the sacrifice is one and the same. Our highpriest is the very same Christ Who has offered the sacrifice

---

[1] *Apost. constit.* 6, 23, 5 (Funk, I, 361).   [2] *Cat.* 23, 8-10.
[3] Loc. cit.   [4] *De sacerdot.* 6, 4.   [5] Ib. 3, 4.
[6] *In 2 Tim. hom.* 2, 4.   [7] *In Hebr. hom.* 17, 3.

which cleanses us. The victim Who was offered then, Who cannot be consumed, is the self-same victim we offer now. What we do is done as a memorial of what was done then. . . . We do not offer a different sacrifice, but always the same one, or rather we accomplish the memorial of it.' Christ 'offered sacrifice once for all, and thenceforth sat down', and the whole action of the eucharist takes place in the heavenly, spiritual sphere;[1] the earthly celebration is a showing forth of it on the terrestrial plane.

Gregory of Nazianzus also brought the eucharistic action into close relation with the Lord's redemptive death. It was, he thought,[2] an outward (cf. τὴν ἔξω) sacrifice which represented as antitype the mystery of Christ's offering on the cross. In a similar strain Theodore taught[3] that the sacrifice of the new covenant was a memorial of the one true oblation, an image or representation of the eternal liturgy which is celebrated in heaven, where Christ, our high-priest and intercessor, now fulfils His ministry. What He offers to the Father in the eucharist is His very self, once delivered to death on behalf of us all. In Theodoret[4] the emphasis is rather on the mystical body; in the eucharist Christ 'does not offer Himself, but rather as the Head of those who offer, inasmuch as He calls the Church His body, and through it exercises His priesthood as man and as God receives what is offered'. He, too, solves[5] the paradox of the uniqueness of Christ's sacrifice and the multiplicity of the Church's offerings by pointing out that in the latter 'we do not offer another sacrifice, but accomplish the memorial (μνήμην) of that unique and saving one . . . so that in contemplation we recall the figure of the sufferings endured for us'. As regards the effects of the eucharist, all the Eastern writers agree that it is a sacrifice of praise and thanksgiving to God for His measureless benefits, and especially for that of our redemption. It is also, however, as Cyril of Jerusalem had indicated, a propitiatory sacrifice for the dead as well as the living. 'It is not in vain', remarked[6] Chrysostom, 'that we commemorate those who

---

[1] *In Hebr. hom.* 13, 1; 14, 1.   [2] *Or.* 2, 95.
[3] *Hom. cat.* 15, 15 f.   [4] *In ps.* 109, 4.   [5] *In Hebr.* 8, 4 f.
[6] *In 1 Cor. hom.* 41, 4.

have gone from us at the divine mysteries and intercede for them, entreating the Lamb Who lies before us and Who bore the sin of the world.'

Western writers before Augustine have little to contribute to the theory of the eucharistic sacrifice, although all of them naturally take it for granted. Hilary, for example, describes[1] the Christian altar as 'a table of sacrifice', and speaks[2] of 'the sacrifice of thanksgiving and praise' which has replaced the bloody victims of olden days, and of the immolation of the paschal lamb made under the new law. According to Jerome,[3] the dignity of the eucharistic liturgy derives from its association with the passion; it is no empty memorial, for the victim of the Church's daily sacrifice is the Saviour Himself.[4] Ambrose's teaching is rather more explicit. It comes out in such a passage as this:[5] 'Now we see good things in an image, and hold fast to the good things of the image. We have seen the chief of the priests coming to us; we have seen and heard Him offering His blood for us. We who are priests imitate Him as best we can, offering sacrifice for the people, admittedly feeble in merit but made honourable through that sacrifice. For even though Christ no longer seems to be offering sacrifice, nevertheless He Himself is offered in the world wherever Christ's body is offered. Indeed He is shown to be offering in us, since it is His word which sanctifies the sacrifice which we offer.' Externally viewed, this oblation consists in the repetition by the priest of Christ's efficacious words;[6] but internally it consists in His perpetual intercession for us before the Father, 'offering His death on behalf of us all'.[7] With this conception of the eucharist as the earthly representation of Christ's eternal self-offering in the heavenly places is conjoined the suggestion[8] that He is also immolated on the altar, so that what we receive in communion is the paschal lamb slain on the cross. Ambrose further teaches[9] that the sacrifice of the altar is an efficacious one, for just as Christ offered Himself veritably on Calvary to procure the

---

[1] *Tract. in ps.* 68, 19.   [2] Ib. 68, 26.   [3] *Ep.* 114, 2.
[4] Ib. 21, 26.   [5] *Enarr. in ps.* 38, 25.   [6] Cf. *de myst.* 54.
[7] *Enarr. in ps.* 39, 8: cf. ib. 38, 25.
[8] *In Luc.* 1, 28; *enarr. in ps.* 43, 36.   [9] *De offic. min.* 1, 238.

remission of sins, so in the eucharist He offers Himself *in imagine* to obtain the same end.

Augustine's conception of the eucharistic sacrifice is closely linked with his ideas on sacrifice in general. 'A true sacrifice', he writes,[1] 'is whatever work is accomplished with the object of establishing our holy union with God'. Essentially it is an interior transaction of the will, and what is conventionally termed the sacrifice is the outward sign of this: 'the visible sacrifice is the sacrament, i.e. the sacred symbol (*sacrum signum*), of the invisible sacrifice'.[2] The supreme and uniquely pure sacrifice, of course, is the offering of Himself which the Redeemer made on Calvary.[3] This is the sacrifice which all the sacrifices of the Jewish Law foreshadowed; it is the memorial of it that Christians celebrate to-day in the eucharist.[4] 'This sacrifice', he remarks,[5] 'succeeded all those sacrifices of the Old Testament, which were slaughtered in anticipation of what was to come. . . . For instead of all those sacrifices and oblations His body is offered, and is distributed to the participants.' The Christian supper presupposes the death on the cross.[6] The self-same Christ Who was slain there is in a real sense slaughtered daily by the faithful, so that the sacrifice which was offered once for all in bloody form is sacramentally renewed upon our altars with the oblation of His body and blood.[7] From this it is clear that, if the eucharistic sacrifice is essentially a 'similitude' or 'memorial' of Calvary, it includes much more than that. In the first place, it involves a real, though sacramental, offering of Christ's body and blood; He is Himself the priest, but also the oblation.[8] In the second place, however, along with this oblation of the Head, it involves the offering of His members, since the fruit of the sacrifice is, precisely, their union in His mystical body. As Augustine puts it,[9] 'The whole redeemed community, that is, the congregation and society of saints, is the universal sacrifice offered to God through the great high-priest, Who offered Himself in His passion for us, so that we might be the

[1] *De civ. dei* 10, 6.   [2] Ib. 10, 5.   [3] E.g. *enarr. in ps.* 149, 6.
[4] *C. Faust.* 6, 5; 20, 18.   [5] *De civ. dei* 17, 20, 2.
[6] *Serm.* 112, 1.   [7] *Ep.* 98, 9: cf. *c. Faust.* 20, 18; 20 21.
[8] *De civ. dei* 10, 20.   [9] Ib. 10, 6.

body of so great a Head. . . . When then the Apostle exhorted us to present our bodies as a living victim . . . this is the sacrifice of Christians: we who are many are one body in Christ. The Church celebrates it in the sacrament of the altar which is so familiar to the faithful, in which is shown that in what she offers she herself is offered.' Or again:[1] 'The most splendid and excellent sacrifice consists of ourselves, His people. This is the sacrifice the mystery whereof we celebrate in our oblation.'

Ib. 19, 23, 5.

NOTE ON BOOKS

Baptism and Confirmation. A. d'Alès, *Baptême et confirmation* (Paris, 1928; Eng. trans., 1929); B. Neunheuser, *Baptême et confirmation* (Paris, 1966); D. Stone, *Holy Baptism* (London, 4 ed. 1905); G. W. H. Lampe, *The Seal of the Spirit* (London, 2 ed. 1967); A. J. Mason, *The Relation of Confirmation to Baptism* (London, 2 ed. 1893).

Penance. É. Amann, 'Pénitence' (art. in *Dict. Théol. Cath.*); P. Galtier, *L'Église et la rémission des péchés* (Paris, 1932); R. C. Mortimer, *The Origins of Private Penance in the Western Church* (Oxford, 1939); B. Poschmann, *Die abendländische Kirchenbusse* (Munich, 1928); *La Pénitence et l'onction des malades* (Fr. trans., Paris, 1966); O. D. Watkins, *A History of Penance* (London, 1920).

Eucharist. K. Adam, *Die Eucharistielehre des hl. Augustins* (Augsburg, 1908); P. Batiffol, *L'Eucharistie: la présence réelle* (Paris, 1905); J. Betz, *Die Eucharistie in der Zeit der Griechischen Väter* (Freiburg, 1955); P. T. Camelot, 'Réalisme et symbolisme dans la doctrine eucharistique de s. Augustin' (art. in *Rev. sc. phil. et théol.*, 1947); G. Dix, *The Shape of the Liturgy* (London, 1945); H. M. Féret, 'Sacramentum—res dans la langue théologique de S. Augustin' (art. in *Rev. sc. phil. et théol.*, 29, 1940); A. Gaudel, 'Messe: le sacrifice de la messe dans l'Église latine' (art. in *Dict. Théol. Cath.*); C. Gore, *The Body of Christ* (London, 1901); F. Kattenbusch, 'Messe' (art. in Hauck's *Realencyk.*); J. H. Srawley, 'Eucharist (to the end of the Middle Ages)' (art. in Hastings' *Encyc. Relig. Eth.*); D. Stone, *A History of the Doctrine of the Holy Eucharist* (London, 1909).

PART IV

EPILOGUE

CHAPTER XVII

THE CHRISTIAN HOPE

I. *The Tension in Eschatology*

FROM the beginning there has been a twofold emphasis in the Christian doctrine of the last things. While stressing the reality and completeness of present salvation, it has pointed believers to certain great eschatological events located in the future. So in the apostolic age, as the New Testament documents reveal, the Church was pervaded with an intense conviction that the hope to which Israel had looked forward yearningly had at last been fulfilled. In the coming of Christ, and in His death and resurrection, God had acted decisively, visiting and redeeming His people. He had 'delivered us out of the power of darkness and translated us into the kingdom of the Son of His love'.[1] Christians now shared by anticipation in Christ's risen life through the indwelling of the Spirit, and had already 'tasted . . . the powers of the age to come'.[2] In other words, history had reached its climax and the reign of God, as so many of our Lord's parables imply, had been effectively inaugurated. Interwoven, however, with this 'realized eschatology' (to use the iargon of modern scholarship) was an equally vivid expectation that the wonderful outpouring of grace so far accomplished was only the beginning and would in due course, indeed shortly, receive its dramatic completion. The Lord Who had been exalted to God's right hand would return on clouds of glory to consummate the new age, the dead would be raised and a final judgment enacted, and the whole created order would be reconciled to God. The Christian hope, as delineated by the Biblical writers, was thus a twofold consciousness of blessedness here and now in this time of waiting, and blessedness

[1] *Col.* 1, 13.　　[2] *Hebr.* 6, 5.

yet to come; and the final denouement was conceived realistic-
ally as a series of events to be carried out by God on the plane
of history.

Although our chief concern in this chapter will be with the
futurist elements in this eschatological faith, a word must be
said about its other and, in some ways, more characteristic
aspect. It is not infrequently alleged that after the first generation Christianity underwent a radical transformation. The assurance of living in the Messianic age and enjoying the first-
fruits of the Spirit, so powerfully evident in the Epistles, is held
to have yielded place to the conception of God's kingdom as a
region or state, located exclusively in the future, which is reserved as a prize for those who have struggled manfully in this
life. Here and there traces of this weakened consciousness of
God's present redemptive action undeniably appear, along with
the implied alteration in the eschatological perspective. Clement
of Rome, for example, speaks[1] of St. Peter and St. Paul, and
other nameless Christians as well, being granted a place in
heaven as a reward for the trials they endured on earth; while
for the author of 2 Clement[2] entrance into the kingdom is
earned by good works and charity. Justin, too, regards[3] the
kingdom of heaven as a prize for virtuous conduct to be
obtained after death; its blessings will be enjoyed by those 'who
have lived in accord with Christ's splendid precepts'.[4] In a
similar strain Tertullian represents[5] Christ as having proclaimed a new law and a new promise of the kingdom of
heaven; He will come again in glory to conduct His saints to
the enjoyment of eternal life and of the heavenly benefits in
store for them. In thought of this type the Christian's confident
and joyous assurance that the age to come has already broken
into the present age has faded into the background. He looks
upon God, not as the divine Father to Whom he has free
access, but as the sternly just distributor of rewards and penalties,
while grace has lost the primarily eschatological character it
had in the New Testament and has become something to be

[1] *Ad Cor.* 5 f.   [2] 9: cf. 6.   [3] *Dial.* 117, 3.
[4] *1 apol.* 14, 3.   [5] *De praescr.* 13.

acquired. It is unnecessary to multiply instances, for the temptation to degenerate into a pedestrian moralism in which the 'realized' element in its authentic eschatology finds no place was one to which Christianity was as much exposed in the patristic as in every other age.

Nevertheless it is misleading to concentrate on such one-sided expressions of the Christian faith. In the early centuries, as indeed in other epochs, wherever religion was alive and healthy, the primitive conviction of enjoying already the benefits of the age to come was kept vividly before the believer's consciousness. In part this was the result of the Church's attachment to Scripture and the apostolic tradition, in which salvation was expounded in terms clearly suggesting that God had intervened once for all in human history. It was thus inevitable that the fathers, when interpreting their present experience of grace, should look back to those mighty acts of revelation as well as forward to the future climax which they foreshadowed. Even more decisive, however, were the doctrine and practice of the sacraments. 'In baptism', as a modern writer[1] has put it, 'the faithful receive the guarantee of the promised inheritance; they are sealed for the final redemption of soul and body at the Parousia. In the eucharist the eschatological bread of heaven is made available within the present order.' The account of the sacramental teaching of the early Church given in the preceding chapter supplied detailed illustrations of the ways in which these rites were regarded as imparting to Christians a foretaste of the blessedness in store for them. True enough, the resurrection and judgment, along with the Saviour's second coming, lay ahead in the temporal future. But already, through baptism, the faithful catechumen participated in the resurrection; he had died and risen again with Christ, and now lived the life of the Spirit.[2] The age of fulfilment had thus effectively dawned; and, as further proof of the fact, the new people of God were already feasting in the eucharist on the eschatological banquet prophesied by Isaiah

[1] G. W. H. Lampe (see Note on Books).
[2] E.g. Cyril Hieros., *cat.* 20, 5 f.

(cf. 25, 6¹), the banquet which Wisdom herself spread out.² By their incorporation into Christ they were enabled to enjoy, while still on earth, a foretaste of the supernatural life. So the tension characteristic of the New Testament remained, as it must always remain, a feature of the eschatology of authentic Christianity.

2. Second-century Conceptions

Four chief moments dominate the eschatological expectation of early Christian theology—the return of Christ, known as the Parousia, the resurrection, the judgment, and the catastrophic ending of the present world-order. In the primitive period they were held together in a naïve, unreflective fashion, with little or no attempt to work out their implications or solve the problems they raise.

We are living in the last times, writes[3] Ignatius; and according to Hermas[4] the tower, which in his symbolism signifies the Church, is nearing completion, and when it is finished the end will come. The hour of the Lord's appearing is uncertain, but it will be heralded by the manifestation of Antichrist disguised as God's Son.[5] 'Barnabas' is satisfied[6] that the scandal of the last days is actually upon us, and thinks[7] that the creation story in Genesis gives a clue to the timing of the Parousia. The six days of creation represent six thousand years, for Scripture reckons one day of the Lord as equal to a thousand years. The universe must therefore last six thousand years, of which the greater portion has already expired. When it is stated that God rested on the seventh day, the meaning is that Christ will appear at the beginning of the seventh millennium in order to dethrone the Lawless One, judge the ungodly and transform the sun, moon and stars. Even so, the precise date remains veiled, and in this the early writers are all agreed.[8] It is hardly a fair question whether they seriously expected the Lord to return in their

---

[1] Eusebius, dem. ev. 10, 31-3.
[2] Origen, comm. in Cant. 2, 4 (Baehrens, 185 f.); Cyprian, test. 2, 2.
[3] Eph. 11, 1: cf. Barn. 4, 9; 6, 13.   [4] Vis. 3, 8, 9.   [5] Did. 16.
[6] 4, 3; 4, 9; 21, 3.   [7] 15.
[8] Cf. did. 16, 1; 2 Clem. 12, 1; Hermas, vis. 3, 8, 9.

own lifetime, for their standpoint was not the empirical one of modern men. When He came, however, it would be in majesty and power, and He would be clothed in purple like a king.[1]

The Parousia will be preceded, states[2] the *Didache*, by the resurrection of the dead. The author appears to restrict this to the righteous (cf. οὐ πάντων δέ), but the normal teaching was that good and bad would alike rise. Ignatius cites[3] Christ's resurrection as a prototype of that of believers, and 'Barnabas' reproduces[4] the Pauline argument that the Saviour arose in order to abolish death and give proof of our resurrection. We should observe that both he and the author of *2 Clement* insist[5] on the necessity of our rising again in the self-same flesh we now possess, the idea being that we may receive the just requital of our deeds. Clement, too, teaches[6] that Christ's resurrection foreshadows ours, and is a pioneer in devising rational arguments, of a type later to become classic, to make the idea of a resurrection plausible. The transition from night to day, he urges, and the transformation of dry, decaying seeds into vigorous plants supply analogies from the natural order, as does the legend of the phoenix from pagan mythology; in any case it is consistent with divine omnipotence, and is abundantly prophesied in Scripture (e.g. *Pss.* 28, 7; 3, 6; 23, 4; *Job* 19, 26). The insistence of these writers is probably to be explained by the rejection of a real resurrection by Docetists and Gnostics, who, of course, refused to believe that material flesh could live on the eternal plane. Polycarp had them (or possibly Marcion) in mind when he roundly stated[7] that 'he who denies the resurrection and the judgment is the first-born of Satan'.

With the Parousia and resurrection, we notice, the judgment is closely linked, and the dogma that Christ will come again as 'judge of quick and dead' had already acquired the fixity of a formulary.[8] Here and there, it is true, there are hints of the idea of an individual judgment immediately after death. Clement, for example, speaks[9] of St. Peter and St. Paul as having

---

[1] *Barn.* 7, 9 f.: cf. *2 Clem.* 17, 5.   [2] 16, 6.   [3] *Trall.* 9, 2.
[4] 5, 6.   [5] Ib. 21, 1; *2 Clem.* 9, 1-4.   [6] *1 Clem.* 24-6.
[7] *Phil.* 7, 1.   [8] E.g. *Barn.* 7, 2; *2 Clem.* 1, 1; Polycarp, *Phil.* 2, 1.
[9] *1 Clem.* 5, 4-7; 6, 1; 50, 3.

departed straight to 'the holy place', finding there a great company of martyrs and saints 'made perfect in charity'; and the Smyrnaean elders know[1] that the dead Polycarp has already received 'the crown of immortality'. Generally, however, the judgment is conceived of as universal and in the future; God, Who sent His Son as Saviour, will send Him again as judge.[2] He will separate the good from the bad, and will sort out the confusion in which they have lived on earth.[3] 'Each will receive', writes[4] 'Barnabas', 'according to his deeds. If he be good, his righteousness will go before him; but if he be evil, the recompense of his evil is in store for him.' Destruction and death will be the lot of the wicked, the impenitent, false teachers, and those who have rejected God; they will perish eternally.[5] The righteous, on the other hand, have 'incorruptibility and life eternal' laid up for them;[6] their reward is 'life in immortality',[7] and they 'will be made manifest in the visitation of the kingdom of God'.[8] They will dwell with the angels, and will have ever-lasting joy to crown their sufferings and trials.[9] At the same time, according to *1 Clement*,[10] heaven and earth will melt away like lead melting in a furnace; while Hermas proclaims[11] that the present world must perish by blood and fire. The cosmic order as we know it must be transformed, and so made fit for God's elect.[12]

3. *The Development of Dogma*

About the middle of the second century Christian eschatology enters upon a new, rather more mature phase. The general pattern, indeed, remains unaltered, all the key ideas which form part of it being accepted without question. To take but a single example, Justin teaches[13] on the basis of Old Testament prophecy

---

[1] *Mart. Polyc.* 17, 1.   [2] *Ep. Diog.* 7, 5 f.
[3] *1 Clem.* 28, 1; *2 Clem.* 17, 4–7; Hermas, *sim.* 3; 4, 1–3; Polycarp, *Phil.* 7, 1 f.
[4] 4, 12.
[5] E.g. Hermas, *vis.* 3, 7, 2; *mand.* 12, 2; *sim.* 4, 4; 9, 18, 2; Ignatius, *Eph.* 16, 2.
[6] Ignatius, *Polyc.* 2, 3.   [7] *1 Clem.* 35, 2.   [8] Ib. 50, 3.
[9] Hermas, *vis.* 2, 2, 7; *sim.* 9, 27, 3; *2 Clem.* 5, 5; 7, 2 f.; 11, 5; 19, 4; 20, 2.
[10] 16, 3.   [11] *Vis.* 4, 3.   [12] Ib. 1, 3.
[13] *1 apol.* 52; *dial.* 40, 4; 45, 4; 49, 2; etc.

that, in addition to His coming in lowliness at His incarnation, Christ will come again in glory with the angelic host; the dead, both just and unjust, will be raised,[1] and in the general judgment which follows the former will receive an eternal reward, while the latter will be consigned, body and soul, to eternal fire and torment;[2] and a universal conflagration will bring the world to an end.[3] Theologians like Irenaeus, with his strongly Biblical bias, reproduce the same themes, though with appropriate embroidery. On the other hand, new emphases and fresh lines of thought begin to appear, partly for apologetic motives and partly as the result of growing speculation. The clash with Judaism and paganism made it imperative to set out the bases of the revealed dogmas more thoroughly. The Gnostic tendency to dissolve Christian eschatology into the myth of the soul's upward ascent and return to God had to be resisted. On the other hand millenarianism, or the theory that the returned Christ would reign on earth for a thousand years, came to find increasing support among Christian teachers.

We can observe these tendencies at work in the Apologists. Justin, as we have suggested, ransacks the Old Testament for proof, as against Jewish critics, that the Messiah must have a twofold coming. His argument[4] is that, while numerous contexts no doubt predict His coming in humiliation, there are others (e.g. *Is.* 53, 8-12; *Ezek.* 7 f.; *Dan.* 7, 9-28; *Zech.* 12, 10-12; *Ps.* 72, 1-20; 110, 1-7) which clearly presuppose His coming in majesty and power. The former coming was enacted at the incarnation, but the latter still lies in the future. It will take place, he suggests,[5] at Jerusalem, where Christ will be recognized by the Jews who dishonoured Him as the sacrifice which avails for all penitent sinners, and where He will eat and drink with His disciples; and He will reign there a thousand years. This millenarian, or 'chiliastic', doctrine was widely popular at this time. 'Barnabas' had taught[6] that the Son of God, appearing at the beginning of the seventh millennium,

---

[1] *Dial.* 80, 5; 81, 4.
[2] Ib. 45, 4; 120, 5 f.; *1 apol.* 8; 28.
[3] *1 apol.* 45; 60; *2 apol.* 7.
[4] *1 apol.* 50-2; *dial.* 14; 31; 32; 34.
[5] *Dial.* 40; 51.
[6] 15, 4-9.

would reign with the just until a new universe was called into
existence at the commencement of the eighth; and the heretic
Cerinthus had expatiated[1] on the material, sensual enjoyments
with which the saints would be rewarded in Christ's earthly
kingdom. Papias looked forward[2] with wide-eyed wonder-
ment to the literal fulfilment in that epoch of the Old Testament prophecies of unprecedented fertility of field and vineyard.
Justin writes[3] in a kindred strain of the idyllic millennium, when
Jerusalem will be rebuilt and enlarged and Christians, along
with the patriarchs and prophets, will dwell there with Christ
in perfect felicity. He confesses that he knows pious, pure-
minded Christians who do not share this belief, but like others
he considers it plainly authorized by the predictions of Isaiah,
Zechariah and the prophets, not to mention *Revelation*, and it
clearly counts in his eyes as an unquestioned article of orthodoxy.

In treating of the resurrection the Apologists stress its reasonableness. Justin, for example, after appealing to the truth that
nothing is beyond God's power, finds[4] an analogy to it in the
way in which the human sperm develops into a living body,
complete with flesh and bones; while for Tatian[5] and Theophilus[6] the resuscitation of a dead man is no whit more marvel-
lous than his original coming into existence out of inanimate
matter. Athenagoras argues[7] that the idea of God's raising the
dead conflicts in no way with His knowledge, His power or His
justice. A resurrection is indeed logically demanded by the fact
that man is a composite being made up of body and soul; since
the end God has assigned him is plainly unattainable in this
world, a future life is necessary, and body as well as soul must
participate in it.[8] He presupposes the idea of a natural immortality, thinking that God created man to live for ever.[9] The
Apologists generally, in spite of a good deal of confusion, are
on their guard[10] against the current Platonic theory of immortality, with its assumption that the soul is increate in contrast to the Christian dogma that it has been brought into being

[1] Cf. Eusebius, *hist. eccl.* 3, 28, 2; 7, 25, 2 f.
[2] Cf. Irenaeus, *haer.* 5, 33, 3 f.   [3] *Dial.* 80 f.   [4] *1 apol.* 18 f.
[5] *Or. ad Graec.* 6.   [6] *Ad Autol.* 1, 8.   [7] *De resurr.* 1-10.
[8] Ib. 18-25.   [9] Ib. 12 f.   [10] E.g. Justin, *dial.* 5.

by the divine fiat. In a similar way, in order to rebut objections to the last judgment, they point to[1] parallels in pagan mythology. Further, since they desire to combat fatalism, they insist strongly on free will and responsibility, deducing[2] from them the reasonableness of a system of rewards and penalties. In the last resort, however, they justify this article by the theodicy implied in Theophilus's dictum,[3] 'When I call Him Lord, I call Him judge'. What they have in mind, like their predecessors, is usually the general judgment at the Parousia, but Justin seems to allow[4] for a particular judgment at death which assigns the souls of the righteous to a more comfortable, and those of the wicked to a less comfortable, place of waiting.

The great theologians who followed the Apologists, Irenaeus, Tertullian and Hippolytus, were primarily concerned to defend the traditional eschatological scheme against Gnosticism. The monotonous thesis of the latter was that, matter being intrinsically evil, the flesh could not participate in salvation, which must therefore be the prerogative of the soul;[5] and so, if the resurrection is a fact, it must be an exclusively spiritual one, consisting in the illumination of the mind by the truth.[6] Imprisoned in the body, the soul alone is saved; and the characteristic terms used by Gnostic teachers were those which expressed its return to the Pleroma[7]—ἀνατρέχειν, ἀναδραμεῖν, ascendere, resipere.[8] Against this Irenaeus vigorously affirms that the realm of bodies is subject to the Word, and that salvation must affect the entire man, body as well as soul.[9] God's power must be sufficient to effect the resurrection, seeing that He formed man's body in the beginning.[10] Being superior to nature, He has the might, and since He is good He has the will; and it accords with His justice that the body which cooperated with the soul in well-being should be conjoined with it in its reward.[11] Further, Christ's rejoinder to the Sadducees plainly

---

[1] E.g. Justin, 1 apol. 8, 4; Theophilus, ad Autol. 2, 36-8.
[2] E.g. Justin, 1 apol. 57; 2 apol. 7; 9; dial. 141. [3] Ad Autol. 1, 3.
[4] Dial. 5, 3.   [5] Eg. Irenaeus, haer. 1, 6, 2; 1, 27, 3; 5, 1, 2.
[6] Id. 2, 31, 2.   [7] See above, pp. 23 f.
[8] Id. 1, 30, 3; 2, 12, 4; Clement Alex., paed. 1, 6, 32, 1; Hippolytus, c. Noet. 11.   [9] Haer. 5, 2, 2 f.; 5, 20, 1.
[10] Ib. 5, 3, 2.   [11] Ib. 2, 29, 2.

implies the resurrection of the body;[1] and the cures and resuscitations He carried out demonstrate His power as well as presaging our resurrection.[2] But the most convincing proof is the incarnation itself, since if the Word assumed flesh He must have done so in order to save it.[3] Tertullian reacts very similarly against the Gnostic disparagement of the flesh, dwelling[4] on the facts that it is God's handiwork, that Scripture extols it (he cites *Is.* 40, 5; *Joel* 2, 28; *1 Cor.* 3, 17; 6, 15; 6, 20; *Gal.* 6, 17), and that God cannot abandon what His beloved Son took to Himself. The divine power, exhibited in the periodical renovation of the natural order, guarantees the possibility of the resurrection;[5] and, since body and soul are so intimately united in all their activities, the divine justice requires that both should come together to judgment.[6] Both for him,[7] however, and for his contemporary, Hippolytus,[8] the decisive proof consists in the massive evidence of Scripture.

Two further points in the teaching of these thinkers merit attention. The first is their heightened interest in the lot of the soul pending the resurrection and judgment. Irenaeus criticizes[9] the Gnostic idea that it passes to heaven immediately after death, pointing to the example of the Saviour, Who descended to hell (i.e. the place of the departed) for three days. His conclusion is that, since no disciple is above his master, 'the souls [of Christians] go to an invisible place designated for them by God, and sojourn there until the resurrection. . . . Afterwards, receiving bodies and rising again perfectly, i.e. with their bodies, just as the Lord Himself rose, they will so come to the sight of God.' Only the martyrs, it seems, are excused from this place of waiting.[10] Tertullian, too, basing himself on Christ's descent, teaches[11] that, with the exception of the martyrs, all souls remain in the underworld against the day of the Lord, which will not come until the earth is destroyed, the just being meanwhile consoled with the expectation of the resurrection, and the sinful receiving a foretaste of their future condemna-

---

[1] *Haer.* 4, 5, 2.
[2] Ib. 5, 12, 5; 5, 13, 1.
[3] Ib. 5, 14.
[4] *De resurr. carn.* 5-11.
[5] Ib. 12 f.
[6] Ib. 14-16.
[7] Ib. 18-end.
[8] E.g. *de antichr.* 65 f.
[9] *Haer.* 5, 31, 1 f.
[10] Ib. 4, 33, 9.
[11] *De anim.* 55-8: cf. *c. Marc.* 4, 34.

tion. The same doctrine appears in Hippolytus,[1] although he is more explicit about the penalties inflicted on the wicked and the blessedness enjoyed by the righteous. Secondly, they are all exponents of millenarianism. Irenaeus, for example, treats[2] the hope of a resplendent earthly Jerusalem as traditional orthodoxy, and protests against attempts to allegorize away the great texts of the Old Testament and *Revelation* which appear to look forward to it. Tertullian likewise, after establishing the reality of Christ's heavenly kingdom, adds[3] that this by no means excludes an earthly kingdom also. In fact, the latter is due to come before the former, and it will last for a thousand years, centred in the new Jerusalem (he cites *Phil.* 3, 20) which will come down from heaven. But he also shows signs of a tendency to spiritualize the doctrine, for elsewhere he speaks[4] of the new Jerusalem as really signifying the Lord's flesh. Hippolytus defended millenarianism in his *Commentary on Daniel* and *De Christo et Antichristo*. Opposition to the doctrine, however, was gathering force, the leader of the reaction at Rome being the priest Caius. In face of this Hippolytus departed from Irenaeus's exegesis of the key-passage, *Rev.* 20, 2–5. The thousand years there mentioned, he now explained,[5] are not to be taken as referring literally to the duration of the kingdom, but are a symbolical number which should be interpreted as pointing to its splendour.

4. Origen

While the theologians we have been studying repeat and elaborate the familiar eschatological themes, there is a further theme, that of the deification of the Christian, which is interwoven with their teaching and which was to have a profound influence on subsequent theology. According to this, the final flowering of the Christian hope consisted in participation in the divine nature and in the blessed immortality of God. The eternal salvation of the righteous, stated[6] Justin, will take the

---

[1] *C. Graec.* (PG 10, 796–800).   [2] *Haer.* 5, 33–6: esp. 35, 1.
[3] *C. Marc.* 3, 24: cf. ib. 4, 39.   [4] *De resurr. carn.* 26, 11.
[5] *Cap. c. Caium* (GCS 1, Pt. 2, 246 f.).   [6] *1 apol.* 10; 52; *dial.* 124.

form of that incorruptibility and impassibility which fellowship with God will impart; and on Tatian's view,[1] when the
divine image and likeness have been restored in a man, he
becomes capable of 'seeing perfect things', and after the resurrection will receive a blessed immortality. The grace of the
Spirit, Irenaeus taught,[2] already at work in us, will, when fully
given, 'make us perfect according to the Father's will; for it
will restore man to God's image and likeness'. After the resurrection God will cause Him to share in His own privilege of
incorruptibility. This will be the effect of the vision of God
which, out of sheer goodness, the Father will bestow on the
elect; for 'those who see God are within God, sharing His
glory'.[3] In the third century Origen developed these and
kindred ideas, interpreting the kingdom of God either as the
apprehension of divine truth and spiritual reality,[4] or (this in
explanation of *Luke* 17, 21) as the indwelling of the Logos or
the seeds of truth implanted in the soul,[5] or as 'the spiritual
doctrine of the ensouled Logos imparted through Jesus Christ'.[6]
'The intelligence (νοῦς) which is purified', he wrote,[7] 'and
rises above all material things to have a precise vision of God is
deified in its vision'; and since true knowledge, on his view,
presupposes the union of knower and object, the divine gnosis
of the saints culminates in their union with God.[8] But Origen's
reflections on eschatology are so far-reaching that they deserve
a closer scrutiny.

First, let us take his teaching about the resurrection of the
body; he preferred this form, for reasons which should become
clear, to resurrection of the flesh. In harmony with his Platonism,
Origen believed in the spirituality and immortality of the soul,
but he was sincerely determined to defend the Christian dogma
against pagan jibes.[9] He was acutely conscious of its difficulties,
as popularly presented,[10] and of the obvious objections to it;[11]
and he accepted Celsus's point that it was a mistake to appeal to

[1] *Or. c. Graec.* 13 f.   [2] *Haer.* 5, 8, 1.   [3] Ib. 4, 20, 5 f.
[4] *Sel. in ps.* 144, 13.   [5] *In Ioh.* 19, 12, 78.
[6] *In Matt.* 10, 14 (Klostermann, 17).   [7] *In Ioh.* 32, 27, 338.
[8] Ib. 19, 4, 23 f.   [9] Cf. *c. Cels.* 5, 14; 8, 49.
[10] E.g. ib. 5, 18; 7, 32.   [11] E.g. *sel. in ps.* 1, 5.

the divine omnipotence.[1] His task was the twofold one of expounding the truth against (a) the crude literalism which pictured the body as being reconstituted, with all its physical functions, at the last day, and (b) the perverse spiritualism of the Gnostics and Manichees, who proposed to exclude the body from salvation. The explanation he advanced[2] started with the premiss that the 'material substratum' (τὸ ὑλικὸν ὑποκείμενον) of all bodies, including men, is in a state of constant flux, its qualities changing from day to day, whereas they all possess a 'distinctive form' (τὸ χαρακτηρίζον εἶδος, or τὸ σωματικὸν εἶδος) which remains unchanging. The development of a man from childhood to age is an illustration, for his body is identically the same throughout despite its complete physical transformation; and the historical Jesus provides another, since His body could at one time be described as without form or comeliness (Is. 53, 2), while at another it was clothed with the splendour of the Transfiguration.

From this point of view the resurrection becomes comprehensible. The bodies with which the saints will rise will be strictly identical with the bodies they bore on earth, since they will have the same 'form', or eidos. On the other hand, the qualities of their material substrata will be different, for instead of being fleshly qualities appropriate to terrestrial existence, they will be spiritual ones suitable for the kingdom of heaven. The soul 'needs a better garment for the purer, ethereal and celestial regions';[3] and the famous Pauline text, 1 Cor. 15, 42-4, shows that this transformation is possible without the identity being impaired. As he explains the matter,[4] when the body was at the service of the soul, it was 'psychic'; but when the soul is united with God and becomes one spirit with Him, the selfsame body becomes spiritual, bodily nature being capable of donning the qualities appropriate to its condition. To make plain what he means by 'distinctive form', Origen equates it with the principle of energy which, according to Stoic principles,[5] maintains the body's identity in the flux of

[1] C. Cels. 5, 23. [2] Sel. in ps. 1, 5. [3] C. Cels. 7, 32.
[4] De princ. 3, 6, 6: cf. c. Cels. 3, 41 f.; 4, 56 f. [5] See above, p. 18.

ever-changing matter. It is a 'seminal reason' (λόγος σπερματικός) inherent in each body which enables it to be resuscitated,
although with a different set of qualities, exactly as the seed
buried in the earth, as the Apostle showed, survives death and
decomposition and is restored as a blade of wheat.[1] Later
critics[2] charged him with affirming that 'in the resurrection
the bodies of men rise spherical' (σφαιροειδῆ). He may well
have done so, on the Platonic theory[3] that the sphere is the
perfect shape, but the evidence is not compelling.

Secondly, in his treatment of the judgment we meet with the
same characteristic tension between the desire to retain traditional dogma and the desire to reinterpret it in a manner palatable to intelligent believers. 'God's righteous judgment', he
declared,[4] 'is one of the articles of the Church's preaching'; indeed, it is a cardinal motive for moral conduct and a convincing
evidence of free will. Immediately after death, Origen seems to
believe,[5] a provisional separation is made between human souls,
and to prepare them for their eternal destinies they pass to an
intermediate state, of longer or shorter duration, which serves
as a probationary school (cf. *quodam eruditionis loco . . . auditorio
vel schola animarum*). The judgment itself will be enacted at the
end of the world, and a definitive separation will then be made
between good and bad.[6] This is the day of wrath of which the
prophets spoke, and it has no doubt been postponed so that the
full consequences of men's actions may be revealed.[7] The Gospel, too, fixes the Master's return 'at the consummation'.[8] Each
will be judged according to his deeds, and this is why the judgment is reserved to God; only He can accurately assess the good
and evil mixed together in men's lives.[9] The framework of all
this is the traditional imagery of the law-court, and Origen
admits[10] that the whole Church accepts the picture of a glorious
Second Coming, with Christ sitting on His throne and separat-

---

[1] *De princ.* 2, 10, 3: cf. *c. Cels.* 5, 18 f.; 7, 32; 8, 49.
[2] Cf. Justinian's letter to Mennas in Mansi, IX, 516D and 533C.
[3] Cf. Plato, *tim.* 33 b.   [4] *De princ.* 3, 1, 1.   [5] Ib. 2, 11, 6.
[6] Ib. 2, 9, 8; *c. Cels.* 4, 9.   [7] *In Rom.* 2, 4.   [8] *In Matt.* 14, 12 f.
[9] *In Rom.* 2, 1 f.: cf. ib. 2, 4; 9, 41; *in Matt.* 14, 8.
[10] *In Matt. comm. ser.* 70.

ing the good from the bad. Even when he starts rationalizing it, he hastens to reassure[1] his readers that he has no wish to belittle, much less deny, the truth of the popular accounts of the Parousia. He is aware, however, that that account, with its spatio-temporal presuppositions, bristles with difficulties, and he propounds[2] a spiritual reinterpretation of it. According to this, all the vivid imagery of the Gospel predictions is explained away as symbolism. The real meaning of the Parousia, we are told, is the manifestation of Christ and His divinity to all mankind, good and bad, which will result in the disclosure of their true character. The Saviour will not appear in any given place, but will make Himself known everywhere; and men will present themselves before His throne in the sense that they will render homage to His authority. They will see themselves as they are, and in the light of that knowledge the good and the bad will be finally differentiated. Needless to say, there is no room here for millenarianism, and Origen castigates[3] the follies of literalist believers who read the Scriptures like the Jews and cherish dreams of dwelling in an earthly Jerusalem after the resurrection, where they will eat, drink and enjoy sexual intercourse to their hearts' content.

Thirdly, believing as he does[4] that the kingdom inherited by the righteous is the contemplation of divine truth, Origen translates the sufferings of the damned into similarly spiritualized terms. 'Each sinner', he states,[5] 'kindles his own fire . . . and our own vices form its fuel.' In other words, the real punishment of the wicked consists in their own interior anguish, their sense of separation from the God Who should be their supreme good. Further, all such punishment, even the pains of hell, must have an end. Origen appreciates[6] the deterrent value of the Scriptural description of the penalties of sin as eternal. He is satisfied, however, that in fact they must one day come to an end, when all things are restored to their primeval order. This is his doctrine of the *apocatastasis*, in which his eschatology, as

[1] *In Matt.* 12, 30. [2] *In Matt. comm. ser.* 70: cf. *in Matt.* 12, 30.
[3] *De princ.* 2, 11, 2. [4] Ib. 2, 11, 7.
[5] Ib. 2, 10, 4: cf. Jerome, *in Eph.* 5, 6.
[6] *C. Cels.* 3, 79; 6, 26; *in Ierem. hom.* 19, 4.

indeed his whole theological system, culminates, and which postulates[1] that the conclusion of the vast cosmic evolution will be identical with its beginning. Two guiding principles, the free will of man and the goodness of God, dominate his formulation of it. The former leads him to conceive[2] of successive cycles of worlds, with the infinity of rational creatures passing through different phases of existence, higher and lower, according as from time to time they choose good or evil. On the other hand, St. Paul has shown (1 Cor. 15, 25) that all things will eventually be brought into subjection to God, Who will be all in all as at the beginning. So far as rational creatures are concerned, however, this will not be achieved by force or necessity (for their free will demands respect), but by discipline, persuasion and instruction.[3] God's chastisement, we observe, has a medicinal purpose, and will cease when this has been accomplished.[4] Even the Devil, it appears, will participate in the final restoration. When Origen was taken to task on this point, he indignantly protested, according to his later champion Rufinus,[5] that he had held no such theory. But the logic of his system required it, since otherwise God's dominion would fall short of being absolute and His love would fail of its object; and the doctrine is insinuated, if not explicitly taught, in his writings[6] as well as taken for granted by his adversaries.[7]

5. Later Thought: Resurrection of the Body

For the later fathers, both Greek and Latin, the resurrection remained an unquestioned article of the Church's faith; they assumed its universality, and also the identity of the risen with the natural body. The majority resisted the temptation to speculate, contenting themselves with reaffirming the traditional dogma and defending it, chiefly by means of appeals to the divine omnipotence. There is no need to provide samples

[1] E.g. de princ. 1, 6, 2.
[2] Ib. 1, 6, 3; 3, 6, 3 (in Jerome, ep. 124, 3; 124, 10): cf. Jerome, c. Ioh. Hieros. 19.
[3] Ib. 3, 5, 7 f.: cf. ib. 3, 6, 6; 1, 6, 4.
[4] E.g. in Ezech. hom. 1, 2.
[5] De adult. lib. Orig. (PG 17, 624 f.).
[6] E.g. de princ. 1, 6, 3.
[7] E.g. Jerome, c. Ioh. Hieros. 16.

of their teaching. On the other hand, there were two groups of theologians in this period whose thought about the resurrection merits attention—(I) those who led a revolt against Origen's rational analysis of it, claiming that his theories amounted to a virtual denial of any real resurrection; and (II) those constructive thinkers who strove, some of them along cautiously Origenistic lines but omitting what was most characteristic of Origen's teaching, to understand the mystery at a deeper level than the crude popular faith allowed.

(I) The best-known representatives of the anti-Origenist reaction in the East were Eustathius of Antioch[1] and Epiphanius.[2] In fact, however, both these teachers were indebted for the bulk of their arguments to the classic onslaught delivered against Origen by Methodius of Olympus († *c.* 311) several decades earlier.

Reduced to essentials the latter's critique fastened, first, on the radical dualism between soul and body presupposed by Origen, which he showed[3] to be inconsistent with the theory that the soul sinned in its pre-incarnate state, and, secondly, on Origen's idea that the permanent element which is restored at the resurrection is the 'bodily form', not the body as such. If this is so, argued Methodius, there is no real resurrection since what is raised is not the body; and indeed, since Origen had used the same concept of the 'form' or 'seminal reason' to explain the appearance of Moses and Elijah at the Transfiguration, Christ would not seem, on his account, to have been 'the first-begotten from the dead'.[4] In Methodius's eyes this 'form' is no more than a mould quite external to the body, like the tube through which water passes;[5] and so far from surviving the flesh, it perishes before it, just as the form of a bronze statue is the first to disappear when the metal is melted.[6] His own positive views, though not entirely clear, are firmly based on the resurrection of Christ Himself considered as restoring the work of creation which sin had marred. Christ, however, was raised in exactly the same body as He bore upon the cross, as

---

[1] *De engast. c. Orig.* 22 (PG 18, 660).   [2] *Haer.* 64, 63-8; *ancor.* 87-92.
[3] *De res.* 1, 29-33.   [4] Ib. 3, 5.   [5] Ib. 3, 3.   [6] Ib. 3, 6.

His dialogue with doubting Thomas demonstrates.[1] Our resurrection bodies will indeed have heightened qualities, for they will return to the impassibility and glory which the human form possessed before the Fall; but they will be *materially* identical with our present earthly bodies.[2] As for the objection that once the particles of a body have been dispersed, they become inextricably mingled with other substances, Methodius has no difficulty in pointing[3] to cases where men, or even nature itself, succeed in separating substances which seem hopelessly mixed up with each other; and the power of the Almighty is, of course, infinitely greater. The most unsatisfactory feature of his account is his assumption[4] throughout that the soul must be a corporeal substance.

A century had to elapse before the most prominent of Western critics of Origen's ideas about the resurrection took the field. This was Jerome, who until 394 was an ardent adherent of Origenism, supporting[5] among other doctrines the master's theory of the disappearance of the natural body and the transformation of the elect at the resurrection into purely spiritual beings. After that date, however, he made a complete *volte-face*, and began to stress,[6] with crudely literalistic elaboration, the physical identity of the resurrection body with the earthly body. Not all Christian teachers, as we shall see, shared this literalism, still less delighted in the paradoxical corollaries which its champions sometimes liked to draw from it. But the critics of Origenism, from Methodius to Jerome, were successful at least in securing that, whatever view was taken of the resurrection body, it had to be regarded as in some way identical with the natural body itself and not merely with its 'form'.

(II) Cyril of Jerusalem provides a good example of a constructive attempt to deal with the problem. He was familiar[7] with the hackneyed scientific objections, based on the putrefaction of corpses, the fact that they may be consumed by fish or

---

[1] *De res.* 3, 12-14. [2] Ib. 3, 16. [3] Ib. 2, 27 f.
[4] Ib. 3, 18. [5] E.g. *in Eph.* 5, 29; *adv. Iovin.* 1, 36.
[6] E.g. *c. Ioh. Hieros.* 33 [7] *Cat.* 18, 2 f.

vultures or animals, their annihilation by fire, and so on, but thought that God's omnipotence could be relied upon to reunite the dispersed particles. He conceived, however, of the resuscitated bodies as being transformed and, in a way, spiritualized. As he expressed it,[1] it is this very body which is raised, but it does not remain such as it was. The bodies of the righteous, for example, will assume supernatural qualities, while those of the wicked will become capable of burning eternally. The formula he thus employed, τοῦτο, οὐ τοιοῦτο, based on the Pauline distinction (1 Cor. 15, 44) between the 'psychic' body and the 'pneumatic' body, and the cautious type of explanation implied in it, seem to have enjoyed a wide currency.[2] Didymus was developing it later when he argued[3] that the resurrection body will be a celestial one; life will not destroy our earthly tabernacle, but will absorb it, imparting superior qualities to it. On the other hand, Gregory of Nyssa advanced a more daring solution along lines reminiscent of Origen. Like his master, he distinguished[4] between the material elements composing the body, which are forever in flux, continually coming into being and passing away, and the bodily 'form' (εἶδος) or 'type', which never loses its individuality. This 'form' is known by the soul, and indeed sets its stamp upon it during its mortal life; consequently the soul can always recognize the physical elements which belong to it, however much dispersed they may be, and at the resurrection will draw to itself such of them as it requires; the mere quantity of matter which entered into the composition of the body will be of no importance. Gregory was careful, we observe, to allow the terrestrial body its proper place in the resurrection, but he also pointed out[5] that this will involve our restoration to the primitive state lost through Adam's sin. The resurrection body will be exempt from all the consequences of sin, such as death, infirmity, deformity, difference of age, etc.; and so human nature, while remaining true

---

[1] Ib. 18, 18 f.
[2] Cf. Amphilochius, frg. 10 (PG 39, 108); Epiphanius, expos. fid. 17; Isidore, ep. 2, 43; etc.   [3] In 2 Cor. 5, 1; 5, 2 (PG 39, 1704).
[4] De hom. opif. 27; de anim. et resurr. (PG 46, 73-80; 145 f.).
[5] De anim. et resurr. (PG 46, 148 f.).

to itself, will ascend to a spiritual, impassible state.

In the West Hilary's teaching closely resembles that of Cyril of Jerusalem. In raising the bodies of the departed, he suggests,[1] God will reconstitute the identical matter of which they were once composed, but will alter their quality and will impart to them a splendour and beauty appropriate to their new condition. Ambrose justifies[2] the rising again of the body as such on the ground that it shares in the actions initiated by the soul and so should come with it to judgment, and points out[3] that the term 'resurrection' itself implies that what is raised is the very body which died and was buried. Nevertheless, while the body remains identically the same, it will undergo a transformation and spiritualization at its resuscitation.[4] For Augustine[5] the resurrection of all men at the last day is an undoubted dogma of the Christian faith; and he is convinced[6] that 'this identical flesh will be raised which is buried, which dies, which is seen and touched, which must eat and drink if it is to go on existing, which is sick and subject to pain'. Norwithstanding this identity, however, the bodies of the elect and the damned alike will be clothed with incorruptibility, in the case of the latter that their chastisement may be everlasting.[7] To solve the hoary problem of bodies which have been devoured by fire or wild beasts, or reduced to dust or dissolved in liquid, Augustine simply appeals[8] to the omnipotence of the Creator; but he also dismisses[9] as extravagant and unnecessary the supposition that every fragment of bodily matter must be restored to exactly the same position as it formerly occupied. The resurrection bodies of the saints will be perfect and entire, with all their organs, and only what is ugly or deformed will have disappeared;[10] and he favours the view[11] that, when children are raised, they will have the mature bodies of adults. His interpretation[12] of the Apostle's promise that the risen body will be spiritual is, not that its substance will have undergone change,

[1] *Enarr. in ps.* 2, 41.   [2] *De excess. Sat.* 2, 88.   [3] Ib. 2, 87.
[4] *Enarr. in ps.* 1, 51; *expos. ev. Luc.* 10, 168; 170.
[5] E.g. *enchir.* 84-7; *serm.* 241, 1.   [6] *Serm.* 264, 6.   [7] *Enchir.* 92.
[8] *De civ. dei* 22, 20, 1.   [9] *Enchir.* 89.
[10] *De civ. dei* 22, 19.   [11] *Serm.* 242, 4.   [12] *De civ. dei* 13, 20.

but that it will be in complete subjection to the spirit, and will thus rise superior to all sluggishness, weakness and pain.

6. *Later Thought: Parousia and Judgment*

The resurrection must, of course, be preceded by the Lord's Second Coming, a dramatic event which looms large in the preaching and thought of the fourth- and fifth-century Church. For the most part its setting is the awe-inspiring but magnificent imagery supplied by Old Testament prophecy and New Testament apocalypse, but there is little to suggest that it was taken otherwise than literally.[1] Only occasionally, as we shall see when we consider the Last Judgment, are there hints that more reflective writers were inclined to spiritualize the crudely realistic pictures associated with it. On the other hand, the influence of millenarianism had all but disappeared in the East and was rapidly on the wane in the West. Men like Methodius,[2] it is true, had done their best (he was writing towards the end of the third century) to keep the old-fashioned beliefs alive in a modified form; but Origen's critique of them proved decisive. His disciple, Dionysius of Alexandria, a generation before Methodius, used the full weight of his authority to discredit them, linking his attack with a rejection[3] of the authenticity of *Revelation*; and in the fourth century only Apollinarius[4] could be found to champion them among Eastern writers. For Ambrosiaster,[5] however, the collapse of the Roman empire was the sign of the approaching end of the world. Antichrist would then appear, only to be destroyed by divine power, and Christ would reign over His saints for a thousand years. Jerome had little use[6] for the millenarian ideal of an earthly kingdom. Augustine confessed[7] that he was attracted by it at one period; but later, repelled by the gross dreams of carnal indulgence

---

[1] E.g. Cyril Hieros., *cat.* 15; Chrysostom, *in Matt. hom.* 79, 1 f.; Cyril Alex., *in Zach.* 105; Hilary, *in Matt.* 25-8.

[2] E.g. *symp.* 9, 1; 9, 3; 9, 4; 10, 5 (Bonwetsch, 114; 117; 119; 127).

[3] Cf. Eusebius, *hist. eccl.* 7, 24 f.   [4] Cf. Basil, *ep.* 263, 4.

[5] *In* 2 *Thess.* 2, 8 f.; *in* 1 *Cor.* 15, 52.

[6] *In Is.* 18, init. (PL 24, 627 f.).   [7] *De civ. dei* 20, 7, 1: cf. *serm.* 259, 2.

conjured up, he changed his attitude and favoured an allegorical interpretation of the vision of the seer of Patmos. The first resurrection, according to this,[1] is our restoration from the death of sin and our summons to the Christian life, while the reign of Christ and His saints is to be understood as the Church carrying out its apostolate here on earth. The thousand years are to be explained either as the final millennium preceding the judgment or, preferably, as the total duration of the earthly Church.

Closely associated with the Parousia is the Judgment, which occupied an equally, if not more, impressive place in the imagination of the period. 'Each of us', declares[2] Athanasius, 'will have to render an account of his deeds in this life on the day of judgment'; and Gregory Nazianzen describes[3] how God has noted all our conduct down in a book. Other writers elaborate the theme of judgment in greater or less detail. For its justification they appeal fairly generally to the principle that, since there is no proper distribution of rewards and punishments in this world, it is only fair that there should be one in the next. So Chrysostom can say,[4] 'If God is such as He indeed is, it follows that He is also just, for if He is not just He cannot be God. But if He is just, He requites each man as he deserves. But we see that people do not all receive their deserts here. We must therefore look for another requital, so that each may duly receive what he merits and God's justice may stand revealed.' As in the case of the Parousia, the Biblical descriptions of the judgment seem to be usually taken at their face value, but some Eastern theologians, without going the whole way with Origen, show signs of trying to understand it in a spiritual fashion. Cyril of Jerusalem, for example, referring to *Rom.* 2, 15 f., explains[5] the inquisition in terms of one's own remorseful self-accusation, 'It will be in the light of your own conscience that you will be judged'; while for Basil[6] the judge's countenance is the divine illumination which sheds light on our guilty hearts. At the judgment our only accusers will be our own sins, which

---

[1] *De civ. dei* 20, 6, 1 f.; 20, 7, 2; 20, 9, 1.   [2] *Apol. c. Ar.* 35.
[3] *Or.* 19, 15.
[4] *De diab. tent. hom.* 1, 8: cf. Cyril Hieros., *cat.* 18, 4; Ambrosiaster, *in Rom.* 2, 3-6.   [5] *Cat.* 15, 25.   [6] *Hom. in ps.* 33, 4.

will rise up before us in our memory.[1] The true meaning of the judgment, writes[2] Gregory Nazianzen, is the heaviness or, alternatively, lightness of the weight which presses upon each man's conscience; on 'the day of visitation' (*Is.* 10, 3) we shall be arraigned by our own past thoughts and deeds, and shall be hauled away condemned by our own selves.[3]

Latin thought is on the whole closely aligned with Greek, although its general flavour tends to be more archaic. We should notice, however, the peculiarly Western tradition[4] according to which, while all will appear before Christ at the last day, only those wayward Christians whose lives have been a mixture of good and evil will in the strict sense be judged. Of the other two groupings into which men fall, the righteous need no judgment, and the wicked have been judged already. This doctrine found support in texts like *Ps.* 1, 5 (Lat. vers. 'the wicked shall not rise again in the judgment'), and *John* 3, 18 ('he that believeth on Him is not judged, but he that believeth not is judged already'). Ambrose's conception[5] of the judgment as taking place in the sinner's own conscience and as the result of God's knowledge of the heart reflects the influence of Greek thought. So does his idea[6] that the judges ranged on the bench and the open books symbolize our consciousness of guilt, and that the thrones of the divine Judge and the apostles, His assessors, are to be taken metaphorically, and that the sentence pronounced merely signifies the ratification in eternity of the respective merits of each individual. But it is Augustine, as usual, who best represents the balanced thought of the West. God's judgment, he affirms,[7] is a permanent feature of history, but since the fact of it is not always obvious God must have a day on which His combined wisdom and righteousness will be vindicated before every eye. For confirmation of this, and to fill in the picture, he turns[8] to the New and the Old Testaments. Both teach that the judgment belongs to Christ;[9] and if

---

[1] Ib. 48, 2.   [2] *Poem. mor.* 34, 254 f.   [3] *Or.* 16, 8.

[4] E.g. Hilary, *tract. in ps.* 1, 15-18; Zeno, 2 *tract.* 21; Ambrose, *enarr. in ps.* 1, 51 and 56; Ambrosiaster, *in 1 Cor.* 15, 51-3.   [5] *Ep.* 2, 9 f.; 73, 3.

[6] *Enarr. in ps.* 1, 51 f.; *expos. in Luc.* 2, 60; 2, 82; 10, 49.

[7] *De civ. dei* 20, 1-3.   [8] Ib. 20, 4 f.   [9] Ib. 20, 30.

Augustine is prepared to allegorize His coming, from certain points of view, as consisting in His reign in the Church, he also looks forward[1] to His triumphal advent at the end of time. All mankind, the righteous as well as sinners, will be subjected to this judgment,[2] and he expressly rejects[3] the idea that certain categories will be immune. By the book which will be opened he understands[4] the conscience of each individual, whose sins will come flooding in on his recollection; but in general he seems content to accept the literal significance of the picturesque language of Scripture.

So far we have been considering the general, or final, judgment, but what of the soul's lot immediately after death? On this matter great uncertainty, not to say confusion, seems to have prevailed among the Greek fathers. Cyril of Alexandria is typical. When discussing the parable of Dives and Lazarus, he decides[5] that the story must prefigure the future judgment at the resurrection; but in other passages[6] he presupposes the immediate entry of the souls of the righteous into heaven and the immediate chastisement of those of the wicked. Perhaps the most consistent is Chrysostom, who explicitly allows for[7] two moments of divine retribution, one at death and the other at the resurrection. So he can speak[8] of a 'tribunal' before which the dead are instantaneously haled; and he reads[9] the parable of Dives and Lazarus as implying that sanctions are applied to good and bad immediately they depart this life. The Latin fathers have more definite ideas on the subject. The righteous, according to Hilary,[10] rest in Abraham's bosom, while the wicked begin to pay the penalty which the Last Day will ratify. Ambrose is quite clear[11] that there are 'storehouses' (*promptuaria*: cf. 2 Esdras 7, 32) where the souls will await the doom which will be pronounced at the judgment, and while they wait will receive a foretaste of its quality. No theologian

---

[1] *Ep.* 199, 41-5.   [2] *De civ. dei* 20, 21, 3; *ep.* 193, 11.
[3] *De agon. Christ.* 29; *tract. in ev. Ioh.* 19, 18; 43, 9.
[4] *De civ. dei* 20, 14.   [5] *In Luc.* 16, 19.
[6] E.g. *de ador. in spir. et verit.* 6; *hom. pasch.* 1, 2; *in ps.* 48, 16.
[7] *In 2 Tim. hom.* 3, 3.   [8] *In 1 Cor. hom.* 42, 3.
[9] *De Laz. hom.* 1, 11; 2, 2 f.; 5, 3; 6, 6; 7, 4.
[10] *Tract. in ps.* 51, 22 f.; 57, 5: cf. ib. 2, 48.   [11] *De bon. mort.* 45-7.

so far, however, had taken the step of describing this provisional allocation of rewards and punishments as a judgment.
The first to do so unambiguously was Jerome, who stated[1] that
'what is in store for all at the day of judgment is fulfilled in
individuals on the day of their death', but was also on occasion[2]
prepared to identify the day of judgment with the day of a
man's falling asleep or departing this life. Augustine's explicit
teaching[3] was that in the intermediary period between laying
aside the body and later resuming it human souls either undergo
torture or enjoy repose, according to their previous conduct in
this world. His language[4] indicates that he regarded this as the
consequence of the divine judgment, while reserving[5] the term
'day of judgment' in the strict sense to the great assize at the
end of the world.

As regards the fate of the wicked (that of the blessed will be
treated in the next section), the general view was that their
punishment would be eternal, without any possibility of remission. As Basil put it,[6] in hell the sinful soul is completely cut
off from the Holy Spirit, and is therefore incapable of repentance; while Chrysostom pointed out[7] that neither the bodies of
the damned, which will become immortal, nor their souls will
know any end of their sufferings. Neither time nor friendship
nor hope nor the expectation of death, not even the spectacle of
other unhappy souls sharing their lot, will alleviate their pains.[8]
Yet Basil has to confess[9] that most ordinary Christians have
been beguiled by the Devil into believing, against the manifest
evidence of Scripture, that there will be a time-limit. Among
these must be included Gregory of Nazianzus, who on occasion seems to wonder[10] whether eternal punishment is altogether worthy of God, and Gregory of Nyssa, who sometimes
indeed mentions[11] eternal pains, but whose real teaching[12] envisages the eventual purification of the wicked, the conquest

---

[1] In Ioel 2, 1.   [2] E.g. in Is. 13, 6-9.
[3] De praedest. sanct. 24: cf. enchir. 109.
[4] E.g. serm. 109, 4; de civ. dei 20, 1, 2.   [5] De civ. dei 20, 1, 2.
[6] De spir. sanct. 40.   [7] Ad Theod. laps. 1, 9 f.   [8] In ps. 49, 6.
[9] Reg. brev. tract. 267.   [10] E.g. or. 40, 36.
[11] De castig. (PG 46, 312).
[12] Or. cat. 26; 35; de anim. et resurr. (PG 46, 72; 104; 105, 152; 157.)

and disappearance of evil, and the final restoration of all things, the Devil himself included. The influence of Origen is clearly visible here, but by the fifth century the stern doctrine that sinners will have no second chance after this life and that the fire which will devour them will never be extinguished was everywhere paramount.[1]

Western thought, which also succumbed to the influence of Origenism at the end of the fourth and the beginning of the fifth century, exhibits subtler nuances than Eastern. Older writers, like Hilary,[2] maintained the traditional doctrine of the eternity of hell-fire; but shortly afterwards we find Ambrosiaster teaching[3] that, while the really wicked 'will be tormented with everlasting punishment', the chastisement of Christian sinners will be of a temporary duration. Jerome develops the same distinction, stating[4] that, while the Devil and the impious who have denied God will be tortured without remission, those who have trusted in Christ, even if they have sinned and fallen away, will eventually be saved. Much the same teaching appears in Ambrose, developed in greater detail. In Augustine's day a wide variety of opinions were in vogue,[5] some holding that the pains of hell would be temporary for all men without distinction, others that the intercession of the saints would secure their salvation, others that salvation was guaranteed for those, even heretics, who had been baptized and had partaken of the Lord's body or at any rate had received these sacraments within the Catholic Church, others that all who had remained Catholics, even if they had lived disgracefully, must be saved, others that only those sinners who had neglected to practise almsgiving when alive were destined to eternal chastisement. The motive behind these ideas, Augustine claims,[6] is a misplaced conception of God's compassion, and Holy Scripture contradicts them: 'the everlasting death of the damned, i.e. their alienation from the life of God, will abide without term'. He concedes[7] that the undying worm of which the prophet

---

[1] E.g. Cyril Alex., *in Ioh.* 3, 36; 9, 29; Theodoret, *in Is.* 65, 20.
[2] E.g. *tract. in ps.* 51, 19; 55, 4; *in Matt.* 4, 12. [3] *In 1 Cor.* 15, 53.
[4] *Ep.* 119, 7; *in Is.* 56, 24. [5] *De civ. dei* 21, 17-22.
[6] *Enchir.* 112 f. [7] *De civ. dei* 20, 22; 21, 9, 2; 21, 10, 1.

speaks (*Is.* 66, 24) may be interpreted metaphorically of the gnawing of anguished remorse, but holds that the inextinguishable fire is real and material. The pain endured will vary in severity in proportion to the guilt of the sinner, and that of children dying unbaptized will be 'most mild of all';[1] but for all the chastisement will be eternal. Nevertheless he is led by certain texts of Scripture (*1 Cor.* 3, 13-15; *Matt.* 12, 32) to allow that certain sinners may attain pardon in the world to come. These are people who, although Christians at heart, have remained entangled in earthly loves,[2] and it is natural that after this life they should undergo purification by 'purgatorial fire'.[3]

7. *Life Everlasting*

It is fitting to conclude this book with some account of the ways in which the fathers conceived of the blessedness to be enjoyed by the saints in the world to come. Origen's picture of it is expressed in intellectual and mystical terms. When they reach heaven, he explains,[4] the redeemed will apprehend the nature of the stars and the reasons for their respective positions. God will disclose the causes of phenomena to them; and at a later stage they will reach things which cannot be seen and which are ineffable. Finally, when they have made such progress that they are no longer bodies, nor even perhaps souls but pure intelligences, they will contemplate rational and intelligible substances face to face. In this blessed state their free will is destined to continue unaltered; but if it be asked what will prevent it slipping back on occasion to sin, the Apostle supplies the answer with his sentence, 'Love never faileth'. When the creature has learned to love God purely and wholeheartedly, that very love, which is greater than anything else, will prevent it from relapsing.[5] Thus 'there will then be only one occupation for those who have come to God through His Word, namely, the contemplation of God, so that, being formed in the knowledge of the Father, they may all become in the strict sense Son, just

---

[1] *Enchir.* 93; 111; 113; *de civ. dei* 21, 16.
[2] *De civ. dei* 21, 26, 2.
[3] *Enchir.* 69. [4] *De princ.* 2, 11, 7.
[5] *In Rom.* 5, 10.

as now it is the Son alone Who knows the Father. . . . It is no error to say that no one knows the Father, be he apostle or prophet, except he has become one with Him, as the Father and the Son are one.'[1] This doctrine should not be caricatured, as Jerome caricatured[2] it, as a species of pantheism, as if Origen understood St. Paul's dictum that God would be all in all as implying the absorption of all creatures in the divine substance. He is never weary of repeating[3] that the end will be like the beginning, so that it would be paradoxical to suppose that he thought of the *apocatastasis* as involving the abolition of the original distinction between God and created spirits.

The creed which Cyril of Jerusalem expounded contained the clause 'eternal life', and he pointed out[4] that the attainment of this was the goal of every Christian's striving. The Father is Himself our veritable life, and thus 'eternal life' can be succinctly defined as being for ever with the Lord.[5] Other fathers expatiate in glowing language on the life of heaven. Basil states[6] that after the resurrection the elect will be counted worthy to behold God face to face; they will blossom like flowers in that brilliant demesne,[7] enjoying friendship with one another and with God. He compares[8] the calm and unending delight they will derive from contemplating God with the sudden, rapturous flashes of awareness of His being which occasionally come upon mortals in this life. According to Gregory Nazianzen,[9] heaven is a perpetual festival, illuminated by the brightness of the Godhead of which here we can only catch obscure, fleeting glimpses, and it will be our joy to gaze upon the Trinity of divine Persons; the understanding can scarcely grasp the magnitude of the blessings that await us, for we shall become sons of God and shall in fact be deified. In Gregory of Nyssa the stress on deification is even greater; in addition to immortality, our human nature will find itself adorned with divine qualities of glory, honour, power and

[1] *In Ioh.* 1, 16.
[2] *Ep.* 124, 10; 124, 14.
[3] E.g. *de princ.* 1, 6, 2; 3, 6, 3.
[4] *Cat.* 18, 28.
[5] Ib. 18, 29.
[6] *Hom. in ps.* 33, 11.
[7] Ib. 28, 3: cf. *hom. 1 in ps.* 14, 1.
[8] Ib. 32, 1.
[9] *Or.* 24, 19; 43, 82; 7, 23.

perfection.[1] Chrysostom affirms[2] that the most intense delight of the saints will be to see God, i.e. to possess a clear and perfect knowledge of Him. The absolute intelligibility of the Godhead was, however, a tenet of the Eunomians,[3] and so Chrysostom was careful to distinguish his doctrine from theirs. Thus, while claiming[4] that the elect will see God as far as it is possible for them to see Him, he denied that they will be able actually to comprehend the divine essence. 'What God in His innermost being is', he declared,[5] 'neither prophets, nor even angels or archangels, have seen.' This is a privilege which has been uniquely bestowed on the Son and the Holy Spirit, and which no creature could ever usurp. According to Cyril of Alexandria,[6] the process of deification which is our redemption will attain its climax after the Parousia and the resurrection, when the union of the elect with their Lord will be indissoluble. Our intelligence ($\nu o\hat{u}s$) will then be filled with a divine, ineffable light, and the partial knowledge we have enjoyed hitherto will give place to 'a more blinding gnosis'. Freed from all shackles 'without needing any figure, riddle or parable, we shall contemplate, as it were with face uncovered and unencumbered mind, the beauty of the divine nature of our God and Father';[7] and this 'perfect gnosis of God', this 'species of divine knowledge', will fill us with happiness.[8] Our resuscitated bodies, having discarded their corruptibility and other infirmities, will participate in the life and glory of Christ.[9]

Theodoret points out[10] that, since there are many mansions in the Father's house, the felicity of the blessed will be graded in proportion to their merits. This idea reappears in the Latin fathers;[11] in Ambrose it is coupled with the suggestion[12] that there is a gradual progression towards the full possession of blessedness. Like the Greeks, they depict heaven as a realm of

---

[1] *De anim. et resurr.* (PG 46, 156 f.).
[2] *In Rom. hom.* 32, 3; *in 1 Cor. hom.* 34, 2.   [3] See above, p. 249.
[4] *De beat. Philog.* 6, 1.   [5] *Hom. in Ioh.* 15, 1 f.   [6] *In Mal.* 4, 2 f.
[7] *In Ioh.* 16, 25: cf. *glaph. in Exod.* 2 (PG 69, 432).
[8] *In Ioh.* 14, 4: cf. *glaph. in Exod.* 2 (PG 69, 429).
[9] *In Luc.* 5, 27; *in 1 Cor.* 6, 15.   [10] *In Cant. Cant.* 1 (PG 81, 61).
[11] E.g. Hilary, *tract. in ps.* 64, 5; 64, 17 f.; Ambrose, *ep.* 7, 11; *expos. in Luc.* prol., 6; 4, 37; 5, 61.   [12] *Expos. in Luc.* 5, 61.

unsullied happiness, where the elect are exempt from corruption, decay and death as a result of their union with Christ. For Ambrose[1] it is a region of supreme rest, eternal light and imperishable glory. His chief thought,[2] however, is of the blessed fellowship which the saints have with one another and with God, and of the mutually sympathetic charity which binds them together. Indeed, what they experience is not simply union with God, but adhesion to Him. The prospect of meeting and conversing with the saints in heaven played a great part in Western ideas about the future life at this epoch. It was characteristic of Ambrose,[3] and Jerome dwelt[4] on it with eager eloquence, pointing out that in heaven he would meet the Blessed Virgin, St. Anne and other blessed ones whom he had never known on earth. While brought to its fulness after death, this intimacy between the saints and their ardent lovers on earth has its beginning even now.[5] Hence Niceta was able to promise[6] his catechumens that in the Church they would attain, among other privileges, to 'the communion of saints', and a mention of this supernatural blessedness soon found a place in the Western creed.

As with so many other doctrines, it was Augustine who set the seal on Western teaching regarding eternal life. In searching for the supreme good, he came to the conclusion[7] that no finite end can satisfy the heart of man. The Platonists were right at least in this, that 'in knowing God they discovered where lay the cause of the created universe, the light by which truth is perceived, and the fountain from which blessedness is drunk'.[8] In fact, it is God, Who is unchanging goodness, Who is our *summum bonum*, and both our moral perfection and our final happiness consist in knowing and loving the divine Trinity.[9] And it is this beatitude which the redeemed, both men and angels, enjoy in heaven, their true fatherland. Augustine is at a loss to give a precise and meaningful description of it, for it

---

[1] De ob. Theod. 30; 32; de bon. mort. 47.
[2] De ob. Theod. 29; 31; 37; 39.
[3] E.g. de ob. Val. 71; 77; de instit. virg. 113.   [4] E.g. ep. 39, 6.
[5] Ib. 39, 7.   [6] De symb. 10.   [7] De beat. vit. 11; confess. 1, 1.
[8] De civ. dei 8, 10, 2.   [9] Tract. in ev. Ioh. 26, 5; de trin. 8, 4-8.

transcends all sensible experience, but he is satisfied that 'in the body they will see God'. All his life he was exercised by the problem whether this beatific vision would be mediated to the saints by means of their actual physical eyes. In his earlier days he had rejected[1] the idea with scorn, but in later life he came to think it plausible.[2] He now realized that their eyes would be transfigured and glorified as a result of their resurrection, and with them they might well see God everywhere present in the new heaven and earth, just as men here and now distinctly apprehend the life of other persons in and through their bodies. The chief enjoyment of heaven, or the city of God, will lie in praising God: 'He shall be the end of our desires Who shall be contemplated without ceasing, loved without cloy, and praised without weariness'.[3] There will be degrees of honour there, based on merit, but there will be no jealousy; and free will will not only continue to be exercised by the saints, but will be the more truly free because liberated from delight in sinning.[4] In fact, eternal life will for the redeemed be a perpetual Sabbath, when they will be filled with God's blessing and sanctification. The Psalmist's words will at last find fulfilment, 'Be still, and know that I am God'.[5]

[1] E.g. *ep.* 92, 6.   [2] *De civ. dei* 22, 29, 3-6.   [3] Ib. 22, 30, 1.
[4] Ib. 22, 30, 2 f.   [5] Ib. 22, 30, 4.

NOTE ON BOOKS

L. Atzberger, *Geschichte der christlichen Eschatologie innerhalb der vorni-cänischen Zeit* (Freiburg i.B., 1896); H. Chadwick, 'Origen, Celsus and the Resurrection of the Body' (art. in *Harvard Theol. Rev.*, 1948); O. Cullmann, *Christ and Time* (Eng. trans., London, 1951); H. Eger, *Die Eschatologie Augustins* (Greifswald, 1933); L. Gry, *Le Millénarisme dans ses origines et son développement* (Paris, 1904); W. L. Knox, 'Origen's Conception of the Resurrection Body' (art. in *Journ. Theol. Stud.*, 1938); G. W. H. Lampe, 'Early Patristic Eschatology' (essay in *Scottish Journal of Theology Occasional Papers*, No. 2); A. Michel, 'Résurrection' (art. in *Dict. Théol. Cath.*); J. Rivière, 'Jugement' (art. in *Dict. Théol. Cath.*).

CHAPTER XVIII

MARY AND THE SAINTS

1. *The Martyrs and Saints*

A PHENOMENON of great significance in the patristic period was
the rise and gradual development of veneration for the saints,
more particularly for the Blessed Virgin Mary. Its full flowering, and the formal definitions sanctioning it, belong to later
ages, but the formative beginnings call for a brief treatment.

Earliest in the field was the cult of martyrs, the heroes of the
faith whom Christians held to be already in God's presence and
glorious in His sight.[1] At first it took the form of the reverent
preservation of their relics and the annual celebration of their
'birthday'.[2] From this it was a short step, since they were now
with Christ in glory, to seeking their help and prayers, and in
the third century evidence for the belief in their intercessory
power accumulates.[3] In arguing for it Origen appealed to the
communion of saints, advancing the view[4] that the Church in
heaven assists the Church on earth with its prayers. With the
cessation of persecution early in the fourth century the cult was
extended to include, in addition to martyrs, other Christians
(e.g. confessors, ascetics, virgins) who had been examples of
heroic sanctity. By the middle of the same century, according
to Cyril of Jerusalem,[4] the patriarchs, prophets, apostles and
martyrs were commemorated in the liturgy 'so that by their
prayers and intercessions God may receive our supplications'.
When God chastizes men, Chrysostom remarked,[5] they should
appeal to His saints since they have efficacious access to Him—
more efficacious than when they were alive, as Gregory

[1] I *Clem.* 5, 4; Hermas, *vis.* 3, 2, 1; *sim.* 9, 28, 3.
[2] *Mart. Polyc.* 18, 2: cf. Cyprian, *epp.* 12, 2; 39, 3.
[3] E.g. Origen, *orat.* 31, 5; Cyprian, *ep.* 60, 5; also funerary inscriptions.
[4] Esp. *in Iesu nave* hom. 16, 5.   [5] *Cat.* 23, 9.   [6] *Adv. Iudaeos* 8, 6.

Nazianzen pointed out,[1] because they are now closer to Him. In the following century Leo the Great in the West extolled[2] the Church's confidence in the prayers and patronage of the saints, whom God had appointed both as an example and as a defence to Christians.

As it steadily established itself, the devotion paid to saints and their relics could not fail to attract the biting censure of critics, pagan (e.g. Julian the Apostate) as well as Christian (e.g. Vigilantius). In defending it Jerome argued[3], as other Christians since Origen had done, that if the apostles and martyrs prayed for their fellow-Christians when still alive, it was natural to believe that they would do so all the more now that they were crowned with heavenly glory. While the technical distinction between the *latria* due to God and the *dulia* permissible to the saints was only beginning to emerge[4] in the patristic epoch, the consistent teaching of the Church, voiced as much by Polycarp's devotees[5] as by theologians like Augustine[6] and Cyril of Alexandria,[7] was that while the saints and martyrs deserved honour and devotion, only God could be worshipped. As Theodoret expressed it,[8] after listing benefits commonly sought from the martyrs, Christians do not invoke them as gods, but as godly men who can be their ambassadors and plead for them.

2. *Mary in the Ante-Nicene Period*

Devotion to the Blessed Virgin developed more slowly, being overshadowed by the enthusiastic cult of the martyrs for the first three centuries at anyrate. It also took rather different forms. Thus reliable evidence of prayers being addressed to her, or of her protection and help being sought, is almost (though not entirely) non-existent in the first four centuries. On the other hand, her role in the working out of God's redemptive plan was relatively early recognized.

[1] *Orat.* 18, 4.　　[2] *Serm.* 85, 4.
[3] *C. Vigil.* 6: cf. Origen, *exhort. ad mart.* 38.
[4] For the distinction see Augustine, *quaest. in Hept.* 2, 94: cf. *de civ. dei* 10, 1, 2; *c. Faust.* 20, 21.　　[5] *Mart. Polyc.* 17, 3.　　[6] *Serm.* 273, 7; *de vera rel.* 108.
[7] *C. Iul. imp.* 6 (PG 76, 812).　　[8] *Graec. affect., cur.* 8, 63.

The affirmation, embedded in Scripture and primitive tradition, that Jesus had been born of the Virgin Mary was the inevitable starting-point, but as time went on not only were the obvious references in the gospels called in aid, but a host of other passages in the Old and New Testaments were interpreted as pointing to her unique experience and role. The first orthodox writer to give her theological prominence was Ignatius of Antioch. While the other Apostolic Fathers made no mention of her, he was emphatic[1] that Jesus had by God's design[2] been carried in Mary's womb, stressed[2] the reality of her child-bearing, and made the cryptic remark[3] that both it and her virginity, like the Saviour's death, had escaped the notice of the Prince of this world, these being three mysteries of loud proclamation which were accomplished in God's silence. His primary concern was to safeguard the actuality of the incarnation against the Docetists, but he was already linking the Virgin and her miraculous conception with God's redemptive purpose.

The apocryphal literature (late first and early second century) on the fringe of the 'great Church' eloquently attests the preoccupation of certain circles with the Blessed Virgin. Thus in the *Ascension of Isaiah* we find the earliest affirmation[4] of the belief that she was a virgin not only in conceiving Jesus but also in bearing Him ('virginity *in partu*'): 'her womb was found as it was before she became pregnant'. The same idea of a supernatural birth involving no physical travail recurs in the *Odes of Solomon*.[5] But the work which most richly embroidered the gospel narratives and was destined to exert a tremendous influence on later Mariology was the *Protevangelium of James*. Written for Mary's glorification, this described her divinely ordered birth when her parents, Joachim and Anna, were advanced in years, her miraculous infancy and childhood, and her dedication to the Temple, where her parents had prayed[6] that God would give her 'a name renowned for ever among all generations'. It made the point[7] that when she was engaged to

---

[1] *Eph.* 18, 1. [2] *Trall.* 9, 1. [3] *Eph.* 19, 1. [4] *Asc. Is.* 11, 8–14.
[5] *Od. Sal.* 19, 6–10. [6] *Protev. Iac.* 6, 2. [7] Ib. 9, 2.

Joseph he was already an elderly widower with sons of his own; and it accumulated evidence both that she had conceived Jesus without sexual intercourse and that her physical nature had remained intact when she bore Him.

These ideas were far from being immediately accepted in the Church at large. Irenaeus, it is true, held[1] that Mary's child-bearing was exempt from physical travail, as did Clement of Alexandria[2] (appealing to the *Protevangelium of James*). Tertullian, however, repudiated[3] the suggestion, finding the opening of her womb prophesied in *Exodus* 13, 2, and Origen followed[4] him and argued that she had needed the purification prescribed by the Law. On the other hand, while Tertullian assumed[5] that she had had normal conjugal relations with Joseph after Jesus's birth, the 'brethren of the Lord' being His true brothers, Origen maintained[6] that she had remained a virgin for the rest of her life ('virginity *post partum*') and that Jesus's so-called brothers were sons of Joseph but not by her. Indeed, from her life-long virginity he concluded[7] that she was the first-fruits and model of chastity for women, just as Jesus Himself was for men. In contrast to the later belief in her moral and spiritual perfection, none of these theologians had the least scruple about attributing faults to her. Irenaeus[8] and Tertullian[9] recalled occasions on which, as they read the gospel stories, she had earned her Son's rebuke, and Origen insisted[10] that, like all human beings, she needed redemption from her sins; in particular, he interpreted Simeon's prophecy (*Luke* 2, 35) that a sword would pierce her soul as confirming that she had been invaded with doubts when she saw her Son crucified.

The real contribution of these early centuries, however, was more positively theological, and consisted in representing Mary as the antithesis of Eve and drawing out the implications of this. Justin was the pioneer, although the way he introduced the theme suggests that he was not innovating. Both Eve and

---

[1] *Dem.* 54: cf. *haer.* 3, 21, 6; *frg. Arm.* 8 (TU 36, 1a: p. 127).
[2] *Strom.* 7, 93, 7–94, 2.   [3] *De carne Chr.* 23.   [4] *Hom. in Luc.* 14.
[5] *Adv. Marc.* 4, 19; *de monog.* 8; *de virg. vel.* 6.   [6] *Hom. in Luc.* 7.
[7] *Comm. in Matt.* 10, 17.   [8] *Haer.* 3, 16, 7.   [9] *De carne Chr.* 7.
[10] *Hom. in Luc.* 17 (GCS 49, 105–7).

Mary, he pointed out,[1] were virgins, but whereas the one contravened God's command and as a result brought forth disobedience and death, the other responded meekly to the archangel Gabriel and so made the birth of a Redeemer possible. Tertullian and Irenaeus were quick to develop these ideas. The latter, in particular, argued[2] that Eve, while still a virgin, had proved disobedient and so became the cause of death both for herself and for all mankind, but Mary, also a virgin, obeyed and became the cause of salvation both for herself and for all mankind. 'Thus, as the human race was bound fast to death through a virgin, so through a virgin it was saved.' Irenaeus further hinted both at her universal motherhood and at her cooperation in Christ's saving work, describing[3] her womb as 'that pure womb which regenerates men to God'.

3. *From Nicaea to Ephesus*

Interest in the Blessed Virgin increased markedly in the century following Nicaea, but while the treatment of some Marian themes made substantial progress, that of others remained in certain quarters relatively static. In East and West alike a powerful influence was exercised by the immense and growing prestige of virginity in ascetic circles.

To start with the East, the title *Theotokos*, or God-bearer, applied quite naturally to Mary by Alexander of Alexandria,[4] was now becoming widely current except in Antiochene circles—so much so that Julian the Apostate mocked[5] Christians for their incessant use of it. We need not infer, however, that the full doctrine of 'divine maternity' was already being read out of it. The title 'ever-virgin' ($\dot{\alpha}\epsilon\iota\pi\acute{\alpha}\rho\theta\epsilon\nu\sigma\varsigma$) was also coming into vogue;[6] but we should note that, while Cyril of Jerusalem was silent on the point, not only the Antidicomarianites attacked by Epiphanius[7] and the Arian Eunomius[8]

---

[1] *Dial.* 100.   [2] *Haer.* 3, 22, 4: cf. 5, 19, 1; also Tertullian, *de carn. Chr.* 17, 2.
[3] *Haer.* 4, 33, 1.   [4] *Ep. ad Alex. Thess.* 54.
[5] So Cyril Alex., *adv. lib. Iul.* 8 (PG 76, 901).   [6] E.g. Athanasius, *or. c. Ar.* 2, 70.
[7] *Haer.* 78.   [8] Philostorgius, *hist. eccl.* 6 (summary by Photius) (GCS 21, 71).

openly taught that the 'brethren of the Lord' were Mary's sons by Joseph, but Basil of Caesarea, when criticizing[1] the latter, implied that such a view was widely held and, though not accepted by himself, was not incompatible with orthodoxy. Athanasius, however, stoutly defended Mary's virginity *post partum*, and in addition held her up as the ideal pattern for Christian virgins.[2] While Epiphanius still maintained[3] that 'the Only-Begotten opened the virginal womb', we are not surprised to find Chrysostom[4] at one with Gregory of Nyssa[5] in proclaiming Mary's virginity in bearing her child as well as after His birth. It was indeed Mary and her virginity, according to Gregory,[6] that finally halted the long reign of death.

The ancient parallel between Eve, the cause of death, and Mary, the cause of life, continued to be everywhere exploited[7] and was sometimes given fresh nuances. Epiphanius, for example, contended[8] that Mary rather than Eve deserved to be called (*Gen.* 3, 20) 'the mother of all living'. We even find Epiphanius reluctant[9] to affirm or deny her death, and wondering whether she should be identified with 'the woman who had borne the male child' of *Rev.* 12, 14 (speculations in which some have detected an anticipation of the idea of her bodily assumption). On the other hand, almost all Eastern theologians, so far from acknowledging her spiritual and moral perfection, followed Origen in finding her guilty of human frailties. Basil, for example, reproduced[10] Origen's interpretation of the sword prophesied by Simeon as signifying her loss of faith at the crucifixion. Chrysostom went much further, pointing out[11] that her pushfulness at Cana and her desire to make a show of the authority she had over Jesus had brought down on her His well deserved censure. Only in Syria, where Marian devotion was particularly fervid, do we find Ephraem delineating[12] her as free from every stain, like her Son.

[1] *Hom. in sanctam Christi gen.* (PG 31, 1468 f.).
[2] Cf. *Le Muséon* 42, pp. 89–91 (trans. of Coptic text).   [3] *Haer.* 78, 19.
[4] *In Matt. hom.* 5, 2 f.; *in Gen. hom.* 49, 2 (PG 57, 56–9; 54, 446).
[5] E.g. *vita Mos.* 2, 21; *or. in cant. cant.* (Jaeger vi, 388 f.).   [6] *De virg.* 14, 1.
[7] E.g. Cyril Hier., *cat.* 12, 5; Greg. Nyss., *hom. in cant.* 13; Chrysostom, *expos. in ps.* 24, 7 (PG 55, 193).   [8] *Haer.* 78, 18.   [9] *Haer.* 78, 11.
[10] *Ep.* 260, 9.   [11] E.g. *hom. in Matt.* 44, 2; *in Ioh.* 21, 2.   [12] *Carm. Nisib.* 27, 8.

In the West Mariology evolved more slowly at first, but reached greater heights by the early years of the fifth century. Hilary, for example, violently denounced people who held that Mary had not remained a virgin after Jesus's birth, and was emphatic[1] that the Lord's 'brothers' were children of Joseph by an earlier marriage. But he still regarded[2] the birth as a natural one; he also took it for granted[3] that Mary would have to face God's judgment for her sins. By contrast his younger contemporary Zeno of Verona was confident[4] that she had preserved her virginity intact both in conceiving and in bearing her child, as well as after His birth. He also took up the antithesis between Eve and Mary, elaborating it by equating Mary with the Church.[5] But it was Jerome, Ambrose and Augustine who contributed most to Mariology in the West. Jerome, we should note, for long frankly rejected[6] Mary's virginity *in partu*, while fiercely championing her virginity *post partum*. He was responsible for the theory,[7] later to become prevalent in the West, that Jesus's 'brothers' had in fact been His cousins, and that Joseph as well as Mary had been a lifelong virgin. For him Mary was the new Eve through whom life had been restored to mankind;[8] she was also the archetype and model of virginity.[9] As for Ambrose, despite early hesitations about her virginity *in partu*,[10] he became a powerful advocate of Mary's perpetual virginity.[11] His intense veneration for her sprang from the twin facts that she was the ideal virgin, showing no trace of imperfection but exhibiting all the virtues appropriate to the virginal state,[12] and that as the mother of God[13] she was endued with a special grace,[14] and was associated with man's salvation.[15] He elaborated[16] the contrast between her and Eve, and found[17] a kinship between her and the Church, both being virgins and both mothers by the operation

---

[1] *Comm. in Matt.* 1, 3 f. [2] *De trin.* 10, 47. [3] *Tract. in ps. 118,* 3, 2.
[4] *Tract.* 2, 8, 2: cf. 2, 9, 1. [5] *Tract.* 1, 13, 1.
[6] *Adv. Helvid.* 18 f.: for his later view see *Dial. c. Pelag.* 2, 4.
[7] *Adv. Helvid.* 15; 19; *comm. in Matt.* 12, 47. [8] *Ep.* 22, 21.
[9] E.g. *ep.* 107, 7. [10] *Expos. in Luc.* 2, 57. [11] E.g. *ep.* 42, 4–6.
[12] E.g. *de virg.* 2, 6–15. [13] *Hexaem.* 5, 65; *de virg.* 2, 13.
[14] *Expos. in Luc.* 2, 9; 17. [15] *Expos. in Luc.* 2, 17; *epp.* 49, 2; 63, 33.
[16] *Epp.* 42, 3; 63, 37. [17] *Expos. in Luc.* 2, 7.

of the Holy Spirit. Christ's words from the cross to Mary and John (*John* 19, 26 f.) were really addressed to the Church, with which she was virtually identified, and to its members.[1]

Augustine drew together and refined the now established themes of Mariology. He was an eloquent exponent[2] of her permanent virginity, arguing[3] that since the risen Christ could enter through closed doors there was no reason why He should not emerge from her womb without violating it. Like Ambrose, he stressed[4] the special relationship between Mary and the Church, the one a virgin who brought forth Christ and the other a virgin who brings Christ's members to birth. The question of her sinlessness arose in the course of his debate with Pelagius, who had cited the Blessed Virgin as an example of a human being who had remained wholly untouched by sin by her own free will. Augustine denied the possibility for all other men (the saints themselves would have been the first to avow their sinfulness), but agreed that Mary was the unique exception; she had been kept sinless, however, not by the effort of her own will, but as a result of a grace given her in view of the incarnation.[5] On the other hand, he did not hold (as has sometimes been alleged) that she was born exempt from all taint of original sin (the later doctrine of the immaculate conception). Julian of Eclanum maintained this as a clinching argument in his onslaught on the whole idea of original sin, but Augustine's rejoinder[6] was that Mary had indeed been born subject to original sin like all other human beings, but had been delivered from its effects 'by the grace of rebirth'.

There is evidence, sparse but persuasive, that a genuine cult of the Virgin was emerging about this time, and that prayers were beginning to be addressed to her. Thus Epiphanius, writing in the 370s, describes[7] a sect, the Collyridians, who celebrated a form of worship in connection with her. He was at pains to refute such heretical practices, protesting[8] like other orthodox writers that, while Mary was beautiful, holy

---

[1] Ib. 7, 5.   [2] E.g. serm. 186, 1; 215, 3.   [3] Serm. 191, 2.
[4] E.g. serm. 192, 2.   [5] De nat. et grat. 42.
[6] Opus imperf. c. Iul. 4, 122: cf. enarr. in ps. 34, 3.   [7] Haer. 79.
[8] Haer. 79, 4; 7.

and deserving of great honour, worship should be confined to Almighty God alone; but the existence of the sect, and the vehemence of his denunciation, suggest that this was no isolated phenomenon. Nestorius's remark,[1] half a century later, that he had no objection to people calling the Blessed Virgin *Theotokos* provided they did not treat her as a goddess can also be taken as implying a tendency in some circles to do precisely that. For prayers there are two illuminating scraps of testimony. The first is Gregory Nazianzen's story[2] of a virgin who implored Mary to assist her in her hour of peril. He relates it in an entirely matter-of-fact way, as if there were nothing extraordinary about it. The second is a papyrus fragment,[3] from the fourth century or perhaps later, which contains the appeal, 'Mother of God, [listen to] my petitions; do not disregard us in adversity, but rescue us from danger', and which may reflect a current in popular piety.

The Christological debates of the mid-fifth century, with the councils of Ephesus and Chalcedon in which they culminated, marked the climax of Mariological development in the classic patristic period. It was not their concern, of course, to do honour to the Blessed Virgin, but rather to clarify and define the union of divine and human in the incarnate Lord. But the generally agreed conclusion that this could only be achieved by recognizing that Mary was in a real sense *Theotokos*, mother of God, finally brought out the full significance of her role, and in doing so inevitably enhanced her status, integrating Mariology firmly with Christology. Nevertheless, although churches were now increasingly dedicated to her, feasts in her honour multiplied, and her name gradually inserted into the liturgy, the process of her theological exaltation was in fact far from complete. After Ephesus, admittedly, her divine maternity and perpetual virginity seem to have been accepted without question in East and West; but the old doubts about her sinlessness and moral perfection continued to be widely held. In the East the tradition going back to Origen

---

[1] Frg. III (Loofs, 353).   [2] *Or.* 24, 11 (date 379).   [3] P. Ryl. III, 470.

which stressed her human frailties and lack of faith in her Son was remarkably slow in dying; in the West the conviction that only Christ has been ideally good, and Augustine's more recent teaching about original sin, remained as stumbling-blocks even longer. Indeed, centuries had to elapse before the doctrines of Mary's exemption from original sin (in the West only) and actual sin, of her position as intercessor and mediator of graces, of her corporeal assumption into heaven and elevation there above cherubim and seraphim, could become elements in the day-to-day faith of Catholic Christians, much less be formulated as dogmas.[1] Only many generations after its first utterance, as an unknown writer of the fourth (?) or fifth (?) century aptly noted,[2] was the Virgin's own prediction (*Luke* 1, 48) that all generations would henceforth call her blessed to find its complete fulfilment. But at least the necessary premisses from which, as they reflected about them, theologians felt entitled to draw these momentous conclusions were established in the four creative centuries surveyed in this book.

NOTES ON BOOKS

H. von Campenhausen, *Die Idee des Martyriums in der alten Kirche* (Göttingen, 1936); H. Delehaye, *Les origines du culte des martyrs* (Bruxelles, 1912); W. Delius, *Texte zur Geschichte der Marienverehrung und Marienverkündigung in der alten Kirche* (Berlin, 1956); *Geschichte der Marienverehrung* (München/Basel, 1963); H. C. Graef, *Mary: A History of Doctrine and Devotion*, Vol. I (London and New York, 1963); G. Jouassard, 'Marie à travers la patristique' (art. in *Maria: Études sur la Sainte Vierge*, Vol. I: ed. H. du Manoir, Paris, 1949); P. Séjourné, 'Saints (Culte des)' (art. in *Dict. Théol. Cath.*, Vol. XIV (1)); H. Thurston, 'Saints and Martyrs (Christian)' (art. in Hastings' *Encyc. Rel. Eth.*, Vol. XI: Edinburgh, 1920); C. Vagaggini, *Maria nelle opere di Origene* (O.C.A. 131: Roma, 1942).

[1] Her immaculate conception, denied in the East although Andrew of Crete and John of Damascus had approximated to it, was declared a dogma by Pius IX in 1854, and her assumption by Pius XII in 1950.

[2] Origen, *comm. in Luc.*, frg. 101 (GCS 35—1st ed., 1930, p. 279). The text is manifestly not from Origen, although it may contain an Origenistic nucleus; the date is quite uncertain. My attention was drawn to it by H. Chadwick.

INDEX

Acacius (Homoean leader), 251
Acacius of Beroea, 328
Achamoth, 24, 27, 235
Ad Diognetum, 190
Adam, 9, 148, 167–9, 170–83, 187, 347–58, 362–5, 367 f., 370–3, 377–379, 388, 394 f.; Second Adam. 297, 312, 318, 377, 380 f., 385, 388 f., 395, 398
Adoptionism, 115-19, 140, 316 f. *See* Paul of Samosata
Adultery, 217, 218, 219, 436, 439
Aenesidemus, 15
Aetius, 249, 256
agennetos (ἀγέννητος), 46, 84, 92, 224, 226, 228, 229, 230, 244, 266
Agrippinus, bishop of Carthage, 218
Albinus, 9, 20, 128
Alexander, bishop of Alexandria, 224 f., 227, 230, 232, 234, 255, 318
Alexandria, 6, 7, 8, 25, 53, 54, 60, 338, 406, 444; allegorical exegesis of, 8 f., 70, 72 f., 213; catechetical school of, 126 f., 132; council of (*362*), 253, 259, 288, 289, 290, 302; synod of (*378*), 296
Alexandrian Christology, 153-8, 281, 284, 288, 289, 290, 295, 302, 304, 309, 311, 312, 313, 318-23, 326, 327, 333, 338, 341, 342
Ambrose: on baptism, 355, 425, 430, 432, 435; Christology, 335 f.; Church, 409; confirmation, 432 f., 435; eucharist (consecration), 426; (presence), 445 f., 448, 450; (sacrifice), 453 f.; grace, 356; last judgment, 481-4; life everlasting, 487 f.; Mary, 496; original sin, 353–5; penance, 437 f.; redemption, 387, 389; resurrection, 478; Roman see, 417 f.; sacramental grace, 422; sacraments, number of, 423; Scripture, 62, 74; soul's origin, 345; Trinity, 269; washing of feet, 355
Ambrosiaster: on baptism, 356, 432; eternal punishment, 484; eucharist (presence), 446; Fall, 353, 354, 355 f.; grace, 356; judgment, 355;

millenarianism, 479; redemption, 387 f., 389, 392
Ammonius, Bishop, 133
Amphilochius of Iconium: on Christology, 300 f.; on Trinity, 266
Anastasius, bishop of Thessalonica, 420
Ancyra, Synod of (*358*), 250, 259
Andrew of Samosata, 325, 328
Angels, 7, 95, 257
Anomoeism, 249
Anselm, 375
Antichrist, 462, 479
Antioch, 282, 302, 327, 406; catechetical school of, 55, 60, 230; council of (*268*), 117, 158 f., 235, 282, 290; (*325*), 231; (*341*), 238, 247 f.; (*344*), 238; (*379*), 296; exegesis of, 60, 72, 75-8, 348; Second Creed of, 247 f.
Antiochene Christology, 281, 282, 283, 288, 290, 293, 298, 301-9, 310, 311, 312, 318, 319, 320, 322, 323, 325, 327, 329, 333, 338, 341, 342
Antoninus Pius, Emperor, 84
Apocalypse of Adam, 22
Apocalypse of Peter, 59, 60
Apocatastasis, 473, 486
Apocrypha, 53-6
Apollinarius, Apollinarianism, 159, 280, 281, 289-95, 296, 301, 304, 307, 311, 319, 322, 323, 327, 328, 333, 404; on millenarianism, 479
Apostasy, 217, 218, 436, 439
Apostles, authors of N.T., 60; composition of creed by, 44; pattern of episcopate, 204 f.; source of tradition, 30 f., 35-47
Apostolical Constitutions, 436, 440
Apuleius, 13
Aquarians, 215
Arians, Arianism, 45, 47, 226-33, 236-240, 244-51, 255 f., 262, 274, 280, 311, 404, 405, 427; Christology of, 281 f., 283, 284, 286, 287, 289, 304, 335
Aristides (Apologist), 84, 145, 190
Aristides the Sophist, 13
Aristobulus, 8

Aristotle, Aristotelianism, 5, 6 f., 19 f., 84, 116, 268, 274, 281
Arius, 223, 224, 226-31, 243, 246, 249, 255. See Arians, Arianism
Artemas (al. Artemon), 116 f., 140, 160
Ascension of Isaiah, 492
Asclepiodotus, 116
Asclepius, 13
Athanasius, 231, 238, 269, 319, 407; Arians, his critique of, 233, 243; on baptism, 430 f.; chrismation, 433; Christology, 282, 284-9, 322; Church, 403 f.; Dionysius Alex., 134; eucharist, 441, 442; Fall and original sin, 346-8; grace, 352; heretical baptism, 427; homoousios, meaning of, 239, 245 f., 253-5; judgment, 480; Mary, 495; Paul of Samosata, 119; redemption, 377-80, 381, 384, 397, 398; Scripture (Apocrypha), 54 f.; (authority), 42, 47; (canon), 60; Son (Word), relation of to Father, 239, 243-7, 252-5; Spirit, homoousion of, 255-8, 259; tradition, 31, 42, 45, 47; Trinity, 233, 258, 263 f.
Athenagoras: on divine transcendence, 85; free will, 166; resurrection of body, 466; Spirit, 102, 103 f.; Word, 99 f.
Atonement. See Redemption
Atticus, 19
Attis, 12, 25
Augustine, 14, 270, 359, 370; on baptism, 429, 430, 432; Christology, 336 f.; Church, 402, 412-17; confirmation, 432 f.; correptio secreta, 439 f.; eternal life, 488 f.; eucharist (presence), 440, 446-9, 450; (sacrifice), 454 f.; Fall and original sin, 174, 357, 361-6, 430, 499; free will, 367-369; grace, 352, 357, 365, 366-9; judgment, 481 f., 484 f.; man's nature, 344 f., 361; Mary, 497; penance, 437 f., 439 f.; predestination, 366-9; redemption, 390-5; resurrection, 478 f.; Roman primacy, 419; sacraments, 422, 423, 425, 427 f.; Scripture (Apocrypha), 55 f.; (exegesis), 75; (inspiration), 63 f.; (O.T. and N.T.), 69; (sufficiency), 43, 46; soul's origin, 345 f.; Spirit, double procession of, 275 f.; tradition, 47; Trinity, 252, 271-9; virgin birth, 365
Augustus, Emperor, 11

Aurelian, Emperor, 13
Aurelius, Emperor Marcus, 19

Bahram I, 13
Baptism: teaching of Ambrose, 355, 422, 423, 430, 432; Ambrosiaster, 356, 432; Athanasius, 427, 430, 431; Augustine, 364-6, 423, 425, 427 f., 429 f., 431, 432; 'Barnabas', 194; Basil Caes., 427; Chrysostom, 405, 430, 431; Clement Alex., 207, 318; Clement Rom., 194; Cyprian, 176, 206, 210 f.; Cyril Hieros., 423, 425, 427, 428 f.; De rebaptismate, 210; Didache, 89; Didascalia Apostolorum, 219; Didymus, 427, 429, 431; Eusebius, 427; Gregory Naz., 425, 430; Gregory Nyss., 431; Hermas, 194; Hilary, 409, 432; Hippolytus, 208; Ignatius, 194; Irenaeus, 195; Jerome, 429, 430; Justin, 33, 89 f., 194 f.; Novatian, 209 f.; Optatus, 411, 424, 429; Orange, council of, 372; Origen, 208; Pelagius, 359, 366, 430; Pope Stephen, 210; Tertullian, 39, 209; Theodore Mops., 403, 430-2; Theophilus, 195; Zosimus, 370
'Barnabas': on baptism, 194; Christology, 143 f.; Church, 190; Fall, 163; God as Creator, 83; redemption, 164-6; resurrection of body, 463; Scripture (canon), 52, 56; (exegesis), 66, 70; tradition, 31; Trinity, 91 f.
Baruch, Book of, 22, 25
Basil of Ancyra, 238, 250, 259
Basil of Caesarea: on Apollinarianism, 296; baptism, 425; chrism, 434; Christology, 300 f.; Fall and original sin, 350, 351; judgment, 480 f.; life everlasting, 486; Mary, 495; penance, 436, 439; punishment of sinners, 483; redemption, 381, 383, 385; Spirit, 45 f., 260 f., 262, 266; tradition, 45 f.; Trinity, 252, 265 f.; 268
Basilides, 25, 27
Baucalis, 226
Bible. See Scripture
Boniface (African bishop), 448

Caecilian, bishop of Carthage, 410
Caius, Roman priest, 469
Callistus, Pope, 121-5, 144, 201, 217, 218
Candidianus, 327

Canon. *See* Scripture
'Canon of truth'. *See* 'Rule of faith'
Capharnaites, 449
Carpocrates, 25
Carthage, Council of (*418*), 361, 369; synod of (*397*), 56
Cassian, John, 46, 371
Categories, Aristotle's, 16, 274
'Catholic', meaning of, 190
Celestine, Pope, 324, 325, 328, 407
Celestius, 357, 361
Celsus, 20, 213, 470
Cerdo, 57
Cerinthus, 466
Chalcedon, Council of (*451*), 339–342, 406
Chrism, chrismation, 207, 423, 432–436
Christ, as Second Adam, 297, 312, 318, 377, 380 f., 385, 388 f., 395, 398; human soul of, 146, 148, 153, 155–7, 159–61, 281 f., 283 f., 287–9, 290, 292 f., 296 f., 298–301, 302–4, 310, 319, 322 f., 329, 335, 336, 339; pre-existence of, 87, 91, 92, 93, 94, 95, 96. *See* Christology
Christology: teaching of Ambrose, 335 f.; Apollinarius, 289–95, 296; Arians, 281 f., 283, 284, 286, 287, 289, 304, 335; Athanasius, 284–289; Augustine, 336 f.; Chalcedon, council of, 338–42; Clement Alex., 153 f.; Clement Rom., 144; Cyprian, 144; Cyril Alex., 317–23, 324–326; Didymus, 301; Diodore, 302 f.; Eustathius, 281–4; Eutyches, 331–4; Gregory Naz., 297 f.; Gregory Nyss., 298–300; Hilary, 334 f.; Hippolytus, 149 f.; Irenaeus, 147–9; Justin, 145–7; Leo, 334, 337 f.; Malchion, 158 f.; Methodius, 160 f.; Nestorius, 310–17; Origen, 154–8; Tatian, 145; Tertullian, 150–52; Theodore Mops., 304–9; Union Symbol, 328 f.
Chrysostom, John: on baptism, 424, 430, 431; Church, 402, 403, 405; eucharist (presence), 405, 426, 444, 450; (sacrifice), 424, 451–3; Fall and original sin, 349, 351; grace and free will, 352; image of God, 348; judgment, 480, 482; life everlasting, 487; Mary, 495; penance, 423, 438; Petrine texts, 407 f.; redemption, 381, 384, 385 f., 391 f.; sacraments, 422, 423; Scripture (Apocrypha), 54; (authority), 42 f.;

(exegesis), 76, 78; (inspiration), 62, 63; sufferings of damned, 483; tradition, 45
Church, as Christ's mystical body, 189 f., 192, 200, 202, 203, 207, 401–417, 446–8; as mother, 191–2, 200, 201, 206; invisible, 191, 202 f., 402, 413–16; teaching of Ambrose, 409; Athanasius, 403 f.; Augustine, 402, 412–17; 'Barnabas', 190; Chrysostom, 402, 405; Clement Alex., 201 f.; Clement Rom., 190; Cyprian, 203–7, 402; Cyril Alex., 402 f., 405 f.; Cyril Hieros., 401 f.; Gregory Naz., 403 f.; Gregory Nyss., 404; Hermas, 189, 191; Hippolytus, 200 f.; Ignatius, 189; Irenaeus, 191–3; Justin, 189 f.; Optatus, 411 f.; Origen, 202 f.; Polycarp, 189; Tertullian, 200 f.; Theodore Mops., 403; Theodoret, 402
2 Clement, 27, 35, 56, 91, 144, 165 f., 191, 194, 460, 463
Clement of Alexandria, 27; on baptism, 207 f.; Christology, 153 f.; Church, 201 f.; eucharist, 213; Fall and original sin, 179 f.; Scripture (Apocrypha), 54; (authority), 42; (exegesis), 4 f., 74; (N.T.), 56; tradition, 43, 44, 47
Clement of Rome: on baptism, 194; Christology, 144; Church, 190; eucharist, 214; God as Creator, 83; Parousia, 464; penance, 199, 217; redemption, 164; resurrection of body, 463; Scripture, 52, 58, 65; tradition, 31, 32, 34, 35; Trinity, 90 f.
Cleomenes, 120, 123
Communicatio idiomatum, 143, 283, 295, 298, 300, 301, 311, 316, 322, 326, 329, 336
Communion of saints, 459, 488, 490
Concupiscence, 364, 365, 366, 373
Confirmation, 209, 210, 423, 430, 432–6
Constans, Emperor, 238
Constantine, Emperor, 5, 231, 233, 237
Constantinople, 310, 318, 324, 406, 437; council of (*381*), 88, 238, 263, 296, 302, 406; (*553*), 303, 307, 343; (*680*), 343; creed of, 339 f., 402; Standing Synod of, 331, 340, 341; synod of (*360*), 238, 251
Constantius, Emperor, 238, 253
Cornelius, Pope, 209 f.
Cornutus, L. A., 8

Correptio secreta, 439 f.

Councils or synods: Alexandria (*362*), 253, 259, 288, 289, 290, 302; (*378*), 296; Ancyra (*358*), 250, 259; Antioch (*268*), 117, 158 f., 235, 282, 290; (*325*), 231; (*341*), 238, 247 f.; (*344*), 238; (*379*), 296; Carthage (*397*), 56; (*418*), 361, 369; Chalcedon (*451*), 339-42, 406; Constantinople (*360*), 238, 251; (*381*), 88, 238, 263, 296, 302, 406; (*553*), 303, 307; Elvira (*303*), 219; Ephesus (*431*), 49, 326 f., 328, 331, 361, 406; (*449*), 334; Hippo (*393*), 56; Jamnia, 52; Nicaea (*325*), 5, 44, 45, 46, 138, 231-7, 280, 281, 406; Nicé (*359*), 238; Orange (*441*), 435; (*529*), 371 f.; Philippopolis (*342*), 238; Rome (*377*), 295 f.; Serdica (*343*), 242; Sirmium (*357*), 238, 250; Toledo (*589*), 439

Creeds: Athanasian, 273; of Antioch (*341*), 238, 247 f.; Constantinople (*360*), 238, 251; (*381*), 339 f., 402; *Ecthesis macrostichos*, 119, 238, 248; Nicaea, 45, 231-7, 238, 339; Nicé, 238, 251; Old Roman, 144; Philippopolis, 238, 248; Serdica, 242; Sirmium, 238, 248 f.

Cross, Sign of the, 39, 211; symbolism of, 66, 169

Cybele, 11, 12

Cyprian: on baptism, 210 f., 427 f.; Christology, 144; Church, 203-7, 402, 412, 415, 418, 419; eucharist (presence), 211-13, 440, 449; (sacrifice), 215 f.; original sin, 176; penance, 217 f.; redemption, 178; Roman see, 205 f., 418, 419; Scripture (Apocrypha), 54; (authority), 42; tradition, 42

Cyril of Alexandria, 4, 45, 307, 333, 340; anathemas of, 324 f., 326, 327, 328, 329; at Ephesus, 326 f.; on baptism, 429, 431; chrism, 433 f., 435; Christology, 307, 311, 312, 313 f., 315, 317-23, 324 f., 329 f., 331, 333, 341, 342, 444; Church, 402 f., 405 f.; eucharist, 318, 444; Fall and original sin, 372; judgment, 482; life everlasting, 487; Petrine claims, 408; redemption, 321, 396-9, 487; Roman see, 324, 407; sacraments, 423; Scripture (exegesis), 74; (inspiration), 63; tradition, 48 f.

Cyril of Jerusalem: on baptism, 425, 428 f.; Church, 401 f.; confirmation, 432 f.; eucharist (presence), 426, 441, 442 f., 450; (sacrifice), 451, 452; Fall and original sin, 349; homoousion, 249 f.; judgment, 480; life everlasting, 486; resurrection of body, 476 f.; sacraments, 423; Scripture (Apocrypha), 54 f.; (authority), 42, 46; Spirit, 256, 258

Damasus, Pope, 295, 419

Decentius of Gubbio, 434

Decian persecution, 204, 218

Dedication Council (*341*), Creed of, 247 f.

Definition, Chalcedonian, 339-42

Demeter, 12

Demiurge, 16, 21, 27, 67 f., 84, 86 f., 235

Demons, devils, 167-9, 175, 180-2, 185 f., 194

De rebaptismate, 210

De sacramentis, 445

Devil (Satan), 167, 171, 176, 179, 180 f., 183, 187, 208, 229, 353, 363, 366, 394, 429, 474, 484; theory of ransom to, 173 f., 185 f., 375-7, 382-4, 387, 391-3, 395 f., 399; ultimate restoration of, 382, 474, 484

Didache, 60; on baptism, 89; God as Creator, 83; eucharist (presence), 197; (sacrifice), 196; Parousia and resurrection, 463; penance, 199; redemption, 164; tradition, 44

Didascalia Apostolorum, 219, 426

Didymus: on Christology, '301; resurrection of body, 477; soul's origin, 345; Trinity, 263, 266 f.

Diocletian, persecution of, 410

Diodore of Tarsus: on Christology, 290, 302 f., 305; Scripture (exegesis), 75-8

Dionysius of Alexandria, 74, 133-6, 230, 231, 479; on *homoousios*, 135, 235

Dionysius the Areopagite, 435

Dionysius of Corinth, 45

Dionysius of Rome, 133-6, 224, 225, 235, 241, 492

Dioscorus, 331, 334

Docetism, 141, 142, 147, 197, 198, 280, 330, 463, 492

Donatism, 409, 410-12, 413, 415, 416, 424, 427, 447

Dulia, 491

Ebionism, 139 f.

'Economy', 104, 108, 109, 110, 112,

114, 122; 'economic Trinitarianism', 108, 109, 241
Ecthesis macrostichos, 119, 238, 248
Elvira, Council of (*303*), 219
Ephesus, Council of (*431*), 49, 326 f., 328, 331, 341, 361, 406, 498; Robber Synod of (*449*), 334
Ephraem, 495
Epictetus, 19
Epicurus, Epicureanism, 15
Epigonus, 120, 121
'Επίνοιαι, 128
Epiphanius: on baptism, 436; Christology, 295, 300; Homoeousianism, 249; Mary, 494 f.; Petrine texts, 408; resurrection of body, 475; Scripture (Apocrypha), 54; (exegesis), 74; (inspiration), 63; Spirit, 263; tradition, 45 f.
Eschatology, 459-89
Eucharist (presence): teaching of Ambrose, 422, 426, 446, 448, 450; Apollinarius, 295; *Apostolical Constitutions*, 440 f.; Athanasius, 441, 442; Augustine, 422 f., 424, 440, 446-9, 450; Chrysostom, 405, 426, 444, 450; Clement Alex., 213 f.; Cyprian, 211 f., 449; Cyril Alex., 318, 444; Cyril Hieros., 426, 441, 442 f., 450; Eusebius Caes., 441 f.; Eustathius, 441; Evagrius, 442; Gregory Naz., 441, 443; Gregory Nyss., 426, 443, 448, 450; Hilary, 446, 450; Hippolytus, 411; Ignatius, 197; Irenaeus, 198; Jerome, 445; Justin, 33, 198; Nestorius, 318, 444; Origen, 213 f.; Serapion, 441; Tertullian, 211, 212 f., 446, 449; Theodore Mops., 426, 444, 450; Theodoret, 445; (considered as a sacrifice): teaching of Ambrose, 453 f.; Augustine, 454 f.; Chrysostom, 424, 451-3; Clement Alex., 214; Clement Rom., 196; Cyprian, 215 f.; Cyril Hieros., 451, 452; *Didache*, 196 f.; Gregory Naz., 452; Hilary, 453; Ignatius, 196; Irenaeus, 196, 197; Jerome, 453; Justin, 170, 196, 197; Theodore Mops., 452; Theodoret, 452
Eudoxius, 282
Eunomius, 249, 256, 494; Eunomians, 427, 487
Euphranor, 133
Eusebians, 238, 240, 241, 246
Eusebius of Caesarea: on Christology, 160 f.; eucharist, 441, 442;

Father and Son, relation of, 224, 225 f., 231, 233, 243; *homoousios*, meaning of, 233, 235 f.; Origen, 160; Paul of Samosata, 140; redemption, 384; Spirit, 255 f., 263; tradition, 45; Trinity, 256
Eusebius of Dorylaeum, 311, 331, 334
Eusebius of Nicomedia, 227, 230, 237 f.
Eustathius of Antioch, 238; on Christology, 281, 282-4, 288, 290, 302; eucharist, 441; *homoousios*, meaning of, 236; resurrection of body, 475
Eustathius of Sebaste, 259 f.
Eutyches, Eutychianism, 298, 331-4, 339, 341
Evagrius Ponticus, 263, 264, 268 f., 442
Eve, 9, 167, 179, 180, 182, 347, 348, 353, 493-6
Exomologesis, 216, 217, 438
Exuperius of Toulouse, 56

Facundus of Hermiane, 306
Fall: teaching of Ambrose, 253-5; Ambrosiaster, 353, 354, 355 f.; Athanasius, 346-8; Augustine, 174, 361-6, 430; 'Barnabas', 163; Basil, 350, 351; Cassian, 371; Chrysostom, 349, 351; Clement Alex., 179 f.; Cyril Alex., 372; Cyril Hieros., 349; Gregory Naz., 349 f.; Gregory Nyss., 349-51; Irenaeus, 170-2; Justin, 167 f.; Methodius, 182 f.; Origen, 180-83; Pelagius, 358 f.; Tertullian, 175-7; Theodore Mops., 373 f.; Theodoret, 373
Father, Gnostic doctrine of, 24, 25; original meaning of, 83, 85, 100, 112, 120, 121, 227; teaching of Alexander Alex., 224 f.; Apologists, 95-104; Apostolic Fathers, 90-95; Arius and Arians, 227-31, 249, 487; Athanasius, 243-7; Augustine, 272-9; Cappadocians, 263-9; Clement Alex., 127 f.; Dionysius Alex., 133-6; Dionysius Rom., 133-136; Eusebius Caes., 225 f.; Hippolytus, 110-15; Irenaeus, 104-8; Modalists, 119-23; Nicene creed, 232-7; Origen, 128-32; Tertullian, 110-15; Victorinus, 270 f.
Faustus of Riez, 436
Felix of Aptunga, 410
Flavian of Constantinople, 331, 332, 333, 334, 340, 341
Fornication, 217, 218

Free will, 166, 171, 175, 179, 180–2, 183, 349, 350, 351, 352, 355, 356, 357 f., 362, 364, 365, 366–9, 370, 373, 374, 467, 472, 475, 485

Gabriel, Archangel, 7, 494
Gaius, Emperor, 8
Galen, 116, 117
Generation, Eternal, 105 f., 125, 128, 130, 225, 231, 243
Gnosticism, Gnostics, 5, 14, 22–8, 36, 37, 38, 57, 59, 69, 86 f., 109, 110, 139, 141 f., 147, 179, 180, 191 f., 195, 198, 235, 280, 463, 465, 467, 471; Christian Gnostics, 22 f., 25, 67, 70 f.
Grace, 357–61, 365 f., 366–9, 370, 371, 372, 374, 412, 460, 470
Gratian, Emperor, 251
Gregory of Nazianzus, 260; on Apollinarianism, 290, 296 f.; baptism, 425, 430; Christology, 297 f.; Church, 403, 404; Eden, Garden of, 348; eternal punishment, 483; eucharist (presence), 441, 443; (sacrifice), 452; Fall and original sin, 349 f.; Godhead, simplicity of, 268; grace and free will, 352; heaven, 486; judgment, 480, 481; Mary, 498; penance, 436; redemption, 381, 383, 385, 452; Scripture (Apocrypha), 54; (authority), 46; (inspiration), 61; Spirit, 259, 261; tradition, 45 f.; Trinity, 252, 264–8
Gregory of Nyssa: on Apollinarianism, 290, 296 f., 404; baptism, 431; chrism, 434; Christology, 296 f., 298–300, 301; Church, 404 f.; creation of man, 348; Devil, restoration of, 484; eternal punishment, 483 f.; eucharist (consecration), 426; (presence), 443, 448; Fall and original sin, 349–51; Mary, 495; ordination, 423; penance, 436, 439; redemption, 380–2, 384, 404; resurrection of body, 477 f.; 'sacrament', meaning of, 423; Scripture (inspiration), 61; soul's origin, 345; Spirit, 261, 262 f.; Theotokos, 300; tradition, 45; Trinity, 252, 261, 264–8
Gregory Thaumaturgus, 133

Hadrian, Emperor, 84
Hegesippus, 45
Hell, 473, 483 f.
Heracleitus, 121
Heracleon, 25, 70 f.

Heretics, Baptism of, 206, 207, 210 f., 410 f., 412, 415, 427 f.; exegesis of, 39–41
Hermas: on baptism, 194; Christology, 143 f., Church, 189, 191; eschatology, 462, 464; God as Creator, 83; origin of evil, 163; penance, 198 f., 217; redemption, 164; tradition, 33; Trinity, 92, 93–95; Shepherd of, 59, 60
Hermogenes, 175
Hilary of Aquitaine, 370
Hilary of Poitiers: on baptism, 430; chrism, 433; Christology, 280, 334 f.; Church, 409 f.; communion of saints, 410; eucharist (presence), 409 f., 446, 450; (sacrifice), 453; grace, 356; homoousios, meaning of, 253, 254 f.; judgment, 482; man, original state of, 353; Mary, 496; redemption, 386, 387, 388, 392; resurrection of body, 478; Roman see, 417; 'sacrament', meaning of, 423; Scripture (Apocrypha), 55; (exegesis), 74; soul's origin, 345; sufferings of damned, 484; tradition and Scripture, 47; Trinity, 252, 253–5, 269
Hippo, Synod of (393), 56
Hippolytus, 22, 139; on baptism, 208; Christology, 144, 149 f.; Church, 201; eschatology, 467, 469; eucharist (presence), 211; (sacrifice), 214; Modalists, 120–22, 123 f.; Monarchians, 120; penance, 216, 217; redemption, 178; Scripture (Apocrypha), 54; (inspiration), 63; Trinity, 110–15
Holy Spirit, Homoousion of, 252, 255–63; inspirer of Scripture, 61–4, 75, 88, 91; procession of, 262 f., 265, 275 f.; teaching of Alexander, 255; Arius and Arians, 255, 256; Athanasius, 255–8, 259; Athenagoras, 102, 103; Augustine, 75, 272–9, 366 f.; Basil Caes., 259, 260, 261, 264–6, 483; Clement Alex., 207; Clement Rom., 91; Cyprian, 207; Cyril Alex., 325; Cyril Hieros., 256, 258; Didymus, 263; Epiphanius, 263; Eunomius, 256; Eusebius, 255, 263; Eustathius of Sebaste, 259, 260 f.; Evagrius, 263 f.; Gregory Naz., 259, 260, 261, 262, 264, 267; Gregory Nyss., 261, 262, 263, 265, 266, 267; Hermas, 94; Hilary, 335; Hippolytus, 111–

115; Ignatius, 92; Irenaeus, 105, 171, 470; Justin, 102, 103; Marcellus, 241; Monarchians, 115-19; Novatian, 126; Origen, 74, 129, 130-2, 255, 298; Sabellians, 119 f.; Tatian, 102; Tertullian, 176; Theodore Mops., 308; Theophilus, 102, 103, 104, 168; Tropici, 256 f.; Victorinus, 270 f.

Homicide, 217, 219

Homoeans, 251

Homoeousion, Homoeousians, 238, 246, 248 f., 250, 252, 253, 254, 255, 264, 269

Homoousion, ὁμοούσιος, 46, 130, 134, 135, 233, 234-7, 238, 239, 240, 243, 245, 246, 249, 250, 252, 253, 254, 255, 259, 264, 267, 270, 280, 290; homoousion of the Spirit, 255-63, 267

Hypostasis, ὑπόστασις, 7, 21, 129, 135, 136, 140, 155 f., 224, 229, 239, 241, 242 f., 247, 248, 250, 253, 254, 264 f.; use of, in Christology, 293, 294, 300, 301, 306, 313, 318, 319, 320, 324, 328, 331, 340, 341
'Hypostatic union', 312, 313, 314, 320, 322, 324, 326, 328, 341, 342

Idolatry, 217, 218, 219

Ignatius: on baptism, 194; Christology, 141, 142 f.; Church, 189; eschatology, 462, 463; eucharist (presence), 197 f.; (sacrifice), 196; Mary, 492; redemption, 164, 165, 166; Scripture (N.T. canon), 56, 58; Scripture and tradition, 31, 33, 35; Trinity, 88, 92 f., 96

Impeccantia, Pelagius's doctrine of, 360

Innocent I, Pope, 56, 419, 434

Irenaeus: on Christology, 142, 147-9; Church, 191-3; eucharist (presence), 198; (sacrifice), 196, 197; Fall and original sin, 170-2; Gnostics, 22, 27, 28; God as Creator, 86 f.; last judgment, 465; Mary, 493 f.; millenarianism, 469; redemption, 172-4, 188, 376; Scripture (inspiration), 61; (N.T.), 56, 58; (relation of O.T. and N.T.), 68 f.; tradition and Scripture, 36-41, 43, 44, 47; Trinity, 88f., 90

Isidore of Pelusium, 402

Isis, 11, 12

Jamnia, Council of, 52

Jerome: on Arian triumph, 238; baptism, 429 f.; confirmation, 433;

eucharist (presence), 445; (sacrifice), 453; grace and free will, 356; heaven, 488; judgment, 483; Mary 496; Origen, 426, 486; punishment of sinners, 484; redemption, 390; resurrection of body, 476; Scripture (Apocrypha), 55; (exegesis), 75; (inspiration), 62 f.; soul's origin, 345

Jerusalem, 140, 406, 465, 469

John of Antioch, 325, 327, 328

John of Damascus, 55, 396, 499

Jovinian, 429

Judaism, influence of, 6-11; Judaizing Christianity, 139 f.

Judgment, Last, 461, 462, 463 f., 465, 467, 468, 469, 472, 473, 479-85

Julian, Emperor, 5, 253, 302, 491, 494

Julian of Eclanum, 350, 361, 363, 370, 419, 497

Julius I, Pope, 242, 407

Justin (Apologist): on baptism, 33, 89 f., 194 f.; Christology, 145-7; Church, 189, 190; Docetists, 141; eucharist (presence), 198; (sacrifice), 170, 196, 197; eschatology, 460, 465, 467, 469 f.; Fall and original sin, 167 f.; Logos, 96-8; Mary, 493; penance, 198 f.; redemption, 168-170; resurrection of body, 466; Scripture (O.T. and N.T.), 52, 56, 58, 65 f., 68; tradition and Scripture, 31, 32, 33, 34, 35; Spirit, 102, 103; Trinity, 88, 96, 102 f.

Justin the Gnostic, 25

Lactantius, 178

Laodicea, Forty-eighth canon of, 434

Latria, 491

Laying on of hands, 195, 207, 209, 210, 211, 433, 434, 435, 438

Leo I, Pope, 312, 333, 334, 406, 420; *Tome* of, 334, 337-42, 408

Logos: teaching of Philo, 9-11; Stoics, 10, 18 f., 285; *endiathetos*, 10, 18 f., 96, 99, 111; *prophorikos*, 10 f., 19, 96, 99, 100; *spermatikos*, 18, 96, 145. *See* Word

Lucian of Antioch, 75, 230

Lucianists, 230

Macarius of Egypt, 441

Macedonians, 259 f.

Macedonius of Constantinople, 259

Malchion, 158 f., 282

Man, doctrine of, 166 f., 171-3, 175 f., 344-9, 353-66, 370-74. *See* Fall, Free will

Mani, 13 f.
Manichaeism, 13 f., 344, 349, 358, 401, 427, 471
Marcellus of Ancyra, 118 f., 122, 407; on homoousion, 238, 239; theology of, 240-2, 250
Marcian, Emperor, 238 f.
Marcion, 57 f., 59, 67 f., 71 f., 84, 87, 142, 175, 463; Marcionism, Marcionites, 68, 141, 401
Marcus (Valentinian Gnostic), 26
Martyrs, devotion to, 490 f.
Mary, Blessed Virgin, 139, 140, 144, 145, 150, 167, 173, 177, 285, 294, 298, 300, 320, 322, 331, 332, 491-9; title Theotokos applied to, 48, 283, 298, 300, 311, 312, 316, 318, 321, 323, 324, 329, 340, 341, 494, 498
Maximilla, 62
Maximus the Confessor, 402, 408
Meletius of Antioch, 249, 302
Melito of Sardes, 45, 54, 145
Menander the Gnostic, 25
Methodius of Olympus: on Fall and original sin, 182 f.; homoousios, meaning of, 235; millenarianism, 479; redemption, 187 f.; resurrection of body, 475 f.
Middle Platonism, 9, 10, 21, 127, 131, 231, 241
Millenarianism, 465 f., 469, 473, 479, 480
Mithras, 11, 12
Modalism, Modalists, 115, 119-26, 129, 133, 136, 140, 274. See Callistus, Marcellus of Ancyra, Sabellius
Monarchianism, Dynamic, 115-19
Monarchy, Divine, 104, 115, 134
Monophysitism, 331, 341, 342, 444
Monothelite controversy, 343
Montanism, 59, 62, 63, 199, 200, 427
Montanus, 59, 62, 239
Muratorian Fragment, 59, 190 n.
Murder, 436, 439
Mystery religions, 12, 22

Naassene tractate, 25
Nazaraeans, 139
Neo-Chalcedonianism, 343
Neo-Platonism, 9, 20-2, 127, 128, 136, 231, 249, 270
Nestorianism, 324, 326, 330, 333, 339, 342. See Nestorius
Nestorius, 48, 307, 310-17, 318, 320, 322, 324, 325, 326, 328, 340, 407, 444; condemnation of, 328, 329, 330
New Testament, allegorical exegesis of, 70 f.; canon of, 31, 35, 56-60, 88; inspiration of, 63; relation to O.T., 64-9, 71, 72; relation to tradition, 30, 33, 34, 40
Nicaea, Council of (325), 5, 44, 46, 138, 231-7, 280, 281, 406; creed of, 45, 231-7, 238, 280, 339
Nicé, Synod of (359), 238; creed of, 251
Niceta of Remesiana, 410, 488
Noetus of Smyrna, 120 f., 123
Nous (Gnostic aeon), 23 f., 25
Novatian, 115 f., 125 f., 134, 152 f., 158, 206, 209; Novatianist schism, 204, 436 f.

Odes of Solomon, 492
Old Testament, canon of, 52-6; Gnostic exegesis of, 67 f.; inspiration of, 60-4, 91; interpretation of, 64-78; Marcion's attitude to, 57, 67; relation to N.T., 31, 32 f., 34, 35, 66-9, 71, 72
Optatus of Milevis, 411, 412, 418 f. 424, 429, 433
Orange, first council of (441), 435; (529), 371 f.
Origen, 5; influence of, 132-6, 158-161, 224-6, 230 f., 241, 484; on apocatastasis, 473 f., 486; baptism, 208; chrismation, 208; Christology, 154-8, 281; Church, 203 f.; Devil, restoration of, 382, 474, 484; eucharist (presence), 213 f.; (sacrifice), 214 f.; Fall (pre-cosmic), 180-183; homoousios, his use of, 130, 234, 235; judgment, 472 f.; life everlasting, 485 f.; Mary, 493; millenarianism, 473, 479; penance, 217; punishment of sinners, 473 f.; redemption, 184-7, 376; resurrection of body, 470-3, 475, 476, 477; Scripture (Apocrypha), 54; (authority), 4, 42; (exegesis), 72, 73 f., 75; (inspiration), 61 f.; (O.T. and N.T.), 69; soul's origin, 128, 155, 344 f.; Spirit, 129, 130, 255, 263; tradition (rule of faith), 43; Trinity, 127, 128-32, 133
Original sin: teaching of Ambrose, 353 f.; Ambrosiaster, 353-5; Athanasius, 346-8; Augustine, 361-6, 499; Basil Caes., 350, 351; Chrysostom, 349, 351, 352; Clement Alex., 179 f.; Cyril Alex., 372; Cyril Hieros., 349; Gregory Naz., 349, 350, 352; Gregory

Nyss., 349, 351; Irenaeus, 171-3;
Justin, 166-70; Methodius, 182 f.;
Origen, 180-2; Pelagius, 358 f.;
Tatian, 168; Tertullian, 175-7;
Theodore Mops., 373 f.; Theo-
doret, 373 f.; Theophilus, 168
Ossius, 231, 236, 237
Ousia, οὐσία, 129, 140, 142, 158,
159, 233, 234, 247, 248, 249, 250,
253, 254, 264-8

Pacian of Barcelona, 437, 439
Pamphilus, 160
'Pantheos', 13
Papias, 33, 37, 466
Parmenianus, 411, 418
Parousia, 461, 462, 463 f., 465 f.,
472 f., 479-83
Patripassianism, 120
Paul of Samosata, 117-19, 140, 158-
160, 230, 290, 311
Paulianists, 427
Paulinus of Antioch, 288, 290, 302
Pelagius, Pelagianism, 324, 344, 345, 357-
61, 369, 370, 371, 373, 390, 419,
430, 497
Penance, Sacrament of, 193, 198 f.,
201, 211, 216-19, 360, 423, 436-40
Persephone, 12
Persona, 112, 113, 114 f., 125, 169, 171,
174 f., 336, 337
Peter, St., foundation of episcopate,
205 f.; prototype of papacy, 407 f.,
412, 417, 418-21
Philippopolis, Council of (*342*), 238;
creed of, 248
Philo, 8-11, 62, 63, 66, 70, 73, 96
Phoebadius of Agen, 269
Photinus, 241 f.
Photius, 154
Phusis, φύσις, 224, 282, 290-5, 297,
299, 301, 310-42
Pierius, 133
Plato, 15 f., 17, 20, 22, 29, 84, 85, 102,
103, 169
Platonism, 10, 14, 15, 72, 74, 85, 129,
131, 213, 231, 281, 287, 321, 346,
348, 375, 377, 378, 379, 381, 386,
397, 466, 470, 472, 488
Pliny, 143
Plotinus, 20 f., 127, 270, 274, 275
Plutarch, 8
Pneumatomachians, 259 f.
Polycarp, 68; on Church, 189; Doce-
tists, 141, 463; eschatology, 463;
forgiveness of sins, 199; Scripture
(Apocrypha), 54; (N.T.), 54; tra-

dition and Scripture, 31, 33; triadic
formula of, 90
Porphyry, 22, 275
Praxeas, 121, 124
Preaching of Peter, The, 190
Predestination, 359, 360, 366-9, 370,
371, 372, 416
Priscilla, 62
Priscillian, 345
Prosopon, πρόσωπον, 112, 114 f., 124,
265, 293, 299, 306, 307, 313, 314,
315, 316, 317, 325, 326, 328, 329,
331, 340, 341; 'prosopic union',
308, 315-17
Prosper of Aquitaine, 370
Protevangelium of James, 492 f.
Pseudo-Basil, 266
Pseudo-Didymus, 351, 427, 429, 432,
434, 435
Pseudo-Dionysius, 422
Ptolemaeus, letter of, to Flora, 25, 67 f.
Purgatory, 484 f.
Pyrrho of Elis, 15
Pythagoras, 12

Recapitulation, theory of, 170-4,
178, 187 f., 376 f., 388, 389, 395
Redemption, 147, 163-88, 375-99;
considered as enlightenment, 163 f.,
165, 168 f., 178, 184 f., 187, 384;
exemplary aspect of, 393 f.; Gnostic view of, 141 f.; 'physical' theory
of, 172-4, 375, 376, 377-81, 384,
386, 391, 396-8; 'ransom' theory
of, 173 f., 183, 185 f., 375 f., 377,
382, 383, 384, 387 f., 390, 391-3,
395; 'realist' theory of, 164 f., 170,
173 f., 177 f., 186, 376, 377, 379 f.,
382, 383, 384, 385, 386, 389 f.,
392 f., 395, 398; teaching of Ambrose, 387, 389; Ambrosiaster, 389;
Athanasius, 242, 377-80; Augustine,
390-5; 'Barnabas', 163, 164, 165,
166; Cappadocians, 380-4, 385;
Chrysostom, 381, 384, 386; Clement Alex., 183 f.; Clement Rom.,
164; Cyril Alex., 396-9; Cyril
Hieros., 384 f.; Eusebius Caes.,
384 f.; Hermas, 163 f.; Hilary, 386-
388; Ignatius, 164, 165; Irenaeus,
172-4; John of Damascus, 396 f.;
Justin, 166-70; Methodius, 187 f.;
Origen, 184-7; Pelagius, 390; Tertullian, 177; Theodore Mops., 395;
Theodoret, 395 f.; Victorinus,
386 f., 388
Relations, Augustine's theory of, 274 f.

Resurrection of the body, 461, 462; teaching of Ambrose, 478; Athenagoras, 466; Augustine, 478 f.; 'Barnabas', 463; Clement Rom., 463; Cyril Hieros., 476 f.; *Didache*, 463; Didymus, 477; Epiphanius, 475; Eustathius, 475; Gregory Nyss., 477 f.; Hilary, 478; Hippolytus, 468; Ignatius, 463; Irenaeus, 467, 468; Jerome, 476; Methodius, 475 f.; Origen, 470-2, 475, 476; Tatian, 466; Tertullian, 468; Theophilus, 466

Roman Creed, Old, 144

Rome, Church or See of, 4, 44, 46, 56, 57, 120, 123-6, 191, 192 f., 205 f., 341, 357, 406-8, 411, 413, 417-21

Rome, Council of (377), 295 f.

Rufinus, 55, 130₂ 181, 235, 474

'Rule of faith' (*regula fidei*), 39, 40, 43, 44, 88 f., 142, 192

Sabellius, Sabellianism, 119, 121-3, 124, 133, 224, 236, 238, 239, 240, 241, 246, 253, 254, 255, 256, 269

Sacraments, 193-9, 423-55; number of, 423 f.

Sacramentum, 193, 423, 433

Saints, veneration of, 490 f.

Satornilus (Saturninus), 25

Scepticism, 15

Scripture, canon of, 52-60; exegesis of, 30, 32, 40, 57, 66, 69-78; inspiration of, 60-4; relation to tradition, 29-53

Second Coming. See Parousia

Semi-Arians, 249 f.

Semi-Pelagians, 370 f.

Seneca, 19

Septuagint, 16, 53

Serapion of Antioch, 141

Serapion of Thmuis, 256, 426, 433, 435, 441

Serapis, 11

Serdica, Creed of, 242

Severian of Gabbala, 76

Severus of Antioch, 343

Sextus Empiricus, 15

Simon Magus, 22

Sin. See Original Sin

Siricius, Pope, 419

Sirmium, Council of (357), 238, 250; creed or 'Blasphemy' of, 248 f.

Smyrna, 58, 189, 464

Socrates, 239 f., 407, 437

Son, Sonship: teaching of Alexander Alex., 224 f.; Apostolic Fathers, 90-5; Athanasius, 243-7; Augustine, 272-6; Basil Caes., 264 f.; Callistus, 124 f.; Clement Alex., 127 f.; Didymus, 263 f.; Dionysius Alex., 133-6; Dionysius Rom., 133-136; Evagrius, 263 f.; Gregory Naz., 265, 267; Gregory Nyss., 265, 267; Hippolytus, 110-15, 123; Irenaeus, 104-8; Modalists, 119-23; Nicene creed, 232-7; Novatian, 125 f.; Origen, 128-32; Sabellius, 124; Serdican creed, 242 f.; Tertullian, 110-15, 125; Victorinus, 270 f.; Zephyrinus, 124

Soul, Origin of, 128, 155, 158, 344-6

Sozomen, 407

Stephen, Pope, 206, 210

Stoics, Stoicism, 10, 15, 17 f., 19, 20, 83, 84, 99, 114, 129, 146, 166, 175, 471; Stoic idea of Logos, 285

Substantia, meaning of, 114, 136

Symphronianus, 437

Tatian: on Christology, 145; free will, 166, 168; resurrection of body, 466; Scripture (N.T.), 58; Spirit, 102; Word, 85, 98 f.

Tertullian: on baptism, 209; Christology, 144, 149, 150-3, 334; Church, 200, 201; Ebionites, 139; eschatology, 460, 467, 468, 469; eucharist (presence), 211, 212, 440, 446, 449; (sacrifice), 214; Fall and original sin, 174-7, 180; penance, 217, 218; redemption, 177; Scripture (Apocrypha), 54; (relation of O.T. to N.T.), 69; soul's origin, 175, 345; theology, 4 f.; tradition and Scripture, 36-40, 41, 43, 44, 47; Trinity, 109, 110-15, 121, 124, 125, 241, 269

Theodore of Mopsuestia: on baptism, 430-2; Christology, 302, 303-9, 310, 311, 314, 330; Church, 403; eucharist (presence), 426, 444, 450; (sacrifice), 452; free will, 373 f.; original sin, 373; sacraments, 422; Scripture (exegesis), 75, 77 f.; (inspiration), 61, 64

Theodoret: 334; on chrism, 433 f.; Christology, 325 f., 328, 330, 331 f., 338 f.; Church, 402; eucharist (presence), 445; (sacrifice), 452; grace, 374; life everlasting, 487; original sin, 373; Petrine texts, 408; redemption, 395 f.; saints, 491; Scripture (Apocrypha), 55; (exegesis), 76, 78; tradition. 49

Theodosius I, Emperor, 251, 296, 302
Theodosius II, Emperor, 324, 326, 334, 338
Theodotus (banker), 116, 121, 140
Theodotus (leather-merchant), 116 f., 140
Theodotus, bishop of Laodicea, 289
Theognostus, 132 f.
Theophanies, O.T., 96 f., 273
Theophilus of Antioch, 27; on baptism, 195; Fall, 168; free will, 166; judgment, 467; resurrection of body, 466; Scripture (O.T. and N.T.), 69; Spirit, 102, 104, 106; Trinity, 85, 109; Word, 99
Theoria, 76 f.
Toledo, Third council of (589), 439
Toura commentary, 301
Tradition, authority of, 30, 36; fathers as interpreters of, 48-51; meaning of, 30 f.; oral, 37, 45; relation of apostles to, 29 f., 36-42; relation to Scripture, 29-51; written, 45 f.; teaching of Athanasius, 31, 45, 47; Basil Caes., 45; Clement Alex., 34, 43; Clement Rom., 32 f., 34, 35; Cyprian, 42; Cyril Alex., 48 f.; Epiphanius, 45 f.; Eusebius, 45; Gregory Naz., 45; Irenaeus, 36-9; Justin, 33; Papias, 33; Polycarp, 33; Origen, 43, 47; Tertullian, 36, 39-41; Vincent of Lérins, 49-51
Traditor, 410
Traducianism, 175, 345 f.
Trinitas, Tertullian's use of, 113
Trinity, Holy, baptism in name of, 194, 195, 411, 424, 425, 432; coinherence of Persons in, 264 f.; first use of term, 102, 111; position of Spirit in, 255-63; teaching of Alexander Alex., 224 f.; Ambrose, 269; Arius, 229; Athanasius, 256-8; Athenagoras, 99 f.; Augustine, 271-279; 'Barnabas', 91 f.; Basil Caes., 264, 265, 266, 268; Callistus, 123-5; Clement Alex., 127 f.; Clement Rom., 90 f.; Didymus, 263; Dionysius Alex., 133-6; Dionysius Rom., 133-6; Eusebius Caes., 225 f.; Eustathius, 259, 260; Evagrius, 263, 264, 268, 269; Gregory Naz., 259-268; Gregory Nyss., 261-8; Hermas, 93-5; Hippolytus, 110-15; Ignatius, 92 f., 96; Irenaeus, 104-8; Justin, 96-8, 102 f.; Marcellus of Ancyra 240, f.; Noetus, 120; Nova-

tian, 115 f., 126; Origen, 128-32; Paul of Samosata, 117-19; Praxeas, 121; Sabellius, 121-3; Tatian, 98 f., 102; Tertullian, 110 f., 113 f.; Theophilus, 99, 102, 104; Victorinus, 270 f.; Zephyrinus, 125
Tropici, 256 f.
Typology, 69-75, 76

Unction, 195, 207, 208
Union Symbol, 328 f., 330, 331, 334, 342
ὑπόστασις. *See* Hypostasis
Uriel, 7
Ursacius, 248

Valens (Arian bishop), 248
Valentinus (Gnostic), 23-5, 27, 150
Victor, Pope, 116
Victorinus: on grace, 357; redemption, 386 f., 388; soul's origin, 345; Trinity, 270 f., 273
Vigilantius, 491
Vincent of Lérins, 43, 371; on tradition, 50 f.
Vitalis, 295

Wisdom, 7, 10, 86, 95, 106, 109, 111, 117, 132, 224, 228, 283, 299, 462; Sophia, 23, 24
Word: teaching of Apologists, 84-6, 95-104; Antiochene fathers (268), 158 f.; Arius, 226-31; Augustine, 336 f.; Chalcedon, 338-42; Clement Alex., 127, 153 f.; Cyril Alex., 317-23; Dionysius Alex., 134 f.; Eusebius Caes., 160, 225 f.; Hippolytus, 111-15, 149 f.; 201, 202; Ignatius, 92; Irenaeus, 104-7; Justin, 145-8; Leo, 337 f.; Marcellus of Ancyra, 240-2; Modalists, 119 f.; Nestorius, 311-17; Novatian, 152 f.; Origen, 128-32, 154-8, 184, 186, 187; Paul of Samosata, 140; Tertullian, 111-15, 150-52; Victorinus, 270. *See* Logos
'Word-flesh Christology', 146, 161, 281, 282, 285, 287, 289, 290, 291, 301, 302, 304, 310, 319, 322
'Word-man Christology', 281, 283, 285, 302, 304, 310

Xystus III, Pope, 328

Zeno of Citium, 17
Zeno of Verona, 496
Zephyrinus, Pope, 117, 120, 121, 123-125
Zosimus, Pope, 369 f.